THE FORGING OF
THE MODERN STATE

Early industrial Britain 1783–1870

Foundations of modern Britain

General editor: *Geoffrey Holmes*

THE FORGING OF THE MODERN STATE
Early industrial Britain 1783–1870

Second Edition

Eric J. Evans

LONGMAN
LONDON AND NEW YORK

Longman Group Limited,
Edinburgh Gate
Harlow
Essex
CM20 2JE, England
and Associated Companies throughout the world.

Published in the United States of America
by Longman Publishing, New York

© Longman Group Limited 1983, 1996

First published 1983
Thirteenth impression 1994
Second edition 1996

ISBN 0 582 08953 0 PPR

British Library Cataloguing-in-Publication Data

A catalogue record for this book is available from the British Library

Library of Congress Cataloging-in Publication Data

Evans, Eric J.' 1945–
   The forging of the modern state: early industrial Britain,
1783-1870 / Eric J. Evans. --2nd ed.
      p.   Cm. -- (Foundations of modern Britain)
   Includes bibliographical references and index.
   ISBN 0-582-08953-0
   1. Great Briatin--Economic conditions--1760-1860. 2. Industrial
revolution--Great Britain. 3. Great Britain--Politics and government--
1760-1820. 4. Great Britain--Politics and government--19th century.
I Iitle. II. Series.
HC255.E89   1996   95-14488
338.0941--dc   CIP
                                             AC

Set by 7 in 10/12pt Times
Produced through Longman Malaysia, GPS

Contents

PART FOUR: EARLY INDUSTRIAL SOCIETY, REFINED AND TESTED, 1846–1870

COMPENDIUM OF INFORMATION

List of maps

Editor's foreword

So prodigious has been the output of specialized work on British history during the past twenty years, and so rich its diversity, that scholars and students thirst continually after fresh syntheses. Even those who read for the pure pleasure of informing themselves about the past have become quite reconciled to the fact that little can now be taken for granted. An absorbing interest in local situations, as a way to understanding more general ones; a concern with those processes of social change which accompany economic, educational and cultural development, and which often condition political activity too: these and many other strong currents of modern historiography have washed away some of our more comfortable orthodoxies. Even when we know *what* happened, there is endless scope for debate about *why* things happened and with what consequences.

In such circumstances a new series of general textbooks on British history would not seem to call for elaborate justification. However, the six volumes constituting *Foundations of Modern Britain* do have a distinct rationale and they embody some novel features. For one thing, they make a serious attempt to present a history of Britain from the point at which 'Britain' became first a recognizable entity and then a Great Power, and to trace the foundations of this state in the history of pre-eighteenth–century England. The fact that five of the six authors either have taught or are teaching in Scottish universities, while one has held a chair in the University of Wales, should at least help to remind them that one aim of the series is to avoid excessive Anglo-centricity. The first two volumes, spanning the years 1370–1660, will certainly concentrate primarily on the history of England, emphasizing those developments which first prepared the way for, and later confirmed her emergence as an independent 'Commonwealth', free from Continental trammels whether territorial or ecclesiastical. But the reader should also be aware, as he reads them, of England's ultimate role as the heart of a wider island kingdom in which men of three nations came to be associated. During the period covered by volumes 3, 4 and 5, 1660–1870, this 'United Kingdom of Great Britain' became not only a domestic reality but the centre of an Empire and the possessor of world-wide influence. Space will allow only limited treatment of Ireland and of Anglo-Irish relations until after the Union of 1801. It is appropriate, however, that in the final volume of the series reasserted nationalism should figure almost as strongly as the erosion of imperial status in the story of Britain's slide down the slippery slope from palmy greatness to anxious mediocrity.

As well as paying more than mere lip-service to its own title, the present series adopts an irreverent attitude to time-honoured chronological divisions. Those lines of demarcation between volumes which dominated virtually every English history series conceived before 1960 (and, with a few exceptions, have displayed a remarkable capacity for survival subsequently) are seen as a quite unnecessary obstacle to readers' understanding of the way modern historiography has reshaped whole vistas of our island's history in the past forty years. Years such as 1485, 1603, 1689, 1714, 1760 or 1815 established themselves in textbook lore at a time when they accurately reflected the heavily political and constitutional emphasis of traditional history teaching. Even on those terms they have become of limited utility. But equally seriously, the conventions which such divisions perpetuate often make it extremely difficult for authors to accommodate fundamental aspects of social and economic development within their allotted compass. The brutal slicing off of 'Tawney's century' (1540–1640) at 1603 is perhaps the worst of these atrocities; but it is not the only one.

All dates are to some extent arbitrary as lines of division, and all present their own difficulties. It is hoped, none the less, that those selected in this series to enclose periods which are in any case a good deal longer than average, may prove less inhibiting and confusing than some of their predecessors and much more adaptable to the needs of British history courses in universities and colleges.

In one further important respect the authors have kept in mind the practical requirements of students and teachers. Their approach eschews lengthy narrative wherever possible and concentrates, within chapters short enough to be rapidly absorbed, on the development of themes and the discussion of problems. Yet at the same time they attempt to satisfy their readers' need for basic information in two ways: by providing, at appropriate stages, skeletal 'frameworks' of events, chronologically ordered, within which the subsequent analysis and interplay of argument can be set; and by placing at the end of each volume a 'compendium' of factual data, including statistics, on a scale much greater than that of normal textbook appendices.

These compendia are essential companions to the texts and are designed for ready and constant use. The frequent references to them which punctuate so many chapters in this series will be found within square brackets, e.g. [B]. They should be easily distinguishable from the numerous arabic numbers within round brackets inserted in the text, e.g. (117). These refer readers to the Bibliography, in which most items are thematically arranged and serially numbered. Where necessary, specific page numbers (in italic) follow the main reference in the round brackets. Superior numerals are for the references which appear at the end of the relevant chapter.

Geoffrey Holmes

Introduction to the Second Edition

It is nearly fifteen years since most of the original edition of this book was written. The author who is fortunate enough to be asked to produce a second edition of a well-used text must perform a delicate balancing act. On the one hand, there is a duty to help readers keep up with the frantic pace of modern scholarship. On the other, and especially within the framework of an established series, a second edition cannot be an excuse to write a new book. I have retained that format of short chapters with distinct sub-headings which readers of syntheses clearly prefer. I have also seen no reason to change the overall titles of those parts, or the value judgements which such titles make. Others must judge how effectively the overall balance has been struck. However, even a cursory examination will reveal that this new edition is somewhat longer than the original and its bibliography very substantially so. It may help to explain to readers familiar with the first edition where they may expect to find the most substantial changes.

Firstly, I hope that I have responded to some justified criticism from colleagues that my treatment was in places excessively Anglo-centric. In addition to providing a wider range of non-English references throughout and reflecting a more recent research interest, I have framed a new chapter (Ch. 41) which discusses the extent to which the four constituent national elements of the United Kingdom were genuinely 'united'. Secondly, there are extensive changes to Part Two, which owe much to some fundamental rethinking by colleagues about the nature of social change during the industrial revolution, including the airing of the useful heresy about whether Britain actually experienced what one might call an 'industrial revolution' in the late eighteenth and early nineteenth centuries at all. What is now Chapter 12, for example, has been entirely recast in the light of this debate, though most of the other chapters in Part Two have undergone substantial revision. Within this revision, I have tried to take due account of much fruitful work in the last decade and a half by scholars researching the history of women. Though I have changed much, I firmly decided against the crass and patronizing ring-fence of 'a chapter on women'. On the other hand, it is interesting to note that my original scepticism about the extent to which Britain can be considered a 'class-conscious' society in the middle of the nineteenth century has been shared by many writers since 1983. Thirdly, although I have in general sustained the judgements I originally made about the leading political figures of the period, I now feel that I was too kind to Sir Robert Peel. Chapter 28 takes a less enthusiastic view of him overall, while also attempting to incorporate some very useful new work on the Whigs in the 1830s. Readers will find many other changes and I was in some ways disconcerted to discover that no chapter emerged from the revision process entirely unscathed.

For the rest, I have made myriad minor changes and I am extremely grateful to reviewers and others who wrote to me with corrections, comments and suggestions for improvement. I have tried to incorporate as many of these as possible. A few readers will be glad to know that this product of the humanities sixth of an early 1960s grammar school, who gave up all formal science at Adrian Mole's age of thirteen and three quarters, can now get 'centripetal' and 'centrifugal' the right way round. Doubtless, corrections will need to be set against fresh errors, and for these I acknowledge sole responsibility. Naturally, I hope that this new edition, though longer than its predecessor, produces a net balance in favour of greater accuracy.

The debts which I acknowledged in the first edition remain undimmed by the passage of time. To these I would like to add now three special thanks. Andrew MacLennan had to wait very much longer for this second edition than the first, but he bore all excuses and prevarications with much greater sensitivity, and much less outward sign of irritation, than I deserved. I am extremely grateful to him for his insight and his urbane forbearance. Jessica Marquis fought against ferocious odds to make me computer literate. Her partial success in my case represents total triumph measured against any realistic set of objectives. Jen Carr offered much sensitive and pertinent advice on what historical and political allusions undergraduates and sixth-formers might not pick up. She also helped in the thankless task of changing every reference to harmonize with the totally recast bibliography. I owe her a huge debt. The many friends and colleagues whose work is listed in the Bibliography will know how much I owe to their insights and will, I hope, be willing to accept my thanks and indebtedness to them collectively. I do, however, owe a special debt to Lancaster University generally, and to colleagues in the History Department there particularly, for continuing to provide such a sympathetic and stimulating environment within which to work.

Geoffrey Holmes, the Series Editor, did not live to see the second edition of this book completed. Severe illness during the last years of his life also prevented him from offering his characteristically shrewd, sympathetic and detailed comments on my redrafting. Yet his influence pervades what follows. I was as grateful for his first suggestion that I might have something to offer to the Series as I have been enormously in his debt for inspiration and guidance thereafter. I dedicate this second edition to the memory of a genuinely great scholar and a humane and civilized friend.

Eric Evans,
Lancaster, December 1994

Acknowledgements

We are grateful to the following for permission to reproduce copyright material: Cambridge University Press for Table D.ii.1; Dr V. A. C. Gatrell and the *Economic History Review*, Blackwell Publishers, for Table D.v.2; Leicester University Press and Pinter Publishers for Tables D.ii.2, D.ii.3 and D.ii.5 Copyright © Leicester University Press 1979, second edition Pinter Publishers, a Cassell imprint, London; Macmillan, London and Basingstoke, for Table D.vii.2 and Oxford University Press for Table G.ii.

Abbreviations

The following abbreviations are used in both footnotes and bibliography:

Add. MSS   Additional Manuscripts, British Library
Ag.H.R.   *Agricultural History Review*
B.L.   British Library
Ec.H.R.   *Economic History Review*
E.H.R.   *English Historical Review*
Exp. Ec. Hist. *Explorations in Economic History*
H.J.   *Historical Journal*
I.R.S.H.   *International Review of Social History*
J. B. S.   *Journal of British Studies*
J.Ec.H.   *Journal of Economic History*
J. Soc. Hist. *Journal of Social History*
P.P.   *Parliamentary Papers*, House of Commons
P. & P.   *Past and Present*
Parl. Hist.   *Cobbett's Parliamentary History of England*
P.R.O.   Public Record Office
R.O.   Record Office (prefixed by name of county or town)
Soc. Hist.   *Social History*
T.R.S.H.   *Transactions of the Royal Historical Society*

The Reader should note that the place of publication is London unless otherwise stated.

Note on the framework of events

The rationale of this feature is explained in the General Editor's preface. Readers of this volume are reminded, however, that additional, and more detailed, chronological information on the major developments in social legislation and on foreign affairs, diplomacy, wars and the colonies is to be found in the Compendium of information under [C] and [F] respectively; [G.i] lists the main developments concerning religion.

I have tried to use the framework additionally to indicate the main scientific, cultural and sporting developments which so often appear, if at all, as separate entities, divorced from time.

PART ONE

Reconstruction and the challenge of war, 1783–1815

FRAMEWORK OF EVENTS, 1783–1815

1783   Treaty of Versailles. Britain recognizes USA independence (Sept); Fox–North coalition resigns, Pitt the Younger appointed Prime Minister (Dec).

1784   General Election secures Pitt a parliamentary majority. Pitt begins reductions in customs duties and attacks smuggling. India Act creates a Board of Control. Cort's puddling process revolutionizes wrought-iron manufacture.

1785   Pitt's motion for parliamentary reform defeated. General Chamber of Manufacturers formed. Boulton–Watt rotary steam engine in operation in a cotton-spinning factory. Paley, *Principles of Moral and Political Philosophy* published. *The Times* founded.

1786   Pitt's sinking-fund established; excise scheme begun. Cornwallis becomes Governor-General of India. Eden Anglo–French trade treaty signed. Penang becomes first Britain Settlement in Malay Peninsula. Burns Scottish dialect *Poems*.

1787   Hannah More, *Thoughts on the Manners of the Great* published. Impeachment of Warren Hastings. MCC moves to Lord's Cricket Ground, Dorset Square, Marylebone. Wilberforce's Proclamation Society founded. Brighton Pavilion begun.

1788   Anglo–Dutch alliance (Apr) joined by Prussia in Aug to secure Triple Alliance for European peace. First signs of George III's mental instability. Trial of Warren Hastings begins.

1789   Pitt's Regency bill quickly followed by the King's recovery. Bentham, *Introduction to the Principles of Morals and Legislation*; William Blake, *Songs of Innocence*. Bill to repeal Test and Corporation Acts fails. C. J. Fox acclaims fall of Bastille. Mutiny on H.M.S. *Bounty*.

1790   Burke and Fox take opposite sides on reaction to French Revolution; Burke's *Reflections on the Revolution in France*. First steam rolling-mill in England. General Election. Spain capitulates to British claims for compensation over attack on British fishing vessels at Nootka Sound (W. Canada).

1791   Ochakov crisis over Russian seizure of Turkish port. Canada Act divides Upper from Lower Canada. Joseph Priestley's house attacked in Birmingham by anti-reforming crowd. Paine, *Rights of Man*, Part I, published; Burke, *Appeal from the New to the Old Whigs*; Mackintosh, *Vindiciae Gallicae*. Boswell, *Life of Samuel Johnson*. Pitt announces Britain's intended neutrality in any European action against the French revolutionaries. *Observer* founded.

1792   Revival of British reform movements with foundation of London Corresponding Society and the Whig Friends of the People. Paine, *Rights of Man*, Part II published; Mary Wollstonecraft, *Vindication of the Rights of Woman*. John Reeves anti-radical Association Movement formed (Nov); Manchester radicals attacked by loyalist crowd (Dec).

1793   Britain enters European war against France (Feb). Trial in Scotland of the radicals Muir and Fysshe Palmer. Board of Agriculture founded with Arthur Young as secretary. William Godwin, *Enquiry Concerning Political Justice* published.

1794   Habeas Corpus suspended by Pitt (May); twelve leading radicals arrested but acquitted or released. Split in Whig party finalized (July). Most join Pitt, leaving Fox with small opposition group. Paine, *Age of Reason*, advocating deism, published. Jay treaty between Britain and USA. Howe wins naval battle in the Channel. Britain occupies Corsica.

1795   Speenhamland expedient for poor relief begun. Warren Hastings acquitted of treason. Food riots and widespread economic distress; high prices. Pitt introduces Treasonable Practices and Seditious Meetings Acts (Dec) against public meetings and political organizations. Joseph Bramah invents the hydraulic press. Acquisition of Cape colony. Acquisition of Melaka.

1796 Peace proposals between Britain and France fail. Edward Jenner begins vaccination against smallpox. Spain enters war against Britain. Britain takes Ceylon from the Dutch. Fanny Burney, *Camilla.*

1797 Economic crisis; Bank of England suspends cash payments (Feb). Naval mutinies at Spithead (Apr) and the Nore (May). French landing at Fishguard, but invasion plans not followed up. William Wilberforce, *Practical View of the Prevailing Religious System of Professed Christians.* Edmund Burke dies. S. T. Coleridge, *Kubla Khan.* Henry Maudslay invents carriage lathe. Pitt Act against Unlawful Oaths.

1798 Newspaper regulation, and newspaper taxes increased. Irish rebellion led by Wolfe Tone. T. R. Malthus, *Essay on the Principle of Population;* W. Wordsworth and S. T. Coleridge, *Lyrical Ballads.* Nelson wins Battle of the Nile; Second Coalition against France begun to be constructed.

1799 Income tax levied for the first time. Church Missionary Society founded. London Corresponding Society, United Irishmen and other named societies proscribed.

1800 Act of Union with Ireland passed (Mar). Robert Owen's 'model' factory at New Lanark founded. Combination Act (together with one passed in 1799) completes illegality of trade unions. Richard Trevithick invents light pressure steam-engine; Henry Maudslay invents precision screw-cutting lathe.

1801 Pitt resigns over Roman Catholic emancipation (Mar); succeeded by Addington. Economic distress and high food prices. Habeas Corpus suspended again. Nelson wins Battle of Copenhagen. First full census. 'Horne Tooke Act', clergy of the Church of England not permitted to sit in Commons.

1802 Peace of Amiens concludes first stage of French Wars. Cobbett's *Political Register* and Whig *Edinburgh Review* founded. First Factory Act (without inspectors to enforce it). John Dalton compiles Table of Atomic Weights. J. Bentham, *Civil and Penal Legislation* published (one of the foundation-stones of Utilitarianism).

1803 Hostilities with France resume. Building of Caledonian Canal begun. Joseph Lancaster's *Improvements in Education* published. John Dalton describes his Atomic theory.

1804 Addington's government falls (Apr); replaced by Pitt's second ministry (May). British and Foreign Bible Society founded. Spain declares war on Britain. William Blake, *Jerusalem* published. Richard Trevithick's steam locomotive for the Penydafren iron works.

1805 Formation of the Third Coalition against France. Trade dispute with USA. Nelson wins Battle of Trafalgar, which gains for Britain undisputed control of the seas; Nelson killed in action (Oct). British Institution for Development of Fine Arts founded.

1806 Pitt dies (Jan); 'Ministry of all the Talents' formed (Feb) – Grenville Prime Minister; Fox Foreign Secretary (first office since 1783). Fox dies (Sept). Humphry Davy isolates the elements sodium and potassium. Continental system of trade embargo against Britain begun by Napoleon (Nov). Congreve rocket-boats used to attack French fleet. General Election strengthens Grenvillites (Dec). Gas lighting installed in a Manchester cotton mill.

1807 Britain declares reciprocal economic blockade on France and her allies. 'Talents' ministry falls (Mar); Portland becomes Prime Minister. General Election produces more supporters for the gvt Britain isolated in the war after Treaty of Tilsit. Slave trade abolished in British territories. Wordsworth, *Ode on Intimations of Immortality.*

1808 Peninsular campaign begins when Wellesley sent to Portugal. Royal Lancasterian Institution founded to advance the education of the poor.

1809 Curwen's Bribery Act passed; restricts opportunity for sale of parliamentary seats. Wellesley becomes duke of Wellington after victory at Talavera. Resignation of Portland; Perceval succeeds as Prime Minister. Tory *Quarterly Review* founded. 2,000 Guineas run at Newmarket for first time.

1810 USA resumes trade with Britain. Wellington's defensive action at Torres Vedras. Strikes begin in part in reaction to effects of gvt's economic policy. George III's mental incapacity recurs; now to prove permanent.

1811 Prince George assumes title of Prince Regent. First Luddite attacks in Nottingham. Handloom weavers form headquarters in Glasgow to co-ordinate activity in defence of apprenticeship. Nash begins work on Regent Street.

1812 Widespread economic distress; Wheat price rises to 126s. (19th-century peak); year of greatest Luddite outbreaks; gvt makes frame-breaking a capital offence. Gvt revokes Orders of Council, thereby hoping to resume more normal trading patterns. Perceval assassinated (May); Liverpool succeeds as Prime Minister. Formation of Baptist Union of Gt Britain. Central London streets first lit by gas. Nash begins oriental conversion of Brighton Pavilion.

1813 Decisive victories in Peninsula. Methodist Missionary Society founded. East Indian trade monopoly in India ended. Statutes protecting apprenticeship repealed. Hedley's 'Puffing Billy' steam locomotive runs on smooth rails at Wylam. Robert Owen, *A New View of Society* published; Jane Austen, *Pride and Prejudice* published.

1814 Defeat of France. Anglo-USA hostilities in Great Lakes ended by Treaty of Ghent. MCC move to current Lord's Cricket Ground. Stephenson builds steam locomotive. Actor Edmund Kean makes debut as *Shylock*.

1815 Napoleon's 100 days end with defeat by Wellington at Waterloo (June). Congress of Vienna brings European peace. Humphry Davy invents miners' safety lamp. First Gurkha regiments of British army formed. Corn Law prohibits imports of foreign corn unless domestic price exceeds 80s.

CHAPTER 1

Britain in the early 1780s:
I Society and economy

I

> If we were to form an estimate of the circumstances of the inhabitants of London
> from the daily gains of the artisans, that people might be thought very rich in
> comparison of the Parisians, the price of work being almost double to what it is at
> Paris . . . the inhabitants of London eat and drink well, and are handsomely cloathed. . . .
> The distant counties of England are . . . the same thing with respect to London, as the
> provinces are with regard to Paris . . . though in England the country people seem
> greatly to have the advantage, as they taste the felicity which was enjoyed by the
> people of Israel in the days of their prosperity.[1]

This assessment by a much travelled and perceptive French lawyer in the mid-
1760s is typical of the views of many diplomats and visitors to Britain. Grosley, it
is true, was taken aback at the high level of prices in the capital which rendered
the relative balance of advantage for the Londoner over the Parisian less great.
High prices, however, as envious British tourists to Switzerland, much of Germany
or Scandinavia in our own day are well aware, are frequently indicative of superior
general levels of prosperity. Grosley confirmed that ordinary Englishmen ate more
meat than their French counterparts, consuming far less bread in consequence and
increasingly confining themselves to the superior wheaten varieties. Although in
the generally harsher and colder climate of Scotland, oats were the staple arable
crop, many Scots enjoyed the benefits of economic growth, especially from the
1740s onwards. Scottish farmhouses in the second half of the eighteenth century
increasingly sported additional rooms and slate roofs, while Scottish town-
dwellers, like their English counterparts, were established tea-drinkers. It is
tolerably certain that Britain in the early 1780s was already the most advanced
nation in the world and that its superiority was reflected in higher living standards
and more diverse patterns of consumption than elsewhere.

In Britain, as elsewhere, land was the basis of wealth and prestige. Compared
with the rest of Europe, however, land was much more closely integrated with
commerce and industry. The opening up of a money market at the end of the
seventeenth century had provided alternative sources of investment for wealth
without diminishing the attraction of a solid landed estate as the tangible symbol of
status. Oppotunities in trade and business provided profitable employment for
younger sons of great landowners in addition to more traditional occupations such
as army officers or dignitaries in the Church of England. Constructive cooperation
between the worlds of agriculture and business was a pronounced feature of that
increase of national wealth which took place in the century before the Industrial
Revolution.

Aspiration to respectable landed status maintained a steady flow of new wealth from business to land, even during the first half of the eighteenth century when returns on investment in land were not good. All extremely wealthy men sought and obtained landed estates, though they sank less of their total fortune in them than their sixteenth- and seventeenth-century forebears had done. Samuel Whitbread, founder of the London brewing firm and father of the Foxite Whig of the same name, bought an estate in 1762 in the Bedfordshire village where his seventeenth-century ancestors had been smaller gentry. By the mid-1790s, when his brewing capital comfortably exceeded £250,000, he had acquired over 12,000 acres of good farming land in Bedfordshire and adjacent counties. Though his rents brought in over £12,000 a year his main income still derived from beer. In the manner of many successful entrepreneurs, he bought himself into Parliament, in 1775, as Member for the borough of Bedford. Though he coveted the extra status traditionally accorded to MPs representing county seats the established county gentry, far less wealthy than he, frustrated Whitbread's ambition to sit for Bedfordshire. Britain was more 'open' to both wealth and talent than any European society, but fine gradations of hierarchy and status survived. Money bought the Whitbreads into Parliament, but it was not a passport to any position. Samuel Whitbread junior firmly believed that his ambition to lead the Whig party after Charles James Fox's death was frustrated by snobbish disdain at his commercial origins.

A generation of students has been taught to believe that the large landowners in England, and particularly the aristocracy, consolidated their position at the expense of smaller men in the first half of the eighteenth century. 'The general drift of property in the sixty years after 1690 was in favour of the large estates and the great lord . . . it clearly marks one of the great changes in the disposition of English property.' The Habbakuk thesis[2] has the attraction of suggesting economic and social parallels to the increasing grip of the eighteenth-century political system held by the great magnates. Farms were certainly getting larger. In a sample from Staffordshire and Shropshire at the beginning of the Hanoverian period three-quarters of all farms were between 20 and 200 acres with only one-fifth exceeding 200 acres. By the late 1770s the proportions had moved to three-fifths and one-third respectively, while even more dramatic developments in the direction of larger farms took place between 1780 and 1830. It is also true that large landowners favoured consolidation of estates in areas where their social influence was already strong.

The weakness of Habbakuk's case, however, lies in the assumption that the land market was sluggish and that great men took advantage to buy out lesser landowners less protected against an adverse agricultural climate. A high degree of turnover of smaller estates has always characterized land purchases in the modern period and the trend was maintained during the eighteenth century. As recent studies have shown, land was snapped up by men whose wealth had been accumulated either in London or the rapidly growing provincial towns (185). Typical purchasers of estates, each sustaining the dynamic link between land and industry, were merchants, bankers and lawyers. They offered no threat to the social supremacy of the 'great lords', but they found niches in English landed society readily enough.

Very few hereditary peerages were created between the Glorious Revolution and the beginning of our period. Thus, the 200 or so aristocratic families at the apex of British society were set apart while the fortunes of most of them grew appreciably. By 1780 some of the richest – the Bedfords, Devonshires, Derbys and Rockinghams – had incomes touching £50,000 a year, making them far wealthier than most German princes, for example. Their wealth came from rents, which were moving upwards from the later 1750s after a longish period in the doldrums, but increasingly from other sources as well. The pickings from patronage and government office could be lavish. Most of the richest landowners also owned mines which became more profitable as the pace of economic change quickened; some invested heavily in transport improvements to maximize returns on business ventures (see Ch. 12).

Nor should acquisition via strategic marriage be forgotten. Many eighteenth-century aristocratic marriages were as carefully calculated for their strategic and social advantages as were those of European royal families. Marriage between a duke, or the heir to a dukedom, and a well-connected heiress was the ideal acquisitive partnership. The marriage of William Cavendish, fourth duke of Devonshire, to Lady Charlotte Boyle, the only surviving daughter of the third earl of Burlington was particularly advantageous to the Devonshires. The Cavendishes – already one of the two or three wealthiest families in Britain – acquired by it Lismore Castle in County Waterford (Ireland), Londesborough Hall and Bolton Abbey in Yorkshire, together with two of the most fashionable residences in London, Burlington and Chiswick Houses.

The splendours of the great eighteenth-century country mansions – Chatsworth in Derbyshire, Castle Howard in Yorkshire, Blenheim in Oxfordshire, Wimpole Hall in Cambridgeshire and the rest – symbolized the uniquely powerful position of the aristocracy. They were built, not only as a testament to refinement and Palladian taste, but as a statement about power. So vast were their estates and so extensive their grounds that no one passing near could doubt the extent of the social and political influence which their owners wielded. An architect of genius, like Robert Adam, whose classical designs so enhance the surviving beauty and grandeur of buildings such as Syon House and Kenwood, in London, Kedleston (Derbyshire), and Hopetoun House, near Edinburgh, needed substantial aristocratic patronage to realize his ambitions. Adam's career flourished first under the Scottish patronage of the duke of Argyll and Lord Minto and later under the first duke of Northumberland, whose interest in, and knowledge of, the visual arts was remarkable.

Eighteenth-century aristocratic grounds were also designed, and redesigned, at vast expense. The duke of Devonshire, referred to above, spent thousands of pounds in the early 1760s to redesign the park and gardens of Chatsworth, removing the formal French-style gardens put in place by his great-grandfather the first Duke seventy years earlier, and replacing them with the freer 'landscape' style so characteristic of Lancelot 'Capability' Brown and his acolytes. Civil engineers as well as gardeners were required, and the duke spent over £900 in only sixteen months in 1760–61 in massive earth-moving activities.

Great wealth could be greatly expended in a wide variety of ways, only some of which survive to delight the eye of the modern tourist. Aristocratic entertainments, food and drink bills and the patronage of London's leading gaming establishments all indicated that great fortunes could be lavished as readily as they could be acquired, while money spent by the Whig oligarchy on court attendance, political duties and even the occasional expensive electoral contest could stretch the deepest pockets.

Some aristocrats, like the earl of Egremont on his model farm at Petworth, played at being gentlemen farmers when away from the House of Lords during the long summer and autumn recess. Smallish estates were kept in hand for the purpose, on which might be tried the latest experiments in crop rotation, artificial grasses or sheep and cattle breeding. The real work of the aristocratic estate, however, devolved on highly professional estate stewards. Some of these became influential figures almost in their own right, like the duke of Sutherland's agent, James Loch, who entered Parliament under his employer's patronage.

The landed gentry comprised an amorphous but not undefinable group of perhaps 12,000 or 13,000 families in 1780. Between them they owned half of England's land. They ranged from southern baronets worth £2,000 a year to northern gentlemen farmers living on no more than £250 or £300. Some northern gentry families, of course, were very wealthy. William Blackett, of humble origins in Durham in the late seventeenth century, became a successful merchant and entrepreneur in Newcastle-on-Tyne, with interests in coal and lead mining. He founded a successful Northumberland family. His third son received a baronetcy in 1690 and the Blacketts were frequently either mayors of Newcastle or high sheriffs of Northumberland during the eighteenth century. Sir Walter Blackett transformed Wallington Hall into the imposing Northumberland residence which testified to the powerful relationship between land and commerce in northern, as well as southern, England.

Most of the upper gentry were figures of first importance at county level sitting in Parliament either as knights of the shire or, like several from the Blackett family in Newcastle, for the large town which sustained their wealth. Most in the middle ranks were Justices of the Peace and as such the only representatives of established authority which ordinary country folk had dealings with in the course of their lives. Government for most people was overwhelmingly local government, concerned to uphold game laws prohibiting poaching or to administer poor relief to those whose incomes were insufficient to support their families. The wealth of the gentry had diversified somewhat since the late seventeenth century; some dabbled in government investments ('the funds') or associated with various business enterprises. But most of the gentry remained gentlemen farmers or, more frequently, gentlemen of some leisure yet modest pretensions and few of the social connections exploited by their betters.

Aristocracy, upper and middling gentry had better, or at least more profitable, things to do with their time than farm their own land. A minority took an active interest in agricultural developments; some even contributed articles on improved husbandry or stock-breeding to one of the specialist journals, like *Annals of Agriculture* or *Farmers Magazine* which proliferated from the 1780s. Most, however, sought reliable tenants to farm their lands. As the eighteenth century progressed ever more land was leased out. By 1790 only 10–15 per cent of all the cultivated land of England was owner-occupied. The remoter Highlands of Scotland, Wales and North-west England apart, Britain was a country substantially without peasant proprietors. Their successors, the tenantry, though wealth and status varied greatly, all held one thing in common which distinguished them from that peasantry which was numerically dominant in Europe: their horizons were bounded by the market, not by domestic production. They required to make a profit according to the terms of their leases and this necessitated productive agriculture.

Landlords usually provided farm buildings and funds for their upkeep in addition to the lands they leased. Tenants supplied working capital, farm stock and agricultural implements. The landlord–tenant relationship in eighteenth-century Britain stimulated productivity. Agriculture was perhaps 40–50 per cent more productive in 1800 than a century earlier with wool and mutton output doubled and grain production more than keeping pace with a population increase of some 70 per cent (180). Perhaps the most impressive aspect of British agricultural development at the time was its labour productivity. This was achieved by making more use of animals and fertilisers. The fact that Britain remained a net exporter of grain until the 1790s is powerful evidence for its agricultural efficiency. Specialization, which saw the emergence of Bedfordshire and Hertfordshire grains, Gloucestershire and Wiltshire cheeses, Lincolnshire and Leicestershire sheep, Kent hops, Somerset apples and vegetable production by market-gardening methods, was a response to growing pressure from urban markets.

Changes in agricultural organization profoundly affected its labour force which formed the wide base of the rural pyramid. Some small owner-occupiers and tenant farmers had been forced to sell up during the long run of low prices between 1730 and 1755. Most of these sank to swell the growing number of mere wage-labourers. As farming profits picked up, the varying fortunes of the landed (including the tenantry) and the non-landed became ever more apparent. It may be permissible to employ a crude geographical distinction here to qualify the generalization. In western parts of Britain, particularly the highland zone where pastoral agriculture predominated, relations between farmers and their labourers remained tolerably close, with many of the latter retaining some economic security as 'farm servants' hired for a specific, renewable period, usually of a year. Most farm servants lived in on the farm, eating at the same table as their employers. In eastern Britain, particularly those parts of the Midlands and East Anglia where arable agriculture had been most improved, the ratio of labourers to farmers, standing nationally at 2:1 in 1780, was higher and the labourers' circumstances less enviable. Improving tenant farmers were reluctant to employ labourers except at times such as haymaking and harvest when their labour was in most demand. In southern East Anglia, the South Midlands and those parts of the South-east outside the centripetal pull of London, underemployment of agricultural labourers was an increasing feature of the rural scene, and one exacerbated by population increase. After 1775 expenditure on poor relief began to rise alarmingly. As the rector of Barkham (Berkshire), David Davies, noted in 1787, labourers in his parish earned no more than 7–8s. (35–40p) a week; they were finding it increasingly difficult to make ends meet when prices rose.[3]

II

Labourers' living standards were directly dependent upon the extent of non-agricultural activity. Domestic industrial production was widespread in Britain but dominated by cloth manufacture based on wool and various woollen-based mixtures. Spinning and weaving in the home provided an important addition to the family budget and it is misleading to calculate living standards merely on the basis of the wages of the adult male. High-quality traditional woollen textile centres were long established in many parts of the country, particularly around Devizes, Melksham and Trowbridge in Wiltshire. Such centres of 'short wool' manufacture, producing broadcloths and white cloths, had been the backbone of Britain's premier export industry; in 1700 more than half of Britain's domestic exports had been of woollen cloth, though traditional broadcloths and kerseys were already being supplanted by lighter fabrics since European import duties on these were much lower. Late-seventeenth and eighteenth-century expansion involved a distinct shift towards long wools, serges and worsteds with greater regional concentration in production. Devon, early on, then East Anglia and, particularly, Yorkshire became the new centres. The small 'maisters' of the West Riding took an increasing share of the markets by producing narrow cloths and 'kerseys', diversifying later in the century into better-quality broadcloths and worsteds. As early as the 1720s Daniel Defoe enthused over the extensive employment for the entire family provided in the villages and out-townships around Halifax.[4] Yorkshire was almost entirely responsible for the woollen industry's growth rate of 13–14 per cent per decade between the 1740s and the 1770s. By 1780 wool provided employment for at least 750,000 people. Linen was Scotland's main manufacturing industry for most of the eighteenth century, its total production increasing about six-fold between 1730 and 1800 (19, i, 5).

Great expansion was also apparent in the metal trades. Iron had been smelted with coke since the early years of the century in Coalbrookdale on the banks of the Severn where the Quaker ironmaster Abraham Darby perfected the process. Iron technology made strides also in the Furness district of Lancashire, in South Wales and, from 1759, in the famous Scottish works at Carron near the mouth of the Forth. Ambrose Crowley's slitting-mill and forges for bar-iron manufacture in Sunderland used local fuel from the coalfields of Northumberland and Durham. Steel was made in coal-fired reverbatory furnaces from bar-iron and charcoal in South Yorkshire and on Tyneside. Exports of iron and steel manufactures increased eightfold during the first seventy years of the century. The major metal-working towns of Birmingham and Sheffield were important in their own right as respectively the third and eighth largest towns in England in 1775 [E.iii]; they were also important distributive centres for the industrial villages of the Black Country and Hallamshire with their wide variety of skilled nailmakers, chainmakers, cutlers and the like. Non-ferrous metals also offered expanding employment opportunities. Cornwall provided copper and tin; Derbyshire, Yorkshire, North Wales and Cumberland extracted lead. Iron smelting took place on the coalfields of South Wales and Lancashire.

Industrial advance usually implies urban growth. Britain experienced significant town development in the century before 1780, but by no means all of it was attributable to manufacturing. Provincial towns such as Bath, Cheltenham and Warwick grew both as leisure and luxury trading centres to accommodate the growing wealth of gentry, moneyed men, fund-holders and the professional classes. Bath, with 21,000 inhabitants in 1775, was the twelfth largest town in Britain at the beginning of our period [E.iii]. Ports expanded rapidly to cater for both overseas and domestic trade. It should be noted that it was far cheaper to transport bulky goods by sea to other parts of Britain than overland. Newcastle was predominantly a coal port, supplying London with most of its needs. Tin and copper also came to the capital by sea. West coast ports grew particularly fast, reflecting the enormous relative shift in overseas trade towards the Americas. Bristol almost doubled its population (30,000–55,000) between 1725 and 1775 while Liverpool, entrepôt of the slave trade between Africa and the West Indies, grew even faster (15,000–35,000).

In Scotland, Glasgow, which was not significantly involved in the slave trade, nevertheless expanded rapidly on the profits of the burgeoning tobacco trade, especially after the town landed a French re-export contract in the 1740s. By the early 1790s, Glasgow's population had risen to more than 60,000, and though it would not overtake Edinburgh for a further thirty years, it was already at the beginning of our period the third largest city in Britain and included an upper middle class of great wealth and increasingly apparent cultural diversity.

Only seven English towns had populations in excess of 30,000 in 1775; five were ports. Little Whitehaven, the late-seventeenth-century creation of the Lowther family stuck away on the remote Cumberland coast, profited immensely from handling Virginia tobacco in addition to Irish cattle and local coals. For a few years in the third quarter of the century the shipping tonnage it cleared was the third largest in Britain. Such success stories are exceptional, of course, but a growing trend towards a national economy could be perceived in these changes. Huge though it remained, the relative importance of London declined as provincial centres, both at the ports and inland, took over many of the functions which had been previously channelled through the capital. Not autonomous but interlocking regional economies were emerging. Even before the seismic shift represented by the Industrial Revolution, therefore, the relative centre of industrial and commercial gravity was moving towards the North and the West. In these years also experiments in business partnership, to maximize investment opportunities, were being developed; the lessons were to bear much fruit after 1780.

The first three-quarters of the eighteenth century witnessed on extraordinary degree of industrial development, albeit only at roughly half the pace which would be achieved after 1780. Most of those areas which were to form the great conurbations of mature industrial Britain – central Scotland, the North-east, South and West Yorkshire, South Lancashire, the West Midlands and South Wales – were already intimately involved in the changes. The term 'pre-industrial' is a grotesque misnomer for Britain in 1740 or 1750, let alone 1780. The developments sketched above provide the essential springboard for industrial take-off. More sources of employment alternative to agriculture emerge; these have a buoyant effect on general wage levels, thus improving living standards and purchasing power for ordinary workers; they stimulate the use and circulation of cash through all sectors of society; they necessitate the development of ever more sophisticated marketing and distributive centres. Even as early as 1700, only a minority of the population was solely dependent on agriculture as a source of employment. In short, Britain was the most developed nation on earth.

---

1. M. Grosley, *A Tour to London, or New Observations on England and its Inhabitants* (2 vols, 1772), i, pp. 66–7.
2. H. J. Habbakuk, 'English landownership, 1680–1740', *Ec. H. R.* 1st ser., x (1939–40), pp. 2–17.
3. D. Davies, *The Case of the Labourers in Husbandry* (1795), pp. 8–13.
4. D. Defoe, *A Tour through the Whole Island of Great Britain* (Everyman edn, 2 vols, 1962), ii, pp. 193–203.

CHAPTER 2

Britain in the early 1780s:
II Politics and government

I

Local and central government in England naturally reflected the social dominance of a landed aristocracy. Local government, from county level down to the parishes, was subject to little control from Westminster. The county Lord-Lieutenant was head of the local militia, but the post was also coveted because it symbolized social leadership. Lord-Lieutenants were usually the great magnates whose influence frequently spread across several counties. The second earl of Egremont was Lord-Lieutenant of Cumberland in the 1750s though he rarely visited his estates in the North-west; the third earl became Lord-Lieutenant of Sussex, where the main family holdings were situated. Family influence consolidated the major county appointments. While the duke of Portland was Lord-Lieutenant of Nottinghamshire, his son, the marquis of Titchfield, occupied the post for Middlesex. That great political manipulator of the eighteenth century, Thomas Pelham Holles, duke of Newcastle, held no fewer than three lord-lieutenancies, those for Middlesex, Westminster and Nottinghamshire while his heir, Henry Clinton, effectively inherited Nottinghamshire having already held Cambridgeshire for more than twenty years.

The Lord-Lieutenants controlled appointments to a wide range of subordinate offices in the shires and access to the great was a decided advantage for those seeking posts. In local as in central government most appointments were decided by patronage. A word in season to a man of influence was worth far more than merit or qualification and thus it was that an intricate filigree of clientage was fashioned from the top of society almost to the bottom and certainly to the level of clerk, overseer of the poor or vestry official in a particular parish. Men were appointed by personal recommendation; the value placed on that recommendation was determined by the social weight of the recommender. It was a profoundly conservative system depending on the stability of personal relationships and the acceptance of an intricate hierarchy of influence and power. At whatever level, a man who wanted a job implying status, however modest, needed a patron. Hence the frequency of 'begging letters' by or, more usually, on behalf of a prospective employee. To eighteenth-century men of property such approaches were not 'pushy'; they were as natural and appropriate a means of recruitment as the situations vacant columns in the quality press of our own day. Nor was the system so inimical to the advancement of merit as might be supposed. A man who recommended a client unqualified for the post to be filled lost credit with those upon whom he himself might have later cause to depend. The system was well suited to an oligarchy; it rewarded loyalty and it treated outsiders with suspicion.

However, it was sufficiently flexible and its operators on the whole sufficiently sensible to accommodate talented but indifferently connected aspirants for office. Ability, particularly if reinforced by the acquisition of a modest degree of wealth, was better satisfied than frustrated, and only rarely was a combination of ability and determination baulked for long provided the aspirant played by the rules.

In local government Justices of the Peace were by far the most important executive officers. In J. H. Plumb's memorable phrase they were the 'restless shuttles' of local administration. They acted not only as magistrates hearing an enormous range of both petty and serious cases but they were the acknowledged leaders of village society. They granted alehouse licences, supervised the workings of the Poor Law and might even fix minimum wage levels. Social leadership and judicial competence were in easy and natural accord. Village squires were automatically JPs, and as the eighteenth century wore on the tendency to appoint better endowed Anglican clergymen to the bench became more pronounced. An Act of 1732 restricted the magisterial bench to men with an estate of at least £100 a year but in most places such a mechanistic computation was otiose. The JPs were the leaders of the local community and Lord-Lieutenants and their deputies considered only men of sufficient weight.

Patronage in central government has been the subject of much greater study, but it was in most respects the natural outworking of principles at work in the shires. Around the great 'political' families – Pelhams, Grenvilles, Bedfords, Cavendishes, Rockinghams and the like – clustered young men anxious for careers in government or administration. Rivalry between these families for political influence also sharpened competition among their clients and, particularly during periods of governmental instability such as the 1760s or the early 1780s, many opportunities for advancement presented themselves. Naturally, an easy entry to the political world was found for kin of the politically powerful. William Pitt the Younger entered Parliament as soon as he was twenty-one and his great rival Charles James Fox, son of one of the most notoriously corrupt Paymasters-General of the Forces of the century Henry Fox, was elected in 1768 while still legally a minor. Able men initially outside the charmed circle could also find their way in. Edmund Burke, a Dublin lawyer who rose through the Rockingham connection to be the leading Whig party theoretician and party propagandist of his day, is only the most illustrious example of the career open to talent through aristocratic patronage.

The exercise of royal patronage had become an increasingly important factor in political life since George III became King in 1760. In the reigns of George I and George II opposition politicians gathered around the Prince of Wales in the expectation of rich reward when the old King died and the new one turned out his ministers. The politicians, however, tended to move in family groups. George III was determined to avoid 'faction politics' and exercised much more independent patronage than his grandfather and great-grandfather had done. Thus John Robinson, George III's official Secretary to the Treasury and unofficial election manager in the 1770s, and Charles Jenkinson, whose career would continue to flourish under Pitt the Younger and whose son and successor as earl of Liverpool would become one of Britain's longest serving Prime Ministers, made careers largely outside aristocratic patronage as 'king's servants'. Both men, however, had started in more orthodox fashion. George III's beloved earl of Bute had been Jenkinson's patron and Robinson had successfully managed Sir James Lowther's burgeoning electoral interests in Cumbria before moving to higher things.

Patronage granted favours but it also implied loyalty. When William Windham recommended the talents of Dr Horseley to his patron and now Prime Minister, the marquis of Rockingham, in April 1782 for the vacancy of Master of the Temple he was careful to assure the marquis that 'I can hardly have any wishes distinct from those of your Lordship'.[1] When Charles Abbot, later Speaker of the House of Commons, showed a disposition to support Pitt's proposals for increased taxation in 1798 he received a sharp reminder from the duke of Leeds, previously Pitt's Foreign Secretary but now replaced, that the duke's patronage had put Abbot into Parliament. 'Such being my opinion of this ill-judged, impolitic and violent measure, it must be needless to point out the conduct I most certainly wish any parliamentary friend of mine to adopt . . . I flatter myself with the hopes that you, my dear Sir, will not think it necessary to support it with your vote any further.[2]

II

By the early 1780s aristocratic politicians and their clients had been forcibly reminded that an eighteenth-century monarch need be no figurehead. Within broad limits the magnates had dictated to the first two Georges, who in any case had German as well as British concerns to occupy them. George III's determination to rule as well as reign was not totally successful, but he forcibly demonstrated how little statutory circumscription of royal power had been effected by the Revolution Settlement. In theory George could veto unpalatable parliamentary legislation, though he never did. More practically the Settlement left the monarch with the responsibility of choosing ministers and thus, by implication, policies. George had learned during the 1760s that he could not appoint men in whom Parliament had absolutely no confidence and he was embarked on the more subtle and fruitful manoeuvre of appointing ministers for whom parliamentary approval could, with skill in the management of royal patronage, be engineered. The policy implied a struggle between the King and those political landowners who had had things mostly their own way between 1714 and 1760 and in the early 1780s the outcome was uncertain. The main opposition group, the Rockingham Whigs, could undermine parliamentary support for the King's faithful servant Lord North, but in the face of royal disapproval they could not form a stable ministry themselves.

Stable ministers needed the support both of King and Parliament. Within Parliament, though it may seem paradoxical in view of the importance of the aristocracy, the more important House was the Commons. Commons influence was firmly grounded in economic power. Though most of the leading offices of State were held by peers who sat in the Lords, control over finance and taxation was vested in the Commons, its enduring and crucial reward for success in the seventeenth-century constitutional struggles with the Stuarts. Throughout our period, ministries led from the Lords faced difficulties which perhaps only Lord Liverpool's successfully surmounted. Chancellors of the Exchequer, though the office admittedly did not achieve the kudos it holds in the modern political system until the 1850s, were necessarily commoners. Most important of all, control over State revenue gave the Commons its ultimate sanction over ministers and the Crown, since no monarch's independent lands or private fortune could begin to rival the power to tax. The King could appoint, but it was not in his independent power to sustain. Stable government depended on a working relationship between monarch and Commons.

The paradox of Commons predominance in an age of aristocratic oligarchy is easily explained. The composition of the House of Commons was to a large extent determined by the patronage of the great landowners. The Commons was not democratically elected; indeed, a substantial proportion of its members never faced an election throughout their parliamentary careers. There was no uniform franchise, except the famous '40-shilling freeholders' of the English and Welsh counties which returned only 92 of the 558 members who sat in Parliament in 1780 [B.iv]. In the boroughs voting qualifications varied enormously from a tiny handful, like Westminster, Preston and Coventry, where most, if not all, adult males qualified to the far larger number in which voters numbered less than 100. In only 7 seats in 1830 did the electorate returning 2 borough members exceed 5,000 while in 77 seats it was below 100 (74, *19–20*). A small number of voters did not automatically mean a moribund political structure, however. In many constituencies, vigorous political life was sustained in meetings, through the local press and on the hustings. Far more people were actively involved in the representative process than might be assumed by counting lists of voters (31, 75). It was not wise to discount their contribution to local political life. An MP, however powerful his patron, needed to be aware of local concerns and often to minister to them if he wished for continued success. Charles Abbot was re-elected by the nineteen voters of Helston (Cornwall) in 1796, having agreed to contribute the handsome sum of 100 guineas towards rebuilding the Cornage Hall 'in a more convenient part of the town'. Eighteenth-century politics was rooted in patronage and 'influence'. However, it is at least arguable that, because of the lively political culture which was encountered in many English boroughs, a wider range of interests were accommodated before the parliamentary Reform Act of 1832 than immediately after it.

Nevertheless, the proportion of actual voters before 1832 was undeniably small. In 1780 it is doubtful if one Englishman in eight could vote; elsewhere in Britain the proportion was much lower. Much of Scotland could be considered a composite 'rotten borough' controlled by government election managers. Nor did seats reflect the distribution of population. The South, and particularly the South-west where the government controlled many small-port 'revenue boroughs', was grossly over-represented. Cornwall sent forty-four members to Westminster (one less than Scotland); Lancashire, on the threshold of its industrial revolution, sent just fourteen. None of Birmingham, Leeds, Manchester or Sheffield returned an MP, though it should be said that Birmingham's commercial interests frequently influenced the nomination to one of Warwickshire's two county seats.

The election of members from those seats with small electorates, therefore, was usually a matter of influence by the 'borough-monger', either peer or wealthy commoner. Frequently a contest was pointless since the borough was entirely at the disposal of one man. Between 1784 and 1831, fewer than one-third of all elections were contested [B.vii. 1]. Namier estimated that at the election of 1761, 111 Commons seats were either nominated to or heavily influenced by a peer and a further 94 by commoners (26, *148–9*). The Tory writer J. W. Croker calculated in 1827 that no fewer than 276 members were directly nominated by patrons. Estimates vary, but it is safe to assume that in the 1780s about half of Britain's MPs sat in Westminster because a patron had put them there. At the election of 1784 eight of the ten seats in Cumberland and Westmorland were controlled by the colliery magnate and landowner Sir James Lowther.

Such 'nominee' MPs were the nucleus of the House; from their number were drawn the professional politicians. The independent MPs, who numbered 200 or so, and who cast their votes entirely according to reason and conscience, tended to arrive late for the anyway short parliamentary sessions and to return early to their estates once spring turned to summer and the crops ripened. County members tended to be independent of political allegiance, proud to represent the landed property of their community. Their natural predisposition was to support the government if convinced of its general competence, but withdrawals of support could be decisive as Lord North found between 1778 and 1782 when the Rockingham Whigs converted many of them to motions highly critical of his administration.

Most MPs were men of substantial means. The most homogeneous social group was probably the sons of peers nominated to seats on their fathers' influence. Between 1780 and 1830 they comprised pretty steadily a fifth of the members, a far higher proportion than early in the eighteenth century. Other families, like the Blacketts of Newcastle whose fortune lay in coal and the brewing Whitbreads of Bedford, bought themselves into Parliament on the profits of their trade. There was always room for 'new men' who had succeeded in trade or commerce though few came from such humble origins as Benjamin Hammet, MP for Taunton from 1782 to 1800, who seems to have been the son of an ordinary tradesman of that town before making a banking fortune in London (25, *155*). About 100 MPs were returned whose primary source of income was the professions. Roughly 30 of the 558 in 1780 were practising barristers with 55 army and 25 navy officers. About 200 substantial landowners, not members of the aristocracy or their clients, were members; many of them representing county seats as 'knights of the shire' like Sir George Savile who served his Yorkshire constituents continuously and with sturdy independence for almost twenty-five years.

Despite its obviously, and intentionally, undemocratic basis the late-eighteenth-century House of Commons represented the various kinds of property effectively but not in equal proportions. Despite royal and aristocratic influence and management, no one group of politicians could ever control it by these means alone. Patronage and the profits of office were powerful bonds to party loyalty, but no government commanded enough to secure a parliamentary majority thereby. Governments needed to propitiate the independent MPs since votes were swayed by argument. In certain respects the unreformed Commons held important advantages over its modern successor. Its control over the executive was stronger, if rarely exercised, and its members were spared the mind-numbing tyranny of the three-line whip. If eighteenth-century elections only rarely effected significant changes of political complexion after 1715 an incompetent government could run into severe trouble from independent-minded men between elections.

Eighteenth-century party allegiance was tortuous and complex. A few crude generalizations must do duty for full discussion of the topic here. While political parties existed they lacked both the organization and the permanence of their late-nineteenth-century successors. They also depended far more on family connections. Allegiance to 'Whig' and 'Tory' which had been surprisingly, even frighteningly, tenacious between 1689 and 1714 on a range of political, religious, diplomatic, financial and constitutional issues slackened thereafter. The Tory leadership gambled heavily and unconstitutionally on a Stuart rather than a Hanoverian succession in 1714; in losing, the Tories were shunted to the wings of the political stage by the victorious Whigs.

Recent research has quite properly stressed that eighteenth-century Toryism retained both adherents and causes in the bleak Walpole-dominated years of the first two Georges, but the real struggle for office and its attendant pickings lay between feuding Whig magnates, from Sunderland, Stanhope and Walpole in the 1710s and 1720s through to Bedford, Grenville and Rockingham in the 1760s and 1770s (5). The battle for supremacy in Parliament was particularly fierce from the mid-1750s as Walpole's system, a mixture of crude and crafty corruption unique both in its command and its unsavouriness, was broken by the new pressures of the Seven Years War (1756–63) and the accession of George III (1760). George, who regarded party politics as the highest evil, was paradoxically responsible for strengthening party allegiances. Whig politicians, tasting extended opposition for the first time since 1714, branded the King's ministers and advisers Tories, hoping to condemn both them and him as the inheritors of a discredited tradition. Thus Lord North, the first Prime Minister to provide George III with a ministry which commanded both his support and a workable majority in the House of Commons, was called a Tory, though he always repudiated the title.

During the North government of 1770 to 1782 the role and functions of the opposition became much clearer. Led by the Rockingham group which included Fox, Portland and Burke, the opposition espoused a reform programme plausibly presented as a principled Whig attack on familiar targets: royal patronage and excessive monarchical power. For a few years before 1783 it could almost be said that an unusually large and united Whig opposition, with more than 100 adherents in the Commons, challenged a government, recognizably Tory at least in its concern for monarchical rights. Squabbles between the Whig lords which had characterized so much eighteenth-century 'debate', were pushed into the background by the great issues of the day – the War of American Independence and the role of the monarchy. The re-emergence of great issues after 1756 was also responsible for the growing vigour of political interchange outside Westminster, not just in London, but among both middle ranks and skilled working men in provincial towns like Birmingham, Sheffield and Norwich. The enervating poisons injected into the body politic by Walpole's system of 'management' were beginning to wear off; after 1760 the political nation was astir.

Just as Britain stood on the threshold of an industrial revolution which would change the face of the world more dramatically than any other event its army was losing a war to uppity American colonials who had the temerity to challenge the mother country's right to rule them. Far from bowing to superior military, naval and economic power, the colonists had maximized the advantages of fighting their kind of war on home terrain. When General Cornwallis surrendered his force to George Washington at Yorktown in October 1781 the last hope of preventing American independence vanished. Defeat profoundly affected political life. North, for twelve years the guarantor of George III's conception of proper government, resigned in March 1782. His departure initiated two years of grave instability during which the respective rights of King and Commons were unsettlingly rehearsed. Military reverses and the increased taxes to which war inevitably leads had loosened old allegiances; the resurgence of the Whig opposition and the brief efflorescence of parliamentary reform associations between 1778 and 1782 were both largely attributable to discontent provoked by war.

Worse, the war threatened the commercial well-being of the country. The volume of British exports, so buoyant for much of the century, declined by almost 20 per cent between 1772 and 1780; exports to the North American mainland, Britain's largest market outside Europe, fell off by almost a half. It is hard to say whether imperial pride or commercial complacency suffered the greater jolt from the turn of events in America. It is certain that military disasters and mercantile setbacks induced in those who did not stand to benefit politically a state of lugubrious introspection. Things were not so bad as they seemed, but to contemporaries the inheritance of William Pitt the Younger, called unexpectedly to office at the height of the crisis, was a sickly one indeed.

---

1. British Library, Dept. of Manuscripts, Add. MSS 37,873, ff. 1–2.
2. *Diary and Correspondence of Lord Colchester* (3 vols, London, 1861), i, pp. 124–6.

CHAPTER 3

'A nation restored': I Politics and finance under Pitt, 1784–1790

I

On 15 December 1783 Charles James Fox's bill to reorganize government and administration in India was defeated by eight votes in the House of Lords. Three days later, following a second adverse vote, George III, who had been fostering opposition to his own ministers in the Lords, dismissed the 'infamous' Fox–North coalition. Eight months earlier the King had accepted only with the most profound reluctance the necessity for such a ministry, an ill-assorted alliance between Lord North, the King's faithful servant from the 1770s, and the Rockingham Whigs, his most steadfast critics. His detestation of it never wavered and he now gave it immediate notice with a deep sense of satisfaction.[1] The Rockinghams took what they saw as this unwanted exercise of royal prerogative with aplomb. They believed their control of Parliament secure enough to prevent the formation of any alternative ministry not favourable to them. They awaited the trial of constitutional strength in the belief that the King's powers of appointment and dismissal of ministers would be revealed as an empty sham. The world would be safe for Rockingham Whigs; the King would be openly declared a cipher, a reluctant tool of the most politically determined faction among the great aristocratic families.

On 19 December William Pitt the Younger, son of the great Chatham, accepted the King's commission to form an administration. Surprised as they were by this expression of royal effrontery, the Rockinghams mingled astonishment with mirth. The new first Lord of the Treasury, despite his high political pedigree, was just short of twenty-four years and seven months old. He had been a Member of Parliament less than four years, nominated on the influence of the duke of Rutland for Sir James Lowther's Westmorland pocket borough of Appleby in December 1780 and taking his seat early in the following year. His ministerial experience was limited to the nine months from July 1782 to March 1783 that the earl of Shelburne's ministry survived; here he had served promisingly as Chancellor of the Exchequer. Promise was no substitute for experience, however, and Whig wags pointed delightedly to

A sight to make surrounding nations stare;
A Kingdom trusted to a school-boy's care[2]

Eighteenth-century wit soon supplied an appropriate sobriquet for the new ministry; Pitt's government was termed the 'Mince-Pie Administration', unlikely to survive the Christmas season.

Certainly, the auguries were less than favourable. The initial choice for Home

Secretary, Pitt's cousin Earl Temple, resigned office after four days and the Cabinet list published on 23 December inspired no confidence that the First Lord's inexperience would be appropriately counterbalanced by tried and weighty ministers. The irascible and unpredictable Lord Chancellor Thurlow apart, it had a mediocre and threadbare aspect. All, save Pitt, sat in the Lords [A]. More importantly, the Fox–North coalition remained in arrogant control of the Commons. Fox's India bill had passed the Lower House in November by a majority of more than 100 and the majority opposed to the King's new minister was variously computed at between 70 and 100. The Rockinghams mulled over their Christmas claret the most favourable moment to bring the young upstart down.

George III, never so politically inept as some historians believe or as contemporary political opponents incautiously calculated, was by the early 1780s an experienced operator. He postponed the dissolution of Parliament for three months after Pitt's appointment. This calculation set a considerable risk against a great opportunity. The risk was that the coalition's Commons majority would rapidly overbear the beleaguered First Lord and bring him expeditiously and impotently to resignation. George wagered that Pitt's ability as a clear-headed debater would enable him to stave off immediate embarrassment to buy time for opportunity. In the first three months of 1784, while Pitt showed his mettle in the Commons, the King's agents could exercise his still formidable electoral influence in his new minister's interest. If the ploy worked Pitt would face the electorate with a double advantage: the King's electoral clout would be silently put at his service and the First Lord could show the voters if not immediate achievement at least promise of future performance in the teeth of massive opposition.

The King's instincts proved sound. He continued his campaign against the Rockinghams in the Lords, urging peers personally that support for his position was vital for the continuation of constitutional government. The duke of Marlborough's support was canvassed in December 1783, for example, since victory for the opposition would 'reduce the Sovereign to a mere tool in its hands' (34). Pitt, meanwhile, was engaged in a war of nerves against Fox in the early weeks of 1784. The new Prime Minister concentrated on persuading independent members to resume their normal stance and support the administration. This task required both skill and tenacity in the circumstances, but if Pitt could chip away at the opposition majorities he could face the electorate at a time of the King's choosing with every prospect of success. He knew well enough that no Hanoverian government had actually lost an election; the longer he survived the more credible would be his case. Fox, knowing an election to be imminent, concentrated on the constitutional issues, particularly the impropriety of the King's flouting the septennial convention by calling an election before the 1780 Parliament had run much more than half its allotted span.

Pitt kept his nerve in the face of heavy initial defeats in the Commons. Support from independent members and also from some supporters of Lord North progressively cut opposition majorities of more than fifty until by early March 1784 Fox's attempt to postpone the Mutiny bill – effectively bringing government to a standstill – passed the Commons by only a single vote. In the face of inevitable defeat on the next occasion Fox let the bill pass. Though Rockingham adherents had remained reasonably solid as party allegiances hardened at a time of constitutional crisis, the Fox–North coalition was done.

The election of 1784 which followed at the end of March, hard upon Fox's capitulation, was a dual triumph [B.v]. Firstly, it confirmed George III's prerogative to choose his own ministers, even in the teeth of hostile opposition in Parliament, and have that choice confirmed by the electorate. John Robinson, the 'ratcatcher' with an unrivalled expertise in wheedling votes and fixing seats, having deserted his former master Lord North, managed this election in the King's interest. Secondly, and more important for subsequent developments, the 1784 Election demonstrated the importance of public opinion outside Westminster. The 'political nation' was stirring 'out of doors' and opinion for or against the King polarized on hustings throughout the land. Pitt's reputation as reformer and new broom helped him, rather than Fox, to take the lion's share of the radical vote. He had introduced a bill in 1783 to strengthen independent county representation in Parliament and stood pledged to return to the question as Prime Minister [B.i]. Pitt's greatest triumphs occurred in 'open' constituencies with large electorates, and particularly in Yorkshire, Norfolk and Berkshire where radical attacks against North's administration had been strongest between 1780 and 1782. By contrast, considering the scale of the national triumph, Robinson must have been a little disappointed at Foxite tenacity in certain 'manageable' boroughs. Nevertheless, the new government gained about seventy seats. Viscount Carmarthen opined that 'the elections went more favourably for government than its most sanguine friends could have imagined' (24, *154*).

It would be wrong, therefore, to see this election as a triumph for monarchical reaction. Fox's manoeuvres towards the sovereignty of the Commons had been unequivocally rejected; more than 100 of his supporters – 'Fox's Martyrs' – lost their seats in 1784. Pitt, however, stood both for the stability of government and for reform. There was no contradiction in this platform and voters perceived none. The healthy government majority was as much pro-Pitt as pro-George and more anti the old political gang than either.

Throughout his career, Pitt always asserted that he was not a 'party man'. He argued that the nation disliked government in the hands of party factions and cited the ministerial instability of 1782–84 as powerful evidence of its preference for honest dealing and patriotic appeal. Accordingly, in his public utterances Pitt frequently emphasized his service to the nation, his loyalty to the King and his distrust of faction. Unlike Rockingham, Fox and Portland, he never attempted to build up a party. His description of himself as an 'independent Whig' was more a statement of generalized support for the principles of the Glorious Revolution of 1688 than a specific commitment to a political party. During the eighteenth century, support for 1688 was generally taken to encompass liberty, patriotism and a viable working relationship between King and Parliament.

Pitt informed the King when the new Parliament met at the end of May that Fox was unable to muster even 150 votes against the government. George replied that this 'gives the most flattering appearance that business may be carried on with decency instead of that violence which disgraced the late Parliament and nearly overturned the Constitution'.[3] 'Decency' for George III implied absence of party wrangles; from 1784 until the unexpected outbreak of hostilities over the Regency issue in 1788 Pitt's decisive victory put party into the background. The Rockingham connection survived, even improving its organization in readiness for future battles, but party conflict paled before Pitt's determination to continue the King's government and rebuild the nation's fortunes. Fox, almost unseated after an enquiry into irregularities at the poll in his Westminster constituency, concentrated increasingly on local issues, recognizing the futility of attempting to repeat the contests of January to March 1784. As so often in the Hanoverian period, the fires of party division, which flared briefly on great constitutional issues, were dampened by cool ministerial expertise as Pitt maintained normal administrative and executive service.

II

Initially, Pitt owed much to George III. Quite apart from his electoral influence, George's household officers formed the nucleus of a government party in the Lords which usually outvoted the opposition by about two to one. Prominent also among the regular voting strength of the majority were the bishops, mostly trained political animals as in the days of Walpole and Bishop Gibson in the 1730s. Pitt's majority was buttressed also by the King's willingness to create new peers, a privilege specifically denied the Rockinghams in 1783. The new creations were mostly strong government supporters (30). No fewer than 119 new peerages were created or promotions within the peerage made during Pitt's administrations, these to an Upper House containing only 212 temporal peers at the end of 1783. Dilution there obviously was, but alarmist opposition propaganda that Pitt was ennobling time-serving hacks of little property or pedigree can be discounted. The bulk of the new creations were prosperous landowners becoming steadily richer with rising agricultural prosperity. Many, like Harewood, Pelham or Delaval, were also important borough-mongers who could consolidate Pitt's position in Lords and Commons alike. Sir James Lowther was created earl of Lonsdale in 1784. He effectively owned Whitehaven and the substantial mineral deposits underneath it as well as extensive lands in Cumberland, Westmorland and Surrey; it should also be recalled that it was he who provided Pitt with his first parliamentary seat before the Prime Minister settled to represent Cambridge University after 1784.

The new creations, which gratified ambition after a long period of frustration, ennobled few moneyed men or stock-jobbers who were not already substantial landowners. There was, of course, the usual small leaven of distinguished sailors (Howe, Collingwood and Nelson), soldiers (Dorchester and Wellesley), diplomats (James Harris and William Eden), colonial administrators (George Macartney) and lawyers (Lloyd Kenyon and Sir John Scott). Honours enabled Pitt both to reward service and to require loyalty. Few creations were so cynical as William Grenville's sudden elevation to the Lords in 1790 to supply secure leadership in the Upper House and pave the way for the troublesome Thurlow's eventual removal from office.

In view of the fact that the 1784 Election represented a rout of the King's enemies, it may seem surprising that George III so rarely occupied the centre of the political stage thereafter. The King had, after all, been active in various ministries since 1760 and his influence at particular points during the ministry of Lord North had been so great as to be of doubtful constitutional propriety. Relations with Pitt were to be of an altogether different order. If George was anyway content with a minor role, his new Prime Minister had no intention of relying on him more than constitutional practice necessitated. The relationship between the two men was correct, punctilious and distanced. Cabinet minutes reached the King punctually; the King responded in courteous fashion, rarely suggesting new initiatives or questioning decisions. By the mid-1780s, George III was a dutiful and experienced, if limited and obstinate, monarch. Pitt knew on what matters the King was not to be crossed and usually found it unnecessary to compromise either his programme or his principles by doing so. For his part, the King knew enough of bad ministries by 1784 to recognize a good one when he saw it and was wise enough not to interfere. He did not even jib at Pitt's institution of a statutory enquiry into the management of Crown revenues in 1786–87, an initiative which brought the civil list under greater parliamentary control than ever before.

George saw in Pitt a long-term salvation from the pretensions of the Rockinghams; Pitt knew well enough that he still needed royal support and was grateful that the enjoyment of it did not significantly impede his actions. The occasional conflicts were more usually over personality than policy. Pitt persuaded a reluctant monarch to drop Lord Thurlow from the Cabinet in 1792; George, however, stuck both to his prerogative and his better judgement in refusing to make Pitt's old tutor, Bishop Tomline, archbishop of Canterbury in 1805. It is ironic that Pitt's resignation in 1801 should have been on one of those rare issues of principle – the religious question in Ireland – on which the two differed.

George continued to support Pitt on almost all essentials though mental instability reduced his direct contribution after 1788. Not surprisingly, he was in close agreement after 1793 on the need to humble republican France and preserve the remaining crowned heads of Europe from the fate of Louis XVI. By the time the Prince Regent took over in 1812, reforms in the patronage system, begun by the Rockinghams in the 1780s to curb royal influence and continued by Pitt in his unremitting search for administrative efficiency, had permanently deprived the monarchy of that 'means to reward services' on which eighteenth-century government had so largely depended. This dismantling of the old patronage network permanently deprived the monarch of a central, directing role. Although Fox's doctrine that the Commons had sole right to make and unmake ministries seemed to have been decisively rejected in 1784, therefore, it was *de facto* practice long before George III was dead. Paradoxically, in view of the reasons for William Pitt's accession to power, the First Minister himself was largely responsible. It may seem bizarre, and it is certainly too simple, to argue that Pitt the Younger destroyed the powers of the monarchy, but the observation contains more than a grain of truth.

From 1784 to 1788 Pitt assumed an easy command over Parliament. On most major issues of policy opposition was muted, though automatic endorsement could never be guaranteed. Between 1784 and 1786, the Prime Minister was defeated on four issues. He failed to persuade the Commons that the scrutiny of the Westminster election result was anything more than a hounding of Fox; the Dublin Parliament refused to endorse reciprocally lowered customs duties with Ireland; George III used his influence against Pitt's moderate parliamentary reform proposals in 1785 [B.i.1]; and an expensive proposal by the duke of Richmond to strengthen dockyard defences in 1786 was outvoted. This last defeat was the less surprising since at least three of Pitt's Cabinet opposed the measure. These reverses show that Pitt's power was not unlimited; they also suggest that after his baptism of fire from December 1783 to March 1784, the First Lord served an apprenticeship during which he learned that proposals to which he attached considerable personal importance were not essential to his long-term strategy. Professor Ehrman is perhaps over-sanguine when he argues that the defeats 'are significant not because they threatened his position, but rather because they suggested how he might buttress its strength' (35, *236*); Pitt felt his defeats keenly but learned from them not to make the same mistake twice. The politician whose early reputation had been made as a supporter of parliamentary reform, for example, was not tempted to promote the question again from the Treasury benches; by the 1790s he had become one of its most steadfast opponents.

III

Particularly in view of his later reputation as a defender of the established order it is important to remember that Pitt brought to his tasks the vigour of youth and the mind of a cautious reformer. He rapidly acquired a detailed knowledge of the country's administrative machinery, an accomplishment rare in eighteenth-century politicians. This mastery of detail made him a formidable opponent in debate and enabled him to embark on his task of reconstruction with confidence.

Pitt's reforms in finance and administration were aimed at making Britain stable and creditworthy. In 1783, government expenditure exceeded income by £10.8m. Though expenditure on the armed forces, the lion's share, would fall with peace terms concluded, it was worrying that income to the Exchequer was actually falling, largely because excise duties had fallen by almost £1m. in the last year of the American War [D.i.1]. It was also increasingly difficult to raise loans; a total collapse of confidence precipitating national bankruptcy was not out of the question.

Pitt's initial priority was to raise revenue, his first target the smugglers. It is impossible precisely to quantify the extent to which contraband cheated the revenue, but most recent estimates suggest that between 3 and 4½m. tons of tea alone found their way illegally into the country each year in the early 1780s, undermining the finances of the East India Company in the process (178). Perhaps one-fifth of all imports were smuggled. Pitt extended rights of search over suspect cargoes but also moved to reduce the attractiveness of smuggling at source. He embarked on a massive reduction of duties. Acting on a plan conceived when he was Chancellor in Shelburne's government, he reduced the duty on tea from 119 per cent to a uniform 25 per cent by his Commutation Act in 1784. The revenue thus lost was recouped partly by a graduated rise in the tax on windows aimed primarily at luxury dwellings. Revenue would also increase as far more tea entered the country by orthodox channels: between 1786 and 1788 the amount passing through customs more than doubled.

The Commutation Act presaged further reductions in duty, especially on wines and spirits, and a general tightening up on revenue agencies, with more business transferred to the excise department. By 1790 the yield to the government on wines had increased by 29 per cent, on spirits by 63 per cent and on tobacco by 39 per cent. By 1792, when Pitt presented his last pre-war budget, he could claim that his period in office had seen an extra £1m. added to the revenue by destroying the profitability of smuggling, £1m. by the imposition of new taxes and £2m. by additional consumption 'attributed to the best of all causes – a general increase in the wealth and prosperity of the country'.[4] In that year total net income was 47 per cent higher than in 1783 and the Exchequer enjoyed a surplus of £1.7m. Tax revenue increased over the same period by about 50 per cent, and the proportion raised by direct taxation declined slightly. At about 17 per cent, direct taxes produced as small a proportion as at any time in the eighteenth century.

The new taxes to which Pitt referred represented little more than a shuffling of the Hanoverian pack; innovation lay in the increased efficiency with which they were collected. Pitt accepted prevailing orthodoxy on taxation: all should bear a share, but the poor should not be overburdened. Taxes should fall disproportionately on luxuries. Thus the odd, but characteristic, imposts on pleasure horses, hackney carriages, gloves, servants and hair powder. Pitt's only true innovation in this area – a tax on shops levied in 1785 – failed. It occasioned disturbances in the capital, provoked burnings of the Prime Minister in effigy and was withdrawn in 1789.

Pitt had inherited huge debts when he took office. More worrying than the size initially, however, was the fact that an increasing proportion of Britain's debts were short-term unsecured, or, unfunded, debt. Bills issued by the government to cover these obligations were marked at a discount of more than 20 per cent. The fact that Pitt was able to 'fund' so much of this in 1784–85 by persuading investors to buy government stock at 5 per cent indicates how much business confidence was revived by the mere fact of peace. The size of Pitt's election victory, promising stable government, also undoubtedly helped.

With unfunded debt back to manageable proportions, Pitt could afford a longer-term policy. Interest charges on the national debt amounted to about a quarter of government expenditure in the 1770s and Pitt wished to reduce its total burden by redemption through a sinking-fund. By this device, annual sums were set aside for government stock to pay off debts. Naturally, the scheme depended on a regular surplus of income over expenditure and this Pitt could begin to guarantee by 1786 when the fund came into operation. As in other areas of public finance, Pitt made other men's ideas work. A Hanoverian sinking-fund had been fitfully in operation from 1716 to the early 1770s, but it was never proof from raiding by ministries in need of ready cash and did not significantly reduce the size of the debt. The transfer of regular annual sums was of the essence for Pitt who had been much influenced by Richard Price's *Appeal to the Public on the Subject of the National Debt* (1772). In this work Price, a leading Unitarian intellectual, had examined the principles of compound interest whereby a regularly supported and inviolate fund would rapidly diminish and eventually extinguish the debt. Pitt did not adopt Price's elegant but potentially unpopular refinement of increasing taxes to finance upward conversion of stock in order to run down the capital of the debt more quickly. The intellectual progenitor of the Pitt sinking-fund, however, was Price: the exchequer was required to give priority to the fund in making its dispositions; a separate body of commissioners was established to manage it; and the fund was to be inviolable, enabling compound interest to work its miracles.

Pitt's plan was all too successful: £10¼m. of stock was rapidly acquired and the debt began to run down. Disarmed by the seductive logic of compound interest, the government forgot that the entire scheme was predicated on the provision of a regular annual surplus. Foolishly, and in Pitt's case probably obstinately, it continued to believe that the magic could still work as wartime deficits mounted. After 1793, the sinking-fund survived only as an anachronistic talisman, redundantly repaying debt when far larger sums were required on less favourable terms. It expired in the 1820s, unlamented and in an advanced state of decrepitude. Yet its unfortunate end should not obscure the important role it played in restoring the confidence of investors in Britain's recovery during the later 1780s.

Pitt's restrained reformism is nowhere better in evidence than in the sphere of administration. Government posts had provided much of the lubrication for the patronage machine. 'Offices of profit' were often rewards for political service or pledges for compliant behaviour to come. If relatively few were absolute sinecures, the need for government to dig deep into patronage resources to cover the maximum variety of political contingencies ensured that posts should be in reasonably plentiful supply, though never enough to ensure satisfaction for all suitors. The result was grossly inefficient deployment of resources. Over-administration in some departments was on such a scale as to make even National Health Service Trust managers in the mid-1990s blink; others, such as excise, were rather thinly manned and badly deployed. Since the system had developed to satisfy political rather than administrative criteria, the end-product is not surprising. A thoroughgoing radical would have hacked at it root and branch and the Rockinghams showed some signs in 1782 that they might wield the axe when revenue officers and those holding government contracts were debarred from sitting in Parliament.

Pitt's methods were more circumspect. He built up efficient departments piecemeal by giving them more work to do and transferring officials from one branch of the service to another when opportunity arose. The Board of Taxes, stiffened by transfers from the Treasury, and the Excise Board, whose central establishment was increased by 35 per cent between 1783 and 1792, were favoured in this way. Men with talent, which Pitt was quicker than most Prime Ministers to spot, like Richard Frewin at customs, Corbyn Morris and Samuel Mead, were advanced and encouraged to formulate their own policies. Frewin was the guiding light behind the consolidation of customs duties in 1787, perhaps the most valuable administrative reform of all since it cleared the decks for much keener control. Customs and excise together, with central staffs totalling about 600, were responsible for collecting two-thirds of government revenue. Frewin's career continued almost until the end of the reign, during which time he introduced further refinements to increase revenue.

Pitt did not tilt at windmills. He understood the entrenched power of vested interest and preferred to bypass it rather than mount a frontal challenge. Thus, though he abhorred waste, he did not deal with overmanning by wholesale sackings. Though urged by the public accounts commissioners in 1786 to abolish 180 redundant sinecure offices, Pitt preferred to wait for their occupants' death when each office automatically lapsed. By 1792, twenty-eight of the offices had fallen vacant. Pitt was to remain in office for eleven of the next fourteen years; by his death most had been wiped out and the logic of his long-term strategy was inexorably apparent. He had avoided the danger of a humiliating reverse at the hands of a league of patronage-mongers, yet their power was still perceptibly reduced. Lord Liverpool, the next long-serving Prime Minister, was to remark that Pitt had all but destroyed the patronage network, and in consequence had put government on an entirely different footing. Most important of all, royal patronage was no longer sufficient either to elevate or to sustain a minister not already powerfully supported in Parliament.

Any reform of administration which left the armed services untouched would be a botched job. The cost of army, navy and ordnance was more than two and a half times greater than the combined cost of all civilian administration. Here, too, there was considerable tightening, with particular concentration on the navy which Pitt rightly saw not only in military but in commercial terms. As with the excise department the First Minister would spend rather than save when he could do so without waste. The naval establishment was raised from 15,000 to 18,000 and between 1784 and 1790 thirty-three new ships of the line were built. Though Pitt took a close personal interest in naval administration, he relied heavily on its Comptroller, Sir Charles Middleton, one of the great public servants of eighteenth-century England, and a protégé originally of Lord North. Middleton, later Lord Barham, was largely responsible for reorganizing a navy equipped to surmount its severest challenge in the French Wars of 1793–1815 and Pitt was prepared to back his judgement against that of the First Lord of the Admiralty, Lord Howe. It was over a dispute with Middleton that Howe resigned in 1788. The navy would have been subject in all probability to still more radical reform – promotion by merit and seniority, salaries instead of fees and perquisites, a fortified Navy Board – had not the Regency crisis (see Ch. 7) diverted Pitt from adopting Middleton's proposals on these lines.

In establishing his position was Pitt merely the lucky beneficiary of circumstances? Certainly the independent country gentlemen were willing to throw their support behind any minister who represented a clean break with the constitutional affronts of 1782–83. Certainly, too, the underlying strength of the British economy, masked by the dislocations of war, became apparent once the Treaty of Versailles was signed; commercial prosperity was a much more important factor than financial dexterity in helping Pitt to balance the books. The young minister came into a more powerful inheritance than was apparent in December 1783.

Almost the lucky beneficiary, therefore, but not quite. Pitt's gifts exactly matched the needs of the first decade of his premiership. His amazingly – and to opponents alarmingly – professional grasp of the complex administrative and financial issues of the day enabled him to harness the energy and dynamism of the British economy. Though industrialists and financiers might take issue with him on particular matters – taxing shops, or giving reciprocal trading concessions to Ireland – they grew to acknowledge that he, more than any other politician, understood the terms of trade and sought to run an administration which would not hinder their pursuit of profit. That same grasp of detail, allied to a clearheaded, even glacial, delivery made him a formidable opponent in debate. His phenomenal capacity for work enabled him to take on talented but more dilettante opponents almost single-handed. It was soon perceived that Pitt's administration, anyway overloaded with peers, included a number of commoners unable to pull their weight on the floor of the House; yet with Pitt present it did not matter. The Prime Minister's watchword was efficiency, his bane, waste. Such concerns inspire respect rather than love both in admirers and the politically uncommitted. Yet they were perfectly attuned to Britain's needs as the country recovered from a disastrous war and began to realize its industrial and commercial opportunities.

---

1. The marquis of Rockingham died in July 1782. The political alliance of which he was the head retained cohesion through the 1780s, however, and it is convenient to retain the title 'Rockingham Whigs', the more so since nominal leadership passed to the duke of Portland, and the term 'Portland Whigs' is used to describe the group which allied with Pitt in 1794.
2. *Criticisms on the Rolliad*, p. 21, quoted in J. Ehrman, *The Younger Pitt: The Years of Acclaim* (1969), p. 128.
3. A. Aspinall, ed., *The Later Correspondence of George III* (5 vols, Cambridge, 1966), i, p. 83.
4. *Parl. Hist.*, 1st ser., xxix col. 830.

CHAPTER 4

'A nation restored': II Overseas trade and foreign affairs

I

Britain's prosperity depended on overseas trade. As an island protected by Europe's largest and most potent navy whose efficiency was a prime concern of successive governments, it could afford to give lower priority than its rivals to dynastic and strategic struggles on the mainland of Europe. Britain was thus well situated to develop colonial markets and commercial trade routes outside Europe. Directors of the East India and South Sea Companies and the Committee of West Indian Planters and Merchants all had ready access to powerful politicians to press their interests. London merchants remained an important lobby as they sought to preserve that mutually beneficial alliance with the Whigs which had survived since the late seventeenth century. The 'sugar interest' or the 'shipping interest' could prove decisive, as Walpole had found to his cost when reluctantly driven to declare war with Spain in 1739.

Indeed, Britain's involvement in each of the four wars fought between 1739 and 1783 was primarily for commercial ends; its rivals could rarely claim as much. In the third of these – the Seven Years War masterminded by Chatham – the distinction was all important. While the Continental powers were fighting primarily for European political and dynastic prizes, Britain took the opportunities offered both in the West and the East. By 1763, Canada had been won from the French; British influence in India was paramount; naval supremacy guaranteed British dominance of the lucrative slave, sugar and carrying trades between West Africa, the West Indies and the mother country; the mainland American colonies were protected from damaging incursions by France or Spain. Britain had emerged as the first trading nation of the world.

Yet twenty years later all seemed set at hazard. The American colonists' successful struggle for independence threatened to deprive Britain of its leading market for manufactured goods. The loss of America was widely regarded as an unmitigated disaster which threatened to unhinge the entire complex of interlocking colonial and commercial activity outside Europe. Within Europe, Britain's isolation was forcibly emphasized not only by French and Spanish aid for the Americans from 1778 and 1779 respectively but by the 'Armed Neutrality' of the northern powers in defiance of Lord North's attempts to redress the diplomatic balance. It is true that in 1783 Britain ceded little to her European adversaries [F.i]; the balance of colonial power, shifted in Britain's favour by the Peace of Paris in 1763, was not much affected. But little solace was taken from the fact; Pitt's inheritance overseas seemed as uninviting as that at home.

31

II

The end of the American War had left Britain starkly isolated in Europe. This isolation was emphasized by the establishment of a close French alliance with the Dutch in 1785 involving the overthrow of the Anglophil House of Orange and threatening European markets via the Scheldt. In so far as Britain possessed a consistent European strategy it was to challenge any French incursions in the Low Countries. Since the Prussians, allies of 1755–63, felt a similar unease, a concerted effort to revive the fortunes of the House of Orange was easily managed. A successful Prussian military incursion into Holland in 1787 was followed by the signing of a Triple Alliance between Prussia, the United Provinces and Britain [F.i]; this gave Britain a diplomatic standing in Europe it had lacked since the Seven Years War. The death of Frederick the Great and the succession of the far less able Frederick William II helped Britain to sway Prussia and employ the alliance as a sword of Damocles over the Bourbon Family Compact which held France and Spain in increasingly flaccid alliance. The solidity of the Triple Alliance enabled Britain to assert itself in the North Pacific in 1790 when Spain attempted to recapture its old authority in the New World and seized ships from a British trading base for fish and furs at Nootka Sound, off western Canada. The resolution of the crisis, which briefly threatened war, saw the ships returned, trading rights confirmed and Spain humiliated. This crisis also confirmed France's inability to aid its family ally. Louis XVI's attempts to equip his navy to support Spain were nullified by the French National Assembly, which refused to intervene.

There is some evidence that Pitt's able diplomatic envoys, particularly Sir James Harris at the Hague and William Eden in Paris, harboured delusions of a British hegemony in Europe founded on the successes of the Triple Alliance and the eclipse of France during its financial crisis in the 1780s and the early stages of the revolution which followed. Such fanciful notions may even have turned Pitt's head for it is difficult to find a rational basis for his threats to Russia in 1791 over the Black Sea port of Ochakov, which that country had captured in December 1788 during a brief war with the Turks. Britain, fearing Russian expansion through the Black Sea into southern Europe and the Mediterranean, used the alliance to demand Russian removal from the port. Catherine the Great was an altogether wilier and tougher antagonist than Pitt had yet encountered and she called British bluff. By the time she made her own, unforced, peace with Turkey, British threats had long been humiliatingly withdrawn.

Most unusually, Pitt left his domestic front unguarded. Fox was able to capitalize on the Russophil sentiments of the Whigs. For a couple of weeks in April, during which the duke of Leeds resigned as Foreign Secretary in protest at Pitt's surrender, Fox believed himself in realistic contention for office. A friend informed Auckland in May 1791 that: 'The country throughout have told Mr Pitt they will not go to war.' A party leader with cleaner hands than Fox would have had 'little difficulty in getting into office'.[1]

The Ochakov incident in itself is trivial. Yet, in broader context, it contributed towards increasing British hostility towards Russia. Fear of Russian expansionism would dog and pervert British foreign policy for much of the nineteenth century. It also curbed the ambitions and influence of Harris and James Ewart, the Ambassador to Berlin who exaggerated it into a major disaster and it put the Triple Alliance into realistic perspective. Within months the greed of Prussia, Austria and Russia in pursuing the further dismemberment of Poland, begun in 1772, destroyed the alliance altogether. Britain remained isolated, though diplomatically of more weight, in 1793 as in 1783.

Britain's partial rehabilitation in Europe is one thread in the Continental policy of this period; trade is the other. Pitt's policies over trade were not novel except in the scale on which he worked. Envoys were despatched to all the leading courts of Europe to negotiate reciprocally lowered tariff duties. The Foreign Secretary, Carmarthen (later duke of Leeds) spoke dismissively and uncomprehendingly about 'the present Rage for Commercial Treaties' (35, *478*). He feared that scrabbling in the market-place would reduce the nation's *gravitas* on the world stage. The fact that most of the embassies came to nothing, despite eight years and more of negotiation with Spain, Portugal and Russia, is evidence enough that British-protected markets would not be relinquished without adequate counter-attractions. There was no headlong rush along the new highway of free trade.

The Eden trade treaty with France, signed in September 1786, is the only solid achievement of the policy and that a temporary one. For just over six years, till war destroyed the fragile experiment, French wines entered Britain at the same preferential rates as the Portuguese. Manufacturers' opposition kept the market for silks heavily protected. France was opened to British manufactured goods in a general tariff reduction of 10–15 per cent. It was a small enough concession, but one which the northern manufacturers were well placed to exploit. Within three years, French manufacturers were moaning that the treaty had been unfairly weighted in favour of their traditional enemies. It seemed so because of the keen competition from British ironmasters and mill owners in the early stages of industrialization. Though the virtual collapse of the French economy in the mid-1780s was a hindrance to British exporters, the Eden treaty gives the first hint of that concealed monopoly which Britain was to enjoy as it became the world's first industrial nation. The liberalization of trade was bound to favour the most efficient producers; Britain's later commitment to free trade by no means represented an intellectual conversion to a persuasive doctrine. British manufacturers were backing a horse which could not lose. Significantly it was those manufacturers using new techniques which supported the treaty. Even as early as 1786, fears of the smaller and more specialist producers in the South that freer trade would harm them split the General Chamber of Manufacturers and destroyed its effectiveness as a pressure group.

The General Chamber had come into being in March 1785 to protest against Pitt's determination to establish a customs union between Britain and Ireland. With duties to be set at the lower, Irish, rate, Pitt explained to the duke of Rutland, Lord-Lieutenant of Ireland: 'We open to Ireland the chance of competition with ourselves, on terms of more than equality, and we give her advantages which make it impossible she should ever have anything to fear from the jealousy and restrictive policy of this country in future'.[2] Pitt's plan was part of a grand design to secure 'permanent tranquillity' in Ireland on the basis of mutual commercial interest. What English manufacturers saw was a threat, particularly to the wool trade, from low-wage Irish competition. The establishment of this first industrial pressure group was the result. It is not without irony that its first chairman was the master potter Josiah Wedgwood, a passionate exponent of freer trade with Europe, where the balance of advantage was more obviously tilted in Britain's favour. Though the *coup de grâce* was delivered in Dublin by the Irish Parliament's refusal to contribute to the costs of imperial defence, industrial opposition would have made the plan extremely difficult to operate. Irish problems after this setback were to bedevil Pitt periodically during the rest of his career.

Though the Eden treaty undoubtedly stimulated trade, more important factors were the return of peace in 1783 and the early exploitation of Britain's industrial potential. Northern and Midland industrialists could undercut the world in a range of manufactured goods. The value of British trade to Europe almost doubled between 1783 and 1792 during which time a trading deficit of £2½ m. was converted into a surplus of almost £2m. The value of the diplomatic scurrying between the courts of Europe in enthusiastic pursuit of commercial accord may be doubted. The motivating principle, in any case, was not economic liberalism but self-interest.

The commitment to 'Empire' remained central to British government policy for most of the eighteenth century. Here, as in much else, Pitt continued the policies of his predecessors (150). For much of the century, press discussion about the value and virtue of empire had concentrated upon colonies as essential for commercial prosperity, and commercial prosperity as the foundation of national power and self-esteem. Hence the extraordinary care lavished by successive governments on the navy; naval supremacy was rightly perceived as the linchpin of that profitable imperial-commercial nexus which had grown with such extraordinary vigour since the Treaty of Utrecht ended the wars with France in 1713. Hence also the importance attached to administrative efficiency at the Navy Board throughout the century and the commitment to naval expansion during the decade after the loss of the American colonies. Despite the considerable taxation and debt burdens produced by the American war, Pitt's government committed itself to restocking the navy during the 1780s. Commercial tonnage also expanded rapidly. Between 1760 and 1792, British-owned shipping tonnage increased from 600,000 to 1.5m. (156, 88) and by 1787 Lord Hawkesbury, Pitt's President of the Board of Trade, could draw the obvious strategic conclusion: 'The navigation of this country is so well protected at present by the laws that are made to favour it, as well as by the excellence of our ships and sailors that nothing in my judgement is to be apprehended from the rivalship of the French in this respect' (156, 96). Pitt, therefore, placed more reliance on the solid base of the mercantile marine than on ephemeral trade treaties. Ultimately, his trust lay in solid oak not diplomatic parchment.

III

In the trade expansion of the eighteenth century the Americas had assumed a pivotal role. The old colonial system, based on heavily protected markets and rigidly regulated trade between colonies and the mother country for the benefit of the latter, was threatened by the liberation of the eastern seaboard states. The assumption was that the newly independent colonies must be cut out of the imperial economic system. After 1783, the United States were seen as a threat to British naval and mercantile supremacy in the New World. Thus, when West Indian sugar planters, threatened by moves to bar US shipping from their ports, petitioned the government in 1784 to allow trade to continue in 'all such lumber, provisions and other produce . . . as might legally have been so imported or exported . . . before the late war',[3] they were rebuffed. Orders in Council prohibited direct trade between the sugar islands and the mainland and Pitt's new Committee of Trade, under the influence of Charles Jenkinson, George III's political adviser, rejected the ideas of Shelburne and the new school of economists who wished to reduce trade barriers. Trade with the USA was not to be reciprocal. Any threat to British naval and mercantile supremacy in the New World would be strenuously resisted. West Indian merchants were to be cut off from their main timber supplies and could trade their molasses only in British ships.

The sugar interest, whose importance was in decline after a century at the very heart of commercial concerns, learned that its well-being came second to that of shipping. The West Indies remained a secure market for British manufactured goods – metals and high-priced luxuries for the planters, cheap textiles for their slaves; annoyance at inflexibility in London could to a degree be braved. The shipping interest, however, required nurture after American independence. About one-third of the British merchant fleet in the early 1770s had been built in the thirteen colonies. Britain had therefore lost not only a substantial source of revenue; the United States retained an important shipping interest of its own.

The interests of the planters were not entirely ignored, of course. Their desperate need for provisions could not be met by the Canadians, as the government had fondly hoped, and from 1787 a 'free port' system was introduced to permit small American vessels to trade in carefully regulated necessities, mostly raw materials. The concession benefited Britain in that it stimulated recovery in the West Indies, thus enabling planters to take more from Britain. After virtual stagnation in the 1780s, exports to the West Indies trebled in the 1790s.

Jenkinson's orthodox protectionist policy towards trade in the Americas was further indicated by the passage of the last great Navigation Act in 1786. Its purpose was to encourage domestic shipbuilders by confining colonial trade to British ships and defining 'British' strictly. Its prime aim was to disadvantage United States' carriers particularly in those northern states which, like Massachusetts, had precipitated the War of Independence. Jenkinson's calculations were commercial rather than vindictive. If the USA could be prevented from developing a mercantile marine of threatening proportions, so the argument ran, the effects of colonial deprivation might be turned to positive account. As Jenkinson told the Commons, 'if proper means could be devised to secure the navigation trade to Great Britain, though we had lost a dominion, we might almost be said to have gained an empire' (35, *339*).

The Navigation Act was one of many issues which preserved glacial diplomatic relations between Britain and the USA after 1783. Commercial advantage on both sides of the Atlantic, however, pulled in other directions. Before independence the seaboard states had been the largest market for British manufactured goods. The Treaty of Versailles, as the Americans quickly discovered, did not alter economic facts; indeed, the speed of Britain's development in its early industrial phase only confirmed the pattern. No country could match British variety, quality and cost. By 1785 British exports to the USA were back to the levels achieved in the early 1770s. American protection in the late 1780s and early 1790s acted only as a minor irritant, though tariffs were used to exercise political leverage on Britain as well as to rectify an alarming trade deficit. After 1793, with Britain involved in a European war which had colonial implications in the West and with Jenkinson (now ennobled as Lord Hawkesbury) overshadowed by the influence of Grenville and Dundas, the Americans discovered more sympathetic ears in Whitehall. The Jay treaty of November 1794 opened certain markets to American shipping and ended mercantile discrimination for a period of ten years. Before long, the prized West Indian markets were further opened to the Americans. The effects were dramatic; Britain's exports to the USA more than doubled between 1793 and 1799 (152, 227–8). Crucial also was the development of the cotton trade which at last provided the United States with a secure market for its raw materials [D.ii.2; iii.1]. By 1800, the USA was taking more than a quarter of British exports; the Americas together accounted for about a half. Economic logic, as much as the exigencies of war, dictated a more liberal policy towards the USA.

Canada, though still British, offered less glittering prizes but its furs, fish and, above all, its timber were not to be despised. Though its scattered population of 300,000 offered a smaller market for the British manufacturer it did contain a significant number of *émigré* Loyalists. Canada assumed greater strategic importance after 1783 as a barrier to possible American expansion and as a counterweight to Anglophobia in the United States. Grenville's separation of Upper and Lower Canada in 1791 [F.iv.2] reflected growing British concern for the colony and also an imprecise but genuine desire to mingle colonial direction with a measure of local self-determination. More precise was the desire to stifle any possible independence movements north of the Great Lakes.

IV

It was natural that the loss of the American colonies should focus government attention on the East, where markets were less well developed but possessed great potential. Britain imported large quantities of cotton, spices and tea from India, the East Indies (where Dutch influence prevailed) and from China. The China tea trade was crucial as that beverage earned its status of national drink towards the end of the century; average annual consumption per head was about 1½ lb. a head in 1800, a five-fold increase over the century. About 7m. lb. of China tea was imported to London in 1750; this had almost quadrupled to 25m. lb. by 1815 (154). As imports by volume from the East were less than two-thirds of those from the West and exports under a third it was an area in which progress could be made.

The fulcrum of the East was India where all British activity was controlled either by East India Company officials in the subcontinent or from that company's London offices in Leadenhall Street. Its trade monopoly extended throughout the East, though 'private' traders were permitted under strict licence. As interested merchants were not slow to note, a trading monopoly no less than the company's continued military activity was an evident anachronism after 1763. American trade was in the hands of private merchants; the Royal African Company and the Levant Company monopolies had ceased in the 1750s. East India Company activities, though vast, were ramshackle and its independence of action a source of growing worry to successive governments. Naturally, company patronage was enormous and its unfettered distribution the source of scandalized gossip even among hardened borough-mongers. Worst of all, its finances were precarious. Yet such was their importance that any erosion of confidence could have dire effects on investment in the London money markets.

It was vital to get a grip on India. Pitt's India Act [F.iv.1], though a compromise wrung from company directors scared out of their wits by Fox's more radical proposals, offered a basis for more businesslike relations. Though the company kept its patronage, effective political and strategic control passed from it. Indian affairs became the responsibility of Henry Dundas, apprenticed in the arts of Scottish patronage and now the ideal man to prune the more luxuriant growth of the Orient. In India itself Earl Cornwallis, having negotiated himself larger powers than originally laid down by the Act of 1784, effected substantial reforms as Governor-General from 1786 to 1793. Sinecures were suppressed and able recruits enlisted. Effective British administration, based on colonial control and native assistance, dates from the Cornwallis era. The Governor-General was unable, however, to secure government control of company troops.

Nor did Dundas have all his own way. His plans to reduce the company's £14m. debt ran into trouble and ambitious schemes to liberalize trade between the Indies and Spain came to nothing. Company opposition, secured by the experience of monopoly over two centuries, was not to be overridden in a decade. The true achievement of Pitt's government was to school the company to think in terms of dual authority, thus enabling a relatively painless eventual transfer of power. Improved relations with local princes, itself a reflection of greater government involvement, also reduced dangers of foreign intervention. When the company's charter was renewed in 1792, Dundas did not feel it necessary to press his earlier intentions of reorganizing military control. The company retained control over transports to Britain, while ceding some independent trading rights in the East. From its protected revenues the company was to pay the Exchequer an annual sum of £500,000. The creation of the new office of President of the Board of Control symbolized the increasing powers of government; the post naturally fell to Dundas.

Trade in the East in these years was generally buoyant [D.ii.5], but exotic schemes to extend its geographical limits met with mixed success. Pre-eminent among these was a plan to reduce the enormous deficit on the China tea trade by inducing the Emperor to break with tradition and import western manufactured goods. Lord Macartney's famous embassy to Peking in 1792 was elaborately staged by Pitt and Dundas (company directors jibbed at footing the bill) and received great publicity. The Emperor remained inscrutably impervious to the blandishments of western civilization, but some progress was made. Indian raw cotton, Asian spices and, *sub rosa*, opium entered the Chinese market to the further benefit of a Company trading account already swollen by a much larger share of the European tea market following Pitt's Commutation Act (154).

Negotiations with the Dutch over the South Pacific had both strategic and commercial aims. Pitt was prepared to guarantee Dutch monopoly of the spice trade in return for naval bases in Ceylon and the Malayan archipelago which could check the French. Complex missions by Harris and Auckland petered out in the confused European situation after 1789 despite a further, but perhaps not entirely serious, offer to the Dutch of a share in the Indian market.

Domestic exports almost tripled in the twenty years after 1784 [D.ii.3]. Imports, stimulated by the massive increase in demand for textile raw materials, particularly cotton, more than doubled [D.ii.2]. The Industrial Revolution is much more responsible for this than any grand design of the Pitt administration. Government initiatives were more consolidatory than innovatory. Neo-mercantilism, encompassing genuinely reciprocal reductions in tariff, was the order of the day.

The loss of the American colonies proved anything but disastrous for the British economy. The mother country did not withdraw from direct colonial involvement in favour of an 'informal commercial empire'. There was, however, a determination to avoid heavy-handed and centralized controls in the remaining colonies as in those outposts – like Cape Colony, Trinidad or Ceylon – which were added to the British Empire as the spoils of war after 1793 [F.iii]. Nor is there convincing evidence of a 'swing to the East', as used to be thought, in conscious reaction to failures in America[4]. British trade involved a world-wide search for markets, with the emphasis on raw materials for import and manufactured goods for export [D.ii.2, 3].

Lack of government resources in any case prohibited the emergence of a global commercial grand design. Economical reform in 1782 had suppressed both the Presidency of the Board of Trade and the Secretaryship of the Colonies. Though the Presidency returned to the Cabinet with Hawkesbury in 1791 a separate Secretaryship for the Colonies did not reappear until Palmerston's government in 1855; from 1801 the post was usually a minor part of the Secretary for War's duties [A]. Commercial matters, other than those concerning India where Dundas was characteristically to the fore, usually devolved on under secretaries in the Home Department. Some, like the efficient Evan Nepean, acquired influence by mastery of their brief; the work of such men pointed to the future development of the Civil Service and was a fruit of Pitt's administrative reforms. Nepean's abilities were to win for him influence and perquisites in the West Indies, a knighthood and, eventually, the governorship of Bombay (150).

Pitt himself rarely needed to give colonial matters priority but he sustained conventional imperial objectives. He aimed to secure continued supplies of cheap raw materials and an accommodation of mutual interest with the United States. In Europe he moved cautiously towards reciprocal reductions of tariffs. Such inducements sufficed for manufacturers to recoup with interest the losses of the American War. Pitt's policy also helped to give Britain a degree of financial security which was to be vital in her strategy for its next, and much greater, wars against the French (Chs 9 and 10).

———————

1. *Journal and Correspondence of Lord Auckland* (4 vols, 1861–62), ii, pp. 388-9.
2. V. T. Harlow and F. Madden, *British Colonial Developments 1774–1834* (Oxford, 1953), p. 179.
3. *Ibid.*, p. 256
4. V. T. Harlow, *The Founding of the Second British Empire 1763–93* (2 vols, 1964) ii.

CHAPTER 5

The new political economy and the early impact of *laissez-faire*

Only rarely does an idea, still less a body of theory, come to dominate the economic and social life of an age. Yet such a claim can be fairly made for the notion of free trade put forward in Adam Smith's *Inquiry into the Nature and Causes of the Wealth of Nations*, first published in 1776. Smith challenged the assumption on which traditional economic policy had been based: that a nation thrives by protecting its manufactures against competition from others. The paraphernalia of protection – tariffs on foreign imported goods, bounties on domestic manufactures of exportable commodities, monopolies, tolls and the like – was assembled to ensure that the protecting nation acquired a favourable balance of precious metals. Such dominance of the main media of exchange, so the argument ran, ensured political strength as well as economic hegemony. What Smith called the 'mercantile system' was founded on political power through economic predominance.

Smith's view was that tariffs and the like hampered the growth of world trade and held back living standards in all countries, whether or not they had a favourable balance of trade. Free trade and an end to controls on production saw prices regulated by the only true arbiter: demand in an open market. Competition ensured best-quality goods at lowest practicable prices; the search for an adequate share of the market under conditions of perfect competition ensured the adoption of efficient means of production and a rational deployment of labour. The conflicting self-interests of producer and consumer to sell in the dearest market and buy in the cheapest were reconciled to the benefit of all parties. Britain's adoption of the broad principles of *Wealth of Nations*, cautiously in respect of foreign trade, eagerly in regard to the organization of labour and production, formed the basis of nineteenth-century economic liberalism. By 1850 free trade had become an unshakeable tenet of government faith, relevant alike to social conditions and economic policy. Rarely, if ever, has a political or economic philosophy achieved such general assent from such a large proportion of educated minds.

Wealth of Nations is a pinnacle of the late-eighteenth-century Enlightenment. It is a logical, cogent, rational, powerful yet deeply humane book. But neither its logic nor its humanity explains its influence; political actions are rarely swayed by power of argument alone. None knew better than Smith the extent to which people respond to self-interest. The book issued from one of the most educationally advanced nations in Europe (Smith was Professor of Moral Philosophy at Glasgow University) and one which had been since the Union of Scotland and England in 1707 part of the most potent commercial force in the world. *Wealth of Nations* spoke directly to the self-interest of commercially minded men; its beautiful reasoning is only a minor factor in its success. If free trade puts a premium on efficiency, it naturally offers a head-start to those who are already more efficient or have the resources rapidly to become so. Industrial developments from the last quarter of the eighteenth century vastly increased Britain's already considerable economic advantages. *Wealth of Nations* showed how to maximize them; it was perfectly in tune with the needs of the age.

Smith is popularly considered the supreme apologist of free-enterprise capitalism. His true concerns were much broader. He is best characterized as one of the ablest sons of the Enlightenment, a widely travelled and broadly educated academic; his aim was to foster the understanding of man as an ethical, social and economic being. The removal of the fetters from the economy was part of the much grander design to liberate mankind from the restrictive and archaic panoply of arbitrary government. He took from the French Physiocrats their concern to shift discussion from producers to consumers and their tripartite division of wealth into rent, profit and wages; he hoped to give back to the Enlightenment a fully integrated study of man in society. *Wealth of Nations* should thus be seen as the economic counterpart to Smith's earlier ethical study, *Theory of Moral Sentiments* (1759). Though he did more than anyone to establish the science of political economy, it was his nineteenth-century successors, David Ricardo, J. R. McCulloch and Nassau Senior, who concentrated on, and deepened, the economic analysis. Smith's interests were eclectic.

The most far-reaching aspect of *Wealth of Nations* is the thesis that the activities of the individual in a free market, motivated by self-interest, nevertheless benefit society as a whole. He 'generally neither intends to promote the public interest, nor knows how much he is promoting it', but in seeking 'his own gain . . . he is . . . led by an invisible hand to promote an end which was no part of his intention' (220, i, *400*). Such a profound fortuity, however, obtains only in a free market. Under protection prices are pushed up and the miraculous machinery of the market malfunctions. Since Smith also believed, with the socialist thinkers who were to follow him, that 'labour . . . is the ultimate price which is paid for everything' (220, i, *173*), labour should be used with optimum efficiency since the prices of the inefficient would be undercut. The free market further aids the proper allocation of economic resources; labourers will be enticed from unprofitable to profitable sectors by the higher wages producers in those sectors can afford and will need to pay. Market forces contain their own dynamic for redistribution and development. Absence of constraint not only satisfies the consumer with low prices; it offers opportunity for investment, development and further economic growth which benefits producer and consumer alike.

The other great foundation stone for classical economics was Smith's analysis of the division of labour. This, the point of departure in *Wealth of Nations*, argues that specialization of productive functions is determined by demand. Producers will develop their manufacture, using more sophisticated processes and training more men to perform a smaller range of tasks more efficiently, in response to demand for their product. The contention that economic growth was largely dependent upon technological specialization in the manufacturing sector was further evidence of its attraction for a nation on the threshold of an industrial revolution.

It is too often forgotten both that Adam Smith's concern was primarily with the consumer and that he had a profound distrust of merchants and manufacturers. It was a great virtue of the free market in his eyes that it clipped the wings of what subsequent generations called the capitalist classes. If this seems a paradox in the prophet of *laissez-faire* liberalism it is so only while people are content with a superficial image. Smith believed that producers and dealers conspired to distort the market with controls and tariffs. From these, only producers and dealers benefited. As Smith noted, 'to widen the market and to narrow the competition is always in the interest of the dealers'. The ultimate aim of such perversions was monopoly production with consumers forced to pay whatever price was demanded. Smith was especially scathing about those large commercial incorporations, like the East India Company, which were not only intrinsically powerful but also exerted pressure on government to protect their narrow interests. *Wealth of Nations* is liberally spiced with anti-mercantile abuse. Smith spoke of their 'impertinent jealousy', 'mean rapacity' and 'monopolising spirit'. They represented 'an order of men whose interest is never exactly the same with that of the public, who have generally an interest to deceive and even to oppress the public' (220, i, *436, 231–2*).Their natural acquisitive interests were best tempered by the independent arbitration of a genuinely free market. It is not surprising that the tobacco merchants of Glasgow, struggling with a trade depression in the mid-1770s, found little in Smith's writings to their taste (16, *348*).

Wealth of Nations is anything but an unqualified endorsement of merchants and manufacturers, yet their nineteenth-century successors regarded it as their lodestar. As invariably happens to those rare seminal works of political or economic science, their adherents simplify, if not distort, the message. Unpalatable observations tend to be ignored. Thus the capitalist classes forgot Smith's insults since many of them stood to profit from freeing the market; nor did they recognize his more or less explicit espousal of a labour theory of value while pressing the government not to implement ancient wage-regulation statutes. Landowners were mostly content for the market to fix labourers' wages. As we shall see, however, they would not be prepared to accept Smith's view that 'even the free importation of foreign corn could very little affect the interest of the farmers of Great Britain' (220, i, *405*). Nor did a government of property owners draw attention to the class implications of his injudiciously honest observation that 'civil government . . . is in reality instituted for the defence of the rich against the poor, or of those who have some property against those who have none at all' (220, ii, *203*). Smith's message was assimilated selectively, the selection based on just that rational self-interest which was at the root of his psychological and economic thinking.

It is worth noting that Adam Smith's commitment to *laissez-faire* was less total than that of some heedless or dogma-driven 'privatisers' in the 1980s and 1990s. The State should liberally provide those services which individuals or companies would not. Smith asserted not only external defence but also internal security to be necessary charges upon the State. Likewise a State education system. Smith's reservations about full *laissez-faire* in overseas trade, however, had greatest impact. Where there was clash of interest between the needs of national security and those of trade the former should have priority: '. . . defence is of much more importance than opulence' (220, i, *408*). This led him to a defence of the Navigation Acts which could be considered the very bedrock of the mercantile system. Smith was also prepared to countenance limited protection of goods with obvious defence value such as British-made sailcloth and gunpowder (220, ii, *22*). Such exceptions should not undermine the view of Smith on free trade, of course, or his distrust of colonial developments with their strong monopolist implications. However, it is possible to agree with the Whig politician and part-time political economist Henry Brougham that Smith's acceptance of the primacy of national defence distanced him from Physiocrat free-traders, if not putting him midway between them and out-and-out mercantilists on the colonial issue (160, *27*). Certainly, Smith's ambivalent views proved embarrassing to later anti-colonial economists like Ricardo and McCulloch.

II

William Pitt knew and admired Smith; he derived great intellectual stimulus during his unprecedentedly brief youth from reading *Wealth of Nations* in the company of his cousin and future Cabinet colleague, William Grenville. As was seen in Chapter 4, however, the direct impact of liberal economics on trade policies in the 1780s was limited. It might almost be argued that Pitt was more taken with Smith's exceptions to the free-trade rule than with the broad sweep of his argument. He could certainly find warrant for the 1786 Navigation Act in Book IV of *Wealth of Nations*. Such a view does scant justice to Pitt's intellectual appreciation, but it recognizes his strengths as a practical politician. Had Shelburne survived longer in office there can be little doubt that Smith's policies would have been more rapidly translated into action.

Shelburne, an intellectual in politics if ever there was one, was an ardent convert to the new thinking and Pitt's reputation as a man committed to free trade derives substantially from his early connections with him. Pitt's career was less influenced by Shelburne than some writers supposed.[1] Pitt was a practical politician to his fingertips; Shelburne was not. Shelburne was dominated by the heady world of ideas; Pitt, though his acute mind assimilated them rapidly, was not. Like most successful Prime Ministers, Pitt was a pragmatist (which is not to say that pragmatists invariably make successful Prime Ministers). His commitment to free trade was always tempered by diplomatic and commercial realities as by the need to treat new concepts cautiously. His policy of reciprocal trade agreements might have borne more fruit in the 1790s had not the French Wars driven him back to protection. In any event, British colonial successes had been achieved by protection; Pitt was not the man to ditch it in a decade because of the intellectual attraction of a new system. In consequence, little of the free-trade highway which Huskisson was to open up in the 1820s was cleared by Pitt.

Smith's ideas continued to provoke thought throughout the war years. With varying degrees of insight Edmund Burke, Frederick Eden and the Revd Thomas Malthus sought to apply his lessons to the problems of scarcity and high prices. Smith wrote for an expansive age; his successors struggled with crisis. The foundation of the *Edinburgh Review* in 1802, a scheme of bright young men like

Henry Brougham and Sydney Smith, was to bring the message to a wider audience. The *Review* eventually became the intellectual house-journal of the Whig party; it championed both the new political economy and liberal causes such as the abolition of slavery and law reform. Some of the most pungent free-trade criticisms of the government's protectionist economic policies in response to Napoleon's Continental System appeared in its pages, mostly the work of Brougham.

III

Malthus's contribution was distinctive. His *Essay on the Principle of Population* (1798) does not compare with the work of Smith either in breadth of learning or depth of analysis, yet its influence is in some ways comparable since it deals with that most basic of economic questions, the relationship between population and the means of subsistence. Malthus offered the first cogent evidence that population growth was not intrinsically beneficial, and the evidence of the first official census in 1801, together with the extrapolations of eighteenth-century growth made by its first director, John Rickman, gave greater point to his analysis. If population had almost doubled in 100 years, which modern research confirms, the fears which suffused Malthus's book seemed all too likely to be realized.

He worked from the basic hypothesis that the capability of man to reproduce himself is greater than the capacity of man to increase the means of subsistence. Population, when unchecked, increases in a geometrical ratio (1, 2, 4, 8, 16, 32, 64). Subsistence increases only in an arithmetical ratio (1, 2, 3, 4, 5, 6, 7).' (221, *71*) The famous 'Malthusian checks' were vital since they operated to keep population and the means of subsistence in reasonable balance. They were of two types. Positive checks resulted from epidemic, famine or war as population broke through the margin of subsistence. Preventive checks, emphasized when Malthus reworked his ideas for the second edition in 1803, resulted from conscious choice: delayed marriage resulting from economic pressure, sexual abstinence or primitive means of contraception. Malthus thought positive checks by far the more important, with all their implications for human misery. Recent demographic researches, however, lay increasing stress on man's ability to operate preventive checks.

Malthus saw his work as a counterblast to what he considered the superficial and incautious Enlightenment ideal of the perfectibility of man. 'It is, undoubtedly, a most disheartening reflection that the great obstacle in the way to any extraordinary improvement in society is of a nature that we can never hope to overcome.' The 'perpetual tendency' of mankind was 'to increase beyond the means of subsistence' (221, *198–9*). To practical men the downward pressure of real wages in the countryside seemed a lugubrious vindication of Malthus's notion. What could be done?

It was largely because Malthus offered so little for the comfort of his fellows, in a generation that was experiencing an unprecedented rate of population growth, and frequent scarcity, that economics was branded 'the dismal science'. He condemned the Elizabethan Poor Law, the basic institutional remedy for distress, and the evidence of his second edition suggests that his condemnation became rounder as his ideas developed. He took the view that all mechanisms which provided artificial assistance exacerbated the very problems they were designed to alleviate. Thus Pitt's Poor Law bill of 1796 embraced 'the great and radical defect of all systems of the kind, that of tending to increase population without increasing the means for its support' (221, *100–1*). If the poor were aided artificially to buy bread they were cushioned from reality; they would respond by marrying earlier and producing more children. At best, their benefactors merely shifted a yet more serious problem on to the next generation. The iron law of subsistence was not to be bent for the satisfaction of the tenderhearted, the incautiously charitable or for the wretches under their care.

When the poor asked Parson Mathus for bread, therefore, he gave them a stone: no parochial relief, no job-creation schemes, not even workhouses. The market must dictate wage levels and without supplementation; the poor must cut their cloth accordingly. They were exhorted to be more provident and more self-reliant; above all they must restrain their appetites, both carnivorous and carnal. Malthus admitted later that the Poor Laws no longer worked and consequently did not stimulate population growth. This did nothing to assuage his hostility to all forms of regulated relief.

After 1805 Malthus took up residence in the new East India Company college at Haileybury where he occupied the first Chair of Political Economy in Britain. Thence issued a series of waspish denunciations of all objections to his iron law. He deeply resented charges by Southey or Cobbett of inhumanity or lack of Christian charity, but considered them ignorant pinpricks which did not begin to puncture the secure ramparts of his population fortress. Though critics carped at the specifics of his differential ratio, the general imbalance between population and subsistence was undeniable. His strictures on poor relief for interfering with the laws of nature found general assent among political economists. David Ricardo, though he disagreed with Malthus on many issues, was at one with him in condemning the Poor Law as 'in direct opposition' to the 'obvious principles' by which 'wages should be left to the fair and free competition of the market, and should never be controlled by the legislature'. By 1820 there was immensely strong intellectual underpinning for a programme of radical reform of the Poor Laws on *laissez-faire* lines.

IV

Parliament was growing similarly reluctant to permit the exercise of old statutes regulating wages and other relations between master and man. Here free-trade economics as much reinforced ancient prejudices as converted MPs to new modes of thought. By the 1790s there was a general view that Elizabethan wage-regulation statutes were anachronistic and impractical. The new generation of writers on poverty, men like Thomas Ruggles and Frederick Eden, exhorted the poor to sturdy self-reliance. Charity must be generated and administered locally; paternalism could not be nationalized. In any event, the resources of government were quite inadequate to cope with the complexities any State interference would throw up. As a Buckinghamshire farmer told Arthur Young in 1795: 'I see so many different cases of distress in this and the adjoining parishes, that I think one general rule will do more harm than good.'[2]

During the two great food crises of 1795–96 and 1800–1 Parliament refused the plea of Samuel Whitbread, the leading Foxite Whig, to set a minimum wage for labourers. It is noticeable that Whitbread himself rejected wage regulation as a general rule; it 'operated as a clog to industry ... the price of labour, like every other commodity, should be left to find its own level'. Minimum wages should be set by local Justices of the Peace only in periods of the most exceptional hardship. Nevertheless, the whole idea was rejected by Whitbread's erstwhile colleague, Edmund Burke, whose *Thoughts and Details on Scarcity* (1795) pushed non-intervention several crude stages further than Smith in a diatribe which, it has been fairly said, transmuted the latter's 'system of economic liberty into a dogmatic faith which the author might scarcely have recognized' (325, *53*). William Pitt offered an altogether more temperate invocation of the 'ample testimony' of the truth of the 'most celebrated writers upon political economy'.[3] Pitt's own solution fared no better. His plan in 1796 to reform the Poor Laws by creating 'Schools of Industry', by giving additional relief to large families and by stimulating self-help through subscriptions to friendly societies, was withdrawn in the face of severe criticism. Even in 1800, when food prices rose even higher [D.vi.3], there was no parliamentary move to alleviate distress beyond pious exhortation to temperate consumption among the gentry and half-hearted measures to increase foreign supply. By 1809 even Whitbread had given up the struggle; he refused to lend support to a petition from Scottish weavers for a minimum wage. The weavers were told by a Commons select committee that their claim was 'wholly inadmissable in principle'; other skilled workers received similarly dusty replies in the first decade of the nineteenth century.

The Combination Acts of 1799 and 1800, though inspired by political considerations during an anti-Jacobin purge (Ch. 8), represented another move in the same direction. Specific associations of workmen to secure better conditions or higher wages had been proscribed by separate pieces of legislation dotted through-out the eighteenth century; many, like that of 1726 against combinations by woollen workers, long pre-dated the works of Adam Smith. Now combinations generally were banned, with notice served that Parliament would sanction no interference with a manufacturer's unfettered right to fix wages according to their market price.

Pressure to enforce clauses in the 1563 Statute of Artificers specifying a full seven-year apprenticeship to trades was likewise nugatory. Eighteenth-century prosecutions of employers for non-observance had been rare and unsuccessful, but with the massive expansion of the textile trades after 1780 the dilution of the labour market by unskilled and semi-skilled workers assumed critical proportions. Richard Sheridan, speaking on behalf of journeymen calico printers in 1807, told of young men taking jobs at 6s. or even 4s. a week in a trade which, when properly regulated, had offered up to 25s. When Yorkshire and west of England weavers had the temerity to petition Parliament in 1802 to enforce apprenticeship regulations and secure the livelihood of skilled workers the response was a six-year suspension of the relevant laws, followed by abolition in 1809.

The calico printers' case evinced much righteous indignation. The leading cotton manufacturer, Sir Robert Peel sen., rose from a sickbed to make his only contribution of the parliamentary session deprecating the pretensions of journeymen attempting 'to give the law to the masters'. He even affected to believe that master manufacturers were considering emigration 'to some country where their property would be better protected, and their trade be more free from restriction'. Henry Erskine argued that the men's petition 'was against the first principles of civil liberty, as well as against all the commercial maxims which had hitherto been received'.[4]

Parliament needed little persuasion to remove the few remaining obstacles to free trade in labour. The repeal of the wage-regulation (1813) and apprenticeship (1814) clauses of the Statute of Artificers was the natural culmination of the process. In each case, Parliament acted in defiance of the wishes of a majority involved in the trades concerned, expressed by the traditional means of loyal petition. In April 1813, 32,000 signatures appeared on a petition calling for apprenticeship regulation to be made more effective. By the end of the French Wars paternalism sanctioned by legislation was dead; relations between masters and men were determined 'objectively' by market forces. A decade before the frontal attack on tariffs, it was the first triumph of the new political economy and a talisman for the new age.

---

1. Disraeli suggested that Pitt could only be understood by first appreciating Shelburne's influence on him, *Sybil* (1845, Penguin edn, 1954), pp. 26–9.
2. *Annals of Agriculture*, xxv (1796), cols 484–5.
3. *Parl. Hist.*, xxxii (1796), col. 706.
4. Hansard, 1st ser., ix (1807), cols 532–3.

CHAPTER 6

The new moral economy: Wilberforce, the Saints and New Dissent

I

The development of early industrial Britain rested on two pillars, free trade and a new moral order. Between 1780 and 1830 the dominant behavioural ethos of Britain underwent a remarkable transformation. The aristocratic hegemony of the eighteenth century was characterized by an expansive, bucolic and roistering culture. Its lavish entertainments and expensive hobbies could be sustained only by a large income. Gambling debts run up on the turf or at the table ran into thousands of pounds; Charles James Fox's losses caused financial embarrassment for even such a hugely wealthy figure as the fifth earl of Carlisle of Castle Howard who frequently stood surety for him. Mistresses were flaunted as a badge of status, a source alike of public approval and private pleasure. George III's sober domestic circumstances were attributed to the personal idiosyncrasy of a dull fellow; they did not persuade men to change their own habits and George's eldest son, later Prince Regent and George IV, was working feverishly by the 1780s to restore the faded Hanoverian reputation for licentiousness. All activities, political and social, were washed down by huge quantities of liquor. Both Pitt, who drank himself into an early grave, and Fox attended the Commons in varying states of intoxication, frequently too inebriated to follow closely the arguments of others, sometimes too sozzled to articulate clearly themselves. Nor was insobriety the prerogative of the wealthy. The excesses of the London poor, for whom alcohol offered welcome oblivion from the common round of toil, are preserved for posterity by the genius of Hogarth.

The aristocratic code of honour was buttressed by the hazardous justice of the duel. A serving Prime Minister – Pitt – fought a duel with the acting Leader of the Opposition – George Tierney – beneath the rotting remains of a hanged highwayman on Putney Heath on Whit Sunday 1798 to satisfy honour impugned during a bitter parliamentary exchange on the subject of national security. The incident led to a sharp exchange between Pitt and one of his few close friends, William Wilberforce, the leader of a new and increasingly persuasive pressure group of evangelical Christians. Duelling symbolized what Wilberforce was to call 'excessive valuation of Character' and the evangelicals condemned all extravagant and licentious behaviour in their unremitting search for 'vital Christianity', manifested in a sober and earnest life, the practical outworking of religious faith.

The evangelicals who led a frontal assault on the moral imperfections of the ruling élite were a close-knit group with professional, mercantile and intellectual interests. Wilberforce, county MP for Yorkshire, came from a prosperous trading family in Hull where his grandfather had twice been mayor. His cousin, Henry

Thornton, was a banker. It was Thornton who bought Battersea Rise, a small estate in Clapham where he and his cousin lived during the 1790s and from where the Clapham Sect took its name. John Venn, a gifted preacher and son of a famous evangelical of the 1740s, became vicar of Clapham and a central figure in the group. Intellectual stiffening was provided from Wilberforce's connections, particularly by Dr Isaac Milner, dean of Carlisle and president of Queens' College, who had taught both Wilberforce and Venn, and Charles Simeon, a Fellow of King's. Another Cambridge graduate and close friend of Thornton was Thomas Babington, a substantial Leicestershire landowner who, rather incongruously save for his own severe character, married the daughter of a Scottish Presbyterian minister. Her brother, Zachary Macaulay, made his fortune in the West Indies where he acquired the most intimate knowledge of any of the evangelicals of the slave trade which they united to condemn. Macaulay accepted the governorship of the experimental non-slaving colony of Sierra Leone in West Africa in 1796; his knowledge and ferocious energies were vital to the anti-slavery cause whose first triumph was the abolition of the British slave trade in 1807 (153). He also helped to launch and then edit the influential, though rather humourless and didactic, evangelical periodical *Christian Observer* from 1802. Macaulay's son, named Thomas Babington after the uncle in whose mansion he was born, was educated privately with Wilberforce's son. The evangelicals used their patronage and privileges in recognizably eighteenth-century ways, but to secure what might be termed nineteenth-century ends. Wilberforce's good offices were instrumental in securing the nomination of T. B. Macaulay to one of the two new Yorkshire seats in the 1830 General Election. The young Macaulay naturally ranged himself on the abolitionist side in the campaign to end slavery in all British territories which achieved success in 1833, the year of Wilberforce's death. Ironically, one of Macaulay's earliest antagonists was the young William Gladstone, whose subsequent career was almost an incarnation of all evangelical precepts but whose Liverpool family owed its wealth in significant measure to the slave trade.

The lucid power of Macaulay's speeches on slavery and parliamentary reform was directed at a House of Commons of very different temper from that of the 1780s and 1790s. Though still unreformed in 1830, a new ethos prevailed. Members dressed more soberly; wigs and hair powder were out of fashion. Ostentatious drinking was frowned upon; proceedings were more obviously businesslike. In polite society order, regularity, self-discipline and moderation in personal habits were prized. George IV died in 1830, but his undisguised indulgencies seemed anachronistically excessive during his decade as king. The aristocracy trimmed their public habits. Though Viscount Palmerston, who became Foreign Secretary for the first time in 1830, was one of the most compulsive womanizers among nineteenth-century politicians he usually concealed his peccadilloes from the public eye. Standards of public morality had undergone a radical change at least ten years before the eponymous Queen Victoria came to the throne; Prince Albert and Victoria merely set a royal seal upon it. Victorianism was anticipated by the evangelicals.

II

The Clapham Sect worked to reform the Church of England from within and thus to revitalize the Christian message. Wilberforce's 'vital Christianity' was distinguished from nominal religious observance as his major work's characteristically long-winded title makes clear: *A Practical View of the Prevailing Religious System of Professed Christians in the Higher and Middle Classes of this Country contrasted with Real Christianity* (1797). His thesis was that the moral laxity of the privileged gave an inadequate example to the lower orders whose allegiance to religious and political orthodoxy was under challenge in the 1790s. Though Wilberforce's moral views stemmed from a real religious conversion his message was pregnant with political significance. In its wider implications it was as much about social quietism as moral reform; to this must be attributed the remarkable success of 'Church evangelicalism'. Evangelicalism itself was nothing new; its novelty in the 1780s lay in the receptiveness of the ruling classes to a message which middle-class Puritanism and, for a while, Low-Church Anglicanism had encompassed since the Reformation. They were receptive, as the next two chapters will show, largely because they feared the consequences of continued inactivity.

Politicians perceived an immensely strong link between the Established Church and the State. Most accepted Bishop Warburton's view in *The Alliance between Church and State* (1736) that the two institutions were mutually self-supporting. Edmund Burke devoted an important section of his *Reflections on the Revolution in France* (1790) to a discussion of the importance of an Established Church for the security of the State; he drew dire conclusions from the attack on ecclesiastical property by the revolutionaries. Pitt opposed the removal of political disabilities from dissenters in the same year because the intimate connections between Church and State were such that 'the safety of the one was always liable to be affected by any danger which might threaten the other'.[1] The old Stuart cry of 'the Church in Danger' was a frequent rallying point for men of property against the pretensions of reformers and dissenters who were frequently and wrongly lumped together as agents of misrule.

As Wilberforce and Milner perceived, the problem was that the Established Church was in urgent need of reform. Given the cynical political calculations which governed its birth in the early years of Elizabeth's reign it is not surprising that the Church of England should have developed ambivalent and latitudinarian ways. The political needs of the early Hanoverian Whigs, however, had necessitated ecclesiastical promotion on primarily secular grounds; spiritual leadership was consequently insecure. There were many capable and conscientious Anglican bishops, like William Wake of Canterbury or William Nicolson of Carlisle at the beginning of the eighteenth century or Lewis Bagot of Norwich and Beilby Porteus of Chester and London at its end, but since the 1730s they had had to share the bench with too many time-serving political hacks and, good or bad, the provision of pro-government votes in the House of Lords ate into episcopal time and kept bishops from their dioceses. Episcopal incomes varied enormously. Ambitious and well-connected clerics – for all bishops owed their elevation to birth and patronage – would hope to serve only for a few years in Llandaff, Carlisle or Gloucester, where incomes ran between £1,000 and £2,500 a year early in the nineteenth century, before promotion to the more opulent sees, which in the case of Durham and Canterbury could exceed £20,000. All bishops were pluralists by the mid-eighteenth century and those in poorly endowed outposts could make ends meet by acquiring deaneries and additional rectories. The bishop of Llandaff was also dean of St Paul's, which office more than quintupled his income; the bishop of Rochester added the deanery of Worcester to his list of offices (199).

Princes of the Church added plural livings almost as monopoly players acquire first houses then hotels on desirable sites. The situation lower in the hierarchy was even more worrying. By 1800 the rigid parochial structure was inappropriate to the changing distribution of population. Since it required an Act of Parliament to create a new parish, important areas of the industrializing North were beyond the reach of Anglicanism. There were almost eight times as many people in Manchester in 1818 as seats available for them in local Anglican churches; in London, Marylebone had just over 7,000 seats for a population of 64,000 (361, *287*). As early as 1778 in a non-industrial town like Chester the vicar of St Oswald reported that: 'There are many who absent themselves from this Church out of pure necessity; There not being room conveniently to accommodate so many thousands.'[2] Chester at least had a resident bishop; Manchester and Salford hardly saw him. Nor did Sheffield or the West Riding woollen towns receive much attention from the archbishop of York in whose huge diocese they happened to fall.

It did not help matters that most urban livings were poorly endowed and unattractive to able clerics. Disparities of parochial income were stark. Some rural rectories, like Blithfield in Staffordshire, were amply endowed with glebe and tithes to the value of over £800 a year; such livings were usually in the gift of, if not annexed to, an aristocratic family, in this case the Bagots. Richard Bagot naturally retained the family living when appointed bishop of Oxford in 1829. At the other end of the scale, almost one living in five realized less than £100 a year as late as 1833 [G.v]. Plurality was an economic necessity for many clerics and plurality meant non-performance of duty. Episcopal pluralism could be criticized, as it was both by evangelicals and anti-clerical radicals like John Wade, whose thoroughly researched *Black Book* (1820) drew attention to the problem, but what of a man like the Revd James Hakewell whose four Oxfordshire livings realized £117 *in toto* in 1786?

Non-residence was endemic. Inadequate stipends and unfit parsonage houses were the main reasons for the alarming fact that 60 per cent of livings were served by non-resident incumbents in 1808.[3] Too much should not be made of statistics of this kind, however. Much non-residence was literal, rather than practical. The Salisbury diocesan visitation records of 1783 reveal that only 90 of 232 parishes were served by resident clergy (364, *19*). Since 119 more lived within five miles of their parishes it is reasonable to assume that many of these were served with passable efficiency. Shortage of manpower was not the difficulty. The Church of England sustained a large and grossly underpaid army of unbeneficed temporary, assistant and stipendiary curates who plugged the biggest holes while they waited desperately to catch the eye of the patron of a vacant living. The acute but not unkindly skills of a Jane Austen can poke gentle fun at such spectacles, but they only strengthen the view that the sprawling and irrational agglomeration of patronage and endowment which was the Church of England by law established was coming apart at the seams. It operated with fitful propriety in the countryside where many beneficed heroes ministered capably to their flocks on secure incomes of £300–£500 a year to set alongside those whose names have survived for other reasons, like the Revd James Woodforde, immortalized by his ingenuous *Diary* of life in Weston Longville, his Norfolk rectory, or the Revd Edmund Nelson, father of our supreme naval commander, who discharged another long and effective Norfolk ministry between 1755 and 1802 in Burnham Thorpe, though holding other local livings in plurality. In the towns the church was too often merely absent.

Evangelical fire concentrated both on the structure of the Church and on its message. Vital Christianity stressed the Christian life in action, the awareness of sin and the need for redemption. Christian precepts must control all responses; earnestness is constantly stressed after the soul is reborn to God through religious conversion. Throughout Wilberforce's *Practical View* the implication is never far from the surface that the Established Church represents nominal Christianity. Shortcomings in religious observance had political consequences: 'To the decline of Religion and morality our national difficulties must both directly and indirectly be chiefly ascribed.' The success of this lumbering book, which sold 7,500 copies within six months, is partly explained by the date of its appearance. In the spring of 1797 a French invasion seemed imminent and Britain's European allies were in full flight [F.ii]. The full horrors of the French Revolution seemed likely to be visited on the British. Small wonder that Burke, who had first warned of its dangers, should spend his last days reading the book. Wilberforce received numerous tributes from influential people anxious to testify to its influence on their lives. Arthur Young, the eminent agriculturalist, underwent a religious conversion; the duchess of Gloucester, whose son the second duke was to become president of the Anti-Slavery Society, was much moved by it. According to Henry Thornton most of the bishops accepted its basic premises and many politicians recognized the errors of their life styles in a dangerous world (58, 59).

As he recognized, Wilberforce's message operated on two levels. It called the great to moral reformation, their improving example percolating downwards to reform society thoroughly. It also offered a means of strengthening the State against political reformers. Vital Christianity rendered 'the inequalities of the social scale less galling to the lower orders, whom she also instructs, in their turn, to be diligent, humble, patient; reminding them that their more lowly path has been allotted to them by the hand of God'. Arthur Young was still more blunt: 'The true Christian will never be a leveller, will never listen to French politics or to French philosophy. He who worships God in spirit and in truth will love the Government and laws which protect him without asking by whom they are administered.' (250, 285)

In 1787 Wilberforce had persuaded influential patrons to support his efforts to enforce royal proclamations against immorality and vice which had first been issued in the 1690s. It was the first stage of the evangelicals' grand design to reform the manners of the great and rekindle in them their sense of duty and leadership. The 'Proclamation Society' actively promoted sabbatarianism, attacked drunkenness and theatrical performances where 'decorum and modesty, and regularity retire, while riot and lewdness are invited to stop.' The Society also attacked dangerous literature, most notably Tom Paine's vigorous anti-Christian tract, *The Age of Reason*. The printer of a cheap edition was prosecuted by the Society in 1797 for publishing a blasphemous and seditious libel. The Society's ample funds enabled them to effect a nice irony by engaging a leading radical Whig, Thomas Erskine, to carry the prosecution case.

Censorship of damaging books was an important element in the moral reformation; counter-propaganda was its complement. The evangelicals' supreme propagandist was Hannah More, the daughter of a Bristol schoolmaster who had undergone the refining process of religious conversion. As a playwright and poet, her work had appealed both to Dr Johnson and to David Garrick. After the anonymous publication of her *Thoughts on the Manners of the Great* in 1787, which plied the standard evangelical message of leadership by example, she put her talents increasingly to countering the assertions of political radicals. A collection of fifty pamphlets known as the *Cheap Repository Tracts* was the result. The tracts, designed to be distributed by the gentry among their labourers, were stuffed with homilies about the virtues of hard work and sober habits and replete with commonsensical scorn directed at those who arrogantly presumed to know better than their betters. 'Will Chip' was one of many who did duty as the level-headed wiseacre who knew that experience and birth were safer guarantors of sane government than the half-baked notions of radical theorists. His rustic good sense soothed the savage brow of any young lad who happened to pick up dangerous ideas. It should be noted that in Will Chip's world the rich invariably did their duty; social cement held fast in Hannah More's constructs.

Anti-radical literature proved extremely popular. About two million copies of titles in the *Cheap Repository Tracts* series were sold. William Jones, a Suffolk curate, had also had considerable success with a series of *Letters from John Bull* in 1792–93. Like More, Jones mixed blood-curdling stories from the French Revolution with simple statements about the importance of religion, practical experience and common sense over the unrealistic and visionary speculations of the radicals. John Bull pointed out to his equally fictional brother, Tom, the true colours of those revolutionary foreigners whose example should on no account be followed in Britain: 'Treason to their King and Ruin to their country! No order! No laws! No Honour! No Justice! King! Religion! or God! – God forbid that *Englishmen* should follow such an example!' (47, *26–7*). The success of such material clearly warns against the assumption that the French Revolution's main achievement in Britain was to radicalize the working population (Ch. 8).

Evangelicals did not promote their views against blanket hostility from the ecclesiastical hierarchy. Seventeen bishops supported the Proclamation society. Bishops Fisher of Exeter and Porteus of London helped to found the British and Foreign Bible society in 1804. More than £65,000 a year was being raised within a decade to promote the evangelical aim of spreading the word of God around the world.

Social historians have tended to emphasize the reactionary role of the church evangelicals in aiding the forces of order during the French Wars. Such a concentration distorts the range of their message. Most in addition to personal piety of somewhat glutinous sort, were extraordinarily generous and saw in vital Christianity an imperative to charitable benefaction. Henry Thornton gave away five-sixths of his banking income when he was a bachelor; the More sisters were liberal in their support of unemployed miners; Wilberforce was a noted philanthropist and also supported a range of 'social' causes from the attempts of Sir Robert Peel sen. to regulate child factory labour to Howard and Romilly's campaigns to reduce penalties for trivial crimes. Institutional benefaction was more cautious. As John Venn indicated, the credentials of applicants to Wilberforce's Society for Bettering the Condition of the Poor were carefully examined: 'Before any relief is granted, information should be particularly sought concerning the moral character of the applicant, particularly if he is accustomed to attend public worship.' (361, 79) Reformation of character was inseparable from amelioration of condition, a further didactic trait which many historians have deprecated.

Episcopal reformers like Porteus and Richard Watson, the absentee bishop of Llandaff, also agreed with evangelicals on the broad strategy for institutional reform of the Church. From 1803 to 1818 a series of Acts were passed promising action on the worst excesses of pluralism, disparities of income and the weaknesses of the urban ministry [G.i]. Those bishops who contemplated moderate reform were much exercised by the challenge of the dissenters, a consideration which weighed less heavily with the church evangelicals most of whom saw no inevitable conflict between Church and chapel.

III

Dissent made remarkable headway in the last two decades of the eighteenth century though the origins of the 'religious revival' date from the 1730s. Religious revivalism, though in part contemporaneous with industrial expansion, pre-dates it; also, dissenters were by no means exclusively concentrated in the new industrial towns. Religious nonconformity progressed respectably in rural England and most impressively in older urban communities, particularly ports and market towns. Though dissenters were to make greater headway among the new industrial masses than was the Established Church, the majority of such workers remained outside the ministrations of any organized religion. It is a mistake to think of the expansion of dissent as largely the story of the Methodist movement. Though Wesleyan Methodism virtually quadrupled its membership in the first thirty years of our period [G.iii] the successes of the Congregationalists and Baptists are almost equally impressive. These two sects combined held as large a proportion of adherents as the various branches of Methodism between 1800 and 1830; nor should it be forgotten that the Roman Catholics seem to have doubled their membership in the same period, well before the main wave of Irish immigration in the later 1840s and 1850s [G.ii].

The main impulse of nonconformity was, as with the Church evangelicals, a conversionist, vital faith; the emphasis was on hearing and preaching the word of God. In most sects, also, laymen were more centrally involved in organization and direction. The Methodist movement, founded by John Wesley in the 1740s, had begun life as an attempt to satisfy all of these desiderata within the framework of the Established Church. Many of Wesley's followers saw earlier than he that the Church would see in his movement an explicit threat to its authority. It was not until the 1780s that its founder conceded the necessity for separate development in the face of unremitting Anglican hostility.

Methodist organization was indeed an implicit rebuke to the failings of the Church. Regular 'class meetings' put the faithful into a caring fellowship through the medium of a discussion group. An integrated organizational structure also developed with each chapel linked to others in the area in a series of 'circuits' (114 in Britain by Wesley's death in 1791) which were themselves later incorporated into districts. Methodism depended on an itinerant ministry; ministers remained in a particular community only for a limited period and at the direction of the Annual Conference. The accent on preaching and conversion was emphasized by the system of 'local preachers' – laymen who followed their temporal calling but were also active chapel members fulfilling preaching duties.

Methodism concentrated on fitting the convert into a social as well as a religious institution; meetings were held on weekdays and the conversionist impulse stressed the impossibility of separating either work or leisure from religion. Methodism made greatest headway where the Church had failed as a social organization. It flourished in the North Midlands and the north of England, particularly east of the Pennines. Staffordshire, Yorkshire's East and North Ridings, Northumberland and Durham, where parishes were large and industrial out-townships common, were fertile ground. In much of the South, Methodism was weaker and the main beneficiaries of Church shortcomings were Congregationalists in Essex and Dorset and Baptists in Buckinghamshire and Bedfordshire. The exception was the extreme South-west; Cornwall, whose tin mines made it a significant industrial county, experienced a massive religious revival in 1814. Methodist success in Lincolnshire is particularly interesting. That county was served by a relatively rich clergy, whose incomes and status had both been swollen by exchanging tithes for land during the recent enclosure movement. Such men made ideal magistrates, and by 1831 47 per cent of all Lincolnshire magistrates were Anglican clergymen (363). Methodist conversions among the labourers probably owed much to the decline of Anglican pastoral concern, symbolized by the exercise over them of judicial functions by its clergy.

Dissent was traditionally attractive to the middle ranks of society. The late-eighteenth-century revival distorted that pattern without destroying it. Old dissenters, Presbyterians and Congregationalists (independents), had taken firm hold in many mercantile and commercial centres between about 1690 and 1720; thereafter, Unitarianism became particularly influential in intellectual circles with the Revd Richard Price and the chemist Joseph Priestley its most famous adherents. The Methodist mission under Wesley was to bring the word of God to those least advantageously placed to hear it; Methodism ministered to the poor. Its most receptive hearers, however, were skilled workers and craftsmen – Cornish tinners, Durham miners, Yorkshire weavers and metal-workers or Staffordshire potters and, on the land, blacksmiths and wheelwrights. Methodism appealed particularly to those outside the traditional Anglican hierarchy of squire, tenant farmer and labourer, though the Primitives, like the Baptists before them, tended to recruit rather lower down the social scale [G.iii.b]. Overall, almost two-thirds of Methodists in the first thirty years of the nineteenth century were drawn from the ranks of the skilled working classes.

Wesley's colossal presence held together a movement with over 50,000 members until his death in 1791. It is a tribute to the power of Wesley's leadership not only that Methodism grew very substantially during the ideologically divisive 1790s but that the movement did not suffer more from splits and internal dissension. The one substantial split was associated with Alexander Kilham, an egalitarian radical firmly in the tradition of the 'free-born Englishman' (Ch. 8). Kilham was strongly opposed not only to the irrational pretensions of the Church of England but to all forms of hierarchical church government. His secession from the main body of Methodism in 1797 took only about 5 per cent of its membership, mostly from the West Riding and Tyneside, but it stimulated an important conservative reaction within the hierarchy of the main body (358). More significant secessions inevitably followed. In 1807 the Methodist Conference condemned revivalist camp meetings on the United States model which had been held at Mow Cop in the Staffordshire moorlands. Within four years Hugh Bourne, a carpenter, and William Clowes, a potter from Burslem, had established a Primitive Methodism Connexion which grew steadily to a membership in excess of 100,000 in 1851 [G.iii]. The Primitives complained that Wesleyanism had become too respectable, forgetting its own emotional revivalist origins in the 1740s. Their appeal was to the non-respectable, with particular success among the rural labourers of eastern and northern England; revivalism remained an essentially rural phenomenon.

In general, Methodist offshoots, including such exotic growths as the 'magic Methodists' of Delamere Forest and the 'Kirkgate screamers' of Leeds, were politically more radical than the parent body. Despite the views of Elie Halevy and E. P. Thompson, however, it would be unwise to infer that Wesleyan Methodism was basically a conservative force (6, 188). Wesley himself was certainly a Tory; his administrative successors Jabez Bunting and Thomas Jackson also opposed all radical initiatives. Many lower down the hierarchy, however, found it perfectly possible to combine personal piety with radical views. Dissent implies criticism and it would have been strange indeed if many articulate working men, trained both in administration and in public oratory by the Wesleyan organization, should not have grasped the full logic of their position. Methodists were vital cogs in the engine of agitation, from trade unionism to Luddism, from pressure for political reform on beyond 1832 to Chartism. Despite well-publicized Primitive involvement in such activities as the pitmen's strikes of the 1840s, Wesleyans were just as active to change the status quo.

Further, Methodism in all its guises was regarded as a serious threat to the social order. The main fear was subversion of the lower orders. Respectable middle-class dissenters with a sizeable fortune, like the Unitarian MP William Smith, offered no threat and eighteenth-century experience had shown that both they and the old dissenters could be safely tolerated. Methodism's appeal to articulate and literate working men was different. Church apologists concentrated on the evils of an itinerant ministry which not only invaded the sanctity of the parish and challenged the authority of its parson but also gave dangerous men the opportunity to spread their poison across the country. Both Samuel Horsley, the pluralist High-Church bishop of Rochester, and George Canning in his articles for the *Anti-Jacobin* magazine laboured the point that Methodism was a cloak for democratic and atheistical activity. Lay preaching was condemned as blasphemous. In 1811, Viscount Sidmouth proposed a bill introducing new restrictions on dissenting ministers; aimed principally at itinerants, it was beaten off only after frantic lobbying by dissenters who emphasized, not for the first time, their unswerving loyalty to the established constitution.

IV

'A state is secure in proportion as the people are attached to its institutions; it is therefore the first, and plainest rule of sound polity, that the people be trained up in the way they should go.' Robert Southey, erstwhile reformer turned defender of the establishment, spoke for many when he indicated the importance of education in achieving the new moral order. By 1815 the argument was not whether education for the lower orders was proper but how much should be provided. The Sunday schools, which grew in such numbers after 1780, were by no means an evangelical preserve. In both Birmingham and Manchester the moving spirits included evangelicals and High-Churchmen as well as both Pittite and Foxite manufacturers and merchants (356). The schools were established to provide instruction in the Scriptures and also to show how to avoid idleness, debauchery and wickedness where parental example was all too often fallible.

More than 2,000 Sunday schools had been founded by the turn of the century; expansion thereafter was even more rapid with 8,000 in existence by 1821 and 23,000 by 1851. Enrolment covered about 10 per cent of children between the ages of 5 and 15 in 1801 and more than 55 per cent by 1851, when 2m. children were on the roll. Perhaps the most telling mid-century statistic about Sunday schools was that 75 per cent of working-class children attended them at least some of the time. In northern working class towns especially, as Laqueur has shown (356), they made a potent contribution to cultural formations. They provided not only instruction on Sundays but the important social penumbra of street parades, Easter and Whitsun outings and, for associated parents of modest means, sick and benefit clubs. By such agencies important 'Victorian' virtues such as industry, sobriety, regularity, and 'improving' leisure could be disseminated – and by no means only by the evangelicals. Even such a crusty High-Churchman as Bishop Douglas of Carlisle appreciated that permanent schools offered a means 'to strike at the root of that ignorant and brutal ferocity, which daily prompts so many unhappy wretches, the pests of society, to acts of horrible outrage, reproachable to good government, and disgraceful to humanity itself' (361, *356–7*). Whether the motive was to educate or to tame there were excellent grounds to support a system of schooling.

Controversy about school methods could be bitter. Hannah More's Sunday schools in the Mendips attracted sustained hostility from High-Churchmen in the so-called 'Blagdon controversy' over the extensive use of laymen. The dispute was a harbinger of more sustained distrust between, on the one hand, 'orthodox' Anglican foundations where laymen were employed sparingly and under strict regulation and, on the other, evangelical and nonconformist institutions where lay direction was much stronger.

All Sunday schools taught their pupils to read; it was accepted that the ability to read the Bible and scriptural homilies was essential. There was more doubt about the wisdom of instruction in writing. The issue split the evangelicals; Hannah More and the philanthropist Jonas Hanway were at one with Jabez Bunting in considering writing a dangerous skill for the poor to acquire. For them the precipice separating the opposed disasters of untamed, brute ignorance and a discontented class with inflated expectations born of inappropriately extensive education was desperately narrow. By the 1820s, however, the 'writers' were in a comfortable majority and both the national educational institutions – the National School Society, founded by High Anglicans in 1811 and the nonconformist British and Foreign School Society – permitted the teaching of writing, though usually within carefully controlled curricula.

The evangelical revival reformed the public morals of the great and helped to subject at least the better-off sections of the working class to a new discipline, congruent with the needs of a society in flux. As vulgar pastimes like cock-fighting, bull-baiting and rumbustious football matches played by whole villages were condemned so Sunday observance and sober recreation were promoted.

Many nonconformists preached total abstinence as the only answer to drunkenness. The emergence of temperance halls, such a feature of the Victorian town, satisfied both ideals: disciplined recreation and self-improving tasks in an abstemious atmosphere. The extent to which middle-class zealots imposed their own morality on reluctant sectors of society above and below can be exaggerated. Ample evidence exists to show both that the late eighteenth-century aristocrats increasingly saw the need for restraint and that artisans anxious to improve themselves eagerly grasped the chance to employ both working and leisure hours more productively. The success of the Puritan ethic of hard work and sobriety, though, owed much to fear of the impact of new ideas in a world of revolutionary economic and political change. Economic liberalism must be tempered by social quietism, and evangelical ideas offered a firm, if limiting, anchor in a world of turbulence. The Victorian age was to be secured by deeply held notions of responsibility and respectability; the pre-Victorian generation taught men to prize such attributes as never before.

---

1. *Parl. Hist.*, xxviii (1789–91), col. 405.
2. Cheshire R. O., EDV Vol. 1, p. 86.
3. *P.P.*, HC 1808, ix, pp. 237–60.

CHAPTER 7

The decline of the Whigs and the emergence of a new Conservatism, 1788–1812

I

This period is rarely considered as a unity yet it witnesses one of the most significant realignments in British political history. During it, the old Whig party, the dominant force under the first two Georges but in almost perpetual conflict with the third, splinters. From the ideological ferment engendered by the French Revolution comes a coalition of Pittites and old Whigs concerned above all to defend property and the old order against rash and speculative political notions like reform and religious toleration. Planted in soil already broken and tilled by expressions of popular anti-reformist 'Conservatism' from the 1770s onwards, the seeds of the modern Tory party germinate in the 1790s, though the naming of its true-blue flowers has to wait until the nineteenth century. The appellation 'Tory', redolent of a discredited opposition two generations earlier, stuck in the throats of the new coalition and was adopted diffidently only by second-generation Pittites during the government of Lord Liverpool after 1812.

The coalition also further weakened the vitality of political independence. The independents were a declining force in Parliament before 1780, but as the great issues of the 1790s, war, reform and religious toleration, polarized opinion, many expressed a consistent preference for the party of order, thus preparing the way for the virtual disappearance of the MP without party allegiance by about 1830. The Foxite Whigs, advocates of moderate reform and opponents of the war with revolutionary France, became an isolated group barely fifty strong in the Commons. Though the confusions of 1801–12 resulted in an accession of strength – the opposition could count on about 150 supporters by 1812 – the Whig split of 1794 effectively consigned the followers of Fox to a generation in the wilderness.

In this period, too, the nature of opposition begins to change. The Foxites were perfectly aware that there was no immediate prospect of office; there was equally little point in propitiating the independents. The climate at least afforded the bleak luxury of adherence to principle. Though the struggle was grossly unequal, it is arguable that Foxite opposition to the Pitt coalition rested more on issues and less on faction than any since 1714. Between 1784 and 1789 the Whigs in opposition had been remarkably cohesive thanks to the centripetal pull of Carlton House patronage and the organizational skills of William Adam, but they lacked ideological homogeneity.[1] This the Foxites of the 1790s could provide, if they lacked every other advantage, and it was a formidable political legacy to the nineteenth century. The complex development of principled opposition must neither be over-simplified nor foreshortened; the Foxites still attacked Pitt as the tool of a monarch who used his executive to trample on the liberties of Parliament, and thus all subjects – the tedious cliché of eighteenth-century opposition. Nor could ideological purity be maintained during the infighting of 1801–12. But the Foxite contribution to the philosophy of opposition should not be minimized. Fox presented himself as a party politician and he offered a separate and distinct party ideology.

II

In a natural anxiety to appreciate the seismic shock to the political system administered by the French Revolution many students have forgotten the tremors of the Regency crisis in 1788–89. This smaller landslip deserves its place, however, since it weakened Whig morale and revealed cracks which the party would not be given time to heal. The story of Whig disintegration properly begins in 1788 not in 1791–92. In the event the Whigs hoped for too much from the unexpected news which reached Pitt in October 1788 that the King had suffered a mental collapse. To George III's attendants, he had become suddenly mad, a diagnosis supported by Pitt after distressing visits to Windsor. Medical research, however, suggests that the King's illness was porphyria, a recurrent, hereditary metabolic disorder with purely physical causes but attended by varying degrees of mental disturbance.[2]

If the King could not discharge his constitutional functions there must be a regency and the obvious candidate was George, Prince of Wales, dissolute eldest son of the King. 'Prinny', a carousing and gambling partner of Fox at Brooks's club, was a committed Whig supporter in so far as he was committed to anything other than the pursuit of his own pleasures. It was an abiding trait of an unlovable dynasty that Hanoverian eldest sons loathed their fathers and built 'anti-courts' to which opposition politicians flocked. Thus the Whigs were adherents to what was known as the 'reversionary interest', one of the most spectacularly unsuccessful attachments in British political history since none of its adherents gained office for more than a week by adopting it.

The crisis seemed to offer unexpected deliverance from what they scathingly called the 'Pitt system', so unjustly triumphant in 1784. Pitt must hope for the King's recovery or the Prince would surely supplant him with Fox. He could capitalize on the constitutional uncertainties which a regency threw up by playing for time in employing his mastery of the Commons in debate and by ensuring that the most clear-headed Whigs were excluded from the committee to examine regency precedents. The House was persuaded in January 1789 to permit Prinny only limited monarchical powers while the permanence of the King's illness remained in doubt (37).

Whig manoeuvres were clumsy and revealed underlying discord, boding ill for the future. Their titular leader, the duke of Portland, disliked the Prince, considering him both irresponsible and a probable electoral liability at a time when public opinion was growing in importance. With characteristic lack of judgement the Prince preferred to listen to the advice of the playwright Richard Brinsley Sheridan, a voluble Whig spokesman with an enormous and misplaced opinion of his political talents whose vulgar showmanship, penchant for backstage deals and theatrical hyperbole all appealed to him. Sheridan aimed to cut through all constitutional knots by a *coup de théâtre* involving immediate installation of a Whig government with himself in a position of greater eminence than either his experience or his pedigree warranted. Portland was further alienated; Fox, who unhappily chanced to be touring Italy with his mistress when the crisis broke, found himself having to mediate between squabbling groups on his return, a task not facilitated by his poor health.

Edmund Burke urged avoidance of backstage activity and a direct challenge to Pitt's interpretation of the question in Parliament itself. Since Fox could, at best, muster upwards of 200 supporters during the crisis the possibility existed that Pitt could be defeated and the Whigs installed. Burke's influence within the party was not strong, however, and Pitt held on in the Lower House with characteristic tenacity. The lack of a united Whig leadership had been manifested well before the King's unexpected recovery in February 1789 ended the crisis as abruptly as it had begun. The Whigs were left dispirited. Fox's skill as a leader had been called into serious question; Portland and many in the party hierarchy now had cause to doubt both the loyalty and the judgement of young Turks like Sheridan; Burke had been pushed nearer the periphery of party affairs. In sum, a severe blow to the party's collective confidence had been dealt. The King's recovery was an outrageous piece of luck for Pitt, but it was luck which his own skill and his opponents' feeble response almost merited. Fox and his party could hardly have been worse prepared for the ferment which the 1790s had in store.

III

The effects of the French Revolution and of the European war it soon provoked dominated British political life for a generation. The ultimate direction of the revolution, however, was veiled from those who wondered at the fall of the Bastille in July 1789. Most British leaders were disposed to afford it a cautious welcome, believing that though the lesson had taken a century to sink into dull Gallic skulls the French had devised a means of establishing their own limited monarchy, along the lines of the Glorious Revolution of 1688. Fox was effusive: 'the greatest event ... that ever happened in the world', but he devoted his energies more to the campaign against the Test Act; Pitt was sure that 'the present convulsions in France must, sooner or later, terminate in general harmony and regular order' (38, 46). Only Burke saw the full implications of a revolution effected, unlike its alleged English counterpart, by the middle and lower ranks against the aristocracy. His *Reflections on the Revolution in France* (1790) was the first and much the most impressive attack on revolutionary pretensions and the incautious application of theories of liberty and natural justice. 'Those who attempt to level, never equalize. ... The levellers can only change and pervert the natural order of things.' The revolution would lead to bloodshed for lack of men of experience at the helm. 'The effect of liberty to individuals is, that they may do what they please: we ought to see what it will please them to do before we risk congratulations, which may soon be turned to complaints.'

The immediate impact of *Reflections* was slight; despite a tearful and public rift between Burke and Fox in the Commons in April 1791, the Whigs were sufficiently united to mount a serious challenge to Pitt over Ochakov (Ch. 4). Burke's *Appeal from the New to the Old Whigs*, which appeared in August, directly attacked Foxites who supported the revolution and invited that majority supporting order and established authority to separate from them. Events in France from mid-1791 seemed to vindicate Burke's gloomy prognosis and by the turn of the year conservative Whigs headed by William Windham and Earl Spencer were advocating resistance to check the French contagion.

Fox, whose main concern was to hold fast to the uncertain middle ground of Whig opinion where the great landowners Portland and Fitzwilliam still supported him, was intensely annoyed by the formation in April 1792 of the Association of the Friends of the People to press for parliamentary reform and to give direction to extra-parliamentary pressure groups already dubbed 'English Jacobins' by Windham and Burke. Though Windham himself perceptively recognized that the Friends of the People had the fundamentally conservative purpose of offering 'timely concessions & changes, temperately and judiciously made, to quiet the minds of the people'[3] the advocacy of an extension of the franchise while the French Revolution moved towards regicide and terror destroyed party unity. Fox's closest younger colleagues, Grey and Whitbread, seemed to be pulling him ever further from the defence of property. By the spring of 1792 Pitt was putting out feelers for a propertied coalition; Portland was consulted on the precise formulation of the proclamation against seditious writings, aimed principally at Tom Paine (Ch. 8). Conservative Whigs were much more alarmed at the prospect of internal sedition than most government ministers, a fact shrewdly exploited by Pitt during the next two years.

In refusing to condemn the September Massacres in France, Fox abandoned hope of holding the party together as a unit to bring down Pitt. As so often in his career, he allowed distrust of monarchy to cloud his wider judgement and his false parallel between the French and British examples had dire consequences. In January 1793 Loughborough became the first Whig defector to join the government when Pitt offered him the Lord Chancellorship, a post he coveted. When Britain declared war against France in February, Pitt characterized the struggle as for survival of civilized European values against the barbarities of a regicide nation. Windham immediately established a 'third party' from among those Whigs prepared to renounce all connection with their leader in the Commons; Fox was left *faute de mieux* with a minority of radicals. When Grey sought to raise the question of parliamentary reform in 1793, a measure Pitt had supported eight years earlier, he could find only forty-one supporters; Burke spoke against him from the Treasury benches.

It may seem surprising that the formal junction between Pitt and the conservative Whigs was delayed for seventeen months after the outbreak of war. Part of the explanation lies in the depth of family and political attachment in the Whig ranks; unlike Pitt's supporters the Whigs were a real party in the eighteenth-century sense. It lies also in the fact that not until early 1794 could the government offer evidence of a real and concerted threat by English Jacobins to the security of the State. The National Convention and the treason trials which followed it (Ch. 8) alarmed Portland and Fitzwilliam more than did the French war. It was vain for Fox and Grey to point out that English reformers asked for nothing more than certain members both of the Rockingham group and of the present government, notably the duke of Richmond, had demanded in the last tottering months of Lord North's administration. What mattered to Portland was not what was demanded but who was doing the demanding. The real key to the political realignment of 1794 was the Whigs' impeccable aristocratic pedigree. In the final analysis, Portland feared the lower orders more than he loved liberty; Fox, though no democrat, did not. Thus, Portland accepted Pitt's offer to meet on 24 May 1794 to agree upon a 'ministerial arrangement' which 'might make us act together as one Great Family' against the Jacobin threat (36, *409*).

Pitt's dispositions were characteristically shrewd. He demoted or dropped those of his followers who did not matter – Chatham, Camden and Stafford – to find room for the most prominent Whigs – Portland, Fitzwilliam, Windham, Spencer and Mansfield. Six of the thirteen Cabinet posts went to those who had opposed Pitt until 1793, a fair reflection of the importance he attached to the new configuration. He was careful to retain trusted followers like Grenville and Dundas in vital positions, bringing the Secretaryship for War out of commission to keep the latter at the centre of affairs once Portland had claimed the Home Secretaryship as his price for joining the coalition [A].

Grenville was delighted that the coalition had annihilated 'all distinctions of parties in this country among those who are attached to the present order of things'[4] It secured Pitt against all parliamentary hazard. Between 1794 and 1801 the opposition could rarely muster fifty votes and after the great set piece on parliamentary reform in 1797 [B.i.1] Fox led his small group into temporary secession, arguing that formal resistance was futile. The new alignment was a true conservative coalition, pledged to defend the principle of aristocratic government. In this important sense Portland could argue that it was he and not Fox who upheld the principles of 1688. The coalition drew ideological succour from the arguments of Burke in *Reflections* and increasing support from propertied opinion outside Parliament which united to resist the malign might of France. The new Conservatism, as yet unrecognized in name and but dimly appreciated in concept, represented a fusion of party cohesion and careful administrative expertise, the legacy particularly of second-generation Pittites like Hawkesbury (later Lord Liverpool), Perceval, Castlereagh, Canning, Huskisson and Peel, most of whom entered politics in the 1790s and 1800s.

The fifty or so remaining Foxites, mostly associated with the Friends of the People, could claim analogous progeny in nineteenth-century Liberalism. In the 1790s they offered passionate and principled, though inevitably nugatory, opposition to the various curtailments of liberty which the government deemed necessary in the interests of national security and the war effort (Ch. 8). Support for the ideals of the French Revolution, though never its later excesses, necessitated opposition to the war, though, after 1794, and with some independent support, they mounted a rearguard action against the strategy, tactics and waste of Pitt's campaigns.

The Foxites believed that the true Whig creed lay in the defence of the liberties of Englishmen and in promoting modest and necessary reform. Since these, together with free trade, were to be the triple bases of Liberalism it is easy to see why Fox is often seen as the bridge from the old political world to the new. His 1792 Libel Act, which made juries responsible for deciding whether written words were actually libellous rather than merely whether they had been written by the accused, lessened the powers of judges and undoubtedly saved many ordinary British subjects from the convict boat and the prison cell in the repressive climate which followed its enactment; it seems to stand four-square in the liberal tradition. But caution is necessary. Fox was an eighteenth-century politician. He saw politics as a struggle by Parliament against the influence of Crown and court and his battles for liberty were waged to limit the power of the Crown. The year 1794 he saw not as a victory for a conservative alliance but as a victory for George III over the politicians. He even saw Pitt as a court dupe. No man was ever more prisoner of the Whig legend than Charles James Fox. The King was still a figure of influence, but Fox was unable to see beyond this to appreciate the full significance of the radicalism of the 1790s. His followers formed the most aristocratic group in Parliament. More than half represented rotten boroughs and owed their positions to aristocratic influence; twenty-five of the fifty-five Foxites identified by Dr Mitchell had direct family connections with the peerage (34). Foxite opposition was forward-looking in its concentration on issues, though even here its fundamental concerns had a conservative base. It sprang unequivocally from the old political world.

IV

Between 1801 and 1812 Britain endured five weak governments. Personal rivalries play a large part in Cabinet-making and the clear party divisions of 1794–1801 do not survive. It would not be true to say, though, that the development of party allegiance is delayed; indeed, by the time that Liverpool becomes Prime Minister after the assassination of Spencer Perceval the outlines of modern Conservatism are much clearer than they had been in 1801. A two-party pattern based on policy divisions that would survive into the post-war world is discernible by 1812.

The most obvious constitutional characteristic of the period, however, is the continuing power of the monarchy to choose ministers. Perhaps the most striking example is the selection of Henry Addington, Speaker of the Commons, to succeed Pitt in 1801, but it is apparent also in keeping Fox out of office in 1804, in the 1807 Election which saw the defeat of many supporters of the recently replaced government and in the Prince Regent's freedom of choice which kept the Whigs out of office once more in 1810–11. Court influence temporarily gained from the confusion of party loyalties, but the situation was largely created by George III when he required Pitt to resign in 1801.

Pitt's resignation neatly illustrated the continuing vitality of two essentially 'eighteenth-century' factors, for this display of royal power was exercised on religious grounds. Pitt argued that the removal of political disabilities from Irish Roman Catholics was crucial for the establishment of harmony in that country and to put the recent Union of the two kingdoms on a secure footing (Ch. 11). George III believed Catholic emancipation to be a breach of his coronation oath and he recalled that the Hanoverian succession had been bedded on a firm Protestant ascendancy in both countries. He brusquely told Dundas that those who supported emancipation 'might be his personal enemies: and he hoped others would rally round him, who were not infected by these factious principles'.[5] It is also possible that he resented Pitt's increasing high-handedness in relations with him and the fact that the Cabinet was much more the Prime Minister's than the King's, a fact emphasized by the refusal of Grenville, Windham, Dundas and seven other ministers to continue in office without their leader. The new administration was desperately short of both talent and experience [A].

Criticism of the choice of Addington initially concentrated more on the lowliness of his birth than on his abilities. Polite society viewed the appointment of the son of a mere medical practitioner, even the personal physician to the great Chatham, as a scandal. The derogatory sobriquet 'The Doctor' which pursued Addington throughout his career was typically snobbish. His ministry was weak in debating talent in the Commons when faced by a rejuvenated Foxite group and by disgruntled Pittites like George Canning, but with Eldon, Hawkesbury and, from 1802, Castlereagh in it, it was not barren of administrative competence. The Peace of Amiens which the government negotiated [F.i] was popular. The 1802 Election occasioned no loss of support and some satisfaction was taken from the defeat at Norwich of the implacably bellicose Windham. It was the return of war in 1803 which undermined Addington. That 'new opposition' led by Lords Grenville, Fitzwilliam and Spencer which had most vigorously criticized the concessions to France at Amiens could now make common cause with most of the Foxites, for Fox himself was convinced that Bonapartism was a dangerous and aggressive antithesis of true revolutionary principles. The alliance of Fox and Grenville in 1804 formed the nucleus of a revitalized opposition and further evidence of the power of aristocratic clientage. Spencer and Windham, who had both been close to Fox before 1789, found it no embarrassment to return to the Whig fold.

Pitt's role was much more equivocal. Though he wished to see the end of an incompetent war ministry he had no taste for political manoeuvres with the Foxites to bring it down. Pitt's determination not to organize his own party in opposition, in fact, contributed significantly to the ministerial weaknesses of 1801–12. A conservative coalition could have been furnished with a strong party base under Pitt at almost any time between 1801 and 1806, yet the leader's disdain for party affiliation only encouraged uncertainty and factious squabbles among his erstwhile henchmen. He remained aloof while Grenville and Fox mounted their assaults, finally bringing Addington down over naval policy in 1804. Pitt's vast experience, moral stature and residual authority made him the natural replacement. While he saw the force of Grenville's contention for a wartime coalition including Fox, George III's veto of his old enemy was decisive. Pitt formed his final administration without Fox and also without Grenville who further strengthened the opposition by refusing to rejoin his old chief on the terms the King laid down [A]. In some respects Pitt was in a weaker position within months than Addington had been. Of the senior Pittites from the 1790s only Dundas (now ennobled as

Lord Melville) and Camden remained. Though Portland did not return to the Whig fold and though Addington was bought back into office with a peerage of his own (as Viscount Sidmouth) to assuage aristocratic taunts, it was not enough. Melville resigned in 1805 following a scandal involving misappropriation of navy funds and by the end of that year Pitt was desperately casting about for new allies. Only his untimely death in January 1806 prevented a governmental collapse as abject as Addington's had been.

Pitt's death removed the King's last prop against the return of the Whigs. There was insufficient talent at senior level among Pitt's adjutants and a coup on the model of December 1783 was now quite beyond George. Grenville was accordingly given an opportunity to construct the grand coalition which had been his aim since 1802. The 'Ministry of all the Talents' which resulted was by no means grand and not especially talented. Its base was the Fox–Grenville axis and its predominant complexion Whig. There were important places both for 1790s Foxites like Erskine and Grey (now Viscount Howick) and returned apostates like Spencer and Windham. A place was found for Sidmouth, however, and the only notable absentees were Portland and rising young Pittites like Hawkesbury, Castlereagh, Canning and Perceval, men outside the charmed Whig circle characteristically dismissed by Lord Holland as 'clerks and secretaries'.[6]

What the Talents gained in comprehension they lost in reforming impulse. There was no talk from Foxites of parliamentary reform and little enough of court influence. The only significant reform during the ministry's brief life was not a government initiative. The abolition of the British slave trade in 1807 was the climax of a long campaign by James Stephen and the evangelicals, though warmly supported by Grenville. The measure had been eased in 1806 by the abolition of the supply of slaves to foreigners, a move craftily justified not on moral grounds but as an aid to the war effort (153). The ministry squabbled about the allocation of offices and about war strategy. The death of Fox in October 1806 only increased a sense of aimlessness. The promotion of Roman Catholic emancipation in Ireland seemed to some to smack of ministerial death-wish and when George III responded in 1807 as he had in 1801, the Talents resigned their seals with little apparent regret.

The installation of the Portland ministry, stuffed full of Pittite 'clerks and secretaries', [A] and the General Election of 1807 which followed it are of first constitutional importance. George III, as ever, wished to secure a ministry which would acknowledge his rights both on choice of ministers and on vital constitutional matters. As we have seen, he placed Catholic emancipation firmly in the latter category. Canning and Castlereagh, who personally favoured emancipation, were prepared to forgo their preferences here to join a ministry which was the King's in terms both of personnel and broad policy. The results of the 1807 Election [B.v] show both the influence which the court continued to exercise in close boroughs and also the national popularity of a 'No Popery' rallying cry. The election was traditional in the exercise of influence, but innovatory in that the Whigs circulated party propaganda nationwide, albeit on a drearily repetitive theme: Crown influence used to trample the liberties of the people. Grenville, his translation to Whiggery apparently complete, supported the appeal, but his influence could not counterbalance the loss of Fox and the Whigs cannot have been surprised at their poor performance. In the 1807 Election it should be noted that the terms 'Whig' and 'Tory' came back to common political circulation to denote both opposition to, or support for, the King's position and alignments on the religious question.

The year 1807 was a victory for 'Toryism' but it brought neither stability nor unity to the Tory governments of 1807–12. The Portland ministry was dogged by charges of corruption and by personal rivalries. The duke of York was forced to resign as Commander-in-Chief in the wake of an army promotions scandal involving sales of commissions organized by his actress-mistress Mary Clarke. There were allegations of East India Company corruption which touched Castlereagh and further charges of electoral malpractice in Ireland. Canning, ambitious for further advancement, schemed within Cabinet for the removal of Castlereagh on grounds of corruption and incompetence in the war effort. Without successes in the war, indeed, no ministry could be secure from more general gripes about excessive taxation, misguided strategy and misuse of funds. That Curwen's much diluted Bribery Act [B.i.1] was the only Whig response to government ineptitude says much for that party's inadequacies. It was now led in the Commons by the instantly forgettable Irish MP George Ponsonby and uncertain how far to trim aristocratic pedigree to catch the first new stirrings of extra-parliamentary pressure for reform.

Portland, incapacitated by a stroke in 1809, gave way to Spencer Perceval, a competent finance minister with few noble connections, many evangelical sympathies and a doughty persistence in debate which had proved more than enough for the sparse Whig talent in the Commons. These attributes were not, however, proof against sniping from non-ministerial Tories like Canning and Castlereagh whose antagonism had cancelled each other out of contention for office. Perceval's ministry was narrowly based, lacking many Pittites of the first rank. He was unable to find a Chancellor of the Exchequer at all, and suffered the ignominy of having the post refused by an obscure Irish peer not yet twenty-five years old. His name was Palmerston. Most significantly, Perceval could not control his incompetently overbearing Foreign Secretary, Marquis Wellesley, Wellington's brother, who never bothered to conceal his contempt for 'Little P' and worked to supplant him.

The ministry staggered through mounting attacks on its economic and war policies during 1809 and 1810. Its salvation, and the prelude to the first truly stable modern ministry acknowledging the description Tory, came unexpectedly courtesy of a second Regency crisis. As in 1788, it was widely assumed that the King's mental incapacity in 1810, which was now to prove permanent, would lead inexorably to the formation of a Whig government. In 1810–11, as in 1789, the Prime Minister of the day strengthened his position through skilful handling of a basically unpromising situation. However, on this occasion the Prince Regent chose to retain Tory ministers and was not removed from the stage by unwelcome parental recovery. Perceval modelled his campaign on Pitt's precedent and rallied independent support by courageous and effective speeches; he achieved the appointment of a limited regency in the first instance. As in 1788, the Whigs miscalculated. They assumed the inevitability of office on their own terms; Grenville and Grey adopted a didactic tone which Prinny resented. He still relied on Sheridan yet he had drifted away from mainstream Whig sympathies since Fox's death. When the Whigs rejected the Prince's suggestion of a coalition with Perceval, he turned instead to investigate the possibilities of a rather more broadly based Tory ministry.

The Cabinet reconstruction of March 1812 brought in Castlereagh and Sidmouth; it also enabled Perceval to sack Wellesley whose own bid for the highest office had fallen flat during the crisis. The most secure administration since 1801 resulted; it was also arguably the most thoroughly anti-reformist since 1714. Sidmouth added reactionary sinew to the basically conservative instincts of Perceval and Liverpool. There was fundamental suspicion of extra-parliamentary agitation and a steely determination to resist its illegitimate importunities. Once Canning had refused office the dangers of a new split on Catholic emancipation receded. It was a true Church and King ministry girded to resist pressure for change. The assassination of Perceval by the deranged John Bellingham only two months later might have thrown all into the melting pot, particularly since the Regent now exercised full monarchical powers. His choice of Liverpool as the new Prime Minister dismayed the Whigs and provoked riots in hard-pressed Lancashire, but it was logical after the recent reconstruction and inevitable once Prinny accepted that Cabinet cohesion would prevail against the attempts of Wellesley, his own first choice, and Canning to storm in on their own terms.

Cohesion, indeed, is the major, if surprising, factor in political life in 1812 after the uncertainties of the previous eleven years. The Tory Cabinet had ideological homogeneity on most issues and successes in the war would soon cement it still further. The Whigs, for all their ditherings, also had cohesion of a kind. Grey and Grenville held the troops together from 1809 to 1812 against a series of attempts from Perceval, Prinny and Wellesley to coalesce with them. Their opposition to the 'Pitt gang' had snobbish undertones, but it had important policy dimensions too. Parvenus like Perceval were the King's choice, not Parliament's; they opposed Catholic rights which the Whigs supported; ministers opposed reform while the Whigs, guardedly, embraced it. The economic dimensions of the war after 1806 afforded further opportunity for principled opposition, on the side of beleaguered traders (Ch. 10). The Whigs faced the electorate in 1812 as a united party with policies quite distinct from those of the government. Though many of the issues in contention have a distinct eighteenth-century feel to them and though both parties had a vested interest in keeping the struggle safely in the control of existing propertied interests, political life had assumed a striking degree of modernity.

---

1. D. E. Ginter, *Whig Organisation in the General Election of 1790* (Berkeley, Calif., 1967), p. lvii.
2. I. McAlpine and R. Hunter, *George III and the Mad-Business* (1969).
3. Windham to John Gurney, B. L. Dept. of MSS, Add. MSS. 37873, ff. 175–6.
4. *Memoirs of the Court and Cabinets of George III* (4 vols, 1853–5) ii, pp. 256–7.
5. *Diary and Correspondence of Charles Abbot, Lord Colchester* (3 vols, 1861), i, p. 232.
6. A. D. Harvey, *Britain in the Early Nineteenth Century* (1978), p. 171.

CHAPTER 8

Radicalism, repression and patriotism, 1789–1803

I

The French Revolution let the genie out of the bottle. After 1789 it was impossible to keep political debate within a privileged circle of propertied interests. Though the British radicals of the 1790s had clear policies, based essentially on government elected without duress by all adult males, what they were was much more important than what they said. Eccentric aristocrats had advocated male suffrage before the revolution and no one had thought of locking them up. However, when shoemakers and metal-workers took the same line they challenged the whole structure of society and their arrogant presumption in calling upon the 'Rights of Man' left few in doubt that they determined to take a share in political decisions. The Revolution engendered a true ideological debate in Britain. In addition to radicalizing important sections of the lower orders, it produced a powerful conservative reaction. This reaction amounted to substantially more than the mere imposition of patrician values on an ignorant population. During the 1790s popular conservatism vied with popular radicalism for supremacy with contending versions of patriotism the main battleground.

The 1790s witnessed the first national political movement since the Civil War which involved the lower orders to a significant degree. The leaders of the popular radical societies were skilled operatives, apprenticed to a trade, independent of the traditional rural social order based on the leadership of the squire and the deference of the village labourer. The societies themselves were overwhelmingly urban; they flourished especially in towns with a large proportion of skilled men. Sheffield, with its cutlers and other metal craftsmen, was the birthplace of the first popular society, the Sheffield Society for Constitutional Information, in 1791; the Norwich weavers had a strong society; London, whose multifarious markets for luxury goods depended upon large numbers of highly skilled men from watchmakers to coachbuilders, printers to tailors and carpenters to cordwainers, was the home of the biggest and most influential organization, the London Corresponding Society (LCS). Skilled men could read and they were encouraged by events in France to think.

The *modus operandi* of the new societies, indeed, depended upon literacy. Most were called Corresponding Societies and they existed to spread the word of political liberty across the nation by circulating letters, pamphlets and propaganda and by inviting orderly debate on the various propositions for reform. The initiative was soon taken by the LCS founded in January 1792 by an expatriate Stirlingshire shoemaker, Thomas Hardy. Hardy's plan of 'informing the public of the violence that had been committed on their most sacred rights' was avowedly didactic.[1] He wished to promote discussion in alehouses throughout the land where workers met and he believed that in rational debate not only would his fellow men be convinced of the justice of the reformers' cause but that by the inexorable power of logic even the aristocracy could be converted to reform. The naive belief in the power of dispassionate reason to sway the minds of men, noble but misguided as anyone who has attended a council meeting or a committee can testify, is characteristic of radical politics from 1792 to 1795. Men like Hardy were to pay a heavy political and personal price for their credulity.

The infant artisan societies owed a great deal to the tutelage of middle-class reformers like John Cartwright, Horne Tooke and the Revd John Jebb who had advocated parliamentary reform in the early 1780s and were galvanized into further efforts after 1789. The Society for Constitutional Information (SCI) revived in the early 1790s and relations between this essentially bourgeois debating club and the LCS were close. Middle-class radicalism, in which dissenters and particularly Unitarians had always been prominent, had taken up the nonconformist cause in a protracted but unsuccessful campaign to repeal the Test and Corporation Acts. Between 1787 and 1790 three motions were introduced into the Commons which, though attracting substantial support among recently elected members from the boroughs, foundered on the argument that Church and State must stand or fall together. Most public offices remained closed to dissenters.

In Manchester the defeat of the reformers was a signal for the formation of a virulent 'Church and King' party in defence of the established order. Religious and political issues were soon fused and confused as opinions polarized. A meeting held by prominent merchants and dissenters in Birmingham to celebrate the second anniversary of the fall of the Bastille provoked five days of rioting by a Church and King mob. This resulted in the sacking of meeting-houses and the destruction of invaluable research materials collected by the Unitarian reformer Joseph Priestley who was also the foremost chemist of his day. Priestley became the first of many reformers to seek sanctuary from persecution in the United States of America. Anglican magistrates in Birmingham offered at least tacit support to the rioters in the early stages, seeing an opportunity not only to harass reformers but to strike down an alternative local élite (245). Similar factors were at work in Manchester in December 1792 when a mob attacked meeting-houses including the Cross Street chapel where the reformist Literary and Philosophical Society gathered. For weeks before the incident the Tory *Manchester Mercury* had been publishing hysterical diatribes. One correspondent urged action to 'crush those insidious vipers who would poison the minds of the people'.[2] The main target was the Manchester Constitutional Society, a mercantile and manufacturing group whose leaders, Thomas Walker and Thomas Cooper, were friends of Horne Tooke and attended meetings of the SCI when in London.

II

Radicalism in the 1790s was nourished from two sources: an older English tradition and the political philosophy of the European Enlightenment. The articulation of the English tradition was less lucid but probably of as much significance. Its talisman was the free-born Englishman. Many radicals fantasized that the Norman Conquest had been the agency of enslavement. The Anglo-Saxon witenagemot was travestied as some kind of proto-democratic assembly and it was not without significance that those who were supposed to have destroyed this liberty were Frenchmen. Believers in the 'Norman Yoke' developed a strong sense of what might be called egalitarian patriotism. Those who succeeded the Normans were no more sensitive to English liberties. Although kingly despotism had been destroyed by the constitutional struggles of the seventeenth century, the main beneficiaries were not ordinary folk but the great landowners. Their system of government depended upon heavy indirect taxation of such necessities as bread and salt. The proceeds of such taxation were used to support a vast army of placemen and other corrupt office holders. Increasingly, during the eighteenth century, they were also used to finance wars from which the lower orders failed to benefit.

The free-born Englishman, therefore, must liberate himself from the corrupt fetters of the state and agitate for a government based on manhood suffrage. Many artisan radicals looked to the Levellers of the 1640s for inspiration. John Lilburne's call for direct representation of 'the poorest he' struck a chord. They shared the view of Thomas Paine that the Bill of Rights in 1689 – that Whig icon of the Glorious Revolution – was in truth 'a bill of wrongs and of insult' because it did nothing to increase the rights of ordinary citizens. The true patriotic response was to agitate for fundamental political reform and to put an end to oligarchical corruption. It was a strain of protest which would continue to inspire radicals for at least another half-century, and into the Chartist agitations of the late 1830s and 1840s (Ch. 29).

Tom Paine is best remembered for his contribution to the second source of British radicalism. The publication of his *Rights of Man* is perhaps the single most important event in the history of British radicalism. Paine, a member of the SCI but with wide experience in America, was a superb propagandist. *Rights of Man* is not a deeply penetrative book, but no other remotely rivalled its ability to crystallize the abstractions of Enlightenment thought and present them in vivid and popular style to an audience of working men avid for a comprehensible interpretation of the significance of the French Revolution. Conceived as a rebuttal of Burke's *Reflections, Rights of Man* was much more rumbustious in tone. Part I, which appeared in 1791, cut great rationalist swathes through Burke's defences of custom and privilege. Each generation must be capable of acting for itself and should not be bound by the precedents of the dead. Universal manhood suffrage was the only means of achieving a properly elected assembly capable of deliberating and acting for the whole of society. Aristocracy and monarchy depended on the arbitrary fortune of hereditary succession and primogeniture; neither institution had any basis in logic. Aristocratic government at best gives undue preference to the interests of one numerically insignificant class; at worst it tramples other interests underfoot. Part II followed in 1792. It offered practical policies for democratic governments to follow. Since war derived only from the conflicting self-interests of monarchies, democracies could afford to decimate the defence budget. The money thus saved could be deployed on social welfare schemes such as free education, family allowances and old-age pensions. Additional support for this anticipation of a Welfare State would come from progressive income and wealth taxes.

Rarely can a book have been so precisely tailored to its market. *Rights of Man* is not a socialist tract; it speaks of equality of rights and of opportunity but there is nothing in it which could be construed as a disincentive to individual effort. Paine's targets were unearned privilege and inherited wealth. He spoke directly to skilled men who looked for advancement to their own talents. The artisans who were the driving force or the new radicalism were, or wished to be, self-made men with aspirations to the status of small master manufacturer. They thus had economic as well as political ambitions; attacks on lazy aristocrats who ruled without 'legitimate' qualification while they amassed vast fortunes by inheritance and the collection of rent, the tribute of other men's efforts, squared with both. It is not surprising that the proselytizing fervour of the Corresponding Societies helped to make Paine's book a best-seller. Part II, immediately produced in a cheap 6d. edition, sold 200,000 copies within a year. It suffused the towns and penetrated even remote villages in North Wales and the Scottish Highlands. Hannah More was alarmed at its appearance in the Mendips, though her own anti-reformist *Repository Tracts* (Ch. 6) were to sell far more (251).

It was the very popularity of Paine's work which exercised the authorities. Part I, selling at 3s. (15p) to middle-class groups, could be tolerated; a cheap edition of Part II to inflame untutored and impressionable minds was quite another matter. The King's Proclamation against Seditious Writings of May 1792 was the first sign of government concern at the spread of radical propaganda and it was directed against Tom Paine. 'We cannot see without indignation, the attempts which have been made to weaken in the minds of his majesty's subjects, sentiments of obedience . . . and attachment to the form of government.'[3]

By this time, Paine had prudently skipped the country and his final legacy to the artisan movement was of more dubious value. His heady words intoxicated carpenters and weavers into believing not only that their reformist cause was just but that justice would prevail. He bequeathed to the radicals his own unbridled belief in the powers of reason. Had he not written in offering Part II of his great work to the world: 'I do not believe that Monarchy and Aristocracy will continue seven years longer in any of the enlightened countries in Europe'? The very success of his book lulled the artisan movement into an unrealistic sense of optimism. Little thought was given to any alternative strategy if aristocrats, rendered redundant by the reasoning of Thomas Paine, sought to combat his reason with their repression to defend not only themselves but European civilization as they understood it. It is frequently remarked how easily authority triumphed over reform in 1794–95; it is less frequently appreciated how ill-prepared were the reformers in Britain for any struggle which spread beyond the comfortable limits of the printed pamphlet or the discussion group.

In terms of membership, the Corresponding Societies never offered a real threat. The LCS at its peak in 1795 numbered about 5,000; provincial radical societies were all smaller and some, for all their pernickety constitutions and their elaborate ground rules for orderly conduct of debate, had memberships in the dozens. Such calculations, however, miss the point. As with nonconformist sects, adherents and sympathizers were far more numerous than formal members and the societies could stage impressive displays of support in the open-air protest meetings which were such a feature between 1793 and 1795. Reformers, whose main charge was the irrationality and corruption of a government based on narrow sectional interest, counted on substantial ancillary support when prices were high and unemployment rife. The trading dislocations of the war together with the largely fortuitous harvest shortages in 1794–95, provoked widespread discontent for the radicals to exploit to embarrass the government.

III

Radical propaganda laid down the gauntlet and the authorities were not slow to pick it up. We should be careful, however, in identifying 'the authorities'. The conservative reaction was not just, or even primarily, a matter of sly counter-propaganda manipulated from Westminster. The counterblast to radicalism in Britain in the 1790s was multi-faceted; it involved the press, the Church of England, local government and the militia among others. It has recently been contended that this counterblast was more effective than government repressive legislation in driving radicalism underground from 1795 onwards. Dickinson has argued that 'radicalism was less popular and less securely based than once thought . . . One of the most significant impacts of the French Revolution on British politics was the enormous boost it gave to popular conservatism' (44, *103*). Especially after the outbreak of war with revolutionary France in 1793, patriotism emerged as a trump card. As Linda Colley has shown, from such unpromising personal material as 'Farmer' George III was created a national icon of common sense, religious propriety, family values and straightforward decency to set against the wild, theoretical speculations of those 'Jacobins and Atheists' in temporary, discordant charge of the destinies of France. Cartoons and sympathetic portraits by the score rammed home the message. In 1809, with the wars far from won, the radical Whig Samuel Romilly reflected that what had 'added tenfold strength to every motive of endearment to the King [were] the horrors of the French Revolution' (23, *208*).

Loyalist political societies also played an important part in counteracting the influence of radicalism. The most famous, John Reeves's Association for the Protection of Property against Republicans and Levellers, was founded in London in November 1792, probably in response to a judicial appeal to the Grand Jury of Middlesex for respectable citizens to mobilize themselves against those who supported 'monstrous and nonsensical' doctrines of equality (47, *155*). Once established, the Reeves Association Movement received government support but perhaps more important was the launching of emulative movements in most British cities. All stressed the need to counteract dangerous radical ideas, support the Church and heighten the nation's sense of patriotic duty. Some accompanied exhortation with threat. One of Reeves's correspondents eagerly offered to cut out the tongues of those who agitated 'seditious and detestable subjects . . . I can be of . . . service in that line, having been a little bit of a farrier in my time'.[4] In most places, loyalist organizations – supported by a vociferous, loyalist press, such as *True Briton*, the *Liverpool Phoenix* and the *Newcastle Courant* – appear to have had greater popular support than did the radical societies. However, in places where artisans and other skilled workers were especially numerous the political battle was more even.

As usual, the Church of England was staunch in support of the authorities. Huge numbers of loyalist sermons were preached while popular writers such as William Jones (Ch. 6) found a ready outlet for their talents. Church writings emphasized the simple virtues of obedience to both religious and secular authority. Patriotic duty was also a frequent theme. Many of the more thoughtful defenders of the established order pointed out that continued obedience from the lower orders necessitated a reciprocal response from their betters. R. B. Nicholls, dean of Middleham (Yorkshire), called for moral reformation and an increase in taxes on the pleasures of the rich to give the poor a good example. During the high-price years of 1795–96, many proposals for aiding the poor were discussed of which the Speenhamland experiment (Ch. 25) was only the most famous. Pitt himself at the end of 1796 proposed to Parliament a generous scheme to revise the poor laws. These involved requiring parishes to provide additional relief and also to increase opportunities for work (36, *472–4*). Though these were rapidly withdrawn after criticism over details, other MPs suggested also that the aristocracy should set a proper example by limiting their own consumption of bread.

Defence of the established order was further buttressed by the success of the Volunteer Movement. This developed in 1794–95 in response to a government plan for the establishment of local companies of volunteers. This involved arming and equipping local forces by public subscription and the response from property owners was enthusiastic. In some places, Association Movements transformed themselves seamlessly into volunteer organizations. The main purpose, without doubt, was propagandist rather than defensive but the numbers involved were substantial. Just short of half a million volunteers had been enlisted by the time of the Napoleonic invasion scare in 1804. There were, however, limits to their enthusiasm. Working-class members of volunteer companies, for example, refused to move against food rioters in the South-west during the dearth years of 1795 and 1801. Many of the lower orders were strongly loyalist but they clearly felt that excessive profits made by middlemen during famine years required an appropriately paternalist response from the authorities.

IV

Loyalist patriotism was dominated by property owners but it was very widespread and it embraced shopkeepers as well as rich merchants and large landowners. It also served its primary domestic purpose. Many radical groups were forced to seek alternative accommodation as magistrates threatened not to renew alehouse licences if premises were used for political meetings. Gilt boards inscribed 'No Jacobins Admitted Here' appeared in many licensed premises in Manchester from late 1792. During 1793 prosecutions of radicals began in earnest. In Scotland, where laws on sedition were tight and juries easily browbeaten by self-righteous Calvinist harangues from the judiciary, the lawyer Thomas Muir and the English Unitarian preacher Thomas Fysshe Palmer were sentenced to transportation to Botany Bay for encouraging Paine's and other disaffected books to be read. A 'National Convention' of British radical societies was held in Edinburgh in November and December 1793. The parallels with the French model were obvious and the more alarming to the authorities since delegates were considering alternative strategies in the light of the recent heavy defeat of their petition for parliamentary reform [B.i.1]. While hardier spirits contemplated the awful prospect of arrogating to themselves the title of true representatives of the nation, the authorities broke up the Convention and arrested its leaders. The LCS delegates, Maurice Margarot and Joseph Gerrald, almost the only English representatives to brave the long journey north, joined Muir and Palmer on the convict boats. Gerrald and William Skirving, the Scottish organizer of the Convention, died soon after arrival.

South of the border a committee of secrecy including Pitt and other leading ministers was investigating the strength and seditious intent of the radical societies. Some evidence of illegal manufacture of pikes and armed drilling on remote West Riding and Perthshire moors was dredged up and given disproportionate prominence in the committee's report. For the most part, societies were discovered to meet and correspond with one another; they sent messages and even 'fraternal delegates' to Paris, asking for support to establish the reign of liberty in Britain. Enough evidence was forthcoming to persuade Parliament of the desirability of suspending Habeas Corpus in April 1794. Pitt's speech on the issue was uncharacteristically violent. He purported to believe that the radical societies threatened a 'whole system of insurrection . . . laid in the modern doctrine of the rights of man; – that monstrous doctrine, under which the weak and ignorant, who are most susceptible of impression from such barren abstract positions, were attempted to be seduced to overturn government, law, property, security, religion, order, and every thing valuable in this country'.[5] Many radicals would have been gratified to think that they cut so much ice with the Prime Minister; more would not have recognized themselves or their alleged influence.

Committee of secrecy evidence was also the basis of the prosecution case against twelve leading London radicals arraigned for treason in May 1794. Hardy, Horne Tooke and John Thelwall, the radicals' leading man of ideas, were among those arrested but, to the undisguised joy of taunting crowds who processed through the streets, the jury found insufficient evidence to sustain a conviction. Even in this triumph the brittleness of radical leadership was apparent. Hardy's pregnant wife was twice violently disturbed – once by Bow Street runners rummaging for evidence and once in an attack on their house by a loyalist mob. She died shortly afterwards. Hardy withdrew from active politics and concentrated on his livelihood. By 1797 he was to be found a respectable small manufacturer in Fleet Street, a freeman of the Cordwainers Company and liveryman of the Needlemakers Company. Respectability had overtaken him. Horne Tooke left the centre of the stage and middle-class support for radicalism cooled perceptibly after the arrests of 1793–94.

After 1794, indeed, artisans relied largely on economic discontent to keep their hopes alive. It is insufficiently realized how far the main threat of radicalism was associated with downswings of the trade cycle and with harvest failure. Skilled weavers, among the aristocracy of labour, were severely affected by a trade depression in 1793 and the early strength of the movement owes much to their grievances. At least 7,000 workers were unemployed in Manchester by May and Sheffield cutlers' wages were cut by up to one-half. Radicals were able to use the war, which they anyway opposed on ideological grounds, to recruit further support by arguing that it disrupted trade and pushed up prices. Nor could the government point to victories to vindicate the nation's sacrifice.

The climax was reached in 1795 when smouldering resentment was fanned into flaming discontent by harvest failure which saw wheat prices rise to more than 75s. (£3.75) a quarter, 23s. higher than the previous year and 70 per cent higher than prices in the last year of peace [D.vi.3]. Massive outdoor meetings were held to call for parliamentary reform and an end to the war; a substantial engine of agitation was constructed with radical societies at the controls. When in October, stones were thrown at the King's coach on his way to open a new session of Parliament, Pitt used the opportunity to launch a new offensive against the radicals. The attack occurred three days after a reform meeting in Copenhagen Fields and the government linked the two incidents, though without compelling evidence. The 'Two Acts' significantly curtailed the liberties of Englishmen. The Seditious Meetings Act prohibited any meetings of more than fifty persons without consent of a magistrate. The Treasonable Practices Act tightened the loose treason laws to encompass not only those who conspired to levy war within the kingdom or to devise evil against the King but also those who spoke or wrote against the constitution. Not even the most benificent London jury could have acquitted Hardy or Tooke if arraigned under the new statute, and Fox rightly pointed out that anyone who advocated the most mild measure of parliamentary reform was liable to transportation under it.

Impressive demonstrations were redundantly staged as the bills passed quickly through their parliamentary stages. Samuel Coleridge inveighed against the curtailing of free discussion: 'Those sudden breezes and noisy gusts, which purified the atmosphere they disturbed, are hushed to deathlike silence. The cadaverous tranquillity of despotism will succeed the generous order and graceful indiscretions of freedom.'[6] Pitt was unmoved and the ranks of the propertied remained unbroken. Only five peers voted against the Treasonable Practices Bill; the bishop of Rochester ensured his place in the annals of liberty by declaring during the debate that 'he did not know what the mass of the people in any country had to do with the laws but to obey them'.[7]

V

Radicalism was silenced in 1795 expertly and with some ease. In truth, the open radical societies had no response once their arguments on reform had failed to sway a Parliament of property owners, and property owners throughout Britain, who were now more or less united in the belief that their patrimony was threatened. Against the might of property the vigorous and optimistic lucidity of Thomas Paine was totally inadequate weaponry. To the extent that radicalism in this early phase offered little effective challenge to the established order it might be argued that Pitt's government over-reacted in its repressions of liberty. It should be remembered, however, that the policy was at least partly designed to frighten property owners into a realization that they must adopt defensive positions to curb the enemy within. This achieved, Pitt could afford not to institute the witch-hunt of prosecutions the legislation of 1795 seemed to presage.

Radicalism after 1795 was driven underground, but its significance in this later phase should not be underestimated. The new generation of radical leaders were perforce plotters; revolutionary machination naturally took the place of organization and open argument. The influence of the disturbed kingdom of Ireland also becomes more manifest. The LCS numbered among its leaders Irishmen like Benjamin and John Binns who looked for salvation to an association between English radicals and the United Irishmen. John Binns was arrested in 1798 along with Father James O'Coigly who was planning a concerted British and Irish uprising with French assistance. Incriminating documents concerning a 'Secret Committee of England' to support a French invasion and urge the Directory to mount one speedily were enough to send O'Coigly to the gallows. The execution of Captain Edward Despard, the son of an Irish landowner, for treason in 1803 effectively ends the second, conspiratorial, phase of the radical movement. Though Despard's personal importance has been overstated by historians the conspiracy which wrongly bears his name bears further testimony to a new radical strategy dependent on initiatives from France (31).

Radical activity after 1795 turned increasingly to the possibility of *coup d'état.* Francis Place was only the most famous of the reformers to be fundamentally out of sympathy with the strategy and to blame it on the 'absurd fanatics' who had taken over the movement. It is beyond dispute that many radical activities in this period were inherently bizarre and self-destructive; additionally, an effective government spy-system ensured that most cadres were penetrated almost at inception. Yet the government was right to treat the threat seriously. The years 1797–98 and 1801–2 were ones of real crisis. Harvests failed again [D.vi.3] and against a background of economic discontent and widespread unemployment the country was nearer military defeat in 1797 than at any time during the wars. A demoralized and underpaid navy mutinied twice and the second mutiny, at the Nore off the Medway towns, showed much evidence of radical sympathy. Its leader, Richard Parker, was a member of the LCS and sought to bring the *Rights of Man* onto the lower deck. Had the French mounted an invasion in the spring or early summer, as they threatened to do, it is difficult to see how it could have been repelled. Even the token force which landed at Fishguard sent shivers of apprehension right up an under-protected west coast. Pitt reneged on government debts in the same year when he suspended cash payments from the Exchequer as a desperate resort to stave off bankruptcy. In such times even 'absurd fanatics' offer a real threat, particularly when they seek help from a powerful enemy.

In 1796–98, as before, local propertied interests were not found wanting. They more or less willingly paid higher taxes, culminating in the first income tax, introduced by Pitt in 1799. A supplementary militia was raised by compulsory ballot in 1796 and local volunteer corps were needed, especially in the North and West of England, as the focus of radical activity shifted away from London. In 1796 a Manchester Corresponding Society was founded in defiance of the Two Acts and with no middle-class support; it remained a reformist working-class organization with some strength in the new cotton factories. Even more pointedly, branches of the United Englishmen, drawing both on the inspiration and the expatriate membership of the United Irishmen, were spreading outwards from Manchester by 1797 (45). The Ancoats area of Manchester was a focus for disaffection, rumours of arms caches and the administration of secret seditious oaths. Spies' reports, actively commissioned by zealous Jacobin baiters like T. B. Bayley and Ralph Fletcher, pointed to a close correlation between economic privation, particularly among self-reliant weavers, and political disturbance. The spate of large protest meetings which greeted the expiry of the Two Acts and return of Habeas Corpus in April and May 1801 lends verisimilitude to stories of much underground preparation earlier. An alarmed government rapidly put the Acts back into operation and Habeas Corpus into commission. One should naturally be suspicious of evidence accumulated by spies, but some historians have too readily discounted it. Much information about secret meetings and plottings can be independently corroborated and neither magistrates nor Home Office officials greatly took to being duped. Spies who believed that their work was paid on piece-rates with no quality control found themselves rapidly removed from the payroll.

We may conclude that a transformed radical movement survived the repression of 1795 and offered a real threat at times when hunger and high prices provided receptive ears for the propaganda of a small number of revolutionary activists. The proximity of Ireland meant that the North-west was a natural haven for agitators though South Yorkshire was also seriously disturbed in 1801–2. Workers in the new factory textile towns were touched by radical ideas at least from 1797. The influence of revolutionaries on hungry workers was not discounted by sane businessmen. As the Bolton factory owner Thomas Ainsworth put it in 1801: 'There is nothing to fear from Jacobinism further than availing themselves [*sic*] of the distracted state of the country . . . if the government does not interfere in respect to the price of provisions every day will grow worse and in the end it will not have it in its power to quell the rising spirit of the people.'

Though the government did not so interfere, lower prices brought respite in 1802. The Peace of Amiens further removed the most potent radical propaganda thrust: war causes distress. Before that, however, the government had needed to pass further legislation against unlawful oaths (1797), to regulate newspapers for the more effective prosecution of seditious writings (1798) and to proscribe named dangerous organizations, including the LCS and all forms of United men. By 1800, Pitt knew that although victories brought loyalist crowds on to the streets the manipulated Church and King mob was already a thing of the past. Nevertheless, the sting of radical agitation had been drawn by 1803. Once war resumed, no one could plausibly maintain that the original ideals of the French Revolution were being sustained by the military dictatorship of another monarch, the Emperor Napoleon I. Radicals no longer looked to France for salvation. Yet a legacy remained. Drawing on the lessons of the 1790s, artisans and factory workers – whose economic interests were beginning to converge – would renew their demands for a more liberal franchise once conditions worsened again towards the end of the war. The Industrial Revolution added ever greater weight to arguments about the over-representation of the rural South and the irrationality of pocket boroughs. Threats of revolution had been easily countered, but the wider reform issue would not go away.

---

1. Thomas Hardy, *Memoir* (1832), p. 11.
2. Thomas Walker, *A Review of Some Political Events which have occurred in Manchester* (1794), p. 44.
3. *Parl. Hist.*, xxix (1791–92), col. 1479.
4. B. L., Add. MSS. 16,919 ff. 5–6, 20–8.
5. *Parl. Hist.*, xxxi (1794–95), cols 498–9.
6. 'The plot discovered', L. Patton, and P. Mann, eds, *Collected Works of Samuel Taylor Coleridge* (1971), i, p. 289.
7. *Parl. Hist.*, xxxii (1795–97), col. 258.

CHAPTER 9

The wars with France: I Pitt's War, Addington's Peace, 1793–1803

The greatest and most costly war Britain had yet fought came upon her almost unawares. On 17 February 1792 Pitt announced reduced defence expenditure during his budget speech to the Commons, asserting 'unquestionably there never was a time in the history of this country, when, from the situation in Europe, we might more reasonably expect fifteen years of peace than at the present moment'.[1] On 1 February 1793 the French National Convention declared war on Britain. That Pitt was prepared to prophesy lasting peace as late as 1792 strongly suggests that he did not envisage the eventual war as a holy crusade against Jacobinism and democracy. True to British traditions in foreign policy no action was taken as first Prussia and then Austria declared war on revolutionary France during 1792. Even the September Massacres, the declaration of a French republic and the arrest and execution of Louis XVI were not regarded as pretexts for war in themselves. Pitt fully shared contemporary horror at these events, but maintained that Britain's interests would not be served by interference in the affairs of a foreign power. He was much more exercised by the French Army's unexpected victory over the Austrians at Jemappes in November 1792 which opened up all her Belgian territories to French occupation. The action was rapidly followed by the freeing of the Scheldt estuary to navigation by foreign ships and a rhetorical flourish offering French 'fraternity and assistance' to all peoples seeking to break the yoke of monarchy and tyranny. The French Revolution was now for export.

Britain's concern with the Low Countries was obvious. Not only was it bound to the Dutch by the Triple Alliance [F.i.2] but a French presence in Belgium threatened domination of the entire coastline of North-west Europe by a hostile power. This prospect was accentuated by evident aggressive French intent towards the Dutch. Domestic security as well as trade were at risk. As Grenville informed the French Ambassador, Chauvelin, in December 1792, England 'will never see with indifference that France shall make herself, either directly or indirectly, sovereign of the Low Countries, or the general arbitress of the rights and liberties of Europe'.[2] It was to contest the ambitions of an aggressor in an area sensitive to British interests rather than to defend the crowned heads of Europe from the ravages of republicanism, therefore, that Pitt took Britain to war.

Pitt's war policy has been the subject of much misinterpretation. It is alleged that he was an inadequate war minister, comparing most unfavourably with his father. His record is cited to buttress the undiscriminating but compelling cliché that constructive peacetime statesmen make inadequate warlords. It is said that his military acumen was slight and that he committed too much of Britain's strained resources to picking off irrelevant French West Indian sugar islands when he should have been striking straight for the heart of the enemy by sustained

Continental campaigns. It is finally asserted that he left the real business in the hands of fickle and weak allies, usually Prussia and Austria, whom he kept in the field only by lavish and ill-considered subsidies, 'Pitt's gold', which slipped wantonly through feckless and fumbling central European fingers.

Such contentions rest in equal measure upon incorrect information and inadequate understanding of Britain's war aims. Much as frightened conservative Whigs like Windham and Burke would have liked to make them see it so, Pitt and his war ministers Grenville and Dundas did not envisage the war primarily as a means of extirpating the Jacobin heresy. When Pitt talked of his aim as 'security' he did not interpret that word in any narrow sense. He knew that reliance on the navy was essential to an island country, but was also alive to the fact that overseas trading interests, particularly in the Americas, offered an opportunity of tilting the balance in Britain's direction. The West Indian islands captured from the French and Dutch between 1794 and 1796 [F.ii.1] were more than peripheral bargaining counters for use in later peace negotiations. They shifted the balance of trade in Britain's direction and Britain was quintessentially a trading nation. As Dundas put it, British victories in the West Indies were 'of infinite moment, both in the view of humbling the power of France, and with the view of enlarging our national wealth and security' (44, *130*). The efforts made by the French to prevent losses in the West, moreover, indicate that the force of the argument was not lost on them.

There were many failures and embarrassments, it is true. Guadeloupe and St Lucia, taken from the French in 1794, were both recaptured by the end of 1795. The immensely valuable prize of Haiti, rich in sugar, coffee and cotton, seemed to have been wrested from the French and Spanish by the capture of coastal towns in 1794; but it was never secured and the government's reluctance to commit further resources in defence of settlements threatened by Toussaint L'Ouverture's Negro rebellion in 1796–97 doomed the enterprise. Worst of all, yellow fever ravaged British troops. With 40,000 men killed and a similar number incapacitated, Britain lost more men in the West Indies than Wellington was to lose in the entire Peninsular campaigns at the end of the war. Yet with more than 50 per cent of all British exports destined for the New World early in the nineteenth century [D.ii.5] and with the wars arguably settled by economic more than military might, Pitt's strategy by no means merited the caustic criticism meted out by such as Burke who wished to see British troops aimed directly at Paris and its hated National Convention. Furthermore, when Holland was overrun and forced to declare war against British as the Batavian Republic, easier pickings appeared in the East. The Cape of Good Hope and Ceylon were taken in 1795; both were to be vital staging-posts for Britain's informal 'empire of trade' in the nineteenth century.

Nor did Pitt offer to Britain's Continental allies the indiscriminate subsidies his critics often suggest. As Professor Sherwig has shown, though Britain released almost £66m. to allies during the French Wars, subsidies were not adopted on a large scale until after Pitt's death (162). Nearly half the total subsidy money was paid during the great push against Napoleon after 1810; only £9.2m. was provided before the Peace of Amiens. European capitals in the 1790s were prone to complain of Britain's unwonted niggardliness in the matter of subsidies since these, in lieu of spilling British blood on foreign fields, had been the customary means of waging land wars. Austria, provided with two loans in 1795 and 1797 rather than the subsidies she requested, complained of ruinous interest charges.

Pitt's subsidies were tuned to a keen strategic awareness. Since Britain had gone to war to preserve the integrity of Holland, he sought to pay those northern European states which might be expected to share his concern at French designs in the Low Countries. The primary beneficiaries were the North German states: Prussia, Hesse-Cassel, Hesse-Darmstadt and, naturally, Hanover. The plan misfired largely because of Prussia's predomiminant interest in picking up more eastern territory from the final partition of Poland. Prussia's sphere of influence remained the Baltic, not the North Sea. The first coalition against the French [F.i.3] was in reality a very loose federation of states with fundamentally different interests. It is not surprising that it crumbled before the fixity of purpose of Carnot's conscripted *leveé en masse*. By 1795 only Austria and Britain remained in the field and relations between these states were notoriously frosty. Austria wished to sever her northern connections by exchanging Belgium for more defensible territory which could consolidate her interests in South-central Europe. British ministers were well aware of this and took little pains to conceal their reluctance to be bound in close accord with her. Grenville moaned in 1794 about 'the difficulty of getting them to adopt any decided line of conduct' and doubted 'very much how far they would cordially concur in the defence of the Netherlands, even though they might consent to do so in the words of their contract'.[3] Crushing Austrian defeats in Italy at the hands of the young Napoleon forced her to peace with France in 1797, leaving Britain totally isolated and facing its greatest crisis of national security between 1588 and 1940. Pitt, however, had never placed much reliance on Habsburg power to avert the storm.

It might be objected in view of the fragility of Britain's allies that Pitt could hardly have done worse by committing more troops to the European mainland. This is doubtful. The army was in no state to sustain a long campaign. So far from there being no Marlborough bestriding a parade ground there was not even a Commander-in-Chief in office at the commencement of hostilities and the army numbered only 13,000 men. The duke of York's expedition in defence of Holland in 1793–94 achieved nothing. Attempts to aid French royalists at Toulon (1793) and in Brittany and the Vendée (1795) [F.ii.1] were spectacularly unsuccessful. Improvements in army organization date only from the duke of York's period in office as Commander-in-Chief after 1795 by which time hopes of a decisive land thrust against ill-organized French forces had long since evaporated.

The most valid criticisms of Pitt paradoxically derive from his peacetime successes. His rehabilitation of national finances was partly at the expense of depleted defence estimates. Rarely had Britain's army and navy been so undermanned as in 1793. Once war broke out, one may further criticize Pitt's flirtations with the French royalists. Limited expeditions such as those to Toulon and the Vendée had failed miserably in earlier eighteenth-century wars. The overall strategy, though not always coherently controlled, was more or less inescapable. In Europe, the more the matter is considered, the less easy it becomes to suggest an alternative. In Europe reliance on others was unavoidable; in the New World there was every prospect of considerable advantage. Above all, and as ever, British defence depended on its navy. Huge sums were spent on re-equipping it in the 1790s; manpower was increased from a woefully depleted 15,000 in 1793 to 133,000 by 1801. Howe's victory over the French fleet off the coast of Brittany in June 1794 prevented reinforcements being sent to the West Indies and facilitated the successes of Jervis's fleet there. It was the first of several vital engagements which preserved Britain's security [F.ii.1]. Duncan's victory over the Dutch at Camperdown in October 1797, with seamen who had mutinied in the Medway only four months earlier (Ch. 8), removed any possibility of northern support for a French invasion fleet based at Cherbourg. It was a potent factor in Napoleon's calculation that France should transfer its major interest for the time being to the Mediterranean. The navy also frustrated this southern strategy since Nelson's decisive victory at Aboukir Bay gave him control there and bottled up French armies in Egypt prior to their eventual defeat on land by Abercromby in 1801. The 'Armed Neutrality of the North' which threatened British trade and especially her Baltic supplies was cowed into submission by Nelson's devastating if insubordinate attack on the Danish fleet in Copenhagen harbour in April 1801.

The British Navy was a formidable, but double-edged, weapon. Its apparent invincibility undoubtedly saved the nation from invasion in the 1790s, but its contribution in Europe was bound to be primarily defensive. The navy could not defeat Napoleon there and its very success encouraged the French to concentrate still more of their efforts on the army, thus increasing pressure on Britain's European allies. Thus by 1801, Britain was no nearer to securing the purposes for which it had entered the war; indeed, France's grip on Europe had tightened steadily. Alarming French triumphs in southern and central Europe, rather than any inspired British diplomacy, made possible a Second Coalition in 1799 [F.i.5] but, despite early successes for the Russians and Austrians in Italy, Napoleon exploited the lack of trust between allies to re-establish French dominance there after the Battle of Marengo and pushed the coalition to rapid collapse. Against French European dominance, therefore, Britain could place control of the seas which had limited French ambitions outside Europe in both West and East. Neither side could defeat the other and both sides knew it. A compromise peace was the natural option in 1801–2, and though Pitt was out of office by this time there is no reason to suppose that his aims would have been any less pacific than Addington's, though he would certainly have insisted on more favourable terms.

Pitt had not been the unbending warlord even in the 1790s. Both overseas and domestic considerations encouraged peace initiatives. Once it had been established that rapid victory was impossible, and this was clear by the end of 1794, opposition mounted at home. The Foxites asserted that the war was unnecessary since no fundamental British interests were threatened; they alleged, wrongly, that Pitt was motivated more by anti-Jacobin spleen than by rational calculation. Such criticisms could have been shrugged off if Pitt had had substantial victories to boast. Without them a Foxite-mercantile alliance was possible since textile manufacturers and workers complained bitterly that war harmed their trade. The crisis of 1795 heightened criticism of war strategy and led to criticism even from so staunch a friend as Wilberforce who believed that Dundas had imbued Pitt with an unwelcome thirst for colonial conquest.[4]

The first serious peace initiatives, in 1795–96, foundered on the dual rocks of Austrian and French bellicosity. A second embassy, headed by Malmesbury in 1797, promised better things with both sides haggling over disputed territories. The *coup d'état* of 18 Fructidor (in the French Republican calendar which operated from 1792 to 1805), however, reasserted Jacobin dominance in the Directory and Malmesbury was packed back to Britain to tell Pitt that no peace was possible unless Britain surrendered all of its conquests while confirming French ones.

The war took a fearful toll of Pitt's vaunted economic rehabilitation. The government, which had borrowed £4½m. in 1793, required £44m. by 1797 (159). Pitt had little alternative to savage increases in direct taxation; indirect taxes, though traditionally favoured, hit the poor too hard to allow much further increase without fears for internal security as the experience of 1795 had shown. Pitt accordingly trebled the 'assessed taxes' on luxuries like servants and carriages in 1797 while placing much greater reliance on the radical remedy of a direct tax on incomes. He announced proposals for an income tax in his 1798 budget speech; collection began in 1799 (218). As a *douceur* to the landed interest, and especially to backbench MPs, the old land tax was to be commuted as a permanent charge on each parish with encouragement given to landowners to redeem charges at current valuations. Given the enormously diverse sources of income and wealth in eighteenth-century England a graduated income tax had long been logical, though politically undesirable since its introduction would stimulate criticism of its inquisitorial aspects particularly from merchants and manufacturers who had hitherto escaped extremely lightly. Since these were vital to the nation's wealth the additional argument could be advanced that Pitt's income tax proposals would kill the proverbial goose which laid the golden eggs.

The nation took to the new tax [D.i.3] with extreme ill grace and on the strict understanding that it should be a wartime expedient only. During the wars, however, income tax was of great importance to the war effort. It raised about 80 per cent of the revenue from the new taxes imposed by government between 1793 and 1815 and 28 per cent of the extra money (new taxes, higher rates of existing taxes and loans) raised for the war (44, *182–3*). Since income tax has attracted such attention as the new impost which eventually came to dominate fiscal calculations, it is worth pointing out that over half of the new tax revenue raised during the wars came from higher rates of existing taxes. One reason why Britain eventually won a ruinously expensive war was that her middle and upper classes were wealthy enough to foot the ever higher tax bills imposed by Pitt and his successors – despite the ill grace with which they were actually paid and the shoe-pinching involved. It is probable that a heightened sense of patriotism, especially from 1797 onwards, militated against widespread evasion.

Like Pitt's war, Addington's peace has had a poor press [F.i.6]. Dr Langford is one of many to find it 'disastrous' (149, *215*). Any defence of the Amiens settlement must be oblique and is wise to steer away from the actual terms negotiated by Hawkesbury (later Lord Liverpool) and Cornwallis. No regard was taken of British victories in Egypt and almost all of Britain's overseas conquests, including all of those taken from France, were handed back with little demur. The strategy Pitt had deployed was utterly vitiated. In Europe, too, French concessions were more apparent than real. Holland, Spain and northern Italy remained effectively under French domination with the remainder of Italy a rich plum ripe for the plucking when it suited Napoleon to stretch out his hand. Despite the efforts of the navy in 1798–1801 British interests in the Mediterranean were anything but secured at Amiens. Canning, never a man to mince words, fulminated against 'the gross faults and omissions, the weakness and baseness, and shuffling, and stupidity, that mark this Treaty' (159, *471*).

Addington, however, knew British political opinion. The nation in 1801 was war-weary, over-taxed and caught in a vortex of rising prices. For this the war was blamed and Pitt's removal from office, though it had nothing to do with the war, created a psychological climate of opinion which strengthened the advocates of peace. Indeed, Addington, when Speaker of the Commons, probably had a sharper perception of backbench feeling than Pitt. As Canning admitted, MPs were in no mood to submit Addington's terms to detailed analytical scrutiny. Almost any terms would have been ratified in May 1802 and Pitt himself fulfilled a pledge to Addington by refusing to condemn them, saying that the peace preliminaries were 'on the whole highly honourable to the country and very advantageous' (49, *126*).

If Addington responded to a deep public mood in 1802 it may be said in further partial exculpation that he was not fooled into believing that Amiens represented a final settlement. The year of uneasy peace was not wasted. The immediate cuts made in army and navy manpower were not so savage as was normal when peace was signed and Addington's revision of the Militia Acts in 1802 added 75,000 'occasional' troops, admittedly of variable quality, to the strength. Troops were left in the West Indies to facilitate the easy reconquest of colonies given back to France at Amiens should the need arise. The reduced taxation of peacetime cooled parliamentary tempers while Bonaparte's obvious preparations to extend French influence once more in Holland and Italy made the recommencement of war politically acceptable. Britain's defences early in 1803 were in sufficiently good order for Addington to take the initiative, declare war himself and take Bonaparte by surprise. The return of war, though not popular, was tolerated, despite the evident fact that Addington was not the man to lead it. The Prime Minister's wretched fall a year later, however, should not obliterate recognition of his modest achievement. In May 1803, for once, Britain went to war tolerably well prepared.

---

1. *Parl. Hist.*, xxix (1791–92), col. 826.
2. J. H. Rose, *William Pitt and the Great War* (1911), p. 99.
3. *Memoirs of the Court and Cabinets of George the Third* (4 vols, 1853–5), ii, pp. 274–80.
4. R. S. and I. Wilberforce, *The Life of William Wilberforce* (5 vols, 1838–42), ii, p. 92.

CHAPTER 10

The wars with France: II Endurance and triumph, 1803–1815

I

The second phase of the French wars entailed far greater sacrifices for the British people than the first. Subsidies to allies were much larger, particularly in the final years when Castlereagh fashioned alliances for victory while preparing for a post-war accord which would bind the nations of Europe to lasting peace. Taxation rose sharply as government income almost doubled between 1803 and 1815. The income tax was made to bite, providing almost a fifth of government income by the end of the war [D.i.1]. Nearly two-thirds of government expenditure went directly on army and navy requirements. By 1815 260,000 men were in the pay of the British Army, four times the number available to Marlborough at the height of the wars against Louis XIV.

The greatest privations, however, were not the result of direct military expenditure. From 1806 the nature of the war changed. Napoleon, having failed to breach British defences by orthodox means, sought to employ his overwhelming superiority in Europe to squeeze the life out of his enemy by a policy of economic blockade. Napoleon's Continental System offers the first major example of economic warfare, very different in scale from the limited mercantilist wars of the seventeenth century. Between 1808 and 1812, when the system was in fullest operation, British exports to Europe were interrupted and civilians suffered high levels of both prices and unemployment.

Faced by an enemy whose ambitions seemed limitless there was little alternative to prolonged resistance. Despite the defeatist tone of Whig opposition pronouncements, little constructive thought was given to how one sued for an honourable peace with an opponent who ignored conventional rules of warfare and diplomacy. Ideological objections to a war with revolutionary France had been dissipated by Napoleon's assumption of the title of emperor. The contrast with the 1790s was stark. When Fox finally returned to government in 1806 his desire to bring France to heel was scarcely less great than that of William Windham with whom he had now made his peace. 'Boney' was characterized as a megalomaniac despot who had extinguished the flame of liberty in France. During this second phase of the war successive British governments employed Press propaganda to bring home to the public the need for a concerted national effort against the forces of darkness. For the first time the British were encouraged to believe that the war effort vitally depended on civilian as well as military contribution. The techniques which Lloyd George and Winston Churchill were to employ on a much grander scale during the two world wars of the twentieth century were not without precedent. Parliamentary opposition to Portland and Perceval after 1807 concentrated much more on British economic policy than on the rationale of the war.

At least until 1810 British strategy was not greatly different from that employed in the 1790s. Events again dictated dependence on the navy with limited military excursions to secure specified objectives. Thus, between 1803 and 1806 Britain reasserted itself in the West Indies and also took the Cape of Good Hope [F.ii.2]. Pitt struggled to reassemble a continental system of alliance against France, though the linchpin of the Third Coalition [F.i.7] was an Anglo-Russian agreement founded on the shifting sands of mutual fear of French ambition in the Mediterranean. Nelson, suspicious of boosting Russian influence in this theatre of war, argued against any combined military operations. Subsequent events, culminating in an ill-fated joint expeditionary force to Naples in 1805–6, were to demonstrate how little trust existed between the two nations (163).

The European monarchs proved as fickle in this period as in the previous decade while the French counter-thrust was yet more decisive. Lack of Prussian enthusiasm vitiated any hope of Russo-Swedish advances towards the Low Countries. Secure in northern Europe, Napoleon could concentrate his forces on the Danube. Decisive blows were delivered first to the Austrians at Ulm in October and then, some 300 miles further east, to a combined Russian and Austrian Army at Austerlitz in December 1805. Here one-third of the 87,000 allied troops became casualties. These celebrated victories, based on speed and concentration of forces, knocked the Austrians out of the war, destroyed Pitt's last coalition and ceded control of South-central Europe to Napoleon. Northern Germany succumbed when Prussia, lured tardily to arms by resentment of French bullying and fear of Napoleon's growing power over the small North German states, was comprehensively defeated at Jena. With Berlin occupied, the Grand Army pushed on into Poland. France was dominant from the Baltic to the Mediterranean and from the Atlantic coast to the borders of Russia.

As in the 1790s also, however, final victory was dependent on the conquest of Britain. Recognizing the lost opportunities of 1797, Napoleon had tried to invade Britain in 1804, before Pitt could fashion a new coalition. A series of strategems was devised to divert Cornwallis's Channel or Nelson's Mediterranean fleets just long enough to permit French men o'war to escort an invasion flotilla from Boulogne across the Channel. In the summer of 1804 more than 80,000 Frenchmen were assembled ready to embark should their navy give them opportunity. Skilled British naval patrols and daring assaults on the invasion ports kept the French on the defensive and no French or Spanish fleet could break Nelson's blockade without risking annihilation. Admiral Villeneuve finally took that risk, leaving the safety of Cadiz on 20 October 1805 in the knowledge that Napoleon had already issued orders for his replacement by a more decisive commander. Nelson's total victory off Cape Trafalgar the following day was the naval obverse of Ulm and Austerlitz. By a nice irony the Battle of Trafalgar was fought the day after the Battle of Ulm. The Franco-Spanish Mediterranean fleet was destroyed; Napoleon was forced to abandon preparations for invasion.

Nelson's death in the hour of his most crushing victory has concentrated attention on him as a glorious martyr. Truly, the naval roll of honour should be much longer. Lord Barham, promoted First Lord of the Admiralty in April 1805 at the age of eighty when Melville was disgraced (Ch. 7) proved himself as able a strategist during the critical months preceding Trafalgar as he had been an effective naval administrator in the 1780s. Admiral Keith, commanding the North Sea fleet, deployed limited resources with consummate skill. Admiral Collingwood, who succeeded Nelson as commander of the fleet, ensured that the initiative secured at Trafalgar would not be squandered. Collingwood's cool administrative brain allied to a total mastery of naval practice kept the French fleet in a state of psychological subservience after 1805. Under his direction the blockade of Cadiz (1805–8) was a major holding operation on which Britain's entire Mediterranean strategy depended. Because of its naval supremacy Britain could contain but not yet subdue the Napoleonic threat. The possibility of an invasion could not be entirely disregarded after 1805, but Napoleon knew as well as anyone that the prospect was remote. He looked for victory thereafter by another route.

II

Prussia's defeat at the end of 1806 enabled Napoleon to mount his economic offensive against Britain. With vastly increased influence in the Baltic he could issue the Berlin Decree, closing all ports under French control to vessels from Britain or her colonies [F.ii.2]. After victory over the Russians at Friedland in 1807 he dictated terms to Tsar Alexander I on the famous raft at Tilsit on the River Niemen, a few miles from the Baltic coast. Russia's accession to the system tightened the noose dangerously. Britain was to be starved to the conference table.

Limited economic warfare was not new. Commercial cargoes of enemy countries were usually treated as valuable prizes and both Pitt (in 1793–94) and the Directory (in 1798–99) had issued decrees aimed at wounding enemy trade and curtailing food supplies. The novelty of the Continental System lay in its scope – the whole of the British Isles was declared blockaded – and in Napoleon's unprecedented control of mainland Europe between 1807 and 1812. He envisaged British 'merchandise repulsed from the whole of Europe, and her vessels laden with useless wealth wandering the wide seas, where they claim to rule as sole masters, seeking in vain . . . for a port to open and receive them'.[1]

Britain retaliated in kind. The Talents ministry issued Orders in Council against traffic between enemy ports, including that involving neutral states. Castlereagh pointed out, however, that this policy merely alienated the neutrals without harming France. Spencer Perceval, Chancellor of the Exchequer in the new Portland administration, was influenced by *War in Disguise* (1805), a treatise by his fellow evangelical James Stephen, and was the moving force behind the retaliatory Orders of November 1807 which stated that all European ports from which Britain was excluded were to be put in a state of blockade. Napoleon promulgated his Milan Decrees as a final counter-retaliation the following month.

Practice belied theory in the waging of economic war. There were two major obstacles to the realization of Napoleon's policy. Firstly, he could never seal off all of Europe; parts of the Baltic remained open to skilled British trading craft as did

Portugal. Much more important, outside Europe Napoleon had no influence whatsoever and it was to extra-European trade that Britain increasingly looked. A report conceded in 1811: 'To keep the English away from the Continent by blockade without possessing fleets is just as impossible as to forbid the birds to build their nests in our country.'[2] Napoleon recognized reality long before he conceded defeat. During the harvest shortages of 1809–10 he permitted the export of French and German wheat to Britain under licence, hoping thereby to provoke a currency crisis. British manufactured goods found devious routes into Europe, particularly along the Baltic coast. From 1810 Russian ports were reopened to British commerce, a great blow to Napoleon which he weighed in the balance when considering his fateful enterprise against the Tsar two years later.

Outside Europe, British entrepreneurs were particularly successful in opening up South America to British goods banned from most of Europe. As the West Indies remained of first importance it is not so surprising as it at first appears that British exports to the Americas outside the USA were more valuable than those either to the States or to Europe between 1805 and 1809. J. R. McCulloch captured the spirit of frenetic trading in new markets: . . . more Manchester goods were sent out [to southern America] in the course of a few weeks than had been consumed in the twenty years preceding; and the quantity of English goods of all sorts . . . was so very great, that warehouses could not be provided sufficient to contain them. . . . Some speculators even went so far as to send *skates* to Rio de Janeiro.[3]

In promoting economic warfare Napoleon was engaging the enemy on its strongest ground. A new industrial nation, the first in the world, full of merchants searching out new trading opportunities and protected by the awesome power of the British Navy would evade a purely European stranglehold, however tight. The British blockade almost certainly inflicted greater damage to France, whose customs receipts dropped by four-fifths between 1807 and 1809, than vice versa. It has even been suggested that Britain's economic crisis of 1811–12 was caused more by incautious speculation in untried markets and consequent industrial overproduction than by the Continental System. This was decidedly not the view of northern and Midland manufacturers who looked to their old protectors, the Whigs, to aid their assault on the Orders in Council. Henry Brougham pictured Birmingham men 'silent, still and desolate during half the week; during the rest of it miserably toiling at reduced wages for a pittance scarcely sufficient to maintain animal life'; they were the sacrificial victims of a mistaken retaliatory assault by the government (51). Fear of industrial unrest in the depressed areas was undoubtedly a factor in the success of the Whig campaign, though the abandonment of the Orders in June 1812 owed something to the removal by assassination of Perceval and to the natural desire of an initially insecure Liverpool administration not to espouse too many unpopular causes.

Though the balance of advantage lay with Britain, economic warfare produced many casualties and much deprivation on both sides. Furthermore, the Orders in Council alienated the United States. Attempts had been made in 1808 to moderate their full effect on the American trade, but relations between the two states, always delicate, continued to deteriorate until the US government passed a Non-Importation Act in 1811. British exports to its largest single market plummeted from £7.8m in 1810 to £1.4m in 1811. Supplies of cotton to the Lancashire mills also suffered; imports in 1812–14 were 45 per cent lower than those of 1809–11. The Anglo-American War of 1812–14 was a confused and inconsequential affair of skirmishes in and around the Great Lakes with neither side able to sustain an advantage [F.ii.3]. Its beginning and end encapsulated the confusion. Had the Orders in Council been suspended only a few weeks earlier the war, which northern states vigorously opposed, would almost certainly not have received Congress approval. The most famous incident of the war, the repulse of a British attack on New Orleans, occurred a month after the Peace of Ghent had been signed [F.i.14], but before news of it reached deepest Louisiana. The peace settled nothing except hostilities; it offered no shift in the balance of forces in the New World. It did, however, permit commercial instinct to reassert itself. The United States resumed its role as chief supplier of cotton to the industrial North of England and the profitable realization of the Great American Dream during the nineteenth century was to be re-interrupted by nightmares about British blockades.

III

Napoleon's attempt to exchange influence for domination in the Iberian peninsula in 1808 begins the critical phase of the war. The revolt in Spain against Napoleon's installation of his brother Joseph as king and abundant evidence of anti-French hostility in Portugal persuaded Castlereagh to send a British expeditionary force of some 15,000 men to the Peninsula to aid the nationalists there. This policy was not new; it fitted the general strategy of offering limited armed support to European adversaries of the French. It thus followed precedents established in the Low Countries in 1793 and in the unsuccessful expeditions to North Germany and to Sicily in 1805–6. Castlereagh initially overestimated the strength of the Spanish insurgents and underestimated Napoleon's power and determination to reinforce his armies in the Peninsula. In consequence, British forces carried more of the burden than the War Office envisaged.

What distinguished the Peninsular campaigns from earlier expeditionary forces was bloody-mindedness and tenacity, bringing eventual success. Here, due in no small measure to the military resource of Arthur Wellesley (created Viscount Wellington in September 1809), Britain was to sustain that vital toe-hold on the European mainland which denied Napoleon full control of the Continent. Important results followed. Napoleon had to deploy more seasoned troops in South-west Europe than he could properly afford when his enemies regrouped in the North and East after 1812. From the Peninsula, too, French soil was first to be invaded when Wellington crossed the Pyrenees after his decisive victory over Joseph Bonaparte at Vitoria. This victory dashed any hopes Napoleon had of concentrating his forces in central Europe to make the victories of Lutzen and Bautzen in 1813 as decisive as those of Ulm and Austerlitz nearly eight years before [F.ii.2].

The Peninsula was a hard slog. Wellington's initial success at Vimiero led only to a pusillanimous accord at Cintra, negotiated by a superior. There was uproar in Britain. Military victories were too rare not to be followed up. Lady Bessborough reported the 'lamentations of all the people we meet with. . . . And certainly, by their account, the terms seem madness.'[4] Despite Sir John Moore's famous rearguard action against Soult at Corunna in January 1809, Napoleon's counter-attack seemed to have been decisive. Before Wellington returned to the Peninsula in April this campaign promised to be no more successful than earlier efforts, or, indeed, than the disastrous Walcheren expedition to the Low Countries was to prove in the second half of the year.

Wellington's campaigns between 1809 and 1813 were a triumph of organization and punctilious husbandry of limited resources against often superior forces. At Talavera most of the effective fighting was done by a British Army approximately half the size of the French, though Spanish reinforcements lay in reserve. This battle, though it earned Wellington his peerage, did not render his forces proof against French reinforcements and his defensive capabilities were tested to their uttermost against Masséna, Ney and Junot as they swept south-westwards after successes at Ciudad Rodrigo and Almeida. Wellington was driven deep into Portugal, but defence of Lisbon at the lines of Torres Vedras during the winter of 1810–11 proved to be a turning-point. Masséna lost 25,000 men in a futile waiting game against defences expertly deployed and manned primarily by Portuguese militia. Though the 1811 campaigning season brought little tangible success it did secure most of Portugal as a base for Wellington's offensive operations in Spain during 1812. The climax of these was the defeat of Marmont at Salamanca, where the French suffered three times the losses of the British and Portuguese, and the subsequent capture of Madrid [F.ii.2]. The decisive thrusts of the following year burst Napoleon's 'Spanish ulcer' with eventually fatal results.

The British Army in the Peninsula at no time exceeded 60,000 men, and though Wellington commanded them with enormous skill the contributions of the Spanish and Portuguese armies and guerrilla brigades were more important than military historians used to admit. Though their training was deficient their nationalist, anti-French fervour was more than adequate compensation. They prevented Napoleon from concentrating his forces on Wellington as he had on Mack at Ulm or Alexander I at Austerlitz. Wellington's organization of food supplies and his meticulous campaigns were both facilitated by the support of Britain's Mediterranean fleet. Just as £18m. of British subsidies kept Spanish and Portuguese forces in the field so naval supremacy ensured better supplies for Wellington's army than those available to the enemy (162, 164). Since life in the Peninsula was extremely gruelling such back-up facilities were doubly important.

IV

By the time Wellington finally broke French resistance around Pamplona and entered South-west France in October 1813 the British government had begun to fashion a system of alliances against Napoleon to finish the job. The Treaty of Reichenbach [F.i.9] provided subsidies for Prussia and Russia to capitalize on the horrible losses Napoleon suffered during his Russian campaign of the previous winter. News of Wellington's victory at Vitoria helped to convince European diplomats that Britain's military commitment was an appropriate counterweight to her financial support. But not until Vitoria and the allied victory at Leipzig [F.ii.2], which smashed the Napoleonic Confederation of the Rhine, did total victory seem close.

Only rarely does diplomacy, as opposed to warfare or economic power, achieve positive changes in relations between nations. Too often its practice merely encourages prevarication, concealment and negative cynicism beneath a baroque veneer of practised *politesse*. The diplomacy of 1813–15 was unique. It settled relations between the major European states for forty years and it facilitated the emergence of 'Great Power' politics. In these negotiations, Britain played the dominant role through one of the greatest of its Foreign Secretaries, Viscount Castlereagh.

The details have long since been definitively described (165) and only the broad issues require discussion here. Castlereagh's objectives crystallized British aspirations during the previous twenty years. The first was to keep the allies together long enough to achieve a total defeat of Napoleon. The second, only superficially a contradiction of the first, was to redraw the map of Europe to satisfy the territorial integrity of all nations, including France. A system of mutual checks to expansionism would achieve the objectives for which Britain had gone to war, since its claims on the European mainland remained in 1815 as they had been in 1793 commercial rather than territorial. It is a measure of Castlereagh's stature that he could persuade the other 'Great Powers' (a term coined during this period) to view the matter from a British standpoint since their own territorial interests were much more compellingly involved. No doubt Britain's economic power, measured in the negotiable currency of unprecedentedly large subsidies, helped.

Separately negotiated treaties, usually under Napoleonic duress, had bedevilled previous attempts at concerted allied action. Now that Napoleon's impregnability had been dented it was Castlereagh's task to keep them together long enough to take allied armies to Paris. The main obstacle was Austria. In 1813 it was tempted by overtures from Napoleon and its cunning Foreign Secretary, Metternich, ran rings round the inexperienced earl of Aberdeen, whom Castlereagh had sent to seek Austria's accession to the Reichenbach accord. With some reason, Metternich feared the aggressive intent of Tsar Alexander as much as he did that of Emperor Napoleon. Only Napoleon's reluctance to play the diplomatic game kept Castlereagh's hopes alive.

Castlereagh knew that a general European settlement could only follow total victory. When he arrived in Basle in January 1814 to conduct negotiations personally, French forces were everywhere in retreat, but Prussia, Russia and Austria were no more trusting of one another's motives. The Treaty of Chaumont [F.i.10], by which the allies pledged to keep 150,000 men each under arms and agreed not to make a separate peace with France, is a splendid example of Castlereagh's skill as a negotiator, but it also shows the new respect which Wellington's victories now commanded for Britain. Unprecedentedly, Britain had 225,000 troops on the Continent in its pay, 70,000 of them British. Castlereagh congratulated himself: 'What an extraordinary display of power. This I trust will put an end to any doubts as to the claim we have to an opinion on continental matters.' (165, *228)*

The peace treaties of 1814–15 [F.i.11–13, 15] showed how precise that opinion was. In his last days of reflective impotence on St Helena, whither he had been banished after his final defeat by Wellington and Blücher at Waterloo in June 1815, Napoleon scornfully dismissed Castlereagh's diplomatic achievements. He 'had the continent at his disposal . . . [yet] the peace he has made is the sort of peace he would have made if he had been beaten'.[5] This spectacular misjudgement reveals a great deal about why Napoleon lost the war and Britain won it. Britain, it will be remembered, went to war in 1793 to preserve its security. As the war progressed it depended more and more on naval strength and on the replenishment which non-European trade and the possession of overseas colonies afforded. Britain neither sought nor required European territory and it would have been a great mistake, which Castlereagh was far too wise to contemplate, to have taken it as the tribute of victory in 1815. Instead he insisted on the very strategy which his tutor Pitt had been working towards: European stability based on the balance of forces. To this Castlereagh added what has been called the Congress System, a formal machinery of diplomacy to consider the operation of the settlement and anticipate any disturbances. France was not to be dismembered or humiliated, though Napoleon's impudence in skipping from Elba and inaugurating his 'Hundred Days' in the spring of 1815, earned for it a temporary army of occupation. France was of far more value to European stability reduced to her pre-revolutionary frontiers. Castlereagh firmly sat on Russian and Prussian attempts to extract more, and shepherded the Bourbon restoration once he had clear evidence that such a solution would satisfy influential French opinion. He insisted on a new United Netherlands as a strong buffer to northern expansion and offered British cash to fortify the Belgian border against France. With Austrian influence in northern Italy still strong and with Prussia sharing a border with North-east France beyond the Rhine, Castlereagh could be content that containment in the West would work.

There was much haggling over dispositions in central Europe at Vienna. Castlereagh's hope of re-creating a Polish kingdom as a buffer to Russian aspirations was thwarted, but the expansion of Prussian territory and the consolidation of Austria in West and central Germany did almost as well. Like Pitt before him, Castlereagh was alarmed at the ease with which a determined aggressor could make progress through the numerous small and weak German and Italian states and he foresaw that future attacks might come from east rather than west. Hence his policy of a strengthened 'strategic centre' based on Prussia and Austria once Napoleon's Confederation of the Rhine had been swept away.

Britain' colonial acquisitions were modest, but they were to be of immense strategic importance to the developing empire of trade which was already becoming the envy of the nineteenth-century world. Malta was Britain's guard dog in the Mediterranean; Guiana, Tobago and St Lucia were all useful acquisitions in the West; the Cape of Good Hope symbolized and facilitated British expansion into the Far East at Dutch expense. Singapore and the Malay peninsula would soon fall into Britain's lap [F.iii.c]. British influence in India was unchallengeable. With Europe settled, such territories would take on much greater significance than had been apparent to most negotiators at Paris or Vienna in 1814–15. The world no longer meant Europe yet Britain was the only European nation equipped to exploit the fact.

Britain defeated Napoleon primarily because of superior economic resources. The country's survival was never dependent on a direct challenge to his military genius since naval supremacy thwarted every attempt at invasion. Even so, Britain's objectives in entering the war might have been lost had not Napoleon proved so unreliable an ally. At different times Prussia, Russia and Austria all sought a lasting arrangement with him in preference to continued resistance, yet none could feel sure of his ultimate ambitions. Between 1812 and 1814 lack of trust in the Corsican upstart gave Castlereagh his opportunity to stitch together agreements with the leading European autocracies. But Britain was still at war in 1812 only because its economy was strong enough and diverse enough to resist a concerted European embargo and because British taxpayers could still support both the navy and an increased military commitment in the Peninsula. Napoleon, whose career had been made possible by France's political revolution, was destroyed by the unprecedented strength his most intractable enemy drew from industrial revolution and commercial expansion. Britain could afford to make a decisive push in terms of subsidies and arms expenditure at a critical time. In 1813–15, £26¼m. was provided to the coalition against Napoleon (44, *142*). Although there may have been capital shortages and a decline in the investment ratio during the French wars, the British economy was much better suited to the long haul than was the French. The iron industry, buoyed by demand for armaments, boomed. American markets and the need for uniforms and greatcoats combined to keep the textile industry booming more often than not. Rapid growth of markets in Latin America provided partial compensation for Napoleon's blockade. Never before had a nation been able to fight a major war while impressively increasing its overall wealth.

In 1799, Henry Dundas, the Secretary of State for War, had written a letter to the First Lord of the Admiralty in which he asserted that Britain's 'power and dignity, as well as the safety of Europe, rests on our being the paramount commercial and naval power in the world' (158, *31*). In 1815, none could contest Britain's right to this title. What Dundas deprecatingly called 'a small spot in the ocean' was now in a position to exercise a predominant influence over world affairs.

---

1. E. F. Hecksher, *The Continental System* (Oxford, 1922), p. 74.
2. *ibid.*, p. 367.
3. J. R. McCulloch, *Principles of Political Economy* (2nd edn, 1830), p. 330.
4. *Private Correspondence of Granville Leveson Gower* (2 vols, 1916), ii, p. 329.
5. H. Nicolson, *The Congress of Vienna* (1946), p. 237.

CHAPTER 11

Ireland: The road to Union, 1782–1801

I

During the last quarter of the eighteenth century Ireland, which the English had both ruled and exploited with a heedless arrogance since James II had tried to recover his throne there at the Battle of the Boyne in 1690, became a problem once more. Any nation in which the vast majority of the land (80 per cent) is owned by a small alien group of a different religion, in this case frequently absentee English aristocrats and gentry, harbours an endemic problem. This is especially so when an equivalent majority, in this case Roman Catholic peasants, are subjected to political, social, religious and educational discrimination to preserve the ascendancy of the minority group. The Irish crisis, however, was precipitated by external factors. Ireland is the backdoor to Britain and a consequent source of concern when Britain stands on the defensive in a major war, as happened twice in the last quarter of the century.

The struggles of the Irish were not spearheaded by the Catholics. Deprived alike of education and aspiration their political will was stunted. Their aims were limited and basic; they sought lower rents and a reduction or abolition of the hated tithe, both tributes to an alien establishment, represented by the Protestant landlord or the Church of Ireland as the Anglican Church in that country was tactlessly called. Their tactics hardly varied; numerous agrarian terrorist organizations, known collectively as Whiteboys, hamstrung cattle, burned ricks and offered gruesome physical violence to those who buttressed the system. Tenants who took over land from those who had been evicted by the landlord were especially prone to vicious attack. Powers of eviction were extensive in eighteenth-century Ireland, except in parts of Ulster, and covert collective intimidation was viewed as the only retaliatory course for those who suffered under them.

The Protestant minority, Anglican or Presbyterian, espoused broader causes. The American War of Independence gave Irishmen an opportunity to stake their claim for concessions from Westminster. Not only was the war unpopular in Ireland since it closed one of the few substantial markets permitted by Britain but many Irish Protestants, particularly the Presbyterians in the North, felt a natural sympathy with American cousins struggling to free themselves from the British yoke. In many cases a kindred spirit was literally appropriate since thousands of Ulster linen weavers had emigrated to the North American colonies when their trade was depressed. Once the French entered the American War pressure on North's government greatly increased. The 'Patriots' in the Irish Parliament, led by the young Dublin lawyer Henry Grattan, drew strength from a Protestant 'Volunteer' movement, established in 1778 to defend Ireland against a possible French invasion but rapidly translated into an agency for increased self-determination. Ulster Presbyterians sought full independence for the Irish Parliament, though under the British Crown; they also hoped for trade concessions. On the latter issue the door was already ajar. In 1779–80, following earlier concessions on fishing rights, Irishmen were at last permitted to export their wool and glass and to trade with all Britain's overseas possessions save those administered by the East India Company.

The crucial psychological concession, however, was the constitutional one. In 1782 the Rockingham administration repealed the Declaratory Act of 1719 which had bestowed full legislative rights on the Westminster Parliament whenever it chose to exercise them. The Irish House of Lords were also given final jurisdiction over legislative matters. But legislative autonomy for the Dublin Parliament was not to be independence for Irish Protestants, still less the Irish nation. During the following nineteen years British governments weighed the constitutional experiment in the balance and found it wanting at almost every point.

The Patriots in 1782 dreamed of separate but equal development for the two nations; some even looked to a pattern of economic progress which would fuse Anglican, Presbyterian and Catholic interests and would foster an Irish State on the precepts of the European Enlightenment. Such fanciful stuff might exercise Dublin coffee-house society, but it evinced no appreciation of the problems of assimilation which would face overpopulated and undercapitalized tenancies in Counties Mayo or Kerry. Nor did it square with the situation as seen from London. Britain had granted parliamentary independence; it had not freed Ireland from its grip on the executive. The offices of Lord-Lieutenant and Chief Secretary were in the gift of the Crown and in practice filled by Cabinet nomination. They executed British, not Irish, policy. After 1782 great care was taken to ensure that the Irish administration was discharged by men loyal to the British interest. Administrators were appointed who had both tenacity and an aversion to further constitutional experiment. The Chief Secretaryship was used as a testing ground for bright young Westminster politicians. Auckland, Grenville and Castlereagh all served apprenticeships there between 1780 and 1800. The two ablest Irishmen to hold office in this period, John Beresford, Commissioner of Revenue from 1780, and John Fitzgibbon, Lord Chancellor after 1789, epitomized both the continuing Protestant ascendancy and complete loyalty to the dictates of Westminster. Significantly, they, rather than British politicians serving short terms in unfamiliar surroundings, became the prime targets of attack from both Dublin parliamentary reformers who believed the constitution of 1782 to offer them independence of action and the extra-parliamentary radicals of the 1790s. During his long period of office Beresford served under eleven Lord-Lieutenants and thirteen Chief Secretaries.

Independence of action was rendered the more difficult because the Irish House of Commons was yet more susceptible to government influence than the British. Fewer than half its 300 members were freely elected by the all Protestant electorate; more than half were placed there by borough-mongers, again mostly English. Opportunities for direct intervention by the executive were thus great and eagerly seized after 1782 when an 'unmanaged' Commons might easily stumble into direct conflict with it to the risk of continuing British primacy. Dublin Castle, where lay the Irish administration, could guarantee a Commons in which one-third of the members were placemen or pensioners. It was a situation which Walpole and Newcastle would have envied richly and it did nothing for the self-esteem of those who thought that their campaigns of the late 1770s and early 1780s had brought tangible reward. One of them, Sir Laurence Parsons, put the situation resentfully in 1790:

> We may pride ourselves that we are a great kingdom, but the fact is that we are scarcely known beyond the boundaries of our shores. . . . A suburb of England, we are sunk in her shade. True, we are an independent kingdom; we have an imperial crown distinct from England; but it is a metaphysical distinction, a mere sport for speculative men. . . . It has been the object of English ministers . . . to countervail what we obtained (in 1782), and substitute a surreptitious and clandestine influence for the open power which the English Legislature was then obliged to relinquish.[1]

II

For those with property a period of economic prosperity during the 1780s assuaged some resentment at the extent of Westminster's residual control. Ireland shared in the 'national revival' engineered by Pitt. Landowners benefited from the 1784 Corn Law which encouraged the production of Irish grain for trans-shipment to Britain. The linen trade's exports tripled between 1781 and 1792, bringing profits for her manufacturers and steady work at respectable wages for her employees in and around Belfast. Britain still loaded the trade dice with Ireland heavily in her own favour, but it will be remembered that it was the Dublin Parliament which rejected Pitt's advances for reciprocal arrangements in 1785 (Ch. 4).

For some in that umbrella category 'the Irish peasantry' who were employed in various branches of domestic industry, the trade boom of the 1780s brought benefits. For the majority who depended solely on the produce of the smallholdings, however, demographic pressure produced the most pitiable consequences. Following the introduction of the potato, which became the staple food of most of the rural poor during the second half of the eighteenth century, the population rose alarmingly. From an estimated 3 million in 1750 it had jumped to 4 million by 1780. Between 1781 and 1801 while the estimated population of England and Wales rose by 13 per cent that of Ireland increased by 29 per cent [E.i]. Whereas the mainland enjoyed economic growth and diversity sufficient to sustain a rise with tolerable comfort, Ireland did not. The Irish tenant bore the full brunt. Landholdings were divided and subdivided until more than half the population, lacking alternative employment opportunities, was shackled to land which no longer sustained normal development. Even the shift away from dairy and pasture farming to more labour-intensive cereal cultivation from the 1780s failed to alleviate the problem. The grain was grown for the English market, but tenants could not afford to buy it anyway and their dependence on the potato became virtually total. Emigration, mainly across the Irish Sea, only scratched the surface of the problem and the Irish were wide open to a potato famine at least sixty years before the disaster of the mid-1840s finally occurred with deadening Malthusian certainty.

Rural incendiarism and terrorism by the Whiteboys increased during the 1780s. Absentee English landlords looked to their Irish estates merely for profit, but it is striking that outrages seem to have occurred most frequently on estates which had been absentee-owned but were inherited or bought by new men determined to exploit land-hunger by pushing up rents and forcing down wages. Nor was that small minority of land-owning Catholics any more indulgent to their co-religionists than the Protestants with whom since liberalizing legislation of 1778 they held equal rights in the purchase and disposal of estates. The effects of poverty impressed themselves on all visitors. Charles Bowden, visiting Tipperary in 1790, was appalled by 'these poor creatures who drag on a miserable existence under an accumulation of woes that it is hard to think human nature can sustain'. Even Fitzgibbon had to admit that the Munster peasantry were 'in a state of oppression, abject poverty, sloth, dirt and misery not to be equalled in any part of the world'. (53, *41, 22*).

III

The French Revolution offered inspiration to Irish reformers while inducing a new sense of wariness in the Protestant ascendancy. By no means all of those who had argued forcefully for the constitution of 1782 were happy to accept the rights of man, still less those of religious equality. Whereas the Volunteers revived in Ulster in the 1790s support for the movement now concentrated among shopkeepers and skilled urban workers rather than among the land-owning classes. The Volunteers of this period in some ways resembled the artisan radicals of England and Scotland, a point underlined in 1791 by the foundation of the Belfast Society of United Irishmen. Among its founders was Theobald Wolfe Tone, a young Protestant lawyer from Dublin. For Tone, radical political reform and nationalist identity went hand in hand. Sectarian division had no place in that political philosophy which, like so many British radicals, he took directly from the European Enlightenment. He drew up the first resolutions of the United Irishmen. They asserted 'That the weight of English influence in the Government in this country is so great, as to require a cordial Union, among ALL THE PEOPLE OF IRELAND ... No reform is practicable, efficacious, or just, which does not include *Irishmen* of every religious persuasion' (44, *87*). The Dublin Society, founded by Napper Tandy a couple of months later, espoused similar nationalist sentiments. The indebtedness of the Irish radicals to French example was made clear in the pages of *Northern Star*, the United Irishmen's journal from January 1792 until 1797.

The United Irishmen thoroughly alarmed reformers of the Grattan school. Not only did they openly espouse 'French principles' but they sought to forge a new and potentially disastrous alliance between the politically literate Presbyterian minority in Dublin and Belfast and the hard-pressed rural Catholic majority. To this alliance, through the medium of the new Catholic Committee, Tone devoted much of his energy before quitting Ireland first for the United States then France in search of allies.

The United Irish mission to the rural underprivileged did not work out as Tone hoped. Lawyers and skilled workers might look to an enlightened republic where sectarian supremacy and bitterness had no place. Catholic political antennae were less sharp but their hatred of Protestant oppressors was acute. They sought to turn events into a struggle for revenge on the Protestant ascendancy. They, rather than the Presbyterian radicals, pointed the way for future struggles in Ireland. Already in the 1790s events had taken a new turn with Catholic 'Defenders' clashing frequently with Protestant 'Peep O'Day Boys' who sought to vitiate recent concessions to the Catholics by frightening them from their lands. Both sides employed secret oaths; both maimed cattle; both terrorized juries; neither hesitated to murder those who infringed the code or who resisted lesser forms of intimidation. After some peculiarly vicious feuding in Armagh late in 1795 the Peep O'Day boys formed an Orange Society in celebration of William III's victories in the 1690s. The north of Ireland was given over to sectarian guerrilla war before the rebellion of 1798. Away from the main urban centres the original United Irishmen's intentions were washed away in a torrent of mutual religious hatred.

British resolve to retain a grip in a deteriorating situation was strengthened by the outbreak of war with France in 1793, not least because republicans like Tone, Tandy and Thomas Addis Emmet pinned their hopes on a French invasion to coincide with the rebellion they were striving for. Pitt fully accepted the advice given to the duke of Rutland when he became Lord-Lieutenant in 1784: 'Ireland is too great to be unconnected with us, and too near us to be dependent on a foreign state, and too little to be independent.'[2] He did not accept the majority view of the Dublin Parliament that Anglo-Irish interdependence could be guaranteed only by continued oppression of the majority. Chief Secretary Hobart, following instructions from London, introduced a Catholic Relief bill in 1793 which admitted Catholics to the franchise on equal terms with Protestants, permitted them to bear arms and allowed them to occupy most civil and military posts. Since restrictions on Catholic education and on Catholics being trained to the law had been lifted in the previous year, virtually the only political disability under which they continued to labour was exclusion from membership of Parliament. Thanks to formidable government patronage, the British government was able to force upon a reluctant Dublin parliament in 1793 a considerably greater degree of civil and political liberty for Irish Catholics than their English counterparts were to enjoy until 1829 (Ch. 23). Protestant domination, of course, continued; the small number of Catholics who could now succeed in becoming army officers or lawyers tilted the socio-religious balance not a whit. It is worth noting that one young Catholic from County Kerry, called to the Irish bar in 1798 at the age of twenty-three, owed much to Pitt's desire for religious equality. His name was Daniel O'Connell. The very fact that *some* Catholics could make significant advances hardened sectarian awareness in Ireland in the 1790s.

The government's aim in 1793, as the future Lord-Lieutenant Camden told the future Chief Secretary Castlereagh, was 'to quiet and satisfy the minds of the moderate men. . . . At the same time we [in England] should take great care not to give from ourselves that command and influence in Ireland, which is essential to both your prosperity and our consequence.'[3] Radicals like Tone scoffed at a sham reform which merely buttressed a 'disgrace to our constitution and our country, the wretched tribe of forty-shilling freeholders, whom we see driven to their octennial market by their landlords' (4, *251*). The prospects of parliamentary reform, in Ireland as in England, in 1793 were nil.

If Catholic relief was Pitt's flimsy velvet glove he was not reluctant to bare the iron fist against direct threats to British authority. Between 1793 and 1796 a Militia Act was passed, a new Protestant Yeomanry formed and an Insurrection Act became law. This last made oath-taking a capital offence and increased the power of magistrates to search for arms. Finally, Habeas Corpus was suspended. The government was determined to destroy United Irish plans for a widespread welcome to any French invasion force. This policy, reluctantly in Pitt's case, necessarily involved strengthening the grip of the Protestant ascendancy. Thus the government played its part in deepening the sectarian divide during the 1790s. At the beginning of 1795 Earl Fitzwilliam, a leading Portland Whig, was sent to Ireland as Chief Secretary, as part of Pitt's recent accommodation with that faction (Ch. 7). His reforming zeal involved the hasty sacking of John Beresford, the influential anti-Catholic Commissioner of Revenue regarded by his enemies as the unofficial 'King of Ireland' in his disposal of patronage.[4] When Fitzwilliam, without any authority from Westminster, promised full Catholic emancipation he was immediately recalled to be replaced by a more dutiful Pittite, Lord Camden. Beresford, whose influence Pitt could not afford to affront however many reservations he might have about his policies, was immediately reinstated. Fox cited the episode as 'the most insulting display of the dependence of the Irish legislature' and proof that, so far from Ireland having gained by the 1782 constitution she had been 'placed in a state of degradation beyond any former period'.[5]

Fox, who was speaking in 1797, also prophesied that government intransigence would lead to civil war between Catholic and Protestant. Though the 1798 rebellion was not precisely this it was far more of a sectarian struggle than the United Irishmen had envisaged. The rising was a prolonged and flabby flop, doomed to failure by the efficient brutality of British counter-measures and by the concentration of so much French military power in Egypt in 1798 (Ch. 9), rendering its rapid movement to aid the Irish rebels impracticable. United Irish attempts to capitalize on their strength in the Protestant North by establishing military organizations in Antrim and Down during 1796 were met during 1797 by a campaign of repression controlled by General Gerard Lake. Lake's militia and yeomanry, nearly all Irish themselves, pursued a course of arson and none-too-discriminate torture to stabilize eastern Ulster. It left only hardened republicans to carry the fight into 1798 with the United Irishmen desperately short of cover from the local community. The rebellion in Ulster in June 1798 was thus kept within manageable proportions. Its two leaders, a Belfast Presbyterian cotton manufacturer Henry Joy McCracken and an episcopalian linen draper Henry Monro, were executed.

The government's spy network hampered rebellious preparations in the South. Most of the Dublin leadership of the United Irishmen were arrested in March 1798. Lord Edward Fitzgerald, their most notable adherent having fought for the British during the American War of Independence and having served in the Dublin Parliament before switching allegiance, was fatally wounded in May trying to escape arrest. He had been directing United Irish military operations and had already given orders for the rising to begin. The date fixed proved to be the day after his death. With such auguries it was a matter more or less of pure chance where the rising took root, if anywhere. The honour fell to the Catholic peasantry of County Wexford, in the South-east, under the leadership of Father John Murphy. Not surprisingly the rising was coloured more by anti-Protestant, anti-landlord hatred than by republican idealism. After initial successes, which owed much to government amazement at rebellion in such an unlikely venue, the Catholics were defeated at Vinegar Hill in June. Other fragmented rebellious outbreaks were dealt with piecemeal.

United Irish reliance on French invasion forces was similarly misplaced. A force of 14,000 French troops was sent to Ireland in December 1796 and a serious attempt to land some 6,000 at Bantry Bay was frustrated by adverse weather and indecisiveness in the French command. When the rebellion was in full readiness the French had embarked on their Mediterranean strategy and could spare only small expeditionary forces for Irish adventures. One such, under General Humbert, marched courageously through Connaught and defeated a British force in the late summer of 1798. However, he failed to rouse the fires of rebellion within the western peasantry and was eventually stopped by Cornwallis *en route* for Dublin. A second small fleet, plus Tone who had been negotiating with the French in Paris, was captured by a British squadron under Sir John Warren in October. Tone was packed off to Dublin to face trial and inevitable conviction. He escaped the hangman's noose by means of a messy suicide inexpertly effected by penknife. The choice of death no less than his importance as the most influential exponent of republican separatism ensure him an honoured place in the embarrassingly large volume of Irish nationalist hagiography.

IV

It used to be argued by historians with a taste for conspiracy that Pitt deliberately engineered the rebellion by harsh repression in 1797 in order to have an excuse to eliminate the Irish Parliament and proceed to Union. The charge is groundless. Pitt would never have deliberately invited disturbance and French intervention at a time when Britain's defences were most stretched and the loyalty of her fleet in question (Ch. 9). Once over, of course, he used the rebellion as his strongest argument to persuade the Protestant ascendancy to surrender its flawed legislative jewel.

The sectarian bitterness of 1798 finally convinced Pitt's government that a Parliament of wealthy land-owning Protestants in Dublin could never represent the Irish nation. An unsettled Ireland, especially in wartime, was a standing threat to

Britain. Pitt hoped to persuade enough Irish MPs that the Dublin Parliament was detrimental to their interests also, since it symbolized a divided nation and might excite further agrarian outrages. Prosperity and full rent rolls could not be produced in such a climate.

The task of persuasion devolved on an elderly Englishman, Earl Cornwallis, and a young Irishman, Viscount Castlereagh. Both were newly appointed to the posts of Lord-Lieutenant and Chief Secretary respectively, in the wake of the rebellion. Their ability to work harmoniously for an end both believed absolutely necessary was to prove invaluable during the protracted and often distasteful negotiations which followed the initial rejection of a bill of Union in Dublin in January 1799. Opposition was strongest among county members representing Protestant landlordism and among those with interests in Dublin where the professional classes feared for their livelihoods if the city lost the legal and administrative benefits accorded to a European parliamentary capital.

Against this, Cornwallis was doubtless right when he reported that, 'The mass of the people of Ireland do not care one farthing about the Union.' (14, *275*) Few could point to direct benefits deriving from the Dublin Parliament; many hated what it represented. Castlereagh made headway in Ulster by arguing that the linen trade in Londonderry and Belfast could only gain from the closer economic association with the British empire of trade which Union would bring. For such advantages, after all, the Scots had voluntarily surrendered legislative autonomy in 1707. The ecclesiastical hierarchy of the Catholic Church was disposed to persuasion since it feared any encouragement to more anticlerical French intervention.

Such accessions of support were valuable, but Union could be won only on the floor of the House of Commons in Dublin. To this end Castlereagh indulged in that vigorous horse-trading which eighteenth-century politicians understood but which Victorians viewed with such high-minded distaste. Even such a hardbitten operator as Lord Salisbury spoke contemptuously of 'bribing knaves . . . and fools'. Twentieth-century historians, as is their wont, have treated the episode with a faintly weary cynicism. Castlereagh used government funds to induce men to change their minds or, more commonly, to leave active politics. No fewer than 20 per cent of the membership of the Commons changed between the two votes on the Union though no general election was held in the interim. Nearly all who left were anti-Union. These interesting facts need to be set against the superficially significant observation that only twelve MPs who opposed the Union in 1799 voted for it in 1800. Far more had been bought off. Pro-Union peers blossomed during patronage's *annus mirabilis*; forty new creations or promotions within it were approved during 1799. The wily archbishop of Cashel was promised the see of Dublin for a change of vote on the Union issue and a few words in season to other ears (54). The value of a borough seat which would disappear on Union was set at £15,000, leaving the Union's most steadfast opponents, the marquis of Downshire and the Speaker of the Commons, John Foster, its most heavily recompensed beneficiaries.

Thus Union was effected though, as Cornwallis cynically observed, fully half of those voting for it in reality detested the measure. One hundred Irish MPs took up seats in Westminster [B.iv] with thirty-two peers added to the House of Lords. Castlereagh's good offices secured twenty years' modest protection for Irish textile manufacturers before full free trade between the countries came about. The Anglican Churches of Ireland and England were united and Ireland was to contribute almost 12 per cent to the United Kingdom budget, though the two Exchequers remained separate until 1817. Though these were imposed terms they were not vindictive. As Professor Beckett argues, they were probably the most generous a British Parliament could have been induced to accept. The sheer size of UK war debts by 1815, unforeseeable in 1800, nevertheless placed on the underdeveloped Irish economy a very heavy burden.

Of all the Unionist politicians Castlereagh, Byron's 'cold-blooded, smooth-faced, placid miscreant', was the most dissatisfied at what he regarded as a half-cock settlement. Genuine loyalty, rather than lowering acquiescence, could only be bought at the price of Catholic emancipation, proper economic provision for both Catholic and Presbyterian clergy and, above all, an accommodation on the tithe question. As he presciently observed in October 1800: 'Those things which, if now liberally granted, might make the Irish a loyal people, will be of little avail when they are extorted on a future day'. (55, *80*) George III's implacable hostility, combined with heavy doubts in Pitt's Cabinet, were enough to blight the prospect (Ch. 7) and both Cornwallis and Castlereagh joined Pitt in resignation when the emancipation question could not be carried. However, Castlereagh's ambition rapidly overbore his conscience; he returned to government as Addington's President of the Board of Control only sixteen months later [A], content not to agitate the Catholic issue further.

Castlereagh's analysis proved correct. Irish Union was a constitutional job carried for British convenience, bought with British determination and mostly British cash. It did nothing to solve the underlying tensions and contradictions of Irish society. As one of its leading opponents Henry Grattan, the hero of 1782, put it: 'There is no identification on any thing, save only in legislature. . . . It follows that the two nations are not identified, though the Irish legislature be absorbed and, by that act of absorption, the feeling of one of our nations is not identified but alienated'(52, *283*). Both Catholic emancipation (in 1829) and tithe commutation (in 1838) had to be 'extorted', and from neither measure did the UK Parliament gain any accession of loyalty. The offices of Lord-Lieutenant and Chief Secretary continued to symbolize Protestant dominance and since the Irish linen industry was, at least from the 1820s, the only one to flourish under the Union, economic discrimination buttressed religious cleavage with Presbyterian Ulster increasingly set apart from the Roman Catholic South.

A 55 per cent increase in population between 1801 and 1841 [E.i] further intensified land-hunger; pressure on landlords from the secret Catholic societies grew accordingly. The UK Parliament's response was further to strengthen landlords by new legislation to extend eviction powers. Each addition to the statute-book confirmed the now unshakeable Catholic conviction that rights would be gained only by force. The Protestants, including even the most fervent opponents of Union in 1800, now looked to it as their ultimate if not their only guarantee of continued primacy. For the opportunities missed in 1800–1 future

British governments were to pay a heavy price. Within a generation, and in direct opposition to the hopes and beliefs of those who created it, the Union had confirmed Ireland's route to sectarian strife. After about 1830, despite the herculean labours of W. E. Gladstone, it is doubtful if the miserably violent destiny of 'John Bull's other island' could have been averted.

----

1. W. E. H. Lecky, *History of Ireland in the Eighteenth Century* (5 vols, 1892), iii, pp. 6–7.
2. E. T. Johnston, *Great Britain and Ireland, 1760–1800* (1963), p. 1.
3. *Memoirs and Correspondence of Viscount Castlereagh* (12 vols, 1848–54), i, p. 156.
4. *Correspondence of John Beresford* (2 vols, 1854), ii. p. 51.
5. *Parl. Hist.*, xxxiii (1797–98) cols 144–5.

PART TWO

The Industrial Revolution and its consequences

CHAPTER 12

The onset of industrialism

I

During the last thirty or forty years of the eighteenth century, the pace of economic growth, already appreciable, quickened markedly. Although economic historians in the past fifteen years have given greater emphasis to continuity rather than change (203, *93–116*) and some have even preferred to talk about a more broadly based 'Industrial evolution', there is little doubt that what began in that period represented the most profound and thoroughgoing change yet experienced by mankind in society. Prodigal as historians now are with the terminology of revolution – political, administrative, financial and legal – it would be pardonable in students to use the term 'industrial revolution' heedlessly and blandly. Pardonable, but unwise. Harold Perkin did well to begin his study of nineteenth-century British society with a chapter on 'The more than Industrial Revolution'. This emphasized that industrial revolutions fundamentally alter 'men's access to the means of life, in control over their ecological environment, in their capacity to escape from the tyranny and niggardliness of nature' (250, *3*).

As Professor Cannadine has shown, fashions in analysing the importance of the Industrial Revolution have changed markedly during the past century (178, ii, *29–70*). Academic fashions can, of course, usefully add to the stock of knowledge. It has been very important to be reminded, by Professor Rubinstein and others in the last decade, that Britain's economy in its classic 'revolutionary phase' was at least as indebted to commerce and the provision of financial services as it was to industrial production. Most of the largest fortunes left by wealthy Britons were by bankers and landowners, not cotton manufacturers or iron magnates. Income tax records after 1842 reveal that, while about 45 per cent of all taxable wealth was earned in London and the Home Counties, only about 20 per cent was earned in the industrial heartlands of Lancashire and Yorkshire (253, *26*).

Vicissitudes of historiographical emphasis, however, can easily enmesh students in labyrinthine detail; clear patterns become obscured in yards of computer-aided macro-economic detail. Even those who argue most strenuously that there was no 'take-off' into industrial growth at the end of the eighteenth century, and that some of the most dramatic changes took place after 1830, nevertheless accept that the cumulative changes in Britain's economic and social structure deserve to be called revolutionary. The message deserves to come across loud and clear: what certainly deserves to be described as an Industrial Revolution happened, and happened first, in late eighteenth-century Britain. Over the century or so covered by this book, it transformed British society utterly.

Industrial societies are readily distinguished from those which have not undergone this transformation. They have larger rates of economic growth than non-industrial ones and are geared to dependence on growth as non-industrial ones are not. Industrial societies have far more towns and a much larger proportion of the population live in them. By the standards of the eighteenth century, Britain was already a heavily urbanized country. About 15 per cent of its population lived in towns in 1750 and 25 per cent in 1800. Yet by 1880 80 per cent of its population was urban. Two-fifths of workers were employed in manufacturing and ancillary occupations in 1801; this had increased to almost two-thirds by 1871. During the same period, workers in agriculture and fisheries declined as a proportion of the total from 35 per cent to 15 per cent [E.vii]. Nearly all production in nineteenth-century Britain was for the market rather than for that domestic consumption which characterizes agrarian and non-commercial societies. Industrial development generates greater wealth which facilitates higher living standards, though the timing of this advance in Britain's case is hotly disputed (Ch. 17). It also promises a vastly increased variety of consumption opportunities. Once living standards rise, smaller proportions of income are spent on food and larger proportions on manufactured goods. Finally, a larger proportion of these higher incomes is diverted from immediate consumption into savings and investment in such high-cost, but vital, capital assets as factories, offices, dockyards, canals and railways. Industrial societies invest much more in the production of goods and services than do non-industrial ones. Between 1760 and 1860, British capital stock increased, while the share of the national capital invested in industry, trade and transport increased from 5 per cent to 26 per cent (178, ii, *208*). Such 'capital formation' probably represented more than 10 per cent of the total national income by 1860 (213).

Cumulatively, therefore, an industrial revolution generates a fundamental, and irreversible, structural change in the economy. It is also possible to characterize an industrial revolution as one associated with technological change which enables faster and more efficient industrial output. It should be clear from the preceding paragraphs, however, that this represents a very partial and instrumental view. Industrial revolutions are about much more than technological breakthroughs. Also, technological change was much more apparent in certain sectors of Britain's rapidly developing economy than in others. In many sectors, more intensive utilization of labour was a much more prominent feature than mechanization. As Professor Crafts puts it, on this definition, 'the "Industrial Revolution" was only *part* of the growth and development process' (201, 7).

Industrial Britain, therefore, was sucked into an accelerating vortex of change affecting every aspect of life. If the primary task in history writing is to chart and explain change over time, then the historian's productivity, like that of the subjects the historian studies, must increase when the industrial period is reached. Not only is there more change to chart, but the numerous variables which interact to produce change make explanation ever more complex. The regional perspective amply demonstrates that not all change represents progress. It has been convincingly argued in recent years that a proper appreciation of the Industrial Revolution necessitates regional study (204). As Professor Hudson says, 'An identifying feature of the [British] industrial revolution was the marked dynamism of certain industrializing regions while in others manufacturing activity and its offshoots stagnated and declined' (205, *101*). While South-east Lancashire and central Scotland exploded into ever more vigorous industrial and commercial life, the Weald of Kent and Sussex, prime suppliers of iron, glass, timber and textiles in the seventeenth century, in effect de-industrialized. The successes of the woollen cloth industry in Gloucestershire, Somerset and Wiltshire at the beginning of the eighteenth century had been easily outstripped by the West Riding of Yorkshire a century later. The West of England cloth trade went into rapid decline.

Given the number and complexity of variables involved, students should not be surprised to find historians of this period borrowing the jargon, if they cannot assimilate the methodology, of the economists, geographers, sociologists, psychologists and even nuclear physicists who study man in an industrial environment.

II

Nowhere has explanation proved more frustratingly inconclusive than in the two most basic questions: 'Why did an industrial revolution occur in late-eighteenth and early nineteenth-century Britain?' and 'Why did it occur first in Great Britain, an island off shore both physically and metaphorically from the main developments of European civilization during the previous millennium?' It is not difficult to isolate factors which seem likely *a priori* to have contributed to industrialism, but such isolation is not necessarily helpful when the phenomenon almost certainly depended upon a complex interaction of many factors. Economic historians have been dismissive in their condemnation of 'monocausal explanations' of the Industrial Revolution. Historians and economists alike still await a convincing 'model of interaction'. Partly because of the rapid development of the discipline of economic history between the 1920s and the early 1960s historians have become too dependent on the theories of the economists. The infallible route to economic growth in twentieth-century Third-World countries, after all, has resembled the quest for an 'economists' stone' both in the frenzy of the search and in the richness of the prize. As social history has experienced a renaissance since the early 1960s so economic historians have become progressively disenchanted with explanations which underplay the human dimension. If no consensus has emerged, yet economic historians increasingly believe that the nature of a given society is more critical to its prospects of generating industrial growth than its 'capital formation profile', banking and interest rate structure or total gross national product.

Emphasis has also been increasingly placed on explanations of economic growth which stress the relatively gradual development of British society and its markets, certainly during the late seventeenth and early eighteenth centuries if not from the Reformation onwards (203, 206). Very broadly, and at the risk of over-simplification, studies such as these argue that the Industrial Revolution occurred because of a wide spread of changes inducing dramatic developments in the exploitation of overseas trading opportunities and in the structure of the British domestic market. They offer a 'balanced growth' theory of industrialism in contrast to studies which, while they acknowledge the importance of adequate preparation in the economy, stress the phenomenal expansion of the cotton industry at the end of the eighteenth century [D.ii.3; D.iii.1] and argue that cottons provided the 'leading sector' which drew the rest of the economy inexorably into industrial production. (210, 12).

The performance of the British cotton industry in particular and textiles in general is remarkable; by the early 1840s textiles provided more than 70 per cent by value of all British exports [D.ii.3], a crazy concentration which might by analogy suggest oil sheikhdoms in the late twentieth century. Such a comparison would be deeply misleading, however, because of the different structures of the respective domestic markets. The British market was both highly developed and diverse in the 1780s and those who embrace the leading-sector explanation have to show how the links between cottons and other sectors were effected to pull 'underdeveloped' areas into industrial production.

The British Industrial Revolution involved a more rapid growth rate in industrial production from about 1.5 per cent per annum from 1700 to 1780 to one between 2 and 3 per cent in the half-century afterwards. This growth was facilitated after 1780 by increasing use of factory production for cotton and woollen textiles; factories facilitated economies of scale in mass-produced goods and the introduction of new technology for accelerating production. However, not all technical innovations depended on factories. Hargreaves's spinning-jenny was predominantly a workshop and domestic implement. The Industrial Revolution was accompanied by factory production but other forms not only survived but flourished. Increased output was frequently achieved without intensive factory production. Between 1780 and 1850 workshop and domestic manufacturers are much more than an adjunct to the factory revolution. Units of production in the building industry remained small but its expansion in the first half of the nineteenth century was remarkable. Brick production, for example, doubled in the period 1815–49 (200, *51*). Until at least 1850, large-scale factory production was very much the exception rather than the rule. From a total labour force of 9.7m. in 1851 [E.vii] only some 6 per cent worked in textile factories and only in textiles had factory production made significant headway before 1850 [D.v.1]. Even in textiles only a small number worked in monster factories; the typical Lancashire cotton operative in 1841 worked in a small factory employing fewer than 100 hands [D.v.2]. Units of production in the early industrial period were far smaller than is generally appreciated.

Since most factories were small affairs before the 1840s it is not necessary to explain the availability of large amounts of capital to establish industrial plants on the grand scale. Factories started small and were enlarged when successful entrepreneurs reinvested large proportions of their profits. Initial investment in buildings and equipment was modest and often provided by smallish loans negotiated with local money-lenders, country banks or by mortgage in local capital markets managed by attorneys which involved funds lodged by widows, clergymen or by friendly societies. The successful Blackburn cotton firm of Cardwell, Birley and Hornby raised over £35,000 between 1780 and 1812 but in 97 mostly unsecured loans, 51 of which were for amounts of less than £100 (222). There were numerous sources of small loans; only as eighteenth-century inventories are examined is it realized how credit-conscious the British were. Men from relatively humble backgrounds could establish businesses and rely on a combination of commercial skill and good fortune for success (Ch. 13).

III

Any explanation of Britain's early Industrial Revolution must stress factors peculiar to the eighteenth century, but she did possess timeless advantages of immense significance when other conditions were right. Britain is a small country with a plenitude of navigable rivers to facilitate movement of bulky goods. Access to the sea, vital for the development of foreign trade, is easy from most parts of the country though those acquainted with the industrial West Midlands will wince at Eric Hobsbawm's assertion that 'no part of Britain is further than seventy miles' from a coastline (212). British uplands, her Celtic extremities apart, are far from impassable to traffic and the fast-flowing streams of the North and North Midlands provided motive power for the early mills. Later, when water gave way to steam, fossil fuel was abundant in the coal seams of South Wales, the East Midlands, South Yorkshire, the North-east and Scotland's central valley. The North-west's damp, mild climate was conducive to the processing of raw cotton. Britain's topography is extraordinarily diverse in a small country and it enabled a rich variety of agricultural specialisms to develop during the seventeenth and eighteenth centuries, rendering the nation proof from the worst effects of crop failure or livestock disease. Each single such advantage could be replicated in other European countries and some could be accentuated, but no other nation enjoyed such a rich combination of natural bounties. Britain's diverse compactness, however, was to prove a hindrance in the second and third generations of industrialism when transport and other technological developments rendered distance a less intractable obstacle and enabled larger nations to maximize the advantages of their bigger coal seams or extensive prairies.

Topographical and mineral advantages operated in late-eighteenth-century Britain upon an economy already extraordinarily well developed. Income per head of each member of the population, which Phyllis Deane has estimated at £12 per annum in 1750 and rising fast, was higher in real terms than that enjoyed by most non-industrialized African and Asian countries in the late twentieth century (203). Explanations of Britain's early Industrial Revolution have lain great stress on the extent of demand for manufactured goods created by rising real incomes in a society dependent on cash rather than in-kind payments and where the bonds tying the worker to the land were less firm than in traditional communities of small or peasant proprietors farming for subsistence. The capitalist organization and market orientation of British farming (Ch. 1) is important not only for itself but in enabling Britain to surmount the challenge of rapid population growth without a decline in living standards.

The substantial growth in the population of Britain during the eighteenth century from about 6¼m. to 10½m. – mostly concentrated after 1740 – is crucial to industrial development in Britain since it provided not only a potential workforce for workshop and factory but also rising demand for industrial goods. Other nations experiencing similar, or more rapid, population growth such as Ireland or Sweden could not channel it into such productive enterprise either because they lacked the commercial superstructure or because their social structure was remorselessly battened down to the stolid conservatism of peasant proprietorship and subsistence farming. Economic growth was the key to escape from the Malthusian poverty trap (Ch. 5), but it would turn only in the well-oiled lock of productive agriculture. The supreme achievement of Britain's agricultural revolution was to provide the necessary precondition for its Industrial Revolution. Industrial progress in the nineteenth century would continue to require back-up from the land and the relationship remained symbiotic.

Stress has been rightly laid on commercial and urban developments in eighteenth-century England. Industrial take-off required both advanced agriculture and a rich diversity of industrial and commercial opportunity. These factors were surveyed in Chapter 1; to them have been added the 'transport revolution', the particular contribution of overseas trade within the general context of commercial advance and, by some historians (especially Hobsbawm, 212), the role of government.

Industry and agriculture alike needed an improved transport network. Landowners, particularly if they owned mines, were in the forefront of investment in canals and turnpike roads. The transport revolution between 1760 and 1820 shows that there was no shortage of capital for high-cost ventures. Not only the ubiquitous duke of Bridgewater but also the Thanet, Egremont, Stafford, Marlborough and Buccleuch families sank capital into canals. The reason is not far to seek. When John Gilbert and James Brindley's first dead-water canal linked the Bridgewater mines at Worsley with nearby Manchester in 1761 it immediately halved the price of coal in that city. If a successful industrial revolution depends on the creation and satisfaction of a mass market then canals and turnpikes were crucial. Mass-produced goods are fiercely price-sensitive and high transport costs before the 1760s were a sizeable hindrance to the development of the market.

Canals soon linked the major rivers, Mersey and Severn, Trent and Mersey, Thames and Severn; by the 1820s, 4,000 miles of navigable waterway were open to trade. During the boom of 1788-95 £8m. was invested at costs which Bridgewater estimated at about 10,000 guineas a mile (13, *115*). As always in booms, some of the investment was unwise. Canals of limited use were built which plunged their backers into debt; however, even dubious investments had their wider uses. Canal mania meant not only high wages for 'navvies' but it increased employment in the construction industry; bricks and iron were in heavy demand. The boom provides a good example of British landowners' sensitivity to investment opportunity outside agriculture. They were unhampered by constraints of custom and caste which so frequently operated in Europe. British landowners were a very entrepreneurially minded lot and the trading and banking origins of so many twentieth-century aristocrats bears eloquent, recurrent testimony to the reciprocal relationship between land, trade and finance. It helped to create the first Industrial Revolution.

Concentration on foreign trade as a prime cause of industrialism is understandable. Trade statistics, though difficult to use with precision, clearly show extraordinary eighteenth-century growth particularly with the Americas. Imports, exports and re-exports (mainly of colonial goods through Britain to mainland Europe) increased by some 240 per cent between 1716–20 and 1784–88 (206, *146*) The growing American market stimulated production both of textiles and metal goods. English exports to Europe increased by a mere 6 per cent between 1700 and 1770 while those to the Americas bounded ahead by 687 per cent, from £461,000 to £3,628,000. Colonial protection was a main cause of the increase since merchants were eager to open up markets denied them in heavily protected Europe. However, independence for the mainland colonists did not break the spell (Ch. 4). Indeed, following the invention of the cotton gin at the end of the century the southern states of the USA became Britain's chief supplier of raw cotton. In the 1770s Britain took a mere 5m. lb. of raw cotton from all markets; thirty years later it was importing 42m. lb. (203, *51, 87*). About two-thirds of all cotton manufactures were exported with the American market taking the lion's share. The shift to the West was remarkable. At the beginning of the eighteenth century about 80 per cent of Britain's exports went to Europe; at the turn of the nineteenth, though figures were artificially low because of the French Wars, less than 33 per cent went there [D.ii.5]. In the first decade of the new century finished textile goods represented three-fifths of Britain's total exports with cottons alone accounting for two-fifths [D.ii.3].

Such figures might suggest that a combination of cotton and foreign trade provided the crucial dynamic to pull Britain out of solid commercial growth into a self-sustaining industrial revolution during the last quarter of the eighteenth century. Some of the large profits made by Glasgow, Liverpool or Bristol merchants also found their way into investment in textiles in Lanarkshire and South Lancashire or iron in South Wales, thus forging another link in the chain of mutually supporting growth. Yet caution is necessary. Foreign trade, though it grew rapidly, did not do so consistently and in the period immediately prior to Britain's take-off overseas merchants had been discommoded by interruptions to trade caused by the American War of Independence. English imports and exports, having grown by 156 per cent in the first seventy-five years of the century, actually declined by 6 per cent in the decade 1775–84. The extraordinary spurt of the last years of the century involved successful penetration of European markets, but it took place during the early years of Britain's industrialization and was not a cause of it. Further, French foreign trade increased at a rather faster rate than Britain's in the period 1700–80, albeit from a smaller base, and the French were not yet on the verge of industrial revolution. Most tellingly, the overseas market remained far smaller than the domestic one. Eversley estimates that the produce of British manufactures was worth some £43m. in 1770 of which only £10m. was exported; by 1811 £40m. of a total output of £130m. went abroad (248, *226–7*). Foreign trade was catching up in the early phase of industrialism but still had far to go. The home market also had a more decisive influence on the range of products produced since foreign trade was increasingly skewed towards cotton textiles.

Governments in eighteenth-century Europe had neither the resources nor the expertise nor the ideology to 'manage' an economy in the way that post-Keynesians use the term. Moreover, since the British was the first Industrial Revolution, no government could possibly have followed policies designed to stimulate one before the model was there to copy. By definition, therefore, the role of government could not have been as direct as, say, that of the German or Russian in the late nineteenth and early twentieth centuries. Yet government might unwittingly have stimulated Britain's Industrial Revolution. Governments used war in the eighteenth century as an instrument of colonial and commercial policy, a luxury permitted by Britain's relatively slight direct concern with events on the European mainland. Britain's successes in the Seven Years War, in particular, enormously strengthened its position *vis-à-vis* France. Wartime production also stimulated the iron industry in the production of armaments and, to a rather lesser extent, the textile industry for blankets and uniforms. The frequent wars of the eighteenth century probably had a beneficial effect on sectors of the economy which were to be vital in the early stages of industrialism; more to the point they certainly benefited Britain more than her European competitors.

Government's failure to uphold various statutes restricting trade also probably had a beneficial effect. Rigid application of the Elizabethan apprenticeship regulations, for example, would certainly have doused the fires of entrepreneurial initiative in many trades. As it was the new metal towns like Birmingham and Sheffield operated almost in conditions of free labour. Weak enforcement of the labour laws ensured easier conditions for the recruitment of a mass workforce, despite the strenuous efforts of skilled men to protect the economic value of their labour exclusivity (Ch. 5). Nor, despite the Bubble Act of 1720 designed to stop the formation of speculative joint-stock companies, did landowners and merchants find it difficult to obtain institutional means of support for large capital projects like canal construction. The absence of internal tolls and tariffs had also made Britain, since the Anglo-Scottish Union of 1707, the largest integrated market in Europe.

The government thus provided indirect assistance to manufacturers in search both of a labour force and a large market. The navy and Britain's protective attitude towards commercial markets provided a firm foundation for commercial growth. *Laissez-faire* policies, which classical economists believed were essential for sustained growth, were developed only gradually in the century after 1760, however, and mostly in response to pressure from an already emergent industrial bourgeoisie (Ch. 5). The role of government, therefore, may have helped in establishing the preconditions for industrial take-off; governments could not have provided the spark.

IV

Perhaps there was no spark, no single dynamic injection to guarantee a transition from economic advance to self-sustaining industrial production. We might conclude that the steady build-up of predisposing factors was such that by the 1780s a 'critical mass' had been reached which would not be contained and

demanded an explosion of industrial productior
dynamic of British society surely demands partict
done on European economies the less secure d
expressed in terms of conventional economic vai
uniquely geared for growth.

Britain's 'open aristocracy' was extensively ir
ventures; this ensured productive use for exten·
of openings were available to men of talent frc
low social ceilings to block advance born of er
in Chapter 1, wealth and profits were transl₄
cotton manufacturer like Jedediah Strutt, who bene .
is the main business of the life of men', could acquire a large ια..
esteemed social position to go with his mills at Belper (250, 86). Such men workċu
in a society 'permeated by a growing economic individualism' with few irritating
regulations and no monopolies to contend with. Many were religious dissenters,
free after 1689 to worship as they pleased but still denied important central or local
government office. It has been plausibly argued that the natural individuality of the
dissenter was thus channelled into productive economic enterprise rather than into
leading judicial, administrative or executive positions. The disastrous seduction of
too many of the most able into the service sector is a feature of Britain's mature,
overripe, industrial period, not of the eighteenth and early nineteenth centuries.

Dissenters played a leading role in the expansion of scientific knowledge,
reflected in the work of the Royal Society in London and leading provincial
organizations like the Literary and Philosophical Societies or Birmingham's
famous Lunar Society, whose meetings attracted Wedgwood the potter, Watt the
engineer, Boulton the metals magnate and Priestley, the research chemist. The links
between science, drawing heavily on the new European learning, and technology
probably have never been closer. Leading manufacturers took a keen interest in
applied science and used their knowledge to perfect techniques pioneered
elsewhere, often in France or the Low Countries. Technological development
during the eighteenth century was by no means a British preserve. It derived from
a West European culture, yet conditions in Britain favoured most profitable and
market-oriented applications here.

A vital stimulus to continued technological refinement and innovation was the
steady development of a mass market in Britain, particularly from the second
quarter of the eighteenth century onwards. It has been shown how agricultural
advance permitted a rapidly increasing population after 1740 to be fed. A run of low
food prices between 1730 and 1755 was only the climax to an extraordinarily low
food price era stretching back to the 1670s. Real wages were raised and demand
generated for a range of cheap consumer goods. The absence of rigid divisions
between the ranks and classes ensured not only that cash circulated lower down the
British social hierarchy than elsewhere but that what Perkin has called 'competitive
spending' enabled quite humble folk to acquire goods which might invite a degree
of status and envy, however modest. The effects of social emulation were seen in
mass production of Lancashire cottons, West Riding worsteds and the bewildering
variety of specialities offered by Josiah Wedgwood's Etruria pottery works.

omas Malthus offered his doom-laden prophecies to the world
ish had already squared his circle by demonstrating how in a
iety rising living standards and a rising population could coexist.
coexistence, however, depended on fruitful partnership between
eur and innovator. The former must organize and develop new markets;
er creates machinery to reduce or eliminate production blockages, reduce
costs and expand the potential market still further. Thus the 'wave of gadgets'
hich revolutionized textile and metal production and controlled sources of power
was not the haphazard bounty of beneficent genius. They appeared, were refined,
duplicated and developed to meet specific demand. Industrialism, it can now be
contended, was the only possible positive response to unprecedented demand
created by significant population growth (about 27 per cent in the forty years
before 1780). It is important to note that most of the preconditions for industrial
growth – transport improvements, technological change, development of internal
and overseas trade, rising living standards – can be discerned in the period
1680–1740, albeit to a less acute degree. Only population stagnated. When this
crucial blockage to increased demand and greater productive capacity was removed
industrial development could proceed; indeed, with hindsight, one is almost
tempted to aver that it was inevitable since population growth was engendered in
an already dynamic society whose urban, commercial and agricultural advance
during the past century provided all the requisite supporting pillars.

CHAPTER 13

Entrepreneurs and markets

I

While it is valuable to chart Britain's industrial progress, so far as is possible, using the conventional indicators of economic growth [D.ii.1, 2, 3] the mere manipulation of figures is not enough. The Industrial Revolution was made by people. Social historians have rightly debated the 'human dimension' to determine how industrialization affected the masses who laboured in the factories and swelled the towns of nineteenth-century Britain. In conscious reaction against 'history from above' some have paid less attention than they might to those who built the factories, bought the machines and chased the markets. Britain's Industrial Revolution depended not on governments but on men of initiative, determination, ambition, vision, resourcefulness, single-mindedness and (not infrequently) good, honest greed. Many social historians have found in the entrepreneur an ideologically unsympathetic subject and have either neglected or caricatured him. A proper understanding of early industrial Britain must include an appraisal of its mercantile and managerial pioneers and of the markets they developed.

The sheer range of tasks performed by the factory masters and industrial capitalists of the period is staggering. It is a nice irony that while factory organization and discipline depended upon specialization of function among the workforce those who ran the firms were polymaths. Their tasks included: the raising of initial capital for factory or other industrial enterprise; the taking of decisions on how to invest profits or to survive the impact of loss; the determination of the firm's overall objective; the organization of productive capacity to fulfil that objective in times both of boom and slump; the physical planning of the factory to maximize production; the recruitment, training and appropriate deployment of a workforce entirely unschooled in factory life; calculations of market trends and opportunities; the evolution of managerial skills appropriate to new modes of production; the development of new accounting procedures; the selection of talented lieutenants to superintend particular functions once the enterprise grew in scale and complexity. Any one of these tasks (and the list is by no means exhaustive) is today regarded as a full-time job for upper management in large firms. Early industrial entrepreneurs had to cope with all of them or their firms went broke and they lost everything. Both risks and opportunities were awesome.

Here we must acknowledge an insuperable difficulty. The records of successful and larger-scale enterprises survive in disproportionate numbers. In the fiercely competitive cotton trade, expansion was the main route to security. Most of the early profits of what were to be the successful enterprises – Horrocks of Preston,

McConnel and Kennedy of Manchester, Peel of Bury, Owen of New Lanark – were reinvested in more equipment and plant. Though a small spinning-mill could be established with initial capital of £300–£400 the biggest mills as early as the 1790s were valued at more than £10,000. The bigger men found it easier to borrow from London and country banks, though even they had their problems in times of economic uncertainty.

Despite this, the cotton industry was far from being dominated by the Peels or the Arkwrights. As late as the 1840s less than 10 per cent of firms employed more than 500 hands and 43 per cent had fewer than 100 workers [D.v.2]. In Preston at the same time only Horrocks, Miller and Co. qualified as a large textile firm with a rating valuation in excess of £60,000; 21 of the 30 mills assessed were valued at less than £8,000 and 19 of them employed fewer than 150 workers. Concentration in the woollen trade was even less pronounced. Of 581 Yorkshire woollen masters who sent in returns to the 1851 Census, 528 (91 per cent) employed fewer than 50 people and only 13 (2.25 per cent) more than 200. As a Birstal woollen manufacturer commented in 1844: 'The woollen manufacture of this district may still be termed domestic' (178, iii, *98, 109*). Both small 'maisters' and handloom weavers survived well into the second half of the nineteenth century. Both organizational and technological change was more rapid in the worsted industry, which was based on combed rather than long-fibre wool. Merchant-manufacturers dominated this trade from early in the eighteenth century and the transition to factory production was more rapid. More than one-third of Yorkshire worsted and stuff manufacturers employed more than 50 hands by 1851.

Among small firms the fear of bankruptcy was real, but a steady supply of entrants to replace those who went under was ensured by the modest capital requirements necessary and by the lure of profit. Indeed, one might almost say that the vigour of entrepreneurial recruitment depended on the size of the firm remaining manageable. The characteristic entrepreneur did not own more than twenty mills in the 1790s, as Sir Robert Peel sen. did; his initial capital came from local moneylenders or trusts or, more likely, from family and friends; he was vulnerable to trade slumps. Economic growth in early industrial Britain was a matter of fits and starts. The general trend was massively upward, of course [D.ii.1], and most slumps were short-term; but while they lasted they accounted for overstretched, undercapitalized or plain unlucky entrepreneurs in droves.

Evidence was given to a parliamentary select committee in 1816 that only one Manchester mill in five still remained in the hands of the original proprietors. In particularly bad years for the cotton trade, such as 1806, 1826, 1837, 1839 and 1847, not only small proprietors went to the wall (222). One Burnley calico printer estimated that half the local owners had failed during the early 1840s (223, *40*). A West Riding factory inspector testified that only 127 of the 318 woollen concerns in operation in his district in 1836 (40 per cent) still functioned ten years later under the same management. Scarcity of records precludes proper concentration on the small family business which was at the heart of the Industrial Revolution, and it has been contended that if the frailties of most small businesses were properly assessable our view of the quality of entrepreneurship would be less roseate (269). Certainly the inability of most small firms to match up to the multifarious entrepreneurial requirements outlined above may be gauged from the rapid turnover. From the 1830s onwards, the trend towards larger units of production in the textile industry accelerated, although smallish family firms remain of overwhelming importance to the history of textiles throughout the remainder of the century.

II

The revolutionary expansion of the cotton industry was made possible by mechanized production first of the spinning and, about thirty years later, of the weaving processes. With few exceptions the main beneficiaries of technological innovation were not the inventors. James Hargreaves, a Blackburn weaver who invented the spinning-jenny in 1766 which enabled a single workman to spin several threads simultaneously, rendered the spinning-wheel obsolete, but he quite lacked the sense of market opportunity to capitalize fully on his invention. Samuel Crompton's spinning-mule of 1769 which enabled stronger yarns to be spun mechanically brought textile spinning into the factories and has some claim to be viewed as the decisive invention of the Industrial Revolution. Crompton permitted commercial exploitation of his brainchild by others. Edmund Cartwright, who possessed both an Oxford degree and a wide range of knowledge (by no means an infallible eighteenth-century combination) had almost no success in trying to sell his pioneer power-loom after its invention in 1785. The power-loom, which finally redressed the technological imbalance in favour of spinning, was not widely used in weaving cloth until the 1820s and Cartwright died, largely forgotten, in 1823. Even James Watt, who patented a condenser steam engine in 1769 which would provide power for factories, mines and metal-works, needed the business acumen first of John Roebuck and then of Matthew Boulton, the Birmingham metal button and watch-chain maker, to make him his fortune. Watt was far more at home in the worlds of scientific enquiry and Enlightenment philosophy than in the rat race of commercial competition.

The example usually cited of the successful inventor–entrepreneur is Richard Arkwright. He patented a power-driven water-frame for roller spinning in 1769 and a carding machine to prepare cloth for spinning in 1775. He set up a very early water-powered factory at Cromford (Derbyshire) in 1771 where more than 300 hands were employed. He was knighted in 1786, the first cotton manufacturer to be so honoured, and when he died in 1792 he was worth £500,000. The irony is that though Arkwright was a shrewd and determined businessman he was not a great inventor. Much of the pioneer work on mechanized spinning had been done by others but his achievement was the greater. His innovations were in business organization and market penetration, and as such more far-reaching than mere invention. He knew where to borrow money and how to run a factory. Financed initially by the wealthy East Midland hosiers, Jedediah Strutt and Samuel Need, he set the standard for new textile factories.

Given the importance of the market, it is not surprising that some of the most successful entrepreneurs, like Benjamin Gott, should have come to factory production from a mercantile background. Gott had been a successful woollen merchant before setting up his famous Bean Ing Works on the outskirts of Leeds in 1792. Here he experimented successfully with various fabric finishes but, as he confessed, he 'became a manufacturer rather from possessing capital than understanding the manufacture' (268, *43*). By the 1820s this pioneer of woollen spinning factories was employing more than 1,500 men and had a capital comfortably in excess of £100,000. Anthony Bacon, a merchant with London and Whitehaven interests, and Richard Crawshay, a London merchant with important Admiralty connections, provided the capital in the 1760s to found what became one of South Wales's biggest enterprises, the Cyfartha Ironworks at Merthyr Tydfil. In 1830 it had eight steam-engines, three iron forges, eight rolling-mills and it employed 5,000 men; its capital exceeded £200,000. Industrial production in South Wales by the 1830s was indeed a wonder of the modern world. Coal production in Wales was virtually non-existent in 1750. By 1850, almost 7m. tons a year were being produced, about one-eighth of total British production. New docks and a rail link to the coalfields of Merthyr saw Cardiff's population grow from a mere 2,000 in 1801 to 40,000 by 1870. Dominated by the Crawshay, Bailey and Guest families, pig iron production in South Wales increased from 34,000 tons in 1796 to 525,000 in 1840 and 969,000 in 1860. In the 1830s, South Wales was producing more than a third of all Britain's output (21, *220–1*). Birmingham, Britain's largest metals town and the sixth largest overall in 1831 with a population of 144,000, provides an interesting contrast. Much of its production depended on less advanced forms of power. In the early 1830s it possessed only 120 working steam engines.

The vitality and diversity of British society before the 1780s is due in significant measure to the interdependence of land with domestic or outwork industry. The social origins of entrepreneurs are extraordinarily diverse, but many came from just this mixed background (267). Joshua Fielden both controlled the family sheep farm on bleak Pennine moorlands outside Todmorden and worked looms in the farmhouse. From this base he acquired capital sufficient to set himself up in factory production. Latterly, the Peels added weaving to their farming activities. Many of the ironmasters of South Yorkshire came from part-farming, part-metalcraft backgrounds.

Bright, ambitious apprentices with a thorough knowledge of the processes of their trade could also make their way with reasonable luck and, not infrequently, a helping hand from a grateful employer. Engineering apprentices benefited especially from apprenticeship and practical training, like Joseph Bramah, inventor of the hydraulic press, and his pupil, Joseph Clements. Thomas Cubitt, perhaps the most successful building entrepreneur of the early nineteenth century, had been trained as a millwright before making his fortune out of successful organization of a large and disparate workforce. Robert Owen began as a drapery apprentice. William Radcliffe, another whose family had supplemented an agricultural income by domestic spinning and weaving, showed an early eye for business: 'Availing myself of the improvements that came out while I was in my teens ... with my little savings and a practical knowledge of every process from the cotton bag to the piece of cloth ... I was ready to commence business for myself and by the year 1789 I was well established and employed many hands both in spinning and weaving as a master manufacturer.'[1] In 1801, Radcliffe employed 1,000 hands.

Among men 'sprung from the cotton shop', drive and ambition were paramount. For the successful, the desire to sink capital in a permanent monument to their success was marked. Industrial wealth was not all reinvested in expansion and improvement; some was used in the purchase of respect, if not an additional career. Sir Robert Peel sen. bought the Staffordshire manor of Tamworth in 1790 which formed the political base for his own parliamentary career in addition to setting him up as a country squire. The same base bought his son early political advancement [A]. Arkwright built Willersley Castle in his latter days and became High Sheriff for Derbyshire. In the next generation Sir Titus Salt erected a massive mansion overlooking his purpose-built woollen textile community at Saltaire near Bingley in West Yorkshire.

Among the less notable, but still successful, country estates and superior town houses became badges of social status. Few industrial capitalists could match the width of culture or vision of a Josiah Wedgwood or a Matthew Boulton, and envious or scornful observers were not slow to condemn the coarseness of manner and narrowness of interest which characterized successful businessmen whose lives revolved around the pursuit of profits. A portion of those profits were thus used to buy privilege for the next generation. Sons and even daughters were expensively educated; vowels and horizons alike were broadened as the grime and habits of the early industrial town were left behind. Those who found their own efforts derided by snobbish county gentry paid handsomely to ensure respectability and acceptability for their progeny.

Much has been made of the disproportionate prominence of religious dissenters among the early captains of industry. Undoubtedly some of the largest eighteenth-century enterprises developed as they did because of financial support from kin and co-religionists. Many iron manufacturers, like the Darbys, Lloyds and Crowleys, bankers, like the Barclays, Gurneys and Lloyds and brewers, like the Trumans, Bevans and Perkins, were Quakers, though not all remained within the sect once they were well established. These trades were among the most expensive to establish and solid financial backing was essential. Several successful cotton manufacturers, like the McConnels, Gregs and Thomas Cooper, the Bolton radical who campaigned for a repeal of the Test and Corporation Acts in the 1780s, were Unitarians. Many middle-class dissenters were educated at their own academies which provided sound training in the commercial arts and boasted more scientific and 'practical' curricula than their conformist counterparts.

Exclusion from most public offices spurred able dissenters to channel their ambitions in industrial and commercial directions. There may even be validity in the threadbare and oversimplified notion that the Protestant work ethic inculcated seriousness of intent, aversion to time-wasting and determination to succeed. But Protestant nations are not self-evidently more serious minded or profit conscious than Catholic ones, and in the nineteenth century Catholic Belgium would industrialize before Calvinist Holland. In Britain the branches of nonconformity are worth stressing. During the eighteenth century Methodists, Baptists and Independents all expanded their numbers rapidly [G.ii;iii]. Many nineteenth-century Methodists, particularly Wesleyan worsted merchants in the West Riding of

Yorkshire, were to be intimately involved in entrepreneurial activity, but the eighteenth-century pioneers came disproportionately from the smaller sects. Quakers were actually losing members at this time but their industrial and commercial contribution was immense; Unitarianism was a creed with a distinctly intellectual following, yet it exerted more influence than mere size would warrant. The accent should be rather on rank than religion. Friends and Unitarians drew on the upper-middle ranks for much of their membership. When modest wealth was allied to extensive kinship support from co-religionists firms could be established on a sound footing and could the more easily ride the vicissitudes of fortune. It has been suggested that nonconformist businesses seem prominent only because their capital accumulations and creditworthiness enabled large numbers to survive rather than because they were particularly significant (269). This ignores strong evidence of motivation within the middle ranks and of the prevalence of nonconformity in this sector of society.

Wealthy nonconformists formed if not a counter-culture then an independent element in British society of profound importance. Unitarian and Quaker families fraternized; their sons were sent as apprentices within the faith; abiding personal and commercial links were forged in the dissenting academies. A nationwide network of contacts and mutual trust, essential qualities both, was built up. Thus, the merchants who had built the nonconformist chapels in the major trading centres after the toleration of 1689 remained the hub of that great wheel of commercial advance without which the Industrial Revolution could not have been set in motion. Nonconformity mattered; the relationship between dissent and business leadership was no accident.

Aristocratic and land-owning entrepreneurs cannot be ignored. Unlike their European counterparts, they owned the mineral rights on and under their land. It gave them incentives to invest in activities which were already important in 1700 and became more so as the need for steam-power and for coal or coke in furnaces increased. Industrial diversification depended to a great degree on the mining investments of the Delavals and Lambtons in Northumberland and Durham, the Lowthers and Curwens in Cumberland, the Norfolks and Rockinghams in Yorkshire and the Dudleys in Staffordshire. Not only coal but iron, tin and lead all attracted productive investment on a scale which only large landowners could provide. As was seen in Chapter 12, the need to shift bulky cargoes like coal and iron from place of extraction to place of utilization was a spur to land-owning investment in the transport revolution. The interconnection of land with industry is a *leitmotif* in these pages since it explains Britain's primacy. Probably no landed class in history has been more entrepreneurially minded than Britain's in the eighteenth century.

III

An effective marketing policy was *sine qua non* for the entrepreneur. Many entrepreneurs had been merchants who turned to manufacture, like the West Riding worsted manufacturers, to achieve greater influence over both supply and demand.

Efficient organization of factory and workforce (see Ch. 14) was important but subordinate to successful marketing. Over-supply was as certain a route to bankruptcy as uncompetitive prices.

Many merchant-manufacturers employed agents to advise on changing fashions at home and abroad. Oldknow and Arkwright took advice from London buyers on which lines to develop and which to let drop. Fashion was crucial. Cottons, in particular, were almost infinitely adaptable and success in this highly competitive world could depend on sensitivity to quite small changes in buying habits or on recognition of opportunities to make into mass lines cheaper variants on last year's high fashion from the salons of Europe. Early entrepreneurs continued to rely on the specialist marketing skills of the London factors. Though local agents were being recruited, a considerable amount of Lancashire's new factory textiles were sold through established channels.

In this respect, as in many others, Josiah Wedgwood, Etruria's master potter, was ahead of his time in developing his own sales strategy. He appreciated the importance of tapping the aristocratic market. 'Fashion', he wrote, 'is infinitely superior to merit in many respects'. Thus he pandered to royal and aristocratic tastes, knowing that his description as 'Queen's potter' or supplier to the Empress of Russia imparted a distinction to outweigh any disadvantage at which the higher prices his goods usually fetched might set him. Wedgwood missed no marketing trick. Travelling salesmen were engaged, London and provincial sales warehouses opened and advertising space commandeered. His phenomenal success, which made North Staffordshire the ceramic centre of the world, was based on shrewd psychology. A mass market could be created by stressing the approval and patronage of the great.

The rationale of the Industrial Revolution was mass production. What Harold Perkin has called 'competitive spending' was at the very heart of industrial success (250, *92*). As early as the 1780s it was noted that 'Every servant girl has her cotton gown and her cotton stockings' (223), and businessmen worked to ensure that during the next half-century she would be able to buy an ever expanding number of cotton prints, light woollens and worsteds at prices which fell steadily. Increased textile production brought economies of scale which in their turn brought lower prices to attract a still wider market and encourage yet more experiment. Britain's early industrial development was incontrovertibly unbalanced, but her citizens were provided with cotton, flaxen and woollen fabrics of reliable quality and bewildering range: fustians, calicoes, cambrics and sateens, swansdowns and toilinets, bandanna handkerchiefs, poplin shirts, linen sheets, kersey trousers.

Professor Davis has argued that, though foreign trade was not vital to the outbreak of the Industrial Revolution, it was crucial to its consolidation in the generation after 1815 when textile exports stabilized at a high level and helped to provide jobs for the over-supply of labour engendered by Britain's massive population growth [E.i]. By the 1820s the Latin American, and by the 1840s the Indian, markets for finished cotton goods were of first importance. By the 1850s more cottons were sold to the 'new' markets in Asia, Africa, Australia and South America than to earlier established outlets in Europe, North America and the West Indies (161). Foreign trade took up about 55 per cent of the cotton industry's output in the 1820s and more than two-thirds by the 1870s when the Indian market for cheap fabrics was at its peak. By value, however, the home market retained an edge since domestic demand was for the finer and more fashionable fabrics which commanded a higher price (166).

Woollen and worsted textile exports were less valuable than cottons. Only about 40 per cent of the value of cotton exports were sent abroad by the Yorkshire clothiers in the first decade of the nineteenth century and only 30 per cent by the 1850s. Nevertheless, about a third of woollen production was exported and a shift within the export trade – broadly away from heavy woollens to Europe towards lighter worsteds to the Far East, Central and South America – helped to loosen the grip of the great merchant community of Leeds. After 1815, when prices fell and the older North European trade routes failed to revive, entrepreneurial control passed to a new generation of manufacturers in Bradford, Huddersfield or Dewsbury prepared to employ agents to develop new world markets or even send goods on speculation for auction to the highest bidder (264).

IV

Before the 1840s, exports of metals and metalwares were worth only about one-fifth of the value of textile exports [Dii.3;iii.3] though the USA remained profitable to the Sheffield cutlers or the domestic hardware manufacturers of Birmingham and the Black Country. Railways, however, provided the greatest stimulus for metal manufacturers and refiners since by the late 1840s Europe and the United States were avid for railway iron, wheels and rolling-stock.

The 1840s witnesses the transition from the first, heroic, stage of industrial entrepreneurship to the second, consolidating, stage. In the first stage textile production dominated both technological innovation and overseas markets. In the second stage more balanced industrial growth is noticeable. The industrial base widens as metals and coal challenge the primacy of textiles; corporations and joint-stock companies make important inroads; plutocratic industrial concentration is foreshadowed; the heavier initial investment required makes the accumulation of great industrial fortunes from modest beginnings more difficult.

The contrast should not be overdrawn, however, since textile innovation was far from over. Samuel Cunliffe-Lister's mechanical wool comber was introduced in the 1850s and improvements in labour productivity were also achieved. In cottons, the largest nineteenth-century percentage increase in exports of piece goods was achieved in the 1850s, not earlier [D.iii.2].

Still, the railways were a new point of departure. More than 6,000 miles of track were open by 1850 and 13,000 by 1870 [D.iv.1]. The rate of industrial investment was greatly increased. Especially during the railway 'mania' of 1844–47 many unsophisticated middle-class investors – parsons, widows and the like – unwisely gambled savings at the top of the market as inexperienced investors tend to do. At this time railway investment probably accounted for more than a quarter of gross domestic capital formation. Speculation played into the hands of financial manipulators like George Hudson, the 'railway king', who controlled about half the track in Britain at the height of his power in the mid-1840s. Hudson had been a draper's apprentice and his knowledge of railways ran well behind his commercial skill. Financial scandal precipitated his fall in 1849 though he continued to represent Sunderland as its Tory MP for a further ten years. Some indication of the importance attached to railway development may be discerned by the fact that more than 100 MPs had substantial financial interests in railways in the 1850s. The technical heroes of this pioneer age were skilled engineers like Samuel Morton Peto and Thomas Brassey. They also developed entrepreneurial skills in the recruitment and training of a construction army. At the peak of the railway boom about 300,000 'navvies' were employed. Brassey, who built railways in twelve countries, died in 1870 worth £3m., one of the first technological millionaires.

Railways were the biggest business Britain had yet seen. Almost a quarter of the expansion of British national income between 1840 and 1865 was attributable to railway development. It created new towns, like Crewe, Wolverton, Swindon and Ashford, where engines and rolling-stock were built, and it made possible the new heavy industry towns of Middlesbrough and Barrow which grew so fast from almost nothing after 1850 [E.iii].

It may be an exaggeration to say that railways solved the first crisis of capitalism (212) but they boosted the concentration of industry. Engineering and machine-making firms proliferated in the great cities. Important innovations by Joseph Whitworth and James Nasmyth brought precision and standardization to the design of machine tools and further developed an already expanding market for engineering technology. The most dramatic developments were in iron and steel, not only because of railway and shipbuilding but under the stimulus of wars in the Crimea (1854–56) and in the United States (1861–65). Armaments contracts both at home and abroad were fully exploited by men like the Tyneside engineering magnate, William Armstrong. It is interesting to notice a thread of continuity in Armstrong's career. Like so many captains of industry in the previous generation, he invested a substantial proportion of his immense wealth between 1870 and 1884 in erecting a country palace, Cragside, in substantial grounds at Rothbury (Northumberland) thirty miles north-west of Newcastle. It was constructed in massive Victorian Gothic style to the design of the Scottish architect Richard Norman Shaw. The powerful conjunction of land and industry (see Ch. 1) was to be preserved into the twentieth century.

New discoveries of haematite ore in the Furness district of North Lancashire and in West Cumberland were matched by workings of Cleveland iron in the 1850s to make Barrow and Middlesbrough the great boom towns of the later nineteenth century. It is characteristic of entrepreneurial flexibility that the engineer who brought railways to Furness, and would later build them in Italy, was J. B. Fell who had first established himself locally as a coal importer and timber merchant with sawmills at the mouth of the River Leven. He saw better than anyone the practical advantages for trade of a railway spanning both that river and the neighbouring Kent to link what had been one of Britain's most inaccessible areas to the main arteries of communication. Fell's railway construction career was later patronized by the great Thomas Brassey.[2]

Iron-ore production increased from 2½m. tons in 1851 to 12m. in 1870. Iron naturally found a place in the expansion of shipping as Britain consolidated her position not only as the workshop but as the carrier of the world. Between 1840 and 1870 the tonnage of British-built ships increased by more than 180 per cent [D.iv.3b] and the challenge from American and German shipbuilders was beaten off by yards on the Tyne, Wear, Mersey, Clyde and, though now in relative decline, Thames. Steamships made a quiet entry, especially on the transatlantic runs, and sail retained a substantial lead in total tonnage until the 1870s despite massive investment in steam during the 1860s. Isambard Kingdom Brunel's talismanic steamship the *Great Eastern* (1859) made its backers a thumping loss and almost certainly hastened that great constructional engineer's premature death at the age of fifty-three. Nevertheless, a fair amount of iron was incorporated into new sailing-ships and the industry did not suffer from the delayed conversion of the British merchant marine to steam.

Steel, that adaptable but highly priced alloy of iron and carbon, had been produced before the 1850s in tiny furnaces at considerable cost. The inventions of Henry Bessemer, whose converter enabled the achievement of temperatures high enough to eliminate impurities in 1856, and William Siemens, who perfected the open-hearth furnace in 1866, revolutionized steel production and made it a metal of mass production for the first time. The emergence of steel for ships and rails in the 1870s would provide new avenues for investment, though by 1870 iron, and particularly Scottish iron, still dominated the market.

Harold Perkin has argued that from the middle of the nineteenth century traditional entrepreneurship was on the decline, to be replaced by an 'emerging plutocracy' or 'business aristocracy' (250). Certainly, the economic growth of this period required larger units of production and sophisticated management. Intricate forms of delegation evolved in the great iron firms, say, of central Scotland or South Wales which moved well beyond the original entrepreneurial concept of the business partnership. Limited liability legislation, introduced in 1856 and 1862, eliminated much of the earlier 'nerve of risk' and encouraged the giant enterprises which would be owned by public shareholders rather than by a family or small partnership. But the impact of joint-stock and limited-liability legislation was not immediate and family businesses wishing to raise capital on the stock market without losing control of company policy found few legal or financial obstacles in their way. As late as 1885 not more than 10 per cent of companies were limited under the 1862 Act (269). The tenacity, if not always the vitality, of the family firm should not be underestimated in British business well beyond 1870. It is also true, as Perkin states, that second-generation entrepreneurs came disproportionately from the professional and industrial middle classes. No doubt both additional capital and a serviceable education became more important as the scale of business enterprises grew and as technology, particularly in the metal trades, became more sophisticated. But even in the first generation, as we have seen, few successful industrialists came from ranks lower than the skilled craftsman.

Though changes between 1840 and 1870 were crucial to the development of a fully industrialized society one must beware of telescoping too much into too short a time. The fundamental changes on the road to industrial plutocracy and the large corporations still lay ahead. During the generally favourable business climate of the 1850s and 1860s most business ownership remained small scale. Even in the late 1860s armaments magnates like William Armstrong or railway engineering tycoons like Thomas Brassey remained as untypical of their entrepreneurial generation as Richard Arkwright or Robert Peel sen. had been of theirs. A route to advancement for the relatively humble still remained open. Many of those who became Clydeside shipbuilders in the boom of the 1850s had been skilled shipworkers themselves fifteen or twenty years earlier (17, 19). It was not until the end of the 1870s and the 1880s that the massive investment required for efficient steamship construction demanded amalgamation and the growth of the great shipbuilding combines. Down to 1870 it is still possible to argue that entrepreneurship had developed in scale rather than changed in kind since the heroic days of the late eighteenth century. Only in the 1890s was the age of corporate capitalism to dawn.

----

1. G. Unwin, *Samuel Oldknow and the Arkwrights* (Manchester, 1924), pp. 115–17.
2. A. N. Rigg, 'John Barraclough Fell: a social study of a mid-Victorian engineer', University of Lancaster MA thesis, 1969.

CHAPTER 14

The structure and organization of the workforce in early industrial Britain

I

The previous chapters have cautioned against a simplified view of the changes wrought during the first two generations of the Industrial Revolution. Though mechanized production was essential to that revolution, the typical employee in 1850 neither worked in a cotton factory nor minded modern machinery of any kind. The two most populous categories of employment in the 1851 census were agricultural labourer (1.8m.) and domestic servant (1.0m.). In the first of these categories, female employment declined sharply once family labour began to decline on those larger, more heavily capitalized farms which dominated arable agriculture from the second half of the eighteenth century (Ch. 15). Domestic service, growing steadily with the burgeoning middle class, was dominated by women in a ratio of approximately 9:1. Domestic servants comprised more than 10 per cent of the entire labour force in 1851 and almost 40 per cent of the female labour force. Twice as many women were in service as worked in any kind of textile occupation. The cotton and woollen industries as a whole employed only 811,000 in 1851 and almost one-third of these as late as the middle of the century still worked in small workshops or from their own homes. Almost as many male shoemakers (243,000) were identified as male cotton operatives (255,000); coal-miners (216,000) had a comfortable edge over male woollen workers (177,000). Though the balance between rural and industrial workers shifted steadily in favour of the latter between 1800 and 1870 [E.vii] the scale of the enterprise in which the industrial labourer worked was typically small. Paradoxically, the nailmaker from Cradley Heath in the Black Country working on many different kinds of nail or the cabinet-maker from Bethnal Green working to different specifications in London's East End was a more characteristic male operative than a worker in Horrocks's giant Preston cotton factory or Guest's enormous Dowlais Ironworks.

Nor was the shift in population from rural to urban areas dramatically rapid. The north-west of England, it is true, had the largest percentage increase in population each decade until the 1860s [E.ii.1], but all regions grew at a rate of at least 9 per cent per decade until the 1840s. Even in the North-west most population increase owed little to long-distance migration and much more to local immigration sustained by a locally generated natural increase. Though textile towns grew most rapidly in percentage terms, they frequently did so from a low base and the growth both of ports and non-factory manufacturing centres is scarcely less noticeable [E.iii]. The movement northwards and from predominantly agricultural to predominantly industrial centres was more a drift than a flood [E.ii.2]. Quite apart from institutional constraints on movement (Ch. 16), the reason is not difficult to find. Especially in the South of England, and the South Midlands, some rural industries continued to thrive. Straw-plaiting was an important employer of labour in Buckinghamshire, Hertfordshire, Bedfordshire and Essex. Pillow-lace making suffered under foreign competition in the late eighteenth and early nineteenth centuries but revived from the 1840s to the 1870s. Leather-tanning, glovemaking and shoemaking remained staple rural industries. The symbiotic relationship between land and industry was by no means destroyed by Bolton cotton mills, Halifax woollen factories or large pits in County Durham. Indeed, Britain's massive population growth between 1780 and 1870 [E.i] delayed the introduction of mechanization in many metal and clothing industries. With a large pool of labour to draw on there was little incentive to invest heavily and speculatively in machinery. There was no shortage of milliners, seamstresses or tailors effectively forced to work long hours for low pay; these were not called the 'sweated trades' for nothing (231).

The total horsepower equivalent provided by steam-engines in 1870, was about 2m.; from here it would leap to 8m. by 1907. While steam-power was introduced steadily to a range of industrial operations, especially blast-furnaces for iron manufacture and machine tools, its use was still in 1870 preponderantly in textile factories which accounted for almost half the total: coal-mining, the great growth industry of the second half of the nineteenth century, took up another quarter. Human motive power remained vital to the mid-Victorian economy and it has been plausibly suggested that American technological advance, which began to outstrip Britain's, was motivated by her much greater labour shortage. Britain's extraordinary industrial diversity in 1870 was mostly small scale and only partially mechanized.

II

The contribution of women and children to textiles has been massively documented. Immediately after the passage of the 1833 Factory Act [C.i and Ch. 26] they comprised two-thirds of that industry's factory labour force. When the proportion of children began to fall from the 1840s women, rather than men, made up the numbers. Adult females, mostly unmarried or at least childless, made up half the complement of textile factories consistently between 1856 and 1870 [D.v.1]. The 1871 census shows 20 per cent of all employed women working in textiles and a further 16 per cent in non-factory clothing trades. Domestic service (46 per cent) comfortably exceeded this, but there is no denying the vital role women played in all forms of the clothing industry. Employers valued women for particular skills – some directly translated from the domestic environment – including nimble fingers, general deftness of application and the ability to undertake laborious repetitive work. Such skills were not, in general, highly rewarded in the market place. Even Josiah Wedgwood paid female flower-painters on his delicate pottery ware 3s. 6d. (17.5p) a day in 1770, compared with 5s. 6d. (22.5p) a day earned by men (200, *156*, 258, 278). More generally women's wages ran between one-third and one-sixth of those earned by men. After 1844 excessive working hours were prohibited by law, but this indulgence did not extend to workshops until 1867 and then only partially. If the mills offered the staple employment for young women in the industrial North, the worst conditions and lowest wages were encountered further south, especially in London by seamstresses, box- or paper-bag-makers, toy-makers and sundry other crafts still organized on a workshop basis and dependent on abundant supplies of labour.

The 1841 census suggested that 74 per cent, and the 1871 census that 64 per cent, of women were 'unoccupied' in the sense of being non-wage-earners compared with 24 per cent and 12 per cent respectively of men. There are good reasons for scepticism about these figures. Women who helped their husbands in their work, generally in a part-time capacity as they brought up families, tended to escape the census enumerators' notice and to be categorized as unoccupied. The survival of ancillary female occupations, such an important feature of 'pre-industrial' society, has been generally underestimated. At least until the 1880s the Industrial Revolution continued to offer increased opportunities for female employment. They were engaged even in such superficially unlikely locations as the North Staffordshire potteries, the Black Country metal trades or London bookbinding workshops. They were also important in the food distributive trades, whether as respectable shopkeepers, street traders or even porters in wholesale markets. For 'fallen women' and the destitute, of course, prostitution offered a tempting, if squalid and dangerous, escape from the workhouse; growth in the oldest profession cannot be quantified. It is true that the census shows a 40 per cent decline in the number of female agricultural labourers between 1851 and 1871 but, contrary to the views of Eric Richards (277), this was offset by a growth of industrial employment opportunity.

Children had been an essential part of the family economy long before the Industrial Revolution wherever corn was to be gathered or wool carded and spun. The children whose disciplined labours Daniel Defoe praised when he visited the Halifax wool centre in the 1720s – 'hardly any thing above four years old but its hands are sufficient to itself'[1] – were the inheritors of a long English tradition. Examples could be cited before 1780 of children divorced from the family and shamefully exploited as chimney-sweeps, 'climbing boys', or as mine-workers' helpers, but during the early phase of the Industrial Revolution child labour became both more systematic and more prevalent. Cotton factory owners valued the delicacy of touch which child spinners brought to their task; they valued the relative ease with which children could be broken to factory work; they valued, too, their mobility as 'scavengers', moving underneath machinery to pick up loose cotton. Most of all, they valued them because they were cheap and plentiful. In 1821 49 per cent of Britain's population was less than twenty years of age; about a half of this population was between the ages of five and fourteen, years now of full-time education, but much less likely to be so in the first half of the nineteenth century. These facts alone go far towards explaining the importance of child labour in a growing economy. By contrast, only about one-quarter of Britain's population in the 1990s is under twenty.

Dr Andrew Ure calculated in 1835 that boys employed in Lancashire cotton mills earned an average of 4s. 10¾d. (24½p) a week whereas adult males could make 22s. 8½d. (£1.13); children in general earned between one-third and one-sixth of their adult male counterparts. Employers thus had every incentive to use children to the full, the more so since many skilled cotton-spinners extended the family economy into the factory by bringing their own offspring with them. In the late 1830s, about 107,000 children under the age of eighteen were employed in cotton factories, 29 per cent of the total workforce [D.v.1].

Attention has naturally concentrated on the exploitation of factory children, especially on the semi-slavery of the 'pauper apprentices' removed by Poor Law Guardians to the charge of factory owners so that they would not further burden the poor rates. Many were subjected to devastatingly long working hours, harsh discipline, absence of recreation and inadequate food; some became 'factory cripples', permanently deformed by keeping immature limbs in unnatural postures for long periods. The problem was encapsulated by the *Memoir* of Robert Blincoe, a London boy sent at the age of seven to harsh conditions in the waterpowered mills of Nottinghamshire and Derbyshire (251, 269). The typicality of child exploitation has been furiously debated without clear result. But it may be that the worst conditions were experienced early on, and particularly in the remote mills away from the prying eyes of humanitarian investigators or community sanctions. Substantial improvements had been effected in many Lancashire towns by the 1830s, both in the shortening of working hours and in the provision of education for factory children.

It was on child labour in the textile factories and the mines that legislators concentrated [C.i]. By the 1840s the education clauses of the Factory Acts and the growing number of church schools, now in receipt of annual government grants (Chs 26 and 36), was reducing the number of child employees. Until 1867, however, children outside these sectors were largely unprotected yet, arguably, the worst abuses were encountered in the non-factory, metals and 'sweated' trades, where competition seemed to dictate longer hours. Children in the nail-making Staffordshire village of Sedgeley, for example, were working from the age of seven or eight as late as the 1860s and would be expected to produce a thousand nails a day within a couple of years. Punishments might include being 'struck with a red hot iron, and burnt and bruised simultaneously' (354, *46*). It is no accident that the government collected from the 1830s reasonably accurate information about the factories of Bolton or Bradford but not from the ribbon-making garrets of Coventry or the match-makers of London's East End.

The North Staffordshire potteries were not brought under the aegis of the Factory Acts until 1864. Investigation in the early 1860s revealed that 17 per cent of the pottery workforce were still under eleven years of age and that conditions for most were appalling. Boys employed as mould-runners, conveying pots from the wheel to the stove for firing, worked in extremes of temperature which rose to 50°C:

> The boys were kept in constant motion throughout the day, each carrying from thirty to fifty dozen of moulds into the stoves, and remaining . . . long enough to take the dried earthenware away. The distance thus run by a boy in the course of a day . . . was

estimated at seven miles. From the very nature of this exhausting occupation children were rendered pale, weak and unhealthy. In the depth of winter, with the thermometer in the open air sometimes below zero, boys, with little clothing but rags, might be seen running to and fro on errands or to their dinners with the perspiration on their foreheads, 'after labouring for hours like little slaves'. The inevitable result of such transitions of temperature were (*sic*) consumption, asthma, and acute inflammation.[2]

III

Many historical sociologists assert that an inevitable consequence of industrialization is the destruction of most forms of craft skill and the substitution of a basically proletarian workforce alienated alike from the means of production and the system of industrial capitalism which created them. This development had not happened in Britain by 1870. At least as many new skills were created as destroyed; others remained largely untouched. Though the plight of many handloom weavers became desperate once the power-loom was introduced from the late 1820s, the new opportunities for millwrights, machinists and other skilled engineers were obvious. Compositors and shoemakers, skilled men with high average earnings in 1780, remained so in 1870.

Britain's early industrial workforce was highly diverse, comprised large numbers of women as well as men, and manifested important distinctions both of status and earning power across the trades and down the hierarchy within a trade. Very roughly, earnings of 30s. (£1.50) or more in the 1830s placed a man within an 'aristocracy of labour'. Employers in luxury trades, like coachbuilding, bookbinding or clockmaking, could not get skilled men for less; some workers could exploit their labour scarcity in an expanding market to command wages of more than £2 a week. As ever, printers came near the top of the wages league. In prosperous times, carpenters, bricklayers, brickmoulders, wheelwrights and shipwrights earned more than 30s., as did men at the quality end of the tailoring trade. Craft societies were increasingly concerned to protect their privileged members from 'dilution' and descent into the 'dishonourable' sectors of a trade where skills were not prized and where the market was flooded with men prepared to work longer hours for perhaps half the wages producing inferior goods for a wider market. It is important to recognize, however, that an aristocracy of labour was not identified by high wage levels alone. The regularity of those earnings was equally important, as also in most cases was the successful completion of an apprenticeship.

A disproportionate concentration of the old craft skills was found in London and here wages at the top of the market were higher. By no means all skilled men qualified as aristocrats of labour; in most trades journeymen earned between 20s. and 30s. (£1 to £1.50) in full employment. The engineering boom from the 1820s onwards, however, was reflected in wage levels. In 1839 patternmakers, fitters, smiths and millwrights around Manchester were above the 30s. borderline, while the carding overlookers – the most highly paid factory operatives – fell below it at 25s. (£1.25).[3] By the late 1850s furnace-men, puddlers and rollers in the prosperous iron-puddling mills were making between £2 2s. 6d. (£2.12½) and £3, while 'shinglers' who removed impurities from the precious metal could earn an extraordinary £4 15s. (£4.75). One apprenticed mechanic, Thomas Wood, earned 32s. (£1.60) a week in his early twenties making textile machinery at the famous Platt Bros. works in Oldham, where 2,000 men were employed in the early 1840s. He found many of his companions 'wicked and reckless. Most of them gambled freely on horse- or dog-races'. (274, *310*). He preferred the £1 or so he earned in a small workshop for 'country-made tools'.

In 1867 Dudley Baxter's *National Income of the United Kingdom* estimated that 14 per cent of the workforce was skilled. Precise categorization is impossible and Baxter's criteria may have been stringent, but it is safe to assume that no more than 20 per cent was skilled at the end of our period and rather fewer in the 1830s. Semi-skilled or unskilled workers rarely made more than £1 a week. The Durham miners, who averaged 24s. (£1.20) in the late 1830s with peaks of 30–40s., were exceptional even in an occupation which attracted relatively high wages.[4] Power-loom weavers in the cotton factories earned about 17s. (85p) if they tended four looms and wages for women and children there stretched down to 7s. (35p) for 'scutchers' who prepared the cloth by beating it. Male spinners generally earned from 14s. to 22s. (70p to £1.10), thus emphasizing an earnings hierarchy even in the supposedly monolithic factory system.

At the bottom of the ladder were found the agricultural labourers and the handloom weavers and framework knitters, rendered cruelly redundant first by trade recession then by technological innovation. About 250,000 handloom weavers survived into the 1840s to earn a miserly 7s. 6d. (37½p) or so in a grossly glutted trade from which at the turn of the century 30s. or more could be made. Agricultural labourers' wages varied from region to region, according to the availability of other sources of employment. In the South-west they were around 8s.; in Yorkshire and the four northern countries 12s. In the West Midlands they varied between these two extremes with highest rates paid in the industrial counties of Staffordshire and Warwickshire.[5] Everywhere, the general trend was for women to be paid much less than men, often for the same work. Female agricultural labourers, at 4s. (20p) a week, earned roughly half the wages of the menfolk, though the discrepancy was much less for Essex silkworkers and, for a time, Bedfordshire strawplaiters earned more than their male counterparts.

Wage rates may conceal wage values. Agricultural labourers in Devon in 1837, for example, had a cider allowance worth 2s. (10p) in addition to their standard wage of 8s. (40p). Other occupations had in-kind payments, but the balance was more often in the opposite direction. Wage rates are for full and continuous employment, but much nineteenth-century labour fell into neither category. Only recently has the full extent of casual labour been revealed (231, 303). Henry Mayhew estimated that 'there is barely sufficient work for the regular employment of half our labourers' and casual labour was the norm for many not only in the London which he knew so well. As Stedman Jones comments: 'Very few workers could expect a working life of stable employment in the nineteenth century.' Rootlessness, which engendered much sanctimonious moralizing by the Victorian middle classes who saw it as a symptom of a feckless, ill-disciplined spirit, was, paradoxically, a basic requirement for Britain's still immature industrial economy. Demographers should not be surprised at the extent of mobility which analysis of mid-nineteenth-century census returns has revealed. Little economic or environmental incentive to settled domesticity existed for most of the working class. The apparently inexplicable tendency of families to move at frequent intervals, sometimes merely from one side of the street to another, makes sense in the general context of precarious employment opportunities, vigilant rent-collectors and overcrowded, insanitary tenements (see Ch. 26).

If industrialism before 1870 had no general tendency to depress opportunities for the skilled man the developing mass market necessitated a blurring of distinctions between skills and an attack on restrictive artisan practices designed to preserve their labour scarcity. Nowhere was this more evident than in the clothing trade. Characteristically assiduous and perceptive, Mayhew ran to ground a blind tailor who was only too well aware of the reasons for the process. His brief life story is symptomatic:

> It is upwards of 30 years since I first went to work at the tailoring trade in London . . . I belonged to the Society held at the Old White Hart. I continued working for the honourable trade and belonging to the Society for about 15 years. My weekly earnings then averaged £1 16s. a week while I was at work, and for several years I was seldom out of work . . . no one could have been happier than I was. . . . I had my silver watch and chain. . . . But then, with my sight defective . . . I could get no employment at the honourable trade, and so I had to take a seat in a shop at one of the cheap houses, in the city, and that was the ruin of me entirely; for working there, of course, I got 'scratched' from the trade society, and so lost all hope of being provided for by them in my helplessness. The workshop . . . was about seven foot square, and so low, that as you sot [*sic*] on the floor you could touch the ceiling with the tip of your finger. In this place seven of us worked. [The master] paid little more than half the regular wages, and employed such men as myself – only those who couldn't get anything better to do. . . . I don't think my wages there averaged above 12s. a week. . . . I am convinced I lost my eyesight by working in that cheap shop. . . . It is by the ruin of such men as me that these masters are enabled to undersell the better shops. . . . That's the way, sir, the cheap clothes is produced, by making blind beggars of the workmen, like myself, and throwing us on the parish in our old age.[6]

IV

Industrial production demanded discipline. Factory owners investing in new machinery needed, or felt that they needed, to keep it working almost ceaselessly. This implied both a shift system and the recruitment of a labour force prepared to work regular, unvarying hours. As the pace of mass production quickened most employers, whether they owned factories or not, demanded longer hours from their workforce. Regularity and discipline demanded from most workers a fundamental change in attitude; the industrial working class must be imbued with characteristics previously associated mainly with the Puritan middle ranks.

'Work-discipline' in pre-industrial society had minimized the value of timed labour and drew fewer distinctions between work and recreation. Just as fairs and hunting had obvious leisure and economic functions so work tended to be irregularly spaced through the year with hectic activity at harvest and haymaking when days were longest. Similarly, industrial by-employment in rural communities could involve frantic round-the-clock work to finish an assignment for the next market day or for when the master manufacturer's agent came to collect it followed by days of idleness and revelry. In many trades such idleness became institutionalized; skilled Sheffield cutlers, Burton-on-Trent coopers or Birmingham gunsmiths earned enough in four or even three days for their needs and kept 'Saint Monday' or even 'Saint Tuesday' sacred for recreation (281).

The industrial employer had a twofold task. He must inure his workforce to the alien discipline of time and rigidly stratify work so that each hand performed a limited number of tasks with maximum, repetitive efficiency. Josiah Wedgwood's aim was 'to make such machines of the men as cannot err'. Thus, the worker lost any control over the organization of his labour and, in general, his work in the factory became more boring. It is not surprising that only higher wages would entice folk into factories.

The imposition of the new work discipline implied the imposition of middle-class Puritan values on an older, freer but altogether less disciplined culture. The battle was by no means one-sided despite the enormous disparities of wealth which separated the contending parties. Many employers followed Wedgwood's lead by installing 'clocking-in' systems. The Manchester cotton spinners McConnel and Kennedy sacked any workman who had not reported for duty within two to three hours of the commencement of work on a Monday morning. Rules on a gamut of offences from lateness and absenteeism to drunkenness, shoddy work and excessive talking were formulated and maintained by fines and, by some employers on children, beatings. Fines and dismissals were reasonably effective deterrents for unskilled workers who, in a period of rapid population growth, could be easily replaced, but skilled men knew their value. Wedgwood was entirely unable to suppress his potters' 'wasteful' habit of non-attendance during the traditional 'wakes' weeks in North Staffordshire: 'our men will go to the Wakes if they were sure to go to the D . . . l the next. I have not spared them in threats and I would have thrashed them right heartily if I could.' Matthew Boulton quietly re-engaged craftsmen sacked by his perfectionist partner James Watt who had been affronted by their indisciplined and frequently intemperate habits. The implicit conflict between contending cultures would be more or less amicably resolved on an agreed length for the working week, Saturday half-holidays, weeks or fortnights for the annual holidays and (though not until the twentieth century in most cases) paid holidays for regular employees.

Drunkenness was one vice on which most employers took a particularly tough line. It was the only misdemeanour for which dismissal was automatic in Robert Owen's model factory at New Lanark. It raised hackles not because it offended nonconformist codes of behaviour but because it set an insidiously bad example to younger workers both in the waste of hard-earned cash and in the neglect of families. It also courted accidents among dangerous machinery.

The employers had powerful allies in their campaign for industrial discipline.

The evangelical revival (Ch. 6) shared the same ends. The soul reborn to God must be a regular, disciplined spirit forsaking wild ways and immoderate habits. Thus, Hannah More inveighed against 'thou silent murderer, sloth'; Joseph Clayton pointed the way to salvation in the abandonment of wasteful and socially unproductive sports like football. Above all, the concerns of the converted must be with the world to come. A patient and placid acceptance of hardship – 'the narrow way' – in this world prepared the convert for the higher joys of eternal life. Edward Thompson brilliantly, if provocatively, suggested how early nineteenth-century Methodism fitted both economic and religious needs.

One must not assume, however, that factory masters exploited evangelicalism merely to tame and discipline the working class. Evangelicalism was the religious counterpart of the secular values of hard work, self-discipline and thrift which the commercial middle classes had espoused since the Reformation. The inculcation of these values was the concern of factory and Church schools (Ch. 26) and of the purpose-built industrial communities which grew up around the water-powered mills in the earliest phase of the Industrial Revolution. Factory owners needed a disciplined workforce, but the middle classes in general became convinced that the inculcation of a range of disciplines and the adoption of a more sober life style was to the benefit of all classes. Dominant social groups almost invariably seek to impose their mores on others; the attack on pre-industrial culture was a much broader phenomenon than can be explained merely by the needs of the factory masters.

By 1870 the campaign had enjoyed considerable success, though older habits remained tenacious, particularly in the craft centres (321) and though the casual labourers of Mayhew's acquaintance were untouched by its message of sobriety and self-improvement. The second and third industrial generations came to accept as natural the regularity of a working week which the first had resented. The typical mid-Victorian worker probably worked harder than either earlier or later counterparts. In so doing, though extensive hardship and some exploitation was involved, that massive economic growth from which all classes eventually gained was made possible. More immediately, Britain's dangerously swollen population was enabled not only to survive but modestly to improve its living standards. The catastrophic Malthusian collapse visited upon Ireland in its potato famine of 1845 did not touch the mainland. This, in itself, was a significant achievement directly dependent upon economic growth to which the organization of the British workforce contributed.

---

1. D. Defoe, *A Tour Through the Whole Island of Great Britain* (Everyman edn, 2 vols, 1910), ii, p. 195.
2. *Quarterly Review*, cxix (1866), p. 367.
3. *Quarterly Review*, cviii (1860), pp. 86–90.
4. *Westminster Review*, xxxviii (1842), p. 90.
5. *Jnl. Royal Statistical Soc.*, xxiv (1861), pp. 328–73.
6. H. Mayhew, *London Labour and the London Poor* (6 vols, 1851), i, pp. 342–3.

CHAPTER 15

A living from the land: Landowners, farmers and improvement

I

The landed interest was far from eclipsed during the first phase of the Industrial Revolution. Land remained a thoroughly worthwhile investment not only for social recognition (Ch. 1) but also for economic return. Agricultural rationalization, which had already made Britain the most advanced farming nation by 1780, continued, spurred initially by the huge profits which could be made during the French Wars (1793–1815). The great landowners with, say, more than 10,000 acres consolidated their position and, through the medium of their professional estate stewards, encouraged further improvement by the tenantry who did most of the practical farming. Much of this consolidation was at the expense of gentry estates and the smaller landowners; by the time of the New Domesday of landownership in 1873 over 80 per cent of the United Kingdom was owned by 7,000 of her 32m. people. In England a mere 363 people owned more than 10,000 acres and one-third of these were commoners (236, 29). By this time 0.2 per cent of the population – a genuine and exclusive aristocracy – controlled 43 per cent of the land. What might loosely be termed 'the gentry' – those owning between 300 and 3,000 acres – comprised about 12,000 families. These families were responsible for a further 26 per cent of ownership. Thus, at the end of our period, fewer than 14,000 families owned about 70 per cent of Britain's land (236, 29 & 185, 547). Most English counties had between 15 and 30 per cent of their land owned by great landowners. Some, like Northamptonshire, acquired a reputation for aristocratic exclusiveness and it is generally true that a more substantial aristocratic presence was to be found in the 'gentler' South of the country. There were exceptions however. The most 'aristocratic' county of all was Northumberland with 51 per cent in 'great landownership'. The duke of Northumberland's vast estates radiating out south, north and west from Alnwick Castle were mostly responsible. Only the implacable North Sea prevented similar extension to the east.

For nineteenth-century businessmen, like the banker Alexander Baring in Hampshire, the iron magnate Sir John Guest in Dorset or the armaments king William Armstrong in Northumberland, the acquisition of substantial landed property was as natural and necessary a route to social leadership as ever. Also, as readers of the political novels of Anthony Trollope will know, the great political parties of the 1850s and 1860s were as effortlessly controlled by the big landowners as they had been in the days of Charles James Fox. Indeed, in the early phase of the Industrial Revolution a capitalist, if not actively entrepreneurial, aristocracy was strengthening its grip on the levers of political power.

The continued prosperity of the landed interest is hardly surprising. The rising population and the transport revolution offered gilt-edged opportunities for efficient tenant farmers to exploit growing and more concentrated markets while landowners took the opportunity to raise rents. Particularly in the first thirty and last twenty-five years of our period much capital was sunk into the land to finance improved husbandry. More productive crop rotations were effected, reducing the amount of land left fallow; clovers and sainfoins enriched weak soils; 'new crops' such as turnips and swedes enabled more animals to be fed and raised the quality of animal nutrition with consequent advantage to the quality of meat and dairy produce; scientific breeding, though it could produce those freaks of ovine and bovine nature which stare uncomprehendingly from the illustrative pages of the agricultural magazines, generally strengthened animal strains. None of these developments was new in 1780, but implementation became more widespread. From the late eighteenth century almost all counties and large market towns established agricultural societies and organized shows; new agricultural journals appeared to publicize latest advances. Some prominent politicians took a keen interest. Viscount Althorp tramped the country in the late 1820s proclaiming the virtues of the mangel-wurzel as a root crop for animal feed, just before becoming Chancellor in Grey's Whig Cabinet [A]. As Earl Spencer in 1837 he presided over the foundation of the Yorkshire Agricultural Society and became the Royal Agricultural Society's first president in the following year. Local farmers' clubs, active from the 1830s, correspondence between larger tenant farmers and the practice of sending away some farmers' sons to effective apprenticeship in other parts of the country all enabled diffusion of knowledge to take place both from one area to another and from the bigger farmers to the smaller (192, 193). This process was also advanced by formal agricultural research. Sir John Bennet Lawes founded the Rothamsted research station in 1843, and the Royal Agricultural College, established in 1845, was in place in time to contribute to improving understanding of the possibilities opened up by 'high farming'.

Until the 1850s, agricultural advance received relatively little help from mechanization. The technology was available, but a combination of cumbersomeness, unreliability and a ready supply of cheap farm labour prevented its widespread application. Thus, Andrew Meikle's threshing-machine, which separated corn from straw by flails, appeared in 1786 but made early headway only in counties such as Lancashire where farm labour was relatively scarce and dear. The machine, despite symbolizing the southern labourer's revolt in 1830–31 (see Ch. 16), remained a comparative rarity in the South-east until the 1850s. Jethro Tull's seed-drills and horse-drawn hoes, well publicized in the agricultural magazines, made little progress, especially on heavy soils. The Ipswich firm of Ransome produced a range of wrought-iron ploughs, but wooden ploughs were still common in the 1860s.

Successful experiments with steam-powered ploughs were reported in the *Journal of the Royal Agricultural Society* in 1859 and 1863, but more general introduction of mechanical mowers and reapers emphasized the trends towards greater mechanization in the 1850s and 1860s and a reduction of dependence on unreliable seasonal labour. Once the agricultural labour force began to decline after 1851 and with more children being introduced to the concept of regular schooling the premium on investment in agricultural machinery was greater. Mechanical mowers apparently cut the cost of harvesting by 30 per cent but, as ever, the agricultural magazines complained of tardiness by the smaller farmers who would not or could not adapt to the new opportunities (194).

Three broad developments stand out from the general improvements of the period: the parliamentary enclosure movement which encouraged intensive farming and the breaking of previously unproductive land to the plough; the growing importance of sheep and cattle farming after the long, unchallenged supremacy of 'King Corn'; and the heavy investment in drainage, manures and feedstuffs after about 1840 designed to increase output both of corn and cattle sufficient to render farmers proof against falling prices: 'high farming'. The general trend of these developments, however, was to increase the amount of land under arable cultivation. Whereas at the beginning of the nineteenth century, roughly 11.3m. acres of English and Welsh land were arable and about 16.8m. pasture, by mid-1854 the totals were roughly 15.3m. and 12.4m. respectively. The arable-grass ratio changed from about 0.68 to 1.23 (236, *31*). The great imperative of British farming was bread for its growing population. Rising livestock prices after 1850, however, also had important implications for the national farming network. The natural livestock areas – the highland zone of the North and West where, with well-defined exceptions such as south-west Lancashire or Cumberland's Eden valley, arable husbandry was not commercial – prospered. Here were produced the meat and dairy items which enriched and varied the British diet in the second half of the century. The natural arable areas of the South and East, which had long produced the staple wheat grain for southern Englishmen, now moved towards 'mixed farming' (grains and livestock). Once the railway network was developed, mixed farming received additional stimulus since the despatch of fattened animals to urban slaughter-houses was both easier and unaffected by that profit-destroying weight loss contingent on packing them off 'on the hoof'. New markets grew up at strategic railheads like Lockerbie (Dumfries) and Ludlow (Shropshire) for border and marcher cattle respectively. The old drove routes, already jeopardized by enclosures which fenced off previously open common from the trekking animals, fell into further decline (193).

The flexibility of mixed farming in lowland Britain was much more easily obtained on well-drained light soils. For much of this period, and certainly after 1813 when grain prices plummeted [D.vi.2], farmers of the stiff, cold, ill-drained clay-lands, which predominated in many parts of the East Midlands and East Anglia, were fighting a desperate battle. Fodder crops, like turnips, grew badly on clay; hay had to be used for winter feed, allowing less opportunity for summer grazing. Opportunities for effective mixed farming here were contingent on heavy investment and many of the cries of anguish about 'agricultural depression' after 1813 came from the clay-lands. Unless they were owned by men of great wealth with able estate stewards, as in the case of the marquis of Stafford with his 35,000 acres at Trentham (Staffs) and Lilleshall (Shropshire), the prospects were bleak. Stafford's formidable agent, James Loch, however, was able to offer real aid to hand-picked tenants in the form of drainage investments and advice on the best crop rotations.[1]

II

The parliamentary enclosure movement has been the subject of more fundamental misapprehensions than any subject in modern British history. It used to be thought that it initiated those major changes known as the agricultural revolution, whereas parliamentary enclosure between 1760 and 1820, came towards the end of a much longer period of far more gradual modernization. It used to be thought that enclosures, more or less alone, killed off the smallholder and replaced him with the large, remote capitalist farmer, whereas their effects here were relatively marginal and came at the end of a much longer period of consolidation. Most misleading of all, it has been contended that the enclosure movement sounded the death knell of the English peasantry and released thousands of erstwhile peasant proprietors to work the factories as a new race of alienated industrial labourers. The effects of enclosures on society's lower orders will be considered in Chapter 16, but it can be said here that the contention is, at best, an absurd over-simplification.

Considered in their proper context, however, enclosures were important agents of change. The 4,000 or so Acts of enclosure passed between 1760 and 1820 represented a massive investment in the land. Many rural experts, including Arthur Young and Sir John Sinclair, the first secretary and president respectively of the Board of Agriculture established in 1793, propagandized ceaselessly and not always accurately for enclosure as the only effective means to convert incompetently farmed open fields into yield-enhancing independent units capable of feeding a growing population. Enclosure was also the best means of making the wastes and rough grazing areas fully productive. During the French War years (1793–1815), when roughly half the parliamentary Acts of enclosure were effected, the most unlikely scrubland and hillsides were broken to the plough. Much of it fell out of cultivation during the subsequent fall in prices.

About one-quarter of the cultivated acreage of England was enclosed between 1700 and 1900. Enclosure offered several benefits. The fencing of land gave each proprietor greater independence and flexibility. The documentation deriving from enclosure awards resolved any ambiguities about ownership. Open-field farming was nearly always inconvenient to the improving proprietor since it involved accommodations and compromises with the owners of adjacent strips. Too often improvement could proceed only at the pace of the slowest. Open-field enclosure was concentrated on a great swathe through the Midlands, East Anglia and what are now the northern Home Counties. Further north enclosure tended to be not of existing arable fields but of commons and waste ground in order to make them productive. In large areas both in the Midlands and the South land had been enclosed either in the Tudor period or earlier, while enclosure by agreement, which did not need the formality of parliamentary enactment, had been proceeding steadily since the early eighteenth century. Parliamentary enclosure, therefore, was a novelty more in the legal than the agricultural sense.

It is often said that parliamentary enclosures were effected to increase arable output and meet the demands of a rapidly increasing population for its staple food. This is broadly true of East Midland and East Anglian enclosures; corn output increased by about two-thirds between 1750 and 1820 as a result both of extended acreages under the plough and improved yields per acre. In important areas of the West Midlands, however, such as the Vale of Evesham or south-east Warwickshire, enclosure was followed by massive conversion of land to pasture farming. Enclosure gave a stimulus to rationalization and specialization according to the nature of the land.

The tenant farmer presented with an enclosed estate could experiment with improved crop rotations to increase output. The landlord enclosed because it was profitable. By 1800 an enclosed farm was letting for at least twice the rent its unenclosed counterpart fetched and sometimes three or four times. Enclosure was a valuable investment during the French Wars even though the cost of the change was increasingly high. The best bargains had often been struck earlier when landlords had bought out smaller men prior to effecting enclosure by agreement. By 1780, parliamentary enclosure was often preceded by a policy of consolidation. Two of Warwickshire's largest landowners, Lord Leigh and the marquis of Hertford, entered the land market just before their lands were enclosed. Hertford bought extensively and determinedly in Binton between 1770 and 1778; when enclosure was effected in 1779 he and the rector of the parish were the sole proprietors (196, 197).[2]

Enclosure by agreement was often the culmination of a long-term policy of land consolidation. Many parliamentary enclosures were of land on which complexities of ownership precluded tidy agreements or on which there had been disagreement about the wisdom of, or necessity for, enclosure. Many enclosures which were not effected until the 1790s or later, therefore, were either complex or contentious. It is not surprising that enclosure costs went up significantly even when allowance is made for the inflationary trend of the times. By the 1790s the Board of Agriculture's own estimate that it cost 28s. (£1.40) an acre was certainly too low; costs regularly exceeded £3 an acre in the 1790s and could rise as high as £12 when the unavoidable costs of fencing were added (196).

Enclosure costs are a critical consideration when the long-term effects of the movement on land-ownership patterns are considered. A 100-acre farmer would not find it easy to raise, say, £300–£400 to finance enclosure even in the 1790s when profits were high and credit relatively abundant. Many farmers were forced to sell parts of their holdings to meet costs and some were left with farms too small to work effectively except in the best years. Others who kept their heads above water during the profitable times were forced to sell up after 1813 when mortgage debts still hung like millstones from their necks. Unit costs of fencing, ditching and road-making fell disproportionately heavily on the smaller landowner. A further consideration is relevant. Old tithe rights were frequently exonerated at enclosure by grants of land to rector, vicar or lay owner of the tithes. The expense of allotting and fencing the tithe owner's land, which could amount to one-fifth of the total, was borne *pro rata* by the remaining proprietors (199). Tithes were considered a fundamental barrier to improvement and farmers would pay the Church a high price to remove it. Once again, the cost in terms of higher expenses and smaller allotments fell most heavily on the small landowner.

This evidence hardly squares with Professor Mingay's optimistic assertion that 'small owner-occupiers were not very seriously affected by enclosure' (242). In

Buckinghamshire, almost 39 per cent of owners (once adjustment has been made for family inheritance) disappeared in parishes enclosed between 1780 and 1820; in parishes enclosed earlier the decline in the same period was less than 20 per cent. In a Warwickshire study of parishes enclosed between 1770 and 1825 the number of landowners with 10 to 50 acres declined from 401 to 285 between 1780 and 1825 while the average holding of the 27 largest landowners in 1825 was 10,227 acres compared with 8,185 acres by the 26 largest in 1780 (196). Enclosures were doubtless not the only factor involved, but the evidence is telling.

Despite the scrupulous fairness of the administrative procedures adopted by most enclosure commissioners, the odds were heavily weighted in favour of the larger proprietors. Size of property rather than weight of numbers determined whether enclosure went ahead; one owner of 7,500 acres could ride roughshod over the wishes of twenty-five owning 100 acres each. The bigger men could spread the considerable costs more easily around their various interests and were more likely to have commercial and business interests to cushion the blow of price falls after 1813. They also stood to gain more from wholesale rearrangement and improvement. Enclosure was a 'property job' whose main beneficiaries were the large landowners, their substantial tenants whose scope for experiment and rational improvement was greatly extended and the Church of England which enjoyed a quite unmerited windfall as landowners fell over themselves to reap its full benefits unencumbered by anachronistic ecclesiastical imposts.

III

Between 1790 and 1813 the average rise in land rents was about 80 per cent. It may well be that landowners did better than tenant farmers (187), but many farmers, protected from price rises by long leases, lined their pockets and rebuilt their property in substantial stone. Price fluctuations, indeed, sounded the death knell of the long lease, which had been considered half a century earlier the most secure guarantee of good farming. Almost all the Spencer estates in Northampton-shire were held by yearly agreement in the 1820s, and the light upland soils of Lindsey, in North Lincolnshire, were converted from rough grazing to mixed farming between 1790 and 1830 by tenants with no long leases (183). As leases fell in on the Stafford estates, they were immediately replaced by annual tenancies.

Once corn prices fell farmers needed to be more flexible. The cries of agricultural distress which engendered parliamentary select committees on the subject in 1821–23 and 1833–36 and which Lord Ernle wrongly considered symptomatic of a general crisis in British agriculture[3] came mostly from the clay-lands. It is true, however, that complaints also came from those with the not unjustified hope of reductions in taxation. As James Loch caustically remarked in 1814 'no set of men cry so loud or so soon as the farmers'. The first response to falling prices by a Parliament of landowners in 1815–16 had been the abolition of income tax and the war malt duty as well as the passing of the most famous of the Corn Laws, designed to keep out foreign grain and keep up prices to the consumer (see Chs 19 and 20). Nor is it coincidental that two further substantial measures of relief for the landed interest – a new Poor Law bringing lower poor rates (1834) [C.iii; D.vii.l] and rationalized tithe payments through commutation (1836) – came in two of the five lowest years for wheat prices in the first half of the century.

Prices after 1813, in fact, were low only in the immediate context of the two preceding decades; post-war levels generally were higher than in the 1770s and 1780s. Those who were broken by them were mostly labouring under the double disadvantage of unwise speculation at the top of the market and farming heavy, unyielding soils. On light lands flexible rotations produced yields high enough to compensate for lower prices, while dairy prices actually rose slightly. It is a superficial paradox only that wheat yields per acre actually increased by 16 per cent in the twenty years or so of 'depression' after 1815 (193).

Some years were indubitably difficult, however, and between 1821 and 1823, when dairy as well as arable farmers suffered, landlords gave rent reductions. Good tenants were too valuable to lose to freak seasons and many landowners extended credit by permitting rental arrears to accumulate until prices picked up. Increased landlord expenditure on farm repairs and other improvements was also a feature of the later 1810s and 1820s, the calculation being that tenants would be thus encouraged to purchase manures and feedstuffs to increase output. Adjust- ments were much easier on the great estates – especially the lighter lands – and the overall situation, though the subject of less attention than enclosure receives, continued the squeeze on the small proprietor.

The performance of Scottish agriculture during the early industrial period varied according to region. Much of lowland Scotland experienced substantial improve- ment, the most advanced areas being the Lothians and Berwickshire. Rental values were as much as eight times higher in 1815 than they had been in the mid-eighteenth century. Moreover, the fact that oats, not wheat, contributed about 75 per cent of Scottish arable output cushioned the blow of falling arable prices after 1815 since wheat prices were much more volatile. Dairy farming boomed in the middle years of the nineteenth century. Ayrshire beef, for example, fed the middle classes of Liverpool as well as Glasgow (17).

The Highlands enjoyed a brief respite from social and economic crisis in the late eighteenth and early nineteenth centuries caused by general rises in agricultural prosperity and the widespread planting of potatoes. Potato monoculture briefly and artifically extended the lease on subsistence farming in Britain's most remote region. Both the drive to profitable, market-oriented agriculture and Protestant, anti-clan triumphalism after the Battle of Culloden (1746) which ended the Jacobite rebellion, had already contributed before 1780 towards that desperate movement known as the Highland Clearances (5, *219–21*). Depopulation and emigration from the Highlands continued apace during the nineteenth century. The creation of a few new fishing villages on the west coast, such as Gairloch and Plockton, did little to cushion the overall blow. The processing of kelp, an alkaline ash extracted from seaweed, initially offered some hope of secure long-term employment and social stability. Once kelp prices fell in the 1820s, what had been the established pattern of change from the mid-eighteenth century was re-established. Undercapitalized smaller Highland landlords faced increasing debt, lacked the flexibility in a harsh climate to diversify and sold out for whatever price

– usually very low – they could get. The Scottish potato famine, much less celebrated than the Irish but taking place at the same time and having a similar demographic effect, completed the process. Sheep-farming became virtually the only profitable large-scale agricultural enterprise in the Highlands from the mid-nineteenth century and it was controlled not by native Highlanders but by 'incomers', often from Scotland's southern uplands. Though only about 20 per cent of land went out of cultivation specifically to make way for sheep, and though clearances were well underway before intensive sheep cultivation made its greatest impact on the Highlands, the image of a society and a culture ruthlessly pushed aside to line the pockets of 'foreigners' and 'capitalists' is one which evokes a powerful resonance to this day. It is certain that, between 1740 and 1850, traditional Highland society died; in the eyes of many (few of them, it must be admitted, economic historians) it was maliciously and wantonly killed.

IV

Arable prices picked up in most of Britain after 1837 but only temporarily. The agricultural prosperity generally associated with 'high farming' had a different base. As Sir James Caird explained in 1868: 'Since 1850 the price of bread on the average, has remained the same, while that of meat, dairy produce, and wool has risen fifty per cent' (195, *109*). This reflected that diversity from grain staples which is characteristic of rising living standards. Those who had converted to mixed farming systems reaped a rich reward in the 1850s and 1860s. Market gardeners flourished. Those at Sandy (Beds) for example could now use railways to move their perishable produce north to the industrial centres of the Midlands as well as south to established outlets in London. Reclaimed fenland around the Wash in Lincolnshire, Lancashire's Fylde coast and the Vale of Evesham all sent large consignments of vegetables and fruit to urban markets. Market-garden small-holders, against the general trend, not only survived but prospered in the mid-nineteenth century.

Arable farmers, of course, lost the protection of the Corn Laws after 1846 (see Ch. 30). However, Corn Law repeal, though the subject of furious contention, did not significantly affect the landed interest for a generation, though the low prices of 1850–52 brought a spate of rent reductions and premature predictions of agricultural Armageddon. In fact, grain demands within Europe were high thanks to population growth; no huge surpluses accumulated for dumping in Britain at rock-bottom prices. Britain's own growing population, meanwhile, afforded ample opportunity for profit by efficient arable farmers, at least on light lands. It is significant that opposition to Corn Law repeal was much less strident on the light lands than on the clays. European wheat imports, it is true, did double between 1850 and 1870 by which time they supplied more than 40 per cent of domestic needs, but an expanded British market kept prices stable [D.vi.3]. Not until the vast granaries of America's Middle-West were opened to the British market in the 1870s did arable landowners reap the bitter harvest of 1846.

Peel's calculation had been that free trade would create a bigger market which the landed interest could effectively tap by investment in further improvements. To this end, the repeal pill was sweetened by a loan scheme to finance drainage of cold, stiff lands. Mass production of cheap tile or clay drains, begun in the 1840s, enabled proper drainage of wetlands at an average cost of about £5 an acre, rather higher than the going rate for enclosures fifty years earlier. 'Green' crops, such as swedes, could be introduced on drained land and previously heavy land need no longer carry the dead weight of a fallow season. The rewards, therefore, were valuable though the incentive of uniformly high prices – the spur to enclosure – no longer existed. Government loans, at 3½ per cent interest, were made from 1847 under supervision of the Inclosure Commission; by 1870 more than £7m. had been paid over.

Results were patchy. More heavy Midland soils converted to pasture and caught the rising livestock market; loans facilitated intensive farming and higher yields. Criticism from agriculturalists of the 1850s and 1860s, however, reads remarkably like that offered during the enclosure years. Too many small farmers and owner-occupiers remained deeply conservative, would not convert to mixed farming and would not drain or, if they would, botched the job for want of knowledge. As before, the larger tenant farmers achieved most, often chivvied by the great landlords' estate stewards. Many large landowners invested heavily in high farming. The duke of Northumberland spent over £650,000 between 1847 and 1868 for a meagre return of 2 per cent (236, *250*). Some who took government loans saw no return at all before the great price slump of the 1870s rewrote all the agricultural rule books.

Here was the rub. Were the rewards of investment in high farming worthwhile? Unlike the enclosure years, more rational repositories for capital now existed. The great landowners' attachment to agricultural investment still made sense in terms of social leadership and obligation to tenants and labourers. It was also eminently sensible where the rewards of conversion to pasture were substantial. But investment in banking, commerce or industry brought between 4 and 9 per cent on capital in the late 1850s and even those who bought railway shares with the market past its peak would expect more than the 2 or 3 per cent that arable landowners were making. Rents rose generally after the mid-1850s, but often only under the impact of heavy investment in drainage and farm buildings in an effort to attract and retain conscientious tenants. In the traditional pastoral areas of the West and North the gains were greatest. Good tenant farmers were the main beneficiaries of what has been called over-capitalization in agriculture. Despite the obvious counter-attractions of mixed farming, conservatism among the less good ensured that arable acreages began to contract only after 1855, and then slowly.

The folly of over-capitalization would not become apparent until the late 1870s when the price slump began the long process of decline for the landed interest. Those landlords who would weather the coming storm were those who already had substantial industrial or commercial interests or who could easily diversify. Fortunately for them, the ring of a title was sufficient inducement in a fundamentally snobbish society to large public companies which sought aristocrats on their boards of directors, often in a non-executive capacity. Only a few years after the end of our period British landowners were in sore need of such perks. The shabby duke and duchess of Plaza-Toro in Gilbert and Sullivan's *The Gondoliers* (1889) were no Spanish hidalgos but thinly veiled caricatures of the British baronet whose influence and social prestige now exceeded his income and who resorted to various *sub rosa* expedients to make good the difference. Hence the duke's paid patronage of various trading establishments, particularly 'those pressing prevailers the ready-made tailors' and his sitting 'by selection upon the direction of several companies bubble' and the duchess's remunerative advertising assertion that her 'complexion derives its perfection from somebody's soap which it doesn't'. By 1870 the landed interest, whose social predominance had been little challenged during the first century or so of the Industrial Revolution, was about to feel the pinch.

------

1. E. S. Richards, ' "Leviathan of Wealth": West Midland agriculture, 1800–50' *Ag. H. R.* xxii (1974), pp. 97–117.
2. J. M. Martin, 'The small landowner and parliamentary enclosure in Warwickshire' *Ec. H. R.* 2nd ser. xxxii (1979), pp. 328–43.
3. Lord Ernle, *English Farming past and present* (6th edn, 1961).

CHAPTER 16

'Living and partly living': Labourers, poverty and protest

I

The massive agricultural growth and specialization of this period brought little benefit to the folk who tilled the soil, tended the animals and cut the hay. The lot of most rural labourers deteriorated from the 1780s at least until the 1850s. From the 1770s to 1813 prices of foodstuffs rose generally and in some cases spectacularly; the profits of farming were based on bread prices too high for most labourers to maintain their already basic standard of living. After 1815, an era of lower prices caused farmers to retrench and rationalize. Wages were cut and unemployment shot up. Behind both developments lay one intractable and growing problem: the number of labourers. However much rapacious landlords or heartless farmers may be criticized, their actions must be seen against a background of rapid population growth. This was by no means confined to the new industrial areas. Even in the fifteen English counties, mainly in the South and East and least affected by urbanization a total population of 1.5m. in 1750 had grown to 1.9m. by 1780, to 2.9m. in 1830 and to 3.3m. by 1850. This rise of 120 per cent in 100 years was far more than even expanded demands for labour could accommodate. It was ideal for industrial recruitment, but the rural labourers' tragedy was that they remained immobile. A swollen but static population exerted severe downward pressure on wages and it is hard to escape the broad conclusion that rural labourers were poor because they were numerous.

But there was far more to it than this. The increasing poverty of the farm worker was but one element in a developing crisis. The doctrine of paternalist support for the poor by their betters, never so firmly entrenched as might be supposed, was shattered by the increased cost of supporting those who could not support themselves. Poor rates, a compulsory levy on property owners raised in each parish, quadrupled in less than forty years after 1780 [D.vii.1]. Farmers argued that their profits were eaten by indigents whose fecklessness and improvidence, rather than inadequacy in their wages, were the real cause of their distress. When distress turned to the use of force in the so-called 'Swing' riots – after the mythical Captain Swing who was supposed to lead the protestors – the rioters' targets certainly included farmers and landowners whose ricks were burned and whose threshing machinery was destroyed in 1830 and 1831. But also Poor Law overseers, who insisted on harsh or demeaning tests before granting relief, and Church of England clergymen, whose tithe exactions might prevent farmers from raising wages and who symbolized an authority and a social system from which labourers now felt utterly alienated, were also attacked. Agricultural labourers agitated for higher wages but their grievances went deeper. They understood that an old order, in which peasants and labourers held a humble but recognized and unchallenged place, had been supplanted by a new in which they were of little account. That is the true measure of the rural crisis of early- nineteenth-century Britain.

The plight of agricultural labourers varied substantially both across the country and even within individual counties. Raw wage data make the point with crude clarity. It has been calculated from James Caird's mid-nineteenth-century estimates that average weekly wages in northern counties, at 11s. 6d. (57.5p) were 37 per cent higher than those in the South (8s. 5d.; 42p). In 'high-wage' Lancashire, nevertheless, wage levels moved in direct proportion to available alternative labour. Chorley agricultural labourers, near the heart of textile Lancashire, earned 3s. (15p) a day early in the nineteenth century with ale also provided. Those at Bispham on the then remote and bleak coast could make only 1s. 4d. (6.5p) a day even at harvest time (185, *698*). These startling variations notwithstanding, there is no doubt that those in central-southern England and East Anglia fared worst. They were doubly hit by the effects of cost-conscious agricultural specialization and the lack of alternative employment. By the 1780s, farmers were seeking profit through rationalization. The proportion of agricultural workers able to find relative security as farm servants, usually hired by the year and living in with the farmer's family, declined. Farm servants, such as cow-keepers, dairymaids or shepherds, remained in demand in the pastoral counties where changes in farming practice did not accentuate the already considerable seasonal imbalance in labouring requirements. In the corn-growing areas much labour was needed at particular times, notably during the late summer harvest but also for sowing, muck-spreading and, since almost no arable farm was without its few animals, haymaking. Tenant farmers with profits to make on their leases naturally preferred to employ labour 'by the task'.

By the 1780s, the trend towards short-term employment of labourers was well established. Arthur Young had noted in 1770 that average labouring wages were twice as high at harvest time but harvests lasted only about five weeks. At times of low demand, which could stretch to forty weeks a year, day labourers might expect no more than 6–7s. (30–35p) a week. There was little security of employment and once prices began to rise farmers provided less and less in-kind payment, calculating rationally but harshly that their business was better served by retaining more of the food they grew for the market and directing their labourers thither. William Cobbett, erstwhile Tory turned radical paternalist, commented in 1825:

> Why do not farmers now *feed* and *lodge* their workpeople, as they did formerly? Because they cannot keep them *upon so little* as they give them in wages . . . if the farmer now shuts his pantry against his labourers, and pays them wholly in money, is it not clear that he does it because he thereby gives them a living *cheaper* to him; that is to say, a *worse* living than formerly?[1]

Women and children might supplement the main income at haymaking or harvest but unless local industries, such as lace-making or straw-plaiting in Buckinghamshire, survived, southern labourers too often became dependent on a single wage. As farm service declined so did female participation in the labour force. Among farm servants, men outnumbered women by only two to one; among less secure agricultural labourers the ratio was twenty to one (241, *94*). Female farm servant numbers fell dramatically during the first half of the nineteenth century and by no less than 53 per cent between the census years of 1851 and 1861.

The old relationship between farming and outwork industry was best preserved near the industrial centres of northern England where the labour market was in altogether better balance; here the worst excesses of southern labouring life – low wages, structural under-employment, poor housing and general demoralization – were mostly avoided. Those living in the pastoral areas were more likely to make their own clothes and footwear and their diet was more adaptable. The most severe price inflation of the French War period was in wheaten bread. Northern labourers, even as late as 1850, were used to consuming a variety of coarser grains, particularly barley and oatcakes; they also baked their own bread. In the South, substitution of barley bread or potatoes, by now much favoured in Lancashire, seemed not only unpalatable but smacked of attempts to reduce the labourer's self-respect. Demand inelasticity was an important factor in the horrendous shortages of 1795, 1801 and 1812. F. M. Eden convinced himself that the miseries of the labouring poor derived 'less from the scantiness of their income ... than from their own improvidence and unthriftiness'. He contrasted the flexibility of the northern diet with the unvarying dry bread and cheese of the southerner, supplemented by tea, that 'deleterious produce of China'.[2]

The temptation to trade in crude regional stereotypes – hardy, independent, adaptable northerners; effete, inflexible southerners – must be resisted. No symbol of desolation is more potent than the Sutherland peasant forcibly evicted from the family smallholding in 1814 to make way for the marquis of Stafford's profitable sheep. Nor were all southern labourers depressed. Some in regular employment obtained wage rises between 1793 and 1815 which outstripped prices. The loss of men to the army and navy, in fact, caused labour shortages from which workers benefited, albeit temporarily (187, 189).

The chaotic nature of the labour market did not help the rural labourer. Demand increased but supply remained even more obstinately buoyant until the 1850s. Institutional constraints complicated matters. The settlement laws of 1662, though much amended and evaded in the next 150 years, established the basic principle that those whose income was insufficient to support them could obtain parochial relief only where, by birth, residence or apprenticeship qualifications, they were deemed to be settled. Legal wrangles between parishes seeking to avoid upkeep in particular cases were almost as frequent as the removal orders which shunted unfortunate paupers back to their places of origin. A labourer with family responsibilities hazarded much when he left his own parish to seek work elsewhere. The settlement laws exercised some restraints on that mobility of population which could have eased the crisis of oversupply.

There was, nevertheless, considerable movement of labourers desperate to find work. Migrant work became increasingly common during the nineteenth century. Irish labourers, in no danger of being added to the parochial poor relief bill, became exceptionally attractive temporary recruits to harvest the corn in East

Anglia and even in those southern counties where the burden of overpopulation pressed hardest. They were also found on the tramp to seasonal work in the market gardens of Essex, the hop fields of Kent, the fruit orchards of Worcestershire and the potato plantations of south-west Lancashire (190). Agricultural specialization placed ever greater emphasis on the need for intensive short-term labour; migrant labour catered well for this while doing little or nothing for the intractable problems of rural poverty. In some areas, indeed, the arrival of the itinerants was the signal for riot and disturbance directed against 'foreigners' working for low wages. The productivity gains in agriculture, which many economic historians see as crucial to its ability to sustain an increasingly non-agricultural population, included substantial wage savings on permanently employed labour.

A further institutional constraint on the emergence of a rational labour system was the so-called 'close' parish system. Close parishes were controlled by a small and sometimes absentee handful of landlords whose overriding concern was to keep the number of resident labourers to an absolute minimum. The purpose was clear; a parish with few resident labourers could not drag down farming profits by excessive poor rate payments when this expenditure soared after 1780 (Chs 5 and 25). Seasonal labour requirements could be met either by itinerants or, more commonly, by gangs of labourers, including women and children, brought in for specific tasks. It is not surprising that close parishes and the demoralizing gang labour which accompanied it were found most frequently in the corn belt. Nationally about 20 per cent of parishes were 'closed'. In parts of Norfolk, Lincolnshire and Yorkshire's East Riding the proportion was nearer to 40 per cent. Some parishes became closed *de facto* as land use changed and labourers moved away; more were deliberately created by ruthless landowners who pulled down labourers' cottages and drove them off. Lincolnshire, indeed, may be said to have experienced its own 'clearances' at about the same time as the much more publicized ones in the Scottish Highlands. The effect on labourers was devastating, though it is doubtful if much permanent financial benefit accrued to landowners through lower poor rates. Many labourers had to travel long distances to work and the system produced comparably overcrowded and under-supervised 'open' parishes where, according to early Victorian commentators, vice, immodesty, laziness and drunkenness were rife. It was largely to combat the alleged moral depravities of the system that the Union Chargeability Act of 1865 [C.iii] was passed, destroying the rationale of close parishes.

The worst years for labourers were those after 1815 when a market glutted by demobilized servicemen coincided with depressed arable prices. In these years, wages were beaten down and poor-rate expenditure reached its peak [D.vii.1]. Wages fell by about a third between 1814 and 1822 while southern labourers often faced entire winters of dependence on charity and Poor Law allowances. Labourers' cottages, usually the responsibility of tenant farmers to maintain, often fell into ruin as farmers fought to remain solvent. Most unkindly of all in the twenty years – 1811–31 – when employment opportunities were contracting most severely, the population of the worst affected counties in the South and East increased by 31 per cent [E.ii.1]. Lack of mobility in the population polarized the problem. As Dr Eastwood puts it, 'the crude choice faced by most agricultural communities lay between perpetuating a pattern of low wages and low productivity, or reducing the workforce to increase incentives through higher wages'(326, *109*). Neither choice was remotely likely to increase rural cohesion.

The 1830s and 1840s were hardly better for rural labourers, although recent research has suggested that the worst of the labour surplus was over by the end of the 1830s (188). Only after 1850 can unequivocal, if modest, improvements be charted. Even by 1870 living standards remained deplorably low. Between the early 1850s and the early 1870s money wages rose by about 40 per cent, comfortably in excess of price rises. The reasons were not far to seek in an age governed by the economics of *laissez faire*. The era of high farming (Ch. 15) required labour-intensive cultivation, much of it still seasonal, but factors affecting the supply of labour were more important. At last after 1851 the numbers employed in agriculture fell from a peak in that year of 1.8m. A 20 per cent reduction had been achieved by 1871 with particularly dramatic falls among farm servants who lived in. The rural labour market was being appropriately thinned. Emigration societies, established in the desperate early years of the century, had carried some to more rewarding opportunities in America and Canada. The effect of the railways was far more dramatic. They made long-distance migration a practical possibility and it was noticeable that wages in parishes adjacent to railways tended to be higher than elsewhere, since the railway offered an obvious escape route for surplus labour.

While English population as a whole increased by 27 per cent between 1851 and 1871 and that of London and the North-west rose by 36 per cent, the rural areas of the South, the South-west and East Anglia recorded an increase of less than 13 per cent [E.i; ii.1]. After a century and more of distortion the balance between supply and demand for agricultural labour was being restored. Canon Edward Girdlestone did much for the cause of internal migration in the 1860s by publicizing the desperate condition of his parishioners in the Devon village of Halberton and organizing their removal to farms and other occupations in the north of England, where demand for their labour was far greater.

However, modest improvements did not stretch to the quality of housing. The report of Dr H. J. Hunter on the state of rural dwellings, published in 1865, revealed that overcrowding had actually increased between 1851 and 1861. Children and parents frequently slept in the same room and not infrequently in the same bed. Coy references to unnatural sexual practices littered the Victorian commentators' strictures on the situation. Labourers' cottages in Dorset were usually constructed of mud and thatch with no proper grates and a constant danger of fire (346). Housing standards in the South and South-west generally were deplorable and in the South-west wages remained obstinately low. Some improving landlords, like the duke of Northumberland, the duke of Bedford and Lord Leicester, were busy constructing model dwellings which they hoped would set a new standard, but by 1870 their efforts had barely scratched the surface of the problem.

The organization of labour still left much to be desired. Though the drainage of the fens brought opportunities for family labour, the wages of women and children employed on the labour gangs of which farmers made much use stayed extremely low. Children in Norfolk were employed from the age of four or five in turnip pulling at 3d. or 4d. (1½p) a day. A wide range of jobs, from weeding to ploughing was done by children according to their age and strength and discipline was strict. Some gangmasters were not averse to using the whip on their young charges, thus providing juicy anecdotes for witnesses to relate to the Children's Employment Commission of 1867. Thirty years after child labour had been controlled in the factories (Ch. 26) it remained unregulated in the fields. Legislation on the gang system was not passed until 1867 [C.i].

II

The social consequences of the parliamentary enclosure movement have been hotly debated by historians. The early twentieth-century orthodoxy of J. L. and B. Hammond that enclosure was the main agency of rural pauperization was challenged in the 1950s and 1960s by economic and agricultural historians such as J. D. Chambers and G. E. Mingay (180, 242). They argued, not only that the Hammonds had indulged themselves in politically slanted exaggeration, but that the effects of enclosure were actually beneficial since they provided new labour opportunities. Enclosure certainly brought the labourers work but the optimistic picture of their effects has certainly been overdrawn. The case of the enclosure of common and waste land illustrates the problem neatly. Agricultural improvers argued ceaselessly the need to bring the commons under the plough and thus increase the nation's food stock. It is beyond dispute that conversion of commons and waste to arable meant more work for labourers. To enjoy this, however, many had to give up valuable common rights. 'Commoners' enjoyed a wide range of rights on the common, such as cutting turf for fuel, fishing ponds and pasturing animals. 'Squatters' had established *de facto* rights to live on or near common land; frequently they lived rough and performed a variety of semi-agricultural, semi-craft tasks on the fringes of village society. On the open fields, a most valuable common right was that of gleaning, whereby women and children could make use of any corn left behind by the harvesters. These rights may seem trivial, but they formed the very basis of domestic economy for many poor families. Frederick Eden recognized, for example, that gleaners could provide their families with enough corn to make bread for six months to a year, a vital consideration when prices were rising so rapidly.

Common rights, like their few twentieth-century survivors the bridleways and footpaths, were a nuisance to the improving farmer. Their preservation by manorial courts and courts leet was irksome and the prospect of being rid of them at enclosure attractive. Enclosure commissioners were scrupulous in upholding verifiable rights during their proceedings, but common rights, almost by definition, were not verifiable according to the normal canons of evidence. They were either set aside or recognized in such a grudging manner as to be valueless. A cottager could usually make nothing of a quarter-acre allotment in lieu of rights when he had to fence and ditch it at his own expense. Most enclosure awards ignored common rights entirely, much to the frustration even of a leading improver like Arthur Young. By 1800 he clearly saw the dangers of a disaffected rural population whose deprivation derived from a reorganization of which he was otherwise a powerful advocate: 'I had rather that all the commons of England were sunk in the sea than that the poor should in future be treated on enclosing as they generally have been hitherto.'[3] Parliament's reluctance to protect the commoners had long-term repercussions. The allotments and smallholdings movement which gained strength from the 1840s as a means of tying labourers loyally to the land would have been largely unnecessary if common rights had been properly safeguarded at enclosure. Their loss affected the structure of rural society more than is generally appreciated. Most of the few anti-enclosure riots, such as those at Redditch and Sheffield in 1791 or Otmoor, near Oxford, in 1829, were protests against the loss of common rights.

Enclosures probably engendered little overt popular protest because they frequently brought more work, at least in the short term. Most rural workers, after all, had already lost their common rights before 1780 and enclosure came at the end of a protracted period of consolidation by which peasant farmer had been translated into wage labourer. Any notion that enclosure 'created' the labourer is ludicrous. All too many labourers in the 1790s and 1800s were grateful for the extra work created by the operative tasks of enclosure; hedging, ditching, fencing and road-making were all labour intensive. These were all finite tasks, yet in many parishes they took eight or ten years to complete, during which time labour demand was buoyant. The great rush of parliamentary enclosures at this time exacerbated the short-term demand for labour and helped to push wages up, if not so far as to match price inflation.

In the longer term, however, the effects of enclosure were less rosy. Once the necessary spade-work was complete enclosure of open-field arable only intensified those unfortunate features referred to earlier: heavy emphasis on seasonal labour and consequent structural underemployment. Additionally, some of the wastes optimistically enclosed in, say, 1795 were out of cultivation again by 1825 because they were uneconomic to farm when prices were low. It is not necessary to claim that enclosure was the main agency of demoralization for the rural labourer to sustain the view that its long-term effects were not advantageous. Some labourers permanently benefited from more intensive cultivation methods. Some, on the other hand, permanently forfeited valuable common rights and with them a certain acknowledged, if lowly, status. For most, enclosure merely exacerbated trends which were to their long-term disadvantage.

It has recently been shown that migration from recently enclosed midland villages was at a greater rate than from unenclosed or old-enclosed areas. Where enclosure *did* boost employment opportunities, moreover, less regular and less secure forms of work were provided. As during another revolution in employment opportunities – that associated with the superficially 'rational' and market-led ideology of the 1980s and early 1990s – parliamentary enclosure engendered uncertainty, part-time work and substantial demoralization. In both cases, also, labour 'surplus' was created by assaults on customary, 'restrictive' working custom and practice. Parliamentary enclosure, therefore, played its part in ensuring that the rural population became more dependent on charity and on the Poor Law.

III

The rural labourer, then, was depressed but not without a voice. Popular protest grew between 1780 and 1850, a period which sees the demise of what had been its most common expression – the food riot – and the development of other forms of action. Food riots were widespread during the high price years of the 1790s and 1800s, especially in market towns and the main communication and manufacturing centres. In the countryside, their leaders tended to be industrial workers such as Cornish tin-miners (Cornwall was particularly riot-prone until the middle of the nineteenth century) or coal-miners and metal-workers in Staffordshire and Durham. As has been convincingly demonstrated, food riots were no blind hunger disturbances (243, 216). Their main purpose was to reduce the price of the necessities of life and their major targets not the producers but the middlemen – dealers, millers and transportation agents who were suspected of distorting or withholding supplies to raise prices and thus profits for themselves. For this reason, abduction of consignments for resale at 'customary' or 'just' prices was far more common than simple looting.

The food riot symbolized a clash of economic ideologies. The rioters, though they expressed themselves less cogently than subsequent social historians, upheld a marketing system in which the activities of large-scale dealers were circumscribed by local regulations enforced by magistrates on behalf of the community. In the controlled market, for example, as at Exeter in 1795, labourers and other folk were permitted to obtain food for their own needs before the dealers were allowed to trade. Middlemen had been increasingly bypassing this procedure by buying direct from the farmer or landowner and then sending supplies by canal or river to the growing manufacturing and commercial centres. Hence the frequency of riots at the main distribution and transhipment points. The controlled market, of course, suited a small-scale, paternalist society, but late- eighteenth-century Britain was not small scale and its paternalism dwindled by the year. It needed middlemen and retailing entrepreneurs to solve the unprecedented problems of mass distribution at distance from the main sources of supply. A Leeds or a Manchester would have starved if provisioned in the traditional way.

As many magistrates and clergymen recognized, middlemen represented a threat to paternalist controls and influence; rioters were often not prosecuted as vigorously as they might otherwise have been. Sermons were preached and pamphlets written against middlemen who 'forestalled' grain on its way to market or 'engrossed' supplies to distort prices. Samuel Reveley, vicar of Crosby Ravensworth (Westmorland) attributed the 'popular Clamour and plebeian Fury' of the 1801 food riots to dealers and speculators who manipulated the market for their own ends. He quoted Proverbs 11: 26: 'He that withholdeth Corn, the people shall curse him; But blessing shall be upon the Head of him that Selleth it.'[4]

By 1801, however, radical anti-government and anti-war slogans were beginning to mingle with the traditional cries of the food rioters, especially in the industrial parts of the North-west (244). A merging of political with economic grievance characterized protest in early industrial Britain and food riots were inadequate vehicles for it. As first good harvests then better methods of food distribution supervened after the last great food crisis of 1812, protest action turned unequivocally to democratic reform agitation and to trade union activity (Chs 18 and 20). By the 1830s and 1840s food riots survived only in the Scottish Highlands and in Cornwall.

Poaching by rural labourers increased enormously as the vice of poverty tightened around their families. Poachers offended against a proliferating series of enactments known collectively as the game laws. It is difficult to present the game laws, which restricted the right to kill a wide range of animals and birds, as anything other than class legislation, jealously protected and strengthened into the nineteenth century by a Parliament of landowners. Their purpose was to secure the rights of landowners to enjoy their favourite sport – killing birds and animals – against propertyless clods, for whom the acquisition of a rabbit or a pheasant could mean the difference between a child's survival or continued malnutrition leading directly or indirectly to early death. Between a quarter and a fifth of all summary convictions in years of scarcity are estimated to have been for infringements of the game laws, and in 1843 the proportion of total male convictions on this count in Bedfordshire touched 36 per cent. After about 1770 ever harsher statutes were enacted to protect the interests of leisured sportsmen; to which poachers retaliated by hunting in packs and even inciting hard-pressed gamekeepers to trials of strength. Heavy fines, imprisonment and even transportation were prescribed for trivial offences and the Ellenborough Act of 1803 added to the already disgracefully long catalogue of capital offences that of resisting arrest for poaching. Even such draconian punishment failed to deter desperate men who saw nothing morally wrong in hunting wild things to feed their families, the more so since the laws were increasingly protecting only the sporadic pleasures of non-resident landowners who gave nothing back to the community. The contrast between the pleasures of the rich and the privations of the poor could hardly have been drawn more starkly. For a Suffolk clergyman in 1849 poaching symbolized 'the antagonism of class against class in our rural districts' (247). It is entirely consonant with the odious attempts at the preservation of unearned privilege that it was the gamekeepers who suffered at the hands of the poaching gangs active in the 1830s and 1840s, and not the landowners.

English agricultural labourers, therefore, should be seen as resentful but not inert. They could fight back against a society which treated them with contempt. Nor was poaching the only weapon to hand. In East Anglia hardly a year passed without reports of rick-burning, cattle-maiming and destruction of farm outbuildings. The years 1816–17 and 1822 were particularly disturbed. Targets, as with food riots, were carefully selected: farmers who paid below the going rate, harsh overseers of the poor, clergyman-magistrates who relished their judicial, but neglected their spiritual, duties. Community complicity often made it difficult to locate offenders. The Revd Henry Bate Dudley of Steeple (Essex), a local magistrate, was formally thanked at Quarter Sessions in 1816 for his 'prompt and decisive measures' against incendiaries. Only later, apparently, was it thought prudent to add the word 'judicious' to the record after 'prompt'. Chelmsford magistrates asked the Prince Regent in the same year to sanction both a reward and immunity from prosecution for information leading to the apprehension of those sending incendiary letters to a local curate.[5]

The more famous Swing Riots of 1830–31, therefore, had precedents. The *Quarterly Review* was quite right to warn its readers in 1829 that if 'the social plague of poverty and degradation among the peasantry is not stayed . . . it will inevitably draw after it a strong and dreadful explosion'.[6] A poor harvest that year and the next lit the spark and much of southern and eastern England was aflame. Large 'open' parishes totally dependent on agriculture were the most often disturbed and the rioters' leaders, as far as may be judged from prosecution records, tended to be the better-off and possibly better-educated section of the labour force: village craftsmen, specialized farm workers and the like. Something more coherent and far-reaching than a desperate throw by the starving unemployed was involved in the Swing Riots. As in the earlier East Anglian outbreaks, labourers not only destroyed threshing-machines, which threatened one of the few remaining sources of winter work, and demanded higher wages. They also attacked leaders in the local community for failing to discharge the traditional obligations of the well-off in rural society. The riots were in part a protest against the decline of paternalism. The government, fearful of the political disturbances on the mainland of Europe in 1830 and over-anxious to draw inexact parallels, took a firm line. Almost 2,000 arrests were made and government special commissions superseded the normal judicial process. No less than 500 rioters were transported to Australia and Tasmania, 600 were imprisoned and 19 executed (238). The countryside returned to uneasy calm but the riots were not totally without effect. The widespread introduction of threshing machines was delayed for twenty years and in many parishes modest advances in wages were achieved. In a wider context, the riots also contributed to the unrest of 1830–32 which was the backcloth to the passage of the first Reform Act (Ch. 23). Essentially, though, they were only the most widespread and dramatic of many pieces of evidence pointing to the destitution and lowering resentment of the most vital and least regarded sector of Britain's workforce.

---

1. W. Cobbett, *Rural Rides* (Everyman edn, 2 vols, 1912), i, p. 266.
2. F. M. Eden, *The State of the Poor* (3 vols, 1797), i, pp. 495–6.
3. J. L. and B. Hammond, *The Village Labourer* (1978 edn), p. 45.
4. S. Reveley, 'A moral discourse on forestalling and monopoly' (Penrith, 1801) Cumbria R. O. (Kendal), WPR/7.
5. Essex R. O., Q/SBb 381/20–21; P/CM 3.
6. *Quarterly Review*, xli (1829), p. 282.

CHAPTER 17

Standards of living and the quality of life

I

The Industrial Revolution has enormously increased living standards. In the long term, it cannot be disputed that the benefits of economic growth have filtered through society to produce higher per capita incomes and a vastly increased range of consumer choices. Contention on this effect of the Industrial Revolution concerns only timing. Certain periods of rapid advance for the majority – the last quarter of the nineteenth century or 1950–70 – stand out. The question exercising economic and social historians in our period is: were the benefits of industrial advance enjoyed to any important degree by first-generation industrial workers, or were they sacrificed through long hours, vile conditions and uncertain wages to profit hungry employers while, unintentionally, smoothing the path for future generations?

This question has proved intensely frustrating. Firstly, extant data on wages and prices in the early nineteenth century, while much fuller than might be supposed, are open to doubt on grounds of accuracy and typicality. Secondly, those entering the living-standards debate have interpreted the phrase narrowly – trends in real wages and per capita income over specific periods – or widely – including environmental, educational and psychological factors – as the fancy, or the needs of their own argument, took them. Thirdly, and most insidiously, what is an important line of historical enquiry has frequently been sacrificed to anachronistic political point-scoring. It comes as no surprise to discover that Marxist historians, beginning with Marx, argue that early industrial workers' living standards and quality of life deteriorated dramatically between about 1780 and 1850 (though by no means all 'pessimists' are Marxists) or that 'liberal' economic historians, particularly those most influenced by theories of economic growth, emphasize the benefits of industrialism in terms of both of higher wages and richer patterns of consumption. When one samples the salvoes fired off by Eric Hobsbawm and Max Hartwell in the late 1950s and early 1960s, for example (283), it is difficult to avoid the impression that history was being used as a weapon in a contemporary ideological campaign.

Having thus declaimed, this historian should perhaps state at the outset that he sees little point in coming to a view on what has become known as the 'standard of living controversy' on the basis of wages and prices evidence alone. Some 'optimists', thinking that the figures support them, have claimed that standards of living can be calculated on the basis of movements in real wages and per capita income; quality of life, a superficially vaguer phrase in tune with the unquanti-fiable elements which comprise most of its inputs, can be considered almost as a separate issue. This contention seems to me dubious on three main grounds. It is invalid arbitrarily to separate quantifiable from unquantifiable elements in explanations of complex historical phenomena, not least because to do so is often to imply (though rarely to assert openly) that evidence which can be counted is somehow more valuable than that which cannot. Secondly, though wage and price data have been subjected to increasingly sophisticated statistical analyses in recent years they cannot come to grips with the vast diversity of employment opportunities and the short-time and casual working which was such an important part of the labour undertaken in early industrial Britain (Ch. 14). Mean wages and mean prices are little more than statistical abstractions when derived from such variegated sources. Further, as many 'pessimists' have pointed out, these wage and price series show a marked southern, if not London, bias which reduces their value for national generalization. Thirdly, as we know from our own time, people do not consider that their standard of living derives only from movements in real wages. Even though government statistical departments tell them that higher wages more than compensate, folk are likely to feel worse off if mortgages are difficult to obtain or if the interest rate goes up, if council houses are not properly maintained or are vandalized, if the roads are not swept, if their children are being educated in bigger classes in more impersonal schools or if they are forced to accept a series of short-term, temporary jobs when permanant employment is required. People's reactions to their experiences are at least as important as the movement of lines on a graph. Man does not live by the regression curve alone.

One further obstacle should be mentioned. This controversy concerns itself with the first two generations of industrialism, say the 1780s to the 1840s. Since the emergence of an industrial society was incomparably the most important development of these years it is tempting to assume that all changes in living standards should be attributed to the effects of industrialism. But severe qualifications are needed. The exigencies of war at the beginning of the period undoubtedly had an effect both on wage levels and on food supplies; so *a fortiori* did the rise in population. Nor should the effects of government policy on corn supplies (Chs 20 and 30) between 1815 and 1846 be ignored. Changes in living standards have been more closely examined in this period than in any other, with the possible exception of 1918–39. But just as depression and unemployment dominated that later period without being solely responsible for changes in living standards, so industrialism should not explain everything in the former. As has been seen (Chs 12–14) industrialism was still in the relatively early stages by 1850 with important sectors of the economy affected only at second hand.

II

Amid the caveats and uncertainties one point can be advanced with reasonable certainty. Between 1780 and 1850 both prices and wages fluctuated more wildly and over shorter periods than ever before. Harvest shortages, population pressure and uncertainties with overseas supplies all help to explain the enormous variations in the price of wheat between 1790 and 1815 [D.vi.3]; wages seem to have lagged behind the prevailing price of the staple food at this time. Wild variations only make averages more suspect and my own crude calculations from Professor Flinn's assemblage of wage and price data [D.vi.1] should be used with extreme caution. These rough approximates are included in simplified form because they form the kernel of the optimists' case. During the difficult war years prices may have outrun wages, but a substantial price fall occurred between about 1815 and 1830, probably concentrated on the peaceful early 1820s, while wages were not dragged down so far. Though with considerable variations (the 1830s possibly saw slight deterioration), improved real wages were further advanced especially during the late 1830s and 1840s, such that an already healthier position was handed on into the years of mid-Victorian equipoise. Even after 1850, when estimates are somewhat more reliable, it is noticeable that real wages hardly make dramatic headway. G. H. Wood's index [D.vi.1] suggests actual decline between 1850 and 1858 with a 15–20 per cent improvement only after 1862.

The consensus of national statistical material on real wages has been increasingly optimistic. Lindert and Williamson's recent calculations (285) [D.vi.1] show remarkable improvements in wage levels, particularly in the later 1830s and 1840s and particularly for the non-manual sector. Over the period 1781–1851 the wages of skilled workers appear to have doubled and those in the non-manual sector to have increased fourfold. To such 'optimstic projections' should be added the important information that expectation of life at birth rose from 25 to 40 years between 1780 and 1840 – little more than half the expectation nowadays but an important advance none the less. The British population also seems to have been getting taller, which probably reflects some improvement in diet.

These hefty initial statistical advantages, however, do not clinch the optimists' case. They provide, overwhelmingly, evidence about healthy men in generally continuous employment. Though this section of the workforce is undeniably important, knowledge of family employment patterns, unemployment, short-time working and structural under-employment in the late eighteenth and early nineteenth centuries warns against considering it as overwhelmingly dominant. Furthermore, detailed regional studies give a more variegated pattern. Regional studies, though using raw material scarcely more satisfactory than the national estimates, are markedly less optimistic. Dr Gourvish calculates that, in Glasgow, only better-paid workers improved their position between 1810 and 1831, a period on which the optimists set great store; unskilled labourers marked time at best. Dr Neale estimates that labourers' real wages in Bath did not again reach 1780s levels until railway construction in the area increased employment opportunities after 1839. In a novel attempt to extrapolate the experiences of a particular cohort of workers he concludes that 'very few labourers entering the labour market in the 1780s could have received a higher real wage at the end of a thirty-year working life', while men starting work in the 1790s, when real wages were squeezed in Bath as elsewhere, 'would probably have experienced a rise in real incomes during the 1820s' (283, *154–77*). Dr Schwarz's work on London notes substantial falls in real wages not just in the 1790s but in the thirty or forty years before that. Improvement during the 1810s stabilized over the next two decades but 'no sustained and unmistakeable increase in London is identified until the 1840s'

(286). The key factor then, as so often, was not wage increases but substantial falls in grain prices.

Nor do the optimists gain greatly from a study of patterns of consumption. If real wages rose, consumption might reasonably be expected to reflect the development. Yet later basic items such as tea, sugar and coffee remained semi-luxuries by 1850, widely used, it appears, only by the middle classes and by artisans. The balance of probabilities is that meat consumption per capita was less in 1840 than it had been in 1780. The provision of fruit, fresh vegetables and milk to industrial towns was difficult before the railways facilitated distribution. The main market-garden boom came after the 1840s (Ch. 15). Bread supplies, however, held up well after the disasters early in the century to ensure the swollen population of Britain a basic but limited diet. In the north of England, potatoes were increasingly used as a nutritious supplement.

It was a major triumph to avoid starvation given the rate of population growth, but the optimists need to prove more than this. More mileage is to be found in clothing. Much of Lancashire's enormous production of cheap cotton goods was sold at home. Mass production required a mass market and many Lancashire and Yorkshire textile entrepreneurs made their fortunes by bringing cheap and serviceable basic cottons and woollens within the means of the working man. After 1815, it seems that the availability of a restricted range of foods at lower prices enabled a mass market to develop for the most celebrated products of the early Industrial Revolution. This was certainly progress, though the extent to which it represented a significant improvement in living standards is open to doubt.

Attempts to chart improvements in living standards by constructing models of consumption based on what working people might be expected to buy at different times have not been successful. The best they can show is that if labourers consumed according to the precepts of twentieth-century academics then the picture appears rosier by 1840, and certainly by 1850, than it had in 1790. But the number of academics to be found in early-nineteenth-century towns was not large and spending patterns were dictated more by community pressures than by desiccated calculations from a cash-book. Thus, workers in industrial Lancashire spent what to economic historians might seem irrationally large sums on funerals – 'a proper send-off'. Not to have done so would have been disrespectful and risked community condemnation. London working men consumed far more of their income than was 'rational' on beer, though the irrationality is partially explained by the difficulty of obtaining pure water in the teeming metropolis and the fact that a beershop was usually cosier than the damp or draughty cellar or tenement where they brought up their children. Actual consumption bore little relation to abstract constructs; the richness and diversity of cultural patterns defeat even sophisticated computer models.

III

It has been asserted by pessimists that the early stages of industrialism necessarily require substantial movements of income towards investment and away from consumption; hence bigger profits and lower wages. This speculation, too, should be treated with caution. Initial investment requirements in Britain's Industrial Revolution (Chs 12 and 13) were not large and not so large, certainly, as during the 'second Industrial Revolution' after 1840 when, by common consent, living standards were rising. On the other hand, it is beyond doubt that the first half of the nineteenth century witnessed a widening gap between rich and poor, hardly surprising since the spur to entrepreneurial investment was profit not social concern. If the poor were not getting poorer, the rich were certainly getting richer. One estimate, based on income tax returns, has the top 1 per cent of the population by wealth increasing their share of the national product from 25 per cent in 1801 to 35 per cent by 1848 (250, *136*). The accuracy of early tax figures is open to doubt and it should be remembered that the richest men in early-nineteenth-century Britain were overwhelmingly landowners and financiers not industrialists, but the shift seems significant. If the massive increase in national wealth did bring higher wages to working people, their gains were slender beside the rewards of the wealthy. It is significant that income per capita grew more rapidly than real wages, thus indicating that other sources – investment, rents, profits – were more buoyant. The pessimists have rightly pointed to the extent of social tension at a time of allegedly rising living standards. The years 1795, 1800–1, 1811–12, 1829–32, 1838–42 and 1848 were all exceptionally disturbed and Britain came nearer to working-class revolution in the early nineteenth century than at any other time.

Another important, if unsurprising, conclusion to emerge from the substantial recent research on living standards is that the Industrial Revolution increased wage differentials within the working classes. At the risk of oversimplification, it now seems safe to make two clear statements about this. First, wages became more buoyant as economic activity increased. In Manchester, for example, carpenters' wages between 1765 and 1795 increased from 64 per cent to 88 per cent of the rates paid in London. Those in Aberdeen, where coastal and commercial activity was substantial, increased from 33 per cent to 43 per cent. In Exeter, by contrast, where less innovation and development occurred, rates *vis à vis* London were reduced slightly (287, 288). Second, the prospects for skilled workers in key positions during the Industrial Revolution were far brighter than for labourers generally. The Industrial Revolution craved engineers; craftsmen in engineering and railway technology did very well, some of them aspiring to middle-class status by the 1850s. Potters' wage rates in Wedgwood's North Staffordshire increased far more rapidly than did those of general labourers and building craftsmen. Most, though not all, of the bewildering range of craft skills, in printing, building and jewellery among many others, came into still greater demand as national wealth increased; their practitioners, not being rendered redundant by machinery, kept well ahead of the game. So did miners, though particularly towards the end of the period as the demand for motive power accelerated dramatically (Ch. 13). Among factory workers, skilled men like the spinners of fine cotton did well. Women and children, who comprised almost 70 per cent of the factory workforce in the late 1830s [D.v.1], worked for far less, but opportunities for work were greater than before and family income for textile workers almost certainly exceeded the cost of living. Factory hands, after all, were not herded into the new towns at the point of any entrepreneurial whip; they were lured by the prospect of securer work and higher wages than they could earn outside. Domestic servants, though their hours of work were long and their status and earnings alike low, were at least in regular employ in large numbers by the 1840s, as servant-keeping became a necessary badge of status for the more numerous middle classes whose own living standards had risen far more. It is permissible to categorize servants as gainers since for many the only alternatives would have been poor relief or prostitution.

Two groups stand out among society's losers. As was seen in Chapter 16, most southern and eastern agricultural labourers did extremely badly between 1780 and 1850 though there was discernible improvement in much of northern England where alternative employment pushed up wages. In the predominantly rural South and East of England, also, women's contribution to the labour force declined on balance. Family incomes suffered severely in consequence. Even the ending of such humble tasks as sewing buttons onto servicemen's uniforms contributed to deteriorating family incomes after the French wars ended in 1815. Those skilled men displaced by machinery also suffered sorely. The desperation of the handloom weavers, so much in demand in the 1790s, so reduced by the 1830s, is well known. To them we might add the framework knitters, the wool combers and the calico printers. Their misery flowed not only from pitiful wages (6s. or 7s. – 30–35p a week in the 1840s) but from a keenly felt loss of status, for these had been among the aristocrats of eighteenth-century labour. Relatively few workers, however, were thoroughly displaced by mechanization. The great expansion of population made it unnecessary for employers in many trades to buy machines when cheap labour was such a ready substitute. In addition to the farm workers and the dispossessed artisans, industrialization's net 'losers' should include a range of workshop employees, such as those in the metal trades whose hours of labour were increased to meet greater demand but whose rates of pay did not match their efforts. They certainly included garret workers in the silk and other textile trades whose employers worked them excessively hard as they attempted to match factory output. They included also workers in the 'dishonourable' trades (Ch. 14), working under intense pressure to make basic or imperfect goods for a mass market. The Industrial Revolution witnessed massive expansion both of the sweated trades and of under-paid and exploited casual labour.

IV

The optimists' case rests largely on statistics which have been severely criticized, together with some reliance on theories of economic development and their effects. It is relevant to mention a counter-factual point: what would have happened to Britain's teeming population had industrial growth not rescued it from a Malthusian poverty trap? It is difficult to see how a 'check' on an even more catastrophic scale than the Irish famine of 1845–47 could have been avoided, and to this not inconsiderable extent the Industrial Revolution brought the benefit of permitting a much larger population to survive and, in the long term, thrive.

The pessimists have tended to rely on arguments about the deteriorating quality of life, some of which can be quantified but most of which is impressionistic. The great weight of contemporary evidence was severely critical of life in the new or massively expanded cities. Urban monsters were unleashed by the forces of industrialism which it would take decades of patient legislation and the expenditure of huge amounts of ratepayers' money to tame. Put simply, the cities grew far too fast for health and safety. Urban growth rates, at between 23.7 per cent and 29.1 per cent a decade between 1801 and 1851, far outpaced even the rapid general population growth. Some already huge cities experienced further massive, and quite unplanned, growth. Glasgow increased its population by 46 per cent in the 1810s, Manchester by 44 per cent in the 1820s. Previously small towns became huge manufacturing centres within a generation. Bradford's population grew by 63 per cent in the 1810s, by 69 per cent in the 1820s and by 52 per cent in the 1830s [E.iii]. The most beneficent central or local administration could not have kept pace with the unstructured influx; the prevailing ethos among Britain's early-nineteenth century legislators eschewed planning and intervention. In consequence the early industrial cities, whether factory or workshop based, became overcrowded, filthy, insanitary breeding grounds for disease, squalor and degradation. People flocked to them because they offered work but the social costs were enormous. Edwin Chadwick shocked contemporaries when his *Sanitary Report* of 1842 demonstrated how much more unhealthy it was to live as a labourer in an industrial town than in any other condition. A labourer's child was twice as likely to die before the age of five in Liverpool as in the rural county of Rutland. Three children out of every twenty died in Britain in the 1840s in their first year of life; in many northern cities where the infectious and enteric diseases to which infants are particularly prone spread rapidly through overcrowded tenements and courts, the proportion was nearly one in four. In both Sheffield and Manchester more than half the children born alive in the 1830s failed to reach their fifth birthday. As Dr Holland, physician to the Sheffield infirmary, put it in 1843: 'We have no hesitation in asserting, that the sufferings of the working classes, and consequently the rate of mortality, are greater now than in former times' (251, *366*). The differential population growth of the cities was due entirely to migration and a high birth-rate consequent on early marriage; death-rates were higher than the average and probably rising until the 1840s.

Unskilled labourers crowded into airless cellar and tenement dwellings, left for them to occupy at low rents and with vastly increased population density, by the middle classes who moved out. Back-to-back houses, lacking most amenities and all privacy, were erected in huge numbers in northern industrial cities by speculative builders looking for a good return on seventy or eighty dwellings to the acre. As in other areas of Industrial Revolution study, desperate conditions in the 1810s and 1820s were beginning to be improved slightly by the 1840s. The number of occupants per house in Nottingham and Sheffield seems to have fallen a little between 1800 and 1850, though the sanitary conditions of both cities remained appalling. In London and Liverpool, commercial centres which attracted disproportionate amounts of unskilled, migrant labour, a steady deterioration in housing provision was experienced until the second half of the century. Everywhere housing standards for the casual and the unskilled labourers remained unbelievably primitive since it was uneconomic for speculative builders to cater for them. No housing policy would emerge in the heyday of *laissez-faire* (343, 346).

It is hardly surprising that social segregation grew apace. More prosperous suburbs were built to house the superior artisans and middle classes, well out of nose range from the stench of the town centres and the hovels in walking distance of them. It is no accident that most higher-quality housing was placed to the west of towns so that the prevailing winds should not blow the smells in genteel directions. The better off also provided for themselves, as ratepayers, better paving, lighting and water supplies; the inner areas suffered relative neglect. Other employers and professional men moved into the surrounding countryside. As E. P. Thompson caustically notes: '... the working people were segregated in their stinking enclaves, and the middle classes demonstrated their real opinions of the industrial towns by getting as far out of them as equestrian transport made convenient' (251, *355*). The physical distancing only emphasized the lack of paternal relationships and difficulties of control in early Victorian cities. Both actually and metaphorically, the working classes were on their own.

City dwellers had to contend with bad housing, filth and bad water. Increasingly, the food they ate was suspect too. Sharks and swindlers happily filled the gaps in distribution with concoctions and supplements to defraud the purchaser. The addition of alum, a mineral salt, made impure bread look whiter so that it could fetch a higher price. Ash, sloe or elder leaves were offered in lieu of tea while both milk and beer could be watered down. Beer could also be adulterated by the insertion of various dubious substances replacing malt or hops. Red lead found its toxic way into pepper pots. It was no longer possible to enforce the protective medieval Assize statutes of bread and ale, even had legislators wished to do so. When the Assize of Bread was formally repealed in 1815 the parliamentary select committee which had examined the issue reported that 'more benefit is likely to result from the effects of a free competition ... than can be expected to result from any regulations' (273, *111*). The extent of adulteration naturally eludes quantifi- cation, but the matter received wider attention from doctors and chemists after the publication of Frederick Accum's *Treatise on Adulteration of Foods and Culinary Poisons* in 1820. Despite the powerful support of Sir John Simon in the 1850s and extensive evidence presented to a select committee in 1855, effective legislation was not forthcoming until the Disraeli Food and Drugs Act of 1875. The steady poisoning of some and systematic cheating of many is an under-explored aspect of the deterioration of urban life.

The fierce competitiveness which characterized the first phase of the Industrial Revolution brought further misery in the form of periodic crises of over-production. These bankrupted some masters and forced others to lay men off. Other factors were involved in the jerkiness of early industrial development and they combined to bring grim social consequences. The years of most acute social tension were years of high unemployment during short-term depressions. Statistics on unemployment before the 1890s are impressionistic and may not always be representative, but the accumulated weight of contemporary evidence on the effects of depression in the cotton trade is too great to be gainsaid. During the worst of them, in 1842, 60 per cent of Bolton's factory employees were out of work. In

Stockport, 51 per cent of workers had no employment and a further 34 per cent were on short time; in Wigan the figures were 38 and 62 per cent respectively, and in Oldham, where machine manufacture mitigated the worst effects, 26 per cent and 26 per cent (283, *71*). One-industry towns were devasted by cyclical depression, and though recovery was usually rapid there were enough bad years to have serious consequences for standards of living and to make wage rates unrealistic when compared to wages actually paid out.

Nor were factory towns the only sufferers. Though the daily wage rates of London shipwrights, tailors and shoemakers remained steady after 1815 as prices fell, a swollen labour market increased unemployment severely. A minority of skilled men were able to preserve their status and improve their living standards, but others were forced by cut-throat competition for jobs to enter the 'dishonourable' sector of their trades where conditions were worse and wages lower (60). In the mining and metals area of the Black Country unemployment was a recurrent problem throughout the nineteenth century. Short-time working and work-sharing both made wage rates unrealistic guides to actual earnings. Even in the supposedly more prosperous 1850s and 1860s, unemployment remained high and the real wages of miners, iron puddlers and general labourers all showed a marked fall from levels reached in the good year of 1850. Only building workers seem to have made advances in Staffordshire in these decades.

Against equivocal and contested evidence for a rise in real wages between 1790 and 1840 and rather stronger evidence of improvement in the 1840s, therefore, stands testimony of environmental deterioration, lowered standards of public health and the psychological shock of a revolution in work patterns and way of life, all of it supported by multifarious contemporary statements both of alarm and concern. Into these less quantifiable areas, the optimists have stepped gingerly, if at all, though their importance is increasingly acknowledged. Professor Flinn, indeed, asserted that no one 'interested in the impact of the momentous changes in agriculture, commerce and industry that occurred between the mid-eighteenth and the mid-nineteenth centuries believes that "standards of living" are assessable solely in cash terms' (284, *411*). Quite. The first generation of workers in industrial Britain, though their real wages probably improved slightly, laboured in worse conditions than their parents had known. The first fruits of industrial progress were harvested by the middle and upper classes, followed at respectful distance by the skilled workers whose jobs were not threatened by machines, particularly those whose skills industrialism created. Even in the 1850s and 1860s only slender improvements were made by ordinary workers, who would have to wait until the price depression of the late nineteenth century to enjoy measurable and un-equivocal benefits from economic development. By that time, of course, those who lived through the squalor of early-nineteenth-century Manchester were all dead.

CHAPTER 18

Organizations of labour

I

Organizations of labouring men to secure higher wages or better working conditions were in existence long before the Industrial Revolution. Craft societies of skilled workers had operated during the eighteenth century partly as insurance and benefit clubs, partly to coerce employers when trade was good, partly to restrict entry to their trade so as to preserve 'craft exclusivity' and the bargaining powers which went with it. These elements of 'combination' not only survived into the early industrial period, they continued as the basis of successful labour organization at least until the 1870s. Until then, unions were largely the preserve of skilled operatives, though in heady moments like the late 1810s or early 1830s, it seemed that the masses might obtain union protection. Not more than 750,000 of Britain's workforce of about 12m. in 1870 were unionized and most of these were workshop, rather than factory, operatives.

Though many exceptions may be found among union leaders, the predominant disposition of trade unions was defensive rather than expansive, status rather than class conscious. It was considered more important to continued prosperity to restrict entry than to challenge the foundations of industrial capitalism. Unionists calculated that effective pressure on employers could be put on employers only if entry to their trade was restricted. A vital distinction must be drawn between skilled workers. Some, like handloom weavers, framework knitters and, somewhat later, carpenters, shoemakers and tailors looked to combination to preserve their hard-won status against the twin challenges of mechanization and the sheer pressure of numbers seeking entry to their trade. For these, defensive struggles were waged in often vain attempts to prevent dilution, lowered wages and unemployment. These craft societies had been the sturdy, load-bearing branches of eighteenth-century unionism. Economic diversity sapped their vitality; many withered away, depriving their members of support and leaving them to drop into the ever-expanding 'dishonourable' or 'unrespectable' sections of their trade. The future prosperity of trade unionism lay with workers no less skilled but better equipped to profit from industrial production. Some, like the cotton-spinners, worked in factories; others, like jewellers, goldsmiths, cabinet-makers and compositors possessed such rarefied skills catering for luxury markets that the threat of dilution did not touch them. Most were in trades which industrialism either generated or nurtured. It is no accident that ironworkers and engineers figure so prominently in the story of nineteenth-century unionism or that to them should be added the coal-miners and shipwrights who provided the motive power and transportation for the new industrial goods.

Many of the most impressive union leaders, men like Gravener Henson of the framework knitters, John Doherty of the spinners or John Gast of the shipwrights, looked to unions for concerted action against employers as a class, but as they developed their notions of union-generated class struggle they generally lost the support of their membership. Dreams of general unions embracing skilled and unskilled alike assumed a hazy and inchoate reality in the late 1820s and early 1830s, but these stood outside the mainstream of union development which remained cautious, sectional and lacking in class solidarity. Unions which succeeded did so because they could safeguard if not improve the living standards of their members by making capitalism work for them as well as for their employers, and devil take the hindmost. Then, as now, they offered cold comfort to radicals; they deserve a narrower and less honoured place in the history of working-class aspiration than some historians are disposed to afford them.

II

Until 1824, combinations of workmen were unlawful. The Combination Acts of 1799 and 1800, though they owed something to the growing belief that trade and manufacture should be freed from artificial encumbrance (Ch. 5), need to be seen primarily against a background of Jacobin agitation. They did not mark a radical change of policy. Most of the troublesome or prominent workmen's combinations had been individually proscribed during the course of the eighteenth century. The tailors had been forbidden to combine in 1720, for example, and the woollen weavers in 1726. The 1799 Act prohibited all combinations, whether by workmen or manufacturers, on pain of three months' imprisonment. Most anti-union prosecutions, however, continued to be under common law for conspiracy or breach of contract where penalties were stiffer, or under earlier statutes concerning particular trades. Prosecutions of unions were frequent in the early nineteenth century, especially in the Midlands and North where new workforces were being rapidly assembled and where the challenge to many of the old skills was at its keenest. The Combination Acts may have strengthened the climate of propertied opinion against challenges to established authority but they did not prevent the spread of unionism. Paradoxically, unions of skilled workers gained strength during the twenty-five years of blanket illegality.

Some combinations flourished as orthodox labour organizations in the guise of friendly societies which were regarded with benevolence by authority because of their self-help characteristics. Craft societies had long incorporated insurance and benefit principles now fostered by friendly societies, so the distinction between unions and friendly societies was usefully hazy. The unavailing campaign to preserve the apprenticeship laws between 1810 and 1814 spurred union growth. The handloom weavers established a union headquarters in Glasgow in 1811 from which a concerted Anglo-Scottish campaign in favour of the traditional seven-year apprenticeship and restrictions on entry to trades was launched. A bitter strike in 1813 followed rejection of the weavers' parliamentary petition. Meanwhile, London artisans concerted pressure through a General Committee across the trades (60).

Despite frequent disappointments, the war years offered opportunities for many craft workers to put pressure on their employers and to force wages up. In London, the tailors were particularly well organized and the secrecy of their activities frustrated attempts to bring them to book. Building workers and shipwrights, in trades favoured by a steady supply of government contracts, also did well. Elsewhere, magistrates frequently fought shy of interposing the law between master and workman. The important Manchester cotton-spinners' strike of 1818 was not brought to the attention of local magistrates for several weeks. In the lace and stockings centre of Nottingham at least fifty illegal unions were formed, and fifteen strikes endured, in the first quarter of the nineteenth century.

Successful unions helped members to keep abreast of wartime inflation and, incidentally, to put greater distance between themselves and their unskilled and unorganized brethren. Strikes were particularly frequent in 1802, 1808–14 and, after the war, in 1818. In addition to the Glasgow weavers' and Manchester cotton-spinners' disputes, strikes by west of England woollen workers and London shipwrights in 1802, Northumberland and Durham miners in 1810, Sheffield cutlers and East Midland framework knitters in 1814 and Lancashire weavers and calico printers in 1818 all deserve special mention. Well might a harassed Home Office under-secretary report in 1818 that the 1800 Combination Act was 'almost a dead letter while conspiracy is increasing on every side'.

The disturbed year 1818 saw attempts to co-ordinate sympathetic activity across the trades. Out of the Manchester spinners' strike emerged briefly a Philanthropic Society of all trades concerned at 'the Distressed State and Privations to which the Working Class of Society are reduced by their avaricious Employers reducing wages to less than sufficient to support nature' (290). Spinners' delegates established contact with the London trades from which developed the Philanthropic Hercules, under the chairmanship of John Gast, to co-ordinate inter-union activity and, incidentally, to set Gast on a road which would preoccupy him and distance him from the more prosaic objectives of his shipwright members. Partly under the influence of Gast, John Wade, the radical journalist and erstwhile journeyman wool sorter, made *Gorgon* the first pro-union newspaper. *Gorgon* printed several articles in 1818–19 on the state of unionism and roundly condemned 'the folly, inutility and cruelty' of the Combination Acts; it also espoused more general radical causes such as parliamentary reform and opposition to the Established Church. The Philanthropic Societies merit attention, not because of their intrinsic importance (both collapsed within months) but because they anticipate later and yet more ambitious schemes for union co-operation and the restructuring of labour in an industrial world. They flash like meteors across the otherwise grey skies of trade union history and more than one scholar has been dazzled by their coruscations.

III

Though strikes were frequent in these early years, a far more dramatic short-term impact was made by collective action against certain types of industrial machinery. 'Luddism' has entered contemporary political vocabulary in a most unfair way.

Early-nineteenth-century Luddites were no ignorant, indiscriminate despoilers. Historians have disputed their precise significance, but it is now common ground that most Luddites were skilled men who attacked specific targets, particularly those machines which threatened the continued predominance of their skills and consequent labour scarcity. Nor was machine-breaking a new phenomenon in 1811–16, when its concentration in the East Midlands, West Yorkshire and south-east Lancashire so disturbed the authorities. Spinning-jennies, water-frames and carding engines were all attacked in Lancashire in the 1770s. Gig mills and shearing frames were attacked at the same time by the 'croppers' or 'shearmen' in the west of England, whose skills in raising and cutting level the nap of woollen cloth were much valued but now directly endangered.

Resistance to the introduction of new machinery is natural, as our own generation is well aware. The concentration of Luddite activity, however, needs to be seen against its economic as well as its more narrowly industrial background. The period 1811–12 was a crisis point in the French Wars; many businesses were ruined by economic warfare which precipitated a sharp decline in European and American markets (Ch. 10). The peak of Luddite activity in 1812 exactly coincided with the highest point in the alarming rise in bread prices [D.vi.3]. In the hosiery and lace trades of Nottinghamshire and Derbyshire, where Luddite outbreaks began and where they lasted longest, about one-half and three-quarters respectively of their products were exported (251). Thus, though the machine-breakers attacked wide stocking-frames producing 'cut-ups', an inferior product which threatened the respectability of their trade and increased the threat of dilution, they also sought to defend themselves against wage cuts in a shrinking market.

Yorkshire Luddism was organized by the croppers who resisted the introduction of gig mill and shearing frame by manufacturers anxious to make long-term economies and to break the monopoly of woollen cloth finishing exercised by no more than 5,000 highly skilled outworkers. By no means all manufacturers could afford the initial investment and the Luddites' targets were easily selected during a violent campaign in 1812 which culminated in the murder of a prominent Huddersfield manufacturer, William Horsfall. Lancashire Luddism is more difficult to disentangle. Power-looms were attacked by handloom weavers in the spring of 1812, but the number of these as yet expensive and unreliable machines was not large until the 1820s and the threat much less immediate than that to the croppers. In Lancashire machine-breaking was often associated with or grew out of other kinds of disturbance, as in the attack on Burton's power-weaving factory at Middleton in April when colliers from Hollingwood who had assembled in the Oldham market-place and forced the sale of food at 'traditional' prices, thereafter took themselves off with others to the factory; here they were fired upon and five rioters were killed. The next day the manufacturer's house was burned to the ground.[1] Lancashire Luddism also merges confusingly into that radical political agitation which disturbed the authorities in 1812.

The ambivalence of Lancashire Luddism anticipates an uncertainty among historians as to the proper significance of the movement as a whole. Considered narrowly, as an attempt to prevent the introduction of certain types of machinery, it was an utter failure, more so certainly than the Swing Riots (Ch. 16). It did not halt the slow but certain decline of both framework knitters and handloom weavers; the now redundant skills of the croppers were not given an artificial extension of life. The progress of mechanization was affected much more by the structure of the market and the availability of cheap alternatives, like unskilled workers in large numbers, than by desperate nocturnal acts of courage on bleak Yorkshire moors. But should Luddism be so narrowly circumscribed? Some have seen in it a much more heroic strain. Luddism, for E. P. Thompson, was 'a violent eruption of feeling against unrestrained industrial capitalism, harking back to an obsolescent paternalist code, and sanctioned by traditions of the working community' (251). Of local support for the Luddites there can be little doubt. The 12,000 troops stationed in the North and Midlands had relatively little success in policing the seriously disturbed areas and machine-breakers remained well concealed. The mistrust felt by the landed gentry, who comprised a large part of the magistracy, towards *nouveaux riches* factory owners should be stressed, as should the mixture of envy and hostility evinced by smaller manufacturers lacking the cash to revolutionize their own modes of production and often with much residual sympathy for the continuation of easy relations between master and man. Even among a middle class easily alarmed by cries of revolution, the Luddites were not without sympathizers.

But Thompson went further. He saw in Luddism a vital stage in the emergence of class consciousness by working men against a Parliament of landowners which deprived them of traditional controls on the organization of their labour and against employers who used the freedom thus bestowed to impose alien patterns of work constructed for the sole purpose of maximizing profit to themselves. Against these assaults workers armed themselves, literally, in the out-townships of Yorkshire and Nottinghamshire in 1812, fighting the might of industrial capitalism with their own weapons of secret oaths, drillings and revolutionary preparation.

There is a perverse romanticism about all of this which many have found compelling. The evidence left for historians by secret societies, whose every action the courts would find treasonable, is naturally scanty and anyway confused, embellished and distorted by this work of spies and *agents provocateurs*. We shall never *know* how many Yorkshiremen harboured revolutionary designs in Halifax or Heckmondwike in 1812; the extent to which evanescent and opaque Luddite manifestations represented an alternative political tradition will remain a matter for informed speculation. It is worth recalling, however, that industrial capitalism was by no means monolithic in its attitude to Luddism and that the Luddites were far from typical of the generality of working men. Most were skilled men trying to maintain skills which necessitated the exclusion of other workers from their ranks. Some, perhaps many, were developing a wider political philosophy which doubtless incorporated many of the ideas and attitudes which Thompson so lucidly attributes to them. Their sense of grievance is indisputable. Had they succeeded, however, it is difficult to see how ordinary workers would have benefited. Their objectives, however morally justified, were restrictive in a generally buoyant economy needing a greatly expanded workforce. The Luddites spoke and fought for themselves. Though they were not without supporters, their claim to represent a stage in the development of working-class consciousness is tenuous. Nor did their movement properly outlast the economic crisis which brought it to life. As conditions improved in 1813, so Luddism faded away, to reappear, briefly and very locally, in Nottinghamshire and Leicestershire in 1814 as an adjunct to activity by unionists in the hosiery and lace trades against particular employers who would not raise wages.

IV

The repeal of the Combination Acts in 1824 was steered through an apathetic Parliament by Joseph Hume, the radical MP for Aberdeen, and Francis Place, the old London Corresponding Society man whose reforming impulse was now controlled by fervour for the new political economy (Ch. 5). Place's many publications and utterances on the labour question disposed enough MPs to believe his assertion that only the continued illegality of unions alienated working men from their employers. Even so experienced a politician as William Huskisson, President of the Board of Trade, asserted 'that the laws against combinations had tended to multiply combinations, and that they had generally aggravated this evil they were intended to remove'[2] Repeal would put an end to combinations and perhaps even to strikes. The rapid emergence of the former in most of the craft trades and among factory spinners and engineers, and the rash of the latter during a boom when demand for labour was strong provoked hasty legislative revision. MPs were not slow to condemn what a select committee of the Commons called 'the circle of combination'. Workmen were alleged to practise 'every art of seduction and persuasion, every application of threat, insult, intimidation and outrage' to maintain membership. The amending Act of 1825 grudgingly maintained the legality of unions, while delivering a sideswipe against combinations as 'injurious to trade and commerce [and] dangerous to the tranquility of the country'. Any person using threats or coercion 'shall be imprisoned and kept in hard labour'.[3] Trade unions remained subject to the common law covering conspiracy and coercion. As many unions were to discover, the common law relating to conspiracy was frequently an effective ally for those seeking redress against them. The 1825 Act, in fact, re-established eighteenth-century values in labour relations. Combinations were permitted only for the named purposes of negotiating hours of work and wage rates. Owners were left free to run their businesses as they wished without legislative restraint.

The 1825 Act remained the basic legal statement on trade unionism for half a century but it did not remove other legislation which could be invoked. When the famous agricultural labourers of Tolpuddle (Dorset) were organized into a friendly society by the Methodist local preacher George Loveless in 1833, for example, they were transported under legislation against the administration of forbidden oaths. Miners suffered under the 'Master and Servant' Acts under which the breaking of contracts of employment by workers was a criminal offence while similar breaches by employers were deemed civil offences only. The miners' leader Alexander McDonald brought pressure through the Glasgow Trades Council in 1860 for repeal of these Acts; he was partially rewarded by the passage of Elcho's

Master and Servant Act in 1867 (292). The greatest legal setback may be traced to Justices of the Peace in Bradford who declared in 1866 that the town's branch of the Boilermakers' Society could not recover funds withheld by its treasurer since the society's rules included material which was considered in restraint of trade and thus illegal at common law. When the Court of Queen's Bench confirmed the decision in *Hornby* v. *Close* they were effectively striking at the entire basis of all trade union activity. No union could function unless it could protect its funds.

Though the law remained a minefield after 1825, trade union progress was still more affected by economic fluctuations. Thus, 1824–25 were boom years when unions briefly flourished; in the downswing of 1826–28 many fell apart again. It is important not to exaggerate divisions between the political and industrial objectives of working people. It is not surprising that those workers with the ability to organize were able to sustain successful trade union activity during periods of economic recovery such as the mid-1830s. Many educated and skilled workers were able to encompass both union membership and support for radical political movements such as Chartism. However, others drew in their horns during times of depression and waited for the next boom to press their claims for higher wages. In skilled but increasingly vulnerable trades, like shoemaking, carpentry and tailoring, political radicalism was more common. The reasons were not solely economic. Many of those craft skills long associated with radicalism were by the 1830s among those most vulnerable to dilution. The democratic, free-thinking shoemaker is a more convincing stereotype than the radical ironfounder.

The 1820s and 1830s saw developments towards district and national unions among skilled men. The first national union of carpenters was formed in 1827. Scottish ironmoulders joined together in a union-based friendly society in 1829 and the Lancashire printers combined to form the Northern Typographical Union in 1830. Doherty's Lancashire men combined in a Grand General Union of Cotton Spinners which held national conferences in 1829 and 1830. Successful strikes could act as a spur to union development as in West Yorkshire in 1831 when a Leeds weavers' strike led to a Leeds Trades' union with links throughout the county.

A feature of many unions is their grand, rhetorical titles. These were partly self-advertisement and partly, no doubt, to spread alarm through the ranks of the employers by raising the spectre of workers' solidarity. Appearances were all too often deceptive. Just as the major union aims in the 1830s, as before, were defensive if not conservative, so these 'national' unions maintained a loose federal structure at best. Their roots were craft-based and local. Of skilled propagandists and radical leaders, however, there was no lack. Trades and union-sympathizing journals flourished in the 1820s and 1830s, many of them redolent with the sonorities of labour consciousness. As early as 1823 Thomas Hodgskin, an early socialist, and Joseph Robertson founded the *Mechanics' Magazine* in London; Robertson moved on to edit the *Trades Newspaper* in 1825. This strove to alert London's artisans to a consciousness of a common identity based on hostility to employers as a class. Hodgskin's *Labour Defended Against the Claims of Capital*, a vigorous attack on capitalism, appeared in it in serial form. John Doherty established a short-lived National Association for the Protection of Labour in 1830 and published *Voice of the People* as its mouthpiece, believing that 'no individual trade could stand against the combined efforts of the masters of that particular trade: it was therefore sought to combine all the trades' (290). James Morrison, editor of the builders' union journal, *Pioneer*, advised his readers in 1834: 'Your present object must be to change *your wages* into a *fair share of the profits* of the productive concern in which they are employed.'

By the late 1820s, then, unionism had become a most important vehicle for purveying an alternative politico-economic philosophy based on the supersession of capitalism and on co-operation rather than individualism. Its most significant manifestation was Owenism. Owen's ideas were anything but precise and anyway not centrally directed towards trade unionism, but his notions of community development of co-operation based on labour as the source of all wealth struck a responsive chord with artisan leaders who had rather more political sense than Robert Owen himself. Both Gast and Doherty publicized Owenite schemes in their journals while Owen, the wealthy cotton magnate, model factory owner and idealist, seemed uncertain of which direction his ideas could most practically follow. Dr William King published the *Co-Operator* in support of trading associations to ensure that members obtained full value for the labour they gave, rather than less than a quarter of which, he asserted, was all that the capitalist system allowed them (61). Owenite co-operative societies flourished briefly in many towns in the early 1830s, and in 1832–33 equitable labour exchanges, an extension of the same labour-value principle, operated in Birmingham and London.

The apotheosis of Owenism was planned to be the Grand National Consolidated Trades Union (GNCTU), formed in February 1834. This federation of trade unions was to concert strike activity and mount a general strike for a maximum eight-hour working day. It should also embrace all operatives, not merely the skilled. In the spring of 1834 many unskilled and some women workers were recruited, though often only in a casual way. Radical journals gave enormous publicity to the venture but the reality was a good deal less menacing than the propaganda. The GNCTU was disproportionately strong in London and remained firmly anchored to the trades tradition of the tailors and shoemakers. Though it did attract such diverse skilled operatives as jewellers, bookbinders and saddlers, its claims to speak for the working classes as a whole were shown to be empty rhetoric by the speed and abjectness of its collapse in the summer. Even during its brief life it had engendered the usual quota of splits and tactical disagreements which plague visionary movements whose ambitions outrun their means. It appears to have had no more than 16,000 paid-up members, though the number of its wellwishers was undoubtedly far higher.

V

The collapse of the GNCTU hardly represented a watershed in trade union history. Many craft men regarded its pretensions with scepticism if not distrust; spinners and engineers avoided it. With its passing, the focus of union activity reverted to the securer base of organization craft by craft, with cautious moves towards regional then national associations. Though a National Association of United Trades flickered briefly in 1845 it received no more support outside London than had the GNCTU whose militancy it had not attempted to emulate. As the Manchester Stonemasons unromantically recorded: 'Past experience has taught us that we have had general union enough'.

Most unions remained small and local until the 1870s, though some national organizations succeeded and have received a disproportionate share of historical attention. Membership figures are not available, but a significantly increased membership is certain in the 1850s and 1860s. In large cities such as Birmingham, Glasgow, Edinburgh, Sheffield and Liverpool, trades councils had been formed by 1860; these acted as information centres and also provided support across the trades in cases of dispute. They were also used as pressure groups to agitate for changes in trade union law, with considerable success in the 1860s and 1870s. One, the London Trades Council, developed sensitive political antennae and its leaders played a prominent part in the agitation for a second Reform Act (Ch. 39). Most councils shied away from general political activity yet welcomed the opportunity to discuss matters of common concern. From the work of the trade councils developed the Trades Union Congress which met for the first time in Manchester in 1868. Its representatives, significantly, were drawn from the smaller, local unions prominent in the provincial councils.

National unions, providing sizeable sickness and unemployment benefits in return for weekly subscriptions well beyond the means of ordinary hands, flourished mainly in the engineering and building trades. The Amalgamated Society of Engineers, formed at the end of 1850 by the fusion of London and Manchester machine-makers' societies, provided unemployment benefit of almost £20 a year for the hefty weekly subscription of 1s. (5p). With a membership of 35,000 by 1870 it was easily the largest union in the country. The Amalgamated Society of Carpenters and Joiners, established in 1860, quickly established itself while the operative stonemasons developed a national organization first tentatively established in 1833. By contrast, the miners resisted the crossing of geographical barriers. A National Association formed in 1842 by Martin Jude was short-lived, and though the Scottish Miners' Association took root in 1855 it was not until the 1860s that permanent miners' associations appeared at county level in Northumberland, Durham and Lancashire. After the collapse of Doherty's venture, and despite attempts in the 1840s, the cotton-spinners could not secure effective national representation until the 1870s; the weavers were in similar case.

A survey of organized labour in Sheffield in 1859 revealed no fewer than 56 separate unions, mostly in the cutlery trade; some had tiny memberships: 14 corn grinders, 50 plate, spoon and fork filers, 55 scythe-makers.[4] Much union growth in the general expansion of the 1850s and 1860s came from a proliferation of tiny craft organizations whose aims were both to put pressure on employers and to use their strength to keep out undesirables. In defence of the latter aim, violent methods were still employed, as in Sheffield in the late 1850s and 1860s when various outrages were perpetrated against non-union men. One such, Joseph Helewell, a saw grinder, was seriously injured by a gunpower explosion in 1859. Such excesses caused embarrassment to union leaders seeking as far as possible to avoid violence. They turned increasingly to intricate negotiation procedures, conciliation agreements, arbitration and the like. Unions increasingly sought respectability. As the carpenters' leader, Robert Applegarth, put it in 1862, the aim was 'to raise . . . the whole tone and character of trades unionism' (292, *57*).

Though the collapse of the GNCTU was undoubtedly a setback for organized labour, it should not be assumed that the skilled workers who dominated trade unionism eschewed the strike weapon. Skilled workers were not necessarily 'moderates' bent upon avoidance of strikes at all costs. Many local, craft unions struck regularly. No fewer than 141 separate local disputes between printers and their employers were reported to the National Typographical Association in 1845–46, while 44 separate strikes are known to have been held by stonemasons in the North-west between 1840 and 1846 (290, *18*). The bitter and unsuccessful Preston spinners' strike of 1853, which lasted for more than seven months, and the London building workers' strike of 1859–60, which evinced unprecedented solidarity among trades societies, are justly remembered. Both were trials of strength against newly formed employers' associations which began by trying to smash the unions but ended by recognizing that the more profitable way lay in accommodation rather than confrontation. It was not that unions accepted an identity of interest between themselves and their employers. Most of the leaders who gave solid support to a Liberal party committed to *laissez-faire* nevertheless appreciated that the interests of capital and labour were divergent. By the 1860s, however, the resolution of such conflicts was more frequently the task of arbitrators than of strikers or lockers-out. While profits seemed secure and unions were the preserve of skilled workers the arrangement suited both sides.

---

1. J. L. and B. Hammond, *The Skilled Labourer* (1979 edn), pp. 234–5.
2. *Speeches of William Huskisson* (3 vols, 1831), ii, pp. 222–3.
3. Report of the Select Committee of the House of Commons on the Combination Laws and The Combination Act, 1825,
4. National Association for the Promotion of Social Science: Report of Committee on Trades' Societies and Strikes (1860), pp. 564–6.

CHAPTER 19

Class consciousness?

I

When they talked of the major divisions in society, eighteenth-century observers tended to talk of the 'lower orders' or the 'middle ranks'. By the mid-nineteenth century these descriptions, though still used, were being replaced by the categorizations 'working classes' and 'middle classes', or, implying still greater precision, 'the working class' and 'the middle class'. Did the changes wrought by industrialism bring about a class system in which the fundamental facet of social organization was its division based on sources of income: rent (aristocracy or upper class), profit (middle class or bourgeoisie) and wages (working class or proletariat)? Further, was mid-nineteenth-century society 'class conscious'? Did it evince that recognition of conflicting interests which binds together the disparate elements of a particular class in struggle against the others?

Karl Marx, who was one of the best read of all commentators on nineteenth-century British society, believed that the basis of the new economic order was profit. As industrial society developed, conflict between its two basic elements – capital (represented by those whose *raison d'être* was profit) and labour (those whose work generated profit for others) – became inevitable. Just as capitalism subsumed an anyway profit-conscious aristocracy so the multifarious distinctions of skill and status within the ranks of labour would be rendered down to produce a working class united against its oppressors. The majority would triumph in struggle and that Marxist nirvana, the classless society, would emerge pure and impregnable from the refining fires.

Marx's predictions proved wildly wrong. Britain did not generate the revolution he confidently predicted and those countries which did in the twentieth century had histories so different from those Marx had said would produce revolution that to call them Marxist at all requires an effort of intellectual elasticity remarkable even by the standards of political propaganda. But this does not necessarily vitiate Marx's social and economic analysis; the best historians frequently make the worst prophets. Industrialism, of course, enormously increased the power of capital. The organization of work in both factory and workshop placed greater emphasis on regular labour (Ch. 14). Workers' freedom to organize their own time was drastically reduced. Whatever the eventual resolution of the standard of living controversy, it cannot be denied that economic changes during the Industrial Revolution widened the gulf between rich and poor. The degree of independence traditionally enjoyed by artisans who owned their own tools and who were contracted to several master-manufacturers had been severely eroded by 1870. Indeed, independent artisans were largely an anachronism by the end of our period.

Industrial and commercial capital was incomparably the greatest economic force, a fact acknowledged by the many wealthy landowners who secured their own positions in the new order either by ancillary industrial and mining interests or by investment in commerce, banking or railways.

The intimate involvement of land with capital, as Marx realized, vitiates a simplified three-class model of society. The British aristocracy had always had close links with capital; the Industrial Revolution both strengthened and diversified them. Stress has been laid on the entrepreneurial activities of the eighteenth-century aristocracy (Ch. 12). In the nineteenth century big landowners – like the Portlands, Bedfords, and Grosvenors in London, the Norfolks in Sheffield, the Calthorpes in Birmingham or the Ramsdens in Huddersfield – were crucial in urban development (294). Landowners' involvement with the reformed banking system in the 1840s and as directors of the joint-stock companies in the 1850s and 1860s further emphasizes the intimate links between land and capital. A critical element in Whig strategy during the Reform Act crisis of 1830–32 (Chs 23–4) was the creation of a propertied alliance of land and industry divorcing the middle ranks from a disastrous confederation with working men. Viewed at least from the perspective of the 1840s, Marx's two-class struggle of capital with labour looks more realistic than any model positing a separate role for the aristocracy. It is worth mentioning that in a political system still controlled by the aristocracy after 1832 the nineteenth century's two outstanding Prime Ministers, Robert Peel and William Gladstone, had impeccably bourgeois origins in cotton and commerce respectively.

II

The entrepreneurial activities of the aristocracy did not protect it from middle-class attacks on rent and hereditary privilege. Told by David Ricardo that capital was the 'fund by whose extent the extent of the productive industry of the country must always be regulated', businessmen and their acolytes could accuse landowners of idle consumption and dissipation of that national wealth which the drive and effort of the entrepreneur had built up (250, *222*). Indeed, once a Parliament dominated by landowners had legislated in its narrow sectional interest by passing the 1815 Corn Law (Ch. 20) a potent alliance of the 'productive classes', manufacturers and workers, could be fashioned against the 'unproductive'. It was the same alliance which Thomas Paine had anticipated in the 1790s when he prophesied the doom of both aristocracy and monarchy. The apposite concessions of 1832 unhinged the alliance, as they were designed to do, and though impressive entrepreneurial pressure could still be assembled to achieve free trade in corn (Ch. 30) the threat was not what it had been. Significantly, the far more radical proposals for free trade in land to break up the territorial security of the great estates received only limited middle-class support and almost none from the captains of industry.

By the 1820s Earl Grey was calling the middle classes 'the real and efficient mass of public opinion without whom the power of the gentry is nothing'; Sir James Graham agreed that the 'seat of public opinion is in the middle ranks of life'

(39, 101). They included not only the industrialists and prosperous merchants but an unbroken chain of propertied opinion stretching down to the vulnerable shopkeeper, dependent for his profit on the fluctuating fortunes of a working-class clientele.

Included by them also was that section of the middle ranks whose income did not derive from profit at all. Besides expanding opportunities for profit, the Industrial Revolution greatly increased the demand for services which professional middle classes existed to provide. It was no accident that lawyers, doctors, apothecaries, civil engineers and architects, to name but a few, formed or refurbished their professional societies early in the nineteenth century. They set qualifications for entry and established standards of professional practice designed both to consolidate their repute and also, most importantly, to regulate the supply of labour to levels which guaranteed an appropriate remuneration for their work. The professional middle classes, in fact, achieved by examination and entry-regulation what the Luddites had failed to preserve by machine-breaking and parliamentary petition. To these skilled occupations, remunerated by refined fees rather than coarse wages, should be added the Civil Servants in local and central government who were much more numerous by the 1840s (Ch. 32). Since they were not profit-makers a superficial case exists for excluding them from the middle classes altogether, though this would be misguided. Some writers and intellectuals, like John Thelwall in the 1790s or James 'Bronterre' O'Brien in the 1830s and 1840s, supported and directed causes espoused by their social inferiors, but the great majority of professional men claimed identity of interest with the industrial and commercial classes. The specialist services they provided were generally dictated by the needs of property, whether landed or commercial. They have been called 'a specialized sector of the ruling class' (255, *23*) and their superior incomes, degree of independence in the organization of their work, respectable status and good education all compel categorization within the middle classes.

III

On a merely descriptive categorization, the observer must be impressed more by the diversity of working-class occupations than by any uniformity deriving from a common status as wage-earners. If, like Engels in his *Condition of the Working Class in England* (1845), we look to the emergence of mass, steam-powered factory production for the origins of class consciousness then we must remind ourselves what a small proportion of Britain's workforce in, say, 1851 was employed in factories (Ch. 14). Income variations were very wide. What cultural links could exist between the skilled ironworker who commanded regular employment at £4 a week in the 1850s and the unskilled, casual migrant who hung around London's dockland at the same time and who has been rescued from utter oblivion only by the extraordinary investigative talents of Henry Mayhew? Mayhew himself drew attention to the different political worlds they inhabited. 'The artisans are almost to a man red-hot politicians. . . . The unskilled labourers are a different class of people. As yet they are as unpolitical as footmen . . . they appear to have no political opinions whatever; or, if they do . . . they rather lead towards the maintenance of "things as they are" than towards the ascendancy of the working people' (251, *266*). The historic links between the older artisan trades, like tailoring or shoemaking, and democratic radicalism have been pointed out (Chs 8 and 18). Yet their lack of identity with the lower orders is hard to gainsay. As one working-class author remarked in 1873:

> Between the artisan and the unskilled labourer a gulf is fixed. While the former resents the spirit in which he believes the followers of genteel occupations look down upon him, he in turn looks down upon the labourer. The artisan creed with regard to the labourer is, that they are an inferior class, and that they should be made to know, and kept in their place.[1]

This is not the language of class.

Some historians have argued that the 'labour aristocracy', whose aspirations to respectability are carefully fostered by a crafty ruling class, falsified Marx's prediction of revolution by failing to act as tutors to the rest of the working classes and as leaders in the struggle. In fact, even as late as 1870, the artisans remained among the most radical of all working men and saw no conflict between political radicalism and an espousal of allegedly 'bourgeois' values like hard work and self-discipline. Why should they? These attributes were no alien concepts cynically grafted on to superior working men by the bourgeoisie; they were part of a distinctive artisan culture developed within craft traditions dating from the eighteenth century and earlier. This culture had distinctive, idiomatic forms of expression. Besides, was there a proletariat to lead? British working people were variously workshop or factory based and separated by huge discrepancies of income; they lived in very different kinds of community and treasured precise gradations of status. The agricultural labour force was still very significant [E.vii]. Industrialization by the 1860s had fully transformed only the textile industry. Against this a common source of income – wages – was inadequate to sustain the colossal weights of class identity and cultural uniformity.

The social structure of nineteenth-century British cities also varied tremendously. In the great factory towns of Lancashire and Yorkshire segregation was marked. Faucher noted a marked 'absence of the higher classes' in central Manchester in 1844. 'The town . . . is only inhabited by shopkeepers and operatives; the merchants and manufacturers have detached villas situated in the midst of gardens and parks in the country' (250, *173*). By the 1850s the rapidly developing railway passenger network [D.iv.1, 2] was accelerating the process of residential segregation by suburb (300). The resulting lack of leadership to civilize ignorant, squalid and potentially brutal working people was a preoccupying concern of Victorian social commentators. One observer noted in 1856 that the main working-class area of Leeds, south of the River Aire 'is deprived of all those civilizing influences and mutually respectful feelings which are exercised when rich and poor – employer and employed – know more of each other than they possibly can under present arrangements'. Doubtless those 'mutually respectful feelings' were dwindling even in the metal towns of Birmingham and Sheffield which were only beginning to succumb to factories by the end of our period. Here, though, and still more in the county towns, social segregation was much less marked. Its effects, in fact, tended to emphasize status rather than class divisions and indicated distinctions far more subtle and culturally diverse than the separation of bourgeoisie from proletariat. In a specialist cotton-weaving town like Blackburn, accommodation of rented property reflected relatively small differences of earning power within the working community. Weavers married weavers' daughters rather than the daughters of unskilled labourers. In the South London suburbs of Deptford and Greenwich skilled workers also married overwhelmingly into similarly skilled families. Less than a quarter of labourers' sons married skilled workers' daughters in 1851–53. Similar segregation applied to housing. As late as 1887 41 per cent of ordinary labourers occupied a single room as against only 14 per cent of shipwrights. A hierarchy among the skilled may also be discerned with shipwrights, carpenters and engineers enjoying better housing than tailors and shoemakers (304, *110–11*). Residential segregation was clear; skilled men rarely lived in the same street as dock labourers (310, 342, 345).

IV

Working men were generally more aware of gradations of status than they were of their solidarity as a class necessarily and incontrovertibly alienated from the owners of capital. Religion and perceptions of 'respectability' were yet further differentiating factors. Marx himself pointed to what he called 'two hostile camps, the English proletarians and the Irish proletarians. The ordinary English worker hates the Irish worker as a competitor who lowers his standards of life' (205, *213*). Certainly, English workers were encouraged by a wide variety of social commentators to think of Irish Catholics as an inferior species of humanity – living in the worst conditions, filthy, frequently drunk, ignorant, priest-ridden and superstitious. Convenient racial and religious stereotypes abounded and certainly impeded the development of shared culture and values.

Those workers in more or less permanent employment were also prone to emphasize their superiority of status and expectation against casual workers. Those in regular employment by the 1850s could put aside some savings and thus develop a 'respectable' lifestyle in contrast to those living a more hand-to-mouth existence. This contrast between 'respectable' and 'rough' culture in Victorian Britain was sharp – the latter associated by the respectable with debt, drink and debauchery. The prevalence of petty crime and the lack of education and political awareness served to accentuate cultural divisions. As with artisans, it is important to emphasize that respectable working families were not so much aping 'middle-class' lifestyles as developing their own rational strategies first for survival and then improvement. Marx attempts to sustain a coherent working-class, even in the face of these massive social and cultural distinctions, by postulating a working 'class in itself' which experiences alienation and deprivation but has not been educated to the active class antagonism experienced by the 'class for itself'. This is very difficult to demonstrate empirically.

Perhaps all attempts to discern class consciousness passively 'like a patient etherized upon a table' are doomed to failure. In the view of still the most influential historian of class formation, the late E. P. Thompson, 'Class is not this or that interest, but the friction of interests. . . . Class is a social and cultural transformation (often forming institutional expression) which cannot be defined abstractly, but only in terms of relationship with other classes. . . . Class itself is not a thing, it is a happening.'[2] Class formation has been seen in such variegated movements, from the 1790s on, as artisan radicalism, trade unionism, strikes, Luddism, political reform agitation, Owenism, co-operation, the Anti-Corn Law League and Chartism. Some historians, like Thompson, treated what they saw as the steady emergence of class consciousness over a couple of generations (251). One has nailed his colours to the mast in brave isolation: 'It was between 1815 and 1820 that the working class was born' (250). A plausible case can be made for delaying the birth until after the frustrations of 1832. But all views of a middle class and a working class in being and with recognition of antagonistic interest by 1850 face formidable obstacles.

If class identity rests on a 'friction of interests' which unites the diverse interests within that class then the degree of class antagonism which can be identified seems to have a dangerously narrow geographical base and a short time span. Large units of production seem to generate the most overt hostility. The riot for industrial and political reform led by the miners and puddlers in the Welsh iron town of Merthyr Tydfil in June 1831 against the might of the iron magnates, the Guests and the Crawshays, has been seen by its historian as an 'achievement of *working-class* identity, however momentary' (105, *225*). An evidently well-educated Lancashire cotton-spinner talked as early as 1818 of 'two distinct classes of persons': workers and employers. The latter 'with scarcely a second idea in their heads' were 'literally petty monarchy. . . . I know it to be a fact, that the greater part of the master spinners are anxious to keep wages low for the purpose of keeping the spinners indigent and spiritless . . . as for the purpose of taking the surplus to their own pockets' (251, *218–19*). A year later a Manchester newspaper commented: 'Here there seems no sympathy between the upper and lower classes of society, there is no mutual confidence, no bond of attachment.' One study of Oldham has fitted events in that Lancashire cotton town into a Leninist interpretation of revolutionary class consciousness with skilled men forming the necessary 'vanguard' in a concerted attempt to force a maximum eight-hour working day by strike action in 1834.[3]

Even in the heart of industrial Lancashire, however, many small industrial villages survived into the 1840s and here, though political radicalism was a pronounced feature, far less antagonism was manifested between master and man. And, as the spinner quoted above knew, antagonism was localized: 'there is a greater distance observed between the master there and the spinner, than there is between the first merchant in London and his lowest servant or lowest artisan'. He might also have added that a clear hierarchy of labour was emerging even within the cotton factories with mule-spinners maintaining a distinct 'aristocratic' position.

It is also legitimate to ask how deep class consciousness ran if it manifested itself so fitfully even during such periods of deep political disturbance as were common between 1815 and 1850. The Oldham study finds evidence of class consciousness in action only in 1834 and during the worst year of Chartist agitation, 1842. After this Oldham's 'revolutionary vanguard' was 'liberalized' by middle-class stratagem which divorced working-class leadership from its natural constituency. By 1850 revolutionary consciousness had dissipated and, it might be added, the interpretation has moved from the merely unconvincing to the downright mechanistically fanciful: an extreme example of the attempt to fit evidence into a pre-ordained theoretical framework.

In the disturbed years after 1815 industrial unrest was largely organized by and in the interests of the skilled minority which manipulated labour scarcity to its advantage (Ch. 18). Political agitation, though frequently great in extent as in 1819, 1831 or 1842, was directly linked with high unemployment and low wages. The economic recovery after 1842 emasculated Chartism (Ch. 29) and more than one radical leader had cause to remember William Cobbett's dictum that it was difficult to agitate a fellow with a full stomach.

Before 1832 the evidence for collaboration between middle and working classes against 'Old Corruption', represented by aristocratic government and the patronage system, is far greater than for hostility between employer and workman. Radical protest, schooled by Thomas Paine, remained anti-aristocratic rather than class conscious (Chs 20 and 24). Even after the 'middle-class betrayal' of 1832 one is impressed more by the sectional vitality of institutions organized by working men than by any integrated consciousness of deprivation or alienation. After 1842, even Chartism, much the most impressive expression of the political values of working people, shattered into contradictory and feuding fragments, indicative of the extent to which economic and social interests within the working classes continued to diverge.

None of this, of course, prevented writers addressing their readers as if class formation was an accomplished fact. Radical newspapers developed Thomas Hodgskin's argument of 1825 that 'the whole produce of labour ought to belong to the labourer'. *The Voice of the West Riding* in 1833 urged 'the Rights of Labour against the "Competitives"' (250, *236*). George Julian Harney implausibly addressed his *Democratic Review* (1849–50) to 'Brother Proletarians. . . . To the proclaiming of your wrongs . . . the assertion of your rights, the advocacy of your interests, and the advancement of your welfare.' Nothing daunted by all evidence to the contrary he asserted in 1851 (of all years): 'A War of Classes is going on in this country, a war which is daily extending, and which threatens to, ere long, produce the most important results.'[4]

Too much should not be made of all of this haranguing. Both among the skilled and the unskilled, status consciousness was far better developed than class consciousness. In so far as it existed at all, class antagonism – as opposed to democratic political protest or militancy in the furtherance of industrial aims – was localized and short term. The heterogeneity of Britain's industrial base worked against the transmission of shared feelings of deprivation or exploitation despite the best endeavours of bourgeois intellectuals to conceptualize economic development in terms of inevitable class struggle. The ability of British workers to skirt round seductive theoretical pits of categorization dug for them by others is well known. Class consciousness was a transparent veil which could be thrown over, but could not conceal, the immense variety of working organizations and experiences in nineteenth-century Britain. Class is too crude and too misleading a concept to encompass them.

---

1. E. Hopkins, *A Social History of the English Working Classes* (1979), p. 197.
2. E. P. Thompson, 'The peculiarities of the English', *Socialist Register* (1965), pp. 311–62.
3. J. O. Foster, *Class Struggle in the Industrial Revolution* (1974).
4. *The Democratic Review*, i (June 1849); *The Friend of the People*, 11 Jan 1851.

PART THREE

The crucible of reform, 1815-1846

FRAMEWORK OF EVENTS, 1816–1846

1816   Trade depression and widespread unemployment. Provincial reforming Hampden Clubs formed. Riot at Spa Fields when crowd gathers to hear reform speeches. Gvt's attempt to retain income tax in peacetime defeated by backbenchers. Cobbett's *Political Register* reduced in price to attract wide readership. Walter Scott, *Old Mortality* published.

1817   Radical activities: March of the Blanketeers to press for parliamentary reform; Pentrich rising in Derbyshire. Habeas Corpus suspended; Act banning seditious meetings passed. Bank of England begins to resume cash payments (suspended since 1797). *The Scotsman* and *Blackwood's Magazine*. Wooler's *Black Dwarf* (radical journal) founded. Ricardo, *Principles of Political Economy and Taxation* published; Byron, *Manfred*. Select Committee set up to consider high cost of relieving the poor.

1818   General Election leaves Tories still well ahead of Whigs in committed supporters. Congress of Aix-la-Chapelle includes France in concert of European powers. Habeas Corpus reimposed. Byron, *Don Juan*; Keats *Endymion*; Mary Shelley, *Frankenstein*. Invention of miners' safety lamp by Humphry Davy.

1819   Stamford Raffles takes Singapore; Peel's Act to resume bank cash payments passed; Peterloo 'Massacre' (Aug) when yeomanry charge pro-reform crowd in Manchester; gvt. passes 'Six Acts' to suppress radicalism (Dec). Thomas Telford begins to build Menai suspension bridge linking N. Wales to Anglesey. Keats, *Hyperion* written. Victoria (later Queen) and Albert (later Prince Consort) both born.

1820   Death of George III (Jan); George IV succeeds; contingent General Election leaves the Liverpool government in firm control. Cato St Conspiracy to murder Cabinet uncovered; leaders executed. Gvt introduces bill to permit George IV to divorce Queen Caroline and deprive her of her titles. Malthus, *Principles of Political Economy*; Shelley, *Prometheus Unbound*. Keats, *Ode to a Nightingale*. *John Bull* founded. First iron steamship launched.

1821   Queen Caroline not divorced and granted large parliamentary annuity (Jan); not permitted to attend George IV's coronation, causing disturbances in London (July); dies (Aug). Resumption of bank cash payments completed; reductions on some timber duties presage general lowering of tariffs. James Mill, *Elements of Political Economy* published; Constable, *The Hay Wain*; *Manchester Guardian* first published.

1822   Castlereagh commits suicide; Canning becomes Foreign Secretary; 1815 Corn Law slightly amended. *Sunday Times* founded. Congress of Verona shows rifts in European alliance system.

1823   Irish Catholic Association established by O'Connell; Act for prison reform. Reduction of protective duties by Robinson and Huskisson. Charles Macintosh invents waterproof garment. Traditional origin of Rugby football by William Webb Ellis. Lamb, *Essays of Elia*.

1824   Canning recognizes independence of Buenos Aires, Mexico and Colombia. Combination Acts against trade unions repealed. Byron dies at Missolonghi helping Greek independence struggle against Turkey. Benthamite radical *Westminster Review* founded. National Gallery founded. Royal Society for Prevention of Cruelty to Animals established.

1825   Repeal of Combination Acts amended somewhat after rash of union strikes. Catholic Relief bill fails in the House of Lords. Stockton and Darlington Railway opened. John Nash begins extensive rebuilding of Buckingham Palace.

1826   General Election preserves Tory position; Catholic issue important. Canning sends troops to the Tagus to aid Portugal against threat from Spain. Singapore, Melaka and Penang formally incorporated into a British colony as the Straits Settlements. London Zoological Society founded by Stamford Raffles. Telford's Menai suspension bridge, Anglesey.

1827   Liverpool suffers stroke and resigns (Feb); Canning succeeds; Canning dies (Aug); succeeded by Goderich. Russia, Britain and France agree to preserve the autonomy of Greece. Reforms of the criminal law by Peel; reduction in number of capital offences; redefinition of law of property. Brougham founds Society for the Diffusion of Useful Knowledge.

1828   Goderich resigns (Jan); succeeded by Wellington. Repeal of Test and Corporation Acts gives religious liberty to dissenters but gravely splits Tory party. O'Connell, as a Catholic, wins County Clare by-election, but law does not permit him to take his seat. Revision of Corn Law sees sliding scale of duties introduced. Thomas Arnold, reforming headmaster, appointed to Rugby school.

1829   Roman Catholic emancipation granted; splits Tories further. Peel creates new London police force. Grand General Union of Cotton Spinners holds first national conference. Stephenson's *Rocket* wins Liverpool and Manchester Railway competition. First Oxford and Cambridge boat race.

1830   France, Russia and Great Britain guarantee Greek independence (Feb). George IV dies; succeeded by William IV; at consequent General Election electorate's pro-reform sympathies detectable (June–Aug). Riots of agricultural labourers begin in south of England (Aug). Huskisson killed by train at formal opening of Liverpool and Manchester Railway (Sept). Wellington resigns as Prime Minister (Nov); succeeded by Grey's Whig administration. William Cobbett, *Rural Rides*; Charles Lyell, *Principles of Geology*.

1831   London protocols for separation of Belgium as independent nation from Holland (Jan). Russell introduces first Reform bill; after defeats gvt gets dissolution of Parliament and greatly strengthens reform majority in Commons (Mar–May). Second Reform bill passes Commons (Sept); rejected in Lords (Oct), whereupon widespread riots, especially in Bristol and Nottingham. Charles Darwin's voyage on the *Beagle* begins; British Assoc. for the Advancement of Science founded.

1832   Third Reform bill passes Commons (Mar); difficulties persist in Lords and Grey resigns, inaugurating period of constitutional crisis and public disturbance (Days of May); Wellington fails to form gvt; Grey resumes office and Lords agree to passage of first Reform Act (June); Scottish (July) and Irish (Aug) Reform Acts passed. General Election (Dec) produces massive Whig victory. Tennyson, *The Lady of Shalott*.

1833   Slavery abolished in British territories. Britain occupies Falkland Islands. First inspected Factory Act (Aug); first State grant for aid to churches in building schools; East India Company monopoly of China trade ended. John Keble, *National Apostasy Considered*; first Oxford movement *Tracts for the Times* published; marriages may be celebrated in nonconformist chapels.

1834   Grey resigns as Prime Minister; succeeded by Melbourne (July); Melbourne resigns (Nov); Peel forms a minority gvt and issues the Tamworth election manifesto to rally Tory cause (Dec). Grand National Consolidated Trades Union formed to co-ordinate labour activity, but quickly collapses; Dorset agricultural labourers transported for taking illegal oath to join a Union. Poor Law Amendment Act introduces new administrative structure for relief of poverty. Houses of Parliament destroyed by fire (Oct). Hansom cabs first appear in London.

1835   Whig–Radical–Irish agreement (Lichfield House Compact) to defeat Peel (Mar); Peel, though Tories make some gains at General Election, resigns when defeated on Irish Church issue (Apr); Melbourne resumes as Prime Minister. Municipal Corporations Act (Sept) starting-point for much local gvt reform in the urban areas.

1836   Ecclesiastical Commissioners of the Church of England inaugurate series of administrative and financial reforms; Tithe Commutation Act ends practice of tithe payment in kind; London Working Men's Association founded to press to further reform (June). Dickens, *Pickwick Papers* appears.

1837   Civil registration of births, marriages and deaths begins. Death of William IV (June); Queen Victoria succeeds. Tories make more gains at contingent General Election, but Whigs retain majority. Rebellions begin in Canada (Nov). Charles Wheatstone designs electric telegraph.

1838   Durham appointed Governor-in-Chief of Canada. People's Charter with democratic six points published (May). Anti-Corn Law League founded by Manchester business-men (Sept). Irish Poor Law Amendment Act passed. National Gallery, London, opened. Chartist *Northern Star* first published; Dickens, *Nicholas Nickleby*. Public Record Office founded as central gvt archive.

1839   Chartist National Convention opens (Feb); rejection of Chartist petition (July), leads to riots and an attempted rising at Newport (Nov), easily suppressed. Melbourne's gvt resigns (May), but Peel refuses to accept Queen's dispositions over ladies-in-waiting and Melbourne resumes office. Acquisition of Aden. 'Opium' War with China breaks out (July), leading to capture of Hong Kong (Aug). Anglo-Afghan wars. Final agreement of Belgian independence. James Nasmyth designs steam- hammer. Turner painting, *Fighting Temeraire*. Henley Royal Regatta instituted; first Grand National run at Aintree.

1840   Upper and Lower Canada reunited (July); British take over sovereignty of New Zealand. Queen Victoria marries Prince Albert of Saxe-Coburg. Penny post begun in Britain (Jan). Opening of Kew Botanical Gardens; Charles Barry begins rebuilding of Houses of Parliament.

1841   Convention of the Straits guarantees independence of the Turkish Empire and powers further agree to close Dardanelles to all nations' warships (July). Election produces Conservative victory for Peel (July); Melbourne resigns (Aug) and Peel becomes Prime Minister. Newman's *Tract XC* provokes conflict within Church of England. Deep economic distress, especially in cotton areas. Chartism revives. British Pharmaceutical Society founded.

1842   Peel's budget makes important reductions of tariff duty. Second Chartist petition rejected (May); Chartist disturbances in many parts of the country (Aug). Frontier between Canada and USA defined by Webster–Ashburton treaty. End of Opium War, with greater trading opportunities for Britain. Chadwick's *Report on the Sanitary Condition of the Labouring Poor* published. Women and children prevented from working underground in mines. Tennyson, *Morte d'Arthur*.

1843   Growing strength of free-trade case; *Economist* founded to publicize free trade. United Free Church of Scotland formed (May) when Thomas Chalmers leads the Disruption from the Scottish General Assembly. Thomas Carlyle, *Past and Present*; Charles Dickens, *A Christmas Carol*.

1844   Bank Charter Act (July) puts note-issuing functions of Bank of England on modern footing. Factory Act limits hours of work for women and children in textile mills. Royal Commission on Health of Towns. Co-Operative Society founded by Rochdale 'Pioneers' (Dec). Anti-State Church Association founded by Edward Miall. Young Men's Christian Association (YMCA) founded.

1845   Budget abolishes export duties entirely and reduces number of import duties. Increased aid to Catholic seminary at Maynooth (Ireland) alienates many of Peel's supporters; Gladstone resigns from gvt (Jan) but returns (Dec). Beginnings of Corn Law repeal political crisis; Peel attempts to let Russell and the Whigs carry the measure, but Whigs cannot form administration. Beginning of Irish potato famine. Disraeli, *Sybil*.

1846   Peel passes Corn Law repeal (critical Commons debate Feb); Tory party split and Peel resigns (June) when defeated on Irish coercion bill; Russell succeeds as Prime Minister of Whig gvt. 'Peelites' act as separate parliamentary group. Introduction of British standard gauge greatly facilitates railway network expansion. Establishment of a pupil-teacher training scheme expands State involvement in education. Liverpool Sanitary Act passed – a landmark in local sanitary and public health provision, involving appointment of town medical officer of health.

CHAPTER 20

Unprepared for peace: Distress and the resurgence of reform, 1815–1820

I

After Wellington defeated Napoleon in June 1815 in 'the nearest run thing you ever saw in your life' France capitulated with unexpected swiftness. Ministers in Britain had been digging in for yet another long campaign in a war which had seen most of them young men at the beginning. Peace crept up unawares and adjustment to it proved painful.

Even before the war ended Lord Liverpool's government had experienced a taste of what was to come. It had bowed to massive agricultural pressure in March and had passed a new Corn Law whereby no foreign corn be could be sold in Britain until the domestic price reached 80s. (£4) a quarter. The purpose was to protect landowners and farmers against falling prices (Ch. 15). Though Liverpool and his Vice-President of the Board of Trade, Frederick Robinson, argued – not unreasonably – that protection would guarantee continued domestic production, leaving consumers less at the mercy of fickle foreign suppliers (65) their justifications cut little ice either with working men or manufacturers. They saw a landowners' Parliament interfering with a free market in their narrow interest – and setting the operative price at near-famine levels too – while, increasingly, a free market was imposed on others (Ch. 5). The Corn Law was perceived as class legislation and it taught radical politicians a lesson which they would din into receptive ears at least until 1846. London crowds both petitioned and demonstrated against the new law. Politicians' windows were broken, including Robinson's; houses were ransacked and Nicholas Vansittart, Chancellor of the Exchequer, was burned in effigy. The government needed five regiments of cavalry and one of infantry to quell the disturbances (293).

Worse was to follow. In 1816 Britain reeled under the triple blows of a stunted harvest, trade depression and a glutted labour market. As wheat prices rose to 100s. (£5) a quarter at the end of a freak year throughout Europe both for absence of sun and abundance of rain, so many of Britain's biggest works were at a stand. The massive iron manufactures of Shropshire, South Wales and East-central Scotland no longer throbbed to meet the previously insatiable demand for armaments. Declining demand for iron necessarily meant diminished demand for coal. Shipyards in London and elsewhere were starved of work as European markets already grotesquely disrupted by the Continental System (Ch. 10) took time to readjust to peacetime conditions. Onto an unstable labour market was rapidly disgorged a demobilized army of some 300,000 soldiers and sailors. A goodly number failed to find civilian work and returned to their home parishes to push poor-rate expenditure to unprecedented levels [D.vii.1]. Those who found work forced down wages in a now sated labour market. Immigration from Ireland into Lancashire and west-central Scotland further exacerbated the dangerous imbalance in demand for labour in the textile districts. In slumps of 1816–17 and 1819, widespread unemployment and fierce downward pressure on wages among previously 'elite' employees such as handloom weavers contributed to the radicalization of Britain's major industrial areas (68, *14-18*, 275, *54-5*). England's population increased by 18 per cent between 1811 and 1821 [E.i] and the new dependants' mouths were not easily fed.

The government anticipated much of the dislocation peace would bring. Liverpool discussed the situation impotently with his colleagues and Vansittart promoted a pallid Poor Employment Act in 1817 which offered government loans for public works schemes to alleviate unemployment. It achieved little. The Tory *Quarterly Review* in 1816 was stimulated to unusually apposite metaphor:

> The whole annual war expenditure . . . of not less than forty millions was at once withdrawn from circulation. . . . A vacuum was inevitably produced by this sudden diminution, and the general dislocation which ensured may not unaptly be compared to the settling of the ice upon a wide sheet of water: explosions are made and convulsions are seen on all sides. (62, *95*)

The situation was tailor-made for radical resurgence and the radicals were not unprepared. Their frustrating apprenticeship in the 1790s served (Ch. 8), leaders were now schooled in techniques of extra-parliamentary pressure. The crises of 1811–12 (Chs 10 and 18) had important political dimensions which served as hors-d'oeuvre for the meaty main course of the attack on 'Old Corruption' between 1815 and 1820. In these years, the government faced nationwide disaffection as never before.

II

Radical agitation took many forms. It encompassed mass meetings both in artisan and factory towns; petitions for parliamentary reform, relief from distress and for lower taxation; the re-emergence of political clubs; the development of an aggressive, reformist Press; and a few attempts at *coup d'état*. Yet the movement lacked coherent leadership. Too many of its orators were too captivated by the sound of their own overworked voices; not enough bridged the gap between rhetoric and practicality. A few of the national leaders, experienced in how to stay just on the right side of the law or, if on the wrong, how to avoid the more serious charges, inadvertently led provincial followers to acts of daring which ended on the gallows. Above all, the movement never came to terms with the ultimate dilemma which thwarted all radicals between 1789 and 1850. Were they to convert by argument and the pressure of disciplined numbers or should they storm the citadels of privilege by force?

The dormant spirit of reform was roused by Major John Cartwright, brother of the inventor of the power-loom (Ch. 13) and veteran radical leader, whose career stretched back as far as the 1760s. In 1812, and at the age of seventy-two, he embarked on the first of three tours of the Midlands and North most affected by economic distress and by Luddism, which he abominated as self-defeating. His message was of class collaboration and wider politicial rights and a household suffrage. His promptings led directly from 1816 onwards to the establishment of several Hampden Clubs (named after the doughty antagonist of Charles I's personal rule). These provincial clubs, unlike the London gentry and aristocratic debating society from which they took their name, were plebeian in composition and thoroughly democratic in temper. They were particularly numerous in the weaving villages of South Lancashire. One, the Middleton Hampden Club, is credited with directing the societies firmly towards manhood suffrage rather than the household or taxpayer franchises favoured by many middle-class reformers (41). For the first time the northern manufacturing districts were setting the pace with skilled outworkers, badly hit by the trade slump, in the van. The Political Union societies which replaced the Hampden Clubs during the agitation of 1818–19 were well-organized bodies of northern workmen which wished not only to secure the vote but also to educate their members to be worthy of it. Many worked on the disciplined model of the Methodist class meeting and some of their leaders were ministers and local preachers. They helped to organize more than 2,000 petitions for parliamentary reform in 1817 and 1818 alone.

What turned out to be the symbolic climax of the peaceful assembly method of protest occurred in Manchester in August 1819. The mass meeting at St Peter's fields was the fourth organized in large cities that summer, coming after expressions of popular feeling for parliamentary reform in Birmingham, Leeds and London. About 60,000 people, including many women and children, attended the Manchester meeting. The arrest of the main speaker, Orator Hunt, and the forcible dispersal of the assembly by the sabres of the local yeomanry at the instigation of the Tory magistracy was a panic reaction. In Manchester at least, property, in the guise of the manufacturers and shopkeepers who comprised the yeomanry, was prepared to meet the challenge of numbers with force. In dubbing the event 'Peterloo' in sardonic emulation of Waterloo, radical writers successfully evoked the image of a war against repressive, corrupt authority. The government, though much irritated by what it judged the over-reaction of the authorities, closed ranks. The Prince Regent thanked the magistrates and one of the clerical magistrates involved, the Revd W. R. Hay, was rapidly promoted to the rich rectory of Rochdale. The Whig Lord-Lieutenant of the West Riding, Earl Fitzwilliam, was dismissed for calling a county meeting to express disapproval of the action of the Manchester magistrates in forcibly dispersing a lawful assembly. The eleven 'martyrs' of Peterloo raised the political temperature several notches and became a potent symbol of sacrifice in the years to come (263).

In London the radical leadership was divided both as to aims and tactics. Its forte remained the monster political rally, but some of these were now taking on sinister undertones. At the second of three huge meetings held at Spa Fields, Islington, in November and December 1816 to hear reform speeches by the Wiltshire farmer Henry (Orator) Hunt, a leader of an extreme group enticed a small group to loot gunsmiths' shops on their way to attack the Tower of London. The attempt was easily repulsed but it indicated the presence of a revolutionary cadre in the capital. Its ideas derived largely from the writings of a bookseller, Thomas Spence, who had died in 1814 and who advocated common ownership of land. Two of these Spencean Philanthropists, James Watson and Arthur Thistlewood, were acquitted of high treason in 1817, a charge brought as a result of the attack on the Tower. The acquittal owed much to the discrediting of a spy's evidence in court and Thistlewood continued to muse on revolution, whether in prison during the government's periodic trawls of suspected persons, or out of it. He enlisted the support of some London shoemakers and silk weavers in a plan to blow up the entire Cabinet as it sat to dinner in February 1820, at the home of the Lord President of the Council. This 'Cato Street Conspiracy', however, had already been divulged to the authorities by the *agent provocateur* George Edwards. Ironically, this botched job may have worked to the government's advantage. As Thistlewood and four co-conspirators were hanged at Newgate (five others were transported for life) Liverpool could make capital out of it during an unwanted election campaign for which, since it was occasioned only by the sudden if much delayed death of George III, the government was less well prepared than it had been for Arthur Thistlewood.

We may poke fun at failed conspirators. They may be branded extreme desperadoes, their attempts pre-ordained to fail. A few loonies with access to dynamite, moreover, can be guaranteed to brighten the pages of history. But the desperate men of 1815–20 who rejected the long road of persuasion and petition must not be type-cast as comic relief to set readers up for the sterner passages of a long book. The petitioners and the purchasers of radical newspapers, of course, were far more numerous, but it would be unwise to deny that a revolutionary underground existed in Britain. Within six weeks of Thistlewood's conspiracy, Glasgow weavers had been defeated by troops at the 'Battle' of Bonnymuir; West Riding woollen croppers from the villages around Huddersfield had seized arms and tried to take the town; an armed crowd assembled on moorland near Barnsley; an attack on the Attercliffe Barracks in Sheffield was planned.

Close parallels also exist with the actions of handworkers in Lancashire, Yorkshire and the East Midlands in March–June 1817. The handloom weavers' projected march from Manchester to London to present a reform petition implied the use of force. The 'Blanketeers' (so called because of the blankets they carried to warm them on the anticipated long journey) hoped to turn their march into a triumphal procession, gaining adherents as they went to arrive in London in irresistible strength. In the event, very few got further south than Stockport and a brisk encounter with local yeomanry. Concerted action, however, continued in the spring of 1817 in South and West Yorkshire, Derbyshire and Nottinghamshire. Plans for a rising were passed on to the government agent, W. J. Richards, better known as Oliver the Spy. Oliver's disclosures to the authorities enabled potential trouble-makers to be taken out of harm's way. The only men to rise in June 1817 were some 300 stockingers and ironworkers from Pentrich, Ripley and Alfreton in north-east Derbyshire. Their apprehension was an easy matter and the Pentrich Rising's leader, Jeremiah Brandreth, was executed along with two of his adjutants.

These incidents in 1817 and 1820 were accompanied by frustratingly incomplete or uncorroborated allegations of plans for national rebellion. Even if they shook down to action by textile outworkers and a few others in skilled but depressed trades, they should not be taken lightly. Both the Home Office and local magistrates felt the need to employ bevies of informers who penetrated supposedly secret radical committees with ease. The revolutionaries were both credulous and naive, but the authorities' ability to nip trouble in the bud does not mean that the bud was a figment of their imagination. Sidmouth and his henchmen were right to be alert. As Wellington informed his Cabinet colleagues in 1819, a reduced and scattered army now of only 65,000 home-based men could not effectively interpose itself against a concentrated rebellious outbreak. Liverpool's government knew that a majority of the population did not have to favour rebellion for the potential for revolution to exist. If the behaviour of crowds at the public executions of radicals is any guide, those who would not join a rebellion themselves were furious that the extreme rigour of the law should be exercised on those who shared a common deprivation but who reacted more forcefully. In May 1820 a few months before a trade revival kicked away the main prop of radical support, Robert Peel, no friend to political reform, expressed his famous view that 'the tone of England . . . is more liberal . . . than the policy of government' (293, *218*).

Radicalism and political education went hand in hand and in this the Press had a vital role to play. By 1820 the government had far more detractors than sympathizers. One is impressed more by the vigour of their attacks than by any coherence of alternative strategy, but implacable hostility to the status quo was a rallying point. The *Leeds Mercury,* under the editorship of the teetotal nonconformist Edward Baines, appealed to middle-class manufacturers and campaigned against the 1815 Corn Law because it pushed up wages and threatened to deprive manufacturers from the northern mills of their competitive edge in world markets. Baines was hostile to the democratic pretensions of working men and favoured a taxpayer franchise, but his exposure of Oliver the Spy as an *agent provocateur* gravely damaged the government's credibility. It also established overnight the *Mercury's* reputation as the most influential provincial newspaper. The *Sheffield Independent,* founded in 1819, followed a similar radical, free-trade line as would the *Manchester Guardian,* established in 1821 with cotton money under the editorship of John Taylor, a leading opponent of Manchester's Tory magistracy (42).

The circulations of these middle-class journals ranged between 2,000 and 5,000. Against this, the success of papers designed for a working-class readership is most striking. Soon after William Cobbett reduced the price of his weekly *Political Register* from 1s. 0½d. (5p) to 2d. (1p) to broaden its appeal, he was claiming a circulation of 40,000 to 50,000. His 'Address to the journeymen and labourers' in the refurbished first issue of 1816 set the tone in its attack on a government which overtaxed its citizens to provide for a vast army of pensioners, placemen and parasites. The Lancashire radical Samuel Bamford testified to Cobbett's immense influence. His *Register,* he opined with pardonable exaggeration, was 'read on nearly every cottage hearth in the manufacturing districts of South Lancashire, in those of Leicester, Derby and Nottingham; also in many of the Scottish manufacturing towns'. Cobbett 'directed his readers to the true cause of their sufferings – misgovernment'.[1]

Cobbett's journalistic talent is as undeniable as his self-conceit. This self-taught ex-farm labourer from Surrey spoke with passion and authority both about rural conditions and about the arrogance of government. But his knowledge of the industrial areas was not extensive and his prescription was, strictly speaking, reactionary since it looked back to the establishment of a self-governing free peasantry, Cobbett's influence is undeniable, but it could be argued it deflected attention from adequate economic analysis of the poverty which, he rightly asserted, was the only engine of mass agitation. Cobbett was not alone in his championing of the cause of the lower orders. Thomas Wooler's *Black Dwarf* (1817–24) had a cutting satirical edge. William Sherwin's *Weekly Political Register* (1817–19) was widely read among London artisans. When it ceased publication its assets were taken over by Richard Carlile, perhaps the most impressive inheritor of the Painite radical tradition. His *Republican* (1819–25) was published from Dorchester gaol since his republication of Paine's agnostic tract *Age of Reason* led to conviction on charges of blasphemy brought by the Society for the Suppression of Vice. The cartoonists also made a pungent contribution. George Cruikshank was a worthy successor to Hogarth, Gillray and Rowlandson; his characterizations of sharp lawyers, bloated parsons and corrupt ministers hit home as only the best visual messages can. The illustrated *Political House that Jack Built,* published by William Hone in 1819, caricatured the entire system. 'These are the people all tatter'd and torn; who curse the day wherein they were born; On account of Taxation too great to be borne.' Visual representations, perhaps even more effectively than written ones, emphasized what was now the established radical line that the distress of the people was caused by corruption in high places and by the misgovernment of a largely unelected elite.

The Prince Regent had never been far from satirical ridicule and in 1820–21, as George IV, he became its central butt during his unsuccessful attempt to divorce Queen Caroline and his successful attempt to prevent her from attending his coronation. As Lord Colchester was informed, the Queen's cause served 'as a rallying point for the disaffected and Radicals'[2] such was the new King's enormous unpopularity. Support for a queen who was profligate, unattractive, lazy and vulgar against a king who was merely profligate, unattractive and lazy had its synthetic elements, but when the Queen died suddenly in August 1821, three weeks after her debacle at the coronation, a menacing London crowd forced the military to abandon the original plan and take the funeral cortège through the City on its way to Harwich and thence to her family home in Brunswick. The disturbances produced two fatalities and the event was regarded as a propaganda defeat for a beleaguered government trying to avoid demonstrations hostile not only to the preposterous monarch but to his ministers as well.

III

None of these alarms disturbed Lord Liverpool's parliamentary position. His government possessed a Commons majority usually worth about 100 [B.v] and it discovered that a restatement of the Pitt policy towards radicalism (Ch. 8) would still serve. Ministers' response to the growth of radical protest was entirely appropriate to men whose political apprenticeship had been worked against a background of Jacobin terror and excess in republican France. The establishment of committees of secrecy, followed by the suspension of Habeas Corpus and the granting of extra powers to magistrates for the control of public meetings, therefore, exactly mirrored in 1817 Pitt's response in 1794–95. The Six Acts (or 'Whip with Six Strings'), hurriedly passed in November 1819, concentrated on the use of force and, like Pitt in 1798, on the regulation of newspapers. A punitive stamp duty was placed on all cheap papers in a vain attempt to restrict readership and the law was further tightened against seditious or blasphemous matter. Nevertheless, the government could have gone further and was urged to do so by much of its backbench support from the country gentlemen. The Six Acts did not provoke a witch-hunt. The standing army was not increased; the government, even after Peterloo, still reposed confidence in local magistrates as the appropriate agents for controlling their own areas.

Like Pitt, also, though with rather more difficulty, Liverpool found it possible to forge a propertied alliance against the reformers. In recent years, Liverpool's reputation has been reappraised (57, 68). He certainly does not deserve Disraeli's famously dismissive put-down of 'arch-mediocrity', having considerable strengths both as a man-manager and as a nurturer of political talent. Though fussy, fretful and inclined to be swamped by detail, he inspired trust. He also had a determination to survive difficult early years in office, while in later years his very lack of ostentation encouraged abler colleagues to serve together under him rather than feud among themselves for the succession. The speed with which the Tories fell, first upon one another and then apart, after his resignation in 1827 is strong evidence of Liverpool's effectiveness as chairman of a Cabinet (Ch. 23). Unheroic political leaders frequently survive much longer than more mercurial talents believe they should.

In the early years of his ministry, however, government weaknesses were too often embarrassingly apparent. Peel, Robinson and Huskisson were working their passage in low-profile minor office and their superiors did not shine. Government deficiencies showed up in the Commons. The waspish and unpopular Canning was shunted to conveniently minor office [A]. Vansittart, an intimate of Liverpool, was unequal to the office of Chancellor of the Exchequer. He was judged by one shrewd contemporary 'made to be an actuary to an Insurance Office' (65, *165*). Over Bragge-Bathurst and Wellesley Pole, both of whom owed advancement to powerful relatives, history has drawn a sympathetic veil; it would be too harsh to draw it back and reveal the emptiness of their contributions during nine full years of Cabinet office. The burden of defending unpopular policies devolved on Castlereagh, Leader of the House as well as Foreign Secretary. His pugnacious consistency stopped short of eloquence; it won him few friends and only grudging respect but he was worth many independent votes to Liverpool.

In the Lords, where it mattered less, Liverpool had talent enough. Eldon was very able, Westmorland and Harrowby competent and Sidmouth dutiful and watchful if uninspiring. Wellington's appointment to minor Cabinet office in 1819 added prestige at a difficult time. He symbolized strength, determination and courage as successful soldiers are apt to do, even when politically naive and inept.

Like all political survivors, Liverpool had his full measure of luck. His ministry was buoyed up during its insecure early years by victories against Napoleon for which he could claim little credit. The crises of 1815–20 strengthened his hand in Parliament since it brought the independents into line behind what they saw as a determined administration. In terms of committed supporters, the Whig opposition was only a handful of votes behind Liverpool but this was of little account after 1815. The reform issue showed up the weaknesses of the Whigs. Their commitment to reform was real enough but it stopped a good deal short of manhood suffrage. Additionally, many aristocratic Whigs were deeply unsympathetic to movements which they could not control. Even Grey's ardour for parliamentary reform cooled, while Grenville and his followers were among the few who were actively hostile (Chs 7 and 8). Grenville supported the ministry over the suspension of Habeas Corpus and formal connection between him and Grey ceased thereafter. The Grenvillites voted for the Six Acts in 1819, though they did not formally throw in their lot with Liverpool until 1822 when their leader in the Commons, Charles Williams-Wynn, accepted office under him [A].

The *Edinburgh Review* naturally carried the fight to Liverpool, calling his ministers in 1818 'men of whom their own steadfast supporters are daily ashamed'[3], but the issues on which the Whigs could traditionally unite, like personal liberty, seemed both pallid and open to contrary interpretation in 1815–20. A defeat for the government was engineered in 1816 on another issue dear to Whig hearts, retrenchment and reduced taxation, but the temporary Whig alliance with the country gentlemen to defeat Liverpool's proposal to retain income tax [D.i.3] in peacetime was not sufficient to bring the government down. Like Pitt (Ch. 3), Liverpool rode defeats even on important issues and he was to sustain another in 1820 when the proposed divorce of George IV and Queen Caroline was dropped. Again the Whigs failed to benefit. They were perhaps unlucky that another 'Whig' issue, religious liberty, was temporarily of minor importance. Ireland between 1801 and 1820 was tranquil and yet to feel the force of Daniel O'Connell (Ch. 23).

Many able Whigs, like Romilly, Mackintosh and Brougham, devoted increasing time to important issues like education and law reform which were not so politically controversial. Additionally, two of the most promising Whig leaders pursued a literally self-destructive course. Both Samuel Whitbread and Samuel Romilly, in 1815 and 1818 respectively, took their own lives when they could have offered much to the cause; neither was easily replaced. Even mastery of parliamentary debate proved a two-edged weapon. A Vansittart or a Bragge-Bathurst could easily be demolished but, as the Whig leaders in the Commons George Ponsonby (until his death in 1817) and George Tierney (1818–21) found, the demolition often gained the victim sympathy from uncommitted members who respected honesty, sympathized with stupidity in an honourable cause and deeply suspected the sophistries of clever wordsmiths. Brougham, perhaps the ablest speaker of his day though prone to rash and violent utterance, suffered more than most. The Whigs found him a generally uncomfortable colleague; to Liverpool, he must have seemed almost a secret weapon.

One of Brougham's famous intemperate attacks was against the Prince Regent in 1816 for his 'blind and profligate expenditure'. It is well to remember that the monarch still mattered, though his influence was being steadily reduced. One incidental effect of Liverpool's having to do without the income tax was a continued paring down of royal and governmental patronage, thus leaving the King with fewer cards to play. (Ch. 3). But royal hostility to the Whigs, and particularly to Brougham and (less rationally) Grey, strengthened Liverpool's position. George was never close to the Whigs after Sheridan's influence waned and he would not use his royal prerogative of dismissal to unseat a Tory ministry, having installed one in 1812. It is not coincidental that the Whigs did not take office while he lived.

The disturbances of 1815–20, therefore, strengthened Liverpool politically by weakening MPs' certainty of their privileges in rapidly changing times. The true radicals in the Whig party were a tiny handful and the party's ambivalence on reform lessened its appeal in Westminster without much strengthening it outside. Independent parliamentary opinion remained massively committed to holding the line against 'rash innovation and speculative opinions' and they looked to Liverpool to hold that line for them. Even as late as 1820 only a minority in either party perceived that the line could not be held indefinitely.

---

1. S. Bamford, *Passages in the Life of a Radical* (2 vols, 1893), ii, pp. 11–12.
2. *Diary and Correspondence of Charles Abbot, Lord Colchester* (3 vols, 1861), iii, p. 142.
3. *Edinburgh Review*, lix (1818), p. 198.

CHAPTER 21

Liberal Toryism?

I

Lord Liverpool's long administration has traditionally been divided into two unequal periods: a long 'reactionary' phase, 1812–22, symbolized by Sidmouth and the Six Acts, and a shorter 'liberal' phase, 1822–27, associated with the economic policies and other reforms of Liverpool's 'second-wave' ministers, in particular William Huskisson, Frederick Robinson and Robert Peel. The ministerial reshuffle necessitated by Castlereagh's suicide in 1822 thus becomes the natural fulcrum. In fact, the division is misleading (68, *43–9*). Not only were the second-wave ministers serving lengthy and generally dutiful apprenticeships before 1822 but many of the reforms traditionally associated with them had been presaged by their supposedly reactionary predecessors. If turning-points are sought, 1819 is a better candidate than 1822, but Liverpool's government never experienced anything so cathartic as an ideological conversion. The Prime Minister had always favoured free trade and stated his belief as early as 1812 that 'the less commerce and manufactures were meddled with the more they were likely to prosper'[1]. His close relationship with Huskisson, whose influence before 1823 was belied by his minor office, suggests both Liverpool's long-term commitment to the reduction of tariff barriers and his recognition of the need to reconcile the potentially divergent interests of land and commerce for the good of the nation and to the discomfiture of radical political reformers. Huskisson had the respect of businessmen, and his understanding of the complexities of the new political economy (Ch. 5) was more secure than that of nearly all his colleagues. The reverse of the coin is more simply stated. Liverpool and his ministers were no more in favour of a reform of the franchise in 1827 than they had been in 1819. It should not be assumed that because these years saw important initiatives in the direction of the liberalization of trade they saw an analagous growth in trust of the masses.

The government changes of 1822–23 show Liverpool at his modest best. A series of minor but cumulatively demoralizing defeats in 1821 in a House of Commons preoccupied with the apparently inexorable decline in corn prices convinced the Prime Minister that he needed more authoritative performers in the Lower House. George IV, smarting over his ministers' failure to do his bidding on the Queen Caroline question, seriously considered breaking up the ministry and choosing a new Prime Minister. He even toyed, though very briefly, with the idea of sending for the Whigs. The redeployment of posts was deftly handled by Liverpool. Both Sidmouth and Vansittart retained their places in Cabinet, though in less exposed positions. Robinson, the protégé of Castlereagh, went to the Exchequer not because he had a better claim than Huskisson but because Liverpool recognized that Huskisson's appointment would belittle Vansittart by seeming to suggest a direct substitution of a man who had long served in the Prime Minister's kitchen Cabinet and whose counsels were now openly to be preferred, 'a disgrace to which he could never have submitted', as Canning told Huskisson (65, *167*). Huskisson's natural pique was partly mollified by a promise that the Presidency of the Board of Trade would carry Cabinet rank.

Peel's promotion to the Home Office, eased by Sidmouth's desire for a quieter life as he moved into his later sixties, was on merit. Though still only thirty-four in 1822, the future Prime Minister had already packed in a dozen years of efficient service in Ireland and on the finance question. Canning became Foreign Secretary against royal hostility (56). George, with reason, suspected that Canning had been an early model on the rapidly moving assembly line of his unlamented wife's lovers and anyway resented Canning's coruscating cleverness. Liverpool's entreaties on Canning's behalf in 1821 brought him near to dismissal and he wisely left the intermediary work in 1822 to Wellington who used his military talent for browbeating to convince the King that Castlereagh's loss was reparable in no other way. The restored ministerial team proved as dominant in the Commons as its predecessor had been flaccid. The Whigs, disappointed once again in their hope of office, were cast down. Almost no opportunity to embarrass the government presented itself once corn prices picked up. Grey withdrew from political life and by 1827 Brougham exaggerated only slightly when he asserted that the Whigs 'have ceased to act as a party'. Freed from any threat of defeat, Liverpool's bright young men could afford to squabble. The ministerial team of 1822–27, though much abler than that of 1812–22, was a good deal more fractious. The tribulations which the Tories would endure after Liverpool's death could be clearly foreseen.

II

From 1815 to 1820 or so, Liverpool's government was concerned primarily with retrenchment and only secondarily with reform. In the last year of war, government expenditure exceeded income by 45 per cent and servicing the national debt cost £30m. a year. The country gentlemen's refusal to have any truck with a peacetime income tax (Ch. 20) further embarrassed the government since that tax was realizing about a fifth of its income by 1815 [D.i.1, 3]. Expenditure was reduced by almost 50 per cent within three years, wholly because of the reduction in the armed services. Between 1818 and 1827 the government books more or less balanced, a healthy surplus being denied only by the continuing incubus of debt repayment which now accounted for more than half of public expenditure.

In the immediate post-war period Vansittart fudged the finances by continuing to borrow in the London money markets to pay off old debts. As interest rates rose, the government found itself in the ludicrous position of raising 'dear' money to pay off old and 'cheaper' debts, adding to the stock of national debt in the process. The radical newspapers were not alone in their condemnation of 'tax eaters' 'and 'fund holders' who seemed to hold the nation in thrall. Liverpool's natural constituents, the landowners, were peculiarly disadvantaged by the combination of lower agricultural prices and higher interest rates as they struggled with loan repayments on debt contracted in years easy both for profit and credit. Politically as well as economically, therefore, the case for a revised system of finance became unanswerable.

Prodded by minds sharper than his own, most notably Huskisson's from within the government ranks and the Jewish banker and political economist David Ricardo's from outside, Vansittart in 1819 acquiesced in proposals to resume cash payments, suspended by Pitt in 1797 (Ch. 8). As Liverpool told the Lords in 1819: 'no country in the world has ever established a currency without a fixed standard of value. . . . It might be gold, it might be silver. . . . It might be anything that had real value in it. . . . But it could not be paper, which has no value, and is only the promise of value.' (70, *44*) A select committee on currency recommended gradual resumption of cash payments by 1823, but the transfer was completed ahead of time. In 1821 Britain was effectively on the gold standard.

The resumption of cash payments has been characterized as reluctant recognition by an aristocratic government of the increasing power of commerce and capital. Yet it was roundly condemned by merchants and manufacturers in Birmingham, Manchester and the leading textile towns. They argued that the decision was premature and feared the effects on their markets of the deflation necessary to tie the currency to abstract value. Experience was to prove what happy consequences attended international competitiveness backed by industrial supremacy and a stable currency. In course of time Manchester was to give its name to that 'School' particularly associated with the liberal economics of *laissez-faire* and sound money. In 1819, however, and doubtless shortsightedly, it was the agricultural interest which supported cash payments as a means of emphasizing 'proper' currency and a return to the square dealing they understood. In so far as the paper currency symbolized commercial speculation, industrial development and urban excrescence, backbenchers and their squirearchical constituents wanted to see the back of it, little heeding how much their own wartime prosperity had been enhanced by banknotes more or less freely printed.

The government practised rigid economy after 1815 but, since the great bulk of its income derived from customs and excise [D.i.1], it appreciated that the sound money to which it was now committed could be ensured only by sustained economic growth. Liverpool himself was never more a Pittite than in the realm of economic policy, and he looked back to the 1780s (Ch. 3) for the linked inspirations of trade revival and the liberalization of trade. Like Pitt, also, he eschewed adherence to dogma. His famous speech of May 1820, which has been called the first firm and unequivocal prime ministerial statement on 'the advantages of an unrestricted freedom of trade' (3), was in fact hedged with many caveats as to timing and extent. Tariffs were actually increased, especially on wool, between 1815 and 1822 and the business interest was hardly committed to *laissez-faire*. The London merchants were sceptical; their famous free trade petition in 1820 was little more than a piece of unrepresentative wire-pulling organized by the economist Thomas Tooke and taken up by the government to publicize the sense of rationalizing the plethora of tolls in the interests of administrative efficiency. Certainly no merchants' interest in favour of free trade emerged in these years. Merchants saw matters pragmatically, preferring monopoly in areas they had sewn up (like the East Indiamen and the China trade) and free trade in areas where others had a preponderating influence. Thomas Wallace, who was the administrative originator of the commercial liberalization policy between 1820 and 1823, during his period as Vice-President of the Board of Trade and chairman of the parliamentary select committees on trade, hoped that it would ease manufactures out of depression, create employment and stimulate entrepreneurs to search for new markets overseas. In all essentials the policy was Pitt's and ministers saw it as the long delayed return to the *status quo ante bellum.*

The trade revival was well under way by the time Robinson and Huskisson were promoted. In 1824–25 Robinson's reduction of excise duties on a wide range of consumer goods and raw materials, from iron to hemp, coal to rum and books to porcelain, stimulated consumption and helped to increase manufacturers' competitiveness. Reductions in indirect taxation between 1821 and 1827 were spectacular. Excise income dropped by 30 per cent and the politically dangerous arguments of 1815–20, espoused by landowners, businessmen and radical leaders alike, that the nation was overtaxed and wastefully administered were torpedoed. In the encouragement of overseas trade, Huskisson built on Wallace's foundations. Trade Reciprocity Acts encouraged commercial treaties with other nations on the basis of mutual reductions in tariffs. Foreign shipping was also encouraged by easier access to ports and London developed as the entrepôt of world commerce. The Navigation Laws were also relaxed to permit the colonies freer trade with foreign countries while Anglo- colonial trade was to remain tied to British ships. A policy of cautious imperial preference emerged. Trade should flourish with the support not only of formal colonies but of the newly independent nations, especially of South America (Ch. 22), in a kind of informal empire based on commercial relations. Huskisson's policy was based on a hard-headed assessment of Britain's immense potential superiority over other European nations. As he told the Commons in 1825:

> . . . we furnish, in a proportion far exceeding the supply from any other country, the general markets of the world, with all the leading articles of manufacture, upon which I have now proposed greatly to lower the duties. I own that I am not afraid of this country being overwhelmed with foreign goods. Some, I know, will come in . . . but they will not interfere with those articles of more wide and universal consumption, which our manufacturers supply cheaper and better; whilst they will excite the ingenuity of our artists and workmen, to attempt improvements, which may enable them to enter the lists with the foreigner in those very articles in which he had now an acknowledged superiority.[2]

Despite lower duties and a maximum protective tariff of 30 per cent, trade expansion was such that customs revenue increased by 64 per cent between 1821 and 1827 [D.i.1]; during Pitt's peacetime ministry of 1784–92 the increase had been only 36 per cent.

Britain's recovery withstood a severe banking crisis in 1825 and a short depression in 1826, accompanied by loom-breaking in Lancashire, to which the government responded with more limited public works schemes to alleviate unemployment. The collapse of about 100 London and provincial banks hastened the emergence of a more modern scheme of financial administration. The ban on the formation of joint-stock companies, theoretically illegal since the South Sea Bubble crisis of 1720, was lifted in 1825 and the advent of joint-stock banks from 1826 onwards helped to stabilize the system. Banks in England and Wales, whose indiscriminate issue of paper money was alleged to have precipitated the crisis, were forbidden to print notes under the value of £5. After furious lobbying the supposedly more prudent Scots were exempted from this constraint (71).

A liberal economic policy for merchants and manufacturers threw into still greater relief the degree of protection afforded to the landed interest. During the agricultural crisis of 1821–23, indeed (Ch. 15), backbench Tory MPs. such as Edward Knatchbull, Thomas Gooch and Thomas Lethbridge were harrying ministers in what amounted to a guerrilla campaign to secure still greater favours. Their only reward came in 1822 with a minor modification of the Corn Laws which, because of prevailing price levels, never came into operation. Liverpool was now convinced, as from the experiences of 1815–20 he well might be, that a government which indulged farming producers at the expense of working-class consumers or tax-paying industrialists rested on a dangerously narrow base. Agriculturalists were plainly told that their concerns could not dictate national policy, but the power of the landed interest, though neither monolithic nor particularly well marshalled, could not be attacked frontally. The first important modification of the 1815 Corn Laws did not eventuate until 1828, a year after Liverpool's resignation. Even then, the clumsy sliding scale of duties which tapered to nominal rates when wheat prices reached 73s. (£3.65) smacked of compromise and Cabinet disagreement on how to handle the most sensitive economic issue of all. Nor, since the leaps in duty were particularly steep at certain points on the scale, did it discourage speculation or promote steady supplies as Huskisson had hoped.

III

Economic issues occasioned surprisingly little serious disagreement in an increasingly irascible Cabinet. This was partly because the reforms were presented as a continuation of the Pitt legacy and partly because the economic conservatives lacked the intellectual avoirdupois to challenge Huskisson, Robinson and Peel. Peel's reforms at the Home Office were for the most part uncontroversial. Like so much else in his long career, Peel succeeded by making other people's ideas work rather than by creating them himself. Here the new Home Secretary followed up recommendations from a report of a parliamentary committee of enquiry set up in 1819 under pressure from the Whig reformer James Mackintosh. Few Tories, however, took exception to legislation in 1823 to reduce the number of capital statutes which lingered anachronistically on the statute-book, since they almost certainly hampered proper punishment. Juries were well known to be reluctant to convict guilty men on a large number of relatively minor charges which nevertheless carried the death penalty. Though public executions would not be abolished until 1868, the grotesque, yet famously popular, spectacle of watching felons twitch in agony on the end of a hangman's rope began to lose its attraction.

Peel rationalized the rules governing jury selection in 1825. In 1826–27, determined as he put it to 'end the sleep of a century', he introduced two famous statutes which ended many of the legal caprices which resulted from the use of overlapping legislation. Five consolidating statutes, together covering four-fifths of the most common crimes, replaced ninety-two pieces of legislation against theft and other property offences (99, *17–18*).

Peel's cool, administrative brain can also be discerned behind the first serious attempt to rationalize unregulated, insanitary and not infrequently corrupt prisons. After 1823, local magistrates were to make regular prison inspections and to report to the Home Office. Despite recent widespread evidence of threats to the public order, however, Peel was less successful in countering antipathy to the notion of a centralized police force. The Metropolitan Police Act [C.ii] in 1829 was a belated and partial triumph for Peel, who had failed to carry a similar proposal in 1822. The capital was widely felt to be a special case, more prone to regular disturbance and less amenable to traditional means of control. Most of the backbenchers who acquiesced in the appearance on London's streets of blue-uniformed and truncheoned 'Peelers' would have been mortified had they known that these strange novelties formed the advance guard of a professional police force which would appear throughout the country within thirty years (353) [C.ii].

The fragility of Liverpool's Tory alliance was more searchingly examined by the reappearance in the 1820s of the Catholic question. If the general division of his government into reactionary and liberal phases is misleading it has specific validity in religious matters. The reshuffle of 1822 strengthened the previously weak position of those who wished to grant full political rights to the Catholics both in England and Ireland. The Grenvillites were emancipators as, stridently, was Canning. In the Commons, indeed, only Peel stood out as a leading ministerial 'Protestant', committed to the ascendancy of the Anglican Church in both countries as the first bastion of established Tory values. Peel and even Liverpool contemplated resignation when the radical Whig, Sir Francis Burdett's Catholic relief bill passed the Commons in 1825. The emergence in Ireland of the Catholic Association under Daniel O'Connell in 1823 sharpened the issue and the high Tories in the Cabinet looked to the Prime Minister as their only safeguard against what they saw as a disastrous concession (15). Though the Tory line against parliamentary reform could still be held against occasional Whig forays such as Lord John Russell's in 1822 [B.i.1], the more immediate problem of Catholic reform would not go away. It was clear to most of his Cabinet well before Liverpool's fateful stroke at the beginning of February 1827 that only his experienced, emollient presence preserved the unity of the Tory party. Political economy was a rarefied, intellectual issue; the long period of Tory dominance would be ended rather by the gut political issues of religion and, through religion, political reform.

---

1. W. R. Brock, *Lord Liverpool and Liberal Toryism* (1941), p. 42.
2. Speeches of William Huskisson (3 vols, 1831), ii, pp. 344–6.

CHAPTER 22

Influence without entanglement: Foreign affairs, 1815–1846

I

Britain emerged from the long wars against revolutionary and Napoleonic France both victorious and with a much enhanced influence in Europe. The alliance system fashioned by Castlereagh put Britain on to the centre of the diplomatic stage for the first time at least since 1713. Unlike the Treaty of Utrecht, which had ended the early-eighteenth-century French Wars, moreover, the ambitious Congress System (Ch. 10) depended on Britain's full participation in the settlement of European disputes. Castlereagh spoke of the need 'to inspire the states of Europe . . . with a sense of the dangers which they have surmounted by their union . . . to make them feel that the existing concept is their only perfect security against the revolutionary embers more or less existing in every state of Europe'. Britain would not need to intervene frequently since 'the interposition of Great Britain will always be most authoritative in proportion as it is not compromised by being unduly mixed in the daily concerns of these states' (55, *180*). But it is possible to think of Britain's naval and economic power after 1815 fitting the country for the self-imposed role of the world's policeman.

Castlereagh's foreign policy met with harsh criticism both inside and outside Parliament; even Cabinet ministers were uneasy at Britain's apparent commitment to European diplomacy. Greville moaned that 'we are mixed up in the affairs of the Continent in a manner which we have never been before, and which entails upon us endless negotiations and enormous expenses (54, *200*). Frequent chats with Tsar Alexander and the Austrian Foreign Minister, Prince Metternich, could be construed as fraternizing with autocrats who could do Britain little good. Britain's reputation with emergent nations might be sullied if the country was pulled into irrelevant and expensive entanglements. Since Castlereagh, not a gifted communicator outside his small circle of intimates, disdained explanation it is not surprising that his reputation should have sunk low or that his policies have been widely misinterpreted.

Castlereagh was no blind supporter of European autocracies. Nor was his judgement affected, as critics alleged, by hob-nobbing with royalty in the lavish courts of central Europe. He pursued objectives which hardly differed until the 1870s, whichever Foreign Secretary was in office. Castlereagh, like his successors, sought to keep a peaceful balance between the European nations to prevent any becoming too strong and threatening Britain's dominance in trade and commerce. At the beginning of the nineteenth century, obviously, the main threat was France. After 1815 the peace treaties curbed French expansionist tendencies, though with an established Bourbon monarch still reigning in Spain as well as a restored one in

France she had to be watched. Increasingly, Russia was perceived as the growing menace. Russia could threaten Britain's grain and naval supplies via the Baltic and, in the South, might challenge Britain's interests in the Mediterranean via the Black Sea. From there she could threaten Britain's entire empire of trade in the Middle East and in India. The expansion of Russian influence was rendered the more likely by the apparently imminent collapse of one sprawling multi-lingual empire – the Ottoman – and the less obvious but still worrying weakness of another – the Austro-Hungarian. British policy after 1815 was generally directed to shoring up obstacles to Russian aggrandizement.

Castlereagh differed from most of his critics in believing that peace and balance in Europe could not be achieved without more direct British involvement on the Continent. He argued that the Congress System would give the powers an opportunity to appreciate mutual problems and interests at regular meetings. It strengthened the Quadruple Alliance (F.i.15] and thus the peace of Europe. From the outset, however, Castlereagh's victorious allies took a different view of the post-war world. The Holy Alliance of 1815 between Russia, Austria and Prussia was envisaged by its originator, Tsar Alexander I, as a means of keeping the world safe for autocracy against the emergent forces of liberalism and nationalism. Castlereagh viewed distastefully the prospect of a concert of established powers with counter-revolutionary intent and concentrated on a more limited interpretation of the Quadruple Alliance. Events worked against him. Even though at the Congress of Aix-la-Chapelle [F.i.16] he was able to negate Russian proposals for the Great Powers to guarantee one another's thrones and territories, the admission of France to the general concert of nations only confirmed the impression that a league of the mighty was being fashioned to stifle those libertarian aspirations released throughout Europe by the French Revolution.

Britain's gradual disengagement from Congress diplomacy after 1818 was facilitated by the other powers' reactions to liberal movements in southern Europe. Alexander I urged collective intervention against democratic movements in Spain and Portugal; Metternich argued that unrest in Piedmont and Naples, where Austro-Hungarian dominance was at risk, justified retaliatory action. When the Congress of Troppau not only sanctioned Austrian intervention in Naples but also issued a protocol justifying international interference on the terms of the Quadruple (now Quintuple) Alliance, Castlereagh dissociated Britain from it. His brother, who represented him in Troppau, was lectured that 'the extreme right of interference between nation and nation can never be made a matter of written stipulation or be assumed as the attribute of any alliance'. Castlereagh's famous State Paper of May, 1820 made the same point. The Quadruple Alliance was never intended 'as an Union for the Government of the World, or for the Superintendance of the internal Affairs of other States' (176, *201*).

Before the end of his life, Castlereagh was embarked on diplomacy which owed little to Congress ideas. A messy but determined Greek independence movement erupted in 1821 and, though philhellene sympathy naturally ran high with educated Britons who remembered their indebtedness to Greek civilization, Castlereagh was pragmatic. A Greek independence movement which weakened the Turks in the Balkans was an open invitation to Russian intervention in a sensitive area.

Castlereagh sought the aid of Metternich and Anglo-Austrian diplomacy was directed to persuading the Russians against intervention. Castlereagh was not above the entirely cynical argument back to Alexander that independence movements in the Balkans would not need to spread far to infect the further-flung Russian outposts. Clearly, the European powers were shaking down into their respective spheres of influence and using one another as pieces in an alliance system fashioned to meet rather the exigencies of a particular crisis rather than any grand design. With the collapse of Castlereagh's more ambitious enterprise, the British Foreign Secretary began to slip into depression. A sense of frustration undoubtedly contributed to his mental collapse and then characteristically efficient suicide in 1822.

II

The traditional contrast between Castlereagh's foreign policy and that of his successor, George Canning, is overplayed. It derives in part from the obvious differences of personality between the two men which was strengthened by personal rivalry and mutual antagonism. But it also rests on a misunderstanding of Castlereagh. Though Castlereagh was a conservative with no liking for 'abstract and theoretical speculations', as his support for Sidmouth's repressive legislation in 1819 (Ch. 20) and his low reputation with British radicals alike suggest, he was far more concerned to protect weaker nations from any allied intervention which might disturb the balance of forces to Britain's disadvantage. Possibly, Castlereagh's presence at the Congress of Verona, held two months after his death, might have dissuaded the powers from sanctioning French intervention in Spain and might have persuaded them rather to concentrate on the wider implications of the Greek struggle. Wellington's influence at Verona, whither he had been despatched in Castlereagh's stead, was minimal. Metternich's hostility to Canning during the next few years wrote the final, unhappy chapter in the history of Congress diplomacy, but it is doubtful if even Castlereagh's legendary ability to get on better with European princes than with his own Cabinet colleagues could have kept it more than nominally alive.

Canning's foreign policy followed a logic already apparent to Castlereagh in the last years of his life. The presentation of that policy, however, was vastly different. Canning preferred the wider stage of public declamation in the Commons, to his constituents or, through judicious plants in the Press, particularly the *Star*; he disdained closet consultations. Canning had made an early mark as a journalist (Ch. 8) and he exploited his knowledge of the profession to the full. It was not an approach which endeared him to foreign diplomats. He announced loftily to the Liverpool electorate in 1822 that in the struggle 'between the principles of monarchy and democracy . . . England has only to maintain herself on the basis of her own solid and settled Constitution, firm, unshaken, not a partisan on either side, but, for the sake of both, a model, and ultimately perhaps an umpire'.

His interventions were generally based on calculations of likely success. Thus, he would not risk war to keep France out of Spain in 1822 since British power there could only be limited. However, when John VI of Portugal died in 1826, Canning despatched 4,000 troops to the Tagus in defence of a regency threatened by Franco-Spanish assault. Not only did Portugal remain Britain's oldest ally and best guarantee of influence in South-west Europe; British seapower could be deployed there to powerful effect.

Seapower was also the main support for Canning's famous Latin American policy. Trade between Britain and the Spanish and Portuguese colonies in the New World had grown enormously during the French Wars. From a position of total insignificance twenty years earlier, Latin America was taking about 5 per cent of all British exports in 1815 [D.ii.5]. Both Castlereagh and Canning strove to improve this position in the much more delicate conditions obtaining as the erstwhile Iberian colonies asserted their freedom. Canning, far more than conservative colleagues like Eldon or Sidmouth, saw the immense commercial advantages which would accrue from recognition of the new nations, however much recognition might seem to weaken both monarchy and the old order. By the agreed memorandum of 1823 signed with the French Ambassador, Polignac, Canning extracted *de facto* French recognition of British predominance in Latin America, since the French eschewed military intervention there. Much to George IV's displeasure (the King feigned illness to avoid reading the announcement to the Lords), Buenos Aires, Colombia and Mexico were recognized as independent states in 1824, and Britain helped to negotiate the independence of Brazil from Portugal the following year. Trade between Britain and Latin America doubled between 1815 and 1825 and British primacy was now acknowledged by the powers. As Canning expressed it, without tact to the merchants of Glasgow at least: 'Spanish America is free, and if we do not mismanage our affairs sadly, she is English'. Canning's New World policy also had the considerable benefit of choking off Bourbon aspirations in the West. As he told the Commons in 1826; 'if France had Spain it should not be Spain "with the Indies" ' (176, *210*).

By the 1820s, also, British policy-makers were increasingly stressing the more-than-commercial advantages of overseas trade. In British colonies, particularly in India, the aim was to create bases far from the mother country upon which to extend a quintessentially British view of the world. As Cain and Hopkins put it, British colonial activity was beginning to put in place 'a set of "like-minded" co-operative elites who would demonstrate that the British view of the world could, and should, be reproduced elsewhere, and that economic progress was compatible with, indeed required, individual liberty, differential property rights, and political stability'. By the early 1830s, the colonial secretary, Earl Goderich, was advocating transferring 'to distant regions the greatest possible amount both of the spirit of civil liberty and of the forms of social order to which Great Britain is chiefly indebted for the rank she holds among the civilised nations' (151, *98*). This distinctive imperial ethic, furthermore, had resonance in those 'distant regions' which Britain did not directly own but over which her commercial influence grew ever stronger in the first half of the nineteenth century. Canning, Palmerston and Aberdeen all conceived a British interest in the political stability of Latin America and hoped thereby to extend British values in what amounted to an informal empire of commercial influence.

If matters outside Europe were settled to general British satisfaction in the 1820s, the South-east of Europe was becoming increasingly troublesome. Early Greek successes in their campaign for independence had been reversed by 1825 when Mehemet Ali, nominally a vassal of the Turkish Sultan but in reality ruler of Egypt, accepted the Sultan's invitation to suppress the rebellion. He acquired the Morea, on the southern Greek mainland, as his personal prize. Canning, determined not to be trapped between Tory Russophobia – and hence support for the barbaric Turks – and incautious British philhellene sentiment, took the opportunity of Alexander I's death to send Wellington to negotiate with the new Tsar, Nicholas I. A somewhat ambivalent agreement promising Anglo-Russian support for Greek autonomy, under only the nominal sovereignty of Turkey, was signed in 1828 and confirmed a year later [F.i.18].

As events transpired, however, a vital initiative had been handed to Russia. Soon after Canning's sudden death in August 1827, his ambitious but risky policy backfired. A combined Russian, British and French fleet destroyed a Turco-Egyptian force at Navarino in 1827 and a short Russo-Turkish War in 1828–29 ended with an enhanced Russian presence in South-east Europe. The Russians, British and French could still agree on the fact of Greek independence [F.i.19], but by 1830 both the British and French had become alarmed at the Russian advance. Their response was to insist upon restricted boundaries for independent Greece, leaving thousands of Greeks who had fought for their independence and had been enthusiastically supported in their fight by British public opinion, still under Turkish rule and effectively abandoned by the western powers.

III

The year 1830, a year of revolutions, forms a natural watershed in the history of European diplomacy. The fact that revolutions succeeded in France and Belgium, whereas in Poland and the Italian states they were crushed by Russia and Austria respectively is significant. By the mid-1830s, and directly contrary to the aspirations of the Congress diplomats, Europe was divided into two power blocs: autocracy surviving in the East, liberal-constitutionalism emergent in the West. Austria and Russia had moved closer at the Convention of Münchengratz in 1833 when they guaranteed the territorial integrity of the Turkish Empire against the able, insidious aggression of Mehemet Ali. Prussia joined the compact in the next month. The Russians further increased their influence in the eastern Mediterranean.

In the West, negotiations for the appropriate recognition of the independence of Belgium dragged on for much of the decade [F.i.20, 22] and Britain's new Foreign Secretary, Viscount Palmerston, had to contend with instinctive Gallic muscle-flexing in an area which France traditionally sought to influence and which influence Britain had equally traditionally resisted. However, the 'July monarchy' of Louis-Philippe was committed to constitutionalism. Self-interest as well as principle dictated that 'firm and strict alliance' between the two nations which Palmerston had advocated to the Commons in 1832. The Quadruple Alliance of

1834 between Britain, France, Spain and Portugal bound the two former powers to uphold the interest of the female constitutional monarchs of the two latter against autocratic pretenders [F.i.21], but Palmerston asserted that it would also 'serve as a powerful counterpoise to the Holy Alliance of the east'.

After a brief period in the tutelage of the Prime Minister, Earl Grey, in the early 1830s Palmerston began to envince that unique combination of deft and boorish pragmatism in the conduct of foreign affairs which so repelled the courts of Europe and not least that of Queen Victoria, whose family ties with those courts were strong and would grow stronger later in her reign as her extensive progeny married into them. Since Palmerston was to be in control of foreign policy for no less than twenty-five years between 1830 and 1865 it was a style to which all became well accustomed. His guiding precept was the furtherance of British interests, unencumbered by the incubus of ideology (72, 73). He schemed against Russia not because it was an autocracy but because it threatened British interests in southern Europe and in Asia. He supported constitutional regimes not because he was a child of the Enlightenment but because their success usually seemed to offer the best counterweight to Britain's actual or potential enemies. He rattled sabres lustily, but only when he judged that the noise would frighten or subdue those within earshot. Thus, he was determined to get his way over Belgium, where British concerns were directly affected and where the navy could play an effective role. His lack of concern for the aspirations of Polish nationalists, where neither situation was obtained, was indicative of the pragmatism of his policy.

Nor was Palmerston glued to alliance systems. As events developed, so he reacted, self-confidently sure that he could repair short-term damage to any long-term ally if the opportunity arose to do lasting harm to a long-term foe. So he used the crisis in the Near East between 1838 and 1841 to neutralize the threat of the Holy Alliance though, in doing so, he isolated the French. Since Nicholas of Russia had now recognized that any attempt to destroy the Turkish Empire would range all European nations against him, the prospect of at least a temporary accord between Britain and Russia to curb Mehemet Ali seemed attractive to both sides. The latter's activities in Syria threatened not only the integrity of the Turkish Empire but also Britain's Mediterranean and eastern trade routes. Since Ali's Egyptian power base was buttressed by French military and commercial aid, Palmerston judged that Britain was threatened more by this alliance than by Russian long-term objectives. An Anglo-Turkish commercial convention in 1838 enabled British trade to grow substantially and offered further justification for Palmerston's policy. The isolation of France was brilliantly managed [F.i.23] and the resolution of the Middle Eastern crisis at the Convention of the Straits [F.i.24] gave Palmerston all he required, not least a continued guarantee of Turkish independence. His diplomacy was a telling illustration of the dictum he would offer to the Commons a few years later: 'We have no eternal allies, and we have no perpetual enemies. Our interests are eternal and perpetual, and those interests it is our duty to follow'. In the process, war between Britain and France threatened briefly in 1840–41 and it was left to Aberdeen, Foreign Secretary in Peel's new Conservative government [A], to pick up the pieces. Relations slowly improved, abetted by royal visits from Queen Victoria to Louis-Philippe in 1843 and 1845.

Public hostility to France, notably over the question of influence in Spain, remained considerable.

While Russia and Britain edged cautiously closer over the Middle East, Britain's Indian interests emphasized the difficulty of a permanent accord. India, of course, was the jewel in Britain's Oriental crown and the East India Company was gradually expanding its direct rule in the subcontinent at the expense of the local princes [F.iii]. As it did so, trade expanded rapidly; over 20 per cent of Britain's exports went to Asia in the mid-1840s, compared with a mere 6 per cent in 1815 [D.ii.5]. As the British sought 'natural' frontiers in India, so they came up against northern Himalaya states, such as Kashmir and Afghanistan which bordered on Persia. And Russian influence over Persia had been growing steadily since the later 1820s. Russia was seen as a threat to the security of India, and a series of diplomatic and even military initiatives were put in train in these buffer states during the 1830s with the aim of curbing Russian influence. Predictably, Palmerston was an enthusiastic advocate of intervention. In 1839 Britain tried to keep out a pro-Russian claimant as king of Afghanistan but, eventually, British troops were forced to retreat from Kabul and an undignified compromise was reached by which, among other things, the Russian choice resumed power. Pacification in Afghanistan was quickly followed, however, by substantial British advances in Sind and the Punjab. By 1846, Britain controlled the Indus valley and had pushed its north-west frontier as far as the Himalayas.

The occasion of the 'Opium War' with China [F.ii.4] was the China government's attempt to stamp out the opium trade from which many British traders had been making a handsome but illicit profit. Palmerston's vigorous prosecution of a war in the Far East in the teeth of much domestic criticism (the young Gladstone took out an early patent on that sanctimonious censure which was to be his hallmark in later years) was based on his assessment that a successful outcome would free the lucrative China trade from anachronistic oriental constraint. The Treaty of Nanking [F.i.26] gave Britain an important territorial toe-hold in the Far East as well as acknowledged access to specific Chinese ports, a concession hitherto denied to foreign traders. It proved to be a turning-point. Regular commercial intercourse between the European powers and China now began in earnest.

In the 1840s, British relations with the United States remained cool. The northern boundary between the USA and Canada, unresolved at the Treaty of Ghent [F.i.14] (Ch. 10), was still a source of contention and attempts to settle the boundary of Maine by mediation in the late 1820s and early 1830s had foundered on mutual suspicions. A Canadian rebellion in 1837 provoked many border incidents and USA neutrality was inevitably called in question. British ownership of Canada remained the biggest potential threat to USA control of the continent of which she was already far the wealthiest constituent. It was also a permanent reminder of that European control which the founding fathers had so successfully challenged. The eventual agreement of 1842 [F.i.25] owed much to the more gentle diplomacy of Aberdeen and, though it was roundly condemned by Palmerston as 'a most disgraceful and disadvantageous arrangement'[1], the new Foreign Secretary rightly judged that protracted USA enmity and suspicion was too great an encumbrance for British merchants and investors in the New World. In the succeeding years Aberdeen had to recognize the impossibility of limiting USA expansion south and west. He unwisely intervened in the dispute between Mexico and Texas in 1844 from which the USA emerged completely triumphant. There could be no 'balance-of-power' diplomacy in the Americas on lines similar to that traditionally practised in Europe. All the European powers must accept USA domination and seek to reach the most advantageous commercial arrangements they could. The final settlement of the USA–Canada border at the 49th parallel of latitude in 1846 was an early recognition of this fact. In almost his last act as Foreign Secretary before Peel's government fell, Aberdeen settled the boundary question and, in doing so, protected Britain's direct colonial and indirect commercial interests in the New World. In the next ten years, with diplomatic relations at last stabilized, the value of British exports to the USA almost trebled [D.ii.5].

In the generation after Waterloo Britain was learning to use its immense naval and industrial advantages as weapons in the battles of diplomacy. Though the threat from Russia in no way diminished, Palmerston seemed for the moment to have it contained. Congress diplomacy had been succeeded by *ad hoc* arrangements in which Britain, under both Canning and Palmerston, played a dominant role. British trade routes in the wider world were secured and extended. Above all, a few minor skirmishes apart, peace was maintained, enabling massive reductions to be made in defence expenditure. In the later 1830s, at some £12½m., it accounted for less than a quarter of all government spending, compared with more than 60 per cent at the time of Waterloo and almost 40 per cent in the immediate post-war period [D.i.2]. The army, much reduced in manpower, stagnated, but enough attention was paid to the navy to maintain its clear lead over all possible rivals. Sir James Graham, as First Lord of the Admiralty in the Grey government of 1830–34, reduced naval expenditure by a sixth while effecting a thorough reform of naval administration. By the mid-1840s, it is true, naval professionals and politicians alike were beginning to question whether Britain's vaunted supremacy could be maintained in the face of growing French naval power and into the age of steam navigation (172). Palmerston also affected to believe that five years of unnecessarily defensive statesmanship by Aberdeen had weakened Britain's position in the world. Yet in 1846 no nation was in a position to challenge it and no nation likewise could arrange its own diplomacy without taking Britain's probable reaction into serious account. Though the means employed by Canning, and still less by Palmerston, were not those envisaged by Castlereagh when he fashioned the alliances of 1814–15, it is unlikely that he would have deprecated the results.

---

1. J. Ridley, *Lord Palmerston* (1970), p. 390.

CHAPTER 23

The crisis of reform, 1827–1832

I

When Liverpool resigned early in 1827 the cause of parliamentary reform seemed as forlorn as at any time since the end of the Napoleonic Wars. Public interest was muted; the issue hardly figured in the election of 1826. Yet a measure which many Tories believed fatal to the cause of sound government was on the statute-book less than five and a half years later. The speed of the change may seem remarkable and the crowded narrative of events in the interim has its confusions, but three important explanatory factors may be kept in mind. First, the Tory party, that immovable obstacle to change in the eyes of the radicals, was not a monolith; the departure of Liverpool removed the central pillar of the structure. Second, the reform question encompassed more than an extension of the franchise. Concessions to Roman Catholics, and even Protestant dissenters, were viewed by many Anglicans as more damaging to the fabric of English society than the granting of a parliamentary seat to Manchester or Birmingham. Third, the economic boom of the 1820s came to an abrupt halt in 1829. By February 1830 the Whig leader, Earl Grey, was talking of 'a state of general distress such as never before pressed upon any country'. As radical leaders and opponents of reform alike knew, only high prices and unemployment could translate an intellectual case for constitutional change into a mass movement of incalculably threatening aspect.

George Canning's right to succeed as Prime Minister was as certain as the fact that his succession would split his party. Though Canning may have given George IV assurances that he would soft-pedal on Catholic emancipation, the leading Protestants in Liverpool's Cabinet would not serve under him. Deprived of the services of Wellington (who had tried to browbeat the King into appointing him Prime Minister and who had resigned as Commander-in-Chief when denied), Peel and Eldon, Canning used his liberal reputation to fashion an alliance with the Whigs. Tierney, Lansdowne and Carlisle came in [A] and, in doing so, split their party too. Grey would have nothing to do with Canning and vituperatively attacked him from the opposition benches. Great though his abilities were, Canning to the end of his life continued to inspire fission, distrust, envy and hatred. His short ministry emphasized how great had been Liverpool's importance to the stability of government.

After Canning's death, Viscount Goderich briefly showed that the financial talents he had displayed as Chancellor of the Exchequer (and as Frederick Robinson) did not extend to the firm leadership of a divided Cabinet. When he fell in January 1828 party distinctions, which had seemed so clear less than two years earlier, seemed to mean almost nothing. With both parties split, George IV's choice of Wellington to head the new administration had a certain perverse logic. Not only was Wellington an anti-reformer on both Catholic and constitutional questions, he was as indifferent to party politics as any political figure of the day. He saw himself as a national leader who could render party divisions petty and redundant. He had enormous residual prestige as the victor of Waterloo, of course, but as a politician his overbearing manner and pig-headed disdain for subordinate virtues like conciliation and consensus would prove a crippling handicap. When the 'ultra' Tories on the right of the party acclaimed the appointment of a 'strong' leader in 1828 they were wrong on two counts. Not only was he less blindly reactionary than they, but his political misjudgements during the approaching crisis would hand power to a Whig-dominated government committed to the very reform they believed Wellington would prevent. He was, in short, a disastrous leader.

Wellington's government experienced the usual initial differences of view. Huskisson, who brought most of the Canningite politicians – including Palmerston, Dudley and Lamb – into uneasy coalition, favoured gentle change. The Huskissonites wanted to disfranchise the demonstrably corrupt boroughs of Penryn and East Retford, whose cases had been brought to the attention of Parliament after the election of 1826, and transfer their seats to Manchester and Birmingham. When Peel proposed in May 1828 that the East Retford seats go instead to the neighbouring area of Bassetlaw where the duke of Newcastle exercised unchallenged influence, Huskisson voted with the opposition and took his followers out of the government. Wellington was glad to be rid of the Liberal Tories, but their debating talents in the Commons were sorely missed.

The Huskissonite defection coincidentally initiated a much more serious Tory split. Charles Grant's successor as President of the Board of Trade was William Vesey Fitzgerald, who represented the Irish seat of County Clare. By a parliamentary convention not finally removed until 1926, an MP accepting government office had to resign his seat and offer himself to his constituents for re-election in his new guise. The resultant Clare by-election saw Fitzgerald matched against Daniel O'Connell, the leader of the Catholic Association, an increasingly important Irish pressure group for full Catholic rights. O'Connell, as a Roman Catholic, could legally stand for election but could not serve if elected. His success presented Wellington and the still more staunchly Protestant Peel with an acute dilemma. If Catholic emancipation were refused, the well-organized Catholic Association would almost certainly provoke civic disorder by rent strikes against English landlords and tithe withholding from the English Church. Even full civil war was not precluded. On the other hand, Catholic emancipation would destroy what fragile unity the Tory party still claimed. Most backbench squires remained intensely hostile to any concessions and ultra-Tory peers, like Winchilsea and Blandford, pointed out that the 1826 Election had demonstrated widespread English antipathy to the Catholic cause.

The ultras, in fact, had been disturbed by Wellington's repeal of the Test and Corporation Acts in 1828 [G.i], the first crack in the edifice of the establishment (29), but this concession could be rationalized since annual indemnity had already rendered the statutes virtually dead letters. Catholic emancipation was different. Ultras feared not only that it would prove the first step on the road to Catholic expropriation of Protestant land and privileges in Ireland but that it would sensibly weaken the Church and social order in England. Worst of all, it would carry against the expressed wishes of the general population. Though Catholic emancipation was accompanied by a raising of the Irish county voting qualification from 40s. (£2) to £10 to exclude the unreliable peasantry (G.i] itself a dangerous precedent since it tampered with the mystical beauties of the unreformed constitution – the ultras were not assuaged. The dowager duchess of Richmond filled her drawing-room with stuffed rats as a visual display of contempt for apostate ministers (74, *54*). George IV felt betrayed. The aristocracy 'had supported his father' but, with Catholic emancipation, 'everything was revolutionary . . . and the peers and the aristocracy were giving way to it' (249, *398–9*). Peel honourably but imprudently resigned his seat at Oxford University where Protestant sentiments ran high; he was defeated in the by-election. He had to seek the dubious but capacious protection of a leading borough-monger, Mannaseh Lopes, to return for a rotten borough in Wiltshire which had not been contested since 1747.

It is impossible to overstate the importance of Catholic emancipation. It split the anti-reformers beyond repair. If Wellington and Peel could 'rat' on the Catholic question, what value had their assurances on parliamentary reform? Peel's career, indeed, would ultimately be blighted by the lack of trust ordinary country gentlemen had in him (Chs 28 and 30). Extra-parliamentary reformers in England saw what disciplined pressure could achieve: 'a great and bloodless victory', the Birmingham banker Thomas Attwood admiringly called it (43, *192*). Paradoxically, but not irrationally, it converted many ultras to the reform case. They believed that the votes of the rotten borough members had given the government its majority on a measure repugnant to the good sense of honest and decent Englishmen. We should not be surprised to note, therefore, that it was the marquis of Blandford and not the radical Joseph Hume who in February 1830 introduced the first thoroughgoing reform bill of the crisis, calling for the transference of rotten borough seats to the counties and large towns, the disqualification of non-resident voters, the expulsion of Crown office-holders from Parliament, the payment of MPs and a general ratepayer franchise. The ultras argued that a rational and widely based electorate could be relied upon to rally round the 'No Popery' flag.

II

By the time that Blandford rose to address the Commons the economic situation had worsened significantly. The harvest of 1829 was a failure; bread prices were high in 1830; a downswing in the trade cycle also brought unemployment and wage cuts. This was the opportunity radical leaders had been awaiting for a decade. William Cobbett fashioned further variations on his well-worn theme of a nation over-taxed to subsidize the idle and profligate expenditure of the 'tax-eaters'. The West End of London, he told his readers, was 'at once the great corrupter of the nation, and the great devourer of the fruit of its toils'. Westminster was 'a mass of drones and wasps got together, to swallow up the honey collected by the industrious bees'. In April 1831 a National Union of the Working Classes was forged in London from disparate radical elements by William Lovett and Henry Hetherington, editor of *Poor Man's Guardian*. It agitated for complete male suffrage. At the election of 1830, called after George IVs death, 'Orator' Hunt had been returned as Member for Preston, one of the few boroughs with a mass electorate. Cheering crowds processed through the streets bearing banners with menacing slogans (293).

Though the size of many political rallies in 1830 and, particularly, 1831 suggested that working-class support for democracy was stronger even than during the Peterloo crisis of 1819, the response of the radical leaders was predictable enough. More worrying at Westminster was a new determination for reform among many sections of the middle class. Influential provincial journals like the *Manchester Guardian* and *Leeds Mercury* had been pro-reform for some years; by 1831 they had been joined by sections of the erstwhile Tory press, like the *Nottingham Journal*. Shopkeepers and small businessmen had always been torn between a natural desire for political recognition and a distaste for collaboration with working men, whose enfranchisement they wished to see no more than did land-owning Tories. But the ever growing importance of industry and commerce combined with hostility to an unrepresentative Parliament which legislated in its narrow interest (as with the Corn Laws) were swinging the middle classes, for the first time, into the reform camp.

In Birmingham, where factories were rare and relations between masters and men not generally hostile, Thomas Attwood in January 1830 founded 'a General Political Union between the Lower and the Middle Classes of the People' to remedy the abuses and mismanagement of government by political reform. Attwood's primary concerns were more economic than political; he wished to end the deflation and the shortage of capital. Currency reform – the 'Brummagem remedy' – would provide readier credit and bigger domestic markets for Birmingham's small masters. This was no basis for nationwide agitation, however, since the northern textile manufacturers who depended on exports were benefiting from the competitive prices government monetary policy helped to ensure. However, Attwood's Political Union could find common cause with them on the need for parliamentary reform. What form this should take remained necessarily vague since Attwood wished to attract both moderate reformers and democrats.

Attwood's Union was a vital step. Other Unions were founded in the major manufacturing and commercial centres. These were not carbon copies of Attwood's. In Leeds, where class separation between factory owners and employees was far advanced, no fewer than three organizations emerged, one primarily for workmen, one for the middle classes and one which tried uneasily to bridge the gulf (75). The cumulative effect of reform agitation via the Political Unions, however, was more important than any differences of social composition and specific objective. They attracted huge crowds to political rallies; they were organized and generally disciplined; and, most important of all, they served notice on Westminster that the middle classes were prepared to labour mightily in the reformers' vineyard. However justified, it was nevertheless an almost unchallenged assumption among members of the unreformed Parliament that the middle classes possessed a power which, if properly harnessed, must carry all before it. It was not that the landed elite of Great Britain had any clear or focused idea of how to define the middle class, merely that its inchoate power could not be denied. As Lord Holland remarked to Grey: 'If the great mass of the middle class are bent upon that method of enforcing their views, there is not in the nature of society any real force that can prevent them.' Grey himself called them the 'real and efficient mass of public opinion . . . without whom the power of the gentry is nothing' (43). During the late summer and early autumn of 1830, MPs were digesting the combined effects of economic distress, agricultural labourers in revolt throughout the South and East of England (Ch. 16), the growing impact of the Political Unions and successful revolutions in France and Belgium. Very probably the majority still remained opposed to reform on principle. Extra-parliamentary events were, however, drawing them to the unpalatable conclusion of a contemporary pamphlet: 'if Reform is refused, Revolution is inevitable'.[1]

III

Within Westminster itself, the anti-reformers' power to resist was weakening perceptibly. Wellington, in the manner of eighteenth-century Prime Ministers, expected to gain seats at the General Election of 1830 by the judicious deployment of government patronage. That patronage, however, had been wasting away since the 1780s (Ch. 3) and the election showed that, even without reform, governments could no longer rely on 'influence' to bend matters to their will. It was not that the government lost heavily; overall, there was little change [B.v]. But in that minority of constituencies where contests were held and where public opinion could be tested things went extremely badly. Government supporters, like John Wilson Croker and Peel's own brother and brother-in-law, were all beaten. That stormiest of Whig petrels, Henry Brougham, won one of the coveted Yorkshire county seats on an unambiguously reformist platform, even though he had no local connections in a constituency notorious for its aversion to non-Yorkshiremen. The election further distanced Canningites and Huskissonites from the administration. They took understandable umbrage at certain instances of the use of patronage to prevent their supporters' election and were thereby brought an important stage nearer to accepting reform.

None of this apparently made much impression on Wellington, while the more astute Peel, who was not fundamentally opposed to modest reform, was hamstrung by his reputation as a turncoat on the Catholic question. He maintained an opposition to reform which, as he must have realized, damaged his party's interests. Wellington, having failed to broaden the base of his ministry, determined on total defiance. At the height of the Swing agitation and with reform sentiment growing on every side, he announced to the Lords in November 1830 that 'the legislature and the system of representation possessed the full and entire confidence of the country. . . . He was not only not prepared to bring forward any [reform] measure; but . . . as long as he held any station in the government of the country he should always feel it his duty to resist such measures when proposed by others.' This bluff, insensitive pronouncement polarized parliamentary opinion. Wellington forced MPs to consider not only their own consciences but also the strength of feeling 'out of doors'. If the passage of the first Reform Act was a triumph for extra-parliamentary pressure then Wellington, perversely, bears responsibility for educating MPs to be sensitive to that pressure. Huskissonites at last made common cause with the Whigs. The government, with Peel its only effective spokesman in the Lower House, was defeated on a minor financial issue less than a fortnight after Wellington's outburst. Few ministers had the stomach for continued parliamentary buffeting and their resignation left William IV with no choice but to appoint Earl Grey his First Lord of the Treasury.

Grey's government is usually, and properly, considered as a Whig ministry, but it included both Huskissonites (Goderich, Palmerston and Grant) and an ultra-Tory (Richmond) [A]. What united them, apart from that aristocratic interlinkage which characterized virtually all administrations before the 1880s, was a recognition of the necessity for reform. But of what kind? Grey had long held to a determination to refuse office in any administration not pledged to reform and now his apparent radicalism alarmed some of his colleagues. He saw that the disfranchisement of a few rotten boroughs and other modish tinkerings favoured periodically during the 1820s would not do. Extra-parliamentary agitation would not be assuaged; the realities of aristocratic government would remain threatened. Not only should 'untainted' county representation be increased but some movement must be made towards aligning parliamentary boroughs with industrial and commercial reality in the first half of the nineteenth century. Further, a uniform borough franchise must replace the present irrational and arbitrary enfranchisements. In the committee of ministers which Grey appointed to draft reform proposals, there was even support for a secret ballot, that radical holy grail, and for shorter Parliaments.

The first reform bill, which Lord John Russell introduced to the Commons in March 1831, reflected Grey's determination. Though neither secret ballot nor shorter Parliaments survived, the government proposed to get rid of 168 borough seats from 108 boroughs and to replace them with 43 new borough seats for the more populous towns and with an increased county representation tied very loosely also to population distribution. Occupiers of houses worth at least £10 a year to rent were to get the vote in all boroughs. The boldness of the stroke both alarmed opponents of reform and amazed radicals outside Parliament, so much so that only Hetherington of the nationally prominent figures opposed it, on the perceptive ground that the enfranchisement of shopkeepers and the *petit bourgeoisie* would reduce working-class expectations rather than enhance them. Other radicals believed that such a big initial step must inevitably be followed by further concessions from which working men would more obviously benefit.

Much to the surprise of Grey, who had expected a much more decisive outcome, Russell's Bill obtained its second reading in the Commons by only a single vote (302 to 301) in the fullest division lobby yet seen in Parliament. The slender advantage derived from substantial majorities among the English county MPs (51 to 25), those borough members whose seats would remain after reform (111 to 65) and O'Connell's unreliable Irishmen (51 to 36). The narrowness of victory made subsequent defeat on amendment certain but, when that happened, Grey was able to persuade the King to break with convention and dissolve

Parliament. The elections of 1831 became a virtual plebiscite on reform. Though fewer contests were held than in 1830 [B.vii.1], their verdict was decisive [B.v]. Of the thirty-four English county MPs who had voted either against the second reading or for the wrecking amendment which had precipitated the election only six survived the judgement of their constituents. Virtually the only Tories who remained sat for those closed or manageable boroughs which were to be so reduced by the proposed reform.

The House of Lords remained a formidable obstacle even when the Commons carried a strong pro-reform majority. Their rejection of a second reform bill, similar in essentials to the first, in October 1831 unleashed a fury of protest throughout the country. In Bristol, rioters controlled the city for three days, evincing particular hostility to the Recorder there, the ultra-Tory Sir Charles Wetherell. Other West Country riots were experienced in the old woollen towns of Tiverton and Blandford. In Nottingham the duke of Newcastle's castle was put to the fire and in Derby several fatalities occurred. The Political Unions organized massive demonstrations with a strongly anti-clerical tone. It had not gone unremarked in the radical Press that twenty-one of the twenty-six bishops had voted against reform. Had they voted otherwise, it would have carried. The Church of England became a special target of popular abuse, the soft underbelly of Old Corruption.

The outbreaks of October 1831 naturally alarmed the authorities, but their implications were serious too for the extra-parliamentary reformers who sought change by peaceful pressure and argument. Attwood and Place blamed lack of organization and a clearly agreed programme. They feared that control of the movement would pass to revolutionaries opposed to any measure which stopped short of full manhood suffrage. The explosions, however, gave Attwood an opportunity to outflank the democrats. When members of the Political Unions were urged to equip themselves with arms, it was an injunction which middle-class supporters, fearful for their property against mob attacks, were only too willing to accept. Armed property owners could also challenge a legislature which continued to deny reform. Place and Attwood's apparent willingness to countenance force was just enough to preserve middle-class leadership of the extra-parliamentary campaign during its crucial, final months. The threat was taken seriously by MPs, as the Unions intended, but Attwood's objective of drawing the fangs of the revolutionaries should not be forgotten.

The lesson of past disturbances was that threats of violence by the lower orders would be repressed. Now the government reacted very differently. Though special constables were sworn in and the creaking mechanism of national defence was cranked up again, as in 1795 and 1820, ministers were much less confident of success. Melbourne, for one, was said to have been 'frightened to death' by the Bristol riots (293, *223*). Extra-parliamentary pressure was probably responsible both for stiffening Grey's resolve to persevere with reform (though in February 1832 he was confiding that he wished he 'had never touched' the question) and for reconvening Parliament early to debate yet another reform bill. As Grey told the King's private secretary immediately after the riots: 'It is . . . undeniable that the middle classes . . . are activated by an intense and almost unanimous feeling in favour of the measure of reform.'[2]

The final stages of the crisis concern coercion and concession. An increasing number both of commoners and peers believed in early 1832 that another rejected bill would precipitate revolution. The government also had to bring pressure on William IV. The passage of the bill through the Lords might require the creation of a substantial number of Whig peers and the King must be persuaded to sanction this if necessary. The strain of the crisis told on anxious and perplexed ministers. Some of Grey's colleagues, always sceptical, now openly doubted their leader's ability to take them along the narrow precipice to the safe uplands of a reform which would conserve. Ministers feared the countervailing chasms of mob rule or blind reaction and, while Durham argued for an immediate creation of new peers and Melbourne languidly presented the opposite case, sought refuge in letters of resignation which were either not delivered or not accepted. Grey himself was close to despair and, after a reverse in the Lords at the beginning of May 1832 and the King's subsequent reluctance to create fifty peers immediately, tendered his government's resignation.

The crisis of the 'Days of May' which followed make little sense without an appreciation of the pressures generated both inside Westminster and outside. As in October 1831, the future of reform was at stake; Attwood and Place, having rehearsed their parts thoroughly the previous autumn, were well prepared for their theatrical springtime utterances. While Wellington investigated the practicability of forming a Tory administration to promote a more modest and less contentious reform bill, anti-Tory petitions flooded into Westminster. Pro-reform property owners urged to a tax strike; Francis Place advocated a withdrawal of private funds from the banks; 'To stop the Duke, go for gold'. Huge public meetings were held again and it was known that a plan for armed resistance to any new Tory ministry was well advanced, though whether Place and his coadjutors had any real intention of bringing it into effect is a matter of doubt. Certainly, a revolution led by Francis Place would have been an incongruous phenomenon.

The actual violence of May 1832 was much less than that of the previous autumn. Except in the North-east, where labour disputes were rife, the nation remained tense but tranquil. Tory prospects of forming a ministry, never bright, were dished by Peel's refusal to serve in any government which would introduce reform. Sensitive to the last of the effect on his career of being branded a double apostate on both Catholic and reform questions, Peel blocked up the only avenue of escape for the King from capitulation to Grey. In fact, the threatened new peers were not needed. Once Wellington had announced his failure to form a ministry, parliamentary opposition to Grey collapsed. On 4 June, only twenty-two peers voted against the third reading of the reform bill. The King gave his assent, though pointedly not in person in the Lords, three days later. The electoral system of Great Britain and Ireland was radically changed without revolution, though the question of how far the Whig reform would prove acceptable to the nation at large remained an open one. If Whig calculations were correct, however, not only would the nation be spared a revolution; the landed interest would retain its rightful place in control of affairs.

1. *Thoughts on Parliamentary Reform with a Plan for the Restoration of the Constitution* (October 1830) quoted in R. Quinault, 'The French Revolution of 1830 and Parliamentary Reform' *History* 257 (1994), p. 392.
2. *Correspondence of Earl Grey and William IV* (2 vols, 1867), i, pp. 410–11.

CHAPTER 24

'The real interests of the aristocracy':
The Reform Act of 1832

I

Earl Grey protested to a still sceptical House of Lords in November 1831: 'If any persons suppose that this Reform will lead to ulterior measures, they are mistaken; for there is no one more decided against annual parliaments, universal suffrage, and the ballot, than I am. My object is not to favour, but to put an end to such hopes and projects.' Grey, of course, needed to convert peers hostile to any extension of the franchise and still more averse to legislating away their patrimony in the form of managed parliamentary boroughs, but there is no reason to believe that he was being other than completely honest. The Prime Minister who carried reform in 1832 had not essentially changed from the young Whig who had so annoyed and embarrassed his leaders in the 1790s with talk of 'wild and speculative schemes' (Ch. 8). Grey believed, now as then, that the real interests of the aristocracy were best served by a cautiously constructive attitude to reform. He remembered in 1831–32 the words of his old antagonist, Edmund Burke, that a State without the means of correction was also without the means of its conservation. 'The principle of my reform is, to prevent the necessity for revolution ... reforming to preserve and not to overthrow.'[1] Grey aimed to keep power securely in the hands of the property owners and he believed, moreover, that landed property would continue to predominate despite the concessions he intended to make to the growing influence of commerce and industry. The Whig remedy, it may be argued, was a far more conservative prescription than the last-ditch stand mounted by many Tories against change of any kind.

The first Reform Act is legislation of prime importance and those who seek to minimize it by drawing attention to what it did *not* change miss the point. The inescapable fact is that the unreformed Parliament willed its own demise and its replacement by one which redrew the political map of Britain. The map was hurriedly and, in some respects, imperfectly drawn and not all the implications of reform were immediately grasped, but the broad strategy was both clear and successful. Some Whigs believed a revolution to be imminent unless reform were immediately conceded; others doubted this but agreed that the old system now lacked that general support necessary for government by consent. The Whigs in 1832 made concessions to preserve the essentials of aristocratic government and their triumphant success should not be overlooked in the welter of minutiae about constituency boundaries and the size of the reformed electorate. Those middle-class property owners whose loyalty had been in severe doubt in 1831 were detached from dangerous political entanglement with working-class protest; government based on property not only survived but was strengthened thereby. Britain did not experience the revolutionary upheavals which swept through western Europe in the 1830s and 1840s. The challenge of 'mere numbers' was easily repelled. Chartism never had the remotest prospect of success (Ch. 29) once the middle classes had been given what they regarded as their rightful recognition by the legislature. But the reformed Parliament was not only strengthened to resist. Its wider base of support gave it the confidence to embark in the 1830s and 1840s on schemes of reform, notably of the Established Church, the old Poor Law and public health (Chs 25–7) which its predecessor would almost certainly have burked. The 1832 Reform Act, therefore, had dynamic as well as conservative implications. Its whole, viewed in the context of Britain's development during the next generation, was vastly more important than the sum of its constituent parts.

II

The major provisions of the reform legislation and their effect on the electorate are outlined elsewhere (B.ii, iii]. It should be noted, however, that the Scottish Reform Act produced the most radical changes of all, involving the possibility of real electoral contests in the new county seats and in the main cities instead of the forty-five virtual pocket boroughs of the unreformed system (77). Even so, only one adult Scottish male in eight had the vote after 1832, compared with one in five of his English counterparts. In Ireland, which also had a separate Reform Act, the higher voting qualification of 1829 (Ch. 23) was maintained; as a result only about 5 per cent of Irishmen could vote.

The uniform £10 householder qualification was designed as a rough-and-ready means of borough enfranchisement for those with sufficient property to be trusted with the vote. Broadly, it achieved its objective but with inevitable anomalies deriving from variations in rental values across the country. In high-rated London, working-class voters were not uncommon; in remote Cornwall or parts of Wales even some shopkeepers failed to qualify. In northern manufacturing towns, as intended, the hurdle was stiff. Leeds, for example, had only 5,000 voters in a total population of about 125,000 [E.iii] (75). Those householders who 'compounded' for their rates by paying them over as part of their rent to the landlord were made to jump through awkward hoops in order to qualify; only the most intrepid seekers after enfranchisement, armed preferably with law books and the financial resources to do battle with registration officials, would get on to the register. As late as 1866, when the obstacles had been eased and when local party organizations had taken on much of the administrative burden of registration, only about a quarter of compounders who might have qualified actually did so. Against this, the modest workings of inflation were increasing the number of qualified voters year by year such that by the 1860s the proportion had increased slightly (B.iii]. Even so, the larger cities did not have much of a working-class electorate. Coventry stood out with 70 per cent of its electorate working class in 1865. Leicester and Nottingham had about two-fifths; Birmingham, Bristol, Bolton, Manchester and Newcastle had between one-fifth and a quarter; Liverpool, Leeds and Halifax were nearer 10 per cent (89, 141). In some of the old quasi-democratic urban constituencies, like

Preston and Westminster, working-class participation declined after 1832 as existing voters died off. In some constituencies, the decline in the number of voters after 1832 was very substantial. About 2,500 electors, for example, voted in Lancaster in the election of 1831. The electorate had shrunk to about 1,400 by 1852. The Peel family borough of Tamworth likewise lost about 44 per cent of its electorate at the same time (75, 61). As Dr Vernon's recent detailed study has shown, the proportion of adult males entitled to vote went down between 1832 and 1852 in such diverse constituencies as the market towns of Boston (Lincolnshire) and Lewes (West Sussex) and the rapidly growing textile and engineering centre of Oldham in Lancashire.[2]

In the counties, the most contentious change concerned the £50 tenants-at-will enfranchised by the so-called Chandos amendment. Radicals outside Parliament, and not a few Whigs inside, believed that this clause, which increased the county electorate by about a third over that originally envisaged, would strengthen the Tories since tenants would be expected to vote automatically for the candidate of their landlord's choice on pain of eviction. A convention certainly existed that candidates usually avoided sounding out the political opinions of their opponents' tenants. Gladstone was upbraided by Lord Grosvenor in 1841 for this supposed 'offence'. Grosvenor self-righteously asserted: 'I have never, to my knowledge, canvassed the tenant of any political opponent qualifying for his landlord's property, nor would any amount of advantage either to myself or my party . . . tempt me to deviate from this course, the propriety of which I thought spoke for itself.'[3] A large landowner prepared to forgo some rent could also 'create' 40-shilling freehold qualifications for his erstwhile tenants and reap the reward in dutiful, deferential voting. Since the Reform Act increased the number of seats and since the proportion of county seats actually contested was also increasing, this ancient device became more attractive after 1832 [B.vii].

The 1832 Reform Act by no means ended the time-honoured practice of inducements to vote. Radical pressure for a secret ballot having been overborne, the enlarged electorate was every bit as venal as its predecessor. The length of polling was lessened to two days in the counties and, after 1835, to one day in the boroughs so that the extensive orgies of treating, retreating and 'bidding-up' were reduced, but more contested elections and more electors merely meant that the jam had to be spread somewhat more thinly over a wider area. Election expenses running into thousands of pounds remained common, and the author of a *Manual of Election Law* argued in 1852 that, 'Bribery is seen perhaps in fuller action at the moment than ever before.' (74, 227) The notion of a highminded early Victorian middle-class electorate doing its serious and sober duty once every seven years is a fanciful one. The gravy train still ran after 1832.

The new device of a registration of voters, in principle a rational and much needed reform, actually opened the way for more electoral sharp practice. Creation and supervision of a proper electoral register demands a specific bureaucracy and 1832 did not provide one. Into the void in the 1830s and 1840s leaped the local party agents whose most important task was to ensure that as many of their own supporters as possible were on the roll, and as few of their opponents'. As party organizations became more professional and extensive on both sides, the registers became a more realistic statement of qualified voters. Early on, however, many marches were stolen on unwary opponents and on the hapless Revising Barrister whose duty it was to decide on inclusion or exclusion, usually on hopelessly inadequate or biased evidence. In the generation after 1832 many dead men 'voted'; some voted several times each election. Sir Robert Peel rightly referred in 1839 to a 'perfectly new element of political power – namely the registration of voters. ... That party is the strongest in point of fact which has the existing registration in its favour.' (79, *118*)

III

As with the extension of the franchise, the redistribution of seats was a crude but generally effective approximation to precisely recognized criteria [B.iv]. It had been an article of faith with all reformers since the 1780s that the allegedly less corrupt and more representative English county seats should be strengthened. This was done with a 76 per cent increase in the number of county seats, and extra MPs for the more populous counties such as Lancashire and Warwickshire. Still, on strictly arithmetical considerations, the English and Welsh counties remained under-represented with almost 57 per cent of the electorate and only 32 per cent of the seats in the two countries [B.iii]. The reorganization of the boroughs was more far-reaching than most MPs had expected. No less than 87 of the 201 English boroughs of 1831 were affected. Among the 'Schedule A' boroughs which disappeared altogether was Appleby, which had first put Pitt the Younger into Parliament; Midhurst, which had performed the same service for Charles James Fox, lost one of its members. They were replaced by 42 new boroughs, mostly from the new industrial areas.

To an extent, therefore, redistribution accorded with the changing face of Britain. But the government was determined to avoid any appearance of mathematical precision. The ancient constitution must carry over at least some of its irrational mystique into the new. Russell told the Commons in March 1831 that the government 'had never put the measure of Reform on a footing of such perfect symmetry and regularity as to reduce the Representation of the country to exact proportions ... anomalies they found, and anomalies, though not such glaring ones as now existed, they meant to leave.'[4] Thus, Thetford, Reigate, Westbury and Calne, all of which were found in 1833 to have fewer than 200 voters, continued to send members to Parliament while Doncaster, Croydon and Loughborough, with populations in excess of 10,000, remained unrepresented. Some desperate horse-trading took place in 1831 when the final lists of executions and reprieves were drawn up, but through all the frantic activity the government held fast to its resolve to preserve at least some proprietary boroughs. Patronage was not to be destroyed at a blow. Through them bright, though inevitably well-connected, young men found an easy and early route to Westminster where they could learn their trade without frustrating extra-parliamentary apprenticeship. They could thus give their country longer and more experienced service. Less noble objectives have often been espoused by more democratic assemblies.

Such a bright young man was William Ewart Gladstone who, at twenty-three years of age and with substantial Liverpool commercial money behind him, secured the patronage of the duke of Newcastle as candidate for Newark and was returned top of the poll in the first election for the reformed Parliament in December 1832. Some months earlier, when on that grand European tour still regarded as an essential ingredient of a civilized young man's upbringing, he had written of his candidature from Geneva and of the 'Probability of success, considering the tone the Duke has taken'.[5] Norman Gash has estimated that between sixty and seventy members continued to appear in the reformed Commons through patronage, though now sometimes more discreetly deployed (79). No less than 36 per cent of members in the Commons of 1841–47 had first been elected before they were thirty years old. The contrast with modern days is stark.

Given the concerns of the Whigs, and despite Tory alarms, it is not surprising to discover that the social composition of the 1832 Parliament hardly differed from its predecessor. Representatives of the aristocracy (particularly its eldest sons) and gentry still dominated the Commons. Precise categorization is elusive, but between 70 and 80 per cent of the Commons in the 1840s came from the landed interest. Halevy calculated that 97 of the 658 MPs in the Parliament of 1837 were bankers, merchants and manufacturers. A similar proportion had been found in the late-eighteenth-century House of Commons; it should be remembered how accommodating the old system had been to a leavening of middle-class interest (Ch. 2). Althorp had assured the Commons in December 1831 that those 'most likely to be returned under the Bill, as Representatives ... would continue to be selected from the same classes as at present'.[6] Greville's initial impression was that the new Parliament was 'rather differently and somewhat less ably composed than its predecessors', but he conceded that 'matters remain pretty much as they were, except that the Whigs have got possession of the power which the Tories have lost'.[7] Radical influence was not prominent. The idiosyncratic William Cobbett returned as Member for Oldham to replace Orator Hunt, defeated at Preston. Even the nonconformists, among the most steadfast of reformers, did not significantly increase their complement.

The failure of middle-class direct representation to increase alongside its enlarged significance in the electorate as a whole is only superficially perplexing. Aristocratic control over most of the levers of power remained extremely tight, at least until the 1870s. Increased county representation strengthened the gentry and, as we have seen, patronage did not come to an end. The organization of political life in the new urban areas, from which most middle-class representation might be expected to come, was still in its infancy in 1832, and though the Municipal Corporation reforms would provide a much needed fillip after 1835 [C. ii], the direct concerns of many businessmen remained local rather than national. Indeed, from the 1830s to the 1860s local elections generally stirred more political passions than did the less frequent and still often uncontested parliamentary elections [B.vii.2]. The preservation of a £300 property qualification until 1858 deterred some, but it was hardly a barrier to the well-heeled banker or cotton magnate. Much more important was the increased amount of time required of an MP. For reasons which will be examined later (Ch. 32) the parliamentary burden on MPs was growing heavily from the 1830s onwards. For the first time, an MP who was so minded could call his parliamentary job a full-time one. Sessions lengthened; even the landowners' high summers could be eaten into; the length of the parliamentary day grew. Twenty-five volumes of Hansard will take the reader from 1820 to 1830; sixty-three must be slogged through to get from 1840 to 1850. The difference is only partially explained by rather more detailed reporting. Parliamentary commitments necessitated the provision of an independent income to sustain an MP; parliamentary salaries were not paid until 1911. Those industrialists or bankers who had the financial resources often lacked the time to devote to parliamentary duties. Many more lacked time, resources and inclination. When J. G. Marshall of the wealthy Leeds flax-spinning firm declined to stand again for the borough in 1852, after having represented it as MP for the previous five years, he conceded to his brother 'that our concern wanted my personal labour and attention' (89, *19*). The reformed House of Commons was almost bound still to be dominated by gentlemen of leisure.

IV

The apocalyptic visions of the Tories, which filled the pages of their journals and diaries between 1830 and 1832, were not fulfilled. Their class, though not yet their party, retained control. The revolution did not come. John Wilson Croker had believed that 'The reform Bill is a stepping stone in England to a republic. The Bill once passed, goodnight to the Monarchy and the Lords and the Church'. He refused to present himself as a candidate for the reformed Parliament. Lord Eldon, one of the great pillars of the anti-reform Tories, believed, as do most reactionaries in most ages, that 'the work of destruction had [long] been going on in this country'; the reform bill would see that work 'very speedily, fully accomplished'. Wellington himself believed reform a ' "bloodless revolution". . . . We shall be destroyed one after the other . . . by due course of law'. In the twenty years which remained to him during a long life, Wellington was to appreciate the folly of his remarks. He would live to see not only no revolution but the resurgence of that Tory party whose disintegration after Liverpool's death had given the reformers such comfort. Events in the 1830s and the 1840s, in fact, triumphantly vindicated the perceptions of Grey. Not the least of the many reasons for wishing to hitch the middle classes to the aristocratic wagon was the belief, amply justified in the event, that once they had been given appropriate recognition most would show themselves as averse to radical politics as the Whigs themselves. As Michael Brock puts it: 'Most of the new voters wanted, not to challenge the aristocracy, but to win recognition from it: once they had their rightful position they did not favour further adventures'. (74, *319*) The Tories would have sacrificed this immense conservative bulwark, with probable consequences much more akin to the doom they prophesied would result from Grey's policies. Despite Gash's heroic attempts at rehabilitation, never were the Tories more truly the 'stupidest party' of J. S. Mill's later epithet than in 1831–32.

The real losers of 1832 were not the proprietors of Old Sarum or West Looe but the working classes. Their pressure had set the engine of reform in motion but it careered totally out of their control. Reform was therefore bound to sharpen class perspectives and antagonisms. Some of their leaders for a short time believed that increased middle-class representation would lead to rapid additional adjustments to the constitution; they were soon disabused. Others, like Henry Hetherington and Bronterre O'Brien, inveighed against the middle-class 'betrayal' almost immediately and made it into the primary engine of radical agitation in the later 1830s and 1840s. Reform, he wrote in March 1833, would 'detach from the working classes a large portion of the middle ranks' and he gloomily prognosticated that, 'Of all governments, a government of the middle classes is the most grinding and remorseless'. (251, *903*) The decisions taken in 1832 ensured that working men would enter the political kingdom crablike, in sideways motion. In the medium term, their representation would increase, but only when their betters deemed that they had shown sufficient evidence of their good behaviour and amenability to the existing order. They must learn, with such as Gladstone their tutors, that votes were privileges to be earned, not rights to be claimed. History would vindicate Tom Paine (Ch. 8) no more than it vindicated the duke of Wellington.

Great stress has been laid here on what was not changed by 1832, but the Reform Act nevertheless opened the door on a new political world. Despite Grey's conservative intentions and the fact that his success probably gave the aristocracy an extra half-century's lease on power, his necessary concession over reform left constitutional questions available for future amendment. The 1832 Act, not the subsequent Reform Acts of 1867, 1884 and 1918, was the decisive move. Despite what Lord John Russell and other Whigs affected to believe, the first Reform Act could never be the final settlement. Peel later rationalized his objections to the Reform Act by saying that he was reluctant to open a door which he saw no prospect thereafter of being able to close. Though the 1832 Act was profoundly anti-democratic in sentiment, its very passage showed how future pressure might bring further concession until, almost imperceptibly, democracy ceased to be one of Westminster's rude words. The development of a recognizably modern political system was a protracted and unheroic business; the most lasting changes frequently are. However unlikely it may have seemed in 1832, the first Reform Act marked the true beginning of the process.

---

1. Hansard, 3rd ser., i, (1831), col. 613.
2. J. Vernon, *Politics and the People: A Study in English Political Culture, 1815–67* (Cambridge, 1993), p. 38.
3. B. L. Add. MSS. 44358.
4. Hansard, 3rd ser., iii (1831), col. 307.
5. M. Foot and H. G. C. Matthew, eds, *The Gladstone Diaries* vol. i (1968), p. 551.
6. Hansard, 3rd ser., ix (1831), col. 420.
7. *Greville Memoirs* (8 vols, 1888), iii, p. 30.

CHAPTER 25

The condition of England question: I The new Poor Law

I

The Whig government of Lord Grey needed no reminding that its assumption of office and the passage of the Reform Act for which it is best remembered owed much to the social and economic crisis of 1829–32. While it would be grandiose to suggest that the Whigs evolved a 'social policy' to meet it, the conjunction of short-term slump and the recognition of the magnitude of Britain's industrial transformation necessitated a more wide-ranging approach to social problems. It was important that a Whig, rather than a Tory, party faced this challenge. When all allowances have been made for the fragility of party allegiance after 1827 (Ch. 23), it remained true that such prominent Whigs as Brougham, Althorp, Russell, Lansdowne and Spring Rice had assimilated the new political economy now so firmly entrenched in Scotland (Ch. 5) and were, in consequence, receptive to more thoroughgoing ideas of social change. Althorp had been an early member of James Mill's Political Economy Club. The Whig *Edinburgh Review* had been publishing a steady stream of articles on the major social questions of the day since the end of the French Wars. To these, Brougham had been a leading contributor. In 1828, important articles by J. R. McCulloch on the Poor Laws and by Thomas Babington Macaulay on the utilitarian theory of government appeared.

Attention had concentrated on poverty and on how efficiently the Elizabethan statutes governing the administration of poor relief operated. The Poor Law question had been in the forefront of public discussion since poor rates had increased so spectacularly in the last quarter of the eighteenth century [D.vii.i]. Farmers whinged to parliamentary select committees, such as those in 1817 and 1824, set up to consider poverty and labourers' wages. The political economists believed the old Poor Law an irrational hindrance to the emergence of a free market in labour which they deemed essential to future prosperity. Malthus had inveighed against the evils of over-population (Ch. 5). The new generation of *laissez-faire* thinkers, J. R. McCulloch, David Ricardo and Thomas Chalmers composed elaborate variations upon the basic theme. By the 1820s, with Poor Law expenditure already under some check, the dominant intellectual view was that the old Poor Law, based on *ad hoc* schemes of parochial relief, exacerbated the very problems it was designed to alleviate. Those allowances and supplementations in aid of inadequate wages which had become common in southern and eastern England from the 1780s onwards were the subject of particular attack. The 'Speenhamland System', named after the Berkshire village where magistrates drew up relief scales in the famine year of 1795, provided variable amounts of relief according to the size of a labourer's family and the prevailing price of bread. The

mighty weight of political economy came crashing
encouraged large families and hence more labourers fo
labour market (Ch. 16). If parishes supplemented wages as a
should any farmer subsidize his colleagues by paying more
Further, if the parish would provide whether a labouring fa
industrious, assiduous in the pursuit of work or feckless, what inc
for that individual endeavour which was, in microcosm, the very
national aspiration and achievement?

Private charity was thus recommended in preference to a bloated and r
system of institutional relief which, as the 1824 Select Committee put it, co
the previously hardy and independent wage-labourer into 'the degraded
inefficient pensioner of the parish'[1]. By the late 1820s the school of utilitar
reformers, whose mentor was Jeremy Bentham, was coming to prominence no
least because it offered a developed alternative to the old Poor Law. As early as
1796, Bentham himself had supplied Arthur Young with a scheme for pauper
management in workhouses where conditions were less desirable than those which
any labourer who could support himself independently might enjoy. Orthodox
economists like Ricardo had mounted a supremely efficient demolition job on the
Poor Laws, but their logic drove them into the politically unacceptable corner of
complete abolition. The Benthamites, broadly in favour of *laissez-faire* but less
wary of some State initiatives (Ch. 32), presented a more elegant solution. The
Poor Law could be radically remodelled; its pernicious effects and 'debasing
influences' would be eliminated while those genuinely incapable of providing for
themselves, the aged, the infirm and the orphan, would still receive necessary
support (327, 82). The key to the problem lay with the able-bodied poor who,
according to prevailing opinion, were being maintained redundantly at the
ratepayers' expense. Both J. R. McCulloch in the 1830 edition of his *Principles of
Political Economy* and that most energetic Benthamite, Edwin Chadwick,
developed Bentham's ideas in calling for the able-bodied to be kept in workhouses
in conditions 'less eligible' than those which might be enjoyed by the most
wretched independent labourer. Thus would disappear all premiums on idleness
and improvidence, those incentives to redundant procreation. Such a sweeping
objective could only be achieved by a rational administrative structure to replace
the myriad local customs currently in force. The Utilitarians added to the principle
of less eligibility a central supervisory and regulatory body to put the objective into
practice briskly and professionally. Poor Law reform was to be supported by the
pillars of centralization and compulsion.

Since both of these concepts ran clean counter to the general ethos of the British
government it should be enquired how they came to be accepted. The intellectual
confidence, if not cocksureness, of Benthamites like Chadwick offers only a partial
explanation. They did not operate in an ideological vacuum. Other writers saw
local administration of the Poor Law, whatever the practical shortcomings, as
critical to the continuance of aristocratic paternalism. The high Tory David
Robinson, writing in *Blackwood's Edinburgh Magazine* in 1818, offered a
proto-Keynesian defence of the Poor Laws arguing them to be 'the great prop of
wages; abolish them and . . . the body of your British labouring orders will be

of taxed articles' (250, *246–7*). Few
nd timeless scepticism towards ideology
'ons even where they understood them.

ving Riots (Ch. 16) and by the
£7m. in 1831–32. Captain Swing
he labourers were biting or, more
en revolution seemed possible.
he towns, the still unreformed
.o Althorp's establishment of a Royal
.oi Law and suggest changes. The more active
..an Commission were heavily influenced by the new
...ny. Its dominant intellectual figure was Nassau Senior, Professor of
..cal Economy at Oxford, whose *Three Lectures on the Rate of Wages* (1830)
had savaged the allowance system. The lawyer Walter Coulson was a disciple of
Bentham and a member of the Political Economy Club. The Canningite MP
William Sturges Bourne had chaired the 1817 Select Committee which had
recommended abolition of the Poor Law. The two episcopal members, Sumner of
Chester and Blomfield of London, were both noted opponents of the Poor Laws
and the former had adopted a broadly Malthusian stance on social issues. A
significant addition was made in 1833 when Chadwick was promoted from
assistant commissioner, in which post he had already given ample proof of his
abilities and his immense, if blinkered, vigour.

The political battle over Poor Law reform had been won by 1832. Impartial
scrutiny of the old system by the Royal Commission was not likely. Since the
commissioners' task was reform rather than appraisal much historical criticism of
their methods misses the point. The voluminous evidence collected by twenty-six
assistant commissioners who knew what their masters wanted was used to buttress
conclusions already broadly reached. Witnesses were led along prepared
Benthamite paths. The enquiry concentrated specifically on how the old Poor Law
worked and not on any broader economic factors, such as population pressure,
unless these were deemed to flow from the evils of the existing system. Little
attempt was made to quantify or even codify the voluminous material. Indeed, Nassau
Senior had written the main body of the Report before all the evidence was in.

The 1834 Poor Law Report proceeds apparently remorselessly, but in fact by
careful selection of evidence, to the conclusion that the old Poor Law was the
primary cause of poverty. Local evidence supporting the commissioners' view is
quoted with approval: 'The system of allowance is most mischievous and ruinous,
and till it is abandoned the spirit of industry can never be revived'. 'With very few
exceptions, the labourers are not as industrious as formerly.' 'He complained of
their deficiency in industry, arising from their growing indifference, or rather
partiality, to being thrown on the parish.' 'If a system of allowances is adopted in a
parish ... the whole of the labourers are made paupers. ... One impoverished

farmer turns off all his labourers; the rest do the same, because they cannot employ their own shares and pay the rest too in poor rates. . . . All grow poor together.' (335, *146–50*) Each form of allowance in aid of wages was roundly condemned; so were the amateurish, if not corrupt, overseers and land-owning JPs who had corrupted the pristine intentions of the Elizabethan legislators.

Though the Poor Law Commission undoubtedly exaggerated the extent to which the old system created poverty and ignored the extent to which many parishes had tightened up their relief procedures in the 1820s there is little doubt that the old Poor Law imposed artificial constraints on both farmers and labourers from which the latter, in particular, derived little benefit. The commissioners' solution was to reduce poor rate expenditure by making application for relief by able-bodied males a far less attractive alternative than hitherto. They recommended the creation of separate workhouses for the aged and infirm, for children, for able-bodied females and able-bodied males in groups of parishes (or Unions) brought together for that purpose. Their recommendation on the termination of relief outside the workhouse for the fit was quite unequivocal: 'All relief whatever to able-bodied persons or to their families, otherwise than in well-regulated workhouses . . . shall be declared unlawful and shall cease'. (335, *375*) The Benthamite solution of a central board with power to appoint assistant commissioners and to frame and enforce regulations was further proposed. The Poor Law, it seemed, was to be professionalized, rationalized and unified.

The passage of the Poor Law Amendment Act in 1834, based on these recommendations, was singularly trouble-free [C.iii]. A few political concessions were made. The language of the Act was notably less strident than that of the Report; the Report's recommendation that the prohibition of relief to the able-bodied 'should come into universal operation at the end of two years' was quietly dropped. But the momentum of reform was too great to be halted by a few parliamentary speeches from the likes of the now ageing Cobbett and a campaign against the despotic implications of centralization from John Walter of *The Times*. The passage of the Poor Law Amendment Act is perhaps the earliest example of the tyranny of the expert. Did not Senior and Chadwick have all the facts at their command? How could opposition to a rational reform stand against the confident certainties of those who had not only the intellectual conviction but the empirical evidence to buttress their position? The Tory parliamentary opposition was cowed. Wellington could not understand the arguments. Peel who, being one, had a soft spot for experts, was singularly unobstructive. Legislation with greater long-term implications for the well-being of the poor than any other passed before the age of Lloyd George went through the Commons with never more than fifty members voting against any clause or full reading. Within Parliament, indeed, reaction was not only acquiescent but enthusiastic. After all, it promised to save landed ratepayers money, and virtually all MPs were substantial landed ratepayers. The Church of England was compliant. Richard Bagot, the Bishop of Oxford, told the clergy of his diocese in 1834 that 'the new Bill is the result of much patient and diligent investigation . . . [by] persons who . . . have the comfort and happiness of the lower orders at heart' (326, *184*). A few years later, Althorp noted to Brougham, 'So far as my observation goes, the new Poor Law is the most universally popular measure I can remember' (87, *129*). Significantly for future developments, however, the kernel of what parliamentary opposition there was came from the newly enfranchised boroughs of the North-west and the West Midlands.

III

The Poor Law Amendment Act in practice proved to be a very different instrument from that envisaged by the Benthamites as they carefully sifted the evidence thrown up by the Royal Commission. The old political world had at least as much say in its administrative arrangements as the new. Edwin Chadwick, the new-broom expert, was passed over for a place on the Commission. Only Senior's intercession elevated him to the position of secretary in which he chafed, fulminated and infuriated his superiors for several years. The commissioners were patronage appointments. J. G. Shaw-Lefevre was both a loyal Whig and bailiff of the Althorp Spencer estate. For balance, Thomas Frankland Lewis commended himself both as a Tory and a county M.P., who might be expected to allay the suspicions of the country gentlemen. He also drafted the 1817 Select Committee Report on the Poor Laws. George Nicholls was head of the Birmingham branch of the Bank of England but known as a Poor Law reformer through his work in the Nottinghamshire parish of Southwell. The assistant commissioners, whose job it was to supervise the grouping of parishes and the erection of workhouses, were also generally recruited on the patronage network. Many of the twenty-one employed in 1836 were retired service officers, lawyers or estate agents having useful political connections, generally with the Whig party.

The powers of the Poor Law commissioners were also far more limited than opponents at the Act liked to pretend. The 'General Orders' by which the commissioners administered the Act could be challenged in Parliament. Though Poor Law Guardians were elected in each Union, old-style JPs became Guardians *ex officio* and continued to make vital decisions on the administration of relief. In some vital areas the commissioners lacked the power, or the political will, to impose the uniform regulations which the Benthamites had considered crucial to their plans. Most Boards of Guardians, for example, erected one large workhouse rather than the separate houses for separate categories of pauper favoured by Chadwick. No clear central directions were forthcoming and local resources became the determining factor in workhouse provision. The commissioners did not even insist that a workhouse be built; some of the most anguished, though impotent, complaints came from assistant commissioners and inspectors trying to persuade parsimonious Guardians to abandon inadequate pre-1834 accommodation and construct new houses. Of the Bolton workhouse, which would not be replaced until 1854, an assistant commissioner frustratedly reported: 'There is no classification; males and females occupy the same airing grounds and even the same privies. ... the workhouse in its present state cannot be conducted with proper discipline and economy' (338, *50*). No workhouse was built even in Norwich until 1859 because it would have been political suicide for either the local

Whig or Tory party to have incurred the odium of bringing a workhouse test to the city. While rural workhouse building proceeded apace in the 1830s and 1840s, a true workhouse programme cannot be said to have been in train in many urban areas until the 1850s. By 1870, however, about four-fifths of the 647 Poor Law Unions had built new workhouses (337).

Workhouse scandals were also given wide publicity by anti-reformers, but these were almost invariably the responsibility of sadistic workhouse masters or cheese-paring Boards of Guardians. At Andover in 1845 starving paupers were discovered to be eating marrow from the bones supplied to the workhouse for crushing. At Fareham, bed-wetting orphans were placed in the stocks. In neither case could blame be laid at the door of 'those tyrants in Somerset House'. Diversity of local practice, in fact, was just as pronounced after 1834 as before, with central pressure, usually ineffectual, applied more towards improving local inadequacies than to warning against excessive indulgence of provision. The practice of 1834 proved very different from the theory. The ratepayer franchise for Board of Guardian elections, which the Utilitarians favoured to reduce excessive powers of landowners and substantial tenant farmers, often prevented local expenditure on pauper education, medical services or even basic workhouse sanitation. Just as assistant commissioners were learning at first hand the complexity and diversity of the poverty problem which the Poor Law Report had grotesquely oversimplified and suggesting improved provision, so many ratepayers were voting from their pockets to frustrate them.

Diversity rather than uniformity also characterizes that most talismanic feature of utilitarian reform, the abolition of outdoor relief for the able-bodied. In the early years of the Act, of course, insufficient workhouse accommodation was available to make indoor relief a practicable proposition. But outdoor relief continued to be more or less freely available for destitute women and children at least until the 1870s. About 4 or 5 per cent of the population were in receipt of poor relief in the 1850s and 1860s, and of these more than four-fifths were relieved outside the workhouse [D.vii.2]. Official evidence suggests, however, that by the 1860s fit men were finding it difficult to obtain outdoor relief. Even during the depression of the early 1840s, when unemployment was high and workhouse accommodation in the industrial North totally inadequate, large numbers of men were denied relief altogether. Only in 1843 did the total number of able-bodied males given outdoor relief 'on account of want of work' or 'insufficiency of earnings' or 'other causes not being sickness, accident or infirmity' marginally exceed 40,000 (337, *181*).

Though the Outdoor Relief Orders of 1844 and 1852 allowed a considerable measure of local discretion, few local Unions seem to have been keen to relieve fit men outside the House. The numbers of unemployed adult males in receipt of outdoor relief in the 1850s was very small, a minimum of 1,600 in 1853 and a maximum of 12,000 in 1858. Since only 5–7 per cent of the workhouse population were adult males, it follows that most Unions were seeking to avoid making the main breadwinner a charge on the rates. Fit men might find that Chadwick's principle of 'less eligibility' had been subtly transmuted by the local Boards of Guardians into one of 'non-eligibility'. Official figures, however, as some historians might be reminded (337), are exceedingly blunt instruments. The effects of non-relief for able-bodied males might be mitigated by more generous treatment for dependants when local guardians thought it advisable. Guardians did not, in the main, officiously strive to inform the Poor Law Boards of such sleights of hand. Also, as assistant commissioner E. C. Tufnell reported of the Frome Union (Somerset) in 1842, the definition of 'sickness' could be conveniently elastic, enabling 'almost' able-bodied males to be relieved without incurring official displeasure.[2]

Workhouse conditions varied enormously, but scandals such as that at Andover were very much the exception. 'Less eligibility' soon proved unworkable since the condition of many independently supported labourers in the late 1830s and early 1840s was so low that a less eligible diet, for example, would have been both impractical and inhumane. Workhouse food reached a general standard of adequacy if an equal degree of monotony. Local Guardians, however, had ample psychological weapons to keep hordes from the workhouse gates. Workhouse clothing, grinding discipline, demeaning labour tasks, such as oakum-picking and stonebreaking, plus a degree of sexual segregation and denial of basic stimulants like tobacco and alcohol, were quite sufficient to set the inmate apart. As intended, the workhouse came to symbolize degradation, a torch of shame which continued to burn into the souls of the twentieth-century poor right up to the days of Neville Chamberlain.

In some areas the new Poor Law represented a greater break with tradition than in others. The large landowners of Northamptonshire maintained their traditional hold over social policy. They had Union boundaries drawn with remarkable proximity to the boundaries of their own estates, and they filled the important offices either themselves or by proxy. In towns and rural areas without aristocratic domination local Poor Law duties devolved on the professional middle classes, the small shopkeepers, even skilled workers. If diversity vitiated the supreme Benthamite principle of 1834, however, the Act did pass its most important test. It rendered poor relief less expensive. Though many individual exceptions may be cited, including large cities like Leeds in the early years, national poor relief expenditure which had stood at £7m. in 1831 and £6.3m. in 1833 was down to £4.6m. by 1840 with quinquennial averages usually between £5m. and £6m. for an ever growing population between 1840 and 1865 (D.vii.1]. While these results were undoubtedly helped by the emergence of a more mature industrial economy less prone to short-term slumps and massive temporary unemployment and by emigration from the countryside to the town, and while the Commission only grasped the technically complex issue of pauper settlement gingerly and in stages in 1834, 1846 and 1865 [C.iii], it is difficult to escape the broad conclusion that the new administrative structure was more cost-effective than the old and that the philosophy of deterrence, though not operating as the Benthamites intended, did have real effect.

IV

It was on the issue of deterrence and on the alleged inhumanity of the new system that opposition concentrated. The Poor Law was an obvious target both for radical supporters of working-class aspirations and for paternalists who saw in its administration an alien and uncaring shift towards centralization and bureaucracy. The famous anti-Poor Law campiagner Richard Oastler asserted in 1837 that it 'lays the axe to the root of the social compact: it must break up society and make England a wilderness'.[3]

Much of the analysis of the Royal Commission had been concerned with the problem of structural under-employment in the South and East (Ch. 16). Even Chadwick, who thought himself fully equipped with intelligence about both villages and towns, knew little about the specific problems of northern industrialism. It is not surprising, therefore, that the commissioners first went to work in southern England in 1835, incidentally during a period of economic recovery. Even here they met considerable opposition from local JPs, from anti-centralizing clergymen and from labourers themselves. At Bapchild (Kent) in April 1835 the relieving officer and a newly elected Guardian were mobbed and their administrative papers destroyed. The next month a cart taking paupers from the old workhouse in Chalfont St Giles (Bucks) to the new Union workhouse at Amersham was attacked and the inmates removed. Workhouses in East Anglia were damaged by villagers hostile to the new methods of pauper classification and by the segregation of the sexes. Many new workhouses were attacked, including St Clement's at Ipswich, and the relieving officers molested (336). While order was quickly restored and the commissioners could play down opposition in their annual reports, sporadic anti-Poor Law activity continued well into the 1840s as part of the enduring but unfocused tradition of rural discontent. Some of it resurfaced as instances of arson, sheep-stealing and animal maiming. The incidence of theft and maiming increased substantially in the later 1830s and 1840s. In Wales, opposition to the new bastardy provisions was an important element in the Rebecca Riots of 1843–44 during which many workhouses were attacked.

The opposition of the industrial North, however, was of an altogether different order of magnitude. It was not mere northern cussedness which united manufacturers and magistrates in the common conviction that outsiders from London could not possible rival their knowledge of local circumstances. Much *ad hoc* Poor Law reorganization had already taken place in the towns; relief policy had been adjusted to industrial conditions. Of what use was an arbitrary workhouse test to an industrial community where labour shortages alternated with devastating short-term slumps? No workhouse imaginable could have coped with Bolton's or Stockport's unemployed in 1841. The solutions of 1834 were inappropriate here and when the commissioners belatedly, and almost reluctantly, cast their eyes north of the Trent in 1837 they were told so. A whole series of Anti-Poor Law associations sprang up in Lancashire and Yorkshire which briefly united Tory paternalists like Oastler, John Fielden of Todmorden and Parson G. S. Bull of Bierley with radicals like the Salford printer R. J. Richardson, the Bradford metal-worker and tavern-keeper Peter Bussey and the Owenite socialist from Huddersfield, Laurence Pitkeithly.

Anti-Poor Law agitation in the North was part of a continuum of causes in the 1830s ranging from activity to limit factory hours (Ch. 26), in which Bull, Oastler and Pitkeithly were prime movers, through to Chartism (Ch. 29) which split working-class radicals from anti-democratic paternalists. The ferment of this decade meant that the commissioners had to contend with a high degree both of organization and political education. Huge public meetings gave practised demagogues like Oastler and the Methodist preacher Joseph Rayner Stephens excellent opportunities to harangue the crowds on 'centralization', 'pauper Bastilles' and the monstrous injustices of 'less eligibility'. Guardians known to favour the new law were mobbed and stoned. In Rochdale, anti-Poor Law Guardians were elected who solemnly refused to relieve the old township overseers of their traditional responsibilities. In Bradford, Dewsbury and Todmorden Guardian meetings were broken up and rioting occurred. Throughout, many of the most spirited anti-Poor Law protestors were women. Some were angered by the new bastardy provisions and the moral judgements they implied about the poor. Others, with direct responsibility for managing family budgets, could see more clearly than many men the implications of reduced allowances for domestic economy.

The degree of integrated pressure from the industrial north alarmed the authorities in London, and the only sensible reaction from Somerset House was tactical retreat. The main demand of the agitators was met in 1838 when Guardians in Lancashire and the West Riding were effectively empowered to continue as before 1834, with no requirement to implement a workhouse test. No workhouse was built anywhere in the West Riding in the 1840s, though it should be said that old methods were powerless to prevent massive suffering during the slump of 1841–42.

Anti-Poor Law sniping continued into the 1840s, though the stereotype of the inhumane, centralized Commission was constantly belied by countless local and individual variations. Oastler turned his *Fleet Papers* of 1843–44 into an extended diatribe against the Commission. W. R. Baxter published his *Book of Bastiles* in 1841 with evidence every jot as selective as that used by Chadwick and Senior eight or nine years before. The outcry against the Commission generated by the Andover scandal (see p. 235) produced legislative fruit. A new Poor Law Board was created in 1847 [C.iii], subject to clearer parliamentary scrutiny and control than the Commission. Its appearance met at least some of the objections even of hardened critics like Walter of *The Times*. Perhaps ironically, and in the generally less troubled times of the 1850s and 1860s with no Chadwickian bumptiousness to raise hackles, the Board superintended a programme of workhouse construction and relief testing which eventually brought Poor Law administration nearer to the objectives of the reformers of 1834 than is often realized.

---

1. Quoted in M. E. Rose, ed., *The English Poor Law, 1780–1830* (Newton Abbot, 1971), p. 52.
2. P. Randell, 'The nineteenth-century Poor Law in Somerset: The case of Wincanton', University of Lancaster M. Litt. thesis, 1983.
3. J. T. Ward. ed., *Popular Movements, 1830–50* (1970), p. 80.

CHAPTER 26

The condition of England question: II Factory reform, education and public health

I

The Poor Law Commission was the most assertive and obvious example in the 1830s and 1840s of what would come to be called the growth of government, whose wider implications are discussed elsewhere (Ch. 32). The major intellectual influence in all of this was undoubtedly that of the Benthamite Utilitarians, but in the three areas of growing State involvement during the 1830s and 1840s discussed here they faced stern competition. In the campaign for factory reform, moreover, most of the protagonists actively opposed the new political economy. Richard Oastler, a land agent, Michael Sadler, a linen merchant and the Revd George Bull, an evangelical curate, all from the West Riding of Yorkshire, were Tory paternalists. They were sceptical of the benefits presumed to flow from unfettered competition and they saw the State as the natural agency whereby the most brutish aspects of industrial capitalism could be curbed. The State should not shrink from donning the mantle of benevolent concern for its citizens somewhat hazily presumed to have been worn by the landowners of rural England in their dealings with the peasantry. In particular, the State must protect children from exploitation by factory owners.

While child labour, so far from being a nineteenth-century innovation, was an essential aspect of the pre-industrial economy (Ch. 14), the factory system imposed a more regimented and frequently unhealthy regime on children working as much as twelve to fourteen hours a day. Early attempts at regulation by Sir Robert Peel sen. in 1802 and 1819 [C.i] and by the radical MP J. C. Hobhouse in 1825 foundered on the rocks of easy evasion and expensive prosecution. By 1830, however, the factory reform movement, which had begun in Lancashire, had spread into Yorkshire, gaining strength as it went. It was supported not only by humanitarians and anti-capitalists, anxious to find any means of showing the new industrialism in a bad light, but by trade unions. John Doherty, leader of the Manchester Cotton Spinners, had played a leading role in the agitation for the 1825 Act, the spinners believing that, given the organization of the textile factories, any limitations of the working day for children should mean shorter hours for all.

Humanitarianism, not surprisingly, was the focus of the reformers' propaganda. Richard Oastler's famous open letter 'Yorkshire slavery', which appeared in the *Leeds Mercury* in October 1830, spoke of 'thousands of little children . . . sacrificed at the shrine of avarice, without even the solace of the negro slave'. Within a few months, thousands of operatives and sympathetic tradesmen had organized themselves into Short Time Committees. In March 1832, Sadler, who represented the pocket Yorkshire borough of Aldburgh which parliamentary reform would shortly remove and who was as opposed to changing the political system as he was in favour of ameliorating the plight of factory children, introduced a ten hours bill to limit the working day for all people under the age of eighteen (339).

The factory question stirred deep passions. The *Leeds Mercury*, rapidly developing under Edward Baines as the leading mouthpiece of the nonconformist Yorkshire clothing interest, carried numerous articles denouncing Oastler; so Oastler published in more sympathetic local journals the Tory *Intelligencer* and the Radical *Patriot*. The configuration of economic interest by no means precisely represented the contending factions. Paternalist factory masters like John Wood of Bradford, John Hornby of Blackburn and John Fielden of Todmorden were all prominent reformers. On the other side, the Association of Master Manufacturers, which dressed up self-interest in the more acceptable garb of political economy and argued against moves which, it was said, would undermine competitiveness overseas as well as infringing the freedom of the market in labour, was supported by influential landowners like Fitzwilliam and, from within the Whig Cabinet, Graham and Russell. Certain patterns, however, do emerge. Many West Riding Tories were virulently hostile to what they regarded as parvenu industrialists, whose religious dissent added a keener edge to the acrimony of their overwhelmingly Anglican opponents. Also, as political economists like Chadwick and Senior appreciated, many of the industrialist factory reformers were large manufacturers in towns which had already implemented, and even exceeded, the reform now being promoted. Factory reform, they believed, would disproportionately disadvantage smaller manufacturers still dependent on water-power in rural areas, where the problems of labour recruitment were much more difficult.

Sadler's parliamentary campaign enjoyed considerable success. The select committee appointed to consider the factory issue was dominated by his allies and, not surprisingly, it produced a most damning litany of abuse, exploitation, factory cripples, immorality and premature death – all attributable to the factory system. But the parliamentary Reform Act unhinged the Ten Hours chariot. Sadler, dispossessed in Aldburgh, was defeated in the famous Leeds election of 1832 by the prosperous nonconformist flax-spinner John Marshall and the Whig intellectual and free-trade apologist T. B. Macaulay. The parliamentary leadership of the factory reformers passed to Lord Ashley (later seventh earl of Shaftesbury). On a majority of one in February 1833, his Ten Hours bill was set aside and a Royal Commission was set up to investigate the problem. The frenzy of agitation in Yorkshire had already convinced the Whigs that a factory Act was inevitable, but the composition of the Royal Commission ensured that the range of options available to them would be both wider and less uniformly unpalatable to the manufacturers than a Ten Hours bill. Crucially, the Commission's Report was in the hands of Edwin Chadwick.

The Commission suggested that much of the evidence to the Sadler Committee, widely publicized in such polemical Sadlerite journals as the *British Labourer's Protector and Factory Child's Friend*, had been either exaggerated or quoted out of context. The factory masters also grasped the opportunity to state their case. The humanitarian issues, they contended, had cloaked the reformers' true intentions, the reduction of the length of the working week for adults, contrary to all commercial sense and the requirements of the free market. The manufacturers' best apologist was Dr Andrew Ure whose *Philosophy of Manufactures* (1835) defended them against the 'mass of defamation' collected by Sadler in 1832.

Chadwick produced a Report favouring the economic arguments of the manufacturers, but which accepted that children needed protection from those masters who overworked them. Factory children were declared to be 'rapidly increasing . . . a very considerable proportion of the infant population'. Crucially, they were not free agents. A utilitarian case for State intervention was thus advanced while the general inadvisability of the State's interfering with conditions of work (Ch. 5) was upheld. In three important respects Sadler and Ashley had been outbid. The 1833 Factory Act [C.i] entirely prohibited factory work by the under-nines; it also included schemes both for compulsory schooling and for a government-appointed inspectorate to supervise implementation. From this latter, and initially inadequate, innovation, indeed, did a whole government bureaucracy grow during the next two generations (Ch. 32). Althorp also ignored Chadwick's recommendation and circumscribed conditions of work for young people between the ages of thirteen and eighteen.

The Ten Hours reformers had to regroup, diverted now by anti-Poor Law agitation, now by Chartism, while the new factory inspectors were learning at first hand of the weaknesses of the 1833 Act and of the fertility of factory owners in evading the intentions of the legislature. Too many factory 'schools' taught nothing, or very little. Age regulations were widely evaded, sometimes with active parental connivance; before civil registration in 1837 precise evidence of age on which to base prosecutions was difficult to obtain. Factory owners also evinced a wholly unsurprising aversion to the red tape of declarations and form-filling. Perhaps most morale-sapping of all, fines on factory owners rarely offered any disincentive to continued recalcitrance, particularly when so many urban magistrates (some of them now factory owners anyway) shared an antipathy to central controls.

Nevertheless, the very operation of the Act brought abuses to light. Administration was generating its own momentum. When a select committee under Ashley's chairmanship met in 1840 to consider the operation of the Factory Act, one of its most trenchantly constructive critics was the factory inspector, Leonard Horner. Horner's experience had converted him from a position of extreme scepticism to one of warm support for the ten-hour day. The 1844 Factory Act, finally introduced by the Tory Home Secretary Sir James Graham after much prevarication and contention over the education to be given to factory children (see p. 244) embodied many of Horner's ideas, notably the switch to half-day working for children under thirteen [C.i]. By this time, largely under Ashley's harrying, a Children's Employment Commission had also reported, initiating the first restrictive legislation for mines, which also defined adult females as 'unfree agents' for whom the State must provide protection.

'Ten Hours' legislation, still a potent talisman in Yorkshire, was delayed until 1847 when it was guided through Parliament by the millowner, John Fielden, and the Yorkshire Tory squire Busfeild Ferrand, against a background of agitation by the central committees of Lancashire and Yorkshire which recalled the great excitements of 1832–33. Not for the first, or the last, time contentious legislation reached the statute-book at a time when its sponsors could claim that its injunctions were already common practice; a trade recession had already reduced hours of work in most northern mills. Richard Oastler, in a valedictory message published in the *Ten Hours Advocate*, exhorted the labourers on whose behalf he had striven for almost twenty years to use those precious extra leisure hours for 'the service of Almighty God' and 'the improvement of your minds and hearts . . . strive to become good men, good women – useful members of society' (92). Humanitarian concern and stern moral imperatives were naturally yoked in Victorian Britain. Even after 1847, millowners were able to avoid the intentions of the new statute by the use of gangs, relay systems and shifts. The ten-hour day was accepted as the factory norm only after amendments in 1850 and 1853 [C.i].

II

It is no accident that factory reform and educational provision were so often linked, for the factory symbolized an urban Britain far less secure in its civilizing influences than before. The spectre of an irreligious, overcrowded and brutalized working class herded together in monstrously multiplying towns like Salford or Bradford haunted more than the humanitarian reformers. Education for the lower orders, long considered by some an unnecessary if not dangerous indulgence since it might nurture ideas above people's station, became an important question. The Swing Riots and the popular reform disturbances of 1830–32 (Chs 16 and 23) drove the message home in unpleasantly insistent ways. As the *Edinburgh Review* put it in 1831 if the manufacturing population were 'made acquainted with those circumstances which principally determine their condition in life . . . those revolutionary and anti-social doctrines, now so copiously distributed, would be rejected at once'.

Long before 1830 both private and church day schools existed in large numbers and bewildering variety. Anglican and nonconformist school-building programmes had been greatly expanded during the evangelical revival (Ch. 6). Two parliamentary reports of 1818 and 1833 estimated that approximately 7 and 9 per cent respectively of the population were attending day-schools. Allowing for underestimates in the urban areas, perhaps 1½m. pupils were enrolled in the early 1830s. Such statistics reveal important areas of growth, but vast discrepancies were found in the quality of provision. Even in church schools, some children were not being encouraged to read; others were developing only that faculty of memory which enabled them to spew out uncomprehended chunks of the King James Bible of 1611. Among private schools, variations were far greater. Many of the so-called 'dame schools' were educationally worthless. The Manchester Statistical Society reported in 1834 that 'the greater part of them are kept by females, but some by old men, whose only qualification for this employment seems to be their unfitness for any other'. A regular curriculum rarely existed and dame schools served the dual function of providing teachers, more accurately child-minders, with their weekly coppers and keeping children off the streets while parents worked. At the other end of the spectrum, highly competent private schools existed for the children of working parents. In industrial areas, many parents were evidently prepared to pay a little more to send their children to such establishments rather than entrust them to the often heavy-handed and moralistic care of the churches. Some 'model' factory schools were also found, such as those of W. R. Greg at Caton (near Lancaster) or Henry Ashton at Turton (near Bolton), which provided evening classes for adults as well as daytime schooling for children. In few mills, however, was education permitted to interfere with production and the educational clauses of the 1833 Factory Act caused much resentment.

Educational statistics show a steady rise in pupil numbers but the overall quality of education is unmeasurable. It is known that absenteeism was common and that education was frequently regarded as a subordinate function of childhood. As late as 1840, probably one-third of all children never attended a day school. Since the length of education for working-class children rarely exceeded three and a half years, and was commonly less than two, levels of attainment even from reputable establishments cannot have been high.

The lack of control over educational output caused increasing alarm. In the early 1830s, roughly 60 per cent of all schools were private, rather than church, establishments and many feared, as had Davies Giddy MP in 1807, that in these ordinary folk would learn to read 'seditious pamphlets, vicious books and publications against Christianity' (347, 9). Church schools, by contrast, were regarded as safe.

The involvement of the State in education was very much a backstairs operation. After a move by Brougham in 1816 to give State grants to elementary schools had been rejected in Parliament, J. A. Roebuck tried in 1833 to establish compulsory education between the ages of six and twelve, with school fees supplemented by State grant. Despite his timely argument that 'the education of the people ought to be considered as a part of the duties of government . . . as a mere matter of policy', such a radical departure was unpopular. A derisorily small parliamentary grant of £20,000 [C.iv] was shunted through the Commons on a low vote, almost as a consolation prize. William Cobbett managed the characteristic sideswipe that any State support would only 'increase the number of schoolmasters and schoolmistresses – that new race of idlers'. The power of the Church, and particularly the Anglican, educational lobby was apparent in the terms governing the grant. Disbursements would go only to religious societies which could first raise half the necessary cash for school building themselves. The Anglican National Society, able to tap aristocratic and gentry funds, outbid nonconformist industrialists and other professional men under these rules in the ratio of 3 : 1. The State grant, in fact, tended to augment provision in the richer areas, where initial subscriptions could be raised, rather than the poorer areas where the need was greatest.

Anglican determination to dominate educational provision in these years is most evident. The Church of England was under severe attack in the 1830s (Ch. 27). Not only did it fear incursions from the nonconformists, the extent of which the religious census would soon embarrassingly reveal [G.vii] but it faced radical attacks for its great wealth, its tithes and its unearned privileges. Control over education became its surest guarantee of survival with all essential privileges intact, including, of course, establishment status. However vocal liberal and radical dissenting parliamentary voices may have been, their voting power was easily overborne by keen churchmen and country squires for whom 'the Church in Danger' was a tested, and still potent, rallying cry.

The 1830s saw numerous official and private enquiries and, in 1836, the establishment of a Central Society of Education, patronized by Lord John Russell and other leading Whigs. It was Thomas Spring Rice, Chancellor of the Exchequer from 1835–39, however, who was the moving spirit behind Whig proposals to increase state involvement in education. He cajoled his party into extending the fashion for government inspection into the field of education. He also proposed an increase in the State grant to £30,000 and the establishment of State 'normal schools' for non-sectarian education. He also successfully saw off opposition from Lord John Russell to the establishment of a new agency of administration, the bulkily titled Committee of the Privy Council on Education, in 1839. Supporters of Church education reacted with predictable fury to what they saw as a decisive challenge to their control over the education of the poor. They had considerable success in watering down Whig proposals. In the 'Concordat' between Church and State, agreed in July 1840, the normal school idea was dropped entirely and moneys to support it were transferred to the Churches to enable them to establish, or augment, their own training colleges. Perhaps more important, the Church of England secured control over appointments to the inspectorate of State-aided schools. Instructions regarding religious instruction became the responsibility of the two archbishops, and were handed down to the inspectors for implementation. Kay-Shuttleworth, the first secretary of the Committee of Council and the foremost educational administrator of the nineteenth century (Ch. 36), ruefully admitted that after the Concordat 'no plan of education ought to be encouraged in which intellectual instruction is not subordinate to the regulation of the thoughts and habits of the children by the doctrine and precepts of revealed religion' (348, 37). Five of the seven education inspectors in post in 1846 were Church of England clergymen.

The Concordat exacerbated the already acute religious controversy over education. In 1843, combined nonconformist, radical and Roman Catholic agitation delayed Graham's Tory Factory bill and aborted the educational clauses which would have given factory children three hours' education a day in schools under Anglican supervision. By the mid-1840s, Kay-Shuttleworth had ample proofs of his private conviction that State control over the schools its money was helping to build must be extended not only on educational grounds but as an attempt to bridge the sectarian divide. The 1846 pupil-teacher scheme [C.iv] (Ch. 36), began a new phase in State intervention. Governmental influence now began to match its rapidly increasing financial commitment, though still in partnership with the churches. The creation of State schools would be work for a future generation of educational reformers. Almost unnoticed amid the clamour of sectarian warfare, however, government grants to the churches were beginning to squeeze private schools for the lower orders. By mid-century the education of the poor was more in the hands of the Church than it had been even twenty years earlier.

III

It may seem ironic that the most profound social problem of all bore the least immediate legislative fruit. It was in the 1830s and 1840s that the links between dirt and disease were most conclusively established. The work of reforming doctors such as James Kay (the later Kay-Shuttleworth) in Manchester and Southwood Smith, physician to the London Fever Hospital, received wide publicity and the newly established statistical societies subjected industrial cities to minute investigation. It was incontrovertible that typhus was a major killer in areas which, as Kay reported, 'are narrow, ill ventilated, unpaved, or which contain heaps of refuse or stagnant pools'. A doctor reported of Leith, near Edinburgh, in the late 1830s that 'the parts of the town in which it seems to prevail chiefly . . . are the central and most crowded districts in which the number of cases amongst the poor during the last five years have been in the proportion of 1 to 6'. Elsewhere in the town the proportion was nearer 1 to 13 (340, *233*).

Knowledge about the health of towns was greatly enhanced by the establishment of civil registration of births and deaths. The first Registrar-General, appointed in 1837, was a London doctor, William Farr, and one of his earliest decisions was to require doctors to cite causes of death following an official classification. By the mid-1840s it was not open to anti-reformers to deny that the most important factors affecting longevity were an individual's social class and place of residence. This truth was most vividly brought home by Chadwick's famous *Sanitary Report* of 1842 (Ch. 17). Chadwick's interest in public health grew directly out of his work with the Poor Law Commission. He had expected to find workshyness the primary cause of poverty, but by 1838 it had been forcibly impressed upon him that the major factor was frequent illness, particularly from fevers, and premature death, all too often involving dependants for whom the Poor Law Union had to accept reluctant responsibility. His further conviction that much of this illness and mortality had an environmental base, and was consequently preventible given appropriate legislation and resources, turned him into a confirmed interventionist. The *Report*, written from an immense body of information supplied by medical men, Poor Law officials and the like, outsold any previous government publication and its eventual influence on the history of public health was immense (Ch. 33). From Farr's table of causes of death in 1838, admittedly not an unimpeachable source, readers could nevertheless gauge the strength of the environmentalists' case. Deaths from fevers, smallpox, consumption, pneumonia and similar diseases which Chadwick argued were substantially preventible, stood at 8–9 per thousand in the rural counties of Hereford, Lincoln and Yorkshire's North Riding. In Lancashire and Middlesex, the two counties which included the greatest concentrations of population, the rate was 18 and 29 respectively.

Though Chadwick was massively influential, his was by no means the only voice urging reform. The Health of Towns Commission produced two Reports in 1844 and 1845 which largely confirmed his findings and recommended improved local administration to supervise sewerage, drainage, water and paving schemes. In 1840 a parliamentary select committee on the health of towns, under R. A. Slaney, using witnesses many of whom had already been milked by Chadwick, reached predictably similar conclusions. All the informed evidence pointed in one direction, yet mighty obstacles lay in the way of an integrated plan for public health. The most important of these was localism. Reduced to essentials, few MPs in the 1840s would have disagreed with the observation that if Rochdale, say, was found to be dangerously filthy, then the responsibility for cleaning it lay with locally elected councillors not with central government. Central intervention was regarded as a form of dictatorship and not one for which history had prepared Britain's legislators. A second huge obstacle was the proliferation of contending agencies for refuse collection, water supply, lighting, paving, drainage and the rest. Many of these functions remained in private hands and where the enterprise did not pay it was not discharged. Poorer areas thus suffered most. Where services were under local authority control, an immense variety of practice still persisted. Some authorities were jealous of their neighbours; in others, squabbles between the various agencies were commonplace; in still others experts disagreed and no clear policy emerged. The Municipal Corporations Act of 1835 [C.ii] was a vitally important but permissive stage on the long road of administrative reorganization. Before 1848 local Improvement Acts were the more certain agency of administrative reform (Ch. 33).

Chadwick himself may have been a third, though more minor, reason for delay. Few advocates are less persuasive than the self-confident, self-righteous, intolerant, hectoring expert and Chadwick was all of these. His superiors on the Poor Law Commission had been happy to divert his demonic energies into public health enquiry after 1838 since his bullying discomfited them. Nor was Chadwick a man to gain his objectives by stealth. He poured scorn on the marquis of Normanby's efforts when, at the very end of the Whig ministry in 1841, he introduced three bills on urban building and drainage. Though, objectively, Chadwick's contention that these bills were precipitate and too narrow in scope was readily substantiable, his characteristic contempt for them alienated a convinced reformer; and there were few enough of these in the upper echelons of either party. Normanby's successor as Home Secretary, Sir James Graham, was far less sympathetic to State intervention.

Meanwhile, Chadwick ploughed on, trusting to the pressure of facts to compensate for his lack of political subtlety and tactical grasp. Criticism was even-handedly ladled out to those who wished to do nothing and 'trust the ratepayers' and to those who tried to improve but who got it wrong. Typically, the Birkenhead improvers were ticked off in 1844 for supporting an Act which failed to look 'beyond the immediate local experience' and was therefore in ignorance of 'the experience already obtained, as to the causes of disease and the practical means of prevention' (93, 95). There was much of the strident schoolmaster about Edwin Chadwick and it hindered his cause, as it has hindered others who have tried to change the habits of a nation with the methods of the scold.

Between 1832 and 1846 only two significant pieces of central legislation were passed on specific aspects of public health. The Cholera Act in 1832 [C.ii] appeared at the end of the first of four major nineteenth-century epidemics of the disease, which killed over 30,000 people. The spur to action was that cholera afflicted the middle classes and the poor alike. Significantly, cholera epidemics provoked more concerned debates in Westminster than did typhus outbreaks. The Vaccination Act of 1840 [C.ii] was an inexpertly drafted first attempt to curb smallpox, a dangerous and disfiguring disease which killed over 41,000 people between 1837 and 1840 (341). These were small beginnings, but in the next generation (Ch. 33) they would be seen to presage much larger initiatives. The deepest breaches in the dyke of *laissez-faire* would be made through public health legislation.

CHAPTER 27

'The Church in danger': Anglicanism and its opponents

I

In the early nineteenth century the Church of England had ranged itself unhesitatingly, if not unthinkingly, against reform. The vote among the bishops of twenty-one to two against the passage of the reform bill in October 1831 (Ch. 23) was only the climax of a policy of reaction which made it a natural target for attack. Radical writers like Richard Carlile, William Sherwin and the ex-Anglican London clergyman Robert Taylor characterized the Established Church as the corrupt and bloated lackey of the unreformed system. Statistical flesh had been put on the skeleton of anti-Anglican vituperation when John Wade's *Black Book: or Corruption Unmasked* appeared in 1820. His remarkably complete catalogue of church plural livings, absenteeism and gross disparities of income was reprinted during the reform crisis.

The logic of the radical case led to disestablishment of the Church and its replacement by religious organizations, supported entirely by voluntary contributions of the faithful. This 'Voluntarist' line was also taken by some nonconformist leaders, though most contented themselves with calling for the correction of proved abuses and the abolition of church rates. Nonconformist political sympathies were overwhelmingly Whig; towns with a substantial middle-class dissenting presence, like Birmingham, Leeds or Hull, proved generally reliable supporters of the Whig cause in national politics.

The tide had been flowing strongly against Anglican traditionalists since the late 1820s. They viewed Roman Catholic emancipation (Ch. 23) as a damaging threat to church supremacy; the fierceness of anti-clerical hostility during the Swing Riots of 1830–31 (Ch. 16) and during the reform crisis also alarmed clerics. For some parochial clergy, labouring unobtrusively in their rural vineyards, the advent of a Whig government in 1830 seemed to presage total ruin. For were not the new ministers the allies and coadjutors of republicans and atheists? The Whigs seemed 'little better than incarnate fiends' in 1830. As the nineteenth century wore on, also, it is noticeable that one of the most tenacious political alliances was that between the parish clergyman and the Tory party (366).

But the rural rectors need not have worried. Whig attitudes to politics and to religion proved remarkably similar. Whatever the views of their radical and dissenting supporters, most Whigs saw the Established Church not only as a buttress against rash change but also as a reliable educator of the nation's poor. As in politics, they were pragmatists; they did not encourage churchmen to believe that a continuation of the *status quo* was either desirable or possible. Earl Grey, a conservative reformer if ever there was one, was the natural friend of the Church, but he informed the long-serving and anti-reforming archbishop of York, Edward Vernon Harcourt, in 1834 that he was only prepared to countenance an Established Church prepared for 'the removal of some causes of complaint' (368, i, *52*). Perhaps fortunately for the Church, its other two leading dignitaries, William Howley of Canterbury and C. J. Blomfield of London, were not so averse to change. Blomfield, indeed, was an energetic, self-confident man, some of whose ideas on redistributing clerical wealth made conservative High-Church flesh creep. Howley, more pliant, sought to moderate and decelerate the more radical proposals with an emollient word here and a letter of considerate charm there. In his quiet way he was to play an important role in educating his Church to adapt to altered circumstances.

It is not difficult to identify the 'causes of complaint' to which Grey referred. The Church of England was overstocked with clergymen in the wrong places. Its urban ministry, somewhat stronger in 1830 than in 1800, nevertheless remained outmatched by the nonconformists. Too many of its incumbents did not live in their parishes. Too much of the Church's enormous income was redundantly, if not wastefully, enjoyed by a tiny handful of opulent clerical princes while curates and vicars had to make do with incomes which were plainly inadequate. This was what the theologian Edward Burton called 'that blot in our establishment' (357, *282*). It is hardly surprising that the Whigs' first move, in 1832, was to establish an Ecclesiastical Revenues Commission. Its Report [G.v.] vindicated some of the radicals' bitterest complaints. Almost half the Church of England's livings were found to be worth less than £200 a year while just over 2 per cent realized over £1,000 each. Not a few of these wealthiest livings were held in plurality by non-resident clergymen. Despite some improvement during the previous twenty years, only half the Church's 10,000 benefices in 1835 enjoyed the services of a resident incumbent [G.iv]. In the upper echelons, benefices were still distributed by political and social connection. The political involvements of the Established Church infuriated those who believed that its peculiar status militated against effective discharge of pastoral responsibility. R. M. Beverley's *Letter to the Archbishop of York* contended that 'as it is now constituted' the Church 'is a machine of Antichrist, greatly surpassing in the grossness of its abuses all other jobs or systems of corruption that ever have afflicted the Kingdom'.[1] He was doubtless thinking of patrons like the marquis of Bath, who bestowed all three of the livings in his gift on his son. The aristocracy and gentry had a vested interest in clerical abuses. In Norfolk, a county with a large number of wealthy gentry and a powerful aristocratic presence, eleven families held the right to present to at least five church livings each. Of more than eighty livings in the gift of these landowners, only 16 per cent were not held in plurality in the early 1830s (365, *178*). Nepotism was the usual reason. Five of the eight Norfolk livings in the gift of Baron Wodehouse of Kimberley were bestowed on his sons, and one more on another relative.

The dissenters, of course, had practical grievances. They organized impressive petitions to both Houses calling for the abolition of religious tests for admission to the ancient universities. A bill introduced by the Unitarian George Wood in 1834, and supported by some Cabinet members, passed the Commons before being thrown out in the Lords. The main dissenting campaign, however, was against church rates. These were annual levies to provide for the upkeep of Anglican churches. Once approved, the rate was a legal obligation on all property owners, Anglicans and dissenters alike. The vote for a rate at the churchwardens' vestry meeting was open to all; in urban areas of high nonconformist concentration this afforded a splendid opportunity for organized dissent to pack meetings and vote down any proposed rate. This occasioned financial embarrassment to the Church and gave practical vent to the principle that no church should require compulsory support from those of alternative religious persuasions. The refusal of a church rate in Birmingham in 1832 was only the best known of a series of *causes célèbres* during the 1830s and early 1840s, involving imprisonment for up to two years of dissenters' leaders like John Thorogood and numerous well-publicized expressions of anti-Anglican sentiment by the national nonconformist magazine *Eclectic Review* and local newspapers like the *Leicester Mercury* and the *Leeds Mercury*. As Melbourne reported to the King in 1837, church rates had 'produced in many places much unseemly discord and contention and very capricious and unsatisfactory results'.[2] As Melbourne well knew, the longer the church rates controversy simmered the more likely to come to the boil were the more extreme demands for voluntarism and disestablishment. The young Quaker John Bright first attracted national attention in 1840 as a campaigner against the vicar of Rochdale's attempts to impose a church rate. He told ratepayers angrily assembled in the town's graveyard: 'My friends, the time is coming when a State Church will be unknown in England, and it rests with you to accelerate or retard that happy consummation'. (366, *106*)

The Whigs had two bites at the church rate cherry in the 1830s but could not swallow either. Althorp's plan in 1834 to abolish the rate and replace it with an annual sum of £250,000 out of the land tax for church maintenance was roundly condemned by dissenters who not unreasonably argued that they would still have to support an alien church but as tax- rather than rate-payers. Tory support for Althorp's bill only increased Whig fears that they might lose their traditional hold on nonconformist votes and the proposal was allowed to drop. In 1837 Spring Rice proposed a fund in lieu of church rates to be established from a surplus to accrue if church leaseholds were more profitably managed. This idea appealed to dissenters, more than half a million of whom had signed a petition organized by the Church Rate Abolition Society. Church leaders, however, would have none of it, since it breached the crucial principle that a State Church must have State maintenance; if not, a bastion against disestablishment was removed. The reforming impulse of Melbourne's government, never strong, was unequal to church intransigence and, again, a church rate bill was dropped. Many urban clerics in the 1830s and 1840s exchanged their legal rights for parochial harmony by relying on voluntary contributions rather than vexatious rates. Those who would not ensured that the issue would remain a festering sore until Gladstone finally abolished them in 1868 [G.i] (364).

An important excuse for the Whigs in their relations with the dissenters was Ireland. Ireland again became a British problem from the late 1820s and after the General Election of 1835 the Whigs depended upon the support of Irish MPs under their nationalist leader Daniel O'Connell. All church questions in Ireland turned on the uncomfortable fact that less than 7 per cent of Irishmen were members of its Established Church, the Church of Ireland, while both the Catholic majority and Presbyterian minority were compelled to pay tithes to support Established Church ministers. In the west of Ireland, indeed, parishes could be found without a single communicant member of the State Church. After 1830 Catholics waged a bitter battle against tithe payment. Rural secret societies proliferated; tithe cattle were maimed or branded so that they should not be sold. In an affray over tithe cattle in Newtonbarry the local yeomanry killed twelve Catholic peasants. Anglican incumbents were reduced to penury where tithe was their main source of income.

The government passed a Coercion Act early in 1833 which brought the most disturbed counties under martial law, but it recognized the need for reform. Any proposed changes, however, intimately affected the ecclesiastical establishment on both sides of the Irish Sea. Grey's Irish Temporalities bill of 1833 proposed extensive ecclesiastical reorganization. Church of Ireland bishoprics were to be reduced in number; the revenues of Armagh and Derry, the two wealthiest sees, would be diminished; parishes with no practical function would not receive incumbents. The most contentious issue concerned the 'surplus revenues' to be released by these reforms. O'Connell's Irish MPs favoured stipends to Catholic priests. The Whigs envisaged a range of educational and social projects. But the principle of appropriating church revenue for any purpose other than the upkeep of the Church stirred atavistic passions. Most bishops thought it a possibly unretraceable step to disestablishment. Van Mildert called it 'an atrocious measure [which] bodes great evil to ourselves at no distant period' (366, *33*). The Tories hated it. Many Whigs, including Edward Stanley, the Chief Secretary for Ireland, shared their alarm. Irish church affairs both perplexed and weakened the government. It either capitulated on an issue which offered some hope for peace in Ireland or it pawned its future still more heavily on O'Connell and the radical MPs. Not surprisingly, the former course was chosen. The 'Appropriation clause', which dealt with the surplus revenues, was deleted from the bill to preserve the administrative reforms. When Lord John Russell raised the appropriation issue again in 1834 he provoked the resignations of Stanley, Graham, Richmond and Ripon from the government [A]. Grey himself resigned a few weeks later, now seventy years old and anxious anyway to lay down the burdens of office, but precipitated in his decision by Cabinet bickering over Irish church questions and by his colleagues' behind-the-scenes negotiations with O'Connell over modification of the Irish Coercion Act. Melbourne, his successor, was not in such secure control and his reconstituted Whig government, shorn now of the Established Church's most loyal supporters, made King William IV uneasy. He was traditional monarch enough to swallow Anglican propaganda about the inseparability of Church and State.

Irish church reform still foundered on the rock of appropriation. Russell, its most fervent government supporter, revived the question in 1835 in the context of tithe reform but a weakened Whig government could not carry it. The Irish, much to O'Connell's disgust, had to make do with a Tithe Act in 1838 which converted the hated impost to a money payment fluctuating with the price of grain and calculated at only three-quarters of its nominal value. In a feeble attempt to assuage peasant anger, payment was to be made by landlord rather than tenant (15). Arrears of tithe, very substantial by this time, were cancelled. Russell believed the Act the most important legislative contribution to peace in Ireland during his lifetime. However, it left Catholics to contribute to Church of Ireland maintenance. Unsurprisingly, Peel's Tory government of 1841–46 would not countenance appropriation when hardy radical spirits like the Sheffield MP H. G. Ward continued to urge it. Peel ran into substantial trouble from staunch Protestants in 1845 when the government grant to the Roman Catholic seminary at Maynooth was both enlarged and made permanent (Ch. 28). New, nonsectarian university colleges were founded in Belfast, Cork and Galway in 1845 in a generally unsuccessful attempt to broaden the base of university education beyond the Anglican-dominated Trinity College Dublin. The Catholic Church, which would only accept State aid for specifically Catholic colleges, scuppered the plan by discouraging attendance. Presbyterian middle-class students, however, attended Queen's College, Belfast in large numbers.

II

William IV's belief that the Whigs were unsound on the Church was an important factor in his decision to dismiss Melbourne in November 1834 and install a Tory administration in its stead [A]. Peel's minority government lasted barely four months but, in establishing the Ecclesiastical Duties and Revenues Commission in February 1835, it set the Church of England decisively on the road to reform. Peel's initiative was to church reform what Grey's had been to the political system. Both men were fundamentally conservative; both believed temperate reform the best defence of established institutions. As Peel had hinted in his famous Tamworth Manifesto of December 1834 (Ch. 28), his Tory party would be no haven of reaction on ecclesiastical or other questions. He was careful, however, to move slowly and with the approval of Archbishop Howley and Bishop Blomfield. The Ecclesiastical Commission consisted of leading politicians – Peel and Goulburn both sat on it and were replaced by Melbourne and Russell when the government changed hands – the two archbishops and three senior bishops. It functioned semi-independently, considering plans and drafting reports to form the basis of legislation (357). The Commission deliberately distanced itself from premature discussion at Westminster until its plans were ready. Its administrative burdens were borne by Charles Knight Murray, its lawyer-secretary and its reforming strategy was more the responsibility of Bishop Blomfield than of any other individual.

The Commission saw the need to eliminate plurality and non-residence as far as possible, to reduce the disparities in beneficed income and to create a more modern ecclesiastical structure by redrawing the map of episcopal boundaries. It was especially sensible of the need to increase the Church's presence in the towns. Not only must more churches be built; sufficient revenue must be made available to provide adequate stipends for their incumbents. Howley feared that 'the accumulated population of large towns' threatened the claims of the Church to be a 'National Establishment'. Presently it was leaving 'multitudes ... in a state of heathen darkness' (361, *301*). Between 1831 and 1851 the Commission supervised a programme of church building which managed the impressive feat of more than matching the rate of population growth in the major industrial areas of England. In this period the number of Anglican churches in Lancashire increased from 292 to 521 and in the West Riding of Yorkshire from 287 to 556.[3] In the whole country 2,029 new churches were built, overwhelmingly with money from the Church rather than the State. The rate of church building was approximately three times that during the twelve years after the passage of the Church Building Act in 1818 [G.i].

The Commission's work bore legislative fruit between 1836 and 1840 with the Established Church Act, the Pluralities Act and the Ecclesiastical Duties and Revenues Act [G.i]. These rectified the most glaring abuses and helped the Church to meet the challenges of urban society. Perhaps their psychological impact was even more important. The Commission proved that the Church could do what its enemies had believed impossible – reform itself in generally efficient ways. The overwhelmingly Tory clergy improved both in enthusiasm and morale between 1830 and 1860 as they assimilated the essentially Whig message that constructive change was the best defence against radical reconstruction. By 1860 few, apart from noncomformist zealots and a few dogged intellectual secularists, talked of disestablishment. That these groups made a disproportionate amount of noise should not be taken as evidence of the strength of their cause.

Two further reforms by Melbourne's government were equally important. After a long campaign, the dissenters gained the right to use their chapels for marriage services and so avoid the despised Anglican Church. The further right to an entirely civil marriage, though little used initially, would be of considerable long-term significance. Dissenters still moaned at the high cost of a marriage licence and at the need to have a registrar present at dissenters' ceremonies though not at Anglican ones, but the reform exactly met the requirements of the dissenter who had assured Grey in 1834 that most of his fellows favoured not disestablishment but rather the removal of practical grievances which they considered 'an insufferable evil, an arbitrary and despotic power held over [their] conscience and judgment'.[4]

Much the most complex reform was the Tithe Commutation Act of 1836 which the Tory writer J. W. Croker considered the most important measure of the parliamentary session. The payment of a tenth part of the produce of the land to the tithe owner had produced vexation and litigation for centuries (Ch. 15) and, though at least a third of all tithes were in lay hands, the Church had suffered nearly all the odium of the system. The call for the abolition of tithe had become an obligatory part of the early-nineteenth-century radical's checklist of reforms. After 1836, tithes could no longer be demanded in kind and the payment of corn rents, which were to fluctuate with the prevailing price of grain, was to be supervised by a central Tithe Commission and by assistant commissioners who worked locally, closely following the blueprint of the Poor Law Commission. Unlike the earlier institution, however, the Tithe Commission engendered remarkably little controversy. The peaceful settlement of the tithe problem was of enormous benefit to the Church (199).

III

However necessary the reforms in the Church, there was no denying that their implementation necessitated a greater direct interference by the State than at any time since the Interregnum. Many Anglicans felt with John Henry Newman, vicar of St Mary the Virgin, Oxford, that in the face of accommodations with dissent and meddling by a politically unpalatable government: 'We must make a stand *somewhere.* . . . The Church shall not crumble away without my doing in my place what I can to hinder it.' The Oxford Movement began in 1833 in protest against improper interference by secular authority in church affairs. It was so called since most of its leaders were Oxford men. In addition to Newman himself, John Keble, Edward Pusey and Hurrell Froude were all Fellows of Oriel College; all had opposed Peel when he unsuccessfully sought re-election as Member for Oxford University after passing Catholic emancipation in 1829 (Ch. 23); all four dated the decisive backsliding on essential church principles to the disastrous years of Tory government immediately after the death of Liverpool. In July 1833 Keble preached a famous sermon, *National Apostasy Considered*, as a blast against the Irish Church Temporalities bill. The government, he alleged, had 'virtually usurped the commission of those whom our Saviour entrusted with *at least one voice* in making ecclesiastical laws. . . . The same Legislature has also ratified . . . that the Apostolical Church in this realm is henceforth only to stand, in the eye of the State, as *one sect among many.*' 'Under the guise of charity and toleration', he thundered, 'we are almost come to this pass; that no difference, in matters of faith, is to disqualify for our approbation and confidence, whether in public or domestic life'.[5]

To place such reliance on the doctrinal integrity of the Church of England may seem odd, even quixotic, to those acquainted with its early history between, say, 1559 and 1662, but the leaders of the Oxford Movement were sober, serious scholars. They sought to purify from within. They emphasized High-Church traditions – authority, ritual and apostolic succession – and the need to re-establish the inner vitality of the Anglican communion. In the search for self-respect in the Church they opposed State involvement precisely because they thought it essential for clerics to put their own house in order. Pusey saw the Ecclesiastical Commission as a standing threat: 'It will absorb our Episcopate; the Prime Minister will be our Protestant Pope'. (366, 85)

High-Church ideas were disseminated, not very widely at first, in a series of short doctrinal pamphlets called *Tracts for the Times*. More than sixty appeared between 1833 and 1835. Their ideas, and the deeper debates to which they led, split the Church. Church leaders, now fruitfully co-operating with the government, found the 'Tractarians' an insistent, self-righteous nuisance. Anti-Tractarians quite early latched on to the point that the Anglican Church, whose doctrines traditionally possessed what one bishop called 'a sort of elasticity', now harboured within its bosom a group whose doctrinal illiberality pointed inexorably towards Rome. At first both Newman and Keble strenuously denied the accusation and wrote against the errors of Catholicism. But Newman, in particular, became increasingly uncomfortable. His famous *Tract XC* (the use of Roman numerals for Tractarian publications became increasingly uncoincidental) of 1841 attempted to prove that the Anglican Thirty-nine Articles of 1563, on which Church doctrine was allegedly based, were perfectly consonant with Catholic doctrine. Newman's blast was logically elegant but politically clumsy. He was censured by the heads of the Oxford colleges and he provoked an almighty row which deprived the Tractarians of the last vestiges of respect in both the Church and the Tory party. In 1845 one of Newman's disciples, W. G. Ward, was stripped of his Oxford degrees for publishing *The Ideal of a Christian Church*, a critique of Anglicanism which seemed to set up the Church of Rome as a model. Ward joined the Catholic Church almost immediately and Newman was received into it a few months later. Those who remained High-Church Anglicans, notably Keble and Pusey, laboured on for internal reform and a re-birth of spiritual values; but their political influence was nil.

The Oxford Movement, despite its political storms, was one of many agencies which stiffened the sinews of Anglicanism and rendered its clergy more dutiful, devotional and self-confident. Politically, they swam against a rising tide of lay interference. Peel led a resurgent Tory party faithful as ever to its Anglican heritage but determined to see the link between Church and State as a reciprocal, mutually reinforcing partnership. If bishops played their legislative role in the Lords, so Parliament, via the Ecclesiastical Commission, must help to direct the course of its Church by law established. Gladstone, the object of Peel's admiration in other respects as a coming young man of immense gifts, was administered a withering rebuke in 1838 for writing *The State in its Relations with the Church*, a pamphlet which took a stern, if convoluted, Tractarian line. Tories as well as Whigs condemned the Tractarians in 1836 for creating such a fuss against the appointment of a liberal Churchman, Dr R. D. Hampden, to the Regius Chair of Divinity at Oxford. Many saw more than a doctrinal objection. The Tractarians were attacking State involvement in a senior appointment in both the academic and the religious worlds. Leading Tories did not trust the Church to put its own affairs to rights and by the time that Peel won the 1841 election, nearly all were convinced that the Tractarian way would lead to the destruction, not the salvation, of the Church. The Church of England, revived and renewed as it undoubtedly was in the 1830s and 1840s, would remain securely, and subordinately, yoked to the State.

---

1. W. L. Mathieson, *English Church Reform, 1815–40* (1923), p. 64.
2. L. C. Sanders, ed., *Lord Melbourne's Papers* (1889), p. 324.
3. *P. P.*, 1852–53, lxxxix, p. xxxix.
4. *A Letter to Earl Grey by a Dissenting Minister* (1834), p. 7.
5. J. Keble, *National Apostasy Considered* (Oxford, 1833), pp. 2, 15.

CHAPTER 28

The age of Peel? Politics and policies, 1832–1846

I

It is tempting to see the 1830s and 1840s as 'the age of Peel'. Peel's most distinguished biographer, Norman Gash, unequivocally does so (79, 80). In 1832, before Peel had become its leader, the Tory party suffered the most comprehensive defeat in its history [Bvi]. Yet nine years later, with Peel firmly at the helm, the Tories won a substantial electoral victory. The *Annual Register* was disposed to pass all of the credit for this revival onto the leader personally: 'No man, it is probable, ever deserved better of a party than Sir Robert Peel of his. . . . Unassisted by the faculties, the temperate wisdom and the parliamentary tactic and address of their leader in the House of Commons, [the Tories] could scarcely have recovered with such steady rapidity, and with so few reverses from the prostration in which the revolutionary struggle of 1831 and 1832 had left them' (99, *38*). The election victory was but the prelude to a five-year ministry in which the nation's finances were put to rights and sustained economic growth secured by policies of free trade and modest taxation. Peel's policies, on this analysis, provided working people both with securer jobs and cheaper bread. The economic depressions which had sustained radicalism from the 1790s to the Chartists in the 1840s gave way to prosperity; prosperity bred tranquillity and acceptance of the established political order. Along this pathway to prosperity, Peel's Tories become modern 'Conservatives', the changed nomenclature symbolizing a more profound change in support as the party broadened its allegiance from the countryside and cathedral towns to accommodate commercial and industrial interests. Confronted by the supreme leadership which wrought this transformation, the Whigs withered. Only the purblind stupidity of Peel's backbenchers, which led them into the ultimate folly of opposing the repeal of the Corn Laws (Ch. 30), offered them a fortuitous and unmerited return to power in 1846.

It is, of course, possible to personalize a historical period, but it is rarely sensible to do so. To call this the 'age of Peel' is to ignore several salient points. First, the Whigs, under first Grey (1830–34) and then Melbourne (1834–35 and 1835–41), were actually in power for almost twice as long as Peel's Tories were. Second, as we shall see, the Whig record during a difficult period in office was far from contemptible. Despite a disastrous final three years in office when debts mounted and morale sagged, the Whig governments deserve the rehabilitation they have recently received (86, 87, 91). Third, though he could pass effective legislation, Peel lacked the broader power to control the flow of events. He was a far more effective administrator than politician and he treated the equivocal, but necessary, political arts of conciliation and dissimulation with contempt. There is a strong case for saying that his self-confident stubbornness was the rock on which his party sundered, sacrificing majority government thereby for almost thirty years in the process.

Simple categorization of this period into one of Whig embarrassment and, until the apocalypse of 1846, Tory triumph also flies in the face of complex political reality. Party allegiances, contorted into weird shapes after the resignation of Lord Liverpool in 1827 (Ch. 23) were not immediately disentangled after the Reform Act. Though the Tories had lost the 1832 election, they had done so as the party which had seemed to oppose reform into the last ditch. Similarly, the 'Whig' victors were anything but a united party in the modern sense. They were a loose coalition of diverse interests which happened to coalesce (though for widely different reasons) about the importance of parliamentary reform. They agreed about little else. Both Whig and Tory leaders strived to sustain existing patterns of government into the new political age against assault from what they considered dangerously wild radicals on the left and atavistic, industry-hating Tory squires on the right. The malt tax, which was a central feature of the budget passed by the Whig Chancellor, Viscount Althorp, in 1833, was opposed both by ultra-Tories like Sir Edward Knatchbull and the idiosyncratic democrat William Cobbett. Peel, as he was to do on no fewer that forty of a possible forty-three occasions during that parliamentary session, supported the government. He was scarcely more popular with the ultras than he had been when he deserted them over Catholic emancipation.

Far from seeing two clearly demarcated and opposed political parties vying for supremacy, therefore, Westminster politics in the 1830s are better characterized as an informal alliance between the two party hierarchies to secure their vision of moderate, 'established' leadership in a new and dangerous age. Frequently, the main challenges to this vision came either from the radical diaspora of dissenters, democrats and nationalists well to the left of the Whig aristocrats who held most of the high positions in government or from a discontented, dispossessed and embarrassingly anarchronistic squirearchy for whom Peel – their nominal leader – openly evinced little patience. Students seeking clear-cut divisions between the parties will more readily find them in the heated battles for town hall supremacy between Liberals and Tories which the passage of the Municipal Corporations Act of 1835 made possible.

Nevertheless, some degree of party realignment at Westminster did take place in 1834 over the Church question (Ch. 27). The resignation of the Stanleyites from the government over Irish Church reform in May [A] did not push them straight into the arms of Peel since Stanley harboured delusions that he might be asked to form a government of moderate reform. It did, however, presage their eventual absorption into the Tory party. Church affairs became the central pillar of the Tory revival. Support for the Established Church could unite moderate reformers and hardened reactionaries as no other issue could. The Tories were also aided by William IV's decision to dismiss Melbourne's government at the end of the year (Ch. 27). The King acted in conscious emulation of his father, George III, in 1784 (Ch. 3) in the hope that he could secure a government more to his liking. The incident marks a constitutional watershed. Never again would a British monarch dismiss a ministry. Also when Peel asked for a dissolution to improve his party's miserable representation his request was readily granted, although the Parliament was barely two years old. Since 1834 the sovereign's assent to a prime ministerial request for a dissolution has never been withheld. Government was now unequivocally parliamentary.

Peel used his windfall well. He had been travelling in Italy when the King dismissed the Whigs and the fact that Wellington had established a caretaker administration [A] until his return suggested to many a reversion to unpalatable ultra-Toryism. It was to correct this impression that Peel issued his Tamworth Manifesto in December. A statement of beliefs to one's constituents was not novel and Peel was merely repeating much of what he had already said in different places over the past two years. What gives the Tamworth Manifesto its importance is the wide circulation it received through the Press and the convenient consolidation of Peel's political philosophy. For the first time a party leader was presenting a programme to a national electorate.

The Tories could not inhabit the new political world without adapting to it. Peel now offered 'a careful review of institutions, civil and ecclesiastical . . . combining with the firm maintenance of established rights, the correction of proved abuses and the redress of real grievances'. Radicals, by contrast, favoured 'a perpetual vortex of agitation . . . [where] public men can only support themselves in public estimation by adopting every popular impression of the day'. Peel offered church reform to extend 'the true interests of the Established religion' and a fresh look at institutions of local government. Promises were kept on the former question (Ch. 27) while he and Wellington exerted massive pressure on the Tory majority in the House of Lords to accept the Whig Municipal Corporations bill [C.ii].

Peel therefore openly promised reforms in order to conserve the essentials of the constitution – a strategy which until 1834 had appeared to be the prerogative of the Whigs. It was also a strategy designed to give the Tories a broader base of support. As the long-serving backbench MP Sir John Walsh recognized, the new Conser- vative party comprised 'all that part of the community who are attached to the Constitution in Church and State, and who believe that it is threatened with subversion by the encroachments of democracy' (80, *80*). But within this broad alliance the differences between country squires, who distrusted not only democracy but most forms of industrial change, and the moderate reformers, who occupied the main positions of influence, were never truly reconciled. Conservative strength grew very substantially between 1835 and 1841. However, far more of this support came from rural and small-town England rather than from either the industrial North of England or the remainder of the United Kingdom. Its base remained much narrower than is frequently supposed.

Immediately, however, Peel's short minority government of 1834–35 showed sufficient signs of ability in adversity to win wide respect and to evoke memories of the younger Pitt before the election of 1784 (Ch. 3). Conservative morale was boosted and boosted even more by the manner of the government's fall. In February 1835 leaders of the Whig, radical and Irish opposition groups met at Lichfield House to concert their forces. Melbourne, in particular, was dubious for he knew that the Whigs could be severely damaged by too close an accord with democrats and Irish nationalists. The so-called Lichfield House Compact used its parliamentary majority to get rid of Peel, but it also marked the beginnings of a turbulent long-term alliance between the Whigs and various pressure groups well to their left. In a sense it marks the beginnings of the Liberal party, and they were hardly auspicious. The election in January had already produced about eighty more seats for the Tories, nearly all won from Whigs rather than the radical groups [B.vi]. Melbourne's government returned shakily to office in April amid a barrage of criticism. A 'Conservative Whig' accused it of selling itself to Daniel O'Connell's Irishmen who were under the influence of 'mob and priesthood'.[1] The King, in an interview with Grey, 'inveighed against the notion of junction with dangerous men, meaning OConnel [*sic*] and others'.[2] The young Benjamin Disraeli offered a typically extravagant attack on the Whigs who were 'only maintained in power by the votes of the Irish and the Scotch members'. The Tories were now 'the national party', while the Whigs struggled to establish 'an oligarchical republic and concentrate the government in the hands of a few great families'.[3]

Tory revival stirred in the counties and smaller English boroughs. The Whig MP for Buckingham, Sir Harry Verney, reported in 1836 that 'at the present moment the fault found with government is that they are too much influenced by O'Connell' (40, *131*). When William IV's death in 1837 brought another premature election, Peel's renewed defence of traditional institutions brought the Conservatives to within thirty seats of their opponents [B.vi]. In Buckingham, Verney, having lost most of the Anglican vote, was forced into second place. About forty MPs, reformers in 1832, had crossed the floor to join the Tory opposition by 1837 (84).

After the 1837 Election Whig dependence on Irish votes was total and the preoccupation with Irish questions at Westminster further strengthened the Conservatives' claim to be the patriotic party of England. The new Poor Law (Ch. 25) was also proving to be an electoral liability while growing Conservative sympathies in the constituencies meant that many radicals who had hung on in 1835 were dumped in 1837. The Whigs lacked vigorous leadership. Melbourne presented a posture of languid, aristocratic amateurism in a political world increasingly made for professionals. Particularly once the Stanleyites were firmly hitched to the Conservative wagon after 1837, the Whigs were out-debated in the Commons by Peel, Stanley, Graham and William Gladstone, that 'rising hope of the stern and unbending Tories' as Macaulay called him in 1839.

Greville believed Melbourne's government by 1839 to be 'in a wretched state of weakness, utterly ignorant whether it can scramble through the session', while Lord Holland, far from a hostile critic, feared that it 'was fast assuming the fatal character of Mediocrity and narrowness of views. . . . I perceive a want of energy, boldness, and decision'.[4] In May Melbourne determined to resign when the government's majority fell to five on a bill for the government of Jamaica and advised the Queen to send for Peel. Victoria, not yet twenty years of age but already wilful if politically naive and totally committed to Melbourne as her mentor, refused to sacrifice certain Whig ladies of the bedchamber to permit the appointment of some Tory sympathizers. Peel refused to take office in these circumstances and Melbourne, who had developed a forte for acting against his not derisory better judgement, agreed to resume office and save the Queen from a constitutional crisis with which he knew she could not cope. Peel profited as Melbourne reeled under the predictable accusation that he had clung to office on the petticoats of the monarch. The radicals pressed their claims for secret ballots to the government's further discomfiture, and a government reshuffle in 1839 [A] only made things worse since it involved the loss of Grey's son, Viscount Howick, one of its more competent ministers. The Whigs slowly subsided, shorn of energy, competence and, ultimately, authority.

It would be harsh to judge the Whigs by the disasters of 1839–41. They attempted to remain true to their general traditions of reform in order to conserve. However controversial, the new Poor Law (Ch. 25) was far from a negligible achievement; the Municipal Corporations Act (Ch. 26) revolutionized local government; church reforms tumbled forth between 1836 and 1840 (Ch. 27); factory and educational reforms (Ch. 26) were also put in train. Not all of these were the brainchild of the Whigs; others depended on bipartisanship in the Commons which Peel arranged in the dual interests of safe and efficient government. Yet they are a substantial legacy to the Victorian age, and the Whigs, who fell prematurely under the shadow of Peel's immense presence, deserve more credit for them than they have been given. Their growing unpopularity owed less to their incompetence than to the logic of the new political world. That world's electorate had both property to conserve and a vested aversion to further radical change. Overwhelmingly, it was an English electorate, deeply attached to its State Church and profoundly suspicious of 'foreign' influences. Once the Whigs accepted alliance with radicals, Irishmen and other undesirables and once Peel had demonstrated his determination to swing the Tories behind modest change to strengthen, rather than shake, the existing constitution, a pronounced swing in political fortunes was inevitable. After a period of turbulence, the electorate craved calm and consolidation and believed that the Conservatives could provide it.

These advantages were maximized by shrewd leadership. Nor should the influence of improved organization be ignored, although at least in the elections of 1835 and 1837 the major parties seem to have been evenly matched with the Liberals rather better organised in many boroughs, the Conservatives decidedly so in the counties. F. R. Bonham acted as Conservative party agent in the 1830s and 1840s and the Carlton Club became the nerve centre of operations after its foundation in 1832. The same service was performed for the Liberals by Joseph Parkes, a Birmingham lawyer, and the Reform Club founded in 1836 by radicals who hoped to convert the Whigs to thoroughgoing reform but which the Whigs soon dominated. Parliamentary candidates continued to be provided by patronage, but the emergence of professional party machines was a crucial development in the modern British political system. Local organizations, generally run by solicitors, busied themselves with electoral registration (Ch. 24) and subscriptions, but the co-ordinating activities of the central party offices implied at least a measure of direction from above. Bonham did not hesitate to either prod dilatory local organizations or to urge appropriate parliamentary candidates upon them. The professionalization of the parties was an important factor in the decline of the independent MP. Within ten years on either side of the Reform Act the independent

MP, such an important factor in eighteenth-century politics, became a rarity, squeezed out by polarization on issues, the increased size of the electorate to which he had to appeal and the ever wider political ground occupied by new party organizations.

The sixth successive premature General Election – and the seventh in fifteen years – came about in 1841 when Melbourne lost a vote of confidence after Sir Francis Baring's budget had been rejected. With the financial deficit mounting and Melbourne palpably without a policy, the death of the government was a merciful release. The 1841 Election was the first in which one government was replaced by another solely by choice of the electorate. According to *The Times*, 'the world has never known an instance of a party being installed in power . . . solely because the nation pledges confidence in their capacity and disinterestedness' (98, *266*). No other election between the Reform Acts caused a change of government, and an existing viable majority in Parliament would not be overthrown by the electorate until Disraeli replaced Gladstone in 1874. The 1841 Election, however, was no popular plebiscite. Almost 100 fewer contests were held than in 1832 and more than half of Britain's MPs in 1841 were returned unopposed [B.vii.2].

The 1841 Election gave Peel a majority of 76 seats [B.vi] but his strength was far from uniform. The victorious Conservative party was overwhelmingly English and very strongly rural. The rush back to Toryism in the English and Welsh counties, evident in 1835 and 1837, was virtually completed in 1841 when the Liberals could manage only 22 seats to the Conservatives' 137. The Liberals hardly figured in the southern shires. By complete contrast, Scotland stayed Liberal by 31 seats to 22 and in Ireland O'Connellites and Liberals outnumbered Conservatives by 62 to 43. Peel's gains in the boroughs, important for his majority, were less impressive than might appear. More headway was made in established cities and ports than in the new industrial towns. Things went very well in Bristol, the City of London (where Lord John Russell came within 9 votes of defeat) and Liverpool (where anti-Catholicism was already bringing the Tories rich rewards from the bigoted and the fearful), but no better in 1841 than 1835 in the larger manufacturing centres. It is often overlooked that, though Peel made a net gain of 7 seats in urban constituencies with populations over 10,000, 19 seats which had previously been Conservative went Liberal in 1841. Generally, towns with large dissenting populations (Ch. 27) stayed loyally Liberal. The bulk of the Conservatives' borough triumphs came from the small towns, some of which had narrowly escaped elimination in 1832; here landlord influence remained rife (Ch. 24).

In view of the cataclysmic events of 1845–46, it is worth also noting how much political opinion was swayed during the 1841 elections by the issue of the Corn Laws (Ch. 30). The Whigs had promised their supporters that they would reconsider the existing levels of protection for corn. Such news was dynamite in the counties and many smaller boroughs where the landed interest was immediately perceived to be in danger. The *Buckinghamshire Herald* portentously informed its readers in June 1841 that 'the great struggle of the general election will arise from the question, of whether the Agriculturalists of the Empire shall or shall not retain that protection which is virtually necessary to their existence'. The *Canterbury Journal* put it even more starkly: 'Shall the Corn Laws be abolished – aye or no?

The Ministers ... go to the country upon THIS question' (87, *308–9*). Peel's position on the Corn Laws was much closer to that of the Whig ministry than he would ever admit to the rank and file. It could be argued that he allowed the Tories to fight the election of 1841 on the false prospectus of staunch support for agricultural protection. The case that he misled not only the electorate but his own party is very strong; many of Peel's troubles with his backbenchers can be ascribed to the consequences of this tactical duplicity.

II

Peel relied for his majority on MPs who interpreted good government as protecting the Anglican Church from spoliation by dissenters, Catholics and infidels and protecting the land as the supreme property. It was an uncomfortably narrow base from which to conduct the administration which Peel had in mind. During the next five years Peel conducted national policies and he expected dangerously parochial troops to follow him obediently into the division lobbies. Peel, it is vital to remember, had been a leading Liberal Tory (Ch. 21) and he aimed to revive British prosperity with measures similar to those which had brought success in the 1820s. His Cabinet reflected a concern for administrative efficiency above political calculation. The only conciliatory gesture to the agricultural protectionists was to give the Privy Seal to the duke of Buckingham, an incompetent minister lately president of the Society for the Protection of Agriculture; he resigned within months [A]. Peel furnished himself with a government of experts.

In administrative, though not political, terms Peel's government ranks alongside Gladstone's of 1868–74 as the ablest of the nineteenth century. It was assembled under the direction of a leader supremely confident of his own abilities and of the direction he must follow. Upon colleagues who served their political apprentice-ships under him, pre-eminently Gladstone, his philosophy of government left an indelible stamp. In total contrast to Melbourne, style counted for nothing; achievement was all. He prided himself on never introducing to Parliament a measure which he failed to carry on to the statute-book. His achievements were founded on hard work, utter dedication, the natural administrator's effortless mastery of detail which others find tedious or unimportant and, controlling the rest, a quite extraordinary intellectual ability. No natural orator, unlike Stanley, he nevertheless dominated the Commons by knowledge and brainpower. Of other nineteenth-century Prime Ministers only the younger Pitt and Gladstone can stand comparison with him.

His first task, like Pitt's, was the reconstruction of the economy. Peel had come to power during an economic crisis (Ch. 17). Chartism flourished and briefly threatened the social order (Ch. 29). The government's deficit had been mounting steadily since 1837 and stood at £7½m. early in 1842. Peel perceived the short-term crisis but was more concerned with the damage which depression did to social harmony. He needed to reduce the financial disabilities under which working people laboured. His means reflected the dogma of the classical economists (Ch. 5): the stimulation of trade and consumption by lower tariffs. The 1842 budget lowered duties on imported corn by almost one-half the levels set in 1828. Tariffs generally were lowered and, to make up the immediate deficit, Peel reintroduced income tax on the moderately well off [D.i.3]. Within two years the economic recovery which this piece of liberalism aided had turned a government deficit into a surplus of £1.2m.

Peel's other famous budget, that of 1845, moved even further towards complete free trade. Export duties on British goods were abolished; import duties on most raw materials, including cotton, were also ended; the controversial sugar duties, which the government had not been bold enough to touch in 1842 and had lowered against fierce backbench Tory resistance in 1844, were further reduced. Income tax, Peel announced, would remain permanent since it was more important to reduce indirect taxes which 'in our opinion press more onerously on the community' (98, *464*). The government's other major economic initiative increased confidence in the banking system. The Bank Charter Act of 1844 confirmed Peel's commitment, first displayed in 1819 (Ch. 21), to a secure currency. The Bank of England's powers to issue banknotes were linked to bullion reserves and securities; weekly statements of note issues were to be published. The rights of existing private banks were severely curtailed and new banks could not issue promissory notes. This rigid monetarist policy would prove itself during the coming expansion. During the next eighty years the Bank had to apply to exceed its stated quota of note issues on only three occasions. Banks had business confidence as never before.

Peel moved far and fast between 1841 and 1845 but he did nothing to quiet the disordered spirits of his backbenchers. He had reduced the protection given to the products of their land; he had eased the tax burdens on an industrial and commercial class which many of them abominated; he talked of a national interest which they understood little and sympathized with not at all; he closeted himself with his administrative cronies and paid backbenchers little heed. Perhaps worst of all, he showed every sign of treating their ignorant but passionate pretensions with contempt.

They gave him fair warning. Ninety-five Tories voted to support a ten-hour day during the debate on Graham's Factory bill in 1844. They felt that the proposed legislation was too favourable to the industrialists. In the same year the protectionist Bristol MP Philip Miles persuaded more than sixty Tories to support a Whig amendment opposing the reduction of sugar duties (99). The argument was twofold. A duty reduction would break faith with colonial sugar producers whose costs had risen sharply since the abolition of slavery and who needed continued protection against competition. Further, if a Tory government could ditch the powerful and long-established colonial interest, why should it not similarly desert the agricultural interest when occasion demanded?

Neither of these assertions of backbench independence threatened Peel's government directly. As so often in these years, it was religious policy which brought matters to a head. Peel had long believed Irish discontents to be a haemorrhage draining away the life blood of national prosperity. He sought to outface O'Connell's increasingly popular campaigns for a repeal of the Act of Union by building an Irish middle class attached to, and benefiting from, the

British connection. This meant treating Catholics as absolute equals and giving more practical effect to the liberation which Catholic emancipation had achieved (Ch. 23). The decision to treble the annual grant to the Catholic seminary at Maynooth in 1845 and to make it a permanent charge on the Exchequer was a plank in this policy. It horrified zealous Anglicans. Sir Robert Inglis declared that Peel was endowing the Church of Rome from the pockets of the British taxpayer. *The Times* charged Peel with deceit. Gladstone, the tortured conscience of high Anglicanism, was affronted by the Maynooth bill and resigned before it was presented [A]. The legislation squeezed through the Commons only with Whig support: 149 Conservatives voted against the measure, 148 for it.

In the wake of the Maynooth fracas Graham accurately reported that 'our party is shivered and angry and we have lost the slight hold we ever possessed over the hearts and kind feelings of our followers (84, *193*). Peel's natural arrogance vented itself privately in a letter to his wife at the end of 1845: 'How can those who spend their time in hunting and shooting and eating and drinking know what were the motives of those who are responsible for the public security who have access to the best information and who have no other object under heaven but to provide against danger, and consult the general interests of all classes.' (84, *202*) Thus, when Peel took the fateful decision to repeal the Corn Laws he was relatively unconcerned about the reaction of his backbenchers, though he undoubtedly underestimated its ferocity. The economic logic of his government pointed towards this further move to complete free trade; he had known that at least since 1843. Repeal was necessary to secure what he loftily told the Commons in 1846 was 'the greatest object which we or any other government can contemplate ... to elevate the social condition of that class of people with whom we are brought into no direct relationship by the exercise of the elective franchise' (98, *590*). The onset of the Irish potato famine precipitated by no more than a few months a decision which Peel had already taken in his own mind.

The economic factors in Corn Law repeal are considered elsewhere (Ch. 30). After Stanley had resigned from the Cabinet rather than compromise his protectionist beliefs, Peel thought it better to resign in December 1845 to give the Whigs, among whom the issue was far less contentious, the opportunity of passing repeal with the help of Conservative free traders. Lord John Russell consulted his colleagues, found Lansdowne and Grey in particular difficult, recognized that he had no parliamentary majority for a stable administration and refused the Queen's commission to form a government. Peel, to the alarm of some of his colleagues, accepted the call to continue in office with tranquil defiance. He would not back down on a measure he was convinced was in the national interest.

The bitterness of the Tory sense of betrayal is well displayed in the debates on the Corn Laws. The protectionists discovered two ill-assorted and unlikely champions. Lord George Bentinck, son of the duke of Portland, had until 1845 been a largely silent backbencher best known for his crusades against corruption on the turf. Now he proved a most tenacious, if rough-hewn, prejudiced and violent opponent of Peel, learning his economics on the floor of the House as he sat through interminable debates. The oratorical brilliance was provided by Benjamin Disraeli, far more intelligent than he was scrupulous and motivated in equal part by revenge on his party leader for his failure to find him a place in government (though in 1841 he had only four years' parliamentary experience) and by the yawning opportunity which now presented itself to climb several rungs up the ladder towards power in the party. Disraeli's contributions were invariably shrewd, often distasteful and occasionally ineffably obnoxious; they rallied the protectionist troops splendidly. Peel was dubbed a betrayer, a statesman with a whip to lash his followers into line, even 'an inefficient and short sighted Minister'. In February 1846 the repeal bill received its second reading by 339 votes to 242, but of the majority only 112 were Conservative votes. No more than 32 per cent had supported their leader. Eighty-six per cent of Tories sitting for rural and university seats had voted with Bentinck, 63 per cent of those representing the small rural boroughs and 50 per cent of large borough representatives (84). The differential response speaks volumes. Peel was felt by the Tory majority to have betrayed the landed interest and thus to have precipitated the destruction of his party. He got repeal because of Whig votes but was defeated on a new Coercion bill for Ireland in June 1846, the kind of law-and-order measure for which backbench Tory support could previously have been guaranteed. That protectionists were prepared to vote with the Whigs on this of all issues shows the extent of their hatred. Bentinck took seventy colleagues into the Whig lobbies while a further eighty abstained. Peel resigned four days later.

Since posterity has, in the main, dealt kindly with Peel, we should preface any observations of his contribution to British political life with the observation that he was, to most of his contemporaries, both a cold and a controversial character. He inspired devotion among his acolytes – Gladstone in 1853 called him 'my great teacher and master in public affairs' (99, *73*) – but distrust and hostility for much of his political career. Controversy has surrounded both his contribution to the development of the Conservative Party and his responsibility for its break-up in 1846.

It is clear that Peel had a vision of moderate Conservatism which cut across conventional class divisions. He looked to the provision of efficient government which would advance the interests of those who had not been enfranchised in 1832 as well as those who had. Economic growth in a new industrial age was the means of securing this objective. His own political world, however, was anchored in the past. He saw himself, as the younger Pitt had liked to do, as the monarch's minister acting in the national interest. Although he understood the growing importance of party, he never accepted that it had anything other than subordinate status in political affairs. Any conflict between national and party interests would be unhesitatingly resolved in favour of the former.

Breaking up the Tory Party over the Corn Laws on this analysis, therefore, was an affordable price to pay for economic advance and social harmony. As events turned out, the quarter-century or so after 1846 proved to be one of unprecedented prosperity for the United Kingdon with social discontent much more muted, for the most part, than it had been in Peel's day. But does Peel deserve the blame for the break-up anyway? The case for the defence holds that party development, although it advanced significantly in the fourteen years after the passage of the first Reform Act, still had far to go. The leaderships of neither the Whig nor the Tory parties were able to impose any significant degree of discipline on their supporters. Voting against the leadership was common in the 1830s and 1840s. Disraeli's frequent assertions during 1846 that party was the necessarily overriding practical consideration for a politician and that nothing substantial should be ventured unless the party could first be carried might be characterized as anachronistic. All politicians of Peel's experience could remember longer periods when either MPs independent of party allegiance held the balance in the Commons or, as between 1827 and 1834, when party loyalties were fractured. Thus, to put policy before party was a natural, not a precious, preference. Moreover, was not Peel's conception of party development more realistic than Disraeli's in 1846? Peel's party objective was the construction of an alliance between traditional Church and Crown Tories on the one hand and businessmen on the other. He thus hoped to fashion a Conservative Party less dangerously dependent on unpopular causes than the Whigs had become after their dependence on Irish and on assorted radical 'extremist' votes from 1835. If the protectionists were not ready for such an alliance, then what did the Disraelian prescription offer but a reversion to narrow Toryism of probably permanent minority electoral appeal? Disraeli himself was to learn Peel's lesson in the long, frustrating years of opposition which lay ahead (Chs 37 and 39). When the Conservatives next came to power with a workable majority, in 1874 and under Disraeli's leadership, it would not be as the party of protection. By a nice irony, when the landowners appealed to Disraeli for protection against dangerously damaging imports of US grain at the end of the 1870s, they were refused. Though he never admitted it, it was Peelite Conservatism which Disraeli put into practice. Likewise, it was Peel's vision of a broad Conservative alliance – linked, admittedly, to meretricious Disraelian populism – which would carry the Tories into the twentieth century as a smooth-running engine of electoral success.

There is, however, a substantial case to be made for the prosecution. The break-up of the Tory Party could almost certainly have been avoided with more dextrous political management and with a leader who had closer, and more sympathetic, links to his backbench support. In fact the three-year phasing in period for free trade in corn and the £2m. 'sweetener' in the form of a drainage loan were substantial accommodations to the landed interest, though Peel gained no political advantage from them. Indeed, he even contrived to lose support from his backbenchers between the second and third readings of the crucial Corn Law Bill. By May 1846, only 106 Tories were prepared to support their leader; 222 were against him. It is difficult to avoid the conclusion that Peel faced his final political crisis exhausted, irascible and intolerant but self-righteously certain of the correctness of his policy. It might almost be said that he willed the break-up of a party not worthy of the great ends for which he had tried to shape it. Peel's enduring conception of himself as the Queen's minister was at variance not only with the immediate interests of his party. Unlike Disraeli, he failed to appreciate the rapidly growing importance of party allegiance to the efficient discharge of business in early Victorian Britain. His leadership had always been aloof. By 1845, it had become almost contemptuous of his followers. It was as if he never forgave his party for not transmuting itself into the broadly-based coalition of propertied interests he envisaged. Peel entirely failed to make the Conservative Party attractive to the newer industrial and commercial interests of northern England, south Wales and central Scotland. A sectional party of landowning protectionists and Churchmen was poorly led by a free-trade zealot who either (as in 1841) misled his followers as to his true intentions in economic policy or (as in 1844–46) believed that they deserved no more than chastisement, browbeating and threats of resignation. Arguably, he richly merited the treatment his backbenchers meted out in 1846.

Future Prime Ministers learned from Peel's mistake. There is no paradox in the judgement that Peel was the last inadequate politician who nevertheless deserves to be considered a great Prime Minister. His achievements in policy and administration are unassailable and, despite recent revisions, his reputation remains high. His fate in 1846, however, taught all successors that ministers of the crown must carry their political parties with them before they presumed to legislate for the nation. Political black arts being what they are, the most successful political leaders have contrived to hoodwink their electorates into believing that national and party interests are indivisible.

---

1. *Three Letters on the Present State of Parties* (1835), p. 45.
2. A. Kriegel, ed., *The Holland House Diaries, 1831–1840* (1977), p. 285.
3. B. Disraeli, *Vindication of the English Constitution* (1835), pp. 181–3.
4. *ibid.*, p. 410.

CHAPTER 29

The politics of pressure: I Chartism

I

Chartism was much the most important political movement of working men organized during the nineteenth century. Its specific aims were simply stated in the People's Charter, drawn up by the London cabinet-maker William Lovett and the radical master tailor Francis Place in 1838: 'Universal Suffrage, No Property Qualifications, Annual Parliaments, Equal Representation [*i.e.* constituencies of equal size], Payment of Members, and Vote by Ballot'. These objectives, none of them new to the radical movement, were necessary 'to provide for the just representation of the people of Great Britain in the Commons House of Parliament'. Two national petitions, incorporating these famous six points, were presented to Parliament in May 1839 and May 1842 with 1.3m. and 3.3m. signatures respectively. If some were bogus (and a third petition in 1848, alleged to contain 5.7m. in reality comprised fewer than 2m., including the forged signatures of such dubious democrats as Queen Victoria, Robert Peel and the duke of Wellington), the petitions nevertheless represented a peak of working-class organization.

Chartism grew from the revival of artisan and middle-class radicalism in London and Birmingham. The London Working Men's Association (LWMA), founded in 1836, and the Birmingham Political Union, first active during the reform crisis (Ch. 23), both concentrated their attention on the failure of the Reform Act to improve the working man's lot. Early in 1837, the LWMA agreed with six radical MPs, including Daniel O'Connell and J. A. Roebuck, to frame democratic legislation. Meetings to promote a Charter were held in many parts of the country in 1837 and 1838. Large rallies, reminiscent of those during the agitations of 1815–20 and 1830–32, were held during 1838 in Glasgow, Birmingham and Leeds. At Kersal Moor, outside Manchester, at least 50,000 people congregated. By the autumn a strategy had emerged: a national petition and the election of a National Convention to put pressure on the government to accept radical reform.

The National Convention assembled in London in February 1839 but proved unequal to its task. Delegates disputed over the value of violence to achieve their ends. Reconvened in Birmingham, the Convention formulated plans for a 'Sacred Month' (effectively a general strike), concerted bank deposit withdrawals and 'exclusive dealing' (trading only with sympathetic shopkeepers). The authorities in both cities were unimpressed. While temperate Chartists fidgeted uneasily and hardy spirits bragged of revolution, arrests were made in July when supporters defied a ban on meetings made by Birmingham magistrates. One week later a motion even to consider the petition was rejected by 235 votes to 46. The Convention broke up in disorder. Little violence followed, except in South Wales when, in November, about 3,000 armed Glamorgan colliers and ironworkers marched on Newport, probably with the intention of occupying the town. They planned to hold a rally to urge Chartist demands and to protest against recent arrests, especially that of Henry Vincent, the LWMA 'missionary' whose oratory had made a deep impact during his tour of Monmouthshire. There is no doubt that some planned a workers' revolution. Certainly the authorities interpreted it as such; soldiers killed two dozen Chartists in dispersing the crowd (109, 107). John Frost, the incident's leader, was a radical draper and magistrate who had vainly urged caution. He was sentenced to death but reprieved and transported, eventually spending seventeen years in Australia. Talk of a national rebellion was mostly hot air, though active preparations were made in South Yorkshire. Between June 1839 and June 1840 more than 500 Chartists were arrested; most of the movement's leaders spent between twelve and eighteen months in prison.

The National Charter Association (NCA) was formed in July 1840 from the wreckage of the previous year to co-ordinate future activities. Its cohesion, which was for a time considerable, owed much to Feargus O'Connor, the Irish landowner and MP who had lost his seat in 1835. Both his physical presence and his Chartist newspaper, *Northern Star*, dominated the movement during the 1840s. O'Connor's methods, however, alienated many other prominent Chartists and contributed to the NCA's regional concentration on South Lancashire and the West Riding of Yorkshire.

Chartism revived during 1842 and NCA membership grew to 50,000. The second National Convention, organized by O'Connor and restricted to NCA members, presented a second petition to Parliament. Even radical MPs such as O'Connell and Roebuck tumbled over themselves to disavow O'Connor as a malevolent demogogue, while cross-party anti-democratic heavy artillery, in the shapes of Peel, Graham and Russell, fired salvoes for the majority. The Chartists were refused a hearing by 287 votes to 49.

The disturbances which followed were, as the Benthamite radical journal *Westminster Review* called them, evidence 'of a general, bitter, deep-rooted, discontent, pervading a vast proportion of the working population of Great Britain'.[1] They began among North Staffordshire miners and spread rapidly to the industrial North and to Scotland. Strikes were common and plugs were removed from boilers to put out the fires which fuelled the mills; hence the general title the 'Plug Plot'. In the desperate conditions of 1842 industrial and political motives were, and still remain, difficult to disentangle, but it is now clear that links between local trade societies and local Chartist groups were considerably closer than either national leadership appreciated. The venerable Potteries Chartist, John Richards, passed a resolution at Hanley: 'That all labour cease until the People's Charter becomes the law of the land.' (80, *100*) Confused, the NCA executive first endorsed strikes as a weapon to achieve the Charter; then, as they collapsed, O'Connor condemned strikes in the *Northern Star*. The authorities mopped up the confusion in a further wave of arrests. As trade revived, mass support for Chartism dwindled.

The last occasion on which the Chartists offered a direct challenge to authority was in 1848. Riots, again born of economic distress, broke out in Glasgow and Birmingham in March. In its later phases, Chartism attracted substantial support from recent Irish immigrants. Bradford, which had the largest proportion of Irish-born in Yorkshire, generated substantial Chartist activity under the leadership of George White, himself of Irish descent. Probably half the Chartists in the town were Irish. Not surprisingly, Irish immigrants were also prominent in London Chartism during 1848, leading *The Times* to characteristically dyspeptic utterance: 'The present movement', it spluttered in April 1848 after the Irish Confederation had made common cause with the Chartists, 'is a ramification of the Irish conspiracy. The Repealers [of the Union] wish to make as great a hell of this island as they have of their own' (259, *131*). The authorities were concerned that concerted Irish nationalist and Chartist activity might overstretch their defences and they anticipated the mass Chartist rally on Kennington Common in April 1848 with some concern. Appeals to the middle classes produced 10,000 recruits as special constables in London. In the event, the rally attracted far fewer than O'Connor had hoped. The authorities banned the procession and O'Connor, fearful of both bloodshed and humiliation, urged his supporters to disperse peacefully while he was permitted to present the petition alone. Much was made in the establishment press of the triumph of law, order and common sense over a few hotheads. Chartism received a humiliating blow to its morale and never again posed any form of mass threat. The clearing up process was a matter of routine. As on so many occasions since the 1790s, constables and magistrates arrested radical leaders, confident that this action would remove any sting from continuing agitation. By midsummer, most advocates of force in the North were under lock and key, while Ernest Jones and other London Chartists were arrested after meetings in the East End, amid rumours of another insurrection with Irish support, planned for June.

II

The Chartists menaced the authorities less in 1839, 1842 and 1848 than had the radical reformers in 1831–32. Now that the middle classes were securely hitched to the constitution, Members of Parliament intellectually unpersuaded of the democratic case, as at least 90 per cent of them were, had no reason for vote from fear against their convictions. Police developments [C.ii] increased domestic security. Indeed, the increase of State power implied by policing was one of the issues the Chartists most bitterly contested (353, 354). The new railways enabled troops to be moved rapidly to any disturbed areas. Even telegraphy was at the disposal of the goverment in gauging the likely Chartist response in 1848. Disorder on the scale of London in 1780, Birmingham in 1791 or Bristol in 1831 was most unlikely. Lord John Russell's papers as Home Secretary do not suggest that he considered Chartism in 1839 an issue worth spending much time upon. Major-General Sir Charles Napier, a known radical sympathizer, was appointed to command the Northern District in 1839, itself an indication of the government's lack of concern. 'Poor creatures', he wrote of the Nottingham Chartists in 1839, 'their threats of attack are miserable. With half a cartridge, and half a pike, with no money, no discipline, no skilful leaders, they would attack men with leaders money and discipline, well armed and having sixty rounds a man.' (106, *98*).

Chartism should not be judged by the threat it posed but as a critical stage in the political education of working people. It was the culmination of a decade of impressive activity, fed by cheap, illegal 'unstamped' newspapers, such as Hetherington's *Poor Man's Guardian*, Carlile's *Gauntlet* and John Cleave's *Weekly Free Press*, which dilated upon the betrayal of the 1832 Reform Act. Those who mine the rich seams of Chartist literature (and never did a political movement publicize itself so extensively) will find many nuggets of class antagonism. John Mason, a Tyneside shoemaker, warned Chartists in Leicester not to heed Anti-Corn Law League cries of 'Cheap Bread' (Ch. 30): 'Don't be deceived by the middle classes again. You helped them to get their votes. ... But where are the fine promises they made you? Do not listen to their cant and humbug. Stick to your Charter. You are veritable slaves without your votes.' (109, *137*) The most usual reaction of Chartists to the League was suspicion and hostility. In the factory districts, they broke up League meetings. Many, perhaps most, of the leadership believed Chartism to be a class movement with two enemies, the tax-consuming, idle aristocracy and the perfidious middle classes whose betrayal extended beyond 1832 to support for a harsh new Poor Law and a new economic system based on profit via labour exploitation. If Britain's fragmented working class (Ch. 19), whose disunity was reflected in Chartism, prevents the movement from being called an outright expression of class politics, it is necessary to stress that some were 'pervaded by a sense of class – both a positive sense of identification and a negative hostility to superior classes'.[2]

In developing the theme of the political education of working people, it must be remembered that working people included large numbers of women. In many textile districts of Lancashire and Yorkshire, indeed, women comprised a majority in the workforce (Ch. 14). We should not be surprised, therefore, to learn that women's political organizations contributed substantially to the development of Chartism, particularly in its early years. The political road from anti-Poor Law agitation (Ch. 25) into Chartism was probably trodden by as many women as men in Lancashire and Yorkshire. Reporters noted the extensive representation of such organizations at the Kersal Moor Meeting in 1838. Two prominent Chartist leaders, R. J. Richardson (who wrote *Rights of Women* during one of his sojurns in prison) and John Watkins warmly endorsed the view that women should have votes on the same basis as men. The *Scottish Chartist Circular* in December 1839 called for 'the elevation of woman as well as man in the scale of human society' as part of what it defined as politics: 'the science of human progression' (107, *125*).

Women, of course, did not need male advocacy. Several put the case themselves with enviable cogency. Elizabeth Neesom pointed out in 1839 that the British throne had recently been inherited by a woman who presumes 'to rule this nation in defiance of the universal rights of man and woman'. The moral was clear: 'we assert in accordance with the rights of all . . . our rights as free women (or women determined to be free) to rule ourselves' (107, *120*). It cannot be denied, however, that many Chartists were embarrassed by the issue of female suffrage, the more so since it was all but impossible to argue against on grounds of natural rights. Many, however, wondered whether pressing the female case might weaken the argument for adult male suffrage. They found it difficult to divorce their ideal perception of women from the image of supportive domesticity. There was also a practical difficulty. The establishment had redefined a propertied franchise in 1832 (Ch. 24) and had quite specifically excluded women from participating in it. Yet many women, especially heiresses and middle-class widows, were substantial property owners. If the issue were reopened, the authorities would be much more likely to favour the franchise for propertied women over extending the franchise to working men. After all, wealthy women paid substantial sums in direct taxation. They would have a prior claim on a property owners' parliament. Not for nothing was the most central of the six points of the Charter universal *manhood* suffrage.

III

Though London formulated the Charter and though London's Press kept the torch of liberty alight between 1832 and 1837, Chartism culminates the long process whereby radical leadership moved north to the major centres of productive industry. Londoners like Lovett stood in the direct line of rationalist, artisan radicalism, which dated back to the 1790s (Ch. 8) and placed its faith in reason and education. 'Whatever is gained in England by force,' said Lovett in 1838, 'by force must be sustained; but whatever springs from knowledge and justice will sustain itself.' Even in London, the Working Man's Association policy of cooperation with the middle classes ran into furious opposition. In 1838 George Julian Harney formed the London Democratic Association which tried, with only limited success, to recruit from among the capital's depressed handworkers and labourers. London Chartism took proper root only in the 1840s when, organized by the tailor John Parker and the shoemaker William Robson, it operated through local trades societies (60).

London Chartism was, relatively speaking, unimportant. In part this was because the capital was little affected by the ferocious agitation against the new Poor Law (Ch. 25). It is no accident that Yorkshire anti-Poor Law activists, such as Lawrence Pitkeithly and Peter Bussey, should have become influential Chartists. Nor is it surprising that this agitation should bring to Chartism both a wider concern and a philosophy already inured to violence. Joseph Rayner Stephens, the Ashton-under-Lyne Methodist minister disowned by the Methodist Conference, urged working men to arm themselves to defend their constitutional rights against the violence of authority which attacked them with a new centralizing confidence. The theme was taken up by the Salford Chartist, R. J. Richardson. He treated the National Convention in 1839 to a learned disquisition 'to show the advantage and propriety of arming the people as the best guarantee of the liberties of a country' and cited such diverse authorities as Aristotle, Queen Elizabeth and Dr Johnson to support his contention (111, *63*). Stephens and Bussey advocated, and possibly even planned, rebellion to achieve the Charter. In Yorkshire, anti-Poor Law agitation shaded imperceptibly into Chartism in 1837–38. *The Northern Star* first appeared in November 1837, six months before the Charter. It was published in Leeds and its early issues stoked the fires of the anti-Poor Law campaign.

Chartism was a mass movement only in times of depression. It is evident that the peaks of activity coincided with troughs in the economy. As at Copenhagen Fields in 1795 and St Peter's Fields in 1819 the great crowds trudged on to Kersal Moor in 1838 because they were hungry, out of work or on short time. There, as previously, they were told that the source of their misery was misgovernment by an unrepresentative minority and that their remedy was political reform. The 1838 harvest was the third bad one in succession. Wheat prices were 64 per cent higher than they had been in 1835 and the 1839 price was the highest since the Peterloo year of 1819 [D.vi.3]. In 1841–42, the main cause of distress was unemployment; in 1847–48, high food prices again.

Nevertheless, dangers lurk in an uncritical reading of J. R. Stephens's assertion that Chartism was 'a knife and fork question, a bread and cheese question'. The effects of the depressions of 1837–39, 1841–42 and 1847–48 were not uniform in a still fragmented economy (Chs 13 and 14) and not all active centres of Chartism were depressed areas. Tyneside suffered little from the trough of 1837–39, yet it generated a Working Man's Association, led by the pitman's leader Thomas Hepburn, and *Northern Liberator*, an impressive and influential Chartist journal. Western Scotland similarly shared the North-east's relative prosperity. It had a shipbuilding boom and its handloom weavers were not yet so badly affected by mechanization as their Lancashire counterparts. In 1838–39 Glasgow became the nerve centre of a substantial Chartist agitation.

Nevertheless, the heartland of Chartism was industrial Lancashire and Yorkshire. Broadly, the movement appealed more to industrial outworkers than to factory operatives and more to textile operatives – especially weavers – than to others. Living standards among textile outworkers were lower than those of factory workers, whether they worked in an expanding area such as Rochdale or Halifax or a contracting one such as Trowbridge or Melksham in Wiltshire. Among such erstwhile aristocrats of labour a strong tradition of political literacy persisted which suggested a sophisticated political direction for their economic grievances. Thus, weaving villages such as Brindle and Padiham produced more fierce, committed Chartists than factory-based Blackburn nearby. In the hosiery trade, the framework knitting towns and villages west of Leicester, Hinckley and Earl Shilton, and to the north, Loughborough and Barrow-on-Soar were noted Chartist centres. In rural East Leicestershire, by contrast, Chartism barely existed (109). In all purely rural areas, Chartism was a sickly plant, desperately lacking nourishing soil.

The nominations to the NCA's General Council in 1841, which Dr Jones analysed (108), indicates the preponderance of skilled outworkers among Chartist leaders. Of 853 nominations, no less than 130 (15.2 per cent) were described as weavers, closely followed by shoemakers and cordwainers (14.8 per cent together), then tailors (6.8 per cent) and framework knitters (3.9 per cent). Craft skills also predominate among the smaller categorizations.

The composition of the Chartist leadership, however, would have looked rather different before the Newport 'Rising'. Delegates to the first Convention included more middle-class democrats and even a few landowners, such as Patrick Matthew who represented Perthshire, and an Anglican clergyman, Dr Arthur Wade, sitting for Nottinghamshire. It was the middle-class representatives who tended to be most alarmed at the rhetoric of violence which enveloped that Convention. Harney, who had told Derby Chartists in 1839 to 'Arm for peace, arm for liberty . . . and the tyrants will no longer laugh at your petitions', attracted particular apprehension. Revolutionary preparations during the summer drove many out of the movement for good. Also, in those areas where economic conflict between master and man was not so far advanced as in the new factory towns, more modest forms of Chartist activity were espoused after the catharsis of 1839. Birmingham, long under the influence of Thomas Attwood (Ch. 23), engendered the Complete Suffrage Movement in 1842, led by the Quaker merchant Joseph Sturge. Its aim was to reconcile middle and working classes around a common programme embracing the six points and a repeal of the Corn Laws. It enjoyed brief success in the city and it also found significant support in parts of industrial Scotland. For those who rejected such an openly 'collaborationist' route, more benign forms of Chartism developed which implicitly attacked the inflexibility of a Harney or a Bronterre O'Brien. Scotland became the home of 'Christian Chartism'; about twenty exclusively Chartist congregations had been established there by the end of 1840. The Scottish journal *Chartist Circular* exhorted: 'Let every thousand Chartists . . . in every district, legally and cordially unite and form a Church, in which they and their families will assemble on Sabbaths and worship God with good conscience.' (111, *294*) The call was taken up by many dissenting ministers in England and Wales, though Sturge deflected others into his new organization. In some weaving communities Primitive Methodist Chartist revivalism was a feature of the 1840s. Anti-clericalism, another pronounced Chartist strain, was overwhelmingly directed against Anglican clergy, and 'the Church of a Selfish Aristocracy' as the *English Chartist Circular* put it in 1841.

IV

The distinction between what the contemporary Chartist historian R. G. Gammage called 'physical force Chartism' (implying an appeal to the use, or at least the threat, of violence) and 'moral force Chartism' (implying total reliance on reason and persuasion) was never crystal clear, but the differing routes taken by Chartist leaders after the disappointments of 1839 and 1842 indicates the general validity of the categorizations. Moral force Chartism, more attractive among the aristocracy of labour, expressed itself in forms which implied a continued relationship with the middle classes. William Lovett, with Hetherington and the rationalist James Watson, promoted 'education Chartism' based on schools and lecture halls where the ideals of self-improvement continued the established traditions of London artisan radicalism. Hetherington, Watson and Thomas Cooper were among the founders in 1848 of the People's Charter Union, which explicitly rejected the violence which O'Connor sanctioned and sought democracy 'by peaceable and legal means'. Henry Vincent and Robert Lowery, the North Shields radical who in later years regretted that the 1839 Convention had unloosed the 'whirlwind of popular passion' when it could not be safely controlled, promoted teetotal Chartism to 'Raise the Charter from the Pot House' (111, *100*). The culture of sobriety, self-improvement and religious dissent would carry many moral-force Chartists along the path to radical Liberalism and, improbable though it would have seemed in 1841 (Ch. 28), increasingly close alliance with Mr Gladstone.

Conversely, some physical-force Chartists journeyed into socialism. Brontere O'Brien, probably the movement's most clear-headed strategist who had argued against the 'Sacred Month' in 1839 because it would provoke a conflict with authority for which the Chartists were not yet prepared, believed that the most fundamental conflict in society was that between capital and labour. He wished Chartism to become the agency whereby workers extracted their full 'labour value' from masters who had imposed a system of 'wage slavery'. His journalistic contributions, especially to the *Northern Star*, gave Chartism a kind of intellectual coherence and he was much missed as he drifted from the centre of the movement after disagreeing with O'Connor over the latter's tactical advice to Chartists to vote Tory at the 1841 Election. Chartist socialists enjoyed their greatest influence after 1848 as the movement slipped into general decline. O'Brien and Harney in *Red Republican* and Ernest Jones in *People's Paper* and on numerous provincial tours converted most remaining Chartists to the belief that the Charter would achieve little without extensive social reform. Links with European socialism were forged in the 1850s but they mattered little. The essential Englishness of working-class protest, which combined a strong historical sense with a distrust of theory and dogma, rendered Chartist socialism unattractive to most before the movement's protracted minor-key coda in the 1850s and early 1860s.

The coherence which Feargus O'Connor gave to Chartism was non-cerebral. He dominated after 1840 by force of personality. His brutal denunciation of artisan moderation in 1839–40 dislodged Lovett from his early prominence. His immensely powerful style of outdoor oratory gained him followers by the thousand, as did his proprietorship of the *Northern Star* which regularly outsold all provincial newspapers, with a maximum circulation of some 30,000 copies. Like so many radical leaders, his determination to uphold the Charter concealed an essential intolerance and self-esteem which alienated able coadjutors and engendered much personal criticism. He had little time for education Chartism, temperance Chartism or, indeed, any deviation from the lines drawn by Feargus O'Connor though, as Harney testified, he imposed little censorship on his contributors to the *Northern Star*. Harney was also one of the Chartist leaders who *did* enjoy warm personal relations with him. Among the rank and file, there is little doubting Feargus's enormous popularity. He possessed personal magnetism and he could be both warm-hearted and generous. He was a formidable organizer and the revival of Chartism after the arrests of 1839 owes much to him. There is little doubt that his reputation among historians had sunk lower than it deserves and that Dr Epstein's reappraisal of his contribution was overdue (113).

Fatally for a demagogue, however, O'Connor never drew clear lines between attainable goals and fanciful aspirations. His rhetoric encouraged expectations which his organization could not meet. His mob oratory suggested a revolutionary potential which simply did not exist in 1839 or 1842. As Harney observed in 1846, the people would not embrace physical force as O'Connor thought they should: 'They applaud it at public meetings, but that is all. . . . they will not arm.' His campaign to elect Chartist MPs was similarly misconceived. Though he himself was returned for Nottingham in 1847, he was the only Chartist candidate ever to succeed in a parliamentary election. Chartists were rather more influential in the local politics of certain areas, notably South Yorkshire. Sheffield had twenty-two Chartist councillors in 1849, led by the redoubtable Isaac Ironside, an Owenite Chartist and educational reformer.

His personality and administrative abilities aside, O'Connor made a distinctive contribution to the later history of Chartism through his Land Scheme, launched in 1845. This helped to sustain morale. Its aim was to return labourers to the land by an allotment scheme to which Chartists subscribed via the Chartist Land Company. About 70,000 participated, though only 250 fortunates eventually received land by ballot at five sites in Hertfordshire, Gloucestershire and Worcestershire before the company was wound up in 1851. Characteristically, the first estate, at Rickmansworth, was renamed 'O'Connorville'. The scheme incensed his rivals. O'Brien charged that it extended 'the hellish principle of landlordism'. The general feeling was that the plan was a sideshow, diverting Chartists from their main task of establishing equal political rights for working men in an increasingly urban society. However, the emotional appeal of 'back to the land' in the English radical tradition should not be underestimated. Cobbett's evocations were still fresh in radical minds and the prospect of translation from a Salford or Halifax slum to strawberry cultivation on the Chartist land colony of Great Dodford (Worcs.) could hardly fail to entice, however speculative an investment in the Land Company might be.

Chartism only imperfectly fused its various elements, but the leadership squabbles and the obvious failure of its great set pieces should not obscure the movement's wider importance. Enough of the autodidactic artisan radical heritage passed into the political education of the industrial areas to ensure that a vigorous egalitarian strain would pass into the labour-based politics of working men in the second half of the century. Chartism imbued its adherents with both a cultural identity and a strong sense of hope which transcended immediate failures. Nothing in working-class politics thereafter would be unaffected by the Chartist experience. Ernest Jones's pronouncement in 1852 that 'The result is certain . . . the Charter is secure' (108, *188*) was no mere bombast. It encapsulated a deep truth which the next half-century would reveal.

---

1. *Westminster Review*, xxxviii (1842), p. 396.
2. D. Thompson, ed., *The Early Chartists* (1971).

CHAPTER 30

The politics of pressure:
II The Anti-Corn-Law League

I

The Anti-Corn Law League appeared to possess all the advantages of a pressure group which the Chartists lacked. It represented the interests of an urban middle class whose influence the Whigs had recognized in 1832; the Chartists represented those who had been deliberately excluded from the franchise. The League's campaigns, drawing on commercial wealth, did not lack finance; the Chartists lived hand to mouth. Its objective was precise and limited – the removal of tariffs on the import of foreign corn; Chartism had precise objectives but their implications were limitless. Most important of all, the League advocated in free trade an objective for which many MPs already had considerable sympathy and one with an impeccable intellectual pedigree (Chs 5 and 21); democracy was both loathed and feared in most reaches of respectable society and by about 90 per cent of the membership of the Commons. It might seem that the League in the 1840s was pushing at an open door. Yet when Peel carried Corn Law repeal, the League's influence was at a low ebb. It will not do to characterize the repeal of the Corn Laws as the pre-ordained outcome of that middle-class pressure which the crisis of 1830–32 had taught the aristocracy it was powerless to resist. It is at least arguable that the Corn Laws would have been repealed even had the Anti-Corn Law League not existed.

Agitation against the 1815 Corn Law had never died out. Anti-protectionists made a great deal of fuss in the 1826 Election and, though a rather crude sliding scale had been introduced in 1828 (Ch. 21), the principle that landowners, as the nation's food suppliers, needed specially favourable treatment gained little general acceptance. Nottingham produced an Anti-Corn Law Association in 1833 which was well patronized by manufacturers. Hostility was not restricted to the middle classes. The artisan radicals remained primarily anti-aristocratic into the 1840s and Sheffield had seen the development of a Mechanics' Anti-Corn Law Association in the early 1830s. Working-class anti-Corn Law organizations were founded, often in the teeth of Chartist disapproval, in Manchester, Leeds, Huddersfield, Carlisle and Leicester between 1839 and 1841 (103).

Once food prices rose in the later 1830s, manufacturing free traders could argue that the Corn Laws had damaging effects throughout the economy. British workmen would agitate for higher wages which would be spent on food rather than manufactured goods. Higher labour costs rendered manufacturers less competitive in world markets. Also, since the Corn Laws enabled foreigners to export less grain to Britain than they would like, they earned less British cash and had in consequence less to spend on importing British manufactures. So the textile mills worked at less than full capacity. Unemployment increased; so did the dangers of bankruptcy among entrepreneurs. These avoidable sacrifices, the argument ran, were demanded of British manufacturers and British workers to satisfy the greed and self-importance of an aristocracy whose value to the economy lessened by the year. Richard Cobden rammed the point home: 'Every instance of violence or turbulence in the great multitude of work-people ought to be laid to the charge of the aristocracy, who have drawn the utmost from their labour to spend in wars and extravagance abroad and at home, and neglected to return any portion for the expense of educating them' (103, 69). It is not difficult to appreciate why a class-based economic analysis would hit home during the debilitating economic downswings of 1838–42 since these had profound consequences in the textile districts of the North.

It certainly energized the anti-Corn Law associations formed in Manchester in September 1838 and in Leeds a few months later. The Manchester free traders, many of whom had been active in the recent campaign for local government reform, included J. B. Smith, a cotton dealer, Thomas Potter, a very wealthy cotton manufacturer who would be the town's first mayor, and George Wilson, a starch and gum manufacturer who became president of the Anti-Corn Law League and its abiding administrative genius. In March 1839, immediately after the failure of a motion attacking the Corn Laws presented by the Wolverhampton radical MP Charles Villiers, the Anti-Corn Law League was established as a national organization to co-ordinate the various provincial pressures. Its Manchester leadership was never in question. As Richard Cobden explained, Corn Law repeal was 'a pocket argument which pressed more urgently upon the great spinners and manufacturers of Lancashire than any other class'. Manchester, as the commercial heart of the new industrial world, had symbolic as well as practical importance. London, though it had produced an Anti-Corn Law Association as early as 1836, was as stony soil for Leaguers as for the early Chartists.

The League adopted standard pressure-group tactics in the early years, 'missionary' lecture tours, meetings and rallies, the publication of sympathetic journals and parliamentary petitions. Lecturers met spirited resistance. James Acland's astringent, class-ridden harangues united the landed classes of Suffolk and Sussex against the League. Chartists, in the full flush of physical force rhetoric during 1839, broke up free-trade meetings in Leeds and Manchester in the names of J. R. Stephens and, significantly, the Tory radical Richard Oastler. The League journal, *Anti-Corn Law Circular*, lost money while preaching largely to the converted. Free traders in February 1839 were refused permission to address the Commons from the bar of the House. Though Villiers got 195 votes for repeal, more than four times as many as the Chartists could muster a couple of months later, the majority against him was almost two to one.

Amid the welter of wordage on the Corn Law question, few perceived the reality of the situation. Britain was a net importer of grain, mostly from northern Germany and Poland. Whereas in the second and third decades of the century the Corn Laws undoubtedly succeeded in holding back supplies of cheap grain, by the late 1830s these supplies were no longer available. Britain's deficient harvests were part of a general European dearth. Manchester's cotton magnates would have found the results of repeal by no means so beneficial as the League claimed. The free-trade 1850s produced wheat prices not markedly different from the protected 1830s and early 1840s [D.vi.3].

II

The argument over the Corn Laws was not conducted on this level of practicality. As with Chartism, what the League symbolized became much more important than its specific objective. The League continued to talk the language of class, while becoming increasingly careful to stress that the interests of the middle classes and of the nation were synonymous. John Bright, the Rochdale radical who had become the first Quaker MP when returned for the pre-eminently unQuaker city of Durham at a by-election in 1843, stated in 1845 that 'the agitation now in progress throughout this Kingdom is one of no trivial or common character. . . . I believe this to be a movement of the commercial and industrious classes against the lords and great proprietors of the soil.'[1] Cobden's theme was similar: 'We are going to assert the right of the great mass of the middle and industrious population to the influence which they are entitled to in the government of the country.' (89, *249*) Their appeals were in the main stream of early-nineteenth-century radical politics with its pronounced anti-aristocratic tradition and its concern to identify and contrast the productive and destructive elements in society.

The problem was to translate intrinsically powerful rhetoric into the kind of pressure to which a Parliament of landowners would submit. Violence was unthinkable, since industrial property owners' fear of working-class violence was at least as powerful as their support for free trade. The League's fingers were burned in 1842 when its conference considered such coercive tactics as a tax strike by free traders and an employers' lock-out of their mills until repeal were passed. Bright was in the thick of this and two League lecturers, Falvey and Finnigan, made inflammatory speeches to large audiences in Manchester. It is hardly surprising that such Tories as J. W. Croker in *Quarterly Review* should blame the League, wrongly, for the outbreaks of industrial unrest during the summer (Ch. 29) (80). The League was fortunate that the disturbances petered out quickly, for the accusation that it advocated intimidation was extremely damaging. Cobden, an earlier advocate himself of a tax strike, and Wilson supplied emollient words.

Much more promising to Cobden was the plan to make Corn Law repeal a directly political question in a new way. He sought to use the electoral machinery created in 1832 (Ch. 24) to demonstrate support on this one, powerful issue. In 1840 he told Francis Place, a past master at the game of political influence, 'we shall separate the question entirely from *party* politics & induce as many electors as possible to associate themselves together to form a body pledged only to the abolition of the corn law'.[2]

The League first proved itself an apt pupil of Peel on the subject of registration (Ch. 24). Registers were scrupulously checked and 'improved' by the addition of names known to be favourable to repeal. This was arduous work but it showed tangible rewards and proved just the thing to keep enthusiasts without oratorical or journalistic skills in profitable employment on the League's behalf. Attention was first concentrated on the boroughs, since these were assumed to possess the largest numbers of favourably inclined electors. Cobden, however, was well aware that the term 'borough' encompassed vastly different urban areas and put League activists to work drawing up lists of those boroughs which were already safe, which winnable with appropriate effort, and which a waste of time.

The strategy had hardly begun when opportunity presented itself in a by-election at Walsall early in 1841. League efforts nevertheless forced the Whig candidate, who was an agricultural protectionist, to withdraw from the contest. Though J. B. Smith had to be drafted in from Manchester in default of an acceptable local free-trade candidate, the Tory, Captain Gladstone (William's elder brother), won the seat by only twenty-seven votes. Knowing the propaganda value which by-elections disproportionately give to minority or one-issue parties, Cobden induced most of the League hierarchy to move to South Staffordshire for the campaign. He challenged William Gladstone to a public debate to disprove 'that the corn and provision laws are partial and unjust, that they are calculated for the temporary enrichment of a small part of the community at the expense of the millions who subsist by honest industry'.[3] Though he twisted the knife by calling protection 'a monopoly second in turpitude only to that law which made merchandise of human beings', knowing that the Gladstone family fortune owed more than a little to the slave trade, the offer was declined. In the General Election which followed within months, the League captured Walsall and both the Manchester seats. Cobden himself was elected for Stockport. Disturbingly, however, some prize northern seats, including Bradford, Leeds and Warrington, ignored League propaganda and returned Tories.

The League learned some harsh lessons in electoral politics from attempting to field candidates in every borough by-election. Not only did the policy prove hopelessly expensive but borough patrons, almost to a man protectionists, demonstrated that influence was far from dead after 1832. In three by-elections, at Hastings, Christchurch and Dudley, in the spring and summer of 1844, the League candidates failed to get half the votes of their protectionist opponents. A climax was reached in 1845 when that doyen of free-trade campaigners, Colonel Perronet Thompson, was defeated by the railway magnate George Hudson at Sunderland by 627 votes to 498. Hudson flaunted his protectionist prejudices and defied the League to make electoral capital out of them. The League was also damaged by continued reports of electoral corruption by their agents. These had surfaced as early as the Walsall by-election and were particularly wounding to an organization committed to attacking the improper influence of the aristocracy.

By 1844, Cobden was sure that a new electoral policy was needed. Attention should be concentrated on those county seats which adjoined the great urban areas and in which many resided whose place of occupation was urban. Cobden laid down the gauntlet in *The League* in June: 'In many counties the mass of unrepresented property is enormous; much of it, too, is of a kind, or belongs to a class, comparatively free from the electoral tyranny of landlords.' (116, 78) League sympathizers were encouraged. to buy property qualifying them for a county vote as 40-shilling freeholders. It did not provide cash, but offered both legal advice and formidable administrative facilities. No fewer than thirty solicitors were engaged in electoral activity designed to nullify 'landlord influence'. Cobden addressed shopkeepers and the lower middle classes, but his message was also aimed at skilled men with some capital. Though the purchase price of property which carried a vote, at £30–£60 a time, deterred all but the most prosperous and committed artisans, Cobden's was a vision which transcended mere elections. The League was encouraging property ownership and, thus, an expansion in the numbers of those deemed worthy of trust by the nation's leaders. Cobden's lesson was not lost on Mr Gladstone (Ch. 39). In later years, Bright upbraided Cobden for his continued obsession with this backdoor approach to franchise extension when most radicals looked to a much bigger change. But Cobden never thought much of the ordinary working man. He wrote in 1838 of 'the *opaque ignorance* in which the great bulk of the people are wrapt'. Their education would be a very long job since 'the great body of English peasants are not a jot advanced in intellect since the days of their Saxon ancestors'.[4] Now he appealed only to that small minority he considered capable of complex reasoning and most alarmed by the violence of 1842.

Bright estimated that £250,000 had been invested in freehold qualifications in Lancashire, Cheshire and Yorkshire by February 1845. Purchases were also brisk in Staffordshire, Surrey, Middlesex and even Sussex. Some seats almost certainly changed hands in consequence. A by-election in South Lancashire in October 1845 turned a Tory majority of 600 into a free-trade one of 3,000. In February 1846 Viscount Morpeth, a free trader, was returned unopposed for the West Riding though the Tories had held the seat against him by over 700 votes at the General Election in 1841. An appraisal of the new registers convinced the protectionists that a contest was useless and would only give the League more propaganda.

III

Peel, of course, denied the League its ultimate test by passing Corn Law repeal in advance of a General Election (Ch. 28). As we shall see, this may not have been coincidental. It is difficult to see, however, how the League's electoral strategy, geared to fighting by-elections with maximum publicity, could have been successfully adapted to fighting between 150 and 200 contests simultaneously, the more so since its 'freehold' ploy could only have influenced 20 to 30 seats at most. More likely, the League effort would have been swallowed in a general Whig–Liberal–radical assault on the Tories. Despite its best endeavours, the Leaguers could never successfully pose as a 'one-issue party'. As their critics never tired of pointing out, they were one element in the radical opposition.

The League's campaigns inevitably drew organized replies from the protectionists. A Central Agricultural Protection Society was formed in 1843. Its president was the duke of Richmond, a Whig peer in Grey's government [A] and its vice-president the duke of Buckingham, who had recently resigned from Peel's Cabinet (Ch. 28). It was strongly supported by backbench squires like Charles Newdegate and William Miles of North Warwickshire and East Somerset respectively. Nicknamed the Anti-League, it never aspired to the intellectual heights of classical economics, though it delivered effective counter-punches by demonstrating the self-contradictory nature of League pronouncements on the likely effects of repeal on wage rates and bread prices. Its success in rallying the farmers was undeniable. Cobden and Bright were frustrated to discover that they won far more arguments than they did converts in the rural world. They were not the first, or the last, reformers to learn the bitter lesson that cases are rarely won on the respective power of the contending arguments. The protectionists, despite being outscored in debate, could demonstrate that the League's lecturers were clever outsiders whose practised homilies concealed a deep antagonism not only to landlords but to rural society in general.

So farmers were not detached from 'idle' landlords and protectionists proclaimed themselves the defenders of all rural institutions, not least the Established Church. Anglican clergymen were prominent anti-Leaguers and the organization developed into a country gentleman's association, encompassing also the substantial tenant farmers. It was in perfect accord with that backbench Tory opinion which caused Peel such trouble in 1845–46 (Ch. 28). Much was made of the League's attractions for dissenters, not only nonconformist manufacturers but ministers, 700 of whom had met in Manchester in 1841 to condemn the self-interest of landowning protectionists. It is tempting to characterize the Corn Law debate in terms of two federations: League – urban, middle-class, dissenting, radical and anti-establishment; Anti-League – rural, landed, Anglican, conservative and pro-establishment. This conjunction, however, was far from total. Most towns, like Leeds and Manchester, were split between usually majority Liberals and usually minority Tories. Samuel Smiles regretted that some Leeds manufacturers were protectionist against their self-interest because 'they can only see the corn law question through the medium of party'. In Manchester, the Liberals were split between radicals and non-radicals. The *Manchester Guardian* supported the latter group, which founded a separate Commercial Association against the League in 1845 (89). In 1844 a protectionist Manchester Tory, William Entwistle, had won South Lancashire against strenuous League efforts.

The Whig landowners put up less of a fight for protection than might have been expected. After the Walsall by-election, Russell had persuaded Melbourne to fight the 1841 Election on a pledge to replace the existing sliding scale of duties with a much lower fixed tariff. Melbourne remained at heart a protectionist, but Russell believed that the future of the Whig–Liberal alliance rested on eventual granting of free trade. In this he was supported by a small, but significant, number of Whig aristocrats. One of them, Lord Radnor, helped John Wilson to found the free-trade *Economist* journal in 1843. Another, the earl of Clarendon, established and maintained helpful lines of communication between the Whigs and urban radicals in the years 1842–45 (88, 46). He even read some economic theory to provide intellectual ballast for this political calculation. When in December 1845, reacting to the Irish famine, he rushed out an open letter to his City of London constitutents declaring his opposition to protection as 'the blight of commerce, the bane of agriculture [and] the source of bitter divisions among classes' (97, *427*), the Whig MPs in the Commons rallied behind him readily enough. Protectionist Whig peers allowed themselves to be swayed by Melbourne's appeal for party unity and did not oppose repeal. The radical MP H. G. Ward believed that Russell's free-trade declaration made them 'a *Party* again which we certainly have not been for the last few years'.

The Anti-Corn Law League carried organized pressure to levels of sophistication not yet seen in British political life. No one subsequently seeking to change the law from outside Parliament could ignore either its methods or its lessons. It remained professional and it did not run out of cash from grateful businessmen. It knew how to please its natural constituents. George Wilson was granted £10,000 in 1846 in gratitude for his organizational expertise and Cobden, whose calico-printing business slid near to collapse without his formidable presence, was helped out of his difficulties with a public subscription which raised over £75,000.

Yet it is difficult to contend that the Corn Laws were repealed because of League pressure. That pressure had certainly kept the question closely in the public eye, but interest was not so strong in 1845–46 as it had been in 1843–44, as Cobden was well aware. The Corn Laws were repealed because Peel no longer believed in them. Protection was untenable when Britain's swollen population craved bread. The old argument that protection kept farmers producing for the home market was no longer sufficient. Additionally, Peel knew that a substantial proportion of the landed interest no longer set great store by protection (Ch. 15). The Irish famine brought the provision question, and hence terms of trade, to a head in both parties. Thereafter, the matter was settled not in the assembly rooms and lecture halls of Manchester, Leeds or Birmingham under League banners but on the floor of the House of Commons where the substantial majority of members remained landowners (Ch. 24) and very few were Leaguers. This was not the least source of Peel's satisfaction as he left office. He hated extra-parliamentary pressure and coercion and he would not countenance that either could force legislative change. He could justify 1846 in equally 'conservative' terms as Grey's political 'concession' in 1832. He believed that efficient farmers would benefit from repeal, particularly when linked to the government's drainage scheme (Ch. 15). He believed also that repeal in 1846 would spike radical guns. Men like Bright were anti-aristocrats first and free traders second. Repeal was a staging-post only for an attack on the game laws, which protected brutal rural pastimes, and (far more importantly) on the land laws which kept aristocratic estates intact by invoking primogeniture and by preventing many forms of land scale by the inheritor. For good measure, radical dissenters put church disestablishment (Chs 27 and 34) prominently on their shopping lists. A government coerced into Corn Law repeal, Peel believed, would be in a weaker position to defend the essence of the establishment. Timely concession, and 1846 was timely precisely because League pressure was for the moment less strident, allowed opportunity for the forces of the establishment to regroup, supported now by many of the urban middle classes who espoused free trade for no motive ulterior to profit and self-interest. Peel's actions in 1846, though they were hastened by the Irish famine, completed the process whereby the forces of property were strengthened, not weakened, during a period of monumental change. Both in 1832 and in 1846 the wild men of the right were dragged kicking and screaming from their last ditches while, centre-stage, the scenery was rearranged in preparation for a generation of bourgeois prosperity.

———————————

1. J. Thorold Rogers, ed., *Speeches of John Bright* (2 vols, 1868), ii. p. 275.
2. J. Morley, *The Life of Richard Cobden* (1920), p. 83.
3. B. L. Add. MSS. 44135, f. 1.
4. J. Morley, *op. cit.*, p. 127.

PART FOUR

Early industrial society, refined and tested, 1846–1870

FRAMEWORK OF EVENTS 1847-1870

1847 General Election confirms Liberal control of Commons; about 90 Peelite Tories returned. Wheat prices rise sharply; last food riots experienced in Britain. Charlotte Brontë, *Jane Eyre*; Emily Brontë, *Wuthering Heights*

1848 Chartist meeting at Kennington Common disperses peacefully after threats of violence; Britain insulated from European revolutions. Public Health Act established General Board of Health under control of Chadwick. J. S. Mill, *Principles of Political Economy*; Elizabeth Gaskell, *Mary Barton*; Hunt, Millais and Rossetti form Pre-Raphaelite Brotherhood.

1849 Liberals further reduce duties on West Indian sugar; Navigation Acts repealed. Russell passes Encumbered Estates Act which facilitates sale of Irish land. Christian Socialist movement organized by Kingsley and Maurice. Bedford College for women students founded. Dickens, *David Copperfield*.

1850 Palmerston uses Don Pacifico claim to assert Britain's responsibilities and rights of her citizens overseas (Jan–June). Pope establishes new Catholic bishoprics in England. Ewart's Public Libraries Act enables funds to be raised by local authorities, but little immediate use. Royal Meteorological Society founded. Tennyson, *In Memoriam*.

1851 Ecclesiastical Titles Act (Aug) prevents Catholic bishops from adopting titles derived from British territory. Palmerston resigns (Dec) as government authority weakened. Great Exhibition held under patronage of Prince Albert. Britain's only religious census taken (Mar). King's Cross railway station built by Joseph Cubitt. Owen's College, Manchester (from which Manchester University developed) opens.

1852 Russell's Liberal gvt resigns (Feb); Derby forms a minority Tory gvt. Treaty of London (May) seems to settle Danish succession and territorial problem. Tory gvt defeated over Disraeli's budget and resigns (Dec); Aberdeen forms a Liberal–Peelite coalition with Gladstone as Chancellor of Exchequer for first time.

1853 Relations with Russia deteriorate over Turkish territorial problems. Unsuccessful negotiations lead to mobilization of navy in Dardanelles. Gladstone's first budget continues move towards complete free trade and anticipates abolition of income tax by 1860. Northcote–Trevelyan *Report on Civil Service* criticizes patronage as method of appointment.

1854 Britain and France ally and declare war on Russia (Mar); forces sent to Crimea (Sept) leading to battles at Alma, Balaclava and Inkerman (Sept–Nov). Elgin treaty (June) covers reciprocal trade agreements between USA and Canada. Orange Free State becomes independent. Chadwick dismissed from post at Board of Health; period of reaction against central directions in sanitary legislation.

1855 Aberdeen coalition resigns (Feb), having been weakened by internal dissent and external criticism of Crimean War strategy; Palmerston forms Liberal gvt. Fort at Sebastopol finally falls to the allies (Sept). Florence Nightingale's nursing reforms in Crimea. Stamp duties on British newspapers abolished (June). *Daily Telegraph* founded. David Livingstone discovers Victoria Falls.

1856 Crimean War ended by Treaty of Paris (Feb–Mar). Tension rises in India after Britain annexes Oudh (Feb). Trading disagreements provoke Anglo-Chinese War (Oct). Bessemer process revolutionizes manufacture of steel.

1857 Indian Rebellion (Mutiny) begins against British rule (May); massacres of soldiers, women and children at Cawnpore (June–July) greatly heightens anti-native hostility among British. Liberals increase their majority at General Election (Apr); national popularity of Palmerston. Science Museum, London, founded. Thomas Hughes, *Tom*

Brown's Schooldays; Anthony Trollope, *Barchester Towers. Birmingham Post* founded.

1858   Palmerston's gvt brought down by discontented Liberals in alliance with Tories (Feb); Derby forms second minority Tory gvt. Remaining political restrictions on Jews removed (June); Property qualification for MPs abolished. Indian Rebellion put down; East India Company loses all remaining governing responsibilities in India (Aug). Isambard Brunel's steamship *Great Eastern* launched. Charles Barry designs Covent Garden Opera House. John Hanning Speke discovers Lake Victoria.

1859   Conservative reform bill defeated (Mar); agreement of anti-Tory elements to bring down Derby's gvt (June); Palmerston becomes Prime Minister again, though the outgoing Tory gvt had improved its parliamentary position at the recent General Election (May). J. S. Mill, *On Liberty*; Charles Darwin, *Origin of Species by Natural Selection*; Dickens, *A Tale of Two Cities*.

1860   Cobden-Chevalier treaty liberalizes trade between Britain and France (Jan). Gladstone's budget leaves only a small number of articles subject to duty. Public opinion grows in favour of Italian unification; gvt also favourable though concerned about growing French influence there. Russell's despatch (Oct) commits Britain to Italian cause and provokes diplomatic furore in established states. Debate between Bishop Wilberforce and T. H. Huxley over origins of life as suggested by Darwin engenders bitter controversy in next few years between Christians and some scientists. Open golf championship first played. George Elliot, *Mill on the Floss*.

1861   Gladstone succeeds in repealing paper duties and gains support among politically aware working men for making 'knowledge' cheaper. Britain stays neutral as American Civil War breaks out, though an incident (Nov) when southern emissaries taken off a British ship *Trent* by Unionists threatens relations. Siemens open-hearth process for making steel increases still further prospects of cheap mass production of the alloy. *HMS Warrior* the first all-iron warship. George Eliot, *Silas Marner.* Prince Albert dies of typhoid (Dec).

1862   Gladstone's northern tours cement his popular reputation as a reformer. Further delicacy in relations between Britain and USA as a result of *Alabama*, a British-built Confederate ship which did considerable damage to Unionist fleet. In Britain, interruption of cotton supplies to Lancashire causes great distress – the 'cotton famine'. Gilbert Scott designs the Albert Memorial. First English cricket team tours Australia. Foundation of Notts County, the oldest football club in the League, presages developments in professional soccer.

1863   Schleswig-Holstein dispute between Prussia and Denmark. Palmerston makes empty threat in attempt to deter Prussian designs on the duchies (July). International conference in London on future of the Ionian Islands (July). Charles Lyell, *The Antiquity of Man*; Charles Kingsley, *The Water Babies*. John Stuart Mill, *Utilitarianism*. Football Association formed (Oct). London Metropolitan Railway (pioneer of the Underground) begun.

1864   Conference to settle Schleswig-Holstein question without further hostilities held in London but fails. Gladstone makes declaration in favour of further parliamentary reform. Manchester Reform Union (sponsored by middle classes) formed to press the case. Octavia Hill begins her work to improve housing conditions for the London poor with tenements in Marylebone. Opening of Metropolitan Railway proves great incentive to suburban housing developments for the middle classes in London. Charles Dickens, *Our Mutual Friend*.

1865   General Election held in which personal popularity of Palmerston increases overall Liberal majority (July); Palmerston dies in office (Oct); succeeded by Russell, who pledges to reopen the reform question. Reform League, of middle-class radicals and skilled trade union leaders, founded. William Booth's Christian Mission in Whitechapel is forerunner of the Salvation Army. Atlantic telegraph cable begins to operate. C. L. Dodgson (Lewis Carroll), *Alice in Wonderland*.

1866   Fenian unrest in Ireland (Feb); Habeas Corpus suspended there. Failure of the bankers Overend and Gurney precipitates financial crisis (May). Splits within Liberal party over desirability of reform lead to defeat of Russell's bill and the fall of his gvt (June); Derby becomes Prime Minister of minority gvt for third time; Disraeli leads in the Commons (July); growth of extra-parliamentary agitation for reform when advent of a Conservative gvt seems to threaten reform prospects. Dr Barnardo opens a home for orphans in Stepney. Marquis of Queensbury codifies rules of boxing. Amateur Athletic Association founded.

1867   British North America Act (Mar) creates in Canada first Dominion, self-governing, status. Neutrality of Luxembourg guaranteed at London Conference (May). Second Reform Act passed after many amendments and extensions to original bill accepted by gvt (May–Aug). Factory Act Extension Act and Agricultural Gangs Act greatly extends protection of the law over female and child labour. Irish Fenian disturbances in England arouse anti-Irish hostility in many parts of the country (Nov–Dec). Anthony Trollope, *Last Chronicle of Barset*. Joseph Lister pioneers antiseptic surgery using phenol.

1868   Derby resigns through ill health (Feb); Disraeli becomes Prime Minister for first time (Feb). General Election (Nov) produces substantial Liberal majority and Disraeli resigns before meeting Parliament; Gladstone becomes Prime Minister for first time (Dec). Payment of compulsory church rates abolished. First Trades Union Congress. Royal Historical Society founded; Press Association founded. Wilkie Collins, *The Moonstone*.

1869   Irish Church disestablished; its revenues, after compensation to existing interests, to aid poverty and other social causes. Girton College, Cambridge, founded for women students. J. S. Mill, *The Subjection of Women*; Matthew Arnold, *Culture and Anarchy*; R. D. Blackmore, *Lorna Doone*.

1870   Irish Land Act (Aug) attempts to provide protection for tenants against eviction and compensation for improvements made. Forster's Elementary Education Act provides for local rate-supported board schools to 'fill the gaps' left by church school provision, but elementary education not yet compulsory. Reforms of Civil Service by promoting entry by competitive examination (but not yet to the Foreign Office). Married Women's Property Act (Aug) gives wives a degree of independent protection over their property. Charles Dickens dies (June) leaving last novel *Mystery of Edwin Drood* unfinished.

CHAPTER 31

The zenith of the bourgeoisie

I

Britain in 1860 was demonstrably both more secure and more prosperous than in 1840. In the 1830s and 1840s the ruling classes feared for their safety. Both in 1831 and 1842 Sir Robert Peel's family put Drayton Manor in a state of fortification. No one thought it necessary to defend Gladstone at Hawarden or Disraeli at Hughenden in the 1860s. The worst that Disraeli had to suffer was temporary unpopularity when he raised his tenants' rents and a feeling in the Wycombe district that Mrs Disraeli was not so lavish in her patronage of local tradesmen as might be expected from a lady of the manor.

Not that the British people had forgotten how to riot. They did so over proposals to limit Sunday trading in 1855 (Ch. 34), over reform in 1866 and endemically where the despised Irish immigrants congregated in London and the North-west (Ch. 41). But these were isolated instances, offering no greater threat to the stability of government than the sometimes violent strikes which punctuated industrial life in the 1850s and 1860s (Ch. 18). Industrial society had come of age. Its base was broadening (Chs 14 and 15) as its prosperity increased. Industrial investment reached a peak in the 1850s; business profits rose sharply. The total national product rose by 75 per cent between 1850 and 1870 and the proportion generated by manufacturing, mining, building, trade and transport, which had been more or less static in the 1830s and 1840s at around 53 per cent, rose suddenly to 60 per cent by 1871 [D.ii.1].

By the 1850s Britain knew that it was the world's workshop and revelled in the fact. It revelled not only in having weathered the storms of the previous two decades but in having given to the world unparalleled examples of what could be achieved by hard work and free competition. As the old Manchester Anti-Corn Law Leaguer Absolom Watkin gloated in 1853: 'never . . . have I seen clearer evidence of general well-being. Our country is, no doubt, in a most happy and prosperous state. Free trade, peace, and freedom.' (250, *408*)

We may call this period the zenith of the bourgeoisie for two reasons. Firstly, the dominant values of society reflected the attitudes of the middle classes. Secondly, though most of Britain's MPs remained landowners, they increasingly accepted that prosperity was to be achieved by adopting in free trade and the fullest possible licence to competition – a policy associated with the middle classes. This process was helped by the co-operation which existed between the Whig government of 1846–52 and certain urban radicals. Though the Whigs had no taste for the class-ridden politics of Manchester school radicals like Bright (Ch. 30), they found others much more congenial. John Wilson, editor of the *Economist*, for example, argued that free trade should conduce to general social harmony rather than attacks on 'backward' landowners. In 1847, he became an MP and a year later was appointed Secretary of the Board of Control, eventually rising to become Financial Secretary to the Treasury (88, *47*). The earl of Clarendon approvingly noted Wilson's contribution to diffusing 'correct information upon commercial questions' and the reassurance his presence in government would give to the middle classes. At the local level the middle classes, in all their diversity, directly controlled the destinies of urban Britain. The Preston Council of 1855, for example, included nine cotton manufacturers, fourteen professional men (lawyers, doctors and the like) and no fewer than twenty tradesmen, ranging from wealthy corn merchants to humble shopkeepers.[1] By the early 1850s as many retailers sat on the Leeds Council as did merchants and manufacturers (265).

After 1846 the remaining bastions of economic protection crumbled quite quickly. The Navigation Laws were repealed in respect of foreign trade in 1849 and coastal trade in 1854. Duties on foreign and colonial sugar were equalized in 1854 and gradually phased out over the next twenty years. Gladstone removed the duties on soap in 1853 and on paper in 1861, thereby making cleanliness, if not next to godliness, at least to knowledge since both books and newspapers became cheaper. After the Cobden–Chevalier treaty with France in 1860 the value of British manufactured goods exported to that country doubled in ten years. The age of economic liberalism, preached since the beginning of our period (Ch. 5) had finally arrived. As *The Times* put it in 1859: 'Free trade is henceforth, like parliamentary representation or ministerial responsibility, not so much a prevalent opinion as an article of national faith.' (89, *112*)

The symbol of national self-congratulation was the 'Great Exhibition of the Works of Industry of All Nations', an international gathering held in 1851. It attracted 6 million visitors during its five-month duration and its real emphasis was on Britain. More than half the 14,000 exhibitors were British or British colonists and the achievements which the Exhibition celebrated were British triumphs for foreigners to admire and emulate. It was a celebration, too, of private enterprise. Henry Cole, a leading Civil Servant and member of the Royal Society of Arts who organized the Exhibition with the Prince Consort, Prince Albert, stated: 'A great people invited all civilized nations to a festival. . . . It was carried out by its own private means; was self-supporting and independent of taxes and employment of slaves, which great works had exacted in ancient days.' (297, *24*) Its centrepiece, that enormous glass edifice more than a third of a mile long and 66 feet high known as the Crystal Palace, dominated Hyde Park and carried the symbolism of progress a stage further. Not only did it evoke gasps of awe from visitors (though trenchant criticisms of vulgarity from aesthetes like John Ruskin), it was designed by a man whose enterprise and talent had raised him from humble origins. Joseph Paxton had been a gardener who taught himself human biology and engineering. These skills he allied to a shrewd and varied business acumen to make his way in the world. It was examples such as Paxton's which the Scottish homilist Samuel Smiles had in mind when he produced *Self Help* (1859), one of the great best sellers of the Victorian age. By the time of Smiles's death in 1905, *Self Help* had sold a quarter of a million copies (327, *20*). 'The spirit of self-help is the root of all genuine growth in the individual; and, exhibited in the lives of the many, it constitutes the true source of national vigour and strength.' The Exhibition was held barely two miles from the spot where, three years before, many thought Feargus O'Connor was about to launch a Chartist revolution (Ch. 29). Yet in 1851 all that the reinforced police had to bother about was a rash of pickpocketing. The national mood was one of celebration not agitation.

II

As British society became more complex so the proportion of its members who might be called middle class increased. In the mid-nineteenth century they formed between one-fifth and one-sixth of the total. Their incomes overlapped aristocratic wealth at one end of the spectrum and skilled men's wages at the other. The wealthiest bourgeois were much more likely to be commercial men based in London than cotton manufacturers from Manchester. James Morrison, the warehouseman and merchant banker (d. 1857) left about £5m. and Richard Thornton (d. 1865), an insurance broker and merchant on the Baltic exchange, left £2.8m. (309). At the other end of the scale, some junior clerks started with incomes as low as £20 a year, and the salaries of most Lancashire clerks in the 1860s did not exceed £60–£70. The only definitional umbrella capacious enough to cover such extremes of income and wealth was the absence of grinding, manual labour which characterized middle-class occupations.

The greatest increase between 1850 and 1870 was probably in trading and commercial jobs. Charles Booth's later reconstruction of the census's occupational material indicates an increase of 164 per cent in the numbers of clerks, accountants and bankers and of 53 per cent in the far more numerous category of wholesale and retail traders, among whom the proliferation of small shopkeepers was especially noteworthy. Most professional groups had established their own societies in the first half of the century as a means both of conferring status and restricting entry. The Royal College of Surgeons had been established in 1800, the Law Society in 1825. Civil engineers had a professional body by 1818, architects in 1837, pharmacists in 1841 and mechanical engineers in 1847. Such groups, with teachers and ministers of religion, continued to expand after 1850 but at a generally slower rate than their commercial counterparts.

Medical practice was a special case. Conflicting interest between the profession's 'aristocrats' – surgeons and physicians – frustrated attempts at national regulation until the 1850s. The British Medical Association was constituted in recognizably modern form only in 1856, and the Medical Act of 1858 established a General Medical Council to be the final arbiter both of the qualifying societies' professional examinations and of entrance to, and maintenance on, a medical register. This Act settled who was entitled to charge medical fees, but since these were frequently outside the reach of ordinary families, self-medication via Holloway's Pills or, for keeping babies quiet, the opium-based Godfrey's Cordial, remained enormously popular. Proprietary medicines were widely advertised in newspapers and magazines, usually accompanied by the most grandiose claims. Among those who could afford orthodox medical aid, confidence in the profession, justifiably low in the early 1850s, began to improve. Significantly, the numbers of doctors recorded in the 1871 census showed almost no increase over those of 1861, 'the qualification having been much raised'.

From the admittedly opaque evidence of income tax returns, it seems likely that those with incomes in excess of £150 a year (the normal tax threshold [D.i.3]) improved their living standards more than most between 1850 and 1870. Despite seductive propaganda about 'wealth ... within the reach of all', early industrial Britain was an increasingly unequal society. According to calculations by the statistician Dudley Baxter in 1867, families receiving more than £100 a year (about 10 per cent of the total) had 50.6 per cent of the total national income and those with more than £1000 (0.48 per cent) had 26.3 per cent of the wealth. Early in the century roughly similar proportions of families accounted for only about 40 per cent and 17 per cent respectively. Total income assessed for tax in the period 1868–69 to 1872 was 79 per cent higher than in the period 1848–49 to 1852–53. The impression of growing financial comfort is confirmed by the expansion in the number of servant-keeping families. The domestic servant total of 848,000 in 1851 had risen to 1,310,000 by 1871, an increase of 54 per cent. More than 90 per cent of these servants were female; housemaids, housekeepers and general servants. Servant-keeping became *sine qua non* for middle-class respectability, and was even a feasible goal for established artisans and well-paid manual workers by the end of the period (278).

III

The bourgeois ethic stressed hard work, seriousness, competition and religious observance as the hallmarks of individual and national progress. It was a direct descendant of Puritanism, which had always been culturally more acceptable to the middle ranks and the emphasis on effort and earnestness had been central to the late-eighteenth-century evangelical revival (Ch. 6). By the 1860s both the aristocracy and the 'respectable' elements in working-class society were adept at earnest exhortation, though it should not be thought that such attributes were an alien graft on to working-class stock since working men had evolved their own criteria for improvement. Palmerston, in some ways the most unregenerate aristocrat among leading politicians, told an audience of artisans just before his death in 1865 that 'wealth is, to a certain extent, within the reach of all ... you are competitors for prizes ... you will by systematic industry, raise yourselves in the social system of the country – you will acquire honour and respect for yourselves and your families. You will have, too, the constant satisfaction of feeling that you have materially contributed to the dignity of your country.[2]

The co-operative movement hastily turned its back on 'the Utopian ridiculous mummery of socialism'. Its president believed in 1860 that the 'common bond' of the co-operator was 'self-interest'. W. N. Molesworth noted of the pioneer Rochdale co-operators in 1861 that 'their object and ambition appears to be that the working class should be well fed, well clothed, well housed, well washed, well educated – in a word that they should be respectable and respected' (333, *108*). Respectable artisans were intensely status-conscious. They took pride in their skills, in their literacy, in their separate route to self-esteem and, above all, in their ability to maintain their families in decent independence (304, 305). They subscribed to savings banks and friendly societies. Mutual aid became big business in mid- Victorian Britain. Friendly societies with names redolent of Christian or patriotic imagery such as 'The Royal Order of Ancient Shepherds', 'Hearts of Oak' and 'Royal Standard' proliferated. Most were small-scale affairs but some were worth millions by the 1870s. Friendly societies also acted as social centres, with more than 1¼m. members by 1872, with particular concentration in the North-west. A clergyman meanwhile extolled the penny savings banks for teaching the habits of thrift, independence and self-respect (307). But independent working men were far from being the dupes of the bourgeoisie, however much some historians might have wished them to take up the cudgels on behalf of a separate, alienated working class which did not exist. Engels, who in a private expression of frustration to Marx in 1858 called England 'the most bourgeois of all nations', was only the first of them.

An important distinction in mid-Victorian Britain was between respectability and non-respectability. Respectability consisted in earning a degree of independence by one's own efforts, in self-discipline (especially in sexual and bibulous matters), and in veneration for home and family as the basic social organism from which all other virtues flowed. The non-respectable could not provide for their families without State or charitable aid, were sexually promiscuous, regularly drunk, failed to put enough aside for rainy days and flitted from one rented tenement to another, as often as not to avoid paying their dues. The categories were not mutually exclusive, however, since not all working folk considered by their 'betters' to be respectable were above riotous 'benders' or, as has recently been suggested, subtle role-playing designed to convince those betters when occasion demanded that they deserved well of them (319).

Respectability had a practical aspect which those who concentrate on Victorian 'hypocrisy' sometimes miss. The Victorians lived in the world's first predominantly urban society and cities, though the commercial glory of their creators, were objects of fear both for their size and their potential ungovernability. It was by no means clear, even to those who basked most refulgently in the splendours of the Great Exhibition, that cities could work, divorced as they were from the traditional checks of an older, slower order. In Professor Burn's memorably telling phrase, 'The "good" mid-Victorians did not for a moment assume that the nation was safe on a plateau of godliness.' Moral imperatives were necessary not just for reasons of ostentatiously sanctimonious piety (though the Victorians had their full share of such qualities) but to prevent a grand explosion. The Victorians dubbed those who did not live by their rules 'the dangerous classes' and they meant the phrase to be taken literally. The idle, drunken, rootless lower orders represented more than a moral affront; they threatened progress.

The temperance movement grew in reaction to what its supporters considered the uncontrolled expansion of opportunity for drunken vice. After the liberalizing Beer Act (1830), the number of beerhouses expanded massively. Some 30,000 were registered by the mid-1830s and 50,000 by the end of our period. A well-known statistic from 1876 revealed that, on average and including children, every inhabitant of the UK consumed almost 35 gallons of beer a year. Temperance organizations, which embraced respectable working men and the middle classes, concentrated their fire on the street-corner pubs in working-class districts. By the 1860s the middle classes were drinking at home or in their private clubs. Drink was condemned as degenerate, wasteful and destructive of family life, a message mawkishly reinforced by the proliferation of ballads on the lines of Mrs E. A. Pankhurst's 'Father's a drunkard and mother is dead'. Temperance lifeboat crews, originating incongruously in Staffordshire in 1861, dressed up, marched with model lifeboats to public houses and symbolically cast lifelines to those needing salvation inside. Thomas Whittaker, one of many artisans who believed that his salvation rested on his abstinence, declared that 'the home that had satisfied my wants as a drinker was not in harmony with my self-respect as a teetotaller and I soon put myself in possession of a house rented at twelve pounds a year'. The Liberal party, the natural vehicle for a nonconformist-influenced pressure group, got little support in the London slums after 1867 where the new voters resented the airs and moral certainties of respectable working-class abstainers.

The archetypal Victorian home represented retreat from the pressures of competitive acquisition. All but the wealthiest of the bourgeoisie, for whom clubland beckoned, spent most of their leisure hours – annual holidays excepted – at home and little expense was spared to make it a place of comfort and sober recreation. The piano, its technology recently improved to give greater depth and dynamic range, became a ubiquitous accoutrement. Female children received piano lessons almost as inevitably as being taught reading and needlework; parlour songs around the fireside were a common form of entertainment. Love of tangible objects dictated the furnishing of homes both opulent and relatively humble; to late-twentieth-century tastes, Victorian rooms appear fussily cluttered with a marked preference for sombre colours. A contributor to *Fortnightly Review* in 1868 stated that thrifty workpeople in Lancashire had living rooms equipped with dresser, sofa, 'a couple of rocking chairs' and an 'eight day clock'. The better paid might aspire to engravings, bookcases and a piano.

The Victorian middle-class home was a strict hierarchy in microcosm. The father was all powerful. Until 1870, wives had almost no independent control over their property. Divorce, though more available after 1857, was so on terms deeply humiliating to the female (Ch. 34). It was almost a defining characteristic of respectability that wives did not do paid work (272). Artisans and clerks strove to earn sufficient to avoid the shame of a dual income. The wife's duty was the good ordering of the home and the deployment of servants' tasks. Her other function was the procreation of children in wedlock. At a time when infant mortality, even in middle-class households, remained obstinately high [E.v.b] the female duty to frequent pregnancy was pronounced. Wives were expected to bear their burden gladly, following the example of Queen Victoria, whose German husband's manners and beliefs were quintessentially bourgeois and who saddled her with nine children in less than seventeen years.

Most careers were considered inappropriate for females and as late as 1870 a highly educated woman tended to be the object of suspicion. Eliza Lynn Linton, the daughter of a Lake District vicar who made a career as a journalist on *The Morning Chronicle* in the 1850s and 1860s, was very much the exception to a widely enforced genteel idleness among conformist middle-class women. Nursing had, however, become more acceptable since Florence Nightingale's exploits in the Crimea and it was considered appropriate for ladies to devote their energies to good works and philanthropic activity. Middle-class infants became the preserve of nurses, nannies and governesses, to be paraded before father on his terms and only at his request. Given the frequency of childbirth, the proverb 'children should be seen and not heard' had a utilitarian as well as a moral basis.

IV

No shortage of critics existed who contended that the bourgeois ethic was rotten at the core. In language which carries eerie pre-echoes of attacks on Thatcherism in the 1980s, the *Quarterly Review* denounced free trade in 1849 as a:

> selfish, sordid and degrading creed . . . a mercenary, unsocial, democratising system opposed to all generous notions, all kindly feelings. Based on selfishness – the most pervading as well as the most powerful of our vicious propensities – it directs that impulse into the lowest of all channels, the mere sordid pursuit of wealth. It teaches competition and isolation, instead of co-operation and brotherhood . . . it disregards the distress of the poor. . . . Wealth is its end and Mammon its divinity. (88, *29*)

As has frequently been remarked, of course, Thatcherite ideology was much more an unreflective and philistine reworking of *laissez-faire* liberalism than a valid strain of Conservatism.

Competition is impossible unless there are losers as well as winners. *The Times* asserted in 1859 that 'Ninety-nine people in a hundred cannot "get on" in life but are tied by birth, education and circumstances to a lower position, where they must stay'. Of course, enough examples of 'rags to riches' could be cited to invest Samuel Smiles with the aura of truth. The Welsh explorer Sir Henry Morton Stanley was born illegitimate and had been brought up in a workhouse. The Baptist preacher, Thomas Cook, founded a great travel empire. Sir William Arrol, who built the Forth Bridge, had been a blacksmith's apprentice. But making a business fortune from nothing, never easy, became progressively more difficult as units of production grew (Ch. 13). An ignominious end in the bankruptcy court was much more likely. The Victorians had not yet learned to accept business failure without social stigma. Not until 1893 would W. S. Gilbert put into the mouth of his 'Company Promoter' this cynical but much heeded advice:

> If you come to grief, and creditors are craving . . .
> Do you suppose that signifies perdition?
> If so you're but a monetary dunce –
> You merely file a Winding-Up Petition,

And start another Company at once!
... the Liquidators say,
Never mind – you needn't pay',
So you start another Company tomorrow.

Many thought Victorian society excessively materialistic. A little earlier the Revd Sydney Smith had sardonically observed that 'the major object for which the Anglo-Saxon seems to have been created is the manufacture of calico'.[3] The *Darlington Telegraph* asserted in 1858 that 'one of the most prominent vices of modern society is the aiming and struggling to keep up external appearance. . . . This false and demoralizing habit arises from the over-weening estimate which we form in this country of two things well enough in their place: rank and wealth.'[4] From writers like Dickens, Ruskin and Matthew Arnold came criticisms of the philistinism and lack of finer feelings of a bourgeoisie which reposed excessive faith in machinery and material reward. But artists are contemporary critics or they are nothing and taste is a personal matter. Victorian artistic achievement is now held in considerably higher regard than formerly. It would be excessively harsh to judge the bourgeoisie of Manchester or Bradford as philistine, given their support for Charles Hallé's and Jacob Behrens's subscription concerts. The Manchester Exhibition of Art in 1857 attracted huge numbers and bestowed permanent cultural benefits. So did the Leeds Musical Festival, inaugurated in 1858. They are matters of trivial importance that musical preference was for 'thick' harmonies in sacred oratorios which twentieth-century ears find cloying, that Bach was undervalued, that Mozart was regarded in many quarters as a trial run for the romantic imagination of Beethoven or that Edward Elgar, incomparably Britain's greatest composer, was born too late (1857) to make his distinctive contribution until the very end of Victoria's reign.

The competitive ethic, however, concealed a double standard. It was a good deal easier for the upper middle class male to 'keep up appearances' while breaking the rules. He could drink himself under the table in his single-sex club without losing face. He could sow wild oats with his servants or with the prostitutes who existed in enormous numbers both in London and other commercial centres, while insisting on absolute chastity in his future bride. As Hippolyte Taine noted, 'the "kept woman" ... is carefully hidden. Reserve in this matter is obligatory and extreme.'[5] Pre-marital pregnancy spelt ruin for the respectable lady. Even the suspicion of illicit liaison might end the prospects of marriage to one of equal station. The 'fallen woman' was an extraordinarily powerful symbol.

Among the lower middle classes and skilled workers the maintenance of respectability was a desperately serious business since it defined their position against those immediately below them in the hierarchy. But the opportunities for 'lapses' were far fewer and the chances of being 'caught' by neighbours' prying eyes proportionately greater. Not surprisingly, the most self-righteous and intolerant expressions of rectitude in such matters as temperance and Sunday observance came from these groups, not from those whose position was more secure. Narrow-mindedness and prudery were defence mechanisms.

For those who failed to make the grade, the Victorians partly inherited and vastly expanded an unwieldy safety net in the form of charity. A profound distrust of State aid combined with the conviction that all members of society were free, within broad limits, to choose to prosper or flounder persuaded the Victorians to salve their consciences by contributing to all manner of charities to relieve orphans, widows, mendicants, cripples, the homeless, the colonial heathen and the domestic ignorant. As Dr Stallard argued to the National Association for the Promotion of Social Science in 1868, 'There is not a want, or form of human wretchedness, for which provision is not made in more or less degree. . . . From the cradle to the grave, benevolence steps in to offer aid.'[6] One estimate listed 386 separate charities operating in London alone, exclusive of parish or City company bequests. So little was precisely known about what *Fraser's Magazine* called 'profuse and heedless almsgiving' that estimates of its total value in the capital ranged from £2m. to £7m. It is a reasonable guess, however, that London's private charities alone disbursed at least as much in the middle 1860s as did the Poor Law over the whole country [D.vii.1]. The Charity Organization Society (COS) was formed in 1869 to rationalize what one observer called 'vicarious and indolent charity' which made the giver feel good without necessarily improving the lot of the recipient. And improvement was the key. Private charity could be relied upon to ameliorate most social evils, so the argument ran, but it must be constructively used. Efforts were made to separate the 'deserving' from the 'undeserving' poor, such that charity would be improving and uplifting. Those who took the gifts of others might be taught to mend their ways so that they should not need to look for assistance thereafter. While the COS believed that constructive charity could promote harmony between the classes by inculcating not only gratitude but also the ethic of improvement, they came close to implying that those old enough to support themselves could either learn its lessons, or rot. It is symptomatic of the naive optimism which underpinned the harsh world of Victorian competition that some of its doughtiest champions believed that the 'dangerous classes' could be educated to responsible and respectable citizenship in such a fashion.

---

1. H. N. B. Morgan 'Social and political leadership in Preston, 1820–1870', University of Lancaster M. Litt. thesis, 1981.
2. G. F. A. Best, *Mid-Victorian Britain, 1851–75* (1971), pp. 235–6.
3. R. Bedarida, *A Social History of England, 1851–1975* (1979), p. 56.
4. W. L. Burn, *The Age of Equipoise* (1964), p. 100.
5. H. Taine, *Notes on England* (Freeport, NY edn, 1971), p. 97.
6. *Westminster Review*, xxxv (1869), pp. 437–57; *Fraser's Magazine*, lxxx (1869), pp. 679–703.

CHAPTER 32

The professionalization of government

I

It may seem the supreme irony in the development of modern Britain that the age of classic economic Liberalism exactly coincided with the growth of government. Between 1830 and 1870 the foundations of modern government were laid in the teeth of a gale. The rhetoric of politicians lauded competition, individual enterprise and local self-determination while decrying State aid, State interference and – horror of horrors – State control. When Gladstone introduced free trade budgets his belief was that commerce would flourish as government restrictions were withdrawn. He never abandoned hope of abolishing income tax as the supreme incentive to lean and hungry entrepreneurs who could rely on the cheapest possible government not to cramp their competitive style.

Yet government grew. By 1870 it had assumed almost modern shape. In 1780 government employees numbered only about 16,000; they were recruited overwhelmingly via patronage (Ch. 2) and their most important administrative function was the collection of customs and excise duties. By 1870, patronage was in retreat; the number of government employees had swollen to about 54,000 and their range of duties was far more diverse. Government was now, through the agency of its inspectors and commissioners, a regulator, co-ordinator and, within limits, director of business including Poor Law and prisons, factories and coalmines down to specifics such as alkali works, burial-grounds, anchors and cables, oyster fisheries and lime juice. From the 1830s, it was equipped with a formidable apparatus of fact finding called the Royal Commission of Enquiry. The Census Office not only reported every ten years on the number, nature and concentration of people in the kingdom; it also made recommendations for improvement and further government effort (352). The change was remarkably rapid. Melbourne could still observe, with only slight exaggeration, in 1836 that 'the duty of a Government is not to pass legislation but to rule' (329, 5). Much of the legislation passed in the 1830s and 1840s was indeed the work of backbenchers acting in co-ordination with external pressure groups (Chs 25 and 26). Yet the machinery needed to make this legislation effective would require the intervention of government not anticipated by even its most perceptive promoters.

In 1869 Horace Mann, Registrar of the General Register Office, reported to the Royal Statistical Society on the cost and organization of Britain's Civil Service. His report coincided with the early phase of Gladstone's first ministry when the Prime Minister was engaging in one of his periodically ferocious attacks on waste in public expenditure. It was remarked that the number of Civil Servants had increased two and a half times since 1832. Mann was, therefore, on the defensive but was able to show that though Civil Service estimates had increased by about 52 per cent since 1848 the range of services provided had been in response to public pressure:

> If the public is inclined now to give up the various advantages ... if we should be content with fewer public improvements, less police protection, fewer sanitary safeguards, a harsher poor law, fewer and dearer courts of justice, fewer postal facilities, and fewer and less useful schools for three-fourths of the community – then it will be easy enough to reduce the civil service estimates by abolishing several departments and attenuating others. But if the public really wants the things for which it, and not the departments, has been crying out, it can get them only by paying for them.[1]

To readers at the turn of the twentieth century this appraisal may seem chillingly modern. In fact the Civil Service of the period was remarkably cheap by modern standards. About 0.17 per cent of the population in 1871 were Civil Servants; the proportion was almost nine times as great in 1991. The proportion of government expenditure on civil matters, including posts and telegraphs, in 1869 was 20.5 per cent (compared with 35 per cent for debt charges and 36 per cent for defence). This caused alarm since it showed a rise from 12 per cent in the late 1830s [D.i.2]. In the financial year 1991/92 the British government spent about 77 per cent of its total expenditure on domestic supply services, excluding defence, 9.7 per cent on defence and only about 6 per cent on servicing the national debt.

Mann's recommendations for reducing Civil Service expenditure added fuel to a debate which had been raging for twenty years. He believed that threequarters of Civil Service departmental work was purely mechanical – filing, letter-copying, indexing and the like. Yet it was still performed by clerks recruited by patronage and drawing salaries of £90–£150 a year. Such work, he felt, would be more economically discharged by

> the class which furnishes teachers to our national and British schools. .... There is no doubt that the millions of money bestowed by the Government for the purpose of assisting popular education, have considerably increased the knowledge, and aptitude for official work, of the class which has received it; and there seems no good reason why the State should not reap some return for its expenditure, by obtaining cheaper labour which it has thus rendered effective. (Ch. 36)

Patronage had long been under attack. Utilitarians criticized the system's waste and inefficiency (Ch. 25). Ministers deplored the way in which nomination for office in the Customs and Stamp Office had passed from them to local MPs. As the work multiplied, so demands intensified for efficient reform. Some reforms were initiated departmentally as early as the 1830s. Under the influence of James and John Stuart Mill, the India Office was overhauled on broadly utilitarian lines. The emergence of central boards to administer Poor Law, education and tithe reform in the 1830s (Chs 25–27) enabled commissioners to establish new administrative practices based on efficient deployment of personnel. The Benthamites, Edwin Chadwick and Nassau Senior, persuaded the Poor Law commissioners to appoint their assistants on merit and after competitive interview. The Tithe Commission, which discharged an immense amount of complicated administrative work with much skill in the 1830s and 1840s, appointed relevantly qualified men, such as land agents and valuers, as assistant commissioners (199).

Thus, by the time Sir Charles Trevelyan and Sir Stafford Northcote produced their famous *Report on the Organization of the Civil Service* in 1853, which criticized the service for appointing 'the unambitious, and the indolent or incapable ... whose abilities do not warrant an expectation that they will succeed in the open professions' (332, *112*), their remarks were already inappropriate as to the new agencies of State intervention and less than fair to some of the established departments, such as the Foreign and India Offices (333). Trevelyan, a Civil Servant with long Treasury experience, and Northcote, then the waste-conscious Gladstone's private secretary, wished above all to increase efficiency and reduce costs. The taxpayers deserved value for money and, as the appearance of more than thirty local Financial Reform Associations between 1848 and 1850 had demonstrated, were quite capable of mounting efficient pressure for cuts in public expenditure.

The Northcote-Trevelyan Report recommended a unified Civil Service, recruited openly by competitive examination and within which promotion would be by merit not seniority. It split the Aberdeen coalition (Ch. 37) into its constituent elements. 'Efficient' Peelites, including Gladstone and Graham, supported it; 'old-guard' Whigs, such as Palmerston and Russell, feared that the destruction of patronage would diminish if not utterly extinguish aristocratic involvement with the government machine. In 1855 a Civil Service Commission was established to superintend 'junior situations in the Civil Establishment' but political patronage remained. Some developments in competitive examination, though within a closed and nominated list, took place in the 1860s, largely due to Gladstone's pressure. Not until 1870 did he finally attack the nomination system at its root and introduce open competitive examination. Even then, some departments remained exempt. Between 1840 and 1870 most of the ablest, and virtually all of the most innovative, Civil Servants – Chadwick, Simon, Tremenheere, Taylor – were recruited from established careers in law, medicine, engineering or one of the other professions and went usually to the new boards and commissions not to the established branches of the service.

II

Government intervention was a necessary response to the problems of an industrializing society. The extent of innovative intervention, especially in the 1830s and 1840s, is most striking. My own catalogue of the main developments [C.i–iv] is by no means exhaustive. The Prison Act of 1835 established an inspectorate reporting back to the Home Office on prison conditions and was the first major step on what has been called 'a long, slow struggle to achieve uniformity of treatment and standards by means of centralisation' (330, *170*). The prison system was remodelled in the 1840s and 1850s under the Surveyor-General of Prisons, Joshua Jebb. The government did not assume full responsibility for prisons until 1877.

In the 1840s the railways were brought somewhat limply under government regulation with the creation first of a railway department of the Board of Trade and then, by Gladstone's Railway Act of 1844, of a separate Railways Board with railway commissioners having powers of inspection and accident investigation. Government appeared to accept the view of a select committee in 1839 that 'the general interests of the community must sometimes be at variance with the interests of the railway proprietors ... and it becomes more important that they should be so far controlled as to secure the public as far as possible from any abuse which might arise from this irresponsible authority'.[2] In practice, little compulsion was exercised. George Stephenson's almost equally eminent son Robert calculated in 1856 that 186 separate pieces of legislation pertained to the London and North Western Railway alone yet the practical effect of railway legislation had been to allow 'competition to be obtained, wherever it has been sought'.[3] The 1844 Act obliged railway companies to run at least one passenger service a day with a fixed rate of 1d. a mile and kept an option for the State to purchase any new lines after an interval of twenty-one years, to minimize duplication of services and consequent waste. Few wanted the option to be exercised and the feeling against State-run railway services was immensely strong.

Greater powers were invoked in regulating the transport of emigrants. A series of Acts passed between 1803 and 1842 imposed minimum conditions of cleanliness and hygiene on passenger shipowners. More elaborate regulations followed between 1847 and 1855 to meet the crisis caused by massive emigration from Ireland (324). The most radical interventionist measure of all was introduced by Russell's government in 1849 in the hope of stimulating capital investment in Irish land. One of the many stark facts revealed by the Irish famine was that landowners were frequently undercapitalized, uncompetitive and unable to provide sufficient investment for secure tenancies (15, 314). Russell wished to bring English and Scottish cash to Irish agriculture and his Encumbered Estates Act established a Commission, acting as a court of law, to sell estates upon application from either landowners or any who held any legal claim, such as a mortgage however small, to an estate. The Act cut through the tangle of entails, settlements and other restrictions which still prevented free trade in English land and it alarmed many of Russell's Whig colleagues who feared that its apparent success would strengthen radical demands for an English counterpart. The commissioners used their unprecedented powers to the full. Three thousand estates were sold and about 25 per cent of Ireland's land eventually changed hands. Many of the purchasers were Roman Catholics but few brought much capital or technical expertise with them; many were speculators attracted by the rock-bottom prices which the sudden glut of purchaseable land produced. The injection of Anglo-Scottish aid failed to materialize. In 1869 Irish Poor Law inspectors reported that tenants farming land owned by the new purchasers were exceptionally bitter. Russell's collectivist legislation contributed modestly to the developing Irish rural crisis (14). Overall, Ireland's more substantial landowners remained enormously wealthy and, indeed, benefited from the famine. By

1870, half of the country's land was owned by 800 individuals, who could realise a gross income of £10m. a year (15, 87).

III

Such interference with the operation of the free market may appear at first sight difficult to reconcile with 'an age of *laissez-faire*'. Closer scrutiny suggests, however, that this general description of the period *c*. 1850–*c*. 1870 remains valid. No classical economist, from Adam Smith onwards, had denied that the State must fill gaps which private enterprise could not or would not fill (Ch. 5). The Industrial Revolution had presented unprecedented problems which necessitated the guiding hand of government to prevent chaos. Besides, none knew, or thought they knew, better than those second-generation *laissez-faire* philosophers the Benthamite Utilitarians, how to regulate most efficiently and least wastefully.

Bentham, in one of his few unequivocal dicta, had asserted that 'the greatest happiness of the greatest number is the foundation of morals and legislation'. Bentham's followers submitted institutions to this test of utility. Initially, they thought they could square the interventionist circle. If industrialism had thrown up issues undreamed of by Adam Smith, what better response than the creation of purpose-built institutions run by experts – themselves – as efficiently as possible and hence at the lowest cost to the taxpayer? Cheap, expert government satisfied utilitarian criteria by interfering only so far as to eliminate specific abuses and aberrations which, if unchecked, would hinder the free market from working its miracles of growth. State intervention, as Senior, Chadwick and J. S. Mill originally envisaged it, did not achieve good of itself but prevented greater evils. Mill's statement in *Principles of Political Economy* (1848) was straightforward enough: '. . . people understand their own business, and their own interests better, and care for them more, than the government does or can be expected to do. . . . *Laissez-faire*, in short, should be the general practice: every departure from it, unless required by some great good, is a certain evil'.

The peculiarly Benthamite solutions to administrative problems – central boards, inspectors, expert salaried officials and the like – were applied again and again in the 1830s and 1840s to achieve 'great good'. Surviving the test of practicability, they were also adopted by administrators who had no connection with Bentham. If humanitarians, philanthropists and Tory paternalists were first to bring certain abuses to light it is beyond reasonable dispute that the Benthamites canalized moral and social outrage about poverty, public health and factory exploitation to fit their own criteria. The real dilemma revealed itself later when inspectors appreciated the intractability of the problems they faced. Administration, to be effective, must be dynamic not static. Dynamism implied greater degrees of State involvement: a permanent, self-contained bureaucracy for each field of activity; more inspectors, more reports, more legislation to correct, redefine and sharpen prentice efforts, more expense (329).

Such developments took place at different speeds in different fields of activity between 1830 and 1950. In our period they are most clearly traceable in public health and medicine. The Public Health Act of 1848 [C.ii] was an uneasy compromise between those – mostly medical men and administrative experts – who favoured an element of compulsion and those who believed that disease was a local responsibility. Chadwick's success in obtaining a General Board of Health with some compulsory powers, though not so many as he would have liked, was considerable. But between 1849 and 1854 it produced severe reaction from those who disliked boards and commissions semi-independent of Parliament and who particularly resented Chadwick's dictatorial ways. *The Times* in 1854 spoke of Chadwick and Dr Southwood Smith, the Board's Medical Officer, as 'firmly persuaded of their own infallibility, intolerant of all opposition, utterly careless of the feelings and wishes of the local bodies with whom they are brought into contact . . . these gentlemen have contrived to overwhelm a good object with obloquy and hatred and to make the cholera itself scarcely a less dreaded visitation than their own' (94, *467*).

Chadwick's dismissal in 1854 and the winding up of the Board of Health in 1858 [C.ii] have been presented as a great triumph for the forces of localism, though the truth is more complex. Chadwick by this time openly admitted that his philosophy had centralizing, collectivizing tendencies, though he continued to urge that the powers he sought were essential to prevent waste through frequent illness and premature death. J. S. Mill would soon go further. The real problem for the political economist in the early 1870s, he asserted, was 'how to unite the greatest individual liberty of action, with a common ownership in the raw materials of the globe'.

The mantle of collectivism in public health activity was taken up by Sir John Simon, Medical Officer of the newly established medical department of the Privy Council. He had no Benthamite or Chadwickian associations but his pragmatic assessment of the dimensions of the problem led him to remarkably similar conclusions. Although ever more local authorities were calling upon central government assistance in the implementation of their drainage and other health schemes (Ch. 33), Simon was convinced that not enough was being done. His Report in 1865 might almost have been written by Chadwick: 'the time has arrived when it ought not to be discretional in a place whether that place shall be kept filthy or not. . . . The language of the law besides making it a *power*, should name it also as a *duty* to proceed for the removal of nuisances to which attention is drawn.' (95) The Sanitary Act of 1866 [C.ii] was a landmark. As the *Lancet* observed, 'it virtually enables the Privy Council to supersede the local authorities'. The administrative structure constructed in 1858, however, was not sufficiently coherent to permit the principles of the Act to be put into widespread practice. It took a Royal Commission on Public Health, sitting between 1868 and 1871, to prepare the ground for the effective Gladstone Local Government and Public Health Acts of 1871–72.

In one overridingly important area of public life, therefore, the State was poised to take the decisive hand in 1870. The *Lancet* excitedly asserted in 1868: 'it is only lately that facts have been sufficiently ascertained to enable us to conceive how much legislation may one day do for the health of the people. Every year makes a difference in the boldness of the suggestions for the protection of the public from the causes of disease.'[4] Three Contagious Diseases Acts were also passed, in 1864, 1866 and 1869, to curtail venereal disease by instituting compulsory medical examinations for known prostitutes, though not their consorts (308). It is perfectly possible to see this as a period of substantial State intervention, therefore, and almost impossible not to acknowledge it as the one in which the decisive steps were taken which would result in the modern system of governmental administration. Even the 1850s and 1860s, supposedly a time of retrenchment after the rash of boards, commissions and experts in the previous two decades, witnessed both consolidation and expansion of provision.

But matters must stay in perspective. Chadwick, Simon and the rest signposted a route which none in the next generation could miss, but the prevailing attitude among educated people in 1870 remained one of profoundest scepticism about the role of the State. If individuals knew their own affairs best, so local communities must be presumed to cater more knowledgeably for local needs than could central government. Even worse than central government was the centralized commission: unelected yet assertive, remote yet cocksure. We may be sure that the view of the lawyer J. Toulmin Smith that commissions 'depress individual thought and effort [and] . . . impose upon it under specious pretences of authority' (332, *116*) evoked a more sympathetic response than the certainties of Chadwick. The fate of his Board of Health is testimony to the fact. Still, in 1870 State intervention was accepted grudgingly and only after the accumulation of masses of evidence that continued inactivity did more damage to the free market than did action. Nearly all 'interventionist' legislation conferred powers on local authorities which they could use or not as their councillors thought fit. Since evidence was most easily accumulated in medical and public health matters, and since even the comfortable middle classes were at the mercy of cholera epidemics it is not surprising that the biggest steps were taken here. The prevailing ethos remained one of rugged individualism. Only a few saw in 1870 that, once admitted at all, State intervention contained an internal dynamic which would not be constrained. In the longer term, a State bureaucracy was almost as important a legacy of industrial progress as was economic growth.

---

1. *Jnl. Royal Statistical Soc.*, xxxii (1869), pp. 38–60.
2. W. L. Burn, *The Age of Equipoise* (1964), p. 163.
3. R. Stephenson, *Presidential Address to the Institution of Civil Engineers* (1856), p. 16.
4. *Lancet*, 1 August 1868.

CHAPTER 33

Urban Britain in the age of improvement

I

In the year of the Great Exhibition the census recorded that, for the first time, one-half of Britain's population lived in towns. During the next twenty years or so, constructive adjustments were made to living in an urban society. These years of relative prosperity encouraged the luxuries of urban identification and civic pride. Not that social problems were ever far from the minds of town councillors elected under the new system of local government initiated by the Municipal Corporations Act (C.ii], but the town was seen increasingly as the emblem of political as well as commercial success. As early as 1843 the Congregationalist minister Robert Vaughan enthused that 'our metropolis has become such as the world has not seen' (though he acknowledged London's severe problems) while, 'Our leading towns in the provinces equal the capitals of ordinary kingdoms'. (294, *26*).

Civic pride had a utilitarian base. In the town, people worked to create wealth the benefits of which were diffused, if unequally, through society. Some middle-class radicals used the town as a weapon against the traditional enemy. From Manchester in 1837 Richard Cobden thundered that 'The battle of our day is still against the aristocracy', and urged fellow citizens to adopt the Municipal Corporations Act to 'give unity force and efficiency to the intelligent and wealthy community of Manchester and qualify it by organization, as it is already entitled by numbers to be the leader in the battle against monopoly and privilege'. Edward Baines of Leeds was convinced that the bourgeoisie of that town were moved by 'dislike and suspicion of the rural-based anti-urban aristocracy' (89, *21–2*). John Bright, who represented Manchester in Parliament from 1847 to his famous defeat ten years later and then Birmingham from 1857 to his death in 1889, left his constituents in no doubt that the major sources of their woes, even after 1846, was a 'proud & idle & pauper proprietary. . . . We are the slaves of a privileged class'. (115, *75, 79*)

Yet it would be quite wrong to characterize urban Britain as anti-aristocratic. Large landowners, whose success in remaining at the centre of affairs owes much to their entrepreneurial talents, were important urban developers. The history of early industrial Liverpool cannot be written without extensive reference to the Derby and Sefton families. The same obtains, among many others, for the Sutherlands in Stoke-on-Trent, the Dudleys in West Bromwich, the Butes in Cardiff and the Fitzwilliams in Sheffield. When the contributions of the Grosvenors, Portlands and Russells to the rebuilding of London is considered (as it easily may be since much of their legacy still stands to the immense profit of their successors), the importance of land to almost the entire range of urban development can be clearly seen (302). By no means all landed families took a direct role in urban government, but they took care to ensure that their benefactions of parks, public monuments, art galleries and other civic buildings should be known and appreciated. Aristocratic largesse could be met with reactions uncomfortably close to old-style deference. The entire Potteries mourned the death of the second duke of Sutherland in 1861; Cardiff enjoyed a week's holiday in 1866 to celebrate the coming-of-age of the third marquis of Bute. Such sentimental spectacles were too much for rationalists to bear. Cobden was probably too precise in 1856 when he regretted that 'people in Lancashire are growing conservative and aristocratic with their prosperous trade' (41, *155*). The truth was that most people are conservative most of the time when the wolf is not at the door, and the aristocracy had so much practice in lordly benefaction that its translation to an urban setting presented few problems. A besetting Anglo-Saxon weakness for titles and trappings did the rest.

Those who assumed that efficient political organization in the towns would drive the final nail into the aristocratic coffin were sadly misguided. Political vitality there was a-plenty in mid-Victorian urban Britain but the contests were usually between the middle classes. Almost no concerted anti-aristocratic pressure was to be found after 1846 and the working-class contribution to municipal government, though not derisory, was rarely decisive. The campaign to establish municipal corporations under the legislation of 1835 was a struggle to replace closed, self-elected and frequently corrupt local administrations by openly elected bodies accountable to the ratepayers for their actions. Because the Test and Corporation Acts (at least in theory) prohibited dissenters from holding municipal office before 1828 [G.i] the old authorities tended to be Tory and Anglican while those clamouring for incorporation were primarily Liberal and dissenting. In this battle some working men, already linked to the Tory hierarchy by a common stance against the new Poor Law (Ch. 25), as in Manchester and Sheffield, took the establishment side. They feared an extension of influence by what the Manchester radical Edward Nightingale called 'the tyranny of the bloated rich' (89, *120*).

In practice, when incorporation was won, one group of 'bloated rich' generally replaced another. On balance, perhaps, a few more new manufacturers appeared while some established merchants faded from the scene, but there was little significant change in the social status of the urban governors. The Liberals, strongly supported by the dissenters, were nearly always the victors. In some instances, as in Birmingham in 1838, gerrymandering of ward boundaries ensured that no Tories at all were returned to the first new councils (131). Liberal predominance was maintained in most large cities until the end of our period. In Leeds, though the Tories managed parity once (in 1840–41), in ten of the twenty years from 1851 to 1870 they had fewer than ten councillors from a total complement of sixty-four (265). Leicester and Nottingham were solidly Liberal. Only in Liverpool, where Protestant ratepayers were persuaded to brand the Liberals as pro-Catholic and hence pro-Irish, were the Tories in solid control from the early 1840s, a supremacy also reflected in the city's parliamentary representation. In Manchester, by complete contrast, the Tories largely opted out and the Liberals were left to squabble among themselves. Fewer than one-third of Manchester's municipal elections were contested between 1838 and 1867, a very small proportion. Almost half the MPs at Westminster between the first and second Reform Acts were returned unopposed (B.vii.2]; only about two-fifths of Leeds or Liverpool councillors had similar fortune. Municipal elections were keen affairs.

Defeated Tories liked to assert that the new councils were less well heeled than the old corporations. There is little warrant for this in the early years, though rather fewer of the upper bourgeoisie were appearing by the early 1850s. In Leeds the numbers of craftsmen and retailers increased substantially after about 1845, while the proportion of professional men, merchants and manufacturers declined from about 80 per cent of the total to barely more than 50 per cent. A broadly similar pattern obtained in Birmingham, though there the numbers of professional men increased slowly. Mayors were disproportionately first generation successful businessmen, often dissenters and not infrequently immigrants from other parts of country. The highest municipal office was evidently the ultimate recognition of the worth of the 'new man'.

In some cases, no doubt, as the novelty wore off, established wealthy businessmen found local politics an unprofitable chore. But, as Professor Fraser's analysis of Leeds indicates, the number of merchants and manufacturers offering themselves as candidates did not significantly change between 1840 and 1870. However, more from the lower middle classes were actually being elected. As councils grew and their functions expanded, the burden on the ratepayers increased and the electors' concern with economy grew. If they did not trust the richest citizens, for whom two or three pennies on the rates might be neither here nor there, they might have greater identity with, say, small shopkeepers for whom the lessons of careful husbandry would be carried directly into the council chamber. This explanation will not fit all cases. Birmingham, for example, elected fewer small businessmen in the 1860s as developments in metal technology gradually squeezed the smaller man (Ch. 13), but the concern with economy remained a powerful factor in Birmingham as elsewhere into the 1870s.

II

The building of Leeds Town Hall at a cost of £122,000 in 1858 is the most famous example of municipal conspicuous consumption, not least because the final cost – complete with dome-capped towers and stone lions – exceeded the original estimate, which the 'economists' on the town council had insisted the young architect Cuthbert Brodrick strictly adhere to, by almost 300 per cent. It was far more than a civic building. Its supporters were determined not only that Leeds should show London what proper architecture was but that the scheme should establish Leeds's superiority over pretentious neighbouring Bradford, whose St George's Hall built for concerts and recreation by private subscription a few years earlier, had set new standards. Leeds, as its inhabitants always insisted, was the rightful capital of the West Riding. Its population was 20,000 greater than that of Sheffield, which was in any case almost in Derbyshire. Dr J. D. Heaton, a leading advocate of the Leeds project, saw it as evidence that 'in the ardour of their mercantile pursuits, the inhabitants of Leeds have not omitted to cultivate the perception of the beautiful and a taste for the fine arts'. It would be 'a lasting monument of their public spirit, and generous pride in the possession of their municipal privileges' (296, *165*). The official opening by Queen Victoria was a propaganda triumph.

Architects, civil engineers and builders were kept in gainful employment by town councillors in the 1850s and 1860s. A rash of town-hall construction developed. The huge edifices dominating central Rochdale and Bolton were finally completed in 1871 and 1873 respectively. Smaller structures, grand enough in the context of the town, were more typical and often completed earlier. One such was in Blackburn, whose town hall, complete with Doric porches and Corinthian columns was completed in 1856 at a cost of £30,000, a tidy enough sum for a town of some 55,000 inhabitants.

Libraries combined civic pride with means of rational recreation. The Manchester Mechanics' Institution believed that the recent building of public libraries in both Salford and Manchester would 'expand that public domain for mental culture which is the joint heritage and ought to be the common enjoyment of rich and poor' (296, *197*). Councils could build public libraries under William Ewart's Free Libraries Act of 1850 if ratepayers, on whom the cost would fall via a halfpenny rate, approved. Those in Manchester gave the necessary authority by a massive majority almost immediately, thus following the example of Salford which had acted under a more restrictive Act passed in 1845. Norwich was another city early in the field, but the most famous free library was that opened in 1866 as the Birmingham Free Reference Library. At the opening ceremony the Baptist minister George Dawson, who has been called 'the creator of the municipal doctrine' declaimed that 'a town is a solemn organism through which shall flow, and in which shall be shaped, all the highest, loftiest and truest ends of man's moral nature'.

III

Though Charles Kingsley thought Dawson the ablest speaker in Britain, his high-flown sentiments would have meant little to that majority for whom life was a struggle for very survival and for whom the 'flow of loftiest ends' was a matter of much less immediate moment than the flow, or more often non-flow, of less elevating materials through the city streets. Town growth continued apace between 1850 and 1870. Few towns increased their populations by less than 35 per cent in this period and some, such as Salford, Sheffield and Southampton, grew faster than during the previous twenty years [E.iii]. Overcrowding was exacerbated by the demolition of much city-centre accommodation to make way for warehouses, banks, office accommodation, railway lines and stations. Almost invariably, the homes of the poor were the ones to be thus cleared. Upwards of 20,000 people were displaced from central Glasgow in the mid-Victorian period through railway construction alone; street clearance forcibly removed about 100,000 Londoners between 1830 and 1880 (300, 303). Housing standards improved little before the 1870s. Pressure on urban space saw to it that rents rose proportionately higher than real wages between 1850 and 1870 while severe overcrowding was the norm. In

1861, 26 per cent of Scotland's population lived in one-room accommodation and a further 38 per cent in two-roomed (276, ii, *206*).

Clearances did not destroy slums. They merely moved them a mile or two away. As early as 1841 William Farr was commenting: 'You take down the dwellings of the poor, build houses in their places for which only the middle classes can afford to pay the rent, and thus by diminishing the amount of cheap house accommodation, increase the rents and aggravate the evil you attempt to cure'. The Bethnal Green Medical Officer of Health noted in 1864 that the direct result of the building of Liverpool Street station had been the 'large influx of persons' into his area which 'has aggravated the greatest evil with which we have to contend, and that is overcrowding. . . . Houses even in bad condition are sure to find occupants'. (303, *180, 163*) The working classes still needed to live near their places of work; they could not afford the mobility which the railways so spectacularly brought to their betters, especially between 1850 and 1870 [D.iv.2]. Yet the space available for them near city centres dwindled by the year. Civic identity and the quality of life, especially of the casual labourers (Chs 14 and 17), were frequently in total, if unacknowledged, conflict.

Public health was a local responsibility and it was discharged in such divergent ways that generalization is impossible. The number of different, and differently elected and appointed, organizations with a relevant interest is bewildering. Town councils, elected under the Municipal Corporations Act, might be the prime movers. The ramshackle work of the old local improvement commissions continued to be called upon eagerly in several places and very slowly in others. Select vestries, street commissioners, highway surveyors, water commissioners, and commissioners of sewers all vied for attention. Water and gas companies might remain in private hands or might be taken over by the municipal authority. They might, like the Birmingham Water Works Company, be generally efficient capitalist enterprises or they might be quite incapable of responding to the challenge of expansion, leaving folk without access to water, even in street standpipes, for more than a couple of hours a day. Though there was little limit after 1850 to what authorities *might* do in matters of public health, councillors frequently judged that attractive though expensive schemes would be rejected by the rate-payers. Birmingham's water remained privately owned until 1869 and was only taken over after a long struggle by Thomas Avery, the scales manufacturer, who had been converted from a position of minimal corporate provision of public services to the essentially Simonite view (Ch. 32) that the power of life or death, which the availability of running water so often meant in the poorer areas, should not remain in commercial hands (131). In Lancashire, few authorities rushed to purchase waterworks. Though the pace of public ownership quickened in the 1860s, Blackburn, Bury and Warrington were still privately served in 1870.

The creation of local boards of health under the 1848 Act [C.ii] might be an immense boon to a town or it might merely generate another tier of administration jostling with others – perhaps much older and jealous of their authority – for work. In some places members of local health boards were the same people who administered the local Poor Law, were sewerage commissioners and would run the place whatever new schemes were dreamed up in Westminster. Elsewhere, they were new brooms determined to sweep away the old and the incompetent. Conflict over powers frequently ensued. In most cases, however, there was little immediate rush to take advantage of the new public health provisions. By 1854 182 local boards of health were in operation but only 13 had completed work on sewerage and water schemes (331). By the end of the 1850s only one-sixth of Lancashire's 2½m. people were covered by Board of Health legislation, most of them living in the south of the county within the influence of Liverpool and Manchester.

Even incorporation under the 1835 Act might take time. Merthyr Tydfil was governed by the parish vestry and the Poor Law Guardians until 1850. Middlesbrough, the boom iron town, was incorporated almost at its earliest opportunity, in 1853. Its western counterpart, Barrow-in-Furness, was unincorporated until 1867, with most of its early administration being carried on by a closed vestry in Dalton and by Poor Law Guardians in Ulverston. Burnley, an established Lancashire cotton community, did not take advantage of the Act until 1861 at which time another, nearby Bury (with a population of nearly 90,000), still remained unincorporated.

Some towns did most of their public health work under private, specific Acts of Parliament. It was expensive to obtain private Acts but they did cut clean through complexities and duplications of function. Manchester's Police Regulation Act of 1844 gave the council powers to deal with a wide range of public health matters and powers were extended by ten further Acts before 1858. Manchester men saw this route not only as efficient but also as establishing their indefeasible right to local self-government. In Leeds a battle between largely Liberal 'improvers' and mainly Tory 'economists' held back early improvement schemes until the mid-1840s. But once the improvers were firmly in control rapid headway was made, culminating in a Sewerage Act in 1848 and the transfer of waterworks to full public ownership in 1852. Leicester also had bitter political battles which prevented the adoption of an improvement Act in a town singled out by Chadwick in 1842 for its peculiarly unhealthy environment. Here the battle was not so much between improvers and economists as between those who wished to spend ratepayers' money on prestige projects and those who preferred to lay the proper foundations below ground. Nevertheless, to Leicester goes the honour of appointing the first part-time medical officers of health (MOHs) under a Nuisance Removal Act of 1846, though much of the subsequent improvements came by adopting the procedures of the Public Health Act.

The most celebrated local legislation is the Liverpool Sanitary Act of 1846 which made the council its own health authority. Augmented by various other pieces of legislation, it gave one of Britain's unhealthiest cities the widest sanitary powers. Dr W. H. Duncan, the MOH appointed under the Act, proved invaluable in pinpointing the need for particular initiatives in his annual reports. Unusually, since housing legislation was almost absent from the improvement agenda, the Liverpool Act included dwellings regulations to cover the infamous cellars in which more than one-fifth of the city's population lived. Liverpool's sanitary powers, it will be remembered, were exercised by a Tory authority and any facile attempt to categorize Tories as economists and Liberals as improvers should be resisted. The terms themselves are frequently misleading, as is indicated by the disputes which arose over whether Liverpool should build an extensive system of reservoirs at Rivington Pike near Chorley to meet its growing need for water. Those who opposed the scheme, the anti-Pikists, included both Tories and radical Liberals while both Liberals and Tories were found in the Pikist camp. The anti-Pikists were at pains to point out also that their objections were not solely to the project's cost, but on priorities. They believed that an augmentation of water was possible locally, leaving funds available for other urgent improvements. The Pikists won, yet Liverpool's water supplies would need further development in the 1860s. The anti-Pikists can be more justly charged in hindsight with inaccurate prediction than with parsimony.

London presented a unique challenge, not only by virtue of its size but from its administrative complexity. More than 300 separate bodies claimed some authority over the health of the capital and, encouraged by the ancient Corporation of the City of London (only a tiny fraction of the capital's surface area by the 1840s), they squabbled over demarcation while death-rates soared. Significant rationalizations were made. During the cholera epidemic of 1847 a Metropolitan Commission of Sewers was established and in the following year John Simon was appointed MOH. Chadwick managed to get an Interment Act in 1850 whose purpose was to reduce health hazards from rotting corpses in overcrowded graveyards, but its passage fearfully antagonized the London parish vestries. Tripartite contests took place between the mutually suspicious Chadwickian Board of Health, the Metropolitan Commission and the vestries. They turned on the old shibboleths of local self-determination and central interference. Chadwick failed to get an integrated water scheme. One private company killed about 6,000 inhabitants by supplying them with unfiltered cholera-infected water (94). In 1870 the capital still lacked a constant supply of running water.

The Metropolis Management Act of 1855, which established a Board of Works, represented the final triumph of the vestries over Chadwick. House drainage, which Chadwick had believed essential for proper improvement, was excluded from the general drainage scheme, and engineers of whom Chadwick disapproved, such as Sir Joseph Bazalgette, were entrusted with the work of constructing two great drainage systems north and south of the Thames. They lasted admirably. From the late 1850s the new Board also embarked on extensive street improvements (344). Vestries could regulate domestic overcrowding by the Nuisance Removal Act of 1855, the Sanitary Act of 1866 [C.ii] and the pioneer but generally ineffective Torrens Housing Act of 1868. Some improvements were made but, as both MOHs and vestries well knew, too vigorous a pursuit of clearance schemes – the only way of dealing with overcrowding – only brought yet more serious problems elsewhere since neither local authorities nor government were within two generations of using ratepayers' money to build council houses to approved specifications. Merely efficient operation of existing legislation could not solve the fundamental problem. London's annual death-rate actually increased from 21 per 1,000 in 1850 to 24.1 in 1870.

By the 1860s evidence was accumulating that more and more local authorities were preferring to use the permissive powers of national statutes, expecially that of 1858[C.ii], rather than ploughing their lonely furrows. Suspicion of central boards and of experts lessened somewhat after the regime of Chadwick and a degree of uniformity was beginning to appear. At last, it seemed, some of the lessons which had seemed so obvious to the 'experts' in the 1840s were getting home. Engineers reporting back to the Board of Health in 1849–50 were bemused by the apparent inability of councillors to see the evident connection between dirt and disease, overcrowding and waste. Robert Rawlinson, an advocate of pipe drainage and an engineer whom Chadwick much admired, visited Whitehaven in 1849, when the death-rate during the high mortality of 1846–48 had risen to 49 per 1,000, more than twice the national average. He reported sadly that 'such of the opposing gentlemen as I could prevail upon to accompany me in my personal inspection, declared in the strongest terms that they had no idea of the state of things existing around them. But this I have found in every town I have visited; few beside the medical gentlemen know anything of the utter wretchedness and misery produced by want of proper sanitary regulations.[1] His back-of-envelope calculations of the loss of earnings caused by sickness and premature death indicated that the resulting sum of £22,301. 15s. 'is more than will be required to sewer the town, drain every house, and provide a water closet in each'.

W. A. Guy, another sanitary engineer, had stated bluntly in 1847 that 'the utter failure of the system of local self-government for sanitary purposes is notorious' (332, 79), but local self-government remained dominant until the 1870s, coming only slowly to grips with the adoption of national patterns of provision. Manchester did not think it necessary to appoint an MOH until 1867. Birmingham's councillors underestimated the cost of road and drainage improvements in the 1850s and, like many other towns, spawned an economist group concerned above all things to keep the rates down – the fatal false economy which Rawlinson and Guy, Chadwick and Simon so deplored. Birmingham, Sheffield and Newcastle would not engage MOHs. until compelled to do so by Gladstone's Public Health Act of 1872. Their defenders would say that their alternative provisions were adequate, but the results of a generation of local self-determination in sanitary provision were profoundly unimpressive. The facts supported the centralizers. While *laissez-faire* and localism alike sustained the 'voluntarists' in their campaigns against central direction, the evidence pointed obstinately against them. The mid-Victorians were unprecedentedly generous supporters of a bewildering variety of charities. They were also eager in their patronage of mutual-aid initiatives. However, this generation of mighty alms giving made little impact on the most basic statistic of all. Death-rates nationally were virtually the same in the late 1860s as in the early 1840s [E.v]; infant mortality also remained obstinately unchanged with three children in twenty born alive failing to reach their first birthdays. Only in the next generation of 'collectivism' and 'compulsion' was the decisive breakthrough made. Despite their town halls, municipal libraries, parks and fine railway stations, Victorian cities in 1870 remained for most of their inhabitants desperately unhealthy places in which to live.

---

1. R. Rawlinson, *Report to the General Board of Health: Whitehaven* (1849), p. 4.

CHAPTER 34

Religion and society

I

Rarely has a secular State been so ostentatiously dutiful in its religious observances as was early and mid-Victorian Britain. Church attendance was taken seriously in bourgeois and respectable circles. Church building was the natural accompaniment of urban and suburban expansion. The Church of England built nearly 1,750 new churches between 1840 and 1876, virtually all paid for by private donation (368). Chapel building by the nonconformist sects was similarly rapid with increasingly ornate architectural styles denoting not only the declining fashion for simple services in spartan assembly halls but the increasing prosperity of those middle-class dissenters who footed the bill. To the horror of old-style Protestants the Roman Catholic Church was responding to the challenges and opportunities afforded by mass emigration from Ireland in the late 1840s. The *Protestant Magazine* reported that the number of Catholic places of worship had increased by 35 per cent and the number of priests by an appalling 48 per cent in the single decade 1846–56 (366, *253*). Moreover, the priests seemed to exert a greater influence in their communities than Protestant clerics did in theirs.

Church building was only the outward and visible sign of religiosity. Respectable Victorians kept Sunday in an aggressively holy way. Places of amusement which charged for admission could not open on the Sabbath; a motion in 1856 to open the British Museum on Sundays was defeated in the Commons by a proportion of eight to one. The Sunday post was reduced in 1850 and a move to close London's public houses and shops might have succeeded in 1855 had not riots against it broken out in Hyde Park. Private prosecutions under the Sunday Observance Act (1677) were frequent and punitive. Visitors from Europe made either bemused or contemptuous references to the sepulchral gloom of the English Sunday. What applied to England applied *a fortiori* to Scotland and Wales where Calvinist intolerance lived on.

Religious history in Scotland in this period, however, was dominated by the split within the Church of Scotland which took place in 1843. Evangelicals who wanted church ministers to be selected by the congregation, rather than by landowners, took about 40 per cent of the membership away into a new 'Free Church of Scotland'. Support for the new church was strong among the urban middle classes. It also won a huge following among erstwhile peasants in the Highlands, where landlords were still blamed for the trauma of the clearances. The church schism had little impact on levels of church attendance which seem to have been considerably higher overall in Scotland than in England during the mid-Victorian period.

Secularists enjoyed useful propaganda against the blasphemy laws when they secured the release of an insane Cornishman, Thomas Pooley, who had been imprisoned for twenty-one months in 1857 for scrawling blasphemous slogans on the local rector's gate. The laws themselves, however, remained impregnable. Those who would not swear religious oaths were penalized. The secularist George Jacob Holyoake was not allowed to sit on a jury because he would affirm rather than swear a Christian oath. Atheists could not sit in Parliament until the 1880s unless they swore the oath. Jews were grudgingly admitted after 1858 when Lionel de Rothschild, returned in three successive elections after 1847 but debarred from taking his seat, was finally permitted to swear on the Old Testament only.

The 1857 Divorce Act, which permitted a man to divorce his wife for adultery but a woman to divorce her husband only for desertion or if his adultery were incestuous or sexually perverted, provoked intense theological dispute in Parliament. High-Churchmen, including Gladstone, argued that it weakened the bond between Church and State since law now diverged from Scripture. Though his position was awkward since almost half the English bishops supported reform, the Act was not passed until an amendment was carried allowing any clergyman to refuse a divorcee remarriage in his church. The anguish accompanying this social reform is indicative of the relationship between religion and government. Most educated Englishmen could not conceive a government pursuing moral policies which did not derive from Christian dogma. Government, as the Anglican headmaster of Merchant Taylors' School sharply reminded the rationalist philosopher John Stuart Mill in 1860, was necessarily Christian and its primary purpose was to promote 'so far as it can, the welfare of its subjects in accordance with Christian principles' (367, *219*).

Yet in 1851 the unique religious census of England and Wales revealed that between one-half and three-fifths of the population had not attended any church on the day the census was taken [G.vii]. This hammer blow to the complacent belief that the nation was naturally religious was followed within a few years by deep debate about the extent to which scientific discovery undermined orthodox faith. Between the various religious sects, furthermore, disagreement and antagonism was far more in evidence than Christian co-operation. Nonconformists resented Anglican domination of education (Ch. 36). The disestablishment campaign gained many adherents in the 1840s and 1850s.

II

The religious census enabled reasonably reliable estimates to be made of the strength of the various sects, both nationally and regionally. From these, despite its recent reforms (Ch. 27), Anglicanism drew little comfort. The Church of England was shaken to discover that, even on the most optimistic reading of figures liable to varying interpretations to account for multiple attendances [G.vii], it held the allegiance of only about half the practising believers of England and Wales. That allegiance, furthermore, was concentrated in the compact, rural parishes of southern and eastern England. Only in the rural South-east did it outnumber dissent by anything approaching two to one; in Yorkshire dissent had almost exactly the same advantage over the Church. In Wales, where general levels of attendance were higher than anywhere, the Anglican Church claimed less than one attendance in five. Nationally, two-thirds of the available seatings in Anglican churches were unoccupied on census Sunday.

Dissent was primarily urban in concentration, though rural counties such as Cornwall and Lincolnshire, had seen some notable conquests by the Primitive Methodists. Methodists were much the most numerous of the dissenting communities, though now fragmented (Ch. 6). Their membership, at over half a million in 1851, was considerably greater than the Congregationalists and Baptists combined [G.ii]. Wesleyan Methodists refused to consider themselves dissenters at all, arguing that the Established Church had rejected them, not *vice versa*, and that their founder wished them to remain Anglicans. The Wesleyans outdid the Established Church in their commitment to central authority. Conference expelled ministers in 1849 who refused to support control from the centre and many ordinary members followed the ejected. The Methodists lost about 100,000 members in five years and it was noticeable that those who remained Wesleyans tended to be middle class.

Primitive Methodism was traditionally strong in mining areas, such as Durham, and in the rural areas among village craftsmen such as shoemakers and blacksmiths who preserved a degree of independence from the traditional controls exerted by squire and parson. Anglican clergy in Norfolk and Lincolnshire considered the Primitives a peculiar nuisance, not only for their resistance to parochial ministrations but for their political radicalism.

Among the older dissenting sects only the New Connexion of General Baptists (less than 10 per cent of Baptist membership) made significant headway among the lower orders, mostly in the East Midlands, East Anglia and South Wales. The Congregationalists, administratively strengthened by a Union of independent churches after 1832, maintained their appeal overwhelmingly to shopkeepers, craftsmen and the lower middle classes, though, like the Baptists' great evangelical preacher Charles Haddon Spurgeon, they used hellfire evangelists whose task it was to redeem the fallen and awaken in them a sense of sin. Unitarians and Quakers, numerically insignificant by the 1850s, preserved both an intellectual and a social exclusivity.

The 1851 census provided much ammunition for Anglican-nonconformist bickering about relative strengths, but much the most important revelation was that, in the inimitably ponderous prose of its administrative principal, Horace Mann, 'a sadly formidable portion of the English people are habitual neglecters of the public ordinances of religion'. This was most apparent in the largest cities, especially London. Religious observance varied in extraordinarily close inverse proportion to community size [G.vii]. In part this reflects the inability of both Anglicans and nonconformists to build churches quickly enough to match the extraordinary speed of urban expansion in the early nineteenth century [E.iii], but the true reasons lie deeper. In the words of one of dissent's most perceptive advocates, the Congregationalist Edward Miall, 'here, in Great Britain, we carry our class distinctions into the house of God. . . . The poor man is made to feel that he is a poor man, the rich is reminded that he is rich, in the great majority of our churches and chapels'. The consequence, he argued, followed inexorably: 'The operatives of these realms, taken as a body, and the still more numerous class whose employment is less regular, and whose temporal prospects are still more discouraging and precarious, must be described as living beyond even occasional contact with the institutions of Christian faith and worship.'[1]

In the central areas of the biggest cities it is doubtful if 10 per cent attended church with any regularity. Ministers frequently gave up the unequal struggle of trying to catch the teeming, impermanent, migrant population attracted by prospects of casual work. The civilizing influences of organized religion did not touch the 'dangerous classes' (Ch. 31). In the rural areas the oppressively hierarchical nature of religious observance could alienate folk with any independence of spirit. The young Joseph Arch, leader in the 1870s of the first National Agricultural Labourers' Union, seethed in a sleepy south Warwickshire parish as his parents submissively waited for their betters to take communion before they approached the altar rail. The replication of a temporal social structure in church, reinforced by reserved pews for the gentry and unobtrusive seats for working families at the back, convinced many of the latter that church was not for them, despite the efforts of a new, enthusiastic generation of Anglican parsons. Working-class unease manifested itself usually in absence from church rather than active anticlericalism, but it told its own story.

The Church's efforts to respond were spasmodic and unco-ordinated. The Christian Socialists, active in the later 1840s and early 1850s, alarmed orthodoxy by their determination to make the Church relevant to the poor. But they also hob-nobbed with Chartists and they attacked *laissez-faire*. Their intellectual leader, F. D. Maurice, stated that their objective was to 'convert a nation of competing shopkeepers into a family of loving Christians'.[2] Their best-known member, the Hampshire vicar and author of *The Water Babies*, Charles Kingsley, believed that respectable people antagonized the poor by using 'the Bible as if it were a mere special constable's handbook – an opium-dose for keeping working beasts of burden patient while they were being overloaded' (368, ii, 353). A handful of co-operative workshops were founded with Christian Socialist help in the 1850s and enjoyed modest success for a time. In 1853 Maurice established a non-sectarian Working Men's College in London.

Christian Socialism withered from a surfeit of raw idealism and a dearth of practicality, but some of its objectives were more widely espoused. It was relatively easy for Anglicans to support factory legislation in the 1830s (Ch. 26) and some bishops saw virtue in wider State intervention to secure social reform. Blomfield was an enthusiastic supporter of public health reforms in London and defended the Board of Health in the 1850s when it was unpopular to do so (Ch. 33). Palmerston's episcopal creations in the later 1850s had a distinctly evangelical tinge and many became active social reformers. Robert Bickersteth became bishop of Ripon in 1857 after serving as incumbent in an overcrowded London parish where living conditions, as he later reported, 'made it almost impossible' for the poor 'to be moral, much less religious' (367, *148–9*). He championed slum clearance and housing reforms in the 1860s. If the great flowering of Anglican social concern took place in the last quarter of the nineteenth century, the mid-Victorian period showed that the church reform movement could bear humanitarian as well as administrative fruit.

III

Organized religion's continued inability to capture the poor was due in part to internecine religious warfare. Local politics in the 1830s and 1840s frequently centred on battles between Anglicans and dissenters over church rates (Ch. 27). In Birmingham and Nottingham, dissenters forced the Church to abandon plans to levy a rate (89). Congregationalist and Baptist ministers were often prominent political leaders in the struggle for municipal control, generally fought out by rival groups within the middle class (Ch. 33). Dissenting Liberals were prominent in the campaign to repeal the Corn Laws (Ch. 30).

It was a natural progression for radical Liberal dissenters schooled in agitation to remedy particular nonconformist grievances to mount a more general campaign against the Church itself. In 1844 some 700 nonconformist delegates agreed in London to establish an organization to promote 'the extinction of the union between Church and State'. The Anti-State Church Association, which changed its name to the Society for the Liberation of Religion from State Patronage and Control (colloquially the Liberation Society) in 1853, was the brainchild of Edward Miall, editor of the journal *Nonconformist*. It became a formidable nonconformist pressure group though it never succeeded in converting all dissenters to the virtues of political agitation. As the *Congregational Magazine* asserted in 1844: 'Its design is to employ worldly influence for the advancement of Christian objects, and to use Christian Churches for the promotion of political objects. We think that Christian societies should be used only for Christian ends'. (366, *128*)

Though concerted pressure for disestablishment was not at its greatest until the 1870s, the Liberation Society used its political influence shrewdly. An overwhelmingly Anglican parliamentary Liberal party was increasingly persuaded to promote objectives favoured by rank-and-file Liberalism in which dissent was a powerful force. Of these, the abolition of church rates and, by the late 1860s, Irish Church disestablishment were the most important. From the General Election of 1847 onwards, local political organizations were concerned to select sympathetic Liberal candidates. Miall himself represented Rochdale from 1852 to 1857. In the 1857 Election the significant improvement in the Liberal vote in the counties was in part due to nonconformist political pressure (135). By the 1860s Liberal MPs in areas of nonconformist strength were beginning to understand that they could not rely on dissenters' votes unless they supported agreed reforms. A by-election defeat in the Liberal stronghold of Exeter, where the Liberals had taken one of the two borough seats almost by right at every election since 1832, was generally ascribed to nonconformist abstentions after the candidate, J. D. Coleridge, the future Lord Chief Justice of Common Pleas, refused to support church rate abolition.

Anglican journals were not slow to respond to the challenge. The *Quarterly* and *Saturday Reviews* carried articles in the 1850s attacking dissenters' pretensions and rallying the Church in defence of its privileged status. Pro-Church pamphlets were issued by a newly formed Committee of Laymen of the Church of England and, from 1859, a Church Institution joined the defence of rates and establishment. Incongruously, the Church's most doughty parliamentary champion was Benjamin Disraeli, who saw the campaign as a means of rallying the Tory party, especially in the rural areas where its vote had slipped badly since 1841 (Ch. 39). By 1868, when the counties held up pretty well for the Conservatives in a generally disastrous election (Ch. 40), Gladstone was ascribing Liberal failure in the shires to zealous electioneering by country clergy fearful of disestablishment.

IV

The sharpest religious antagonisms were prompted by the revival of Roman Catholicism. Industrial employment opportunities had brought Irishmen to England in a steady stream since the late eighteenth century. By 1840 working-class Irishmen were a prominent minority in London, Glasgow and Liverpool. During the Irish famine, the stream became a spate and, so righteous Protestants believed, threatened to flood England's green and pleasant land with alien dogma and Popish superstition. The 1851 census showed that more than 500,000 of England and Wales's population of 18m. had been born in Ireland; almost all of these were Catholic. Though the small indigenous Catholic community, well entrenched in Lancashire, deprecated the development almost as much as their Anglican counterparts and heaped scorn on the ill-educated peasant priests who accompanied their flock, general anti-Catholicism was soon a divisive political issue.

Catholics believed that after the return of a Whig government in 1846 they would be able to consolidate the religious liberties recently acquired [G.i] and create a new episcopal structure. In 1850 the Pope sanctioned thirteen new Catholic bishoprics, mostly in densely populated areas such as Birmingham, Liverpool and Salford. Nicholas Wiseman, archbishop of Westminster, was also created a cardinal, England's first since the reign of Mary I. Wiseman celebrated his elevation with an injudicious pastoral letter celebrating the fact that 'Catholic England has been restored to its orbit in the ecclesiastical firmament, from which its light had long vanished' (368, i, *291*).

Wiseman had overlooked the deep well of anti-Catholicism in which English history was steeped. Now the echoes bubbled unpleasantly to the surface. Ultra-Tories like Robert Inglis and J. P. Plumptre were ready with rebarbative utterances and even Lord John Russell, his Whig majority under threat by 1850 (Ch. 37), was ready to pander to anti-Catholic prejudice in an effort to retain the support of loyal Anglican Whigs. His narrow-minded Ecclesiastical Titles Act [G.i] was an attempt to rally his troops and also to stem the flow of anti-Catholicism which had, for example, made traditional Bonfire Night celebrations literally inflammatory in 1850. The dissenters, torn between their vehement dislike of Catholic theology and feelings of sympathy for fellow dissenters from the British tradition, generally opposed Russell. The Quaker John Bright asserted that freedom was the proper weapon with which to attack Catholicism and Russell's Act only buttressed the illegitimate authority of an Anglican Church 'held together only by its vast funds'.[3]

Russell's ill-advised initiative failed on three counts. It did not rally party loyalists; it did not work; and it failed to prevent further anti-Catholic outbreaks. Riots occurred where Roman Catholic minorities were prominent, the most serious being at Stockport in 1852 where a quarter of the population was Catholic and fears of a labour market glutted with unskilled aliens undoubtedly exacerbated religious hostility. Working-class Catholicism in industrial Lancashire and North-east Cheshire had longer-term consequences. Riots continued sporadically into the 1870s and the political expression of anti-Catholicism helped the Conservatives in the area. The Liberals won only thirteen of Lancashire's thirty-four seats in the 1868 Election, a far worse outcome than in any other area (Ch. 40). Militant anti-Catholicism, translated into 'establishment' Tory votes, was an important factor. It is notable also that Wesleyan Methodism, the most pro-establishment and least pro-Liberal of the dissenting sects, was particularly attractive in South Lancashire.

Religion, especially after 1850, was one of the strongest determinants of voting behaviour. But by the end of our period a cloud was darkening the skies of self-confident, if not self-absorbed, sectarianism. The accumulated weight of scientific evidence caused a reconsideration of the Bible as the basis of religious belief. The science of geology, at least since the 1820s, had cast doubt on the plausibility of the Genesis creation story, but in the 1830s and 1840s such discoveries, as yet little understood and not widely publicized except in scientific circles, did not create a crisis of faith. The Professors of Geology at Cambridge, Adam Sedgwick, and of Micrology at Oxford, William Buckland, were both beneficed clergymen in the great line of Anglican scholars. Neither lost his faith and Buckland rose to become dean of Westminster after 1845. Discussion in the 1840s and 1850s of the eighteenth-century zoologist Lamarck's views on evolution by the inheritance of acquired characteristics caused several ripples since they challenged conventional theology on the nature of Man. This process was transformed into turbulence with the appearance in 1859 of Charles Darwin's *Origin of species*, the distillation of ideas which Darwin had been wrestling with for several years but had feared to publish.

For much of the 1860s the debate on Darwin's theory of evolution by natural selection seemed to divide the educated classes into those who accepted it, thus rejecting orthodox Christianity, and those who rejected it, maintaining the corpus of their beliefs aggressively intact. In fact, the distinction was a hopelessly crude one, however much it may have suited Thomas Huxley, by far the most committed anti-Christian among the scientists, to draw it. Many clerics from Bishop Wilberforce in his famous British Association debate of 1860 with Huxley (when he fatuously enquired whether Huxley was descended from an ape on his mother's or his father's side) onwards were prone to dogmatic, irrational denunciation which polarized science versus religion. Only at the end of the decade were more measured responses possible. When the Darwinian dust settled it was seen that most scientists remained Christians; educated Christians found it far from impossible to accommodate evolutionary theories within a still firm faith. Most clerical fears came to centre on the effects a vulgarization of Darwin's ideas would have on simple minds. If a scientist could 'disprove' religion by undermining the Creation story, ordinary people, whose hold on faith was tenuous enough, might abandon it altogether with dire consequences for the social order. The clergy need not have worried. Victorian Britain could not comprehend morality outside Christianity. Church attendance among semi-skilled, unskilled and casual workers was not high, though there is some evidence that women were more dutiful worshippers than men. Overwhelmingly powerful social expectations continued to encompass marriage in church, 'churching' (to purify the female body and to give thanks for safe delivery from childbirth) and infant baptism. Many working-class parents also encouraged Sunday School attendance, if only to give them a rare opportunity for privacy and – not infrequently – further procreation (276, iii, *340*). Children looked forward to church festivals and Sunday school outings (Ch. 35). The cultural influence of Christianity was pervasive, if sometimes distanced.

This lesson was also becoming apparent to the doughty but diminutive band of secularists and freethinkers. Their leader in the 1840s and 1850s, G. J. Holyoake, emulated the Christians in his quest for respectability. His secular journal, *Reasoner*, bowed to none in its earnestness; its appeal was naturally limited to that minority of working people for whom reading and rational dispute were ruling passions (370). This did not mean that secularists did not alarm the authorities. Joseph Barker of Preston was only one of many to be arrested for giving a series of atheistic lectures to an audience of artisans. But it was not to be Holyoake's role, or that of his provincial counterparts, to dechristianize Britain, however nobly he argued about superstition and the implicit tyranny of revealed religion. Nor could his more charismatic successor, Charles Bradlaugh, achieve it though he was responsible in the early 1870s for generating the last significant republican movement in Britain. The churches in 1870 were threatened far more by apathy, absenteeism and alternative calls on leisure time (Ch. 35) than they were by Thomas Huxley or by George Holyoake. Religion still appeared to extend a powerful hold over most aspects of national life. The long march of indifference, however, had already begun.

---

1. D. M. Thompson, ed., *Nonconformity in the Nineteenth Century* (1972), pp. 141–3.
2. D. Bowen, *The Idea of the Victorian Church* (Montreal, 1969), p. 316.
3. B. L. Add. MSS. 43392, f. 75.

CHAPTER 35

Leisure and responsibility

I

How people spent their time when not at work was a matter of increased interest in early and mid-Victorian Britain. There are several reasons why this should have been so. An industrial society sharpens the distinction between work and leisure. Timed work in a factory, for example, is a self-contained operation. Work in the fields or even in a workshop can incorporate elements both of work and leisure. In the latter drink is usually available; work is often divided between members of the family and is done to complete a particular task or assignment. The worker is in much greater control of time (Ch. 14). Because industrial work was rigidly timed the non-working portion of the day was in consequence more clearly delimited. By the 1850s, hours of work especially for skilled men were beginning to be set alongside prescribed holidays and half-day working on Saturday, a development facilitated by the Factory Acts [C.i]. The Inspector of Factories reported in 1859 that a greater clarity obtained 'between the worker's own time and his master's. The worker now knows when that which he sells [his labour] is ended and when his own begins'. (317, *150*) It is probable that skilled workers fortunate enough to have the choice were choosing to forgo additional income by opting for increased leisure.

New leisure opportunities were created incidentally by technology. It was assumed that most railway work would be in freight carriage but the companies rapidly appreciated the profit to be made from passengers, particularly by excursion trips. Many people travelled a long distance for the first time in 1851 to visit the Great Exhibition (Ch. 31). Thomas Cook offered a 5s. (25p) return fare from Leeds to London for passengers travelling on the Midland Railway. A boom in cheap passenger fares followed in the next two decades. Seaside towns, which had been developing steadily before the age of the railway, were given an immense stimulus. The application of technology also made fairs and circuses more varied and more interesting spectacles. This was the age of the mechanical roundabout and many other opportunities for investment in gaudy, catchpenny contrivances did not go unexploited.

Leisure, however, was a subject for concern as well as opportunity, and this aspect of the subject has most interested those scholars who have enormously enhanced our knowledge in the past thirty years or so. Leisure is a growth area in contemporary historical scholarship because it seems to offer a new dimension in our understanding of social relations in Victorian Britain. Many – some would say most – of the recreations of the lower orders in pre-industrial Britain were either violent, drunken, cruel or all three. Crowds flocked to cock-fights, bull-baitings, prize-fights, public executions and fairs. These last usually had rowdy undertones and their many critics asserted that, having lost much of their original commercial function, they had become debauched by the presence of prostitutes and by other opportunities for illicit sexual liaison (316). Even football matches, which were immensely popular, were largely unstructured rough-houses between neighbouring villages played under few ascertainable, and no universally applicable, rules. Hunting and horse-racing, recreations traditionally patronized and controlled by the landed gentry, attracted the lower orders. At virtually every popular amusement drink was available without stint and the additional attraction of gambling was a further inducement to attendance. Though the sums involved were widely divergent, the love of a flutter (a term dating from the 1870s and originally connoting sexual as well as financial speculation) was a common bond between high and low.

As we have seen (Chs 6 and 31) many in the middle ranks of society evinced strong moral disapproval of riotous, licentious, drunken or otherwise uncontrolled pleasure. The 'reformation of manners' had clearly in its sights the innocent and the not so innocent amusements of the poor. Many traditional pastimes were successfully attacked between 1780 and 1850. The Society for the Suppression of Vice was especially active against fairs. The Society for the Prevention of Cruelty to Animals was founded in 1824 and became instrumental in obtaining a Cruelty to Animals Act in 1835 which prohibited animal-baiting. Unheroically, the vast majority of prosecutions which the Society brought were against the lower orders and not against the gentry or aristocracy whose influence over blood sports was far greater.

Traditional Puritanism among the middle classes combined with the success of the evangelical movement ensured attacks on many traditional forms of amusement. However, the attempt to supplant these with what the Victorians called 'rational recreation' had another motive force. Old leisure pursuits were deemed not only anachronistic but dangerous in an industrial society. Whatever its advantages the Industrial Revolution had engendered in demographic terms a much bigger [E.i] and in organizational terms a less controlled, society (Chs 14, 17 and 31). Those amusements which might be tolerable, if offensive, under rural, squirearchical patronage posed threats to public order in the towns. After Peterloo and the Bristol riots (Chs 20 and 23) public opinion was acutely sensitive to the possibility of social breakdown in 'ungovernable' cities. The desire for order, first in the cities and later in rural areas as well, was a prominent factor in the establishment of the new professional, preventive police, who appeared under legislation passed in 1829, 1839 and 1856 [C.ii]. According to Dr Gatrell, the nineteenth-century police were 'intended to be the impersonal agents of central policy' (276, iii, *260*). In reality, as in so much else concerning the growth of government, continuity of personnel and of informal policing attitudes was as important as change until near the end of the nineteenth century. Early constables were usually drawn from the labouring classes and paid the equivalent of labourers' wages. Under the direction of the new Chief Constables, the normal targets were easily identified. Much early policing was directed towards clearing the streets of drunken young working-class males. On average, one adult male in 29 would have been arrested in 1861 and one adult female in 120 – many of the latter for prostitution. The concentration upon drink and sexual offences rather than, say, on larceny is only superficially surprising. The authorities in Victorian Britain prized their version of respectability above all things and they perceived alcoholic and sexual licence as the most public obstacles to its realization. Thieving took place in secret; drunks and prostitutes were all too obnoxiously public. They were an easy touch for the ever strengthening arm of the law. Worse, both might spread if not vigorously restrained (353). As the nineteenth century drew to its close a welter of new local by-laws regulating public entertainment kept the local police increasingly busy.

The attack on fairs, however, continued to the end of our period. Fairs attracted not only legitimate petty traders but pickpockets, pimps, prostitutes and – inevitably – drunks. After 1848, however, crowds as such were less likely to be perceived as a threat to public order and the pressure on fairs began to slacken. The movement to regularize and anaesthetize ancient festivals like Whit Walks and Whit Ales continued. The eighteenth-century Oxfordshire gentry had patronized various Whitsun festivals, some lasting up to a fortnight. Their nineteenth-century successors withdrew that support and transferred it to more 'rational' and much shorter celebrations, often organized by benefit clubs or friendly societies (320).

Another factor working against traditional pastimes was lack of space. Urban developers regarded open spaces as lost opportunities for profit. Both these and the allotments which afforded both recreation and a modest relief to the food bill, came under severe pressure during the nineteenth century. The enclosure of common land (Chs 15 and 16) further restricted access to places previously used for a wide variety of games, gatherings and festivals. More than 600,000 acres of common land were enclosed between 1845 and 1869 under the provisions of the General Enclosure Act and less than 4,000 of these were specifically set aside for recreation grounds or allotments.

II

Rational recreation meant replacing what was deemed unsuitable with amusements which were more improving. Robert Slaney, the Liberal country gentleman and MP for Shrewsbury, first took up the cause of popular recreation in Parliament in the 1830s, fearing that 'the working classes will fly to demagogues and dangerous causes' unless 'safety valves for their eager energies' were provided. Edward Edwards, a librarian at the British Museum, asserted in 1849 that 'the want of some provision, from the public resources, of amusements of a rational and improving character, has led to the introduction, to a large extent in our towns, of brutalizing and demoralizing amusements' (319, 317). A powerful, didactic sense of mission towards the poor was being called for. For rational, middle-class minds the solutions were straightforward: provide food for the mind and recreation for the body, if possible in an atmosphere conducive to gratitude in the recipient. Thus could 'eager energies' be sensibly channelled and the cultural gulf between rich and poor be bridged by what the Manchester banker Benjamin Heywood called a 'community of enjoyment'.

Much rational recreation was, in the literal sense, patronizing. Radical MPs from the 1830s supported the free opening of national exhibitions and art treasures to the public. Slaney chaired a Commons Select Committee on Public Walks which criticized the lack of open spaces. In 1840 a parliamentary grant of £10,000 was made to help local authorities provide parks. Manchester, which had already raised £30,000 locally by private and public donation, was given £3,000. In 1845 Sir Robert Peel gave £1,000 towards the cost of a 'Peel Park' in the city. Private philanthropy proved bountiful in the 1850s and 1860s. Sir Francis Crossley presented a park to the people of Halifax in 1857 as did the Calthorpe family of Edgbaston to Birmingham in 1867. The iron magnate Henry Bolckow put up the cash for Middlesbrough's Albert Park, which opened in 1868 (296). Park construction was also a means of ameliorating unemployment in various Lancashire towns during the 'cotton famine' of the early 1860s. Parks had by-laws emphasizing controlled amusement. Many prohibited ball games; access to the floral displays was strictly controlled; some even prescribed appropriate apparel for walking in parks. The Calthorpe agent upbraided the Birmingham town clerk in 1870 for permitting cycling in Calthorpe Park against the directives of the covenant (294).

Supporters of public libraries and museums also argued that not only was knowledge valuable in its own right but its easy access would reduce the gulf between the classes. The effort to improve would show the individual how social harmony could be achieved through economic growth aided by serious, responsible effort. Legislators paid lip-service to this optimistic view with the Public Libraries Act in 1850 but the reality fell far short of the ideal. Only twenty-four rate-supported libraries were built between 1851 and 1867 and public usage was generally disappointing. Public libraries, even at the end of the century when far more were open, were more effective as expressions of the civic ideal (Ch. 33) than as a means of self-improvement for the masses. Still, libraries and reading rooms did attract considerable legacies and other forms of charitable support while co-operative societies also invested some of their funds for the same purpose.

The temperance movement was a natural response to the call for rational recreation since most traditional amusements seemed debauched or vulgarized by alcohol (Ch. 33). Particularly after 1850 nonconformist churches, most notably the Methodists, embraced the temperance ideal. Temperance halls were a common feature of Victorian towns. In them lectures and discussion groups were held not only, or even primarily, on the evils and waste of demon drink but on a wide range of subjects political, economic, social and cultural. Temperance societies were among the most extensive patrons of railway excursions both to the seaside and to inland beauty spots. The didactic purpose is neatly encapsulated by a Cornish temperance ditty:

Happy Camborne, Happy Camborne where the railway is so near
And the engine shows how water can accomplish more than beer.

Temperance societies quickly learned that to retain audiences they must cultivate the lighter touch. Many concentrated on offering a range of amusements which would appeal to the whole family. Family participation stood in stark contrast to the male domination of the public house.

Mechanics' institutes began in the 1820s to offer basic scientific instruction to the lower classes (351). During the next half-century they established themselves overwhelmingly as vehicles of improvement for the lower middle classes and skilled workers, usually but not invariably under middle-class control. The adult educationist J. W. Hudson stated in 1851 that the purpose of the institutes was

> the creation of intellectual pleasures and refined amusements tending to the general elevation of character. The frequent intercourse of men of different parties and grades of life, for the purpose of promoting one intellectual object . . . is unquestionably an object to be cherished and encouraged. By such means a taste for rational enjoyment may be produced, and those hours generally spent in listlessness and in foolish amusements, may be converted into periods rendered precious by the inculcations of enlightened and elevating principles.

By the 1850s and 1860s, however, the sober buildings which housed the institutes not only saw lectures and classes but more lighthearted activities including such frivolities as Christmas parties. Excursions were also arranged in a conscious attempt to sugar the pill of enlightenment to retain membership.

Some factory owners in Lancashire and North Cheshire offered recreational outlets for their employees. A degree of factory paternalism had been essential in the earlier, remote factories well away from urban centres (Chs 12 and 13), but it was not only translated into the towns but often extended there. Samuel Greg's model mill at Styal had attached gardens and a games playground. Tea-parties and music classes were also provided. While the purpose-built industrial and social community built in the 1850s by Titus Salt as Saltaire, near Bingley (Yorks.), was very much the exception, many larger established firms, such as Horrocks and Miller in Preston or Hornby in Blackburn, assiduously cultivated the 'mill community'. Proprietors spent on day schools and Sunday schools, reading rooms, railway excursions and a variety of 'treats'. The purpose, obviously, was the creation of a loyal and cohesive workforce and to break down the artificial barriers between work and leisure which the factory had itself erected by offering pleasurable yet structured means of filling the latter. Loyalty was expected to have its price. The continued attractions of trade unionism to those able to profit from it (Ch. 18) and the immoderately hostile reaction to unionism displayed by some even of the most 'enlightened' employers suggest that factory paternalism was only of limited value. One historian has claimed that the 'new paternalism' offers a convincing explanation for the decline of social conflict in the North in the 1850s and 1860s (312). This seems dubious, not least in view of the relatively small number of firms, especially outside Lancashire, which were by then sufficiently established to offer the requisite range of 'extra-curricular' activities over a long period and in view of the rapid turnover of proprietorship (Ch. 13). It is dangerous to generalize from the atypical large firm which both succeeded and left usable records for the historian. That factory owners did provide rational recreation, however, cannot be gainsaid. We owe the continuing excellence of many northern brass bands to factory paternalism.

III

'Respectability' had chalked up some notable triumphs by 1870. With a few prominent exceptions – such as the survival in a few places of the long weekend through 'Saint Monday' into the 1870s – leisure time had become formalized. Annual holidays either replaced or grew out of older wakes; Saturday half-holiday was more or less established; the first Bank Holiday Act, a milestone in the regularization of leisure, would be passed in 1871. Yet recent historians of leisure have been more impressed by the continued vitality of vulgar amusements and by their successful adaptation to the new world. It is fanciful to suppose that, because a Slaney or a Hudson said they should, most of the working classes spent their precious leisure time in a nonconformist bible group, a temperance hall, a reference library or even walking sedately in a municipal park.

The pub remained the essential social centre for most working men. Arduous physical labour demanded that a thirst be slaked and, to the continued irritation of temperance reformers, men preferred the slaking properties of beer over those of tea. Worse, they would drink the vile stuff in pubs, away from their families. Alcohol consumption, mostly on beer, increased in the third quarter of the century. The pub had traditionally been a place both of local games and sports, like darts and skittles, and of entertainment, provided either by the drinkers themselves or, increasingly, by singers and dancers in singing saloons, 'speak-easies' and 'penny gaffs'. From these humble origins, semi-professional artists emerged and it was but a small step to the establishment of music-halls, the best-known early example of which was the Canterbury Hall, opened by Charles Morton in Lambeth in 1851. This building was extended soon afterwards to incorporate a library, picture gallery and reading room. The Alhambra in Leicester Square, which had a capacity of 3,500, was opened in 1860. During the following decade, extensive investment made music-halls big business both in London and the provinces. Professional artistes were retained on contract to theatrical managers. The music-halls attracted criticism from superior persons who found the 'turns' vulgar and the general atmosphere both lurid and debased, but many of the middle classes did develop a taste for ribaldry which hall managers could satisfy by differential seat charges keeping them at safe physical distance from the roughs. In the mid-1860s the theatrical critic John Hollingshead thought music-halls 'as lucrative a business as any business we have' (320, *222*). Orthodox capitalism was busy by the end of our period moulding an old tradition of entertainment to its own needs and, in doing so, widening the audience.

A similar story of increased investment could be told of popular theatre, circuses and fairs. For East End Londoners Thomas Wright considered the Britannia Theatre, Hoxton, 'the most popular resort of pleasure-seeking workmen' in the late 1860s (317). 'Lord' George Sanger made himself a fortune from touring the country with an international circus. Theatrical and musical spectacles established themselves as firm attractions for folk with a few coppers to spare. More basic pub entertainments also survived, of course, but it seems reasonable to agree with Dr Bailey that as living standards rose a larger proportion of the working classes were finding drink 'more of an incidental social lubricant and less of a total experience' (319).

Working men also showed themselves capable of moulding 'improving' institutions to their own tastes. Working men's clubs were established in the early 1860s to educate the lower orders to the higher ideals of improvement and social harmony. The first secretary of the Working Man's Club and Institute Union (1862), Henry Solly, aimed to promote a club atmosphere so notably lacking in the pub. He even saw working men as 'New Greeks' whose animal energies, now to be directed in rational ways, would invigorate the whole nation. The clubs flourished and many did indeed establish reading rooms and promote literary lectures. By 1870, when the main lines of future development were already laid, it could be seen that, while they certainly represented an 'improvement' on the street-corner spit and sawdust, they hardly met Solly's grandiose notions. Their fixed points were the sale of beer and the inadmissibility of women, except as visiting artistes on concert nights. They became clean, if basic, refuges from wife and family. Improvement was incidental.

The railway companies were happy to provide excursions both for 'rational' and 'debauched' purposes. The same company would offer cheap fares both for a temperance outing and for a trip to a public hanging. The most spectacular development, however, was in excursions to the seaside. The railway did not create the seaside resort, but it dramatically changed the characters of many. It is often forgotten that the early development both of New Brighton and Blackpool before 1850 was to cater for the middle classes who would either stay for a period or, like Liverpool or Manchester merchants, buy superior villa accommodation as an out-of-town address. Southport in 1851 was almost twice as big as Blackpool and by no means more select (301). The Lancashire coastline was developed rapidly during the next twenty years as demand increased, particularly from unmarried cotton operatives and female weavers whose regularity of employment and generally fewer family obligations enabled them to spend spare cash on trips to the sea (322). Seaside resorts ceased to be the exclusive preserve of the wealthy. As early as the late 1850s, accommodation of a decidedly inferior sort was being provided in parts of Brighton, Blackpool and Scarborough to cater for working-class visitors. Day trips brought increasing numbers of operatives determined to enjoy themselves noisily to the extreme annoyance of established residents. The day tripper was heartily disliked both for rude habits and limited spending power, but could not be kept away from seaside towns with good railway links. Blackpool's population was between 6,000 and 7,000 in 1871 but this small community was already receiving more than half a million visitors a year.

In 1850 the only sizeable seaside resort away from the south coast was Scarborough (Yorkshire), which had long catered for fashionable visitors. In the next twenty years pressure particularly from textile Lancashire saw great growth not only in Blackpool and Southport but in Rhyl, New Brighton and Morecambe. From a very early date resorts developed respectable and non-respectable zones and, more importantly, divided themselves according to clientele. All resorts wanted to attract the wealthy and keep out the riff-raff, but only those in which important families had a preponderating interest could manage it. Blackpool was divided between numerous owners and developed, especially after 1870, as the archetypal working-class resort with a Golden Mile which still in the 1990s, when many erstwhile clients have decamped annually to Torremolinos, offers the most ostentatiously vulgar aspect in Britain. The Clifton family kept Lytham, five miles to the south, select by controlling development. The same service was provided for Southport by the Heskeths and Scarisbricks under the watchful eye of the local improvement commissioners. On the south coast, where the job was anyway much easier, the Devonshires made Eastbourne 'the duke's town' and kept the railway away until as late as 1868; Folkestone was controlled by the earls of Radnor. Brighton, much the biggest and, by south coast standards, one of the most socially mixed resorts had no overriding landed interest.

Historians of leisure have claimed to see evidence in this period either of 'social control' by the middle class over the working class or, somewhat more subtly, of the 'hegemony' of the dominant social group. That many promoters of rational recreation were overt and unrepentant social controllers in aspiration is beyond dispute, but it remains extremely doubtful whether 'social control' is an adequate description of an extremely complex phenomenon (311). If it means the imposition of a given set of values by the middle class on the working class, then it surely fails on two counts. First, it did not work. The working classes proved themselves eminently capable of resisting imposition where they wished to resist it and, as in the case of music-halls, one aspect of 'rough' culture successfully percolated 'bourgeois' sensibilities by the 1870s. Secondly, and more importantly, rational recreation was by no means the exclusive preserve of a dominant, didactic bourgeoisie. Working-class respectability produced its own hard-headed, rational culture. No one can study, for example, artisan radicalism, Owenism, teetotal Chartism or the co-operative movement without appreciating that many operatives, by no means all of them artisans or 'labour aristocrats', shared a passion for self-improvement, hard work, discipline and regularity with the Victorian bourgeoisie. The attack on wasteful expenditiire in the street-corner pub cannot adequately be portrayed as an attack by the 'dominant' bourgeoisie on the 'exploited' working class which must succeed if industrial capitalism is to thrive. It was an attack by respectability on non-respectability (Ch. 31) and it resists crude class formulation. The sober, skilled male operative learning economics in a free library or discussing disestablishment of the Anglican Church in a public lecture hall was no dupe of an exploiting class. He was taking the opportunities offered to fit himself the better to fight his own battles. The battleground might be a labour dispute or a campaign to abolish sectarian education. He might fight it as a socialist, or, much more likely, as a radical Liberal. His political position was not to be pre-ordained by his economic circumstance.

Some history of leisure is written as if it were an attempt to fight the posthumous battles of the underdog. Thus, respectability is derided as a thin smokescreen covering bourgeois domination and naked class interest. Drunken louts who squander their earnings in the beershop, and keep their wives and children short of the bare necessities of life or the pickpockets who thrived at fairs or wakes week celebrations are vindicated as the upholders of a valid culture under threat. True, it is rarely presented as crudely as this and it is frequently clothed in the cumbersome garb of social science jargon, but it properly belongs to the 'goodies and baddies' school of historical writing. The movement for rational recreation was, at least in part, a plea for a change in leisure patterns consonant with a complex industrial society in which, for the first time, work and leisure could be clearly separated. It cut across class barriers, if such barriers are to be defined economically, and it had limited success. It was motivated in part by fears of ungovernability. It also owed much to a hatred of waste and a recognition of the need for discipline. To argue that its basis was the control by a dominant minority over a subservient majority is not only a simple-minded distortion of a complex reality. It is crassly insulting to those members of the working classes who embraced it consciously as an appropriate agency of their own improvement, the political results of which would permanently affect the structure of twentieth-century politics.

CHAPTER 36

Education and the consciousness of status

I

Few aspects of life indicate the hierarchy of Victorian society so starkly as education. The value of education for all classes was all but universally accepted by the 1840s, but there was almost equal agreement among the leaders of society that its primary function was to fit recipients for their proper station in life. Only in exceptional circumstances was it thought desirable to encourage people to better themselves by learning. The three major royal commissions on education emphasized the apparent immutability of social divisions. It was the task of the Clarendon Commission (1861) to investigate how far the education at England's nine great public schools remained appropriate to the training of the nation's leaders. The Taunton Commission (1864) studied the vast range of schools provided for 'those large classes of English society which are comprised between the humblest and the very highest'. The Newcastle Commission (1858) examined schooling for the labouring classes on the understanding that it should be cheap, efficient and should not normally take children beyond the age of eleven.

If schooling was a means of confirming status, it follows that relatively few were much concerned with the quality of education as such. The sons of the aristocracy were not sent to Eton or Harrow to acquire finely honed minds but to carry themselves off as gentlemen. It is one of the more striking characteristics of the English aristocracy that, with rare exceptions, they have never posed either as intellectual giants or as aesthetes, preferring to evince that bluff common sense and preference for physical over intellectual endeavour which can easily be mistaken for the common touch. In this respect, as in most others, Palmerston is a more typical aristocrat than Gladstone. The public school curriculum deliberately eschewed most branches of useful knowledge. Classical language, literature and philosophy were its fundament. At Rugby in the 1860s seventeen out of the twenty-two working hours were spent studying the classics. Science and, particularly, technology were regarded as not fit subjects for gentlemen to study. A few of the ablest pupils, such as Gladstone who was at Eton from 1821 to 1828, thrived on the disciplined training of a classical education and took from it a breadth of cultural reference, an abiding love for the classics and a precision in the presentation of argument which lifted them well above their fellows in intellectual attainment. For most, the dull grind of Latin and Greek primers took second place to apparently endless hours of muscular athleticism on the playing fields. Such athleticism by no means implied orderly team games. Eton and Harrow were both noted for roughness and bullying, cavalierly rationalized as 'character-training'. But being at one of the great public schools was the thing. It indicated superiority and it opened avenues in later life. As Howard Staunton observed in *The Great Schools of England* (1865) 'The Great Endowed Schools are less to be considered as educational agencies, in the intellectual sense, than as social agencies'. (349, *130*)

Public school reforms, associated with Thomas Arnold and his disciples, did not displace the classics but involved some modernity in the shape of compulsory mathematics and modern language teaching. Of greater importance than the curriculum, however, was the attempt to impose disciplined, structured effort within a religious framework. This meant compulsory chapel (two or even three times on a Sunday), a prefectorial system of discipline, and team games played by rules. Rugby football, which developed after 1828, was a godsend. It combined wholehearted commitment to physical effort in the quasi-disciplined structure of the scrum with certain, though limited, opportunities for the deployment of individual skill and flair. It was, and is, an activity in which the merely brawny could pull their full weight for the benefit of the team. In England, the game became a talisman of status. The public schools emulated Rugby and, well beyond the end of our period, grammar schools pathetically aped the public schools by adopting 'rugger' in preference to 'soccer' because of its superior social cachet. Competitive effort was increasingly necessary in the classroom also, since by the 1850s and 1860s greater attention was paid to examinations as a means of entrance both to universities and the professions.

The universities of Oxford and Cambridge, though susceptible of some reform and no longer the scandalously unacademic institutions they had been for much of the eighteenth century, remained open to the charge that they were finishing schools for gentlemen more than seats of serious learning. Some colleges, Oriel and Balliol at Oxford, and some disciplines, the Mathematical tripos at Cambridge, for example, had deservedly high academic reputations, but the majority of undergraduates were young men who had struggled with the classics at their public schools and would continue to struggle in dilettante pursuit of an undistinguished pass degree while devoting most of their time to rowing, gambling, drinking and sport. The pall of Anglican exclusivity hung heavily over both universities. Most tutors were young clergymen, anxious to polish their claims to a cosy rural benefice in the gift of the college they served. After the mid-1850s Oxford undergraduates did not have to take a religious test to read for a degree, but college fellowships remained closed to nonconformists; full religious equality was not established until 1871. Women achieved their first, still insecure, toe-hold with the foundation of Girton College, Cambridge, in 1869.

Probably the best university education, and certainly that most relevant to modern needs, was found away from Oxbridge. The four Scottish universities St Andrews, Glasgow, Aberdeen and Edinburgh – had their faults, but their undergraduate recruitment was wider and their professoriate undeniably more distinguished. Edinburgh's medical faculty was renowned as was Glasgow's science. Oxford got round to building science laboratories only in the second half of the 1850s. English nonconformists had long sent their sons north of the border for a university education, though many others felt that practical knowledge and experiments carried out in the workshop were more valuable than theory.

From the late 1820s an English reaction to Anglican domination of higher education set in. Bentham was instrumental in establishing a non-denominational University College in London in 1828. This was countered by an Anglican foundation, King's College, in 1834. London University, incorporated in 1836, expanded rapidly, but sectarian rivalries vitiated some of the early utilitarian hopes. Durham University, founded in 1832 in the shadow of the cathedral, was an avowedly Anglican institution and the placid tenor of its early years was unshaken either by scandal or by excessive intellectual enquiry. A radical non-conformist, John Owens, left almost £100,000 on his death in 1846 to found a non-denominational college in Manchester which opened its doors with five professors and two other teachers, as Owens College in 1851. By the time it was recognized as the independent Victoria University of Manchester in 1880, its radical departures in higher education had made it an impressive centre of learning. In general, however, university education in this period did little to shake the belief of many businessmen that the practical acquisition of technological skills by apprenticeship was greatly preferable to cultivating the mind by translating Homer. The predominant university response was a withering contempt for practical skills. Thus was enshrined a wholly artificial and deeply damaging divide between 'intellectual' (hence socially acceptable) and 'practical' (hence *sub rosa*) subjects.

II

Education for the middle classes came in a rich range of guises, but between 1840 and 1870 a pattern was emerging which depended critically upon status. As a Taunton commissioner noted: 'The education of the gentry has gradually separated itself from that of the class below them and it is but natural that this class in their turn should be unwilling to be confounded with the labourers they employ.'[1] Since the State made no prescription as to quality, this criterion could have been satisfied by employing a tutor or governess at home. This remained common, especially for girls, but for those who could afford the fees – and many were far from excessive – the fashion developed for sending boys away to proprietary boarding schools, run as private ventures often on the joint-stock basis.

Several factors explain the superficially odd development of flinging children out of the parental nest before they reached their teens. Emulation of gentry practice was one. Ease of access was another. Railways covered most of England by the late 1850s, and some apparently most isolated spots were surprisingly near a station. The need to acquire qualifications also became increasingly important from the 1850s. At Rossall, founded near Fleetwood in 1844 as an Anglican school and northern counterpart to Marlborough, boys had been so efficiently trained in the classics that by the late 1860s several of their best pupils were winning open scholarships to Oxford and Cambridge. Fees were stiff enough – £65 a year and £52 for the sons of the clergy – to ensure a degree of social exclusivity, and the academic achievement was such that the ablest could compete with the best families in the land, for whom entry to the ancient universities was still more or less automatic.

The decline of the grammar schools aided the emergence of fee-paying proprietary schools. Grammar schools, usually endowed with benefactions in the sixteenth or seventeenth centuries, had seen their resources eaten away by inflation and the quality of education had naturally suffered. Thame Grammar School, with two masters and one boy, was described by the Taunton commissioners as 'one of the greatest scandals in the country'. They concluded that 'by far the majority' of the endowed schools 'give no better education than that of an ordinary national school and a very great many do not give one so good'. School buildings, often situated in the centre of grimy cities, tended to be inadequate and the schools' social tone, far more important to many middle-class parents than academic attainments, pretty low. The attractions of a private boarding school in rural surroundings, and buttressed by fees which excluded all but the well-to-do, were considerable. As the Taunton commissioner for Lancashire, James Bryce, commented in 1868: 'When a Lancashire merchant or manufacturer sends his sons from home, he desires as often as not to send them a long way off, partly that they may lose their northern tongue, partly that they may form new acquaintances, and be quite away from home influences'. By 'home influences' he meant socially inferior local connections. The revival of the grammar schools as avenues of advancement would come only in the twentieth century under local authority and State supervision. In the 1850s and 1860s most were totally inadequate to middle-class needs.

The new public schools aped Arnoldian reformism with their emphasis on chapel-going, self-discipline and team spirit. Most developed a modern curriculum alongside the classics. Rossall, for example, introduced physics and chemistry in the early 1850s under the headmastership of the Revd. W. A. Osborne, but only for less able pupils. Though many schools catered for a specialized clientele, Marlborough and Rossall for Anglican clergy sons, Wellington for army and Epsom for medical families, they were drawn together by the need to define a collective role against outsiders. The Headmasters' Conference was established in 1869 and soon developed as the touchstone of social acceptability to prospective parents. It included the nine 'Clarendon' schools and still survives, jealous of its restricted membership, to remind us of the Victorian middle-class educational ethos.

More than 10,000 private schools were believed to exist in 1864, very few of them in the category just discussed. Many were fly-by-night establishments charging extremely low fees and intended primarily for the lower orders. Doubtless, though in the absence of government inspection it is impossible to be sure, many of the schools not in receipt of a State grant designed for small tradesmen's and shopkeepers' children were also educationally valueless. Few have left any record of their existence. The proprietary day schools, however, did make a valuable contribution. About 100 such institutions, of which the Liverpool Royal Institution School (1819) had been the first, were offering an education grounded in mathematics and modern languages, sometimes with science. In the 1850s, and against fierce prejudice, serious schooling for girls was developed. The North London Collegiate School opened its doors in 1850 to be followed by Cheltenham Ladies College three years later.

The Taunton Commission proposed a most radical solution to the problem of educational diversity at the secondary level. It recommended a central bureaucracy to superintend the division of schools into three categories appropriate respectively to: (a) gentry, business and professional men's sons; (b) smaller businessmen and substantial shopkeepers; (c) the sons of tradesmen and superior artisans, 'a class distinctly lower in the scale'. Schools would be distinguished by fees charged and by recommended leaving age. The first group (leaving age 18–19) would prepare boys for university and social leadership, the second (leaving age 16) for commerce and industry, the third (leaving age 14) for no specific professional career but to a level markedly above that of the elementary schools. The Endowed Schools Act of 1869 did not follow this structured lead and was, in fact, an anodyne measure achieving as little as it ventured. That the Commission should even consider such a graduated scheme, however, speaks volumes for the perceived importance of status in education. Education was certainly not to 'lead out' children from one station in life to another since 'class distinctions' were stated to be 'exceedingly mischievous both to those whom they raise and to those whom they lower' (250, *301*).

III

The State's most direct concern with education before 1870 was with that provided for the lower orders. Compulsory education had been prescribed for two categories, pauper and factory children [C.i], while the State's financial commitment to those educated in church schools in receipt of government grants (Ch. 26) increased markedly after 1846. Generally, factory schools disappointed the education inspectors. Most employers remained reluctant to enforce the education clauses of the Factory Acts strictly. Leonard Horner categorized as 'good' only 76 out of 427 schools attended by factory children, 146 as 'inferior' and 66 as so bad as to be 'a fraud upon the poor ignorant parents who pay the school fees' (330, *218*). In places where factory paternalism was taken seriously, however, factory schools could be very good. The Hornbys, Pilkingtons and Hopwoods competed in school building in the 1840s and 1850s in Blackburn, as did the Thomassons and Ashworths in Bolton. It was reported in 1867 that Rossendale manufacturers 'have exhibited the greatest possible interest with the schools which the child employed in their factories attend [*sic*]' (312, *173*). In the 1840s the Guest family provided in their iron town of Merthyr Tydfil infant schools, day schools and evening classes both for employees and their relatives.

Effective pauper education was vitiated by the parsimony of many Poor Law Guardians, by the impossibility of imposing centrally prescribed standards, and by the continued prevalence of outdoor relief (Ch. 25). Most children relieved outside the workhouse could not be 'rescued' from the depravity and slovenly habits which were presumed to be the defining characteristics of parents who applied for poor relief. Some workhouse children did indeed receive good training both in basic literacy and in numeracy, together with practical crafts such as handwork, cookery and needlework on the district-school principle pioneered by Sir James Kay-Shuttleworth at Norwood in the late 1830s. Most Poor Law schools, however, were starved of funds.

It was at Norwood that Kay-Shuttleworth developed ideas for teacher training, which were to be put into practice after 1846. He would have liked teacher training to be free of the denominational incubus which plagued all educational initiatives in this period but had to bend before the continued power of the Church. As the National Society gloated in 1847 it remained 'essential to education that religion pervade the whole teaching of the school' and 'the main direction of education should be left in the care of those who would ... handle. it from a care for the immortal souls of the children' (348, 92). Under the new pupil–teacher scheme pupils would be apprenticed for five years from the age of thirteen, serving under their teacher and receiving a State grant to train before being examined by educational inspectors. In Anglican schools the managers 'must certify that the moral character of the candidates, and of their families justify an expectation that the instruction and training of the school will be seconded by their own efforts and by the example of their parents' (332, 92). Kay-Shuttleworth correctly calculated that the limited career structure of elementary school teachers would prove attractive to able children from the upper working classes who would be 'the pioneers of civilization' in passing on sound moral training. At the apex of the scheme were the teacher training colleges, also State-supported. Scholarships were available for successful pupil-teachers and as 'certificated' they could return to their schools with a modestly increased salary, the increase again funded by the State. By 1858, thirty-five State-grant training colleges were in existence, twenty-six of them Anglican and thirteen open to women.

State funding of elementary education grew rapidly. In the first year of the new training scheme it stood at £100,000. It had reached £189,000 in 1850 and proceeded apace to reach £840,000 by 1862. Despite an attempt to reassert the importance of wholly private schools,[2] the education of the lower orders was increasingly in the hands of grant-aided church schools. Horace Mann calculated that there were 2.1m. day scholars in England and Wales in 1851, a figure which had risen, according to the Newcastle commissioners, to 2.5m. by 1858. Of these, about two-thirds were aided schools, compared with two-fifths in the early 1830s. The impression that education was having an effect is strengthened by the admittedly crude literacy test provided by marriage registers. In 1840 about 33 per cent of men and 50 per cent of women made a mark in lieu of proper signature. By 1870 this proportion had dropped to 20 per cent and 27 per cent respectively.

Much work, however, remained to be done before England could call itself an educated society. The Newcastle commissioners optimistically reported that only about 120,000 English and Welsh children in the late 1850s from a total of 2.7m. in the age range three to fifteen remained beyond the contact of any school. But names on a register were no guarantee of attendance; many of the children counted were notional attenders only. Schooling continued to take second place to help in the home or casual work. Large numbers would spend only three or four years at school. In the 1860s the statistical bases of the Newcastle calculations were torn to shreds by educational inspectors like the Revd D. R. Fearon and J. G. Fitch. They indicated that a disturbing proportion of the nation's children remained without any formal education and hence outside the civilizing influences by which education-alists set primary store. Government-aided schools were attended primarily by the children of workers in secure employment. But evidence was uncovered that church schools were refusing to admit the children of casual labourers or 'roughs' on the grounds that, if they did so, skilled workers' children would be removed. As Fearon reported, those a little higher up the social ladder did not want their offspring to 'associate with the lowest classes of the town, whose habits and language are sometimes filthy, and whose bodies are almost always dirty and often diseased' (350, 55). So large gaps in the system of educational provision remained where they were most needed to be filled.

The steady rise of State expenditure on education disconcerted many, who believed that economies could be made, particularly if aided schools were submitted to uniform tests of efficiency. Hence the Revised Code, the brainchild of Robert Lowe, the Liberal Vice-President of the Privy Council Education Committee. The Code inaugurated in 1862 a system of payment by results. A full grant was available only for a child in regular attendance who could satisfy inspectors of his or her competence in basic literary and numerical tests [C.iv]. Its effect was immediate, both in stimulating attendance and in narrowing the curriculum. 'Fringe' subjects such as history, geography or music which many of the better elementary schools had introduced, often under the initiative of Kay-Shuttleworth in the 1840s, were either downgraded or eliminated since, in practical terms, they no longer paid. The Revised Code established a set of confining measurements by which teachers could be judged both by inspectors and by school managers. Managers not infrequently set pay-levels on the basis of the results. An age equally philistine in its treatment of mass education now calls such measures 'performance indicators', and deems them an integral part of what is described with no sense of either irony or oxymoron an 'academic audit'.

Kay-Shuttleworth reacted with fury that 'his' pupil-teachers should be accused of being 'too highly instructed' and to notions that 'the semi-barbarism of children from coarse sensual homes' could be civilized by crude penny-pinching 'utterly inconsistent with all preceding national policy'. Lowe responded that

> a great many of these schools are receiving under the present system a great deal more than they are entitled to. . . . It must never be forgotten that those for whom this system is designed are the children of persons who are not able to pay for the teaching. We do not profess to give these children an education that will raise them above their station and business in life.' (332, *96–100*)

As so often in mid-Victorian Britain, economy won. The belt was tightened; tax-paying pipers were presumed to demand an educational tune played in unison across a single octave; the State grant declined to £600,000 by 1866. But the Revised Code had some merit. While it encouraged unimaginative mediocrity in teaching and learning it did at least penalize that active inefficiency which too many church schools, operating under well-intentioned but clueless clerical direction, had fostered. It also imposed unashamedly secular standards. It no longer paid a teacher to have his pupils memorize such Old Testament arcana as the weight of Goliath's spear or the dimensions of Solomon's temple.

In educational terms, by the nineteenth century if in few others, Scotland remained a separate land. The pride of the distinct Scottish educational system had been the 'parochial' schools which became a compulsory feature of every parish after legislation passed by the Scottish Parliament in 1696, eleven years before the Act of Union. Eighteenth-century Scots had been undeniably better educated than their English counterparts by salaried dominies in every parish. Facilities for secondary education in established burgh schools (concentrating on the classics) and the newer academies (with a more modern curriculum) were generally superior and certainly reached much further down the social scale than in England and Wales. The Industrial Revolution brought the nations closer together, however, since nineteenth-century Glasgow or Paisley could no more cope with a huge population increase and high population density than could Manchester or Bolton. Ever more children slipped through the net as inadequate private dame schools and the like sprang up to try to meet the need. An Act of 1838 to encourage the building of 'parliamentary' schools had only limited success. The Argyll Commission, established to consider the state of education in Scotland, reported in 1867 that there was much inadequacy, especially in the larger towns.

The educational history of Scotland, at least in its lower levels, closely accords with that of England in this period. Scotland, too, had an education inspectorate, a teacher-training programme, even its own Revised Code. Only the residual strength of the parochial system kept it ahead. Scotland's literacy levels remained higher as late as 1870, though the differential had dramatically narrowed since the beginning of the century, and her access to secondary and higher education remained significantly superior. About 16 per cent of Scottish university students in the mid-1860s were from skilled working families while similar avenues in England were all but closed. Though the more strident claims for overwhelming educational superiority can be discounted by the early industrial period, important areas of Scottish predominance remained in 1870.

IV

Education was such a contentious political issue because of its religious dimension. Middle-class nonconformists, whose direct interest in the educational welfare of the lower orders was limited, nevertheless concentrated on education because they felt that Anglican influence there enabled them to exercise an anachronistic control. Dissenters also objected that their taxes helped to sustain Anglican schools through the grant system. Their response to the problem, however, was a deeply divided one. One school of thought, led with immense energy by Edward Baines of the *Leeds Mercury,* opposed any form of State involvement with education and professed to believe that voluntary action would suffice. Baines adopted the classical liberal position that 'it is not the duty or province of the Government to train the mind of the people'. He told Kay-Shuttleworth as late as 1867: 'I confess to a strong distrust of government action [and] a passionate love for voluntary action and self-reliance'.[3] Voluntarists argued that an Established Church deprived of State aid would wither, producing that religious equality which they craved.

Those dissenters who opposed Baines, led from Manchester by Cobden, took a severely practical view. Armed with statistics collected by Manchester and other Statistical Societies, they had proved by 1860 that voluntarism did not work. Success for Baines, though it would undoubtedly harm the Church, would deprive the most needy of any access to education and the means of civilization. The only solution was State provision of non-sectarian education. By 1867, even Baines was forced to recant in the face of the evident failures of voluntarism. The National Education League, founded in Birmingham by George Dixon and other prominent Midlands dissenters, including the young Joseph Chamberlain, whose first political campaign this was, urged 'for every child, free, compulsory, undenominational, but not a Godless education'. The League attracted many anti-Anglican radicals, many of whom wished to disestablish the Church completely, but its primary concern was with the education of the nation. Baines's voluntarism had put the ecclesiastical cart before the educational horse.

The National Education League posed a severe dilemma for the Liberal party after 1868. Forster's Education Act of 1870 [C.iv] was as much a political as an educational response. Few Liberal MPs supported State control of education. They continued to support *laissez-faire*, not centralism, and they anyway pointed to the apparently impressive achievements brought about by a generation of State aid to private ecclesiastical bodies. Most Liberal MPs were also, like their leader, staunch Anglicans (Ch. 34). It is hardly surprising, therefore, that Forster's strategy was to fill the gaps rather than create an entirely new secular, centralizing structure as demanded by the League. Elementary education was made neither compulsory nor free by the 1870 legislation, and Forster's main concessions to League pressure concerned the way the new board schools would be established and controlled. Specifically, board schools could not purvey characteristically religious, denominational education. The Church of England, however, continued to receive State aid to which dissenters' taxes contributed. The Education Act was an important watershed, in that it gave State recognition to the important principle that schools should be provided in sufficient convenient locations so that no one should lack an education for want of places. It also clearly put eventual compulsion to school attendance firmly on the short-term political agenda. But it was as much conservative as innovative. As Lowe and other leading educational experts wanted, it sustained an infrastructure designed to keep the lower orders in their place and the Church of England at the centre of educational affairs. Education in 1870, and for many years thereafter, still confirmed and even helped to define distinctions of status. Students and intellectuals have a vested interest in the transforming vitality of education. It is perhaps salutary to reflect that the history of education in modern Britain suggests how frequently it confirms rather than transforms.

---

1. W. L. Burn, *The Age of Equipoise* (1964), p. 197.
2. E. G. West, *Education and the Industrial Revolution* (1975).
3. E. Baines, *Letters to Lord John Russell on State Education* (1847), p. 10; Leeds City Archives, Baines Papers, 52/11, Baines to Kay-Shuttleworth, 19 October 1867.

CHAPTER 37

'An assembly of gentlemen': Party politics, 1846–1859

I

The Conservative split on the Corn Law question was attended with exceptional bitterness, sometimes even within families. The protectionist duke of Newcastle used all his formidable electoral influence to block the re-election of his Peelite eldest son, the earl of Lincoln, as Member for South Nottinghamshire at a by-election in February 1846. Lincoln, unopposed at every previous election since the Reform Act, had to scuttle north to win a very close contest at Falkirk and remain in Peel's government during its closing months. Father and son did not speak to one another again until the duke lay on his deathbed in 1851. Similarly, prompt reconciliation between Peelites and Protectionists in Parliament proved impossible, hard though Stanley, who assumed the leadership of the latter as one of the very few with ministerial experience, tried. The Peelites (or Liberal Conservatives as they were sometimes known) and Conservatives acted as separate units and party politics, which had seemed so ordered in the late 1830s and early 1840s, lapsed into confusion.

Between 1846 and 1859, the steady work of grass-roots party organization continued and local issues still generated fervent two-party debate (Ch. 33). Likewise at Westminster, party loyalty among backbenchers remained remarkably strong, proof against disintegration and faction. Disputes among the leaders, however, created a climate of prolonged political instability. Palmerston for example, the dominant Whig–Liberal statesman of the 1850s and 1860s, was approached by Derby (as Stanley had become on succeeding to the earldom in 1851) to join a Conservative government in 1852 and by Disraeli to lead one in 1859. Gladstone, at once the most prized and the most fastidious of the Peelites, was subjected to almost constant overtures in the 1850s either to join an administration, or to remain in one when his mighty conscience was affronted by a colleague's actions, or to stand aloof from a government in the expectation that, without him, it would speedily fall to be replaced by one in which his influence would be greater. Russell's government, which followed Peel's, lasted almost six years [A], but was sustained in office by insufferably superior Peelites fearful of letting protectionists back in and its major achievement was its longevity. None of the four administrations between 1852 and 1859 lasted more than three years and none controlled the Commons exclusively from its own supporters. The Lower House became in the 1850s the arbiter of political fates as it had not been since 1815 and never would be again.

The struggles for power at Westminster were waged by a restricted group of landowners, utterly unrepresentative of the teeming world outside. Britain was ruled, if not by a completely closed, then certainly by a charmed, political circle. The economic well-being of the nation from the later 1840s onwards took the sting out of most domestic political issues. In consequence, politicians were little troubled by clamour from the unenfranchised whose rude aggression had discomfited so many administrations between 1815 and 1846. The decisions of that minority of the population with votes were also relatively unimportant since no government was turned out solely by a general election in this period. Politicians in the 1850s enjoyed the luxury of determining events from Westminster and, despite the recent rifts, this situation encouraged cosy courtesies amid the struggles for office. As Palmerston told the Whigs in 1852, in welcoming the Derby government's public declaration that it would not seek to reimpose protection, 'we are here an assembly of gentlemen and we who are gentlemen on this side of the House should remember that we are dealing with gentlemen on the other side'.[1]

II

The Corn Law crisis created three broad political groupings where previously there had been two, but Peel declared to Sir Henry Hardinge in September 1846, 'I intend to keep aloof from party combinations.' (84, *226*) During the four remaining years of his life he kept to this resolution, preferring the mantle of Olympian greatness which the newspapers and public soon cast over him. While he lived, the ninety or so Peelites would not desert the flag though some, notably Gladstone, were anxious after the 1847 Election [B.vi] for a more central role. Lincoln, Herbert and Graham, among the leading Peelites, had no qualms about refusing office in Russell's Liberal government, while Peel himself gave advice to the Chancellor of the Exchequer, lent his weight on big issues such as the ending of the Navigation Laws in 1849 (Ch. 31) and discussed statecraft with young Prince Albert, probably the ablest member of the royal family in modern times and well worth Peel's superior attentions.

Peel's Indian summer had unsettling consequences. Russell inevitably operated in his predecessor's shadow and the most significant of his government's domestic measures, the increased education grant in 1847 (Ch. 36) and the Public Health Act [C.ii] (Ch. 32), hardly conduced to party unity. Indeed, to talk even of three-party politics after 1846 is an oversimplification. The Liberal radicals owed the new government little allegiance and stated openly in 1848 that they did not consider themselves bound to support it. Russell's Cabinet had twenty-one members, twelve of whom were the sons of aristocrats and five more of whom were inherited baronets (117). No attempt was made to integrate middle-class support at the highest levels. This government was a typical Whig confection of interrelated great families. One of its less successful members, in the exposed position of Chancellor of the Exchequer, was Charles Wood, who owed office primarily to the fact that he was Russell's brother-in-law. Cobden complained in 1857, when Palmerston's government was similarly composed: 'Half a dozen great families meet at Walmer and dispose of the rank and file of the party.' (124, *273*) Not that the radicals themselves were in any way cohesive. Fielden's Ten Hours Act in 1847 [C.i] (Ch.

26) divided 'humanitarian' radicals from 'Manchester school' radicals like Cobden and Bright. Bright was described by factory reformers as a 'heartless Quaker' and a man of 'bile and bad feeling'. They were split also on most foreign policy questions. Cobden and Bright opposed the Crimean War (Ch. 38) as both immoral in itself and bad for trade; Roebuck wanted it prosecuted still more vigorously.

The Conservatives were demoralized by losing nearly all their natural leaders to the Peelites in 1846 and anyway soon divided on issues. From 1849 onwards, Disraeli was urging the abandonment of protection, their great cause, as a certain and continuous vote loser. Not surprisingly, he became an object of lingering distrust and suspicion to his own backbenchers on this as on other issues. Between 1849 and 1852, despite Disraeli's pleas, protectionism enjoyed something of a revival as arable prices tumbled and farmers believed that they were about to experience the disastrous consequences of repeal. Stanley exercised his languid intelligence as party leader almost equally from Newmarket racecourse and from the House of Lords, though with a marked emotional preference for the sport of kings over the sport of politics. This is not to say, however, that Stanley lacked political ambition. His leadership aimed at preserving Tory unity while the diverse range of interests which currently supported Russell fell apart, leaving him to pick up the pieces. Bentinck had been forced out of the leadership of the party in the Commons in 1847 when he voted in favour of admitting practising Jews to Parliament; a year later he died of a heart attack. Granby, the backbenchers' choice as successor, lasted less than a month before throwing in his hand and no leadership was exercised at all for a time until Disraeli was accepted *faute de mieux*. Disraeli, of course, had voted with Bentinck on the Jewish question, but such was the Tories' paucity of talent that he was the only man in the Commons who could string together half a dozen coherent sentences on fiscal policy to answer Chancellor Wood, let alone Chancellor-in-waiting Gladstone.

Opposition also cramped the Peelites' distinctive style. They were trained for executive office and, deprived of it, they lacked purpose. Free to vote according to their consciences, they showed themselves between 1846 and 1852 no more united than the rest. They split almost equally on the Factory Act; they divided about two to one against Jewish emancipation. More centrally, they split on a fundamental economic question in 1849 when Goulburn, Herbert, Gladstone and about two-thirds of the remaining Peelites voted against Russell's proposal to reduce colonial preference on West Indian sugar, while Peel and Graham supported the government. Numerically, the Peelites were soon a declining force. Almost twenty rank-and-file Peelites had moved back to the Tories before their leader's death and numbers continued to dwindle during the 1850s [B.vi]. The Whig MP George Cornewall Lewis accurately observed in 1849 that 'the Peelites were not only small in numbers but disunited among themselves' (132, 56).

III

Though Russell's party was in no worse case than its opponents its good fortune could not indefinitely run ahead of its manifest mediocrity. Wood's budgets were generally incompetent and that of 1851 was mercilessly exposed by Gladstone. Ironically, however, the government's collapse owed most to one of its abler members, Lord Palmerston. Palmerston had been running the government's foreign policy in an aggressively independent way. In 1850 he had scored a major propaganda triumph both in the Commons and in the country when he used the dubious claims against the Greek government of one Don Pacifico, a disreputable Portuguese-Jewish trader who claimed British citizenship, to assert British power of independent action, not only against Greece but against the European autocracies (Ch. 38). It was the beginning of Palmerston's extraordinary hold over a generally chauvinistic public opinion and it boded ill for Russell. The triumph was Palmerston's, not the government's. Russell's irritation against an able, insubordinate colleague was increased by the knowledge that Palmerstonian foreign policy alienated leading Peelites, who disliked both threats of aggression and the populist methods by which they were advanced. By the time that Palmerston's effrontery in underwriting Louis Napoleon's assumption of power in France without bothering to inform the Cabinet made his dismissal unavoidable in December 1851, Russell was already in deep trouble. He had promoted the anti-Catholic Ecclesiastical Titles bill [G.i] (Ch. 34) against the better judgement of many Whigs and most Peelites, whose support for religious liberty was probably second only to their commitment to free trade. Deprived of Peelite support at last, Russell's government lasted only the couple of months it took for Palmerston to arrange his 'tit-for-tat with Johnny Russell' – parliamentary defeat on a Militia bill.

Derby's attempts to persuade the Peelites to a reconciliation in government foundered in the fashion that Disraeli had predicted the year before. 'Every public man of experience and influence, however slight, has declined to act unless the principle of Protection were unequivocally renounced.' (124, *305*) Derby, therefore, accepted the Queen's commission to form a government by nominating one of the least-experienced administrations in history. Only three of its members, Derby himself, Lonsdale and Herries, had held office before [A]. Disraeli became both Chancellor of the Exchequer and Leader of the House. Well might that deaf, but redoubtable, octogenarian, the duke of Wellington, with more than sixteen years high office behind him, bellow 'Who? Who?' as Derby read him the list of names in the Lords seven months before his death.

Derby's 'Who? Who?' administration only just outlived the duke. An election in the summer of 1852 enabled the Conservatives to capitalize on anti-Catholic prejudice in the wake of the Ecclesiastical Titles Act (B .vi]. The Peelite Edward Cardwell was beaten by 'Protestant' Tories in Liverpool, for example, but Derby was some way short of an overall majority. In the circumstances it was important not to offend the Peelites, but Disraeli's budget offended spectacularly. He did not budget for a government surplus and he sought to differentiate between earned and unearned income in the rate at which income tax was levied. These were the cardinal errors in the Peelite canon and Gladstone, the most Conservative-inclined Peelite, nevertheless delivered himself of the most ferocious speech of his career in denouncing it as 'the most subversive in its tendencies and ultimate effects that I have ever known'. Gladstone's language now seems ludicrous. In December 1852 it carried immense weight, and earned him the undying hostility of the Tory backbenchers since it led directly to the rejection of the budget and the fall of the government. However anguished Gladstone's eventual decision not to rejoin the Conservative party, it was by no means certain after 1852 that, despite Derby's sporadic entreaties, he would have been an acceptable colleague.

After Derby's resignation, the only configuration which offered any prospect of secure government was a coalition between Liberals and Peelites and, in the week before Christmas, Aberdeen put one together. The fact that the Peelites, with only about forty MPs, could claim half the places in the coalition, including the prime ministership, calls for some comment. As ever, the Peelites in 1852 had a practical value, as experienced men of affairs, out of all proportion to their size. Their impressive record of achievement between 1841 and 1846 contrasted sharply with the inefficiencies that had followed. They were needed and they knew their price. Aberdeen's acceptability as Prime Minister is similarly explicable. Russell's stock had slumped since 1850 and his obvious rival, Palmerston, was both offensive to the Queen and the object of Peelite suspicion. The Whigs could present no remotely comparable senior alternative to these two and they could see no grave objections to serving under the senior Peelite. Aberdeen, at sixty-nine, was eight years older than Graham, twenty-five years older than Gladstone and had, in fact, been born four years before Peel himself. Though Russell carped and was to prove a disruptively prickly influence throughout the coalition's life (133), decisions on posts were reached with remarkable expedition, particularly once Palmerston agreed to accept a senior post which kept him safely away from foreign affairs [A].

The long-term importance of this coalition is considerable. It showed the Peelites that cohabitation with the Whigs was not entirely distasteful. They found what Newcastle called 'Whig Oligarchical Cliquery' stifling and it could cut across their drive towards administrative reform (Ch. 32), but few Peelites were strangers to silver spoons. The landed backgrounds, for example, of Graham, Herbert (son of the earl of Pembroke) and Newcastle himself were impeccable. The Whigs were also historically linked to the traditions of liberal Conservatism. Men like Palmerston and the much-respected Lansdowne would not be swayed by democratic excess but they saw the value of reform in order to conserve.

On a deeper level, too, this coalition was the natural development. Despite the gadfly presence of Disraeli (itself a sufficient deterrent for some) it is difficult to avoid characterizing Derby's Conservatives in the 1850s as the party of narrow, landed reaction. Important sections of it still resented the loss of protection and it defended its beloved Church of England with the intolerant fervour of one who knows that the tide is running strongly against it and clings desperately to the securest rock. Above all it remained overwhelmingly the party of the land. By 1865 about one-third of Liberal MPs were businessmen, bankers, lawyers and other professionals. Though relatively few of these became ministers of the Crown, their presence testified to the importance of the middle class as a whole to the fortunes of Liberalism. By contrast, landowners outnumbered businessmen by almost five to one in the Conservative party and many backbenchers seemed to have opted for permanent, if watchful, opposition. Despite their Tory origins, this was no party for a group of achievers, and the Peelites were 'do-ers' or they were nothing. The formation of the Aberdeen coalition presaged Peelite fusion with the Liberal party in 1859. No Peelite who took office in the coalition would ever rejoin the Conservatives.

The coalition put in train some useful administrative reforms in 1853 and 1854 and its early success was consolidated by Gladstone's first budget in 1853. This held out the prospect of permanently pegged public expenditure and, by 1860, the total abolition of the income tax. Little of this extraordinary fiscal and intellectual edifice survived an unforeseen war (Ch. 37), but its immediate impact was immense. Some erstwhile Conservatives switched their allegiance to the coalition in recognition of its apparent ability to provide secure, able government and promote prosperity. Disraeli, fretful at losing office and anxious to make a speedy return, was reduced to flirting with Irish Catholics and Manchester school radicals for which he was firmly rapped over the knuckles by Derby. The evident tactical disagreement between the two leading Tories only strengthened Aberdeen's hand.

The collapse of a promising administration owed a little to *prima donna* antics both of Russell and Palmerston as they jockeyed for position and much to the Crimean War which the government was powerless to prevent and proved incompetent to wage. 'Peelism' depended crucially upon peace and retrenchment to provide appropriate conditions for worthwhile administrative reform, and Aberdeen tried to resign as soon as it was clear that he could not avert hostilities. The end came in February 1855 when the patriotic radical J. A. Roebuck, long a supporter of Palmerston's foreign policies, carried a resolution calling for an enquiry into the conduct of the war. Derby tried, though hardly as if his life depended upon it, to forge a Conservative-dominated coalition. Disraeli moaned about his chief yet again. Palmerston was absolved of any direct responsibility for the war and remained secure in the knowledge that public opinion held that if he had been in charge war would have been prevented by a more threatening posture. It believed further that, like the elder Pitt, he alone could remedy the situation. Palmerston refused to serve under Derby. He knew that the Queen would have to swallow her pride and turn to him, though in the event she did so only after not only Derby but Lansdowne, Clarendon and even the discredited Russell had failed to form a government.

IV

Few politicians inspired such dislike in their colleagues as Palmerston. His evident ambition was criticized, his non-gentlemanly foreign policy appalled many, but his greatest fault in their eyes was that he did not play the political game by the established rules. His constituency was not this party grouping or that, but public opinion. He was the first major political figure who learned the value of taking his case to the people. For this he was bitterly attacked by those who believed that his extra-parliamentary appeals involved histrionic exaggeration if not outright duplicity. Bright, who had already felt the force of Palmerston's populist appeal during the Prime Minister's influential visit to Manchester in 1856 (88), called him an 'aged charlatan' with 'unscrupulous ambition'. Disraeli wrote to a friend that he was 'really an imposter, utterly exhausted . . . and now an old painted Pantaloon . . .

[but] he is a name which the country resolves to associate with energy, wisdom, and eloquence' (124, *363*). A marked novelty of Palmerston's politics was his ability to appeal to political opponents. The patriotic card was played to telling effect in gaining support both from the Tories on the right and from the imperialistic, patriotic element in radicalism on the left. Such "poaching" was resented by colleagues at Westminster.

His 1855–58 government began as a reincarnation of the Aberdeen coalition, minus only the old Prime Minister, his Secretary for War, Newcastle, and Russell, whose manoeuvres at the end of the coalition had met with universal condemnation. When Palmerston bowed to parliamentary pressure to continue with Roebuck's enquiry, however, all the Peelites except Argyll resigned after a fortnight believing, in Gladstone's words, that 'we had a right to believe that Parlt. wd. not inflict this Committee on a Govt. which had its confidence.'[2] Palmerston was able to sustain a pure Liberal government thereafter mainly because the Crimean War turned in Britain's favour, and no domestic issue remotely rivalled its importance. As the new Chancellor, Cornewall Lewis, said in August 1855, 'Our domestic politics are entirely dependent on the events of the siege [of Sebastopol].' (138, *46*) Palmerston also exploited the weaknesses of a divided opposition, by no means all of which wanted to turn him out. By April 1856 Sir James Graham was observing a much greater fragmentation than in the days of Aberdeen. 'There is not one man in the House of Commons who has ten followers. ... The Government goes on because there is no organized opposition prepared and able to take its place, and the Government receives a sufficiency of independent support, because all feel that the business of the country must be carried on.'[3]

The ace in Palmerston's pack was electoral appeal and in 1857 he used it when his government, increasingly riven by internal disputes, was defeated on a censure motion by Cobden after Canton had been bombarded in retaliation for the arrest of the Chinese crew of a British ship, *Arrow*, which had been trading illegally in that port. The 1857 Election became a virtual plebiscite on Palmerston and Liberal strength increased markedly [B.vi]. The Tories lost twenty-three county seats at a time of agricultural prosperity in the first election for twenty years at which Protection had not been the central rural issue. Manchester school radicals learned the hard way that Anti-Corn Law League unity among the middle classes was a thing of the past. Most merchants and manufacturers in the North were strong Palmerstonians. They saw commercial advantage in 'gunboat diplomacy' provided it was successful, and under Palmerston it usually was. Cobden lost at Huddersfield to a Palmerston Liberal, while in Manchester itself Bright and Milner-Gibson were beaten by the wealthy Liberal industrialists Sir John Potter and J. A. Turner in a ding-dong struggle between the radical-pacifist Liberalism of the Leaguers and the aggressive and increasingly plutocratic Liberalism of the town's wealthier citizens (89).

The election, however, did not significantly improve the Prime Minister's standing in the Commons. Whig infighting, Peelite disquiet and Tory opposition all had to be faced and, such being the way of nineteenth-century political organization, by-elections brought Bright and Milner-Gibson back to Westminster within months, Bright to begin his long electoral association with Birmingham. It was Milner-Gibson who engineered Palmerston's defeat over a storm in a teacup, brewed when the Prime Minister, judging it expedient to placate the French, introduced a Conspiracy to Murder bill in 1858 when a plot by the Italian republican Felice Orsini to murder Napoleon III was discovered to have had its origins in England. Milner-Gibson, adopting, as Palmerston sardonically noted, the incongruously cynical posture of 'vindicator of the rights of this country against foreign nations', was joined by an ill-assorted but potent mixture of Disraelite Tories (Derby had advised against the attempt), Peelites, Russellite Liberals (Russell had been out of office since a diplomatic blunder in July 1855) and Manchester school radicals. Palmerston went down by nineteen votes.

Derby's second minority Conservative government [A] lasted six months longer than his first. It was not barren of achievement. It removed the property qualification for MPs (the first of the six Chartist points to be achieved), finally won the long battle to admit Jews into Parliament, and ended the East India Company's direct interest in the government of India (Ch. 38). Yet it had, if anything, a less secure parliamentary basis than the administration of 1852. Another General Election recovered some of the English ground (mostly in the smaller boroughs) lost to the surge of Palmerstonian enthusiasm two years earlier, but it did not dent the overwhelming anti-Tory vote in Scotland, Wales and Ireland and it left Derby about thirty seats short of a majority.

Paradoxically, the main effect of the Conservative government was to bring the anti-Tory elements closer together in a search for stability. Russell and Palmerston, though they disliked one another disliked opposition even more, and knew that their protracted feud was harming the Whig cause. The radicals were insufficiently numerous to be other than an irritant and appreciated that their influence was most effectively deployed within a governing Liberal group. Nearly all the Peelites had been convinced that a fusion with the Liberals was the only realistic long-term solution since 1852 and by 1859 they were anxious to bank their wasting assets in a secure government. Gladstone, the least Liberal-inclined of the Peelites, now had cogent reasons for letting his executive head rule his Tory heart. In the matter of Italian nationalism (Ch. 38) he at last found an important issue on which he could agree with Palmerston. He also saw the party of his youth waiting to drop, like ripe fruit, into the palm of Disraeli, a man for whom he felt (as he was later to put it) 'a strong sentiment of revulsion'. A self-interested calculation would also have told him that, whereas he would have to fight the now deeply entrenched Disraeli (only five years his senior) for the Tory succession on Derby's retirement, both Palmerston and Russell on the other side were nearing the end of their careers with no obvious Liberal successor in sight. In these circumstances the advice of John Bright that any course other than junction with the Liberals would blight the career of the ablest politician of his generation must have been compelling.

Under genial chivvying by Herbert the anti-Tory coalition was put together at Willis's Rooms in June 1859, and though the meeting hardly deserves to be described as the true foundation of the Liberal party, as some have suggested, it did end the confusion of parties. Less than a week after the meeting, the new grouping carried by thirteen votes a motion of no confidence in the Derby administration and, as agreed, Palmerston led the Liberal government which took its place, despite the Queen's preference for Granville. Gladstone voted with Derby but agreed readily enough to serve as Chancellor under Palmerston when the inevitable call came. This unlikely combination solidified the new administration and gave it greater authority than any since the resignation of Peel.

1. J. Ridley, *Lord Palmerston* (1970), p. 545.
2. M. R. D. Foot and H. C. G. Matthews, eds, *The Gladstone Diaries* (in progress, 1968–).
3. *Greville Memoirs* (8 vols, 1888), viii, p. 41.

CHAPTER 38

Palmerston and the *pax Britannica*

I

Soon after Derby's brief government of 1852 was formed Palmerston offered a few tips to the incoming Foreign Secretary, the earl of Malmesbury. He adumbrated certain basic principles, such as both the need for, and the perpetual difficulty of obtaining, good relations with France, but referred most particularly to the 'power of prestige England possesses abroad' and to a Foreign Secretary's overriding duty to ensure its safe continuance.[1] In the confident years after 1815 Britain's world-wide influence, buttressed by its navy and commercial supremacy, had been acknowledged on every side (Ch. 22). In the 1850s and 1860s, however, just as the domestic tranquillity which accompanies prosperity was achieved, the first significant blows to Britain's 'power of prestige' were struck. Britain, the self-assured Palmerston included, reacted too slowly to shifts in the balance of forces in Europe after 1848 and found its power to influence Continental affairs substantially reduced. In the wider world, though Britain's trading primacy remained universally recognized, perplexing questions of commercial influence and colonial domination presented themselves. Increased defence commitments were required. According to the classical canons of Gladstonian Liberalism (Chs. 37 and 39), economic *laissez-faire* implied minimal government interference and the lowest taxes possible. Yet in 1869, the first full year of Gladstone's prime ministership, Britain spent £27m. on its army and navy, virtually twice as much as when Palmerston gave his advice to Malmesbury [D.i.2]. Britain's world role did not come on the cheap and Gladstone would never realize his dearest ambition, to abolish the income tax.

Fear of Russia preoccupied British statesmen until the end of the 1850s. Attention still concentrated on the Black Sea and on the slow subsidence of the Turkish Empire from which, it was believed, Russia alone would gain, with consequent hazard to British strategic and commercial interests (Ch. 22). The area was increasingly important because British trade with the Turks increased eightfold in the 1830s and 1840s. Contrary to the belief of many politicians, stridently embellished in the British Press, Tsar Nicholas I had no immediate plans to dismember the Turkish Empire, though its continued decline hardly displeased him. Nicholas had discussed, with Aberdeen in 1844 and with the British Ambassador, Sir George Seymour, in 1853, the possibility of concerted Anglo-Russian action in case of Turkey's collapse. Nicholas wanted to avoid conflict with Britain and would greatly have preferred to capitalize on the long-standing mutual suspicions of Britain and France to forge a firm Anglo-Russian alliance.

Yet events and misunderstandings in South-east Europe pulled the powers in precisely the opposite direction. Britain stiffened Turkish resolve between 1849 and 1852 against pressure from Russia and Austria for the extradition of Polish and Hungarian refugees of the 1848 revolutions and against Russian demands for protection of Orthodox Christians within the Turkish Empire. In 1853 Russia sent Prince Menshikov to Constantinople to press this case. The British envoy, Lord Stratford de Redcliffe, combined an extensive knowledge of Turkey with an implacable hostility to Russia. During complicated negotiations in 1853 Menshikov's brusque demands of Turkey and Stratford's conviction that Russia's concern for Turkish Christians was a cover for territorial aggrandizement soured relations further. Russian occupation of Moldavia and Wallachia in July seemed to confirm Stratford's view. The Aberdeen coalition was split on foreign affairs. Palmerston and Russell combined (for once) to convert Clarendon to a bellicose posture while Aberdeen and Graham were the leading pacifiers (101). By September Clarendon felt justified in breaching the 1841 Straits agreement [F.i.24] by sending warships through the Dardanelles to counterbalance Russian power. He stated that 'the claims put forward by Russia are ... irreconcilable with the assurance that no extended power or influence is sought in Turkey' (157, *152*). After the declaration of war by Turkey on Russia in October and the destruction of the Turkish fleet by the Russian navy at Sinope the following month, Russophobia reached new peaks of intensity in Britain. An Anglo-French alliance was hastily concluded [F.i.28] and the Crimean War began in March 1854.

Palmerston was sure that war should have been avoided. As he wrote to a friend just before it began, 'My belief is ... that if the measures now tardily resolved upon had been taken when I first recommended them six or eight months ago, much of the present difficulty would have been avoided.'[2] Self-justification was never Palmerston's weakest point but an earlier show of resolve might indeed have deterred Nicholas, who continued to labour under the misapprehension that Britain and France would not combine against him. He never understood the importance either of Cabinet government or of public opinion in moulding events in Britain. Aberdeen, whose pacific intentions were clear, could not overbear the increasingly ferocious public mood or the strength of feeling inside the government simply because he was Prime Minister. The desire for war was real. Public opinion increasingly viewed Russia as an intolerant, boorish and aggressive nation ruled by a brutal despot whose evil designs must be thwarted. The mood of expansive British self-confidence, fostered during the Great Exhibition (Ch. 31), had its unpleasantly chauvinistic side. A wealthy nation which had seen no serious hostilities for almost forty years was now tempted to impose its civilized will on lesser nations. As all nations, on this view, were 'lesser' – in wealth, in naval might and in political maturity – Britain claimed not only the right but the duty to intervene for the greater good of all. Now that the territorial integrity of Turkey, a traditional friend, was threatened the *pax Britannica* demanded that she be aided.

The events of the Crimean War [F.ii.5] revealed horrifying unpreparedness and blunders to a British public schooled to anticipate infallibility. Modern communications helped to bring home for the first time the wholly unglamorous and pitiable aspects of war. The pioneer war despatches of William Howard Russell in *The Times* were especially illuminating, not least because the government was not prescient enough to censor them. 'News management' (a weasel phrase designed to gloss the crude fact of misleading reportage) was to be a central feature of all future wars (158, *104*). The Crimean battles, as the rash of Sebastopol Terraces and Inkerman Streets in mid-Victorian towns testify, captured the imagination, none more so than the amazingly courageous charge of Lord Cardigan's Light Brigade against the main artillery of the Russian Army at Balaclava. This resulted from Cardigan's misunderstanding of his commanding officer, Raglan's, order for a far less valiant but considerably more valuable action to stop British guns, captured by the Russians from the Turks earlier in the day, being carried away during a retreat. The charge was indicative of the legendary discipline of the British Army but also of the lack of tactical grasp which beset the joint Anglo-French campaign. The war, designed to teach the Russians a sharp lesson in a limited theatre of war, dragged on for two years until an isolated Russia, under a new tsar, Alexander II, conceded the main points in dispute at the Treaty of Paris [F.i.30]. Clarendon believed it 'a sufficiently good peace . . . having placed England in a very fine position'.[3] At the least, it provided a valuable breathing space until the inexorable decline of Turkey forced the Balkans back to the centre of the European stage in the mid-1870s.

Britain's Crimean difficulties were compounded by a generation of military neglect. In 1854 the British Army totalled about 135,000 men of whom 70,000 were serving in India and the other colonies. It was notably deficient in trained staff and supply services. The exigencies of war produced a new training programme and the government after 1854 channelled its war strategy through a reorganized War Department which took over functions previously exercised with little co-ordination by various ministries. In the agitation for change public opinion, shocked by the privations of the British soldiery, racked by cholera and dysentery during the winter of 1854–55, again had a part to play. After the Crimean War the army did not play second fiddle to the navy; Palmerston's peace-time government in the early 1860s maintained an army of about 215,000 men.

II

The perceptible decline of British influence in Europe is closely bound up with emergent nationalism. European nationalism exercised powerful contrary appeals which Britain could not reconcile. On the emotional level, nations 'struggling to be free' from the shackles of autocracy plucked at a responsive chord in a land which had not been autocratic for 200 years and whose pre-eminence in the concerts of Europe its people were inclined to attribute, at least in part, to its liberal constitution. The claims of Italy to nationhood evinced a particularly powerful response among those whose education and cultural reference were grounded in classical civilization. Since this group included virtually all the nation's leaders (Ch. 36) it could hardly be ignored. Russell and Gladstone were strongly pro-Italian in the 1850s. The emotional claims of nationalism were further advanced since so many nationalists, from Mazzini in the 1830s onwards, made

Britain their place of refuge after failure or while they planned their next attempts. Since autocrats, like Austria's Foreign Minister Prince Metternich, dispossessed after the 1848 revolution fled similarly to Britain this was hardly decisive, but British public opinion assailed by strident opinion in different European accents in the 1850s emerged as strongly pro-nationalist.

On the level of pragmatic political response, from which Palmerston never strayed far, the position was much more opaque. Nationalism was a profoundly destabilizing force and Britain's concerns in Europe were bound up with the stability of contending forces. In 1848, also, as Palmerston clearly saw, the struggle could be characterized as one 'between those who have no property and those who have and wish to keep it'. In any such struggle the British ruling classes had to think very hard before supporting nationalism. The whole problem was symbolized by the difficulties of Austria. Austria, Palmerston reminded the Commons in 1849, 'is a most important element in the balance of European power'. The Habsburg Empire was Britain's security against Russian expansionism in South and central Europe. Nationalist risings affected her dominions in both Hungary and Italy. Palmerston's response is typical. He believed that Austria was wasting its substance in Italy in an 'exertion of military effort' which left her 'less able to maintain her interests elsewhere' (167, *199*). In 1859 he put the matter more bluntly: 'The Austrians have no business in Italy, and they are a public nuisance there.'[4] Austria should concentrate its flagging energies in central Europe since Hungarian independence, unlike Italian, would be 'such a dismemberment of the Austrian empire as will prevent Austria from continuing to occupy the great position she has hitherto held among European powers' (157, *174*). Palmerston's very real disapprobation of Austrian atrocities in both Italy and Hungary did not prevent his working to stabilize the Austrian regime in eastern Europe while encouraging the development of a united northern Italian state powerful enough to repel predatory French advances in an area she had long considered liable to her intervention.

Events worked against that self-interested arbitration in which Palmerston specialized. When Napoleon restored Pius IX to his Roman territories in 1849 after the Pope's earlier overthrow by nationalist forces, he greatly extended French influence in Italy. Such influence Britain had traditionally believed threatened Britain's commercial domination of the Mediterranean, a threat Napoleon III was anxious to employ since his own stability depended, he felt, on score-settling with Britain after the imposed settlement of 1815 [F.i.15].

During the confused Italian Unification crisis of 1859–61 Britain's new Foreign Secretary, Russell, acting generally under Palmerston's direction but capable of initiatives of his own, found the delicate act of balancing popular nationalist aspirations with the contending ambitions of France and Austria too precarious. Both the leading Whig statesmen, 'those two dreadful old men', as Queen Victoria called them, braved royal displeasure in 1859 by not acting decisively to support Austria (and hence a Great Power in the enjoyment of its established rights) against France. By the spring of 1860, however, after France had gained both Nice and Savoy, suspicion of the traditional enemy was uppermost in both of their minds. Russell's enthusiasms outran his judgement, however, when, against Palmerston's advice, he refused joint Anglo-French action to stop Garibaldi's nationalists taking Naples. While the other Great Powers stood ready to condemn nationalist aggression, Russell issued his famous despatch of 27 October 1860 in which, without having consulted most of his Cabinet colleagues, he effectively committed Britain to a united Italy:

> A conviction has spread . . . that the only manner in which Italians could secure their independence of foreign control was by forming one strong Government for the whole of Italy. . . . Her Majesty's Government must admit that the Italians themselves are the best judges of their own interests . . . [and] will turn their eyes . . . to the gratifying prospect of a people building up the edifice of their liberties, and consolidating the work of their independence. (157, *223–5*)

Russell's emotional attachments, which included a fervently pro-Italian wife, undoubtedly aided this pronouncement. But his *coup de théâtre* had momentous international repercussions. The Great Powers saw it as an unprincipled declaration of support for revolutionaries and, therefore, a critical breach in the undertakings made in 1815 at Vienna (Ch. 22). The Prussian Prince Regent icily informed the British Prince Consort that it was tantamount to 'a declaration on the part of England, that, wheresoever there exists any dissatisfaction among a people, they have the privilege to expel their sovereign, with the assured certainty of England's sympathy'. Many noted the uncomfortable consequences of Russell's dictum being applied to India or, still worse, Ireland. Britain's increasing isolation during the 1860s owed much to the belief among the established powers that she could not be trusted to honour the most solemn obligation of all – to uphold 'the Law of Nations as hitherto recognised'.

III

British diplomacy chalked up few triumphs in the 1860s and one reverse as humiliating as any since the end of the Napoleonic Wars. Neutrality was preserved during the American Civil War, though with some difficulty since the North assumed that Britain's economic links with the South, most notably through the cotton trade, would overbear her long-established aversion to slavery. The Polish revolt against Russia in 1863 was briefly encouraged by Britain, and Palmerston suggested that an independent Poland might be established under the superintendence of Austria. British suspicions of France prevented the calling of a general Congress to settle the dispute and Russia, aided by Bismarck, the new Minister-President of Prussia, saw off the Polish threat, confident that Palmerston would, as in the 1830s (Ch. 22), offer the Poles nothing more substantial than words of encouragement and vaguely libertarian sentiments.

The contrast between words and deeds was much more dramatically displayed during the Schleswig-Holstein crisis of 1863–64. This turned on the position of three duchies, Schleswig, Holstein and Lauenberg, which had traditionally been attached to the Danish monarchy, though not to Denmark itself, so long as the royal succession remained in the male line. In 1852, the Great Powers had imposed a settlement on Denmark and Prussia [F.i.27] which satisfied neither state. When the issue was raised again in 1863 no prospect existed of joint action by Britain, France and Russia while Prussia was now much stronger and more assertive. Palmerston told the Commons that if the duchies were seized by Prussia the 'independence and integrity of the Danish monarchy' would be threatened and 'it would not be Denmark alone with which they would have to contend'.[5]

Perhaps the single most important misjudgement of Palmerston's career was his failure to anticipate Prussia's drive to dominate the North German states. Bismarck exposed Palmerston's boast when he annexed Schleswig and Holstein in 1864 amid anguished but inconsequential talk of British intervention. British embarrassment was the greater since only the previous year the Prince of Wales had married Alexandra, daughter of the King of Denmark. Family ties, however, did not prevent Victoria's clear-headed assessment that intervention was useless. The incident weakened British claims to be considered a powerful ally in European affairs. The next year von Moltke, one of the architects of Prussia's military revival, remarked contemptuously but not inaccurately to his brother that 'England is as powerless on the Continent as she is presuming'.[6]

In fact, in the five years after Palmerston's death in 1865, Britain 'presumed' less and less. She stood aside from the Austro-Prussian War and watched while Prussia completed her preparations for pan-German hegemony. Some politicians even applauded this development as the most desirable counterbalance to French pretension. The non-interventionist Edward Stanley, Foreign Secretary in his father's Conservative government of 1866–68, stated a fortnight after taking office that 'if North Germany is to become a single great Power, I do not see that any English interest is in the least degree affected' (167, *44*). It proved to be one of the most spectacular diplomatic misjudgements in history. Britain's only significant initiative was to guarantee Luxembourg's neutrality at an international conference held in London under Stanley's chairmanship in 1867 [F.i.33]. Napoleon III had threatened the independence of Luxembourg, thereby awakening long-established concerns about the preservation of Belgium's territorial integrity (Ch. 22). Gladstone confirmed his government's determination after 1868 not 'to assume alone an advanced, and therefore an isolated position, in regard to European controversies' (112, *318*). Both Conservative and Liberal governments, therefore, groped towards non-intervention and both remained convinced that France, rather than Prussia, represented the major threat. Britain was totally unprepared both for the cataclysm of the Franco-Prussian War late in 1870 and for its outcome.

IV

Benjamin Disraeli, as sharp on all matters as he was shallow on many, offered his Buckinghamshire constituents in 1866 a rationale for Britain's less central European role. Britain, he argued, was the first world power; hence, 'she interferes in Asia because she is really more an Asiatic power than a European'.[7] Taken literally, this was nonsense in both the geographical and the diplomatic sense. European diplomacy preoccupied Britain's diplomats in this period because this was still where the country's major concerns were perceived to lie. Palmerston needed a map to place accurately many of Britain's colonies and trading outlets. Few nineteenth-century politicians travelled outside Europe, even after 1875 when the scramble for colonies properly began. Yet in a commercial sense Disraeli was right; Britain was *the* world power. Between the mid-1840s and 1870 British imports increased in value by 253 per cent and its domestic exports (excluding re-exports of colonial goods) by 215 per cent. In the mid-1850s only 32 per cent of Britain's exports went to Europe, no less than 37 per cent to the Americas, 20 per cent to Asia (including India) and 9 per cent to Australasia, now a rapidly expanding market [D.ii.2–5]. Europe declined steadily in relative importance as a source of national wealth. In 1815 she had taken more than half of Britain's goods and Asia a mere 6 per cent.

Much argument has surrounded the nature of Britain's commercial expansion. The famous Robinson–Gallagher thesis emphasized Britain's 'informal empire of free trade' in which, outside a framework of formal colonialism, Britain established commercial dominance which virtually excluded competition from other Great Powers. This was achieved by a process which has been called 'cultural imperialism', whereby the trading nation unconsciously absorbs Britain's commercial ethos and willingly adapts itself to her requirements in the reasonable expectation of profit for herself. Latin America, where Britain owned almost nothing but dominated trade, seems to fit this case very well (Ch. 22). The thesis has been widely attacked, most notably by Platt, who argued that Britain had no need of an 'informal empire' since until the 1840s Britain could sustain itself adequately from existing European and American markets buttressed, where necessary, by protection. The government's aim was merely to secure favourable clauses in trade treaties to prevent discrimination against British goods (170, 171).

As so often, there is more to be said on both sides of the argument than the protagonists allow. It is difficult to dispute the increasingly close cultural and economic links between Britain and, for example, both Brazil and Argentina in the 1850s and 1860s; these depended critically on a lack of formal colonialism. On the other side, an 'informal empire of free trade' seems an odd concept in the 1830s and 1840s when protection remained an important determinant of policy. It is common ground, however, that colonies between 1815 and 1870 were acquired reluctantly and with no desire for territorial expansion as such. Formal control was significantly extended [F.iii], but the motives were strategic and economic rather than imperial. Singapore, acquired by Stamford Raffles, served in his words as 'a great commercial emporium and a fulcrum whence we may extend our influence politically as circumstances may hereafter require' (168, *342*). Soon linked with Penang and Malacca as the Straits Settlements, it offered a secure base for trading and also an effective buffer to Dutch expansion in the East Indies. British routes to China and control of the Indian Ocean were secured by a string of ports from the Cape, through Singapore and Labuan to Hong Kong and, a little later, Kowloon after the second Anglo-Chinese War, fought, like the first (Ch. 22), to establish British trading rights in a notoriously recalcitrant quarter [F.ii.6; F.i.31].

Acquisitions might also take place on advice from the man on the spot that a direct presence would settle boundary and trading disputes. Extensions of British control in India and Burma come mostly into this category as, in 1861, did the acquisition of Lagos. Lagos was used to continue the long-running fight to abolish the trade in African slaves and also to protect supplies of palm oil, an increasingly important commodity since ever growing supplies of machinery required greasing and other lubrication. Palmerston's concern was the usual one – 'if we do not take this step the French will be before-hand with us and to our great detriment' (168, 267).

Australia, first settled as a convict colony, took in large numbers of non-convict emigrants from the 1830s as fears of British overpopulation grew. Transportation to New South Wales ceased in 1840 and to Tasmania in 1852. First wool then, from the 1850s, gold vastly increased the continent's economic importance to Britain. Territorial annexation [F.iii] followed the need to maintain order when settlers moved into adjacent areas. In New Zealand, pressure from Christian missionaries, alarmed at the effect of rapacious and lawless white settlers on the indigenous Maori population, was an important factor in Britain's assumption of formal control in 1840 [F.iv.3].

From the middle of the 1840s opinion moved in favour of forms of self-government for the settled territories. In this, colonial reformers like Edward Gibbon Wakefield and Sir William Molesworth were prominent. In 1848, Molesworth, who was briefly to become Colonial Secretary in Palmerston's first government before his untimely death at the age of forty-five, argued that the colonies were too expensive to maintain and would be much cheaper if they controlled their own affairs. Some recent acquisitions of limited value, like the Falkland Islands [F.iii], should be abandoned forthwith. Self-government would also promote colonial self-respect and genuine, rather than forced, esteem for the mother country on which future development could be securely based. Internal self-government, however, must not interfere with Britain's strategic needs and, preferably, should not disadvantage the native population. The aim, in the words of the third Earl Grey, was the 'establishment of a civilized polity' under a rule of law in accordance with British traditions of government. The ideal hardly matched the reality. Most attempts at federation either came to nothing or, as with New Zealand after 1853, worked poorly. The only substantial achievement was confederation for Canada under the British North America Act in 1867 [F.iv.2]. This initiative was accelerated by fear of United States' northwards aggrandizement after the Civil War ended. Against this threat, federation seemed to offer the best safeguard.

In the late 1850s and 1860s colonial affairs were further complicated by local uprisings of which that which the British called 'the Indian Mutiny' but which was in reality a rebellion (1857) affecting much of the country, was much the most important and psychologically damaging. India remained by far the most valuable overseas possession and the mutiny, entirely unanticipated, provoked major changes both in policy and in British attitude to the Indian native population. East India Company involvement in defence and government was finally terminated in 1858 [F.iv.1]. Greater reliance was placed on Indian princes as guarantors (however shaky and atypical) of tolerance towards British rule. The annexation of Oudh in 1856 was the last of the great Indian territorial acquisitions (177). But, as the young Charles Dilke observed in the 1860s, 'the sympathy which Englishmen . . .

felt for the natives has changed to a general feeling of repugnance' (168, *226*). Disturbances in places as far separated as Sarawak, New Zealand and Jamaica also helped to shake British complacency in their ability not only to civilize the colonies but to win their love. By 1870, with British influence in retreat in Europe and mounting evidence that the Irish were not alone in their antipathy to foreign rule, mid-Victorian self-esteem had been somewhat deflated.

----

1. 3rd Earl Malmesbury, *Memoirs of an Ex-Minster* (2 vols, 1885), i, pp. 317–18.
2. Palmerston to Laurence Sulivan, 11 January 1854. K. Bourne, ed., 'The Palmerston-Sulivan Letters, 1804–63', *Camden 4th ser.*, xxiii, *Royal Hist. Soc.*, 1979.
3. *Greville Memoirs* (8 vols, 1888), viii, p. 37.
4. R. W. Seton-Watson, *Britain in Europe, 1789–1914* (1937), p. 395.
5. Seton-Watson, *op. cit.*, pp. 441–2
6. Seton-Watson, *op. cit.*, p. 465
7. Seton-Watson, *op. cit.*, p. 478

CHAPTER 39

The revival of reform

I

The Palmerston government of 1859–65 was reasonably harmonious. Palmerston and Russell sank their differences in old age. The few radicals in the government were held firmly in check. The only left-wing Liberal in the Cabinet was the aristocratic radical C. P. Villiers, who was tucked impotently away at the Poor Law Board. Palmerston's many examples of personal kindness helped to keep the government working in good accord. Most importantly, Palmerston, never more than the mildest of reformers and ever a staunch upholder of aristocracy, ventured little. Derby and Disraeli, in a clear minority after the Liberal agreement of 1859 (Ch. 37), found few pretexts for an attempt to turn the government out. Derby was content to see in harness an administration which was Conservative in all but name and Disraeli, his 1850s radical flirtations behind him, was learning the vital parliamentary virtue of patience. Though he would be sixty in 1864, Palmerston would be eighty and Russell seventy-two. He could afford to wait for the inevitably much changed political world when the 'two dreadful old men' were no longer on the scene.

Palmerston's only serious domestic worries concerned W. E. Gladstone. With most of the Peelites dying off in the 1860s the indefatigable Gladstone became the only important standard bearer of a revered tradition. His commitment to free trade and economy in government was undiminished. But the Crimean War and its aftermath (Ch. 38) had engendered an inflated defence commitment which Gladstone wished to reduce. Palmerston and Gladstone clashed on the need for coastal fortifications in 1859–60 and, during the 1860 budget, on the desirability of removing duties on paper in the cause of free trade. The Prime Minister taunted his Chancellor with a proposal of substantial benefit only to radicals whose literature he would make unnecessarily cheap. Gladstone had to wait a year to lose the duties. The struggles between two men of adamantine will were fearsome to behold; for a time, Gladstone's resignation seemed imminent. Had it come, Palmerston would almost certainly not have enjoyed the rare luxury of dying in office as Prime Minister. Gladstone, ironically in the light of his early career, was now considered by radical Liberals the essential man of the government. They would have schemed against any administration without him in it.

The storms had blown over by 1862 and Palmerston left Gladstone a freer hand. The 1860 budget had left only fifty articles subject to any duty, most of them trifling. By 1862 Gladstone was able to budget for government surpluses while reducing the burden of direct taxation. Income tax at 10d. (4p) in the pound in 1860 was progressively lowered to 4d. (1½p) by 1865 and public expenditure was reduced by about 10 per cent between 1861 and 1866 [D.i. 1,2], despite a modest inflation.

Prosperity and the continued popularity of Palmerston combined to give the Liberals a comfortable election victory in 1865 [B .vi]. The Conservatives made no headway either in Scotland or the larger boroughs, yet the main reason for their despondency was the lack of a rousing issue in the shires. Protectionist Tories had rallied round Peel, unwisely as it transpired, in 1841 when the party had won 86 per cent of the English and Welsh county seats (Ch. 28). By the 1860s, with protection dead, the proportion had dwindled to two-thirds. Many counties, like Lincolnshire, preferred an election arrangement whereby two anti-radical Liberals, Sir Montague Cholmeley and George Packe, were returned unopposed with two Conservatives. In an election fought, as Lord Stanley put it, 'on no particular issue except confidence in the prime minister'[1] such demonstrations of rural harmony were fatal to the Tory cause at Westminster.

II

It is significant that Stanley should not have identified parliamentary reform as a contentious question in 1865. Yet a commitment to widening the franchise had been a plank in the Liberals' platform. It may seem that Stanley's judgement was faulty in view of the furious arguments over reform during the next two years, but reform did not figure prominently in the 1865 campaign. Edward Miall's propaganda for the abolition of church rates (Ch. 34) raised the temperature more in the urban seats. Reform was not a strictly partisan issue. The most ingenious of the four reform bills introduced between 1852 and 1860 had been Conservative and, though its defeat in 1859 had precipitated the resignation of Derby's second government, about thirty Liberals had supported it.

Reform became a live, though only occasionally a central, issue in the 1850s for reasons entirely different from those in the period 1815–32 (Chs 20 and 23). The parliamentary radical wing of the Liberal party, perhaps seventy strong, had never accepted the immutability of a settlement which left the aristocracy in control. But the main standard bearer of the reform cause in the 1850s was an aristocrat. Lord John Russell, 'Finality Jack' of 1832, had declared by the end of the 1840s that the question should be reopened. He had not abandoned his abhorrence of democracy (an abhorrence shared by most parliamentary radicals, including John Bright); his argument for widening the franchise rested on the proposition that a larger proportion of the population deserved the vote in view of 'the improvement and intelligence of the people and the general spread of information since 1832' (141, 32).

The reform debate, therefore, was reopened in a period of prosperity, not depression and in an atmosphere of trust, not fear. A wider franchise was a safe move in view of the evident absence of popular rancour and envy against the governors. Inflation, prosperity and the efforts of the registration agents (Ch. 24) all contributed to an increase in the number of voters of about 62 per cent between the first two Reform Acts [B iii]. The Liberal proposals of 1852, 1854 and 1860 would have increased this number by lowering the rental qualifications from the levels set in 1832 [B.i.2].

Characteristically, it was Gladstone who diverted reform on to the path of high moral duty. Between 1860, when he struggled with Palmerston, and 1865, when his Oxford University constituents threw him out for abandoning his old High-Church principles and espousing 'dangerous' causes, Gladstone became 'The People's William'. Radicals appreciated his destruction of the 'taxes on knowledge' – these had been a bone of long-standing contention – and his nationalist sympathies were also generally popular (Ch. 38). Manufacturers and workers in secure jobs undeniably benefited from the buoyancy of overseas trade and general reductions in indirect taxation. Triumphant visits to Manchester, Bradford, Newcastle and Middlesbrough were made in 1862. Gladstone was much moved by the Lancashire operatives' stoicism during the cotton famine and by their refusal to support the Southern, slavery, cause in the American Civil War, though their own livelihoods seemed to depend upon its success. He talked of the 'great lesson' which the middle classes could learn from the 'mature opinions and sentiments' emanating from 'those little tutored but reflective minds'. Though opposed to 'violent, or excessive, or intoxicating change' in the franchise, he delivered himself in 1864 of the famous view that 'every man who is not presumably incapacitated by some consideration of personal unfitness or of political danger is morally entitled to come within the pale of the constitution'. Less often quoted, but equally important, was his rider that 'fitness for the franchise' existed only in a 'select portion of the working class'.[2]

Within Parliament, reform also became a tactical struggle between the parties even before 1866. Conservatives felt, with much justice, that the 1832 settlement loaded the dice against them. Calculations made in the mid-1860s showed that 11½m. people lived in the county constituencies of England and Wales which returned 162 MPs (recently increased from 159); only 8½m. lived in the boroughs, which nevertheless returned 334 MPs [B.iv]. Worse, Tory chances were marred since many county seats included a substantial electorate drawn from town-dwellers who qualified via the 40-shilling freehold and voted in the counties. Conservatives did much better in county seats where 'urban' voters were sparse. The objectives of the Tory bill of 1859 [B.i.2] are explicable largely in terms of assumed electoral advantage.

Two factors notably absent from the resurgent reform issue, at least before 1865, were popular clamour and extra-parliamentary agitation. When Russell agreed to withdraw his 1860 bill he admitted to Palmerston that 'the apathy of the nation is undeniable' (117, *304*). Reform had become, from the all-consuming passion of 1831–32, an interesting, but largely academic, debating topic within the 'assembly of gentlemen'. It is surely indicative that Palmerston's long-standing aversion to tinkering with the representative system was sufficient to dampen the issue down in the early 1860s. In October 1865, however, Palmerston died to be succeeded by Lord John Russell. One old man's aversion to reform was replaced by another old man's enthusiasm for it. As the Secretary of State for India, Sir Charles Wood, correctly prophesied as he walked away from Palmerston's graveside: 'Our quiet days are over; no more peace for us'. (124, *436*)

III

The twists of fortune and the intricacies of debate over reform in 1866 and 1867 are awesomely complex. Students who wish to follow them in full, and who will incidentally sample some of the finest parliamentary debating in the English language, have two studies of high quality to guide them (141, 142). This reform struggle was quintessentially a parliamentary battle and the shape of the Reform Act which finally emerged was dictated by tactics and by party considerations. In stark contrast to 1831–32, external pressure was a subordinate factor. Despite one heroically wrong-headed attempt to suggest that the second Reform Act was dictated by the ruling classes' perception of 'the proximity to revolutionary situations' and, in particular, by fear of working-class wrath after a meeting in Hyde Park in May 1867 (139, *133*), the absence of any such fear among those best qualified to judge is palpable. John Bright, the *enfant terrible* of parliamentary radicalism with his uncomfortable reminders of the power of 'the nation outside this House', conceded privately in 1866 that the 'organization of the multitude is not complete enough to enable them to make a very effective demonstration of strength' (115, *182*). The Reform League, an amalgam of middle-class radicals and trade union leaders under the presidency of the barrister Edmond Beales and the secretaryship of the bricklayers' leader George Howell, resorted to open-air mass meetings in support of manhood suffrage very reluctantly. There was no expectation that they would have the galvanic effect of those in 1816, 1819 or 1831–32.

This is not to deny the reality of working-class pressure for reform in the 1860s or its importance in keeping the issue insistently going when administrations changed at Westminster and when new ministers were gauging the profit to be gained from a new reform initiative. Many organizations sprang up in northern industrial towns, some led by ex-Chartists, which were in the mainstream of the movement for political liberation. The Reform League drew heavily on this tradition. Though the League can still be called, at a stretch, 'an indigenous working-class radical movement' (307, *316*), it was inextricably bound up with the ethic of improvement which linked middle-class radicals with respectable, predominantly skilled, working men (Chs 31, 33). Most of these working-class parliamentary reformers benefited from the culture of the mechanics' institute, the union branch meeting (Ch. 18) and the public lecture room and library (Ch. 35). It was seductively easy, therefore, to espouse reform in the Gladstonian image, as a privilege which the respectable working man claimed by virtue of his superior skills and responsibility rather than as a right to be demanded. Thus, while William Smith, secretary of the Nottingham Manhood Suffrage Association, agitated for the vote as part of a broad attack on aristocratic and middle-class domination, many other Reform Leaguers were given pause when asked directly whether they intended to enfranchise paupers, idlers, scroungers and the vagrant flotsam and jetsam of Britain's teeming cities. Many, on reflection, took John Bright's view, expressed as early as 1851: 'I have never adopted the phrase "universal" or "manhood" in connexion with the franchise ... nor do I think what is expressed by them the best to give a chance of the best government.'[3] The same line was taken by the Reform Union, founded in Manchester in 1864, with middle-class sponsorship and drawing both on the expertise and the subscriptions of old Anti-Corn Law Leaguers, to press for a householder franchise exercised by secret ballot.

Extra-parliamentary activity during 1865 gave Russell confidence that when he unveiled his new reform bill early in the new year it would merit a central place in the government's legislative programme. He also hoped that his government's paper majority of seventy or so would be proof against inevitable defections. His calculations were upset both by bad luck and bad judgement. It was unfortunate that Gladstone, whose task it would be as Leader of the House to pilot the Bill through the Commons and who was anyway less sanguine than Russell about the prospects of success, was deflected at critical moments in his dual capacity as Chancellor of the Exchequer by the financial implications of a cattle plague in 1866, then a poor harvest and then the collapse of the financial house of Overend and Gurney. Russell's bad judgement underestimated the depth of opposition within his own party; he also forgot the supreme lesson of 1846 – that Disraeli was a superb spoiler and parliamentary tactician.

The bill was modest [B.i.2] in the tradition of Russell's earlier attempts. The calculation was that it would increase the electorate by about 400,000 people, by no means all of whom would be working class. Gladstone, whose commitment to the bill grew as he saw the scale of the opposition ranged against it, declared it a safe enfranchisement. Bright and most of the parliamentary radicals were disappointed and would probably have opposed but for two practical considerations. Firstly, it could always be considered 'payment on account' and strengthened later. Secondly, even this instalment would need every assistance since a group of anti-reform Liberals, led by Robert Lowe and the old Peelite Lord Elcho, determined on opposition. Lowe, a brilliant, doctrinaire and abrasively confident man, submitted the bill to the utilitarian tests he had applied four years earlier to the Revised Educational Code (Ch. 36). Would it improve the quality of government? Was it either necessary or desirable, since about a quarter of the electorate were working men already, to increase that proportion further? Was it not dangerous to entrust the choice of the nation's governors to people whose opinions did not command respect at Westminster? Government was a sacred trust; even the secondary participation encompassed by elections demanded qualities of which prospective voters must prove themselves worthy. Lowe's lucidity rallied many Palmerstonian Liberals. Bright, remembering the First Book of Samuel, christened the Liberal anti-reformers 'Adullamites' since David, in escaping from Saul, fled to 'the cave Adullam.... And everyone that was in distress, ... and everyone that was discontented, gathered themselves unto him'. Disraeli cared little for the finer points of Utilitarianism and less for Lowe personally, but grasped this obvious opportunity to defeat the government. A shrewdly chosen amendment, carried in June 1866 after government majorities had been falling steadily, did the trick. Forty-eight Liberals voted with Disraeli, destroying Russell's last hopes of retiring with a substantial legislative achievement under his belt after a long but decidedly patchy career. He resigned the leadership of his party early in 1868, and lived on until 1878. He remained bitter towards the Adullamites until the end.

IV

Though Bright and Gladstone urged an immediate dissolution of Parliament after the defeat, Russell and a majority of his Cabinet, knowing that an 1866 Election could not be a repeat of the plebiscitary election of 1831 (Ch. 23) to give him an unstoppable authority from the people to wave at Lowe and Disraeli, preferred the more orthodox course of resignation. Some Adullamites harboured grandiose designs of posing as latter-day Peelites to support a refurbished Conservative coalition. Negotiations were held but the Adullamites wanted the removal of Disraeli from the centre of the stage which Derby (whose own position was vulnerable) would not concede. Disraeli, naturally, would not be a sacrificial lamb at a feast arranged by Robert Lowe. A less personal consideration was also relevant. As Stafford Northcote had perceptively observed a few months earlier, Lowe's 'dislike of Reform arises much from his fear of letting in the class which will be swayed by passion rather than reason. He might support us, or even join us for a time, as a means of getting rid of the Reform question; but ultimately he would blow us up on Church questions.'[4] The Conservatives soldiered on alone and Derby formed his third minority government [A]. Events were to prove that the Adullamites had been ditched in more senses than one.

After Russell's defeat, the Reform League stepped up its activities. An attempt to prevent the League holding a meeting in Hyde Park at the end of July 1866 led to disturbances and the breaking of railings in the royal park, but the so-called Hyde Park riots were small beer indeed in the context of nineteenth-century agitation, and the evidence is slender to connect this event with Disraeli's advocacy of a Tory reform bill. A heightened political awareness out of doors undoubtedly played its part in convincing both Derby and the Conservative rank and file, who had after all been trooping obediently into anti-reform lobbies in the spring, that reform remained a live issue.

Disraeli's calculations were much more narrowly political. He knew that the Conservative party would never succeed as the party of landed reaction (Ch. 37). His guiding principle, in so far as this most unprincipled of politicians had one, was to prise his party from the clammy grip of permanent minority status. The Tory reform bill of 1867 was presented to the party as its best hope of success. Circumstances were more propitious than in 1859. Few of the Tory leadership now thought it wise to oppose reform in principle and their leaden backbenches were hardly likely to throw up so able a destroyer as Robert Lowe. The perfect boost for Tory morale would be a reform mission accomplished by a Conservative minority government, where a Liberal majority government had failed. For Disraeli personally, it would be the perfect riposte to the insufferably superior Gladstone, a man with whom, in Disraeli's eyes, the fates had dealt all too kindly. In politics – even in Victorian politics – great issues frequently turn less on principle than on personal rivalry. The 1867 Reform Act is a case in point. Disraeli cared little for the details; he hardly understood many of them. Derby explained his own motivation in personal terms also. 'I did not intend for a third time to be a mere stop-gap until it should suit the convenience of the Liberal party to forget their dissensions.' (84, *366*)

The process, lasting from the late summer of 1866 to the early spring of 1867, by which the Conservatives arrived at the presentation of a reform bill is one of the most farcically confused in the history of British politics. One week Disraeli favoured a rate-paying householder suffrage for the towns, the next week a minimum rental qualification. Derby did not know whether a declaration of intent to reform would suffice, followed by a Royal Commission to examine the issues fully and a bill in 1868 not 1867. The proposed bill was altered in Cabinet in February 1867 to accommodate three extremely hesitant reformers, Cranborne (the future marquis of Salisbury and Tory Prime Minister), Peel and Carnarvon; then changed back when Derby and Disraeli gambled that the government could survive without them [A]. On one calculation, the Cabinet made ten material changes to its proposals in the three weeks between 9 February and 2 March 1867 (124).

A bill, hastily drafted and bearing the marks of Cabinet infighting, arrived in the Commons in March. After a fashion, it embodied Disraeli's personal preferences. The 'fancy franchises' of 1859 [B.i.2] were given another whirl; the county franchise for tenants was reduced from £50 to £15; in the towns it was proposed to extend the vote to all occupiers who made personal payment of their rates and who satisfied a two-year residence qualification. Much time was expended on ratepaying since the prevailing wisdom was that those who paid rates in person were the more solid and respectable members of the working classes, whereas those who 'compounded' (i.e. paid a rent for their houses to the landlord which included an amount for rates) were of the poorer, less-established sort, including what Bright and others called the 'residuum'. Compounders, it was felt, were not responsible enough to vote and the vast majority of MPs remained opposed to the principle of giving effective power to the working classes.

Disraeli's concern, however, was not principle but parliamentary arithmetic. A Conservative Reform Act would only reach the statute-book if most Tory backbenchers could be kept in the fold and enough Liberal radicals could be induced to vote for the worthwhile reform they had been denied in 1866 (125). A degree of outbidding of the previous Liberal effort, therefore, was essential. Lowe, who knew a thing or two about the subject, declared in shocked tones to Gladstone that 'The Tory policy has been to break up the discipline of party by placing themselves in advance of the Liberals.'[5] Party morale was best sustained by making every effort to defeat official Liberal amendments; a Commons majority could only be secured by making concessions to the Liberal radicals. Gladstone's great assault on Disraeli's apparently precarious edifice came in April with an amendment to permit householders to vote whether they paid rates personally or not. Gladstone hoped to gain radical support for this proposed extension to the franchise while telling more cautious Liberals that, if his amendment carried, a rental limit would have to be reimposed to prevent urban manhood suffrage which very few MPs wanted. The radicals were not gulled. Forty-five Liberals voted with Disraeli against the amendment, which was defeated by twenty-one votes.

After this 'smash without example' (Gladstone's phrase), Disraeli knew that he could win. But his tactics for the remainder of the session astounded colleagues and disgusted opponents. Radical amendment after radical amendment was accepted, usually with minimal debate or time for Tory backbenchers to catch their breath and reflect where Disraeli was leading them. Acton Ayrton's amendment to reduce the residence qualification from two years to one was carried; Disraeli quickly admitted defeat and accepted the new clause. W. M. Torrens, an Irish lawyer, proposed a franchise for lodgers paying a £10 rent; with a minor change, Disraeli accepted it. In May a Newark solicitor, Grosvenor Hodgkinson, moved to abolish the category of compound householder for franchise purposes, thus proposing the admittance on the electoral register of all urban householders. This proposal alone would enfranchise almost half a million people and would drive a coach and horses through all the intricate calculations of responsibility, respectability and balance which had consumed so much debating time in the previous eighteen months. Disraeli had just fought off Gladstone's amendment which, as it stood, would have had much the same effect. Another Gladstone-inspired proposal stood in the wings. To pre-empt Gladstone, Disraeli accepted the Hodgkinson amendment without debate. Stanley noted impassively in his diary that Disraeli had 'rather imprudently' accepted a large change which 'was not considered in Cabinet and may give trouble hereafter'.[6] Virtually the only expansionist amendment of consequence which Disraeli did not allow in the hectic May of 1867 was John Stuart Mill's proposal for a female suffrage; this was duly rejected. Mill, MP for Westminster since 1865, had no opportunity to press his unfashionable case further for the electors threw him out at the next election.

Tory backbenchers were bounced by Disraeli into a Reform Act (B.ii.2) which bore virtually no relation to their government's bill introduced three months earlier. Few supported it on its merits, but as the third reading proceeded without a division in July, they could reflect that their party had brought off a tactical coup of the first magnitude. It was a triumph of expediency over both principle and rational calculation. Suggestions that the Act encapsulated Disraeli's vision of a Tory democracy (144) to which he must now educate his followers may be discounted. In 1867 Disraeli had no such vision. He was never a democrat and his overwhelming concern for Toryism was to make it, for the first time since 1846, a party of stable government. His success in 1867 rested on the two talents in which he was pre-eminent: parliamentary management and the ability to think more quickly on his feet than his opponents. In July 1867 the mere fact of reform was enough. No one, least of all Disraeli, had the faintest idea how it would actually work.

---

1. J. R. Vincent, ed., *Derby, Disraeli and the Conservative Party: The Political Journals of Lord Stanley, 1849–69* (Hassocks, 1978), p. 232.
2. Hansard, 3rd ser., clxxv (1864), col. 324.
3. B.L., Add. MSS., 43723, f. 10, Bright to Joseph Sturge.
4. *Life, Letters and Diaries of Sir Stafford Northcote* (1891), p. 55.
5. B.L., Add. MSS., 44301, ff. 23–6, Lowe to Gladstone, 21 March 1867.
6. Vincent *op. cit.*, p. 309.

CHAPTER 40

'The principle of numbers': Towards democracy, 1867–1870

I

Among opponents of the 1867 Reform Act prophecies of doom and accusations of betrayal flew thick and fast. Cranborne used the third reading to dampen Tory euphoria and to launch a wounding personal attack on Disraeli:

> I see with enormous astonishment that the passing of this Bill is spoken of as a Conservative triumph . . . if it be a Conservative triumph to have introduced a Bill guarded with precautions and securities, and to have abandoned every one of those precautions and securities at the bidding of your opponents, then in the whole course of your annals I will venture to say that the Conservative party has won no triumph so signal as this. . . . If you borrow your political ethics from the ethics of the political adventurer, you may depend upon it, the whole of your representative institutions will crumble beneath your feet.

Cranborne's ally, Lord Carnarvon, could foresee revolution. 'The Conservative party is in imminent danger of going to pieces now if indeed it does not disappear under the deluge that the Government are bringing on.' (145, *42*) From the Liberal benches Lowe spoke of 'the shame, the rage, the scorn, the indignation and the despair with which this measure is viewed by every cultivated Englishman who is not a slave to the trammels of party, or who is not dazzled by the glare of a temporary and ignoble success'. He loathed the apparent triumph of what he called 'the principle of numbers as against wealth and intellect'.[1]

Even the Act's supporters offered little more than bemused agnosticism. Derby himself used a phrase of Palmerston's in appraising Russell's bill of 1854 when he talked of 'taking a leap in the dark'. Derby offered the Lords in 1867 his confidence 'in the sound sense of my fellow-countrymen' to see that things turned out well. To their Lordships this vacuous statement must have seemed uncomfortably close to John Bright's campaigning slogan in 1866: 'Let us trust the nation'. Many Tories blamed Bright for having put dangerously radical ideas into their leaders' minds. Bright, however, considerably more cautious in public than he appeared on the hustings, confessed to misgivings about the Act. The Liberal Chief Whip and successful banker C. G. Glyn told Gladstone, 'all is new & changed & large & I fear I must say in some respects *dark*' (148).

In fact the 'leap' was not so blind as it might seem. It is indisputable that the number of people enfranchised by 1867 was very large. The electorate almost doubled within three years [B.iii] and went on increasing steadily, especially in the large boroughs, as the efforts of local party agents were rewarded (146, 147).

Birmingham's electorate of 15,000 in 1866 had risen to 43,000 in 1868 and to 62,000 by 1877. Manchester had 22,000 voters in 1866, 48,000 in 1868 and 64,000 in 1877 (141). It was this kind of growth in places least amenable (or so it was thought) to organization and control which most alarmed Robert Lowe. Yet in 1870 less than two Englishmen in five had the vote. The lower rural franchise [B.ii.2] did not have a dramatic effect and in the boroughs the lodger franchise, potentially of enormous significance, in practice gave the vote to very few. Most lodgers had to forgo wages to make personal application during office hours for enfranchisement before the revising barrister. Lodgers did not value a vote so highly. The residence qualification, although reduced (Ch. 39), still kept a surprising number off the electoral register. Rapid changes of residence were a very common feature of nineteenth-century working-class life (Ch. 14). It is worth remarking that, for reasons such as these, only about 60 per cent of adult males appeared on voting registers as late as 1918, a generation after the third Reform Act (1884) had brought the county qualification in line with the boroughs.

Scotland enjoyed the largest proportionate increase in the numbers of voters. The number of electors in the Scottish burghs increased from about 55,000 in 1866 to 152,000 in 1868 (77). The greatly swollen electorate voted in seats which, by the separate Scottish Reform Act of 1868, were subject to some redistribution. Seven of the English seats disfranchised in 1867 were transferred to Scotland, though some care was taken not to maximize the influence of the new working-class voters. Three of the seven new seats went to the counties (where, of course, the voting qualification was more restricted) and two more to the newly created combined university seats of Edinburgh and St Andrews and Glasgow and Aberdeen (77). Only two new seats went to centres of industry, a third in Glasgow and a second in Dundee. In Ireland no change was made at all to the wholly illogical distribution of seats; Irishmen in 1868 were on average only half as likely to possess the vote as Englishmen, Welshmen or Scotsmen.

In Britain as a whole the vital issue of seats redistribution acted as a break on the acceleration of political change which the huge expansion in the number of voters seemed to promise. On the more-or-less rational principle carried on amendment by the Adullamite Samuel Laing, one MP was removed from every borough with a population of less than 10,000 [B.ii.2]. Honiton, Thetford and Wells which had kept their two MPs in 1832 though they had fewer than 500 electors, lost both in 1867. Lancaster, Totnes, Yarmouth and Reigate were all struck off in 1867 for corruption. In all, 52 post-1832 English borough seats were lost. Seven went to Scotland, while 23 of the remaining 45 strengthened the English counties. Liberals thought this a party manoeuvre, since it offered improved chances to Tories in areas of traditional strength, but the redistribution could be defended on the basis of proportions. In 1866 on average one borough MP represented 1,525 electors while one county MP represented 3,412. After reform the differential narrowed to one for 4,303 and 3,957 electors respectively.

Boroughs and counties continued to operate under very different political rules [B.ii.2]. The more populous counties, it is true, received more MPs after 1867 though still, on mathematical grounds at least, considerably under-represented. Variations within the boroughs, though not so glaring as before, remained substantial. Most radical reformers thought the decision to grant only one extra MP to the four largest English provincial cities (none of which in 1870 had populations of less than a quarter of a million [E.iii]) exceedingly stingy, though understandable in a Parliament where the vast majority of members still had as little direct contact with the great cities as possible. The 19 largest boroughs after 1867 returned between them 46 MPs, and their combined populations totalled 5m. Sixty-eight boroughs with populations of less than 20,000 each (totalling 420,000) retained one MP each. Andover, Knaresborough, Midhurst, Northallerton and Petersfield all had electorates of between 750 and 1,000 in 1868 (141). The redistribution saw a net total of 13 seats removed from the 5 most south-westerly counties and a net gain of 9 for Cheshire, Lancashire and the West Riding, but the long-standing bias in favour of the south of England lingered after 1867. Most of the smallest boroughs – Launceston, Liskeard, Calne, etc. – remained in the South-west, as before 1832 (Chs 2 and 24).

Landowners set special store by the preservation of 'influence' and they defended it with remarkable resilience. Professor Hanham has identified 46 British boroughs and 38 counties (12 of them in Ireland) still controlled by patrons in 1868 (147). They had to be more ready to fight elections on behalf of their nominees after 1867 and, like the Liberal earl of Carlisle in East Cumberland, often laid claim to only one of the two constituency seats, leaving the other to opponents; but patronage survived into the 1880s. The borough patrons were a blend of 'old' and 'new' men, strongly reminiscent of the pattern in the 1780s. The marquis of Westminster still controlled Chester, for which borough a Grosvenor sat continuously from 1832 to 1874. Earl Fitzwilliam 'possessed' Malton in Yorkshire, put his son into it and had to contest an election there for the first time since before 1832 to fight off a Conservative challenge in 1874. A Peel represented Tamworth continuously from 1832 to 1880. At Aylesbury, a nineteenth-century banking fortune bought N. M. de Rothschild into politics in 1865, much as a brewing fortune had won a controlling interest for the Whitbreads in nearby Bedford a century earlier. Samuel Whitbread represented Bedford continuously from 1857 to 1895.

II

To a surprising degree, therefore, the old world survived the traumas of 1867. The electorate remained carefully divided between borough and county franchises; regional imbalance was maintained, favourable to the rural areas; no secret ballot had been introduced; at least one-eighth of parliamentary seats were under patronage. Nor did the social composition of Britain's MPs undergo drastic change immediately after 1867. Members of Parliament whose main occupations were industrial and commercial increased from about 90 to 112 between 1865 and 1880 though this calculation does less than justice to the much larger numbers whose base was landed but whose commercial interests, as for example via banks or extensive ownership of railway shares, were extensive and ever more important. Of Gladstone's 'hard hands' in 1870, there was none. The first working-class MPs would appear in 1874. Both would be solid union men; both would be respectable

Gladstonian Liberals. Fears of a civilized Parliament of gentlemen swamped by uncouth manual labourers after 1867 were immediately stilled. George Howell, secretary of the Reform League which, with almost 300 provincial branches, was much the most significant political pressure group of its day, stood for Aylesbury at the 1868 election as a radical Liberal. Campaigning against 'the Farmers, Employers, "Gentlemen", Parsons and a large number of "shops" Tradespeople',[2] he finished 500 votes behind the Conservative who was elected as second MP for the borough. De Rothschild topped the poll as a Liberal, but one who (like so many in the smaller boroughs) was quite amenable to seeing the town's political representation amicably split. That had long been the gentlemanly way.

The 1868 Election was the first to be fought under the new rules and there is a temptation, which should, however, be firmly resisted, to assume that any changes took place because of reform. Reform was a minor issue in 1868, though the new franchise obviously posed immense logistical problems for local party organizations. The election produced a result broadly similar to that of 1865, though the Liberals increased their majority over the Conservatives from about 70 to 110 [B.vi]. Though in disarray in 1866 and early 1867, there was time after the Second Reform Act passed in August 1867 for wounds to heal. The Liberal coalition of interests, substantial but unwieldy, met the electorate in good heart. When Derby rather reluctantly resigned the premiership through illness in February 1868 and advised the Queen to appoint Disraeli, the new Prime Minister formed the fourth minority Conservative government in sixteen years.

Disraeli undoubtedly expected too much from the new electorate and encouraged his followers to believe that simple gratitude for enfranchisement would secure a parliamentary majority. Whether he believed this himself is less certain, but he had no other cards to play. His failure in 1868 made his position as party leader parlous for he did not lack for enemies on his own side. If a 'political adventurer's' adventures misfire he has little to fall back on save his wits. Disraeli's characteristically clever rehabilitation via 'Tory democracy' lies outside the scope of this book. We take our leave of him in 1870, an ageing outsider (now sixty-six) well into the second half of his great political game and in desperate need of at least a couple of late goals to secure further progress in the competition.

Disraeli did at least hang on to the heartlands. After the 1868 Election over 80 per cent of Tory seats were in England. In the English counties, the party captured 75 per cent of the seats; the bulk of the remainder were in the small boroughs. In the larger English boroughs the Liberals captured 125 of the 159 seats; from a total of 194 in Scotland, Ireland and Wales they claimed a massive 150. In view of the fact that many smaller boroughs remained 'managed' and that not much more ground could possibly be captured in the shires, the only realistic prospect for a Tory revival after 1868 was in the larger boroughs. The Celtic lands would remain anti-Tory for as long as the Tory party was pro-Church of England.

Industrial Lancashire seemed to point the way. Against the national trend Lancashire returned twenty-one Conservative MPs and the Liberals only thirteen. The Conservatives took solid industrial seats like Salford (newly enfranchised), Bolton, Preston and Blackburn and, in the process of winning all eight county seats, they defeated Gladstone himself in South-west Lancashire. In truth, however,

Lancashire politics rested far more on the old world than on the new. As we shall see, the great issue in 1868 was religion, and Lancashire had never been particularly strong Liberal ground because of the strong bias against substantial Catholic minorities which settled in the county (Chs 34 and 41). The working men of Salford, for example, voted Tory because they were anti-Irish and the Liberals were traditionally 'soft' on Catholicism.

The other important factor in the Conservatives' success was factory paternalism, and here too the Reform Act only reinforced an existing trend. The Liberal agent in Blackburn, W. A. Abram, resignedly explained in 1868 that the established factory owners exerted their traditional grip over their employees' political allegiances. 'Politics resolve themselves into partisan warfare, and the real objects of political parties are totally forgotten in the zest of local clanships.' (312, *201*) The Tory victory of William Hornby and Joseph Feilden in Blackburn was a victory for Tory mills over Liberal mills. Although factory owners built only about 13 per cent of the town's housing themselves, political wards under the influence of a mill of particular political allegiance voted six or seven to one in favour of that allegiance. Tory success in Preston rested on the immense vote polled in the Fishwick ward where the Horrocks mill was dominant. For many of the new voters after 1867, however galling it was to improving radicals, political allegiance was as unthinking as the sporting allegiance to town football teams which were beginning to be organized professionally at precisely this time.

III

The 1867 Reform Act, then, did not turn the political world upside-down overnight. The same parties contested power; working men would not evolve their own party for another generation. Women would not vote in a parliamentary election for another half-century. But we should not assume that 1867 was another exercise in the manipulation of power largely in the interests of the ruling class. Fundamental changes quickly followed. The secret ballot arrived within five years, equal electoral districts and a uniform franchise within eighteen. No one talked of 'Finality' in 1867 and Lowe's objections were not just fastidiously intellectual. He saw clearly where a household franchise must lead.

Party organization had to adapt to the new electorate and this did not just mean more agents and more envelopes to be licked. It involved the creation of a new kind of party which centralized both electoral effort and decision-making. Less scope would exist for healthy independence and for party direction from the great English country houses. The exclusive world of the duke of Omnium crumbled within thirty years of the second Reform Act; the age of mass politics took its place.

The 1867 Act's so-called 'Minority Clause' (B.ii.2] offered an early test for the power of organization. This clause was inserted against the advice of Disraeli with the intention of guaranteeing strong minority representation. The calculation was that if a large borough had three seats but only two votes to be used by each elector, then one-party exclusivity would be broken. Leeds, Liverpool and Manchester duly split two to one in 1868, but in Birmingham expert organization was deployed to such precise effect that three Liberal MPs were elected, all receiving within 500 votes of one another in a total of 60,000 votes cast. John Bright, the third Liberal, came home almost 6,000 votes ahead of the first Tory. Such electoral wizardry was bound to be emulated. The Birmingham Liberal 'Caucus', controlled in the early 1870s by the radical Unitarian screw manufacturer Joseph Chamberlain, presaged the modern party machine, that most soulless effect of Lowe's 'principle of numbers'.

The influence of those skilled working men for whom Gladstone and others contemplated further reform in the early 1860s is interesting. The trade union leaders of the Reform League gave the election of working-class candidates a fairly low priority. Working men must first be educated by sympathetic tutors before they were ready to assume a direct governing responsibility. As George Howell told the electors of Exeter in 1868: 'I wish the workmen of your good old town could send in a working man, but of course you must first walk and then run'. (116, *312*) Glyn enthused to Gladstone a few months later: 'I should like to show you some of the reports made by the working men. They are so sound and so sensible & in most places their great object is to unite the two sections of the party *for you* & not to put up their own or any extreme men'. (148, *454*)

Glyn quite accurately perceived that skilled men tended not to be extreme radicals, but it should not be assumed that they were happy to follow where established Liberalism, in its traditional wisdom, chose to lead. Howell, Applegarth, Odger and the rest had objectives as precise as those of Miall and the anti-church rate campaigners (Ch. 34). In alliance with middle-class radicals like James Stansfeld they fought against the entrenched positions of Whig – Liberalism. The tutors of the working class were needed, but they must fight for extended political rights, for non-sectarian education and for a less ambiguous declaration of the status of trade unions. Howell's *bête noire* was aristocracy, and one reason why he opposed 'extremist' policies such as disestablishment or the abolition of the monarchy (a briefly popular cause at this time) was because he feared that they would drive 'respectable' middle-class opinion back to a dangerously retrograde dependence on the old Whigs. Gladstonian Liberal working men, anachronistically derided as collaborationists in some quarters, had a clear vision of Liberalism developing into the twentieth century as a radical, rationalist, individualist and essentially anti-aristocratic creed, similar in many respects to the political philosophy of Thomas Paine eighty years before (Ch. 8). Until the catastrophic Liberal split over Ireland in 1886 it was a vision with some prospect of realization. Had it succeeded, it is difficult to see how a Labour party could have squeezed itself into the twentieth-century two-party system, deprived as it would have been both of established trade union support and of most of its radical vitality.

---

1. Hansard, 3rd ser., clxxxviii (1867), cols 1528–9, 1539, 1540, 1550.
2. R W Davis, *Political Change and Continuity, 1760–1885: A Buckinghamshire Study* (Newton Abbot, 1972), p. 209.

CHAPTER 41

Conclusion: Forging a modern state or modern states? Integration and diversity in the United Kingdom

I

The zenith of British power and influence was reached in the 1860s. Despite some diplomatic reverses (Ch. 38), no nation would plan to engage Britain in war without both formidable allies and a very strong navy. Crucial economic challenges were on the horizon but Great Britain in 1870 was still the world's pre-eminent industrial and trading nation. London was the world's financial capital and a significant proportion of the nation's wealth was earned from international banking and insurance – those so-called 'invisible exports' or 'invisibles' which helped to bridge the adverse trade gap between imports and exports. Even at the apex of its industrial might, Britain still imported more goods than it exported or re-exported. The gap in the late 1860s, for example, was about £57,000 [D.ii.4].

Conventional measurements testified to the United Kingdom's lead over other nations in 1870. Its annual output of coal was about 25,000 tons greater than that of its seven nearest competitors combined. Its pig iron production (6m. metric tons in 1870) was substantial higher than the combined efforts of these seven competitors (5.49m.). Raw cotton consumption was almost three times as great as that of the United States. Only the United States could rival the UK's tonnage of merchant ships registered (UK 5.7m.; USA 4.3m.). The combined tonnage of the main European competitors did not reach 4m. (253, 8–9).

Significantly, these indicators of economic and industrial advantage almost invariably use United Kingdom, or at least Great Britain, statistics. The clear assumption given by the economic historians is that the world's greatest power was a united nation, not three, or four, separate nation states. Yet how valid is this assumption? To what extent had industrial might finessed social and cultural distinctions between the constituent nations of the United Kingdom? Or did England's massive demographic advantage carry all before it, laying national cultural diversities steam-roller flat, rendering them of such trivial importance that most foreigners and, apparently, all Americans of non-Irish extraction still use the words 'England' and 'Great Britain' interchangeably? After all, England's 21.6m. people in 1871 represented 69 per cent of the United Kingdom's population and 82 per cent of Great Britain's [E.i]. This balance of comparative demographic advantage, moreover, was widening since the populations of Scotland and Wales were not growing as fast as England's, while Ireland's disastrous post-famine decline continued inexorably. In the thirty years after the Famine, starvation and emigration reduced Ireland's population by more than one-third.

To Ireland's demonstrably special case we shall return at the end of the chapter. It is important first to determine whether that dominant nation called 'Great

Britain' was in 1870 properly one state or three. The constitutional issues may be dispensed with summarily. England, Scotland and Wales had agreed national boundaries, although whether Monmouth was properly part of Wales or England was to remain a matter of contention until the creation of antiseptic Gwent in 1974 resolved the issue in the smaller nation's favour. All three nations returned separately elected MPs to the House of Commons, in very rough proportion to their populations, though Scotland, with 13 per cent of the Britain's population, secured only 9 per cent of its parliamentary seats. This imbalance, interestingly, has been more than reversed in the late twentieth century when Scotland returns considerably more MPs than its strict demographic due, one of the few permanent benefits which the contemporary political system bequeaths to the Labour party.

Constitutionally, also, the Acts of Union joining Wales to England in 1536 and 1543 preserved far fewer separate rights than did that of 1707 which yoked Scotland to England. Scotland not only retained, but gloried in, its entirely separate legal and educational systems. The state church of Wales in 1870 remained the Church of England – an ecclesiastical and cultural affront which was not imposed on Scotland. Both nations, however, nurtured much more Puritanically-Protestant traditions than did England, where the state church was mostly Protestant only in the negative sense of rejecting Papal authority. Its thirty-nine Articles of Faith, dating from 1563, were far more impressive as a piece of Elizabethan *realpolitik* than they were as a system of belief. For many Englishmen, to be a member of the state church was more a necessary part of cultural and political acceptability than an endorsement of belief.

On most political and administrative criteria, Scotland was more distinctively different from England than was Wales. The Welsh, however, had retained their own language. At the end of our period about two-thirds of Welshmen used Welsh as their first language; most of these, indeed, were monolingual. In rural North and mid-Wales the proportion was very much higher – between 80 and 90 per cent. In Scotland, by contrast, Gaelic had been in retreat for three centuries. Attempts to preserve a language spoken in 1870 by perhaps 15 per cent of Scots, mostly in the Highlands, owed more to pre-echoes of 'heritage' which painlessly extracts the incisors from the jaws of national identity. Minority status was no barrier to the disdain of the Registrar-General at the 1871 Scottish Census: 'The Gaelic language may be what it likes, both as to antiquity and to beauty, but it decidedly stands in the way of the civilization of the natives [*sic*] making use of it' (130). Any remaining threats from Highlanders, Jacobites and the Clan system long dispersed, both sentimental Lowlanders and Queen Victoria's court, which regularly decamped to Balmoral after 1848, could wear the kilt, promote Highland Games, patronize bagpipers and reinvent a safe, sanitized and certainly not a separate, North Britain (16, *355*).

Wales was rather different. Frederick Engels was not entirely inaccurate when he asserted that 'The English know how to reconcile people of the most diverse races with their rule; the Welsh, who fought tenaciously for their language and culture, have become entirely reconciled with the British Empire' (21, *301*). He was, however, underestimating the potential of Welsh identity to develop forms which stressed not only 'otherness' but overt antagonism. The touchstone was usually language. When, in 1847, parliamentary commissioners reported on the state of education in Wales, their message was as clear as it was controversial. Welsh was denounced as 'a peculiar language isolating the mass from the upper portion of society'. The language, in the commissioners' view, was the strongest impediment to civilized advance. The Welsh speaker 'is left in an underworld of his own, and the march of society goes so completely over his head that he is never heard of, except when the strange and abnormal features of a Revival, or a Rebecca or Chartist outbreak, call attention to a phase of society which could produce so contrary to all we experience elsewhere' (21, *310*).

Such disdain was bound to provoke reaction in a society which needed no spur to pronounce the value of its identity. *Eisteddfodau* increased in number throughout the nineteenth century in industrial South Wales as well as the more rural North, and the Welsh could celebrate poets and novelists of stature such as William Thomas, Gwilym Hiraethog and Daniel Owen. A Welsh Manuscripts Society was established in 1836; pressure for a separate University of Wales grew. The first University College, at Aberystwyth, opened in 1872 though the University of Wales, incorporating this and colleges at Cardiff and Bangor, had to wait until 1893.

Meanwhile, the Liberal party in Wales was emerging as the increasingly potent counterpart to this cultural renaissance. Wales by 1870 was developing as a stronghold of radical Liberalism and, under the direction of Henry Richard, MP for Merthyr Tydfil, was channelling many pro-Welsh sentiments in significant new directions. Richard spoke not for establishment Liberalism but particularly to ordinary Welshmen, many of whom had been enfranchised in the towns in 1867. The election of 1868 saw a decisive breakthrough for more populist and aggressively non-conformist Liberalism. The Liberal party in Wales, after a long period of virtual parity with the Tories, now held roughly two-thirds of the seats and established the long, and still unbroken, tradition of anti-Toryism in the Principality. Many of the defeated Tories were landowners and evictions of pro-Liberal tenant farmers in 1868–70 served only to emphasize the degree of cultural separation. David Lloyd George, certainly the most famous – and probably the most mendacious and unscrupulous – politician in Welsh history, was only seven years of age in 1870 but the seeds of that radical, anti-aristocratic populism which sustained his early career had already been sown.

II

In a recent book Linda Colley has brilliantly argued that the experience of regular warfare against France – 'the Catholic Other' as she terms it – in the eighteenth and nineteenth centuries was instrumental in forging a Protestant British nation from diverse constituent elements (23). An expanded social and governing elite included increasing numbers of Welsh, Scots and Protestant Anglo-Irish landowners and businessmen. The work of actually governing an increasingly complex State in war and peace brought these elements closer together in a common goal. Among the lower orders, the experience of war, and especially the lengthy and hugely costly wars of 1793–1815, increased political awareness and afforded this expanded elite an opportunity to mould patriotic icons – from the unpromising clay which 'the mad King' George III offered downwards – around which the people could rally. In Colley's view, under a propagandist onslaught 'impressive numbers of Britons did make the step from a passive awareness of nation to an energetic participation on its behalf' (23, *371*).

Colley's thesis is broadly persuasive, though the manufacture of 'patriots' by the elite was in conscious reaction to a powerful radicalization of the skilled workers for whom patriotism represented an attack on the very institution of aristocracy as both wasteful and irrational (Ch. 8). Patriotism in the late eighteenth and early nineteenth centuries was a keenly contested battleground between left and right. It was far from clear until after 1870 that the Conservative interpretation of patriotism, which was basically nationalist and defensive, would win the day. Colley has importantly rescued one form of patriotism – albeit the one which survived for immensely profitable transmutation into a bankable electoral asset by Conservative Central Office from Disraeli in the 1870s onwards.

For Colley, whose own study ends with the accession of Queen Victoria, the engine of patriotism was war. Those attempting to understand Britishness in the 1860s or 1870s need to acknowledge that her dynamic was far less relevant. Britain was hardly ever at war in Europe between 1815 and 1914. Protestant patriotism was important in shaping relations between Britain and Ireland throughout the century, though rarely to the advantage of either state. The question which needs to be resolved, however, is whether a sense of British national identity survived the long period of peace which began in 1815.

In one sense, it self-evidently did. Nationalism in Scotland, Wales and the Celtic fringes of England was more cultural than political. Too many industrialists, bankers and merchants literally had too much invested in the British Industrial Revolution to make any break from England a viable proposition. The nineteenth-century rebuilding of Glasgow as one of the most advanced cities of the British Empire emphasized how handsomely the gamble over dual nationhood with England in 1707 had paid off for its merchants and capitalists. Both Scottish and Welsh aristocratic families intermarried with their English counterparts in the later eighteenth and nineteenth centuries, while generous participation in Britain's economic growth was a sufficient incentive for the burgeoning bourgeoisie of South Wales and the central valley of Scotland. Upper and middle-class Scots and Welsh had a powerful vested interest in union and few perceived significant conflict between their 'smaller' and 'greater' nationhood. The question of national identity, however, remained a controversial one, particularly when language, dialect and accent were regarded by the cultural elite as indicators of superiority or inferiority.

Such indications operated with equal force within England. Until his death, it cannot be said that Robert Peel was a popular politician, and attacks on his Lancashire accent and industrial background were not infrequently made upon him by snobbish opponents within his own party (98, 99). In dissections of English society, so much emphasis has been laid upon class distinction that it is easy to conclude that social and educational background are of much greater importance than perceptions of distinctively English national identity. The Liberal MP James Bryce asserted in 1877, that an Englishman 'has but one patriotism, because England and the United Kingdom are to him practically the same thing'.[1] Plentiful evidence exists of a primary regional, rather than national, allegiance well into the second half of the nineteenth century. Patrick Joyce has argued that industrialization contributed little, if anything, to a developing sense of English identity and notes the importance of the 'link between tight community structures and . . . cultural continuities' and the flowering of dialect, and therefore almost by definition exclusive, literature in Lancashire.[2] Rivalry between different parts of the north, cotton Lancashire and woollen Yorkshire, for example, was frequently keen, as was indicated with the development of professional sport in the 1860s and 1870s.

The standard North-South cultural fault-line offers crude, if powerful, stereotypes invoked to explain differences. Thus, while Lewes (Sussex) is more attractive and eligible than Leeds, it is – in the northern version of the stereotype – the latter town which creates the nation's wealth and stiffens its backbone. From the Industrial Revolution onwards, northerners, might be portrayed as hard-working, practical, serious and good (*i.e.* 'careful') with money and Puritan, whereas southerners were effete, comfort-seeking, frivolous (*i.e.* 'wasteful') with money and Anglican. Those who see the quintessentially 'English' game of cricket as a metaphor for English life will also note its amateur traditions in southern counties such as Hampshire, Kent and Sussex; here amateur players learned their skills by playing friendly fixtures in an amateur spirit. Many of the most successful Lancashire and Yorkshire cricketers, by contrast, were products of highly-competitive, regionally-based leagues.

English national identity is particularly difficult to extract from within a successful British State of which it is much the largest and most powerful element. This is not, however, unusual. Almost all nation states encompass vigorous and not infrequently mutually hostile regional diversities. It is, however, possible to associate a distinct 'Englishness' with a set of values embraced by the ruling classes from the sixteenth century onwards and which could be generalized, if ambivalently as English or British, in the period of imperial expansion which began in the 1870s.

This Englishness drew on a political tradition. Its essential elements were Protestantism and progress. Catholicism was regarded with suspicion as an authoritarian and oppressive faith which sustained authoritarian and oppressive rulers. The defeat of the Spanish Armada in 1588 and James II's forced removal from the throne in the 'Glorious Revolution' of 1688 became talismans of English liberty. Less well remembered, but equally symbolic, was the death of Charles Edward Stuart in 1788. 'Bonnie Prince Charlie' had been, in 1745–46, the last Catholic claimant who took up arms in an attempt to overthrow the Protestant Hanoverian State. The Whig landowners who eventually became the main beneficiaries of the Glorious Revolution first argued, and then assumed, English pre-eminence in developing a superior political system based upon co-operation rather than coercion and liberty rather than authority. England was always politically advanced and it is not surprising that first reactions by the elite to the

French Revolution in 1789 assumed that the dull-witted Catholic French were at last learning lessons in constitutional partnership from the more advanced Protestant English (Ch. 8).

An oligarchy of landowners with country estates and important interests to nurture there naturally embraced localism. It is not surprising that in heavily urbanized England to this day, romantic images of England nevertheless evoke the rural idyll – village greens, warm beer and an ordered, benign and tolerant hierarchy. Centralized states were indelibly associated, to the end of our period and beyond, with Catholicism and lack of liberty. This helps to explain much of the hostility to measures such as the new Poor Law of 1834 and the Public Health Act of 1848 which set up central boards. Dickens's Mr Podsnap in *Our Mutual Friend*, first published in 1864, spluttered in response to a gentle enquiry about better provision for the poor: 'I see what you are driving at. I knew it from the first. Centralization. No. Never with my consent. Not English'.[3] Not the least of the attractions of nineteenth-century *laissez-faire* was its promise of low taxes, a minimal role for the State and therefore local self-determination. Industrial and commercial success during the nineteenth century helped to burnish the image and fit it in the next generation for the purpose of imperial expansion. By the end of the nineteenth century, this variant of Englishness was helping to spread the messages of superiority, progress and liberty to 'lesser breeds without the [English] law'.

III

In the middle years of the nineteenth century the Protestant British had to accommodate themselves to a huge influx of, predominantly Catholic, Irish. At the peak in 1861, the Census recorded 806,000 Irish-born residents in Britain. The impact of the Irish in Britain is certainly more diverse, and probably more complex, than is usually assumed. The Irish immigrant stereotype can readily be read as the obverse of English. It presents Irish immigrants as uniformly lower working-class, entirely lacking both civilized values and the education to understand a rapidly changing urban society. It has them all concentrated in large urban centres like Liverpool, Glasgow and London, where they were disproportionately likely to commit crime. With the enthusiastic warrant of influential commentators, the stereotype further portrays them as a filthy, drunken drag on an improving society – ignorant, illiterate, priest-ridden and with a pronounced tendency to drag down the Englishman's wages. Here is Frederick Engels, on Irish immigrants in Manchester:

> Drink is the only thing which makes the Irishman's life worth living; so he revels in drink to the point of the most bestial drunkenness. The southern facile character of the Irishman, his crudity, which places him little above the savage, his contempt for all humane enjoyments, in which his very crudeness makes him incapable of sharing, his filth and poverty all favour drunkenness ... when he has money he gets rid of it down his throat. With such a competitor the English working-man has to struggle, with a

competitor upon the lowest plane possible in any civilised country, who for this reason requires less wages than any other.[3]

This was the considered judgement of Dr W. H. Duncan, Liverpool's celebrated Medical Officer of Health in 1859: 'The wards of highest mortality are those which contain the largest proportion of Irish of the lowest class, not only the most destitute but the most improvident and the most filthy in their habits' (315, *60*). The ponderous authority of the 1871 Scottish census was placed behind the following value judgement:

> The immigration of . . . a body of labourers of the lowest class, with scarcely any education, cannot but have the most prejudicial effects on the population. As yet the great body of these Irish do not seem to have improved by their residence among us; and it is quite certain that the native Scot who has associated with them has most certainly deteriorated.[5]

The stereotype seems confirmed by periodic outbreaks of violence between Irish immigrants and the English and Scottish working classes. The Stockport Riots in 1852 (Ch. 34), the most famous of these, were used to reinforce messages of xenophobia and fear by a British press already anxious to sell copy on the back of crass categorization, simplification and distortion. It is certainly true that the majority of Catholic immigrants settled first and in greatest numbers in the major towns, simply because these were most likely to afford diverse job opportunities. In 1851, 22 per cent of Liverpool's population was Irish-born, 19 per cent of Dundee's and 18 per cent of Glasgow's. However, dispersal was relatively rapid. By 1871 and directly contradicting the stereotype, more than two thirds of Irish-born lived outside the four major concentrations of Liverpool, London, Manchester and Glasgow. Scotland had a substantially larger proportion of Irish immigrants than either England or Wales, but many of these were not Catholic at all but Ulster Protestants returning to the land from which their ancestors had made the opposite journey in the seventeenth century.

The Irish dispersed widely throughout much of Britain during the nineteenth century. More than thirty towns, including such relatively small places as Bath (then Somerset), Colchester (Essex) and Newport (Shropshire) had in excess of 1,000 Irish-born residents in 1861. In the area around Chesterfield (Derbyshire), as the Dublin newspaper *The Nation* reported in 1872, about 5,000 Irish were found earning good wages in mining. The general condition of the Irish was described as satisfactory: 'There is sufficient church accommodation . . . and . . . the Jesuit Fathers, who serve the mission at Chesterfield, speak in very favourable terms of the conduct, morals and habits of the Irish people, as contrasted with their English fellow-labourers in the mines and works'. Though the Irishman's 'one vice' was drink, Irish 'honour and honesty are remarkable'[6].

Nor does the image of Irish racial ghettoes survive detailed examination. Even among the poorest, there was considerable mobility, while few of those immigrants in skilled and professional jobs lived in areas which could be described as distinctively Irish. Likewise, the proportion of relatively well-off Irish-born was higher than is generally assumed. Detailed research on the census of 1851, 1861 and 1871 reveals that between a third and two-fifths of Irish-born residents in Liverpool, Greenock, Hull and York were in professional or skilled occupations (315, *71*). Even in genuine ghettoes, domestic organization frequently belied the horror stories recounted by Engels or Duncan. *The Nation*, perhaps not surprisingly given its provenance, provides a much more sympathetic picture but so do some perceptive English observers. Henry Mayhew, for example, visited courts and tenements occupied by Irish petty street traders in London in the late 1850s and noted how people with very little disposable income nevertheless thrived 'on the associative principle, by mutual support. In all of the houses that I entered were traces of household care and neatness that I had little expected to have seen.'[7] The Irish, therefore, contributed a great deal more to the burgeoning British economy than cheap surplus labour and helped to augment the profits of more than the brewers.

IV

For William Gladstone, the five million or so Irish who remained in Ireland would dog the remainder of his career. The story is well known (indeed, it has become the hoariest historical cliché of the nineteenth century) that when his favourite physical pastime of tree-felling on his Deeside estate of Hawarden was interrupted at the end of 1868 by the arrival of the telegram in which Queen Victoria confirmed her request for him to form a government, he stated: 'My mission is to pacify Ireland'. It was a mission he would neither abandon nor achieve.

The Irish problem obstinately refused to go away. Though post-famine demoralization and a modest agricultural recovery in the 1850s had dampened down agitation, Ireland's long-term grievances obtruded once more in the 1860s. Its agricultural future lay with pasture farming, which is less labour intensive than arable. During the 1860s, 400,000 Irish acres fell out of tillage. Tenants and labourers had no protection against eviction and unemployment and, except in the area around Belfast, which was becoming one of the United Kingdom's boom towns because of engineering and shipbuilding, little alternative employment was available. Religious grievance compounded economic hardship. Just short of 80 per cent of Ireland's population in 1868 was Roman Catholic but economic advance was largely confined to the predominantly Presbyterian North-east.

Gladstone was convinced that the unswerving defences of Protestant Church establishments, for which he had become famous in the 1830s and 1840s, (Chs 27 and 28) had been misguided. In the 1860s he published typically detailed and anguished recantations and promised to reopen the question of the Church establishment in Ireland. Both the Queen and the Conservatives thought Gladstone traded less in recantation than in cant, since they believed he espoused the Irish Church issue so passionately only because it was the best issue with which to rally the demoralized Liberal troops. A leader of a party whose strength was in Ireland, Wales and Scotland could hardly afford to remain an aggressive champion of intolerant Anglicanism. Furthermore, the English electorate, which usually ignored

Ireland when it could, had been alerted by the activities of the Fenian Brotherhood, an Irish Catholic revolutionary organization which had so alarmed the Irish authorities in 1866 that Habeas Corpus had been suspended there. In late 1867 a policeman was killed when Fenian prisoners were rescued in Manchester; at the attempted rescue of a Fenian in Clerkenwell (London) an explosion killed at least a dozen people. As always, these atrocities evoked short-term anti-Irish revulsion and a longer-term reluctant willingness to reflect why Irishmen resorted to violence.

Gladstone toppled Disraeli by playing the Irish card. His resolutions on the Irish question were carried against the government by a revived Liberal party in the spring of 1868 and the dissolution of Parliament as soon as the new, expanded, electoral registers were in operation became a formality. Gladstone thought Liberal majorities of sixty and more 'wonderful'[8] and gave credit to his 'three *corps d'armée* ... Scotch presbyterians, English and Welsh nonconformists, and Irish Roman catholics' (120, *145*). The marquis of Hartington, whom Gladstone would make Chief Secretary for Ireland in 1870, thought Gladstone's proposed reforms necessary both for 'firm administration' and that 'conciliatory policy [which] shall place the justice of our whole system of government there beyond dispute'.[9] Hartington sat for a Lancashire seat and, like Gladstone, paid for his Irish sympathies with electoral defeat. He quickly found a more hospitable political haven in nonconformist North Wales.

Gladstone's Irish Church Disestablishment Act of 1869 was carried against substantial Tory opposition in the Lords. The principle of disendowing church revenues was pregnant with significance for the security of property as a whole. About two-thirds of the value of that church property went to recompense life interests – the incomes of bishops, clergy and linked charges. The remaining third was eventually put to the relief of poverty and the encouragement of various agricultural and educational schemes. In 1870 an Irish Land Act attempted, though with little practical result, to give compensation to tenants who expended their own meagre capital on land or property improvements and then had to leave their tenancy, and compensation also to those who were evicted, provided they were up to date with their rents. The Tories in the Commons did not oppose it, partly from ignorance of a highly technical subject and partly from an entirely justified belief that the legislation's inadequacies would preserve ample scope for Irish landowners.

In 1870 the British government's major legislative concerns were with the problems of a sister nation which had enjoyed few of the benefits of industrial progress and, in the Elementary Education Act [C.iv] (Ch. 36), with a class whose labour had made that progress possible. The predominantly aristocratic composition of the Gladstone government which passed these Acts [A] would not have seemed alien to Pitt the Younger at the beginning of our period, though the presence of a radical Quaker in John Bright would have required explanation. The nature of the legislation itself, however, would have been inexplicable to Pitt. Both Acts implied, if they did not quite require, a central coercive role for the State in matters concerning the lower orders. In the 1780s, education and 'tenant right' were the responsibility of individuals and private institutions, moderated possibly by local justice and local government. The Industrial Revolution had pressed on the government far greater responsibilities and the 1867 Reform Act ensured that, within a very short space, 'social legislation' would be a matter not just of administrative reorganization but of electoral appeal to predominantly working-class electorates in the towns. The preservation of aristocratic primacy in early industrial Britain has been one of the central themes of this book, but by 1870 it was very near its end. The *Edinburgh Review* observed in 1867 that 'the force of the aristocratic principle . . . is so considerably abated that, in order to retain its social position, the aristocracy . . . is ready to make large and increasing concessions of political influence and power'.[10] Within the Liberal party a struggle for control was in progress between established, Whig, landowners and the middle classes, aided by skilled working men, which the former seemed sure to lose. The Conservatives meanwhile were coming to appreciate that they could shake off their apparently permanent minority role only by appealing directly to the new electorate and by playing down their dependence on the land. Few yet appreciated that in 1870 Great Britain had already passed the zenith both of its economic and, despite the great age of imperial expansion still to come, its international primacy. More, however, now agreed that 'Nations and national governments . . . ought to be the great moving and regulating powers in human life',[11] and understood that for this to happen governments had to be not only responsible to, but more obviously representative of, the people they served. For Robert Lowe, now serving as Gladstone's Chancellor of the Exchequer, who had tried so hard to prevent the widening of the franchise, just as for other members of the government in 1870, the task ahead was to convert the 'principle of numbers' into a responsible ethic of government.

---

1. D. G. Boyce, 'The Marginal Britons: the Irish' in R. Colls and P. Dodd, *Englishness* (Beckenham, 1986), p. 231.
2. P. Joyce, *Visions of the People* (Cambridge, 1991), pp. 279–95.
3. C. Dickens, *Our Mutual Friend* (1864, Penguin edn, 1971), pp. 186–7.
4. F. Engels, *The Condition of the Working Class in England in 1844* (Panther edn, 1969), pp. 124–5
5. J. E. Handley, *The Irish in Modern Scotland* (1947), p. 240
6. *The Nation*, 4 September 1872, quoted in A. O'Day, ed., *A Survey of the Irish in England* (1990), p. 65.
7. H. Mayhew, *London Labour and the London Poor* (Penguin edn, 1985), pp. 56 and 58
8. H. C. G. Matthew, ed., *The Gladstone Diaries*, vi, 1861–1868 (Oxford, 1978), p. 588.
9. B. Holland, *Life of the Duke of Devonshire, 1833–1908* (2 vols, 1911), i, p. 70.
10. W. L. Burn, *The Age of Equipoise* (1964), p. 318.
11. *Pall Mall Gazette*, 17 August 1869.

COMPENDIUM OF INFORMATION

A: BRITISH GOVERNMENTS, 1783–1870

Preliminary Note: The lists of ministries which follow contain only ministers included in the Cabinet. It will be clear that some offices did not invariably carry Cabinet rank. Thus, when ministries change hands during an administration and no successor to an office is apparent it should be assumed that the successor did not sit in Cabinet or, more rarely, that the office lapsed. Similarly, ministers are not infrequently promoted to the Cabinet, though continuing to hold the same office which had previously been outside the Cabinet. In such cases, the date given is that at which membership of the Cabinet began.

1. First administration of William Pitt the Younger Dec 1783–Mar 1801

(a) First period: Dec 1783–July 1794

First Lord of the Treasury and Chancellor of the Exchequer:	William Pitt
Lord President of the Council:	Earl Gower, 1783–84
	Lord Camden, 1784–94
Lord Chancellor:	Lord Thurlow, 1783–92
	Lord Loughborough, 1793–94
Home Secretary:	Lord Sydney, 1783–89
	William Grenville (later Lord), 1789–91
	Henry Dundas, 1791–94
Foreign Secretary:	Marquis of Carmarthen (from 1789 duke of Leeds), 1783–91
	Lord Grenville, 1791–94
First Lord of the Admiralty:	Viscount Howe, 1783–88
	Earl of Chatham, 1788–94
Lord Privy Seal:	Duke of Rutland, 1783–84
	Earl Gower, 1784–94
Master-General of the Ordnance:	Duke of Richmond, 1784–94
President of the Board of Trade:	Lord Hawkesbury, 1791–94
Commander-in-Chief:	Lord Amherst, 1793–94

(b) Second period: July 1794–Mar 1801 (i.e. after the Whig realignment)

First Lord of the Treasury and Chancellor of the Exchequer:	William Pitt
Lord Privy Seal:	Earl Spencer (Jul–Dec 1794)
	Earl of Chatham (Dec 1794–96)
	Earl of Westmorland, 1796–1801
Lord President of the Council:	Earl Fitzwilliam (Jul–Dec 1794)
	Earl of Mansfield, 1794–96
	Earl of Chatham, 1796–1801
Lord Chancellor:	Lord Loughborough
Home Secretary:	Duke of Portland
Foreign Secretary:	Lord Grenville
Secretary for War:	Henry Dundas
First Lord of the Admiralty:	Earl of Chatham (Jul–Dec 1794)
	Earl Spencer (Dec 1794–1801)
Master–General of the Ordnance:	Duke of Richmond, 1794–95
	Marquis Cornwallis, 1795–98

Chancellor of the Duchy of Lancaster and President of the Board of Trade:	Lord Hawkesbury (cr. earl of Liverpool, 1796)
Secretary for War:	William Windham
Commander-in-Chief:	Lord Amherst, 1794–95
Minister without Portfolio:	Earl of Mansfield, 1794–95
	Earl Camden, 1798–1801

2. Administration of Henry Addington (Tory) (Mar 1801–May 1804)

First Lord of the Treasury and Chancellor of the Exchequer:	Henry Addington
Lord Privy Seal:	Earl of Westmorland
Lord President of the Council:	Earl of Chatham, (Feb–July 1801)
	Duke of Portland, (July 1801–4)
Lord Chancellor:	Lord Eldon
Home Secretary:	Duke of Portland, (Feb–July 1801)
	Lord Pelham (July 1801–3)
	Charles Yorke, 1803–4
Foreign Secretary:	Lord Hawkesbury
Secretary for War (with additional responsibility for the colonies):	Lord Hobart
First Lord of the Admiralty:	Earl of St Vincent
Chancellor of the Duchy of Lancaster:	Earl of Liverpool, 1801–3
President of the Board of Trade:	Earl of Liverpool
President of the Board of Control:	Viscount Castlereagh, 1802–4

3. Second administration of William Pitt the Younger (Tory) (May 1804–Jan 1806)

First Lord of the Treasury and Chancellor of the Exchequer:	William Pitt
Lord Privy Seal:	Earl of Westmorland
Lord President of the Council:	Duke of Portland, 1804–5
	Viscount Sidmouth (Addington), (Jan–June 1805)
	Earl Camden, 1805–6
Lord Chancellor:	Lord Eldon
Home Secretary:	Lord Hawkesbury
Foreign Secretary:	Lord Harrowby, 1804–5
	Lord Mulgrave, 1805–6
Secretary of State for War and the Colonies:	Earl Camden, 1804–5
	Viscount Castlereagh, 1805–6
First Lord of the Admiralty:	Viscount Melville (Dundas), 1804–5
	Lord Barham, 1805–6
President of the Board of Control:	Viscount Castlereagh
Master-General of the Ordnance:	Earl of Chatham
Chancellor of the Duchy of Lancaster:	Lord Mulgrave, 1804–5
	Earl of Buckinghamshire (Jan–July 1805)
	Lord Harrowby, 1805–6

President of the Board of Trade: Duke of Montrose
Minister without Portfolio: Duke of Portland, 1805–6

4. Ministry of Lord Grenville (Feb 1806–Mar 1807) ('Ministry of all the Talents' Whig-dominated coalition)

First Lord of the Treasury:	Lord Grenville
Chancellor of the Exchequer:	Lord Henry Petty
Lord Privy Seal:	Viscount Sidmouth (Feb–Sept 1806)
	Lord Holland, 1806–7
Lord President of the Council:	Earl Fitzwilliam, (Feb–Sept 1806)
	Viscount Sidmouth, 1806–7
Lord Chancellor:	Lord Erskine
Home Secretary:	Earl Spencer
Foreign Secretary:	Charles James Fox (Feb–Sept 1806)
	Charles Grey, 1806–7
Secretary for War and the Colonies:	William Windham
First Lord of the Admiralty:	Charles Grey (Feb– Sept 1806)
	Thomas Grenville, 1806–7
Master-General of the Ordnance:	Earl of Moira
Lord Chief Justice of the King's Bench:	Lord Ellenborough
President of the Board of Control:	Thomas Grenville (July–Sept 1806)
Minister without Portfolio:	Earl Fitzwilliam, 1806–7

5. Second administration* of the duke of Portland (Tory) (Mar 1807–Sept 1809)

First Lord of the Treasury:	Duke of Portland
Chancellor of the Exchequer and	
Chancellor of the Duchy of Lancaster:	Spencer Perceval
Lord Privy Seal:	Earl of Westmorland
Lord President of the Council:	Earl Camden
Lord Chancellor:	Earl of Eldon
Home Secretary:	Lord Hawkesbury (cr. 2nd earl of Liverpool 1808)
Foreign Secretary:	George Canning
Secretary for War and the Colonies:	Viscount Castlereagh
First Lord of the Admiralty:	Lord Mulgrave
Master-General of the Ordnance:	Earl of Chatham
President of the Board of Trade:	Earl Bathurst
Secretary for War:	Lord Granville Leveson-Gower (June–Sept 1809)
President of the Board of Control:	Earl of Harrowby (July–Sept 1809)

* Portland's first administration is better known as the Fox–North coalition, 1783.

6. Administration of Spencer Perceval (Tory) (Oct 1809–May 1812)

First Lord of the Treasury and Chancellor of the Duchy of Lancaster:	Spencer Perceval
Lord Privy Seal:	Earl of Westmorland

Lord President of the Council:	Earl Camden (1809–Mar 1812)
	Viscount Sidmouth (Mar–May 1812)
Lord Chancellor:	Lord Eldon
Home Secretary:	Richard Ryder
Foreign Secretary:	Earl Bathurst (Oct–Dec 1809)
	Marquis of Wellesley (Dec 1809–Mar 1812)
	Viscount Castlereagh (Mar–May 1812)
President of the Board of Trade:	Earl Bathurst
Secretary for War and Colonies:	Earl of Liverpool
First Lord of the Admiralty:	Lord Mulgrave, 1809–10
	Charles Yorke, 1810–12
President of the Board of Control:	Robert Dundas (became Viscount Melville, 1811) (1809–Mar 1812)
	Earl of Buckinghamshire (Mar–May 1812)
Master General of the Ordnance:	Earl of Chatham, 1809–10
	Lord Mulgrave, 1810–12
Ministers without Portfolio:	Duke of Portland (Oct 1809)
	Earl of Harrowby (Nov 1809–12)
	Earl of Camden (Mar–May 1812)

7. Administration of Lord Liverpool (Tory) (June 1812–Feb 1827)

First Lord of the Treasury:	Earl of Liverpool
Chancellor of the Exchequer:	Nicholas Vansittart, 1812–23
	Frederick J. Robinson, 1823–27
Lord Privy Seal:	Earl of Westmorland
Lord President of the Council:	Earl of Harrowby
Lord Chancellor:	Lord Eldon
Home Secretary:	Viscount Sidmouth, 1812–22
	Robert Peel, 1822–27
Foreign Secretary:	Viscount Castlereagh, 1812–22
	George Canning, 1822–27
Secretary for War and Colonies:	Earl Bathurst (also Pres. of Board of Trade June-Sept 1812)
First Lord of the Admiralty:	Viscount Melville
President of the Board of Control:	Earl of Buckinghamshire, 1812–16
	George Canning, 1816–21
	C. Bragge-Bathurst, 1821–22
	Charles W. W. Wynn, 1822–27
Master-General of the Ordnance:	Lord Mulgrave, 1812–19
	Duke of Wellington, 1819–27
Chancellor of the Duchy of Lancaster:	C. Bragge-Bathurst, 1812–21
	Nicholas Vansittart, 1823–27 (cr. Lord Bexley, 1823)
Master of the Mint:	W. Wellesley-Pole, 1814–23
	Lord Maryborough, 1821
President of the Board of Trade and Treasurer of the Navy:	Frederick J. Robinson (1818–Jan 1823)
	William Huskisson (Oct 1823–27)

Ministers without Portfolio: Earl Camden (June–Dec 1812)
                                         Earl Mulgrave, 1819–20
                                         Viscount Sidmouth, 1822–24

8. Administration of George Canning (Tory) (Apr–Aug 1827)

First Lord of the Treasury and Chancellor of the Exchequer:	George Canning
Lord Chancellor:	Lord Lyndhurst
Lord President of the Council:	Earl of Harrowby
Lord Privy Seal:	Duke of Portland (Apr–July 1827)
	Earl of Carlisle (July–Aug 1827)
Home Secretary:	W. Sturges Bourne (Apr–July 1827)
	Marquis of Lansdowne (July–Aug 1827)
Foreign Secretary:	Viscount Dudley and Ward
Secretary for War and the Colonies:	Viscount Goderich
Master-General of the Ordnance:	Marquis of Anglesey
President of the Board of Trade and Treasurer of the Navy:	William Huskisson
President of the Board of Control:	Charles W. W. Wynn
Chancellor of the Duchy of Lancaster:	Lord Bexley
Secretary for War	Viscount Palmerston
First Commissioner of Woods and Forests:	Earl of Carlisle (May–July 1827)
	W. Sturges Bourne (July–Aug 1827)
Master of the Mint:	George Tierney (May–Aug 1827)
Ministers without Portfolio:	Marquis of Lansdowne (May–July 1827)
	Duke of Portland (July–Aug 1827)

9. Administration of Viscount Goderich (Tory) (Aug 1827–Jan 1828)

First Lord of the Treasury:	Viscount Goderich
Lord Chancellor:	Lord Lyndhurst
Lord President of the Council:	Duke of Portland
Lord Privy Seal:	Earl of Carlisle
Chancellor of the Exchequer:	John C. Herries
Home Secretary:	Marquis of Lansdowne
Foreign Secretary:	Viscount Dudley and Ward
Secretary for War and the Colonies:	William Huskisson
Master-General of the Ordnance:	Marquis of Anglesey
President of the Board of Trade and Treasurer of the Navy:	C. Grant
President of the Board of Control:	Charles W. W. Wynn
Master of the Mint:	George Tierney
Chancellor of the Duchy of Lancaster:	Lord Bexley
First Commissioner of Woods and Forests:	W. Sturges Bourne
Secretary for War:	Viscount Palmerston

10. First administration of the duke of Wellington (Tory) (Jan 1828–Nov 1830)

First Lord of the Treasury:	Duke of Wellington
Lord Chancellor:	Lord Lyndhurst
Lord President of the Council:	Earl Bathurst
Lord Privy Seal:	Lord Ellenborough (Jan–Sept 1828)
	Earl of Rosslyn (June 1829–30)
Chancellor of the Exchequer:	Henry Goulburn
Home Secretary:	Robert Peel
Foreign Secretary:	Earl of Dudley (Jan–May 1828)
	Earl of Aberdeen (May 1828–30)
Secretary for War and the Colonies:	William Huskisson (Jan–May 1828)
	Sir G. Murray (May 1828–30)
President of the Board of Trade and Treasurer of the Navy:	C. Grant (Jan–May 1828)
	W. Vesey Fitzgerald (May 1828–Feb 1830)
	John C. Herries (Feb–Nov 1830)
President of the Board of Control:	Viscount Melville (Jan–Sept 1828)
	Lord Ellenborough (Sept 1828–30)
Master of the Mint:	John C. Herries (1828–Feb 1830)
Chancellor of the Duchy of Lancaster:	Earl of Aberdeen (Jan–May 1828)
Secretary for War:	Viscount Palmerston (Jan–May 1828)
First Lord of the Admiralty:	Viscount Melville (Sept 1828–30)

11. Administration of Earl Grey (Whig) (Nov 1830–July 1834)

First Lord of the Treasury:	Earl Grey
Lord Chancellor:	Lord Brougham
Lord President of the Council:	Marquis of Lansdowne
Lord Privy Seal:	Lord Durham, 1830–33
	Earl of Ripon (formerly Viscount Goderich) (1833–May 1834)
	Earl of Carlisle (May–July 1834)
Chancellor of the Exchequer:	Viscount Althorp
Home Secretary:	Viscount Melbourne
Foreign Secretary:	Viscount Palmerston
Secretary for War and the Colonies:	Viscount Goderich, 1830–33
	Edward Stanley (1833–June 1834)
	T. Spring Rice (June–July 1834)
First Lord of the Admiralty:	Sir James Graham (1830–June 1834)
	Lord Auckland (June–July 1834)
President of the Board of Control:	C. Grant
Chancellor of the Duchy of Lancaster:	Lord Holland
Postmaster-General:	Duke of Richmond (1830–June 1834)
Minister without Portfolio:	Earl of Carlisle (1830–June 1834)
Paymaster–General of the Forces:	Lord John Russell, 1831–34
Chief Secretary for Ireland:	Edward Stanley, 1831–33
President of the Board of Trade and Treasurer of the Navy:	J. Abercromby (May–July 1834)
Secretary for War:	E. Ellice (May–July 1834)

12. First administration of Viscount Melbourne (Whig) (July–Nov 1834)

First Lord of the Treasury:	Viscount Melbourne
Lord Chancellor:	Lord Brougham
Lord President of the Council:	Marquis of Lansdowne
Lord Privy Seal:	Earl of Mulgrave
Chancellor of the Exchequer:	Viscount Althorp
Home Secretary:	Viscount Duncannon
Foreign Secretary:	Viscount Palmerston
Secretary for War and the Colonies:	T. Spring Rice
First Lord of the Admiralty:	Earl of Auckland
President of the Board of Trade and Treasurer of the Navy:	C. E. Poulett Thomson
President of the Board of Control:	C. Grant
Master of the Mint:	J. Abercromby
Chancellor of the Duchy of Lancaster:	Lord Holland
Secretary for War:	E. Ellice
First Commissioner of Woods and Forests:	Sir John Cam Hobhouse
Paymaster-General of the Forces:	Lord John Russell

13. Second administration of the duke of Wellington (Caretaker administration) (Nov–Dec 1834)

First Lord of the Treasury, Home Secretary, Foreign Secretary, Secretary for War and the Colonies:	Duke of Wellington
Lord Chancellor:	Lord Lyndhurst
Chancellor of the Exchequer:	Lord Denman

14. First administration of Sir Robert Peel (Conservative) (Dec 1834–Apr 1835)

First Lord of the Treasury and Chancellor of the Exchequer:	Sir Robert Peel
Lord Chancellor:	Lord Lyndhurst
Lord President of the Council:	Earl of Rosslyn
Lord Privy Seal:	Lord Wharncliffe
Home Secretary:	Henry Goulburn
Foreign Secretary:	Duke of Wellington
Secretary for War and the Colonies:	Earl of Aberdeen
First Lord of the Admiralty:	Earl de Grey
President of the Board of Trade and Master of the Mint:	Alexander Baring
President of the Board of Control:	Lord Ellenborough
Secretary for War:	John C. Herries
Paymaster-General:	Sir Edward Knatchbull

15. Second administration of Viscount Melbourne (Whig) (Apr 1835–Aug 1841)

First Lord of the Treasury:	Viscount Melbourne
Lord President of the Council:	Marquis of Lansdowne
Lord Privy Seal:	Viscount Duncannon, 1835–40
	Earl of Clarendon, 1840–41
First Commissioner of Woods and Forests:	Viscount Duncannon
Chancellor of the Exchequer:	T. Spring Rice, 1835–39
	Sir Francis Baring, 1839–41
Home Secretary:	Lord John Russell, 1835–39
	Lord Normanby, 1839–41
Foreign Secretary:	Viscount Palmerston
Secretary for War and the Colonies:	Lord Glenelg (C. Grant), 1835–39
	Lord Normanby (Feb–Sept 1839)
	Lord John Russell, 1839–41
First Lord of the Admiralty:	Lord Auckland (Apr–Sept 1835)
	Earl of Minto, 1835–41
President of the Board of Trade:	C. E. Poulett Thomson, 1835–39
	Henry Labouchere, 1839–41
President of the Board of Control:	Sir John Cam Hobhouse
Chancellor of the Duchy of Lancaster:	Lord Holland, 1835–40
	Earl of Clarendon, 1840–41
Secretary for War:	Sir George Grey (Jan–Aug 1841)
	Viscount Howick, 1835–39
	Thomas B. Macaulay, 1839–41
Lord Chancellor:	Lord Cottenham, 1836–41
Chief Secretary for Ireland:	Lord Morpeth, 1839–41

16. Second administration of Sir Robert Peel (Conservative) (Aug 1841–June 1846)

First Lord of the Treasury:	Sir Robert Peel
Lord Chancellor:	Lord Lyndhurst
Lord President of the Council:	Lord Wharncliffe, 1841–45
	Duke of Buccleuch (Jan–June 1846)
Lord Privy Seal:	Duke of Buckingham, 1841–42
	Duke of Buccleuch, 1842–46
	Earl of Haddington (Jan–June 1846)
Chancellor of the Exchequer:	Henry Goulburn
Home Secretary:	Sir James Graham
Foreign Secretary:	Earl of Aberdeen
Secretary for War and the Colonies:	Viscount Stanley, 1841–45
	William Gladstone (Dec 1845–46)
First Lord of the Admiralty:	Earl of Haddington, 1841–45
	Earl Ellenborough, 1845–46
President of the Board of Trade:	Earl of Ripon, 1841–43
	William Gladstone (1843–Jan 1845)
	Earl of Dalhousie (Dec 1845–46)
President of the Board of Control:	Lord Ellenborough (Aug–Oct 1841)
	Lord Fitzgerald, 1841–43
	Earl of Ripon, 1843–46

Secretary for War:	Sir Henry Hardinge, 1841–44
	Sidney Herbert, 1845–46
Paymaster-General:	Sir Edward Knatchbull, 1841–45
Minister without Portfolio:	Duke of Wellington
Chancellor of the Duchy of Lancaster:	Lord Granville Somerset, 1844–46
First Commissioner of Woods and Forests:	Earl of Lincoln, 1845–46

17. First administration of Lord John Russell (Whig) (June 1846–Feb 1852)

First Lord of the Treasury:	Lord John Russell
Lord Chancellor:	Lord Cottenham, 1846–50
	Lord Truro, 1850–52
Lord President of the Council:	Marquis of Lansdowne
Lord Privy Seal:	Earl of Minto
Chancellor of the Exchequer:	Sir Charles Wood
Home Secretary:	Sir George Grey
Foreign Secretary:	Viscount Palmerston, 1846–51
	Earl Granville, 1851–52
Secretary for War and the Colonies:	Earl Grey
First Lord of the Admiralty:	Earl of Auckland, 1846–49
	Sir Francis Baring, 1849–52
President of the Board of Trade:	Earl of Clarendon, 1846–47
	Henry Labouchere, 1847–52
President of the Board of Control:	Sir John Cam Hobhouse (cr. Lord Broughton, 1851) (1846–Jan 1852)
	Fox Maule (Jan–Feb 1852)
Chancellor of the Duchy of Lancaster:	Lord Campbell, 1846–50
	Earl of Carlisle, 1850–52
First Commissioner of Woods and Forests:	Lord Morpeth (cr. earl of Carlisle 1848) (1846–Apr 1849)
Chief Secretary for Ireland:	Henry Labouchere, 1846–47
Postmaster-General:	Marquis of Clanricarde
Paymaster-General:	Thomas B. Macaulay, 1846–47
	Earl Granville (Oct–Dec 1851)
First Commissioner of Works:	Lord Seymour, 1851–52
Secretary for War:	Fox Maule, 1851–52

18. First administration of the earl of Derby (Conservative) (Feb–Dec 1852)

First Lord of the Treasury:	Earl of Derby (Viscount Stanley, succeeded to earldom 1851)
Lord Chancellor:	Lord St Leonards
Lord President of the Council:	Earl of Lonsdale
Lord Privy Seal:	Marquis of Salisbury
Chancellor of the Exchequer:	Benjamin Disraeli
Home Secretary:	Spencer Walpole
Foreign Secretary:	Earl of Malmesbury
Secretary for War and the Colonies:	Sir John Pakington
First Lord of the Admiralty:	Duke of Northumberland
President of the Board of Trade:	Joseph W. Henley

President of the Board of Control: John C. Herries
First Commissioner of Works: Lord John Manners
Postmaster-General: Earl of Hardwicke

19. Administration of the earl of Aberdeen (Peelite/Whig coalition) (Dcc 1852–Feb 1855)

First Lord of the Treasury: Earl of Aberdeen
Lord Chancellor: Lord Cranworth
Lord President of the Council: Earl Granville, 1852–54
    Lord John Russell (1854–Jan 1855)
Lord Privy Seal: Duke of Argyll
Chancellor of the Exchequer: William Gladstone
Home Secretary: Viscount Palmerston
Foreign Secretary: Lord John Russell, 1852–53
    Earl of Clarendon, 1853–55
Secretary for War and the Colonies: Duke of Newcastle, 1852–54
Secretary for War: Duke of Newcastle, 1854–55
Secretary for the Colonies: Sir George Grey, 1854–55
First Lord of the Admiralty: Sir James Graham
President of the Board of Control: Sir Charles Wood
First Commissioner of Works: Sir William Molesworth
Secretary for War: Sidney Herbert, 1852–54
Minister without Portfolio: Marquis of Lansdowne
Chancellor of the Duchy of Lancaster: Earl Granville, 1854–55

20. First administration of Viscount Palmerston (Whig) (Feb 1855–Feb 1858)

First Lord of the Treasury: Viscount Palmerston
Lord Chancellor: Lord Cranworth
Lord President of the Council: Earl Granville
Lord Privy Seal: Duke of Argyll (Feb–Dec 1855)
    Earl of Harrowby, 1855–57
    Marquis of Clanricarde, 1857–58
Chancellor of the Exchequer: William Gladstone (Feb 1855)
    Sir G. Cornewall Lewis, 1855–58
Home Secretary: Sir George Grey
Foreign Secretary: Earl of Clarendon
Secretary for War: Lord Panmure (formerly Fox Maule)
Secretary for the Colonies: Sidney Herbert (Feb 1855)
    Lord John Russell (Feb–July 1855)
    Sir William Molesworth (July–Oct 1855)
    Henry Labouchere, 1855–58
First Lord of the Admiralty: Sir James Graham (Feb 1855)
    Sir Charles Wood, 1855–58
President of the Board of Control: Sir Charles Wood (Feb 1855)
    R. V. Smith, 1855–58
First Commissioner of Works: Sir William Molesworth (Feb–July 1855)
Postmaster-General: Viscount Canning (Feb–July 1855)
    Duke of Argyll (Nov 1855–58)
Minister without Portfolio: Marquis of Lansdowne

Chancellor of the Duchy of Lancaster:	Earl of Harrowby (Mar–Dec 1855)
	M. T. Baines, 1855–58
President of the Board of Trade:	Baron Stanley of Alderley

21. Second administration of the earl of Derby (Conservative) (Feb 1858–June 1859)

First Lord of the Treasury:	Earl of Derby
Lord Chancellor:	Lord Chelmsford
Lord President of the Council:	Marquis of Salisbury
Lord Privy Seal:	Earl of Hardwicke
Chancellor of the Exchequer:	Benjamin Disraeli
Home Secretary:	Spencer Walpole (1858–Feb 1859)
	Thomas H. Sotherton-Estcourt (Feb–June 1859)
Foreign Secretary:	Earl of Malmesbury
Secretary for War:	General Jonathan Peel
Secretary for the Colonies:	Lord Stanley (Feb–May 1858)
	Sir E. Bulwer-Lytton, 1858–59
First Lord of the Admiralty:	Sir J. Pakington
President of the Board of Trade:	J. W. Henley (1858–Feb 1859)
	Earl of Donoughmore (Feb–June 1859)
President of the Board of Control:	Earl of Ellenborough (Feb–May 1858)
	Lord Stanley (May–Aug 1858)
Secretary of State for India:	Lord Stanley (Aug 1858–59)
First Commissioner of Works:	Lord John Manners

22. Second administration of Viscount Palmerston (Liberal) (June 1859–Oct 1865)

First Lord of the Treasury:	Viscount Palmerston
Lord Chancellor:	Lord Campbell, 1859–61
	Lord Westbury (1861–July 1865)
	Lord Cranworth (July–Oct 1865)
Lord President of the Council:	Earl Granville
Lord Privy Seal:	Duke of Argyll
Chancellor of the Exchequer:	William Gladstone
Home Secretary:	Sir G. Cornewall Lewis, 1859–61
	Sir George Grey (July 1861–65)
Foreign Secretary:	Lord John Russell (Earl Russell from 1861)
Secretary for War:	Sidney Herbert (Lord Herbert of Lea from 1860), 1859–61
	Sir G. Cornewall Lewis, 1861–63
	Earl de Grey, 1863–65
Secretary for the Colonies:	Duke of Newcastle, 1859–64
	Edward Cardwell, 1864–65
First Lord of the Admiralty:	Duke of Somerset
Secretary of State for India:	Sir Charles Wood
Chancellor of the Duchy of Lancaster:	Sir George Grey, 1859–61
	Edward Cardwell, 1861–64
Chief Secretary for Ireland:	Edward Cardwell, 1859–61

Postmaster-General: Earl of Elgin, 1859–60
Duke of Argyll (May–Aug 1860)
Baron Stanley of Alderley, 1860–65
President of the Poor Law Board: Thomas Mimer-Gibson (1858–July 1859)
Charles P. Villiers, 1859–65

23. Second administration of Earl Russell (Liberal) (Oct 1865–June 1866)

First Lord of the Treasury: Earl Russell
Lord Chancellor: Lord Cranworth
Lord President of the Council: Earl Granville
Lord Privy Seal: Duke of Argyll
Chancellor of the Exchequer: William Gladstone
Home Secretary: Sir George Grey
Foreign Secretary: Earl of Clarendon
Secretary for War: Earl de Grey (1865–Feb 1866)
Marquis of Hartington (Feb–June 1866)
Secretary for the Colonies: Edward Cardwell
First Lord of the Admiralty: Duke of Somerset
Secretary of State for India: Sir Charles Wood (1865–Feb 1866)
Earl de Grey (Feb–June 1866)
Postmaster-General: Baron Stanley of Alderley
President of the Poor Law Board: Charles P. Villiers
Chancellor of the Duchy of Lancaster: George J. Goschen (Jan–June 1866)

24. Third administration of the earl of Derby (Conservative) (June 1866–Feb 1868)

First Lord of the Treasury: Earl of Derby
Lord Chancellor: Lord Chelmsford
Lord President of the Council: Duke of Buckingham, 1866–67
Duke of Marlborough, 1867–68
Lord Privy Seal: Earl of Malmesbury
Chancellor of the Exchequer: Benjamin Disraeli
Home Secretary: Spencer Walpole, 1866–67
Gathorne-Hardy, 1867–68
Foreign Secretary: Lord Stanley
Secretary for War: General Jonathan Peel, 1866–67
Sir John Pakington, 1867–68
Secretary for the Colonies: Earl of Carnarvon, 1866–67
Duke of Buckingham, 1867–68
First Lord of the Admiralty: Sir John Pakington, 1866–67
Henry Lowry-Corry, 1867–68
President of the Board of Trade: Sir Stafford Northcote, 1866–67
Duke of Richmond, 1867–68
Secretary of State for India: Viscount Cranborne, 1866–67
Sir Stafford Northcote, 1867–68
First Commissioner of Works: Lord John Manners
Chief Secretary for Ireland: Lord Naas (cr. earl of Mayo, 1867)
President of the Poor Law Board: Gathorne-Hardy, 1866–67
Minister without Portfolio Spencer Walpole, 1867–68

25. First administration of Benjamin Disraeli (Conservative) (Feb–Dec 1868)

First Lord of the Treasury:	Benjamin Disraeli
Lord Chancellor:	Lord Chelmsford
Lord President of the Council:	Duke of Marlborough
Lord Privy Seal:	Earl of Malmesbury
Chancellor of the Exchequer:	G. Ward Hunt
Foreign Secretary:	Lord Stanley
Secretary for War:	Sir John Pakington
Secretary for the Colonies:	Duke of Buckingham
First Lord of the Admiralty:	Henry Lowry-Corry
President of the Board of Trade:	Duke of Richmond
Secretary of State for India:	Sir Stafford Northcote
First Commissioner of Works:	Lord John Manners
Minister without Portfolio:	Spencer Walpole

26. First administration of William Gladstone (Liberal) (Dec 1868–Feb 1874) (changes are included only up to 1870)

First Lord of the Treasury:	William Gladstone
Lord Chancellor:	Lord Hatherley
Lord President of the Council:	Earl de Grey
Lord Privy Seal:	Earl of Kimberley (1868–July 1870)
	Viscount Halifax (was Sir Charles Wood) (from July 1870)
Chancellor of the Exchequer:	Robert Lowe
Home Secretary:	Henry A. Bruce
Foreign Secretary:	Earl of Clarendon (1868–July 1870)
	Earl Granville (from July 1870)
Secretary for War:	Edward Cardwell
Secretary for the Colonies:	Earl Granville (1868–July 1870)
	Earl of Kimberley (from July 1870)
First Lord of the Admiralty:	Hugh C. E. Childers
President of the Board of Trade:	John Bright (1868–Dec 1870)
Secretary for India:	Duke of Argyll
President of the Poor Law Board:	George J. Goschen
Postmaster-General:	Marquis of Hartington
Chief Secretary for Ireland:	Chichester S. Fortescue

B: PARLIAMENT AND PARLIAMENTARY REFORM

B.i.1 Major proposals for parliamentary reform, 1783–1830

May 1783: Pitt's objective 'not to innovate, but rather to renew and invigorate the spirit of the Constitution, without deteriorating materially from its present form'.
    (a) Measures to be taken to defeat bribery at elections.
    (b) Boroughs convicted by a Select Committee of the House of corruption to be disfranchised.
    (c) An unspecified addition to the number of MPs representing both counties and metropolitan boroughs.
    Defeated 293–149

April 1785: *Pitt's proposals*
    (a) To 'buy out' voluntarily 36 small boroughs by compensating electors for their lost rights.
    (b) Seats then vacated (maximum 72) would be transferred to counties and to London.
    (c) Forty-shilling copyholders and some leaseholders to be added to the county electorate.
    Defeated 248–174

May 1797: *Grey's motion*
    (a) To increase county representation from 92 MPs to 113, taking the seats from certain small boroughs.
    (b) Extension of county franchise to copyholders and leaseholders.
    (c) Borough members to be elected on a householder franchise.
    (Based on resolutions of the Society of the Friends of the People in 1794.)
    Defeated 256–91

May 1810: *Thomas Brand's motion*
    (a) County franchise to be extended to copyholders.
    (b) Borough MPs to be elected by householders paying parochial rates.
    (c) Decayed boroughs to be deprived, their seats being transferred to unenfranchised larger towns.
    (d) Patrons of deprived boroughs to be compensated.
    (e) Triennial parliaments.
    Defeated 234–115

April 1822: *Lord John Russell's motion*
    The 100 smallest boroughs to lose one of their two MPs, the seats being transferred to counties and unenfranchised towns.
    Defeated 269–164

1809: Curwen's Act to Prohibit the Sale of Seats in the House of Commons passed.

1826: Borough of Grampound disfranchised for corrupt practices: its two MPs added to the existing two for the county of Yorkshire.

B.i.2 Major proposals for parliamentary reform, 1852-1866

February 1852: Russell's bill: Vote to be extended to householders to the value of £20 in the counties and £5 in the towns.
    Bill fell with the Russell government.

February 1854: Russell's bill
   (a) Vote to be extended to £10 householders in the counties and £6 householders in the boroughs.
   (b) Sixty-six small boroughs to be disfranchised and seats transferred – 46 to the counties, 17 to the boroughs, 2 to the Inns of Court and 1 to London University.
   Withdrawn when Crimean War began.

February 1859: Derby's bill
   (a) Vote to be extended to £10 householders to both counties and boroughs.
   (b) A lodger franchise of £20 per year to be introduced.
   (c) Forty-shilling freeholder living in a borough must vote in that borough and not in adjacent county.
   (d) Seventy small boroughs to be disfranchised and seats transferred – 18 to large boroughs, 52 to counties.
   (e) Vote also extended to members of certain professions, government pensioners, university graduates and those with deposits of at least £60 in savings banks. 'Fancy franchises' (John Bright).
   Defeated 330–291. Derby government resigns.

March 1860: Russell's bill
   (a) Vote to be extended to £10 county householders and £6 borough householders.
   (b) Small redistribution of seats.
   Withdrawn June 1860.

March 1866: Russell's bill
   (a) Vote to be extended to £14 county householders and £7 borough householders.
   (b) A lodger franchise of £10 to be introduced.
   (c) Vote to be extended to those with deposits of at least £50 in savings banks.
   (d) Forty-nine small boroughs to be disfranchised. Boroughs with populations of less than 8,000 to be grouped – 26 seats to go to counties, 22 to boroughs, 1 to London University.
   A Conservative amendment carried 335–304 on 18 June. Russell resigned a week later.

Additionally, seven motions to introduce a secret ballot at elections were introduced without success between 1851 and 1864.

B.ii.1 Parliamentary Reform Act, 1832

1. *Changes in distribution of seats in England*
(a) Fifty-six borough constituencies disenfranchised and 30 lose one of their two members.
(b) Twenty-two new double-member and 20 new single-member borough constituencies created.
(c) Yorkshire to have 6 county members; 26 counties elect 4 county members instead of 2; 7 counties to elect 3 members instead of 2; Isle of Wight detached from Hampshire to return a single member.

2. *Main qualifications for the franchise in England*
In county seats:
(a) Adult males owning freehold property worth at least 40s (£2) per annum.
(b) Adult males seized of copyhold land worth at least £10 per annum.
(c) Adult males who lease or rent land worth at least £50 per annum (Chandos amendment).

In borough seats:
(a) Adult males owning or occupying property worth at least £10 per annum, provided that:
    (i) they had been in possession of the property for at least one year and had paid all contingent taxes arising from the property;
    (ii) they had not received any parochial poor relief in the previous year.
(b) Pre-1832 franchise holders kept their rights in their lifetimes provided they lived in or within 7 miles of the borough in which they wished to vote.
    A register of voters to be established in borough and county seats.

B.ii.2 Parliamentary reform and redistribution, 1867–1868

1. *Changes in the distribution of seats in England*
(a) One single-member and 3 double-member boroughs disenfranchised for corruption.
(b) Of boroughs with a population of less than 10,000: 3 lost both members, 35 lost one of their two members and 4 lost their single member.
(c) Two new double-member and 9 new single-member borough constituencies created.
(d) Birmingham, Leeds, Liverpool and Manchester increased from double-member to triple-member constituencies; Merthyr Tydfil and Salford became double-member constituencies.
(e) Ten counties elect 2 additional members each: Lancashire elects 3 additional members; Yorkshire (West Riding) elects 2 additional members.
(f) University of London to elect 1 member.

2. *Main qualifications for the franchise in England*
In county seats:
(a) Those with lands of a clear yearly value of at least £5, owned or on lease of 60 years or more.
(b) Those occupiers of lands to a rateable value of £12 per annum who have paid the relevant poor rates.
(c) Otherwise as established in 1832.

In borough seats:
(a) Adult male owners and occupiers of dwelling-houses, if resident for at least 12 months.
(b) Lodgers occupying lodgings worth at least £10 per annum, for at least 12 months.

The Minority Clause
In county or borough seats with 3 members no elector could vote for more than 2 candidates; in the 4-seat constituency of the City of London no elector could vote for more than 3 candidates.

B.iii Approximate size of the electorate 1831–1869

England and Wales	1831	1833	%increase 1831–33
Counties	239,000	370,379	55
Boroughs	200,000	282,398	41
Combined	439,000	652,777	49

England and Wales	1866	1869	% increase 1866–69
Counties	542,633	791,916	46
Boroughs	514,026	1,203,170	134
Combined	1,056,659	1,995,086	89
Scotland	1831	1833	1869
	4,579	64,447	230,606

Estimated proportion of adult males enfranchised in England and Wales before and after the first two Reform Acts

1831: 439,000 of 3,463,795 (13%)   **1833**: 652,777 of 3,577,538 (18%)
1866: 1,056,659 of 5,373,033 (20%)   **1869**: 1,995,086 of 5,562,508 (36%)

Note: Figures are only approximate. It is impossible to be sure how far plural voting affected total figures of the electorate. Estimations of population derive from census material and extrapolation of trends in inter–censual estimates.

Sources: J. Cannon, *Parliamentary Reform 1640–1832* (2nd edn 1980); F. O'Gorman *Voters, Parties and Patrons: the Unreformed Electorial System of Hanoverian England, 1734–1832* (Oxford, 1989); B. R. Mitchell and P. Deane, *Abstract of British Historical Statistics* (1962).

B.iv The composition of the House of Commons, 1801–1868

1801	England	Wales	Scotland	Ireland	Total
County seats	80	12	30	64	186
Borough seats	405	12	15	35	467
University seats	4	—	—	1	5
	489	24	45	100	658

1833	England	Wales	Scotland	Ireland	Total
County seats	144	15	30	64	253
Pre–1832 borough seats	260 } 323	12 } 14	15 } 23	39	399
Newly created borough seats	63	2	8		
University seats	4	—		2	6
	471	29	53	105	658

1868	England	Wales	Scotland	Ireland	Total
County seats	169	15	32	64	280
1832–67 Borough seats	272 } 290	13 } 14	23 } 26	39	369
Newly created borough seats	18	1	3		
University seats	5	—	2	2	9
	464	29	60	105	658

B.v A note on approximate strengths of parties and groups in the Commons, 1784–1832

It is not possible to offer any clear indication of the state of parties after each General Election in this period. Most elections in any case did not result in any marked change of allegiance between parties; none directly caused a change of government, though the 1830 Election sensibly weakened Wellington's. The two great shifts in parliamentary strength after elections – 1784 and 1807 – reflected massively increased support for new governments already installed by George III.

Nor are party allegiances reliable guides. Though subsequent historians have pinned the label on to him cheerfully enough, the younger Pitt would never accept that he was a Tory. This title was accepted only by his direct political descendants: Liverpool, Canning and Peel. Similarly, the vicissitudes of the Whigs reflect splits as well as loss of support. Some kind of continuity can be claimed from the Rockingham Whigs, through the Foxite reformers of the 1790s and the opposition to Liverpool's long administration to the eventual emergence of Grey's government in 1830. Such continuity, which can be further traced into Liberalism in the 1840s and 1850s, should not obscure the fact that the Portland Whigs who joined the Pitt government did so with no sense of desertion from Whiggery; rather they were defending the true spirit of the 1688 Revolution in an age threatened by 'Jacobins and Atheists'.

In such a situation it is more accurate to talk of groups than parties. The estimates below draw on calculations made by party managers. They frequently got their sums wrong and only limited reliance should be placed on them. Solid quantification is not possible given the fluid condition of party allegiance and the continuing strength of independent MPs. The task is made harder by the fact that very few divisions attracted the votes of even as many of one-half of the members of the Commons. Except for the committed politicians, the general rule as late as 1830 was arrival in London after the parliamentary session had begun and departure well before it finished. This was not infrequently exploited by government managers anxious to smuggle contentious legislation through a thin House early or late in the session. Party strengths, therefore, tended to fluctuate more within a particular session because of absence than between elections as a result of measurable shifts of opinion.

When ministries were firmly established, also, there was a tendency for opposition to become more formal and for opposition support to dwindle. Thus, the Whigs could call upon only between 30 and 60 supporters in divisions immediately before the 1818 Election, though the election itself, fought in a difficult economic climate for the government, resulted in the return of perhaps 175 members favourably disposed to the opposition. On particular issues, too, those affecting taxation and expenditure, opposition and independents could combine seriously to embarrass the government or even defeat it. In 1816, most notably, this combination resulted in a defeat for Liverool by about 40 votes on a government motion to retain Pitt's wartime expedient of an income tax. Even such a severe rebuff, however, did not pose a threat to the government's continued existence. Both parties knew that on any issue of confidence, the independents would return to their natural haven and support the government.

In the computations which follow it is important to remember that in normal circumstances the opposition was the most clearly identifiable group in the Commons apart from ministers themselves. Given the natural predisposition of independents to support the government in the interests of stability, the distinction between administration supporters and independents or uncommitted was hazy. It is safe to assume that the government could hope to entice far more of the uncommitted into its lobby on any issue of confidence than could the opposition. In other words, figures for the opposition should be regarded as near maxima; government support, though more amorphous, was potentially much greater.

Indeed, during the Liverpool administration, those formally committed to the government rarely exceeded 60 or 70, as the power of patronage perceptibly diminished. Government majorities which in a moderately full division fell as low as the size of this formal support were regarded as embarrassing.

Government also had cause for concern if, despite obtaining majorities in the House, its support was falling among county members and those who represented borough seats with electorates sufficiently large to be proof against aristocratic management. It was most noticeable in the ostensibly indecisive election of 1830 that the government fared badly in county and 'open' borough seats. Wellington's obvious lack of public support in those constituencies where it could be effectively expressed was damaging and led to a further erosion of support among those independents who normally voted with the government. His administration lasted barely three months after the results were known.

I have included estimates only for key stages in political alignment.

John Robinson's estimate of the strength of parties on Pitt's accession to power, December 1783

Supporters of the Fox-North coalition	231
Supporters of Pitt	149
Independents leaning towards Pitt	104
Independents leaning towards Fox	74

State of the parties after General Election, March 1784

Pittites	315
Foxites and Northites	213
Independents and doubtfuls	30

These figures include large numbers of independent members who declared themselves either for Pitt or for Fox on the hustings but who would not consider themselves 'party men'. One estimate puts the Whig opposition at 132 after 1784, including over 60 supporters of the Fox–Portland connection and over 50 followers of Lord North.

State of the parties in 1788

Government: Pitt	280
Opposition: Portland-Fox group and followers of North	155
Independent members	122

State of the parties after the Whig split July 1794

Supporters of Pitt plus independent members who generally supported the government on important issues	426	} 503
Portland Whigs	77	
Foxite Whigs	55	

State of the parties at the accession of the Ministry of All the Talents, 1806

Supporters of the ministry	260
Independent, but leaning to the ministry	176
Opposition (Pittites)	108
Independent, but leaning to the opposition	110

State of the parties after the 1806 Election

Supporters of the Talents ministry	308
Independent, but leaning to the ministry	151
Opposition (Pittites)	90
Independent, but leaning to the opposition	102

State of the parties after the 1807 Election

Supporters of the Portland ministry	216
Independent, but leaning to the ministry	154
Opposition (Foxites and Grenvillites)	213
Independent, but leaning to the opposition	71

State of the parties after the Election of 1818

Supporters of Liverpool (Tories)	280
Opposition (Whigs)	175
Doubtful or uncommitted	203

State of the parties after the Election of 1830

Government supporters (Wellington-Peel Tories)	250
Opposition supporters (Whigs, Canningite and Huskissonite Tories)	196
Doubtful or uncommitted	212

State of the parties after the Election of 1831

Pro-reform (Whigs)	370
Anti-reform (Tories)	235
Doubtful or uncommitted	53

Sources: J. Cannon, *Parliamentary Reform 1640–1832* (2nd edn, 1980); F. O'Gorman, *The Whig Party and the French Revolution* (1967); L. G. Mitchell, *Charles James Fox and the Disin- tegration of the Whig Party, 1782–94* (1971); M. Roberts, *The Whig Party, 1807–12* (1939); A. Mitchell, *The Whigs in Opposition, 1815–30* (1967); A. D. Harvey, *Britain in the Early Nineteenth Century* (1978); J. E. Cookson, *Lord Liverpool's Administration: the crucial years, 1815–22* (1975); M. Brock, *The Great Reform Act* (1973)

B.vi General Election results, 1832–1868: An approximation

December 1832

Whigs (reformers)	483
Tories (anti-reformers)	175

January 1835

Whig/Liberals	385
Conservatives	273

August 1837

Whig/Liberals	345
Conservatives	313

July 1841

Conservatives	367
Whig/Liberals	291

July 1847

Liberals	338
Conservatives	227
Peelites	91

July 1852

Liberals	310
Conservatives	299
Peelites	45

April 1857

Liberals	367
Conservatives	260
Peelites	27

May 1859

Liberals	325
Conservatives	306
Peelites	23

July 1865

Liberals	370
Conservatives	288

November 1868

Liberals	387
Conservatives	271

Notes

1. These figures can be used as a rough guide only. Some members included here, especially in the early elections, considered themselves independent of party allegiance. No attempt has been made to separate radicals from Liberals, though the Liberal grouping was rarely cohesive and radicals frequently voted against Liberal governments. Independently minded county MPs have been allotted here to the Conservatives.

2. The 105 Irish MPs, who rejected precise English political labels, have been assigned to the parties they generally favoured. In the 1830s, they supported the Liberals roughly in the proportion 2 : 1. Between 1841 and 1868 support was more evenly split. Usually, the Liberals benefited in the ratio 3 : 2 but in 1859 the parties received approximately equal support.

3. Party labels were particularly fluid between 1846 and 1859 (see Ch. 37) and, though Peelites have been distinguished from the rest, party managers found it peculiarly difficult to distinguish firm support for either large party group. Their estimates frequently differed. Soon after the 1859 Election, the remaining Peelites joined the Liberal party and party allegiance became firmer.

Sources: F. W. S. Craig, *British Parliamentary Election Results, 1832–1885* (1977); J. Vincent and M. Stenton, eds, *McCalmont's Parliamentary Poll Book* (1971 edn); J. B. Conacher, *The Peelites and the Party System, 1846–52* (1972).

B.vii.1 Contested elections in England, 1784–1868

	Number of contests	*Total constituencies*	*Percentage*
1784	72	243	29.63
1790	76	243	31.28
1796	60	243	24.69
1802	73	243	30.04
1806	65	243	26.75
1807	71	243	29.22
1812	57	243	23.46
1818	93	243	38.27
1820	73	243	30.04
1826	88	243	36.21
1830	83	243	34.16
1831	75	243	30.86
1832	188	254	74.02
1835	153	254	60.24
1837	176	254	69.29
1841	138	254	54.33
1847	120	254	47.24
1852	159	254	62.60
1857	131	254	51.57
1859	125	254	49.21
1865	152	254	59.84
1868	195	267	73.03

Average percentage of contests 1784–1831: 30.38
Average percentage of contests 1832–65: 58.71

B.vii.2 Contested elections in Britain, 1832–1868

	Number of contests	*Total constituencies*	*Percentage*
1832	276	401	68.83
1835	224	401	55.86
1837	253	401	63.09
1841	189	401	47.13
1847	166	401	41.40
1852	231	401	57.61
1857	186	401	46.38
1859	164	401	40.90
1865	206	401	51.37
1868	280	420	66.67

Average percentage of contests 1832–65: 52.51

Sources: J. Cannon, *Parliamentary Reform 1640–1832* (2nd edn, 1980); F. W. S. Craig, *British Parliamentary Election Results, 1832–85* (1977)

C: THE GROWTH OF GOVERNMENT

C.i Factory and industrial legislation

1802: Health and Morals of Apprentices Act:
1. Pauper apprentices in textile mills not to work more than 12 hours a day.
2. Inspection may be made by local Justices of the Peace; this provision proved largely ineffective.

1819: Peel's Factory Act: specific to employment to cotton mills; no inspection
1. No child under 9 years could be employed.
2. Maximum working day of 12 hours for children of 9–16 years.

1833: Factory Act: applied to all textile mills except silk and lace
1. No child to be employed under the age of 9 years.
2. Children under 13 years could work a maximum of 8 hours; those of 13–18 years could work a maximum of 12 hours a day.
3. Children under 13 years to receive education for at least 2 hours in each working day; employers may make wage deductions to cover education costs.
4. Four factory inspectors appointed to supervise implementation of the Act.

1842: Mines Act: women and children prohibited from work underground; boys not permitted to work underground until 10 years. Inspectorate established.

1844: Factory Act: Applied to textile factories only
1. Children of 8–13 years could work a maximum of 6½ hours a day.
2. Children to receive education for at least 3 hours each working day.
3. Women not permitted to work at nights and not more than 12 hours in any working day.

1847: Factory Act: women and children 13–18 years could work a maximum of 10 hours a day or 58 hours a week. Precise times of work not stipulated and the 'relay system' survived.

1850: Factory Act: those covered by the 1847 Act could not work before 6 a.m. or after 6 p.m. or 2 p.m. on Saturdays

1853: Employment of Children in Factories Act:
1. Extended to children of 8–13 years the same starting and finishing times as had been prescribed to women and young persons in 1850.
2. Because of factory work organization this established a standard working day for most operatives.

1867: Factory Act Extension Act and Hours of Labour Regulation Act:
1. Extended principles and provisions of earlier factory legislation to non-textile factories and workshops (though some trades, such as potters in 1864, had already been brought under protective legislation)
2. No child to be employed under the age of 8 years; those of 8–13 years must receive at least 10 hours education a week

1867: Agricultural Gangs Act:
1. Prohibited employment of children under 8 years.
2. Prohibited employment of women and children along with men in a field-gang.

C.ii Local government and public health

1829: Metropolitan Police Act:
1. Established a central police department in London.
2. Two police commissioners and an assistant direct the department under control of the Home Office.
3. Commissioners to recruit a professional police force: 'Peelers'.

1831: Establishment of a central Board of Health followed by local boards created by Orders in Council. To deal with cholera epidemic and rapidly disbanded after the end of the outbreak.

1832: Cholera Act: gave local boards of health powers to finance anti-cholera activity from poor rates.

1835: Municipal Corporations Act:
1. Replaced 178 local closed boroughs with a network of elected borough corporations.
2. Councillors elected by rate-paying householders; councillors to elect mayor and aldermen from among their number.
3. Annual elections but councillors serve for 3 years.
4. Corporations could take over duties of local improvement commissions. Few councils took advantage of this permissive clause.
5. Corporations could levy rates.
6. Councils must form watch committees and may establish borough police forces.

1837: Civil Registration established: central Board under Registrar-General registers births, marriages and deaths (including causes of death).

1839: County Police Act: permissive Act and not including boroughs. Counties may establish forces under a chief constable. All police charges to be paid locally.

1840: Vaccination Act: free vaccine against smallpox available on demand through local medical officer.

1848: Public Health Act:
1. Establishment of a central Board of Health with three members, responsible to Parliament.
2. Local boards of health established on petition of not less than 10 per cent of ratepayers. These boards would be under central supervision.
3. No central inspection for those authorities, particularly big cities, which had established boards under separate legislation.
4. Central Board would compulsorily establish local boards of health only in places where the death-rate exceeded 23 per 1,000 (compared with a national average of 21).

1853: Vaccination becomes compulsory for all infants.

1856: County and Borough Police Act:
1. Compulsory establishment of borough and county constabularies.
2. Home Office given greater powers over co-ordination and discipline of local forces.

1858: Local Government Act and Public Health Act:
1. These two pieces of legislation wound up the Board of Health and its compulsory powers were not transferred to replacement bodies,

2. Functions of the Board transferred to the Local Government Act Office and a medical department of the Privy Council.
3. Local authorities empowered to establish their own sanitary authorities, free from central controls.

1866: Sanitary Act:
1. Sanitary powers which had been granted to specific local boards of health under the 1848 Act were made uniformly and compulsorily available.
2. Authorities compelled to be responsible for the removal of 'nuisances' to public health.
3. 'Nuisances' now extended in definition to include domestic property; authorities given powers to improve or demolish slum dwellings.

C.iii Poor Law

1782: Gilbert's Act: permissive legislation encouraging parishes to join together for building workhouses for the aged and infirm. Relief of the able-bodied should be largely provided outside workhouses. Few parishes took advantage of the legislation.

1795: Speenhamland system of relief: only the most famous of many attempts to supplement wages when prices were high. Here the extent of relief was dependent on family size and prevailing price of bread. It was a widely adopted local initiative, not government legislation.

1795: Settlement Act: no person was to be removed to the parish of original settlement until actually chargeable to poor relief funds.

1834: Poor Law Amendment Act:
1. Established a centralized Poor Law Commission to offer general principles governing relief of poverty throughout the country.
2. Poor Law Guardians to be locally elected; they replace overseers of the poor.
3. Parishes grouped into Unions; new workhouses to be built if Unions required them.
4. Assistant commissioners were to supervise the implementation of the Act in the localities.
Note: the Act did not specifically prescribe the ending of outdoor relief or of allowances in aid of wages. Nor did it prescribe a workhouse test based on the principle of 'less eligibility'. The commissioners were left to enunciate general policy and they favoured these developments.

1846: Settlement Act: persons continually resident for 5 years in a parish were not to be removed to parish of settlement if they applied for relief.

1847: Poor Law Act: replaced the Commission with a Poor Law Board under a president, who would be a minister of the Crown, and 2 secretaries. Made administration of poor relief more responsible to parliamentary scrutiny.

1852: Outdoor Relief Regulation Order: acknowledged necessity of outdoor relief for able-bodied males in certain cases. Recipients should be set to work at prescribed labour and at least half the relief awarded should be paid in kind.

1865: Union Chargeability Act: powers over settlement transferred from parish to Poor Law Union. Persons continuously resident for 1 year could not be removed to place of settlement.

C.iv Major developments in education provision

1833: First government grant (£20,000) for building of school houses in England and Wales.

1839: Establishment of the Committee of the Privy Council on Education to superintend use of public funds for promotion of public education. First education inspectors appointed.

1846: Establishment of a pupil-teacher training scheme to replace 'monitors' and improve the quality of teaching. Minimum standards of teaching staff, equipment and discipline prescribed for schools to qualify for training grants.

1862: Introduction of Revised Code in response to the Newcastle Commission Report (1858–61) on elementary education:
1. Grant now to be paid direct to school managers.
2. Size of grant determined by satisfactory performance in three prescribed subjects: reading, writing and arithmetic. No grant for proficiency in any other subject.
3. Two-thirds of the grant determined on the basis of performance in tests; one-third on attendance.
4. Inspectors were to carry out the tests.
5. Effectively, the State was now controlling basic syllabus in schools which were largely dependent on State grants.

1870: Elementary Education Act:
1. School boards established to provide 'public elementary schools' to fill gaps left by the voluntary system.
2. Fees should be paid but might be remitted by school boards in appropriate cases.
3. Boards to be elected by all ratepayers, including women; women could also sit on the school boards.
4. Boards could make by-laws making attendance compulsory between the ages of 5 and 13, though with some exemptions for 10- 13-year-olds.
5. 'Cowper-Temple Clause': no specifically denominational religious education to be provided in board schools.

D: THE ECONOMY

D.i.1 Government income statistics, 1781–1870 (in £000s)

5-year average	Customs (%)	Excise (%)	Land and assessed taxes (%)	Property and income tax (%)	Stamps Post Office (%)	Total income
1781–85	3,285 (24)	6,058 (44)	2,616 (19)	—	530 (4)	13,693
1786–90	3,796 (23)	7,142 (43)	2,939 (18)	—	793 (5)	16,468
1791–95	3,888 (21)	8,807 (47)	2,973 (16)	—	925 (5)	18,606
1796–99*	4,846 (19)	10,708 (43)	4,356 (18)	418† (2)	1,363 (5)	24,875
1801–5	8,177 (20)	15,599 (38)	5,359 (13)	3,543 (9)	2,212 (5)	40,897
1806–10	12,140 (19)	25,280 (40)	7,140 (11)	8,960 (14)	3,400 (5)	63,460
1811–15	14,120 (19)	27,640 (38)	7,700 (10)	13,720 (19)	4,110 (6)	73,380
1816–20	13,300 (21)	26,500 (41)	8,280 (13)	5,900 (9)	4,570 (7)	64,700
1821–25	13,000 (22)	28,860 (48)	7,240 (12)	—	4,580 (8)	59,920
1826–30	19,360 (35)	21,320 (38)	5,220 (9)	—	4,770 (9)	55,880
1831–35	18,780 (37)	17,840 (35)	5,160 (10)	—	4,700 (9)	51,360
1836–40	22,560 (44)	14,820 (29)	3,900 (8)	—	4,690 (9)	51,220
1841–45	23,240 (43)	14,340 (27)	4,400 (8)	2,240 (4)	4,390 (8)	53,960
1846–50	22,120 (39)	14,740 (26)	4,500 (8)	5,480 (10)	4,750 (8)	57,340
1851–55	22,080 (38)	15,920 (27)	3,700 (6)	6,580 (11)	4,630 (8)	58,320
1856–60	23,680 (34)	18,380 (27)	3,160 (5)	11,820 (17)	5,300 (8)	68,640
1861–65	23,360 (34)	18,540 (27)	3,200 (5)	9,800 (14)	6,320 (9)	68,920
1866–70	22,040 (32)	20,600 (30)	3,680 (5)	7,380 (11)	6,920 (10)	69,240

* 1800 figures have been omitted as these are incomplete.
† Income tax was introduced for the first time in 1799. This figure represents 1 year's yield, divided to produce a notional 4-year average.

Notes:
Figures are net for 1781–1801, gross thereafter.
Figures for Great Britain 1781–1800, United Kingdom thereafter.

Source: B. R. Mitchell and P. Deane, *op. cit.,* (1962) pp. 388, 392–3.

D.i.2 Government expenditure statistics, 1781–1870 (in £000s)

5-year average	Debt charges	(%)	Civil government	(%)	Army and navy	(%)	Total expenditure
1781–85	8,048	(31)	1,354	(5)	15,882	(62)	£25,726
1786–90	9,393	(58)	1,583	(10)	4,848	(29)	16,323
1791–95	9,631	(39)	1,722	(7)	12,600	(52)	24,455
1796–99*	14,520	(30)	2,225	(5)	31,470	(65)	48,716
1801–5	19,690	(34)	4,934	(9)	30,413	(53)	57,418
1806–10	23,320	(31)	5,020	(7)	43,040	(57)	75,580
1811–15	26,540	(27)	5,360	(5)	60,640	(62)	97,540
1816–20	31,800	(46)	5,600	(8)	26,940	(39)	68,920
1821–25	31,100	(55)	5,560	(10)	15,360	(27)	56,620
1826–30	29,240	(53)	5,680	(10)	15,660	(29)	54,660
1831–35	28,560	(57)	4,700	(9)	13,300	(26)	50,340
1836–40	29,320	(53)	5,080	(9)	12,600	(23)	55,080
1841–45	29,760	(55)	5,680	(10)	14,060	(26)	54,560
1846–50	28,500	(50)	6,800	(12)	16,340	(29)	56,540
1851–55	28,140	(49)	7,040	(12)	17,680	(31)	57,780
1856–60	28,620	(38)	9,200	(12)	29,660	(40)	74,360
1861–65	26,280	(38)	10,680	(15)	27,640	(39)	70,080
1866–70	26,520	(38)	11,000	(16)	25,200	(36)	69,620

*1800 figures have been omitted as these are incomplete.

Notes:
Figures are net for 1781–1801, gross thereafter.
Figures for Great Britain 1781–1800, United Kingdom thereafter.

Source: Mitchell and Deane, *op. cit.*, (1962), pp. 391, 396–7.

D.i.3 Direct taxation

(a) Land tax
1783–98: Paid at 4s. (20p) in the £ on old valuations of land. In 1798 the tax, which realized about £2m. annually, was commuted by translation into a perpetual charge on the land. Owners could redeem their land from tax at the existing valuation, the sums thus raised being set against the national debt.

(b) Income tax

Years inclusive	Rate in the £ on income of £60+		Rate in the £ on income of £100–£150	Rate in the £ on income over £150
1799–1802	2s.	(10p)		
1804–5	1s.	(5p)		
1806	1s. 3d.	(6p)		
1807–16	2s.	(10p)		
1843–53	—		—	7d. (3p)
1854	—		5d. (2p)	7d. (3p)
1855	—		10d. (4p)	1s. 2d. (5½p)
1856–57	—		11½d. (5p)	1s. 4d. (6½p)
1858	—		5d. (2p)	7d. (3p)
1859	—		—	5d. (2p)
1860	—		6½d. (2½p)	9d. (4p)
1861	—		7d. (3p)	10d. (4p)
1862–63	—		6d. (2½p)	9d. (4p)
1864	—		—	7d. (3p)
1865	—		—	6d. (2½p)
1866–67	—		—	4d. (1½p)
1868	—		—	5d. (2p)
1869	—		—	6d. (2½p)
1870	—		—	5d. (2p)

Note: No income tax was levied in 1803 and between 1817 and 1842.

Sources: W. Kennedy, *English Taxation 1640–1799* (1913) and Mitchell and Deane, *op. cit.*, pp. 427–8.

D.ii.1 Distribution of national income in Britain, 1801–1871 (in £000,000s)

	1801	1811	1821	1831	1841	1851	1861	1871
Agriculture, fisheries and forestry	75.5	107.5	76.0	79.5	99.9	106.5	118.8	130.4
%	(32.5)	(35.7)	(26.1)	(23.4)	(22.1)	(20.3)	(17.8)	(14.2)
Manufacture, mining and building	54.3	62.5	93.0	117.1	155.5	179.5	243.6	348.9
%	(23.4)	(20.8)	(31.9)	(34.4)	(34.4)	(34.3)	(36.5)	(38.1)
Trade and transport	40.5	50.1	46.4	59.0	83.3	97.8	130.7	201.6
%	(17.4)	(16.6)	(15.9)	(17.3)	(18.4)	(18.7)	(19.6)	(22.0)
Domestic and personal	12.8	15.7	16.6	19.2	26.9	27.4	35.0	45.5
%	(5.5)	(5.2)	(5.7)	(5.7)	(6.0)	(5.2)	(5.2)	(5.0)
Housing (rent)	12.2	17.2	17.9	22.0	37.0	42.6	50.3	69.4
%	(5.3)	(5.7)	(6.2)	(6.5)	(8.2)	(8.1)	(7.5)	(7.6)
Income from abroad	—	—	3.0	3.9	6.2	10.4	19.9	39.5
%			(1.0)	(1.1)	(1.4)	(2.0)	(3.0)	(4.3)
Gvt, professional and other	36.8	48.1	38.1	39.3	43.6	59.0	69.7	81.3
%	(15.8)	(16.0)	(13.1)	(11.6)	(9.6)	(11.3)	(10.4)	(8.9)
Total national product	232.0	301.1	291.0	340.0	452.3	523.3	668.0	916.6
Percentage increase on previous decade	—	29.8	−3.4	16.8	32.9	15.7	27.7	37.2

Note: Figures are rounded and do not add exactly to the sum in the total column.

Sources: These figures are drawn from a variety of sources by P. Deane and W. A. Cole, *British Economic Growth, 1688–1959* (2nd edn, Cambridge, 1969) pp. 166–7.

D.ii.2 Imports, 1784–1856 (in £000s)

	Average of years							
	1784–86	1794–96	1804–6	1814–16	1824–26	1834–36	1844–46	1854–56
Textile raw materials	4,680	6,891	13,436	18,113	18,459	29,161	24,663	42,831
%	(21)	(18)	(24)	(25)	(28)	(42)	(30)	(28)
Other raw materials	5,237	8,764	14,373	18,903	17,671	18,498	26,370	46,601
%	(23)	(23)	(26)	(26)	(27)	(26)	(32)	(31)
Food	9,609	18,212	23,953	32,018	26,370	20,680	27,386	54,469
%	(42)	(48)	(43)	(45)	(40)	(29)	(33)	(36)
Manufactures	3,235	4,050	3,796	2,762	3,889	1,926	3,544	7,680
%	(14)	(11)	(7)	(4)	(6)	(3)	(4)	(5)
Total imports	22,761	37,917	55,558	71,796	66,389	70,265	81,963	151,581

Note: Davis's work incorporates important new research designed to overcome the difficulties in presentation of trade statistics according to increasingly unreal 'official' values based, for the most part, on 1696. Davis's figures, therefore, represent estimated real values.

Source: Calculations reproduced from R. Davis, *The Industrial Revolution and British Overseas Trade* (1979), pp. 94–101, by permission of Pinter Publishers, a Cassell imprint, London, England.

D.ii.3 Exports, 1784–1856 (in £000s)

	Average of years							
	1784–86	*1794–96*	*1804–6*	*1814–16*	*1824–26*	*1834–36*	*1844–46*	*1854–56*
All textile manufactures	5,834	11,082	24,391	30,008	26,457	32,715	38,737	47,628
%	(43)	(46)	(59)	(63)	(66)	(71)	(66)	(46)
Cottons	797	3,801	16,339	18,994	17,375	22,398	25,835	34,908
%	(6)	(16)	(40)	(40)	(44)	(48)	(44)	(34)
Woollens	3,882	5,764	6,800	8,722	6,882	7,321	9,534	12,720
%	(29)	(24)	(16)	(18)	(17)	(16)	(16)	(12)
Iron manufactures	1,228	2,228	2,740	874	824	1,021	2,086	5,860
%	(9)	(9)	(7)	(2)	(2)	(2)	(4)	(6)
Food	1,284	2,185	2,867	5,339	2,215	1,571	1,809	5,764
%	(9)	(9)	(7)	(11)	(6)	(3)	(3)	(6)
Raw materials	1,141	1,232	2,048	2,510	1,927	2,539	5,177	13,646
%	(8)	(5)	(5)	(5)	(5)	(5)	(9)	(13)
Total	13,614	24,028	41,241	48,002	39,906	46,193	58,420	102,501
Re-exports	3,601	8,345	9,828	17,725	9,640	10,226	10,794	21,005

Notes: Only principal export items have been included so figures do not add to totals.
Re-exports are not included in the percentage calculations.
Exports from Ireland are included until the 1820s; thereafter they are considered as domestic trade.

Source: Davis, *op. cit.*, pp. 94–109.

D.ii.4 Value of British overseas trade, 1855–1870 (in £000s)

Average of years	Imports	Domestic exports	Re-exports
1855–59	169.52	116.12	23.40
1860–64	235.52	138.40	41.56
1865–70	289.18	184.17	47.92

Source: Calculated from figures in Mitchell and Deane, *op. cit.*, p. 283.

D.ii.5 Value of British exports to particular areas, 1784–1856 in (£000s)

	Average value of years in the middle of the decade							
	1784–86	*1794–96*	*1804–6*	*1814–16*	*1824–26*	*1834–36*	*1844–46*	*1854–56*
Europe	6,272	7,792	17,427	24,672	18,510	17,610	23,251	32,991
%	(46)	(32)	(42)	(51)	(46)	(38)	(40)	(32)
United States	2,838	6,399	10,143	7,348	5,695	9,438	7,162	20,078
%	(21)	(27)	(25)	(15)	(14)	(20)	(12)	(20)
West Indies and Canada	2,131	5,667	8,483	10,152	5,798	6,249	7,146	8,273
%	(16)	(24)	(21)	(21)	(15)	(14)	(12)	(8)
Latin America	7	79	1,125	2,476	5,009	5,047	5,634	8,974
%	(0)	(0)	(3)	(5)	(13)	(11)	(10)	(9)
Africa	489	483	1,187	353	372	967	1,368	2,623
%	(4)	(2)	(3)	(1)	(1)	(2)	(2)	(3)
Asia	1,877	3,601	2,840	2,979	4,326	6,152	12,683	20,071
%	(14)	(15)	(7)	(6)	(11)	(13)	(22)	(20)
Australasia		7	36	22	196	730	1,176	9,491
%		(0)	(0)	(0)	(0)	(2)	(2)	(9)
Total	13,614	24,028	41,241	48,002	39,906	46,193	58,420	102,501

Note: Exports to Ireland are included in the Europe section until the 1820s; thereafter they are considered as domestic trade and excluded from computations. Irish exports represented 7 per cent of total exports in the 1780s and 11½ per cent in the 1820s. Their disappearance from the 1830s, therefore, distorts the total pattern, particularly to Europe, significantly.

Manufactured goods as a proportion of Britain's total exports by value:

1784–86	82%	1824–26	90%
1794–96	86%	1834–36	91%
1804–6	88%	1844–46	88%
1814–16	84%	1854–56	81%

Source: Calculations from data in Davis, *op. cit.*

D.iii.1 Imports of raw cotton, 1780–1870

Decennial averages (m. lb.)

		Percentage re-exported	Percentage increase over previous decade
1780s	15.9	7	205
1790s	29.6	3	85
1800s	61.7	3	109
1810s	105.0	8	70
1820s	189.7	9	81
1830s	354.6	15	87
1840s	606.4	9	71
1850s	927.8	14	53
1860s	1,090.2	26	18

Note: The decennial average for the 1860s is distorted by the 'cotton famine' caused by the virtual stoppage of supplies from the American South during the Civil War. An average of 597m. lb. was imported in 1862–63, less than half the average of 1860–61 (1,324m. lb.).

Source: Calculations from data in Mitchell and Deane, *op. cit.*, pp. 178, 180.

D.iii.2 Exports of cotton piece goods, 1815–1869 (m. yd)

	Annual average	Decennial percentage increases	Percentage increase over previous quinquennium
1815–19	227.5	1820s: 40.7 (over average of 1815–19)	—
1820–24	293.6	1830s: 72.6 (over average of 1820s)	29.1
1825–29	346.8	1840s: 76.9	18.1
1830–34	475.8	1850s: 89.8	37.2
1835–39	629.6	1860s: 28.0	32.3
1840–44	848.4		34.8
1845–49	1,107.0		30.5
1850–54	1,542.6		39.3
1855–59	2,167.8		40.5
1860–64	2,096.6		−3.3
1865–69	2,653.0		26.5

Source: Calculations from material in Mitchell and Deane, *op. cit.*, p. 182.

D.iii.3 Iron and steel exports, 1780–1870

	Decennial averages (000 tons)	Percentage increase over previous decade
1780s	14.3	9
1790s	27.2	91
1800s*	37.3	(37)
1810s*	52.6	(41)
1820s	76.5	45
1830s	180.1	135
1840s	457.6	154
1850s	1,225.1	168
1860s	1,781.5	45

* Figures unavailable for 1809–11 and 1813. Averages do not include these years; the effect is to inflate the averages since 1810–11 represented the peak of the campaign of economic warfare between Britain and France and her European allies.

Note: Figures include exports to Ireland until 1808. The importance of the change in amounts is considerable since about two-fifths of iron and steel exports went to Ireland in the early nineteenth century.

Source: Mitchell and Deane, *op. cit.*, pp. 144–7.

D.iv.1 Railway development, 1830–1870

	Miles of track open	Passengers carried (m.)	Passenger train receipts (£m.)	Freight carried (m. tons)	Freight train receipts (£m.)
1830	98				
1832	166				
1834	298				
1836	403				
1838	743	5.4			
1840	1,498				
1842	1,939				
1844	2,148	25.2	3.4		1.6
1846	3,036	40.2	4.6		2.8
1848	4,982	54.4	5.6		4.2
1850	6,084	67.4	6.5		6.2
1852	6,628	82.8	7.3		7.7
1854	7,157	104.3	9.6		9.7
1856	7,650	121.4	10.6	63.7	11.4
1858	8,354	130.7	10.9	71.9	11.9
1860	9,069	153.5	12.2	88.4	14.2
1862	9,953	170.0	13.0	91.9	14.7
1864	10,995	217.4	14.7	108.5	17.7
1866	11,945	261.2	16.4	121.8	20.1
1869*	13,170	298.6	17.6	n.a.	21.4
1871*	13,388	322.2	18.1	166.5	23.2

* Figures for 1868 are seriously deficient; hence statistics have been included for 1869 and 1871.

Source: Mitchell and Deane, *op. cit.*, p. 225.

D.iv.2 The development of railway passenger traffic in the UK, 1851–1870

No. of passengers travelling in each class (in 000s)

	1st	%	2nd	%	3rd and parliamentary	%	Total	
1851–52	9,210	11.9	28,021	36.3	39,885	52.7	77,116	
1870	31,839	9.6	74,153	22.4	224,012	67.9	330,004	(+327.9%)

Receipts from passengers in each class (in £000s)

	1st	%	2nd	%	3rd and parliamentary	%	Total	
1851–52	2,073	32.0	2,592	38.7	2,032	30.3	6,697	
1870	3,949	24.2	4,926	30.1	7,474	45.7	16,349	(+144%)

Notes: Figures of 1851–52 are from the first half of each year. Season tickets are excluded. While lines available almost doubled between 1852 and 1870, usage of the railways more than trebled. Usage among third-class and 'parliamentary' passengers increased almost sixfold.

Source: *P. P.*, 1852–53, XCVII, pp. 298–9 and 1871, LX, pp. 528–9.

D.iv.3a Shipping, 1790–1870

(a) Shipping registered in the UK: Decennial average

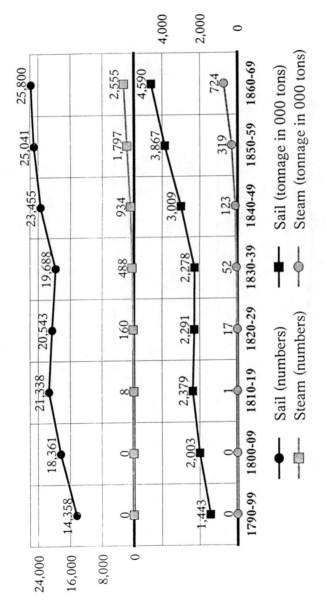

D.iv.3b Shipping, 1790–1870

(a) Ships built and first registered in Britain

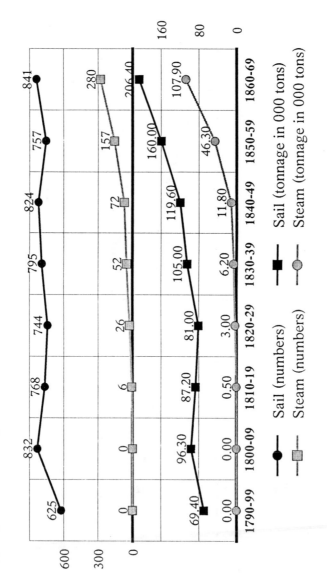

D.v.1 Numbers employed in cotton and woollen factories, 1835–1870 (in 000s)

	Children under 13			Children 13-18			Adult females			Adult males				Totals		
	Cotton	Wool	%	Cotton	Wool	%	Cotton	Wool	%	Cotton	Wool	%		Cotton	Wool	All
1835	29	14	11	56	23	20	119	23	36	100	32	33	1835	304	92	396
1838	12	10	4	95	33	26	146	45	39	113	42	31	1838	366	130	496
1847	18	15	5	94	37	22	182	66	41	134	59	32	1847	428	177	605
1850	15	17	6	37	20	10	189	82	47	142	72	37	1850	383	191	574
1856	24	18	7	39	18	9	222	91	49	157	76	36	1856	442	203	645
1861	40	20	8	41	18	8	269	92	49	183	81	35	1861	533	211	744
1867	41	32	9	34	23	7	240	152	49	161	110	34	1867	476	317	793
1870	43	24	8	38	24	8	272	130	49	178	108	35	1870	531	286	817

Source: Mitchell and Deane, *op. cit.*, pp. 188, 199.

D.v.2 Size of Lancashire cotton firms in 1841

		%
Firms employing fewer than 100 hands	423	43
Firms employing 100–199 hands	257	26
Firms employing 200–299 hands	114	12
Firms employing 300–399 hands	56	6
Firms employing 400–499 hands	40	4
Firms employing 500–599 hands	60	6
Firms employing more than 1,000 hands	25	3
Total	975	

Source: V. A. C. Gatrell, 'Labour, power and the size of firms in Lancashire cotton in the second quarter of the nineteenth century', *Ec. H. R.*, 2nd ser., xxx (1977), p. 98.

D.vi.1 Average indices of price and wage movements, 1788–1850

	Percentage price changes		*Percentage wage changes*
1788/92–1809/15	+74.1	1788/92–1810/14	+63.1
1809/15–1820/26	−29.3	1810/14–1820/24	−10.6
1820/26–1846/50	−16.4	1820/24–1846/50	+ 0.4

Calculations from indices quoted in M. W. Flinn, 'Trends in real wages, 1750–1850', *Ec. H. R.* 2nd ser., xxvii (1974), pp. 404–407.

D.vi.2 Estimates of adult male full-time earnings in various categories, 1781–1851

(Index numbers, for each category: 1850=100)

	Farm labourers	*Skilled workers*	*All manual*	*Clerical etc.*	*All workers*
1781	61.12	48.30	50.19	22.24	39.24
1797	74.50	46.73	53.61	23.45	42.48
1805	74.51	42.55	51.73	20.82	40.64
1810	67.21	42.73	50.04	19.97	39.41
1815	75.51	52.18	58.15	25.49	46.71
1819	73.52	50.26	55.68	27.76	46.13
1827	75.86	66.39	69.25	39.10	58.99
1835	91.67	78.62	83.43	66.52	78.69
1851	100.00	100.00	100.00	100.00	100.00

Source: P. H. Lindert and J. Williamson, 'English workers' living standards during the industrial revolution: a new look' *Ec. H. R.* 2nd ser., xxxvi (1983), pp. 13, 24.

G.H. Wood's index of real wages, 1850–1870 (1850 = 100: some allowance is made for the effects of unemployment)

1850	100	1857	94	1864	118
1851	102	1858	94	1865	120
1852	100	1859	104	1866	117
1853	107	1860	105	1867	105
1854	97	1861	99	1968	105
1855	94	1862	100	1869	111
1856	95	1863	107	1870	118

Quoted in R. A. Church, *The Great Victorian Boom, 1850–1873* (1975) p. 72.

D.vi.3 Average prices of wheat, 1780–1870

Years	Yearly average price per imperial quarter		Standard deviation	Peak price		Year
1780–89	46s. 1d.	(£2.30)	5s. 5d.	54s. 3d.	(£2.71)	1783
1790–99	57s. 7d.	(£2.88)	11s. 8d.	78s. 7d.	(£3.93)	1796
1800–9	84s. 8d.	(£4.23)	19s. 5d.	119s. 6d.	(£5.98)	1801
1810–19	91s. 5d.	(£4.57)	18s. 10d.	126s. 6d.	(£6.33)	1812
1820–29	59s. 10d.	(£2.99)	7s. 0d.	68s. 6d.	(£3.43)	1825
1830–39	56s. 9d.	(£2.84)	9s. 6d.	70s. 8d.	(£3.53)	1839
1840–49	55s. 11d.	(£2.80)	7s. 11d.	69s. 9d.	(£3.49)	1847
1850–59	53s. 4d.	(£2.67)	13s. 5d.	74s. 8d.	(£3.73)	1855
1860–69	51s. 8d.	(£2.58)	7s. 11d.	64s. 5d.	(£3.22)	1867

Note: Inelasticity of demand can result in considerable variations in price from year to year, especially when a decade includes a period of exceptional scarcity. Thus the decennial standard deviations and peak price years have been included.

Source: Calculations from figures in Mitchell and Deane, *op. cit.*, pp. 488–9

D.vii.1 Expenditure on poor relief in England and Wales, 1783–1868

	Average expenditure (in £000)	Per head of population	Percentage increase or decrease
1783–85	2,004	5s. 2d.	—
1803	4,268	9s. 2d.	—
1813	6,656	12s. 5d.	+56 (on 1803 figure)
1814–18	6,437	11s. 7d.	− 3
1819–23	6,788	11s. 2d.	+ 5
1824–28	6,039	9s. 2d.	−11
1829–33	6,758	9s. 8d.	+12
1834–38	4,946	6s. 7d.	−27
1839–43	4,773	6s. 0d.	− 3
1844–48	5,290	6s. 2d.	+11
1849–53	5,198	5s. 10d.	− 2
1854–58	5,791	6s. 0d.	+11
1859–63	5,880	5s. 10d.	+ 2
1864–68	6,717	6s. 2d.	+14

Note: Expenditure on poor relief reached a peak of £7,871,000 in 1818. This was not exceeded until 1871 when the population of England and Wales (22.8m.) was almost exactly double the 1818 figure.

Source: Mitchell and Deane, *op. cit.*, p. 410.

D.vii.2 Indoor and outdoor relief, 1850–1870: England and Wales

	Mean number of paupers relieved in workhouses	Mean number receiving outdoor relief	Total	% of population
1850	123,004	885,696	1,008,700	5.7
1855	121,400	776,286	897,686	4.8
1860	113,507	731,126	844,633	4.3
1865	131,312	820,586	951,898	4.5
1870	156,800	876,000	1,032,800	4.6
Mean for the period 1850–70	129,205 (14%)	817,939 (86%)	947,144	4.73

Source: M. E. Rose, *The Relief of Poverty, 1834-1914* (1972), p. 53.

E: POPULATION

E.i Population of the U.K, 1781–1871 (in 000s)

The figures to the right of the population indicators give the percentage increase in population per decade from 1801–71

	England		Wales		Scotland		Ireland		Total	
1781	7,042		545		1,435		4,048		13,070	
1791	7,740						4,420			
1801	8,319	—	541		1,625		5,216		15,701	
1811	9,491	*14.09*	611	*12.94*	1,824	*12.20*	5,956	*14.19*	17,882	*13.89*
1821	11,205	*18.06*	718	*17.51*	2,100	*15.13*	6,802	*14.20*	20,825	*16.46*
1831	13,008	*16.09*	807	*12.40*	2,374	*13.05*	7,767	*14.20*	23,956	*15.03*
1841	14,872	*14.32*	911	*12.89*	2,620	*10.36*	8,175	*5.25*	26,578	*10.95*
1851	16,812	*13.04*	1,006	*10.43*	2,889	*10.27*	6,552	*–19.85*	27,259	*2.56*
1861	18,834	*12.03*	1,121	*11.43*	3,062	*5.99*	5,800	*–11.50*	28,817	*5.71*
1871	21,370	*13.47*	1,222	*9.00*	3,360	*9.73*	5,413	*–6.67*	31,365	*8.85*

National population growth rates, in percentages:

	England	Wales	Scotland	Ireland	Total
1801–51	*102.09*	*79.44*	*79.66*	*25.61*	*73.61*
1801–71	*156.88*	*108.82*	*108.96*	*3.78*	*99.77*

Note: Irish population statistics are radically affected by the impact of the potato famine of 1845–47. On the eve of the famine in 1845, Irish population stood at an estimated 8.3m. It fell continuously thereafter until 1916 when it stood at 4,273,000, a decline of approximately 48.5%. Total population growth in the UK (which includes Ireland) between 1801 and 1845 is estimated at about 75%.

Sources: English population figures are taken from the extensive recalculations of Wrigley and Schofield, *The Population History of England, 1541–1871* (1981), pp. 534, 588. Welsh figures are taken from the Census. Figures for Scotland are derived from M. Flinn *et al.*, *Scottish Population History from the Seventeenth Century to the 1930s* (Cambridge, 1977), p. 302. Figures for Ireland are derived from S. Daultry, D. Dickson & C. O'Grada, 'Eighteenth-century Irish population: New Perspectives from Old Sources' *Journal of Economic History*, xli (1981), pp. 601-28, W. E. Vaughan and A. J. Fitzpatrick (eds), *Irish Historical Statistics: Population, 1821–71* (1978), pp. 2–3

E.ii.1 English population growth by region, 1801–1871 (in 000s)

	1801	1811	% increase	1821	% increase	1831	% increase	1841	% increase	1851	% increase	1861	% increase	1871	% increase
1. North-west	1,023	1,235	20.72	1,530	23.89	1,895	23.86	2,297	21.21	2,740	19.29	3,200	16.79	3,665	14.53
2. North-east	1,177	1,334	13.34	1,581	18.52	1,848	16.89	2,166	17.21	2,493	15.10	2,885	15.72	3,509	21.63
3. West Midlands	854	972	13.82	1,115	14.71	1,294	16.05	1,498	15.77	1,705	13.82	1,981	16.19	2,204	11.26
4. East Midlands	448	515	14.96	593	15.15	678	14.33	759	11.95	819	7.91	892	8.91	990	10.99
5. East Anglia	1,051	1,159	10.28	1,359	17.26	1,518	11.70	1,659	9.29	1,805	8.80	1,829	1.33	1,942	6.18
6. South Midlands	623	680	9.15	783	15.15	865	10.47	945	9.25	1,007	6.56	1,051	4.37	1,132	7.71
7. London and environs	1,265	1,464	15.73	1,742	18.99	2,048	17.57	2,387	16.55	2,829	18.52	3,343	18.17	3,931	17.59
8. South	935	1,059	13.26	1,235	16.62	1,382	11.90	1,534	11.00	1,666	8.60	1,830	9.84	2,045	11.75
9. South-west	1,103	1,255	13.78	1,467	16.89	1,684	14.79	1,876	11.40	1,983	5.70	2,059	3.83	2,156	4.71

Notes: The following county categorizations have been used.

North-west: Cumberland, Westmorland, Lancashire, Cheshire.

North-east: Northumberland, Durham, Yorkshire.

West Midlands: Staffordshire, Shropshire, Warwickshire, Worcestershire, Herefordshire.

East Midlands: Derbyshire, Nottinghamshire, Leicestershire, Rutland.

East Anglia: Lincolnshire, Huntingdonshire, Cambridgeshire, Norfolk, Suffolk, Essex.

South Midlands: Northamptonshire, Oxfordshire, Berkshire, Buckinghamshire, Bedfordshire, Hertfordshire.

London and environs: London, Middlesex, Surrey.

South: Wiltshire, Dorset, Hampshire, Sussex, Kent.

South-west: Gloucestershire, Monmouthshire, Somerset, Devon, Cornwall.

Source: Calculations from county figures in Mitchell and Deane, *op. cit.*, pp. 20–1.

E.ii.2 Changing regional balance of population, 1801–1871

	Percentages of total English population in given categories			
	1801	1831	1851	1871
North	25.95	28.33	30.70	33.25
Midlands and East Anglia	35.10	32.96	31.30	29.05
South	38.96	38.71	38.00	37.69
Industrial and Commercial counties	44.89	48.49	52.50	57.30
Mixed counties	31.65	29.99	27.97	25.78
Agricultural counties	23.46	21.53	19.53	16.92

Notes:
1. The regional classification derives from the list in E.ii.1. North comprises 1 and 2, the Midlands and East Anglia categories 3–6 and the South categories 7–9.
2. The economic division follows that in P. Deane and W. A. Cole, *op. cit.*, p. 103. 'industrial and commercial' counties are Durham, Gloucester, Kent, Lancashire, Middlesex, Northumberland, Staffordshire, Surrey, Warwickshire and Yorkshire, West Riding plus London. 'Mixed' counties are Cheshire, Cornwall, Cumberland, Derbyshire, Devonshire, Dorset, Hampshire, Leicestershire, Monmouthshire, Northamptonshire, Nottinghamshire, Shropshire, Somerset, Westmorland, Worcestershire and Yorkshire, East and North Ridings. 'Agricultural' counties are the remainder.

Source: Calculations from figures in Mitchell and Deane, *op. cit.*, pp. 20–1.

E.iii Population of towns, 1780–1871

Preliminary note: An attempt is made here to chart the growth of representative British towns. Choice is inevitably subjective; I have tried to include towns both of large and modest growth as also centres of expanding industry and those of relatively stagnant production such as the workshop textile centres of the South-west which were by-passed by factory developments further north. The categories below are not mutually exclusive, but it is useful to distinguish between the major centres of cotton and woollen manufacture (b) and other important towns whose units of manufacturing production remained relatively small (workshop rather than factory dominated) until at least 1850 (c). Category (d) includes market, administrative and leisure centres, although some manufactures were carried on in each of them. Category (e) defines itself; category (f) towns are either 'railway towns' or heavy-industry towns which developed largely because of railway provision.

Population (in 000s)

	Pre-1801	1801	1811	1821	1831	1841	1851	1861	1871
(a) *London*	775	959	1,139	1,379	1,685	1,948	2,362	2,804	3,254
		Rate of growth, 1801–51: 146%							
(b) *Factory textile towns*									
Blackburn	6	12	15	22	27	37	47	63	76
Bolton	12 (1789)	18	25	32	42	51	61	70	83
Bradford	4 (1781)	13	16	26	44	67	104	106	146
Glasgow	62 (1791)	77	101	147	202	275	345	420	522
Halifax	7	12	13	17	22	28	34	37	66
Leeds	24	53	63	84	123	152	172	207	259
Manchester	30	75	89	126	182	235	303	339	351
Oldham	5	12	17	22	32	43	53	72	83
Paisley	14 (1792)	25	29	38	46	48	48	47	48
Preston	6 (1791)	12	17	25	34	51	70	83	85
Salford	8 (1788)	14	19	26	41	53	64	102	125
Stockport	5 (1779)	17	21	27	36	50	54	55	53

Average rate of growth, 1801–51: 299%

Population (in 000s)

	Pre-1801	1801	1811	1821	1831	1841	1851	1861	1871
(c) Other manufacturing towns									
Barnstaple	3	4	4	5	7	8	9	8	9
Birmingham	42 (1778)	71	83	102	144	183	233	296	344
Coventry	15	16	18	21	27	31	36	41	38
Derby	9 (1788)	11	13	17	24	33	41	43	50
Devizes	3	4	4	5	6	7	7	7	7
Edinburgh	85 (1791)	83	108	138	162	166	194	203	242
Leicester	13 (1785)	17	19	26	41	53	61	68	95
Merthyr Tydfil		8	11	17	22	35	46	50	52
Northampton	6	7	8	11	15	21	27	33	41
Norwich	39	36	37	50	61	62	68	75	80
Sheffield	27	46	53	65	92	111	135	185	240
Swansea	4	7	9	11	15	20	25	33	43
Trowbridge	4	6	6	10	11	11	11	10	12
Walsall	4	10	11	12	15	20	26	38	46
Wolverhampton	10	13	15	18	25	36	50	61	68
		Rate of growth 1801–51: 186%							
(d) County and leisure towns									
Bath	21	33	38	47	51	53	54	53	53
Brighton	3	7	12	24	41	47	66	78	90
Chester	15	15	16	20	21	24	28	26	30
Ipswich	12	11	14	17	20	25	33	38	43
Margate		5	6	8	10	11	10	10	14
Scarborough	6	6	7	8	8	10	12	17	22
Shrewsbury	11	15	17	20	21	18	20	22	23
Worcester	11	11	14	17	19	27	28	31	33
York	13	17	19	22	26	29	36	40	44
		Rate of growth 1801–51: 139%							

Population (in 000s)

	Pre-1801	1801	1811	1821	1831	1841	1851	1861	1871
(e) Ports									
Bristol	55	61	71	85	104	124	137	154	183
Cardiff		2	2	4	6	10	18	33	40
Hull	14	30	37	45	52	67	85	98	122
Liverpool	35	82	104	138	202	286	376	444	493
Newcastle upon Tyne	33	33	33	42	54	70	88	109	128
Southampton	5	8	10	13	16	19	21	25	32
Sunderland	16	24	25	31	39	43	65	78	98
Whitehaven	10 (1775)	9	10	12	11	12	14	14	13
Yarmouth, Gt	13 (1784)	17	20	21	25	28	31	35	42
		Rate of growth, 1801–51: 214%							
(f) 'New' towns									
Barrow	—	—	—	—	—	—	0.5	3	19
Crewe	—	—	—	—	—	—	4	8	18
Middlesbrough	—	—	1	2	—	6	8	19	40
Swindon	—	1	1	2	2	2	5	9	12

Sources: The censuses of 1851 and 1871 list of population figures from 1801–71. Pre-1801 estimates mostly derive from C. M. Law, 'Some notes on the urban population of England and Wales in the eighteenth century', *Local Historian*, x (1972), pp. 13–26 and from J. Sinclair, *The Statistical Account of Scotland* (21 vols, Edinburgh, 1795). Estimates are for 1775 except where reasonably accurate local censuses exist; the dates of such censuses are shown in parentheses. Estimates for Barrow in 1851 and 1861 are drawn from J. D. Marshall, *Furness and the Industrial Revolution* (Barrow, 1958), pp. 201, 281. A 1788 estimate of Salford's population derives from J. Aitkin, *A Description of the Country Thirty to Forty Miles around Manchester* (1795), pp. 156–7.

E.iv Baptisms and birth-rates in England and Wales, 1783–1869

(a) Total baptisms 1780–1839 (Anglican)

	Annual average per decade (in 000s)
1780s	237.0
1790s	262.1
1800s	283.5
1810s	321.0
1820s	371.4
1830s	398.3

(b) Total births and birth-rate 1840–1869

	Annual average per decade (in 000s)	
	Births	*Birth-rate per 1,000*
1840s	539.8	32.45
1850s	637.9	34.08
1860s	739.0	35.12

Note: Many children born to non-Anglican parents were not baptized according to the Anglican rite and are not included in Table (a). Table (b) derives from civil registration data and is more comprehensive.

Source: Mitchell and Deane, *op. cit.*, pp. 28–9.

E.v Burials, death-rates and infant mortality in England and Wales, 1783–1869

(a) Total burials 1780–1839 (Anglican)

Annual average per decade (in 000s)	
1780s	189.9
1790s	193.3
1800s	194.9
1810s	200.9
1820s	241.5
1830s	288.6

(b) Total deaths, death-rate and infant mortality rate, 1840–1869

	Annual average per decade (in 000s)		
	Deaths	Death-rate	Infant mortality per 1,000 live births
1840s	375.5	22.57	153.2
1850s	415.6	22.20	154.5
1860s	470.2	22.33	152.9

Note: Infant mortality figures are for deaths of children under the age of 1 year who had been born alive.

Source: Mitchell and Deane, *op. cit.*, pp. 28, 34, 36.

E.vi Age structure of the British population in 1851 and 1871 (in 000s)

		1851	%	1871	%
Males	0–4	1,366	6.56	1,767	6.78
Females	0–4	1,354	6.51	1,760	6.75
Males	5–14	2,349	11.28	2,966	11.38
Females	5–14	2,314	11.12	2,942	11.28
Males	15–34	3,453	16.59	4,148	15.91
Females	15–34	3,721	17.88	4,481	17.19
Males	35–54	2,003	9.62	2,487	9.54
Females	35–54	2,121	10.19	2,729	10.47
Males	55–74	858	4.12	1,138	4.36
Females	55–74	979	4.70	1,293	4.96
Males	75+	128	0.62	156	0.60
Females	75+	170	0.81	206	0.79
Total males		10,157	48.79	12,662	48.56
Total females		10,660	51.21	13,411	51.44

Note: Population figures as from England, Wales and Scotland.

Source: Calculations from figures in Mitchell and Deane, *op. cit.*, pp. 12–13.

E.vii Estimates of the distribution of the British labour force, 1801–1871 (in 000,000s)

	1801	1811	1821	1831	1841	1851	1861	1871
Agriculture, fisheries and forestry	1.7	1.8	1.8	1.8	1.9	2.1	2.0	1.8
%	(35.4)	(32.7)	(29.0)	(25.0)	(22.6)	(21.6)	(18.5)	(15.0)
Manufactures, mining and industry	1.4	1.7	2.4	3.0	3.3	4.1	4.7	5.3
%	(29.1)	(30.9)	(38.7)	(41.7)	(39.2)	(42.2)	(43.5)	(44.2)
Trade and transport	0.5	0.6	0.8	0.9	1.2	1.5	1.8	2.3
%	(10.4)	(10.9)	(12.9)	(12.5)	(14.2)	(15.5)	(16.7)	(19.2)
Domestic and personal	0.6	0.7	0.8	0.9	1.2	1.3	1.5	1.8
%	(12.5)	(12.7)	(12.9)	(12.5)	(14.2)	(13.4)	(13.9)	(15.0)
Public service and professional	0.3	0.4	0.3	0.3	0.3	0.5	0.6	0.7
%	(6.3)	(7.3)	(4.8)	(4.2)	(3.6)	(5.2)	(5.6)	(5.8)
Total	4.8	5.5	6.2	7.2	8.4	9.7	10.8	12.0

Notes: These figures should be used with caution; they are intended to give general indications only. Since occupational categories were not included in the census until 1841 the figures for 1801–31 are little more than extrapolations and, as Deane and Cole put it, 'order-of-magnitude estimates'. Even after 1841 categorization is both imprecise and liable to fluctuation.

There is a small residual category of 'other' employment not included here. Percentages, however, are calculated from the total known or estimated occupied population, and not according to the method employed by Deane and Cole which seems to exaggerate the public service and professional category unwarrantably.

Source: Deane and Cole, *op. cit.*, pp. 141-3.

F: FOREIGN AND COLONIAL AFFAIRS

F.i Leading diplomatic treaties and alliances affecting Great Britain

1. Treaty of Versailles, Sept 1783: ending American War of Independence
(a) The 13 mainland colonies granted independence from Britain.
(b) Certain fishing rights off Newfoundland granted to the Americans and extended to the French.
(c) France gained West Indian islands of Tobago and St Lucia plus Senegal and Gorée.
(d) Spain gained Minorca and regained Florida.

2. Triple Alliance, Apr-Aug 1788
Britain, Holland and Prussia: alliance to preserve European peace.

3. First Coalition against France, Feb 1793
Britain, Prussia (left 1795), Spain (left 1795), Austria (made peace with France, 1797), Holland (defeated 1795), Sardinia (left 1796).

4. Treaty of St Petersburg, Sept 1794
Britain, Russia and Austria against France.

5. Second Coalition against France, June 1799
Britain, Russia (left 1800), Austria (left 1801), Turkey, Portugal (left 1801) and Naples (left 1801).

6. Peace of Amiens, Mar 1802: ending war between Britain and France
(a) All British maritime conquests during the war returned with exceptions of Trinidad (taken from Spain) and Ceylon (taken from the Dutch).
(b) Cape of Good Hope returned to Batavian Republic (Dutch).
(c) France agreed to evacuate southern Italy.
(d) Egypt returned to Turkey; both Britain and France agree to quit it.
(e) Malta handed over to a Neapolitan garrison.

7. Third Coalition against France (Treaty of St Petersburg), Apr 1805
Britain and Russia to liberate North German states. Austria joins in Aug but leaves in Dec after making peace with France at Pressburg.

8. Treaty of Örebro, July 1812
Britain, Russia and Sweden against France.

9. Treaty of Reichenbach, June 1813
Britain, Russia and Prussia against France. Britain agrees to £2m. subsidy to keep Russian and Prussia armies in the field.

10. Treaty of Chaumont, Mar 1814
Britain, Russia, Prussia and Austria against France. £5m. British subsidy to other participants. Signatories agree not to make separate peace with France.

11. Treaty of Fontainebleau, Apr 1814
Allies agree on Napoleon's banishment to Elba.

12. First Peace of Paris, May 1814
(a) France given her pre-war (1792) European territories plus Savoy.
(b) French overseas possessions restored, except Tobago, St Lucia and Mauritius which were retained by Britain.
(c) France recognized independence of the Netherlands and the German and Italian states.
(d) Belgium given to Netherlands, forming the United Netherlands. The Scheldt to remain an open river.

13. Anglo-Dutch Treaty, Aug 1814
(a) Britain retained Cape of Good Hope and Guiana settlements, Demerara, Essequibo and Berbice as part of British Guiana.
(b) Britain to restore Java to the Dutch (handed over in Dec 1816).
(c) Britain paid United Netherlands £2m. to be spent on fortifying Belgian frontier against France.

14. Treaty of Ghent, Dec 1814: ending war between Britain and USA
(a) Both sides revert to status quo ante bellum, except that Britain retains islands in Passamaquoddy Bay (off Maine).
(b) USA did not press compensation claims for wartime commercial loss.
(c) Outstanding problems on fishing rights and navigation unresolved.

15. Congress of Vienna, June 1815 and Second Peace of Paris, Nov 1815: ending Napoleonic Wars
(a) France ceded Saar, Landau and Savoy; army of occupation to stay in France for five years.
(b) Britain retains Malta and Heligoland.
(c) Victorious powers agree to act together to maintain the settlement if France attempted to disturb it. Quadruple Alliance (Britain, Austria, Prussia, Russia) renewed.
(d) Powers to meet in regular conference to discuss the workings of the European settlement.
(e) Britain establishes protectorate over Ionian Islands.

16. Congress of Aix-la-Chapelle, Nov 1818
(a) France joins European concert of nations.
(b) Quadruple Alliance of 1815 renewed to preserve France from revolution.
(c) Powers agree to periodic meetings, but Britain refuses to negotiate strengthened counter-revolutionary alliances.

17. Congress of Troppau, Nov 1820
Britain refuses to accede to declaration by Austria, Prussia and Russia that revolutions in other states could justify Great Power intervention to crush them.

18. Treaty of London, July 1827
Britain, Russia and France recognize autonomy of Greece but under suzerainty of Turkey.

19. London Protocols, Feb 1830
After Russo-Turkish War ends, Greece declared fully independent under protection of France, Russia and Britain.

20. London Conference, Oct–Nov 1831
Britain, France, Austria, Prussia, Russia and Belgium agree on 24 articles enunciating terms for the separation of Belgium from Holland. Negotiations controlled by Palmerston; Holland forced to accept terms after defeat by France in Dec 1832.

21. Quadruple Alliance, Apr 1834
Britain, France, Spain and Portugal. Negotiated by Palmerston to block absolutist candidates to the thrones of Spain and Portugal and secure the constitutional rights of the two infant queens, Isabella of Spain and Maria of Portugal.

22. Treaty of London, Apr 1839
Formal ending of the Belgian question. Belgian and Dutch territories finally confirmed; Luxembourg becomes an independent Grand Duchy.

23. Treaty of London, July 1840
Quadruple Alliance of Britain, Russia, Prussia and Austria to impose settlement in war between Turkey and Egypt, led by Mehemet Ali. Diplomatic initiative to curb growing French influence in the Middle East. British attack on Acre persuades Mehemet Ali to accept terms.

24. Convention of the Straits, July 1841
(a) Mehemet Ali becomes hereditary pasha of Egypt.
(b) Great Powers, now including France, guarantee Turkish independence.
(c) Dardanelles and Bosphorus are closed to warships of all nations during peacetime; this reversed terms of a Russo-Turkish accord in 1833.
    Russian and French ambitions in Ottoman Empire curbed to British diplomatic and commercial advantage.

25. Webster–Ashburton Treaty, Aug 1842
USA and Britain agree frontier between USA and Canada; treaty inaugurates a period of improved relations between the powers.

26. Treaty of Nanking, Aug 1842: ending first Anglo-Chinese War
(a) Britain acquired Hong Kong.
(b) Britain gained access to Chinese ports of Amoy, Shanghai, Ningpo and Foochow.
(c) China paid compensation for confiscated opium and for cost of the war.

27. Treaty of London, May 1852
Britain, France, Russia, Austria and Sweden. Major powers assign succession of Danish throne and Frederick VII of Denmark agrees not to incorporate duchies of Schleswig and Holstein within Denmark.

28. Anglo-French alliance, Mar 1854
To aid Turkey in her war with Russia. Britain concerned about Russian expansionism in the East.

29. Triple Alliance, Dec 1854
Austria joins Anglo-French alliance. Promises to keep 30,000 men in the Danubian principalities to counter Russian threat. France guarantees Austria's Italian possessions.

30. Treaty of Paris, Mar 1856: ending Crimean War
(a) Britain and Russia agree to respect Turkish independence.
(b) Black Sea becomes neutral; Russian fortifications at Sebastopol and Odessa to be demolished.
(c) Danubian principalities cease to be under Russian protection; placed under suzerainty of Turkey with their privileges guaranteed by the powers.
(d) European Commission to control navigation of the Danube.
(e) Russia cedes part of southern Bessarabia to Moldavia.

31. Treaty of Peking, Oct 1860: ending second Anglo-Chinese War
(a) Ships allowed to trade in the Yangtze as far as Hankow.
(b) Eleven more Chinese ports opened to foreign trade.
(c) Importation of opium legalized.

32. Treaty of London, July 1863
Britain, France, Russia and Denmark settle the question of the Ionian Islands. The islands cease to be a British protectorate and become neutral; fortifications on Corfu demolished. Prussia and Austria (1864) and Turkey (1865) approve the agreement. Britain establishes good relations with Greece, which elects a pro-British king.

33. Conference of London, May 1867
Great Powers guarantee neutrality of Luxembourg against demands by Napoleon III that it be incorporated within France. Prussian troops withdrawn from Luxembourg.

F.ii Wars involving Great Britain, 1783–1870

1. War with Revolutionary France, Feb 1793–Mar 1802

1793	July – Corsica occupied; Aug – Adm. Hood captures Toulon but it has to be evacuated under republican pressure in Dec; Sept – British Army under duke of York defeated at Hondschoote.
1794	Apr – Subsidies paid to Prussia and Holland; Seychelles, Martinique, St Lucia and Guadeloupe captured but French recapture Guadeloupe.
1795	Feb – Tr. of Basle: Prussia make peace with France; Batavian Republic (Holland) declares war on Britain; Ceylon captured from Dutch; June–Oct – Unsuccessful attempt to aid counter-revolution in Brittany – Quiberon Bay expedition; June – St Lucia recaptured by French; Oct – Belgium annexed by France.
1796	July – Elba captured; Aug – Tr. of San Ildefonso between France and Spain; Oct – Spain declares war on Britain. Britain captures Demerara, Essequibo and Guiana from Dutch; St Lucia and Grenada captured from French; Britain quits Corsica.
1797	Feb – Battle of St Vincent won by Jervis and Nelson against Spanish Navy; Trinidad captured. Apr–May – Naval mutinies at Spithead and the Nore; Oct – Adm. Duncan defeats Dutch fleet at Camperdown; Peace of Campo Formio between Austria and France leaves Britain isolated.
1798	May – French expedition to Egypt; danger of invasion of Britain recedes; Aug – Nelson defeats French fleet in Aboukir Bay (Battle of the Nile); attempted French invasion of Ireland during Irish rebellion; Dec – Anglo-Russian alliance signed.
1799	Mar–May – Siege of Acre by Napoleon frustrated by British and Turkish force; Oct – duke of York defeated at Alkmaar; naval blockade of Holland begins.

1800   Sept – Britain captures Malta; Dec – 'Armed Neutrality' (Russia, Sweden, Denmark, Prussia) against Britain's right of search of ships.

1801   Jan – British embargo on ships of the Armed Neutrality; Feb – Tr. of Luneville, Austria and France; Mar – France defeated near Alexandria; Mar–Apr – Naval actions against Denmark; Nelson's victory at Battle of Copenhagen forces Denmark to a truce; Prussia joins the Armed Neutrality; June – Armed Neutrality breaks up; Abercromby captures Cairo for Britain; Portugal shuts ports to British ships; Sept – France captures part of Guiana; Oct – Peace preliminaries begin.

2. Napoleonic Wars, May 1803–July 1815

1803   May – Britain places embargoes on French and Dutch ships in British ports; June – France occupies Hanover; Britain takes St Lucia and Tobago; Sept – Britain takes Dutch Guiana.

1804   Oct – Capt. Moore captures Spanish silver convoy on its way to Cadiz and sinks escort; helps to drive Spain to declare war on Britain in Dec.

1805   Oct – Austrians defeated by France at Ulm; decisive defeat of Villeneuve's French fleet by Nelson at Trafalgar, off Cadiz, renders Britain secure from invasion; Dec – Russia and Austria defeated by France at Austerlitz; Austria makes peace with France.

1806   Jan – Britain occupies Cape of Good Hope; Feb – By Franco-Prussian agreement Prussia agrees to bar British ships from her ports; Apr – Britain declares war on Prussia and begins blockade of French coast; Oct – Prussia, fearing French advances in Germany, declares war on France and is defeated at Jena. Berlin occupied; Nov – Berlin Decrees begin the Napoleonic 'Continental System' with aim of closing all Continental ports to British vessels.

1807   Jan – Britain extends naval blockade and declares all ships trading in ports from which hers are excluded liable to capture; June – New alliance between Britain, Russia and Prussia against France; Russians and Prussians defeated at Battle of Friedland; July – By Treaty of Tilsit Russia makes peace with France and agrees to co-operate in economic wartare against Britain; Prussia makes a similar agreement; Sept – Britain bombards Copenhagen to prevent Napoleon using Danish fleet against her; Oct – Denmark declares war on Britain; Nov – France invades Portugal which refuses to support Continental System; Dec – Milan Decrees against British trade extend the System.

1808   Feb – France invades Spain; Aug – British expeditionary force sent to Portugal under command of Wellesley; French defeated at Vimiero but by the Convention of Cintra the French Army was permitted to retire from Portugal intact; Dec – Madrid falls to the French.

1809   Apr – Wellesley returns to Portugal; Orders in Council restrict trade with USA; May – British troops defeat French at Oporto and force their retreat from Portugal; July – Wellesley defeats French in Spain at Talavera; British expedition to the Scheldt to aid Austria in her resumed hostilities with France; British troops land at Walcheren; Oct – Austria makes peace with France; Dec – Walcheren expedition fails and British troops evacuated.

1810   Jan – Sweden joins Continental System; June – French take Portuguese forts of Ciudad Rodrigo and Almeida; Wellington, in retreat, pursues scorched earth policy; July – Britain captures Ile de Bourbon and Mauritius; Oct – Wellington's defences at Torres Vedras prevent French capture of Lisbon; Fontainebleau Decrees order confiscation of British goods found in Napoleonic states; Guadeloupe taken by Britain.

1811   May – Wellington holds off French at Fuentes d'Onoro; Almeida recaptured; Portugal lost to the French; Aug – Britain occupies Java under Sir Samuel Auchmuty.

1812   Jan – Wellington recaptures Ciudad Rodrigo; Apr – Wellington captures Badajoz; June – Russia invaded by Napoleon; July – Wellington defeats French at Salamanca; Aug – Wellington enters Madrid; Sept – Napoleon enters Moscow after defeating Russian troops at Borodino; Oct – Wellington retreats from Burgos; Napoleon's retreat from Moscow begins; Dec – Napoleon returns to Paris with 500,000 casualties from the Russian campaign.

1813   Feb – Prussia and Russia agree on joint attack against Napoleon; May – Napoleon defeats Prussians and Russians at Lutzen and Bautzen; June – Further British subsidies to Russia and Prussia; after Wellington's defeat of the French at Vitoria he holds the entire Peninsula; Aug – Austria declares war on France; Oct – Wellington enters France across the Pyrenees; Napoleon defeated at Leipzig and his Confederation of the Rhine collapses; Nov – Wellington lays siege to Bayonne; France expelled from Holland; Dec – Allies agree to invade France from the east.

1814   Mar – Wellington captures Bordeaux; allies enter Paris.

1815   Mar – Napoleon returns to France from exile and enters Paris; Austria, Prussia, Russia and Britain unite against Napoleon and Britain promises £5m. subsidies; June – Wellington and Blucher defeat Napoleon at Waterloo and this decisive action effectively ends hostilities.

3. War with the United States of America, June 1812–Jan 1815

1812   June – US Congress declares war, claiming harassment by Britain and British support for Indian tribes blocking westward development; Aug – Detroit surrendered to British forces, preventing US attack on Canada; Oct – US defeated by British force under Isaac Brock at Queenston Heights.

1813   Apr – US captures York, Toronto; indecisive naval encounters, involving raiding parties on both sides; US unable to launch decisive attack on Canada; Sept – US reoccupies Detroit; Nov – British force defeats US at Chrysler's Farm, Montreal; Dec – US forces burn Newark; British forces burn Buffalo in reprisal and take Fort Niagara.

1814   July – Indecisive British and US attacks in the Great Lakes; Aug – British force takes Washington, burning main buildings.

1815   Jan – Unsuccessful British attack on New Orleans before news of peace reached the area.

4. 'Opium War' with China, 1839–42

1839   July – hostilities flare up after Chinese confiscation of British opium stocks. Aug – British capture Hong Kong.

1840   Canton and Chusan seized by British and ransomed for 6m. dollars.

5. Crimean War with Russia, Mar 1854–Mar 1856

1854   Sept – British and French troops land in Crimea and win Battle of the Alma but victory not followed up. Oct – Siege of Sebastopol begun. Battle of Balaclava results in allied victory but at great cost, including the loss of the Light Brigade; Nov – further allied victory at Inkerman.

1855   Jan – Piedmont joins allies against Russia; Sept – Sebastopol finally falls.

6. Second Anglo-Chinese War, 1856–60

1856   Oct – hostilities commence after Chinese authorities arrest 12 crew members of a British registered vessel. British squadron bombards Chinese forts in Canton river.
1857   Dec – Anglo-French force attacks and captures Canton.
1858   May – capture of Tientsin.
1860   Sept – Anglo-French attack on Peking, burning Emperor's summer palace.

F.iii Major colonial acquisitions, 1783–1870

(a) Africa
1806, Cape Colony; 1808, Sierra Leone; 1810 Mauritius; 1816, The Gambia; 1821, Gold Coast; 1843, Natal; 1861, Lagos.

(b) The Americas
1797, Trinidad; 1803, Tobago and St Lucia; 1814 Demerara, Essequibo, Berbice; 1833, Falkland Islands; 1858, British Columbia.

(c) Asia
1786, Penang; 1795, Ceylon; 1819, Singapore; 1824, Malacca; 1824, western Burma outside Irrawaddy delta; 1839, Aden; 1842, Hong Kong; 1846, Labuan (North Borneo); 1852, Burma (Irrawaddy delta); 1861, Kowloon.

(d) Australasia
1788, New South Wales; 1804 Van Diemen's Land (Tasmania) settled (declared separate colony 1825); 1829, Western Australia; 1836, South Australia; 1840, New Zealand; 1850, Victoria; 1859, Queensland.
(Britain claims responsibility for whole continent, 1829.)

(e) India
1793, Bengal; 1802, Poona; 1843, Sind; 1849, Punjab; 1853, Nagpur; 1856, Oudh.

F.iv Major landmarks in colonial constitutional development

1. India
(a) India Act, 1784.
    (i) establishment of a Board of Control to superintend British territorial possession in the East Indies;
    (ii) Board of Control, whose members to be ministers of the Crown, to superintend political and military affairs of the East India Company;
    (iii) powers of the Governor-General increased;
    (iv) patronage remains in control of Directors of the Company.

(b) 1813: Renewal of East India Company Charter. Trading monopoly ended but trading and administrative functions retained.

(c) India Act, 1858.
    (i) all territories and properties of the East India Company transferred to the Crown;
    (ii) Governor-General becomes Viceroy of India.

2. Canada

(a) Canada Act, 1791.
- (i) establishment of two separate provinces: Upper (Ontario) and Lower (Quebec);
- (ii) each province to have legislative assembly elected every seven years and empowered to vote annual supplies;
- (iii) each province to have a legislative council appointed by the government; members to serve for life;
- (iv) each province to have an executive council, nominated to assist the Lieutenant-General under the Governor-General.

(b) The Durham Report, 1839.
Recommendations after investigation into disturbances in 1837:
- (i) union of the two provinces;
- (ii) ministers to be responsible for their own legislature;
- (iii) Governor to rule with legislature and Britain not to interfere 'except on points involving strictly imperial interests'.

(c) Canada Act, 1840.
United provinces of Upper and Lower Canada.

(d) 1847: Canada granted responsible government.

(e) British North America Act, 1867.
- (i) established a federal 'Dominion' of Canada comprising Ontario, Quebec, New Brunswick and Nova Scotia;
- (ii) mother country retained control only of foreign relations;
- (iii) Manitoba and Northwest Territories added in 1870, British Columbia in 1871.

3. New Zealand

Treaty of Waitangi, 1840.
- (i) British sovereignty declared;
- (ii) Maoris on North Island ceded sovereignty rights and were granted by Britain full, undisputed rights over their lands and fisheries.

G: RELIGION

G.i Main developments in religious legislation, 1783–1870

1791   Toleration Act (1689) extended to permit Roman Catholics to worship according to its provisions.

1803   Sir William Scott's Act regarding non-residence of Anglican clergy. Bishops to make annual returns about the state of their dioceses.

1809   Initiation of a new series of grants to augment income of poorest livings.

1812   Relief Act: Concessions on registration of dissenters' places of worship. Five Mile Act (1665) and Conventicle Act (1670) repealed. Restrictions remain on meetings of dissenters in unregistered premises.

1813   Toleration Act extended to Unitarians.

1818   Church Building Act. Aims to promote building of Anglican churches in new industrial areas. Separate Act of Parliament no longer necessary to alter parochial boundaries. The first of a series of facilitating measures.

1828   Test (1673) and Corporation (1661) Acts repealed. Dissenters' political disqualifications removed.

1829   Roman Catholic emancipation: Catholics permitted to sit in Parliament. All Irish offices of State, except Viceroy and Chancellor, opened to Catholics.

1835   Peel's minority Conservative government establishes the Ecclesiastical Commission to consider reforms of the Church of England.

1836   Established Church Act. Episcopal incomes equalized at £4,000 except for higher stipends for Canterbury, York, London, Durham and Winchester.

1836   Marriage Act. Dissenting chapels licensed for matrimonial ceremonies for first time; civil marriage permitted.

1836   Registration Act transferred registration of births, marriages and deaths from church parishes to the State.

1836   Tithe Commutation Act. Tithes commuted to cash payments varying with prevailing price of corn. Central Tithe Commission established to supervise the operation.

1838   Pluralities Act. Holding of two livings prohibited if the livings were more than 10 miles apart, if the population of one exceeded 3,000 or if the joint annual value exceeded £1,000. Holding of three livings prohibited. Clergy could not engage in trade or farm more than 50 acres of land without episcopal permission.

1840   Ecclesiastical Duties and Revenues Act. Many non-resident cathedral appointments abolished; money from them put to augment poor livings or create new parishes.

1850   Reorganization of ecclesiastical commission with a permanent, professional estates committee with wider powers to supervise the administration of church property.

1851   Ecclesiastical Titles Act. An anti-Catholic measure designed to prevent Catholics adopting titles for their new diocesan hierarchy which had already been taken by Anglican clergy. No prosecutions issued under it; repealed by Gladstone in 1871.

1868   Compulsory payment of church rates (levied by Anglican churches for upkeep of those churches or to help build new churches in cities) abolished by Gladstone's Liberal government. Earlier dissenting campaigns for abolition in 1810s and 1830s had failed.

1869   Anglican Church in Ireland disestablished.

G.ii Estimated membership of main British churches, 1800–1870 (in 000s)

	Church of England and Scottish Episcopalians	% of total	Scottish, Welsh and English Presbyterians	% of total	Roman Catholics	% of total	Methodists	% of total	Other sects*	% of total	Congregationalists	% of total	Totals
1800	577	46	324	26	129	10	96	8	3	—	55	4	1,244
1810	599	42	361	25	158	11	145	10	4	—	87	6	1,433
1820	622	37	419	25	198	12	208	12	4	—	117	7	1,665
1830	658	33	479	24	250	13	302	15	7	—	155	8	1,977
1840	821	33	554	22	305	12	451	18	11	—	196	8	2,492
1850	953	27	680	20	846	24	513	15	40	1	248	7	3,475
1860	1,078	26	838	20	1,179	28	525	13	25	1	291	7	4,153
1870	1,206	26	953	21	1,213	27	603	13	22	—	313	7	4,564

	Baptists	% of total	Society of Friends (Quakers)	% of total
1800	40	3	20	2
1810	60	4	(19)	1
1820	79	4	18	1
1830	109	6	17	1
1840	138	6	16	1
1850	180	5	15	—
1860	203	5	14	—
1870	240	5	14	—

*Other sects comprise Churches of Christ (formed 1827), Latter-day Saints (1837), Moravians and New Church.

Note: These are estimates only; the surviving evidence does not permit precise quantification. The figures are included mainly to give a general guide to the relative strengths of the various sects and also to show growth over time. Broadly speaking, membership data become more reliable after 1850. Though the presentation offers different categorizations, most of the data derives from material drawn together in R. Currie, A. Gilbert and L. Horsley, *Churches and Churchgoers: Patterns of Church Growth in the British Isles since 1700* (Oxford, 1977), pp. 23–30, 139–49, reproduced by permission of Oxford University Press.

The figures for Church of England and Scottish Episcopalian membership derive from data or estimates of Easter Day communicants. Nominal allegiance to the Established Church, of course, was far higher.

G.iii The growth and social composition of British Methodism, 1781–1871

(a) Membership (in 000s)

	Wesleyan Methodists	Methodist New Connexion (Kilhamites) (from 1797)	Bible Christians (from 1826)	Primitive Methodists (from 1820)	Wesleyan Methodist Association (1837–56) and United Methodist free Churches (from 1851)	Total	% increase per decade
1781	38	—	—	—	—	38	
1791	58	—	—	—	—	58	52
1801	90	5	—	—	—	94	62
1811	146	7	—	—	—	153	62
1821	200	10	—	16	—	227	48
1831	250	11	7	37	—	305	34
1841	329	21	11	76	22	459	50
1851	302	17	13	106	20	459	0
1861	320	23	17	128	53	540	18
1871	347	23	18	149	62	599	11

Note: As figures are rounded sums do not always add exactly to totals shown. Percentage increases are derived from the real, rather than the rounded, figures. The 1851 figures are distorted by a secession from the Wesleyan Connexion after 1849. Many seceders do not reappear until figures for the UMFC are computed in 1857.

(b) Occupational structure of Methodism, c. 1800–1837 (from sample)

	Wesleyans (%)	Primitives (%)
Merchants and manufacturers	1.7	0.5
Shopkeepers	5.8	3.9
Farmers	5.5	5.6
Artisans	62.7	47.7
Labourers	9.5	16.1
Colliers, miners, etc.	7.6	12.5
Others	7.2	13.7

Sources: Currie, Gilbert and Horsley, *op. cit.*, pp. 139–42; A. D. Gilbert, *Religion and Society in Industrial England* (1976), p. 63.

G.iv Non-residence in the Church of England, 1810–1850

	Total no. of benefices	Resident incumbents	%	Non-resident incumbents	%	Curates
1810	10,261	4,421	45	5,435	55	3,694
1814	10,602	3,798	39	6,003	61	4,405
1827	10,533	4,413	46	5,171	54	4,254
1831	10,560	4,649	48	4,983	52	4,373
1835	10,571	5,146	51	4,975	49	4,435
1841	10,987	6,699	64	3,736	36	4,743
1846	11,386	7,445	69	3,366	31	4,690
1850	11,728	8,077	73	2,952	27	

Note: Non-residents not infrequently performed the duties of their parishes though non-resident in their parsonage houses for whatever reason. In 1814, for example 1,990 (33%) were listed as doing duty; in 1831 the percentage was 34 and in 1850, 39. A non-resident was not necessarily a non-performer.

Source: Currie, Gilbert and Horsley, *op. cit.*, pp. 196–7.

G.v Disparities of clerical income in the Church of England

Report of the Ecclesiastical Revenues Commission, 1833

		% of total	
Benefices with income of less than £50	294	2.81	⎫
Benefices with income of £50–£99	1,621	15.53	⎬ 4,861(46.57%)
Benefices with income of £100–£149	1,591	15.25	⎪
Benefices with income of £150–£199	1,355	12.98	⎭
Benefices with income of £200–£299	1,964	18.82	⎫
Benefices with income of £300–£399	1,317	12.62	⎬ 4,111(39.39%)
Benefices with income of £400–£499	830	7.95	⎭
Benefices with income of £500–£999	1,278	12.25	⎫ 1,464 (14.03%)
Benefices with income of over £1,000	186	1.78	⎭

Source: P. P., H.C., 1834, xxiii, pp. 5–7.

G.vi Leading dignitaries of the Church of England, 1783–1870

Archbishops of Canterbury
1783–1805 John Moore
1805–28   Charles Manners Sutton
1828–48   William Howley
1848–62   John Bird Sumner
1862–68   Charles Thomas Longley
1868–83   Archibald Campbell Tait

Archbishops of York
1777–1808 William Markham
1808–48   Edward Vernon Harcourt
1848–60   Thomas Musgrave
1860–62   Charles Thomas Longley
1862–91   William Thomson

Bishops of London
1777–87   Robert Lowth
1787–1809 Beilby Porteus
1809–13   John Randolph
1813–28   William Howley
1828–56   Charles James Blomfield
1856–69   Archibald Campbell Tait
1869–85   John Jackson

G.vii The religious census of England and Wales, 1851

Preliminary note: The tables below attempt estimates of churchgoers in various categories on census Sunday, 30 March 1851. This is a hazardous undertaking since the census enumerated total attendances, including a substantial proportion of believers who attended twice or perhaps even three times on the day in question. This proportion cannot be precisely calculated, but the following estimates make a reduction of one-third on the total attendances to allow for multiple attendance. This rule of thumb probably distorts the ratio of Anglican to nonconformist attenders, since the latter tended to place a higher premium on two or more attendances on the Sabbath day.

For a detailed discussion of the census see K. S. Inglis, 'Patterns of religious worship in 1851', *Jnl. Eccles. Hist*, xi (1960), pp. 74–86 and D. M. Thompson, 'The 1851 religious census – problems and possibilities', *Vict. Stud.*, xi (1967–68), pp. 87–97.

(a) Regional variations in religious attendance (in 000s)

	Population	Church of England attenders	% of popn	Nonconformist, etc. attenders	% of popn	Roman Catholic attenders	% of popn	Total attenders	% of popn
London	2,362	330	14.0	216	9.1	37	1.6	583	24.7
South-east	1,628	426	26.2	227	13.9	10	0.6	664	40.8
South Midlands	1,234	340	27.5	315	25.6	3	0.3	659	53.4
East	1,114	300	26.9	238	21.3	3	0.3	541	48.6
South-west	1,803	457	25.3	413	22.9	6	0.3	875	48.5
West Midlands	2,133	414	19.4	333	15.6	29	1.4	776	36.4
North Midlands	1,215	227	18.7	274	22.6	9	0.8	511	42.1
North-west	2,491	329	13.2	322	12.9	107	4.3	758	30.4
Yorkshire	1,789	233	13.0	402	22.5	20	1.1	656	36.7
North	969	110	11.3	144	14.8	17	1.8	271	27.9
Wales	1,189	126	10.6	523	44.0	6	0.5	655	55.1
Totals	17,927	3,293	18.4	3,406	19.0	247	1.4	6,946	38.8
Adjusted totals*	17,927	3,530	19.7	3,479	19.4	256	1.4	7,264	40.5

*Adjusted totals include estimates to compensate for returns which failed to reach the Registrar's office.

Note: Figures are rounded and so do not add exactly to totals.

The Census Office regional divisions were:

South-east: Surrey, Kent, Sussex, Hampshire, Berkshire.

South Midlands:	Middlesex, Hertfordshire, Buckinghamshire, Oxfordshire, Northamptonshire, Huntingdon, Bedford, Cambridgeshire.
East:	Essex, Suffolk, Norfolk.
South-west:	Wiltshire, Dorset, Devon, Cornwall, Somerset.
West Midlands:	Gloucester, Herefordshire, Shropshire, Staffordshire, Worcestershire, Warwickshire.
North Midlands:	Leicestershire, Rutland, Lincolnshire, Nottinghamshire, Derbyshire.
North-west:	Cheshire, Lancashire.
Northern:	Durham, Northumberland, Cumberland, Westmorland.

(b) Patterns of urban churchgoing (in 000s)

The following figures estimate church attendance in the 61 urban communities with populations in excess of 20,000 at the 1851 census. The figures contrast sharply with figures from small towns and rural areas.

	Population	Church of England attenders	% of popn	Nonconformist, etc. attenders	% of popn	Roman Catholic attenders	% of popn	Total attenders	% of popn
London	2,362	330	14.0	216	9.1	37	1.6	583	24.7
8 towns over 100,000	1,581	171	10.8	204	12.9	72	4.6	447	28.3
18 towns 50,000–99,999	1,169	149	12.7	213	18.3	23	2.0	385	32.9
34 towns 20,000–49,999	1,034	182	17.6	176	17.0	21	2.0	379	36.7
Total urban areas	6,146	831	13.5	810	13.2	152	2.5	1,793	29.2
Total rural, etc. areas	11,782	2,462	20.9	2,596	22.0	95	0.8	5,153	43.7

Note: Figures are rounded and do not add exactly to totals; they do not compensate for omissions in the returns (see (*a*) above).

Source: P. P., 1852–53, lxxxix.

Maps

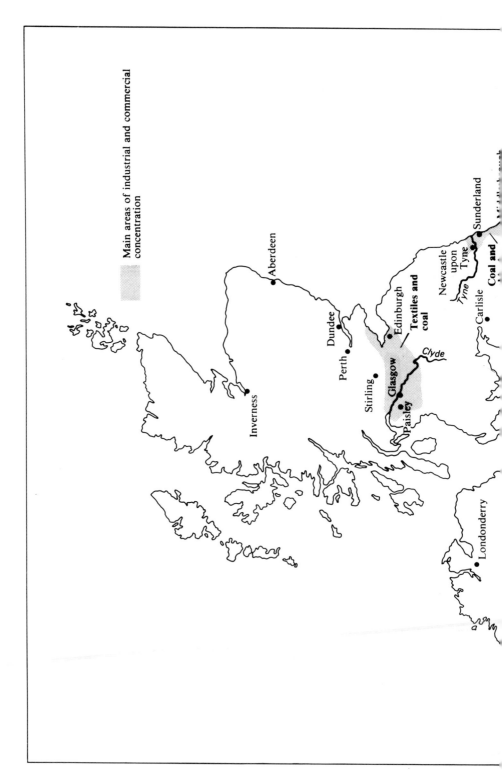

Main areas of industrial and commercial concentration

Inverness

Aberdeen

Perth
Dundee

Stirling
Glasgow
Paisley
Edinburgh
Textiles and coal
Clyde

Newcastle upon Tyne
Tyne
Sunderland
Coal and

Carlisle

Londonderry

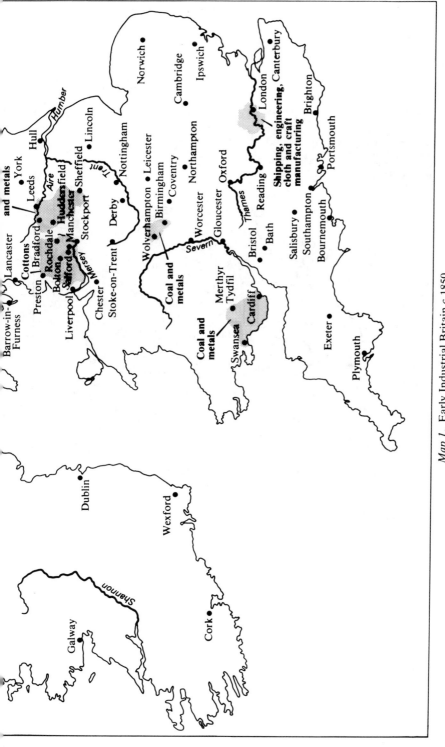

Map 1. Early Industrial Britain c.1850

453

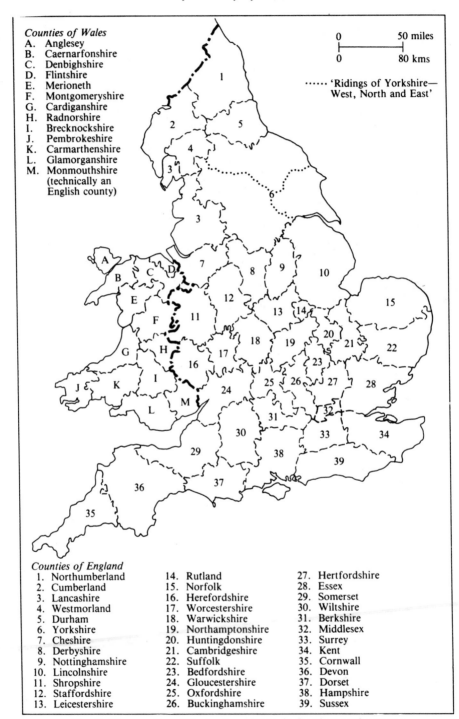

Counties of Wales
A. Anglesey
B. Caernarfonshire
C. Denbighshire
D. Flintshire
E. Merioneth
F. Montgomeryshire
G. Cardiganshire
H. Radnorshire
I. Brecknockshire
J. Pembrokeshire
K. Carmarthenshire
L. Glamorganshire
M. Monmouthshire
    (technically an
    English county)

	0	50 miles
	0	80 kms

······ 'Ridings of Yorkshire—
West, North and East'

Counties of England

1. Northumberland	14. Rutland	27. Hertfordshire
2. Cumberland	15. Norfolk	28. Essex
3. Lancashire	16. Herefordshire	29. Somerset
4. Westmorland	17. Worcestershire	30. Wiltshire
5. Durham	18. Warwickshire	31. Berkshire
6. Yorkshire	19. Northamptonshire	32. Middlesex
7. Cheshire	20. Huntingdonshire	33. Surrey
8. Derbyshire	21. Cambridgeshire	34. Kent
9. Nottinghamshire	22. Suffolk	35. Cornwall
10. Lincolnshire	23. Bedfordshire	36. Devon
11. Shropshire	24. Gloucestershire	37. Dorset
12. Staffordshire	25. Oxfordshire	38. Hampshire
13. Leicestershire	26. Buckinghamshire	39. Sussex

Map 2. The counties of England and Wales in the nineteenth century

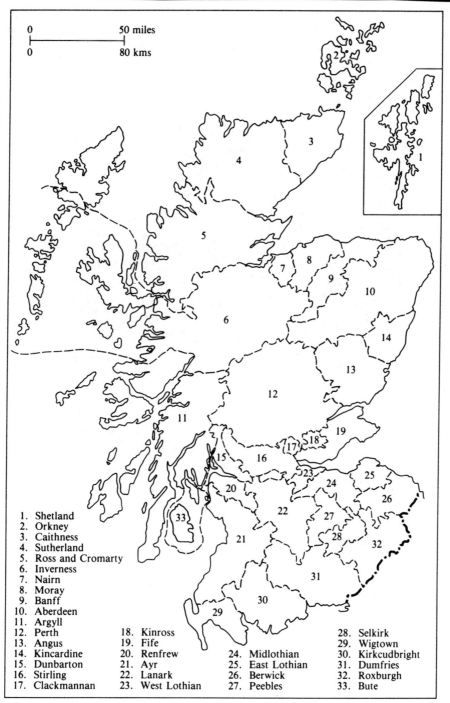

0   50 miles

0   80 kms

1. Shetland
2. Orkney
3. Caithness
4. Sutherland
5. Ross and Cromarty
6. Inverness
7. Nairn
8. Moray
9. Banff
10. Aberdeen
11. Argyll
12. Perth
13. Angus
14. Kincardine
15. Dunbarton
16. Stirling
17. Clackmannan
18. Kinross
19. Fife
20. Renfrew
21. Ayr
22. Lanark
23. West Lothian
24. Midlothian
25. East Lothian
26. Berwick
27. Peebles
28. Selkirk
29. Wigtown
30. Kirkcudbright
31. Dumfries
32. Roxburgh
33. Bute

Map 3. The counties of Scotland in the nineteenth century

Map 4. The counties of Ireland in the nineteenth century

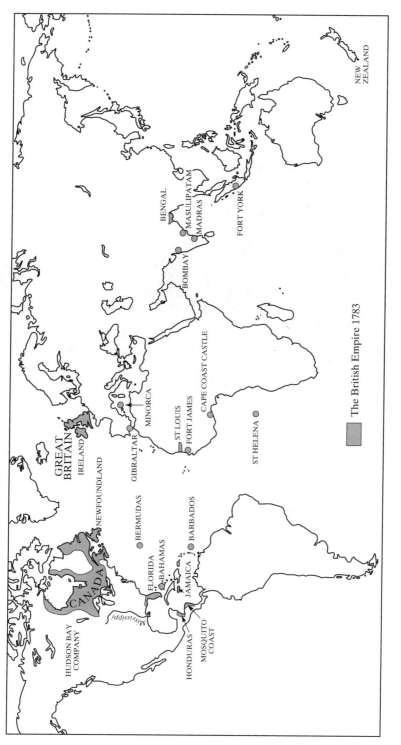

Map 5. The British Empire 1783

The British Empire 1783

Map 6. The British Empire 1870, including dates of independence

5 G. Holmes and D. Szechi, *The Age of Oligarchy: Pre-Industrial Britain, 1722–83* (1993). A magisterial study in the same series as the present volume.

6 E. Halevy, *England in the Nineteenth Century* (6 vols, 1924). Probably the best extended study of the nineteenth century ever written, especially vols i–iii (1815–41). Vol. i looks backwards to provide a splendid extended introduction. Scandalously under-used in recent years.

7 R. Brown, *Society and Economy in Modern Britain, 1700–1850* (1991).

8 R. Brown, *Church and State in Modern Britain 1700–1850* (1991) – 7 and 8 are two bulky volumes which synthesize much recent research.

9 N. McCord, *British History 1815–1906* (Oxford, 1991).

10 E. Royle, *Modern Britain, A Social History 1750–1985* (1987).

11 T. May, *An Economic and Social History of Britain 1760–1970* (1987) – traverses the ground traditionally examined in GCE Advanced level economic and social history syllabuses.

12 C. More, *The Industrial Age: Economy and Society 1750–1985* (1989).

13 P. Mathias, *The First Industrial Nation* (2nd edn, 1983).

14 J. C. Beckett, *The Making of Modern Ireland, 1603–1923* (2nd edn, 1981).

15 K. T. Hoppen, *Ireland since 1800: Conflict & Conformity* (1989).

16 M. Lynch, *Scotland: A New History* (1991) – Part V covers the chronology of this volume in an imaginative and wide-ranging fashion.

17 R. Campbell, *Scotland since 1707: The Rise of an Industrial Society* (2nd edn, 1985).

18 R. Mitchison, *A History of Scotland* (2nd edn, 1982).

19 T. M. Devine and R. Mitchison (eds), *People and Society in Scotland* (3 vols, 1988–90) – vols 1 and 2 cover the period 1760–1914.

20 S. O. Checkland, *Industry and Ethos: Scotland, 1832–1914* (1984).

21 P. Jenkins, *A History of Modern Wales, 1536–1990* (1992).

22 G. A. Williams, *When was Wales? A History of the Welsh* (1986).

SECTION 2

Within the thematic sub-sections which follow the arrangement is broadly chronological. Volumes covering some important themes have been kept together, however, when it was felt that this would be of greater reference value.

In recent years, series of short volumes have been introduced which aim to provide readers with introductions to major themes. These series have considerable value, but it is useful to differentiate them from frequently much more substantial monographs. Volumes in such series are identified below by the following abbreviations after the title:

BHP: British History in Perspective (Macmillan)
HAP: Historical Association Pamphlets
HAS: Historical Association Studies (Hist. Assoc.)
HB: History Briefings (Heinemann: collections of brief articles first produced in the sixth-form journal *Modern History Review*)
LP: Lancaster Pamphlets (Routledge)
SEH: Studies in Economic and Social History (Macmillan)
SSH: Seminar Studies in History (Longman)

A: Politics and biography

23 L. Colley, *Britons: Forging the Nation, 1707–1837* (Yale, 1992).

24 B. W. Hill, *British Parliamentary Parties, 1742–1832* (1985).

25 J. Brooke, *The House of Commons, 1754–1790* (1964).

26 L. Namier, *The Structure of Politics at the Accession of George III* (2nd edn, 1957).

27 J. Brewer, *Party Ideology and Popular Politics at the accession of George III* (Cambridge, 1977).

28 K. Perry, *British Politics and the American Revolution* BHP (1990).

29 J. Cannon, ed., *The Whig Ascendancy* (1981).

30 J. W. Derry, *British Politics in the Age of Fox, Pitt and Liverpool* BHP (1990).

31 F. O'Gorman, *Voters, Patrons and Parties: The Unreformed Electoral System of Hanoverian England, 1734–1832* (Oxford, 1989).

32 F. O'Gorman, *The Emergence of the British Two-Party System, 1760–1832* (1982).

33 E. J. Evans, *Political Parties in Britain, 1783–1867* LP (1985).

34 L. G. Mitchell, *Charles James Fox and the Disintegration of the Whig Party, 1782–1794* (1971).

35 J. Ehrman, *The Younger Pitt: The Years of Acclaim* (1969).

36 J. Ehrman, *The Younger Pitt: The Reluctant Transition* (1983).

37 J. W. Derry, *The Regency Crisis and the Whigs* (Cambridge. 1963).

38 F. O'Gorman, *The Whig Party and the French Revolution* (1967).

39 E. A. Smith, *Earl Grey 1764–1845* (Oxford, 1990).

40 R. W. Davis, *Political Change and Continuity, 1760–1885: A Buckinghamshire Study* (Newton Abbot, 1972).

41 D. Read, *The English Provinces, c. 1760–1960: A Study in Influence* (1964).

42 D. Read, *Press and People, 1790–1960* (1961).

43 J. Cannon, *Parliamentary Reform, 1640–1832* (Cambridge, 2nd edn, 1980).

44 H. T. Dickinson, ed., *Britain and the French Revolution, 1789–1815* (1989).

45 A. Goodwin, *The Friends of Liberty* (1979).

46 C. Emsley, *British Society and the French Wars* (1979).

47 M. Philip, ed., *The French Revolution and British Popular Politics* (Cambridge, 1991).

48 M. Elliott, 'The "Despard Conspiracy" reconsidered' *P.& P.* 75 (1977), pp. 16–61.

49 P. Ziegler, *Addington* (1965).

50 P. Jupp, *Lord Grenville* (Oxford, 1985).

51 R. Stewart, *Henry Brougham: his Public Career* (1985).

52 R. Foster, *Modern Ireland, 1600–1972* (1988).

53 R. Kee, *The Most Distressful Country* (1976 edn).

54 C. J. Bartlett, *Castlereagh* (1966).

55 J. W. Derry, *Castlereagh* (1976).

56 W. Hinde, *George Canning* (1973).

57 N. Gash, *Lord Liverpool* (1984).

58 J. Pollock, *Wilberforce* (1977).

59 R. Furneaux, *William Wilberforce* (1974)

60 I. Prothero, *Artisans and Politics in Early Nineteenth-Century London* (1979).

61 J. F. C. Harrison, *Robert Owen and the Owenites in Britain and America* (1969).

62 J. E. Cookson, *Lord Liverpool's Administration, 1815–22* (Edinburgh, 1975).

63 A. Mitchell, *The Whigs in Opposition, 1815–1830* (Oxford, 1967).

64 H. van Thal, ed., *The Prime Ministers* (2 vols, 1974).

65 B. Hilton, *Corn, Cash, Commerce* (Oxford, 1977).

66 N. Gash, *Mr. Secretary Peel* (1985).

67 N. Thompson, *Wellington after Waterloo* (1986).

68 E. J. Evans, *Britain Before the Reform Act, 1815–32* SSH (1989).

69 P. Catterall, ed., *Britain 1815–1867* HB (1994).

70 B. Gordon, *Political Economy in Parliament, 1819–23* (1976).

71 B. Gordon, *Economic Doctrine and Tory Liberalism, 1824–30* (1979).

72 K. Bourne, *Palmerston: The Early Years, 1784–1841* (1982).

73 M. E. Chamberlain, *Lord Palmerston* (1987).

74 M. Brock, *The Great Reform Act* (1973).

75 E. J. Evans, *The Great Reform Act of 1832* LP (2nd edn, 1994).

76 J. A. Phillips, 'The many faces of reform: the Reform Bill and the electorate' *Parliamentary History* i (1982).

77 I. C. G. Hutchison, *A Political History of Scotland, 1832–1924* (Edinburgh, 1986).

78 K. T. Hoppen, *Elections, Politics and Society in Ireland, 1832–1885* (Oxford, 1984).

79 N. Gash, *Politics in the Age of Peel* (1953).

80 N. Gash, ed., *The Age of Peel* (1968).

81 N. Gash, *Reaction and Reconstruction in English Politics, 1832–52* (Oxford, 1965).

82 N. Gash, 'The organization of the Conservative party, 1832–46' *Parliamentary History.* i (1982), and ii (1983).

83 R. Stewart, *Party and Politics, 1830–52* BHP (1989).

84 R. Stewart, *The Foundation of the Conservative Party, 1830–1867* (1978).

85 T. A. Jenkins, *The Liberal Ascendancy, 1830–86* (1994).

86 P. Mandler, *Aristocratic Government in the Age of Reform, Whigs and Liberals 1830–52* (Oxford, 1990).

87 I. Newbould, *Whiggery and Reform, 1830–41* (1990).

88 G. R. Searle, *Entrepreneurial Politics in Mid-Victorian Britain* (Oxford, 1993).

89 D. Fraser, *Urban Politics in Victorian England* (1976).

90 A. MacIntyre, *The Liberator: Daniel O'Connell and the Irish Party, 1830–1847* (1965).

91 I. Newbould, 'Sir Robert Peel and the Conservative Party, 1832–1841: a study in failure?' *E. H. R.,* xcviii (1983).

92 C. C. Driver, *Tory Radical: The Life of Richard Oastler* (New York, 1946).

93 R. A. Lewis, *Edwin Chadwick and the Public Health Movement* (1952).

94 S. E. Finer, *The Life and Times of Sir Edwin Chadwick* (1980 edn).

95 R. Lambert, *Sir John Simon, 1816–1904* (1963).

96 P. Ziegler, *Melbourne* (1976).

97 J. Prest, *Lord John Russell* (1972).

98 N. Gash, *Sir Robert Peel* (1986 edn).

99 E. J. Evans, *Sir Robert Peel: Statesmanship, Power & Party* LP (1991).

100 D. Read, *Peel and the Victorians* (Oxford, 1987).

101 J. T. Ward, *Sir James Graham* (1967).

102 M. E. Chamberlain, *Lord Aberdeen* (1983).

103 W. Hinde, *Richard Cobden: A Victorian Outsider* (1987).

104 W. O. Aydelotte, 'The House of Commons in the 1840s' *History, xxxix* (1954).

105 G. A. Williams, *The Merthyr Rising* (1978).

106 E. Royle, *Chartism* SSH (2nd edn. 1986).

107 D. Thompson, *The Chartists: Popular Politics in the Industrial Revolution* (1984).

108 D. Jones, *Chartism and the Chartists* (1973).

109 A. Briggs, ed., *Chartist studies* (1959).

110 D. Fraser, ed., *Cities, Class and Communication* (1990) – J. Belchem, 'Beyond Chartist studies: class, community and party in early Victorian populist politics'.

111 F. C. Mather, ed., *Chartism and Society* (1980).

112 D. K. G. Thompson and J. Epstein, eds, *Languages of Class: Studies in Working Class History, 1832–1932* (1982).

113 J. Epstein, *The Lion of Freedom* (1982) – a sympathetic revision of the career of Feargus O'Connor to 1842.

114 N. McCord, *The Anti-Corn Law League* (1958).

115 K. Robbins, *John Bright* (1979).

116 D. A. Hamer, *The Politics of Electoral Pressure* (Hassocks, 1977).

117 D. Southgate, *The Passing of the Whigs, 1832–1886* (1965).

118 I. Newbould, 'Whiggery and the growth of party, 1830–41' *Parl. Hist.,* iv (1985).

119 A. Hawkins, ' "Parliamentary Government" and Victorian political parties, *c.* 1830–80', *E. H. R.,* civ (1989).

120 E. J. Feuchtwanger, *Gladstone* (1975).

121 M. J. Winstanley, *Gladstone and the Liberal Party* LP (1990).

122 H. G. C. Matthew, *Gladstone, 1809–74* (Oxford, 1986).

123 R. T. Shannon, *Gladstone, Vol. 1, 1809–65* (1982).

124 R. Blake, *Disraeli* (1966).

125 J. K. Walton, *Disraeli* LP (1990).

126 B. I. Coleman, *Conservatism and the Conservative Party in Nineteenth-Century Britain* (1988).

127 D. Southgate, ed., *The Conservative Leadership from 1832 to 1932* (1974).

128 W. L. Burn, *The Age of Equipoise* (1964).

129 T. J. Nossiter, *Influence, Opinion and Political Idioms in reformed England: Case Studies from the North-East, 1832–74* (Hassocks, 1975).

130 K. Robbins, *Nineteenth-Century Britain: England, Scotland and Wales, the Making of a Nation* (Oxford, 1988).

131 E. P. Hennock, *Fit and Proper Persons* (1973).

132 J. B .Conacher, *The Peelites and the Party System, 1846–1852* (Newton Abbot, 1972).

133 J. B. Conacher, *The Aberdeen Coalition, 1852–55: A Study in Mid-Victorian Party Politics* (1968).

134 E. D. Steele, *Palmerston and Liberalism, 1855–1865* (Cambridge, 1991).

135 J. R. Vincent, *The Formation of the Liberal Party, 1857–68* (1966).

136 E. F. Biagini, *Liberty, Retrenchment and Reform: Popular Politics in the Age of Gladstone, 1860–80* (Cambridge, 1992).

137 A. Hawkins, *Parliament, Party and the Art of Politics in Britain, 1855–59* (1987).

138 J. R. Vincent, 'The parliamentary dimension of the Crimean War' *T.R.H.S.* 5th ser., xxxiii (1981).

139 R. Harrison, *Before the Socialists: Studies in Labour and Politics, 1861–81* (1965).

140 E. F. Biagini and A. F. Reid eds, *Currents of Radicalism: Popular Radicalism, Organised Labour and Party Politics in Britain, 1850–1914* (Cambridge, 1991).

141 F. B. Smith, *The Making of the Second Reform Bill* (Cambridge, 1966).

142 M. Cowling, *1867: Disraeli, Gladstone and Revolution* (Cambridge, 1967).

143 J. Vincent, ed., *Derby, Disraeli and the Conservative Party* (Hassocks, 1978).

144 G. Himmelfarb, 'The politics of democracy: the English Reform Act of 1867' *J.B.S.* vi (1966).

145 E. J. Feuchtwanger, *Disraeli, Democracy and the Tory Party* (Oxford, 1968).

146 D. A. Hamer, *Liberal Politics in the Age of Gladstone and Rosebery* (Oxford, 1972).

147 H. J. Hanham, *Elections and Party Management, Politics in the Time of Disraeli and Gladstone* (1959).

148 R. Harrison, 'The British working class and the general election of 1868', *I.R.S.H.* v (1960).

B: Foreign policy, commerce and the colonies

149 P. Langford, *The Eighteenth Century, 1688–1815* (1976).

150 J. H. Parry, *Trade and Dominion: The European Overseas Empires in the Eighteenth Century* (1971).

151 P. J. Cain and A. G. Hopkins, *British Imperialism: Innovation and Expansion, 1688–1914* (1993).

152 J. B. Williams, *British Commercial Policy and Trade Expansion, 1750–1850* (Oxford, 1972).

153 R. Anstey, *The Atlantic Slave Trade and British Abolition, 1760–1810* (1975).

154 C. A . Bayly, *Imperial Meridian: The British Empire and the World, 1780–1830* (1989).

155 J. Black, *British Foreign Policy in an Age of Revolutions, 1783–1793* (Cambridge, 1994).

156 J. Black, *A System of Ambition: British Foreign Policy, 1660–1793* (1991).

157 H. Temperley and L. Penson, eds, *Foundations of British Foreign Policy, 1782–1902* (1966 edn).

158 M. E. Chamberlain, *'Pax Britannica'? British foreign policy, 1789–1914* (1988).

159 J. Holland Rose, *William Pitt and the Great War* (1911).

160 B. Semmel, *The Rise of Free Trade Imperialism* (1970).

161 R. Davis, *The Industrial Revolution and British Overseas Trade* (Leicester, 1979).

162 J. Sherwig, *Guineas and Gunpowder: British Foreign Aid in the Wars with France, 1793–1815* (Harvard, 1969).

163 P. Mackesy, *The War in the Mediterranean, 1803–10* (1957).

164 J. Weller, *Wellington in the Peninsula, 1808–14* (1962).

165 C. K. Webster, *The Foreign Policy of Castlereagh, 1812–15* (1931).

166 D. A. Farnie, *The English Cotton Industry and World Markets, 1815–1896* (Oxford, 1979).

167 P. Hayes, *The Nineteenth Century, 1814–80* (1975).

168 R. Hyam, *Britain's Imperial Century, 1815–1914* (1976).

169 E. Ingram, *In Defence of British India: Great Britain and the Middle East, 1775–1842* (1984).

170 A. G. L. Shaw, ed., *Great Britain and the Colonies, 1815–65* (1970).

171 P. J. Cain, *Economic Foundations of British Overseas Expansion, 1815–1914* (1980).

172 C. J. Bartlett, *Great Britain and Sea Power, 1815–53* (Oxford, 1963).

173 M. E. Chamberlain, *British Foreign Policy in the Age of Palmerston* SSH (1980).

174 B. Semmel, *Liberalism and Naval Strategy: Ideology, Interest & Sea Power during the Pax Britannica* (1986).

175 H. W. V. Temperley, *The Foreign Policy of Canning, 1822–27* (1966 edn).

176 K. Bourne, *The Foreign Policy of Victorian England, 1830–1902* (Oxford, 1970).

177 D. K. Fieldhouse, *Economics and Empire, 1830–1914* (1973).

C: The economy

178 R. A. Church and E. A. Wrigley, *The Industrial Revolutions* (11 vols, Oxford, 1994) – this massive compendium includes many articles on the economic and social aspects of industrialization originally published in learned journals. The most important volumes covering this period are 1, J. Chartres, ed., 'Pre-Industrial Britain'; 2 and 3, J. Hoppit and E. A. Wrigley, eds, 'The Industrial Revolution in Britain'.

(i) Agriculture (NB. for works predominantly concerning rural society, see section D below)

179 M. Overton, *Agricultural Revolution in England: the Transformation of the Rural Economy, 1500–1830* (Cambridge, 1987).

180 J. D. Chambers and G. E. Mingay, *The Agricultural Revolution, 1750–1880* (1966).

181 J. Addy, *The Agrarian Revolution* SSH (1972).

182 J. V. Beckett, *The Agricultural Revolution* HAP (Oxford, 1990).

183 G. E. Mingay, ed., *The Agrarian History of England and Wales, vi, 1750–1850* (Cambridge, 1989).

184 C. W. Chalklin and J. R. Wordie, eds, *Town and Countryside: the English Landowner in the National Economy, 1660–1860* (1989).

185 J. V. Beckett, 'The pattern of landownership in England and Wales, 1660–1880', *Ec. H. R.* 2nd ser., xxxvii (1984), pp. 1–22.

186 A. Offer, 'Farm tenure and land values in England, *c*.1750–1950' *Ec. H. R.* 2nd ser., xliv (1991), pp. 1–20.

187 G. Hueckel, 'English farming profits during the Napoleonic Wars, 1793–1815' *Exp. Ec. Hist.*, xiii (1976), pp. 331–45.

188 E. J. T. Collins, 'The rationality of "surplus" agricultural labour: mechanization in English agriculture in the nineteenth century' *Ag. H. R.* 35 (1987), pp. 36–46.

189 E. L. Jones, 'The agricultural labour market, 1793–1872' *Ec. H. R.* 2nd ser. xviii (1964–65), pp. 322–38.

190 E. J. T. Collins, 'Migrant labour in British agriculture in the nineteenth century' *Ec. H. R.* 2nd ser., xxix (1976), pp. 38–59.

191 D. Grigg, 'Farm size in England and Wales from early Victorian times to the present' *Ag. H. R.* 35 (1987), pp. 179–89.

192 S. Macdonald, 'Agricultural improvement and the neglected labourer' *Ag. H. R.* 31 (1983), pp. 81–90.

193 E. L. Jones, *The Development of English Agriculture, 1815–73* (1968).

194 C. S. Orwin and E. S. Whetham, *History of English Agriculture, 1846–1914* (1964).

195 E. L. Jones 'The changing basis of agricultural prosperity, 1853–73' *Ag. H. R.* 10 (1962), pp. 102–19.

196 M. E. Turner, *Enclosures in Britain, 1750–1914* SEH (1984).

197 J. Chapman, 'The extent and nature of parliamentary enclosure' *Ag. H. R.* 35 (1987), pp. 25–35.

198 J. R. Walton, 'On estimating the extent of parliamentary enclosure' *Ag. H. R.* 38 (1990), pp. 79–82.

199 E. J. Evans, *The Contentious Tithe: The Tithe Problem and English Agriculture. 1750–1850* (1976).

(ii) Industrial and technological change

200 M. Berg, *The Age of Manufactures: Industry, Innovation and Work in Britain, 1700–1820* (2nd edn, 1994).

201 N. F. R. Crafts, *British Economic Growth During the Industrial Revolution* (Oxford, 1985).

202 A. E. Musson, *The Growth of British Industry* (1978).

203 P. Deane and W. A. Cole, *British Economic Growth, 1688–1959* (2nd edn, Cambridge, 1969).

204 P. Hudson, ed., *Regions and Industries* (Cambridge, 1989).

205 P. Hudson, *The Industrial Revolution* (1992).

206 R. M. Hartwell, ed., *The Causes of the Industrial Revolution* (1967).

207 E. A. Wrigley, *Continuity, Change & Chance: The Character of the Industrial Revolution in England* (Cambridge, 1988).

208 J. Mokyr, *The British Industrial Revolution* (Oxford, 1993).

209 R. Floud and D. N. McCloskey, eds, *The Economic History of Britain since 1700, I: 1700–1860* (2nd edn, Cambridge, 1994).

210 D. Landes, *The Unbound Prometheus* (Cambridge, 1969).

211 W. W. Rostow, *The Stages of Economic Growth* (Cambridge, 1960).

212 E. J. Hobsbawm, *Industry and Empire* (1968).

213 F. Crouzet, ed., *Capital Formation in the Industrial Revolution* (1972).

214 C. Feinstein and S. Pollard, *Studies in Capital Formation in the United Kingdom, 1788–1920* (Cambridge, 1988).

215 J. Hoppit, 'Understanding the industrial revolution' *Hist. Jnl.* xxx (1987), pp. 211–24.

216 J. Hoppit, 'Counting the industrial revolution' *Ec. H. R.* 2nd ser., xliii (1990), pp. 171–93.

217 N. F. R. Crafts, 'British economic growth, 1700–1831: some difficulties of interpretation' *Exp. Ec. Hist.* xxiv (1987), pp. 245–68.

218 W. Kennedy, *English Taxation, 1640–1799* (1913).

219 M. Berg, *The Machinery Question and the Making of Political Economy, 1815–48* (Cambridge, 1980).

220 A. Smith, *Inquiry into the Nature and Causes of the Wealth of Nations* (1776, 2 vols, Everyman edn, 1910).

221 T. Malthus, *Essay on the Principle of Population* (1798, Pelican edn, 1970).

222 M. M. Edwards, *The Growth of the British Cotton Trade. 1780–1815* (Manchester, 1967).

223 S. D. Chapman, *The Cotton Industry in the Industrial Revolution* SEH (2nd edn, 1987).

224 R. Church, *The History of the British Coal Industry, 1830–1913, Victorian Pre-eminence* (Oxford, 1986).

225 J. R. Harris, *The British Iron Industry, 1700–1850* SEH (1988).

226 M. W. Flinn, *British Population Growth, 1700–1850* SEH (1970).

227 E. A. Wrigley and R. S. Schofield, *The Population History of England, 1541–1871: A Reconstruction* (1981).

228 N. L. Tranter, *Population and Society, 1750–1940* (1985).

229 T. R. Gourvish, *Railways and the British Economy, 1830–1914* SEH (1980).

230 G. R. Hawke, *Railways and Economic Growth in England and Wales, 1840–70* (Oxford, 1970).

231 R. Samuel, 'Workshop of the world: steam power and hand technology in mid–Victorian Britain' *Hist. Workshop Jnl.* iii (1977), pp. 6–72.

232 R. Church, *The Great Victorian Boom, 1850–1873* SEH (1975).

233 M. Collins, *British Banks and Industrial Finance in Britain before 1939* SEH (1990).

D: Society and social structure

234 J. V. Beckett, *The Aristocracy in England, 1660–1914* (Oxford, 1986).

235 G. E. Mingay, *The Gentry* (1976).

236 F. M. L. Thompson, *English Landed Society in the Nineteenth Century* (1963).

237 K. D. M. Snell, *Annals of the Labouring Poor: Social Change and Agrarian England, 1600–1900* (Cambridge, 1985).

238 E. J. Hobsbawm and G. Rudé, *Captain Swing* (1969).

239 B. Reay, *The Last Rising of the Agricultural Labourers: Rural Life and Protest in Nineteenth-Century England* (Oxford, 1990).

240 G. E. Mingay, ed., *The Victorian Countryside* 2 vols (1981).

241 A. Armstrong, *Farmworkers: A Social and Economic History* (1988).

242 G. E. Mingay, *Enclosure and the Small Farmer in the Age of the Industrial Revolution* SEH (1968).

243 E. P. Thompson, 'The moral economy of the English crowd in the eighteenth century' *P.& P.* 50 (1971), pp. 76–136.

244 A. Booth, 'Food riots in North-west England, 1790–1801' *P.& P.* 77 (1977), pp. 84–107.

245 R. B. Rose, 'The Priestley riots of 1791' *P.& P.* 18 (1960), pp. 68–88.

246 D. J. V. Jones, *Rebecca's Children: A Study of Rural Society, Crime and Protest* (Oxford, 1989).

247 D. J. V. Jones, 'The poacher: a study in Victorian crime and protest' *H.J.* xxii (1979) pp. 825–60.

248 E. L. Jones and G. E. Mingay, eds, *Land, Labour and Population in the Industrial Revolution* (1967).

249 J. C. D. Clark, *English Society, 1688–1832* (Cambridge, 1985).

250 H. J. Perkin, *The Origins of Modern English Society, 1780–1880* (1969).

251 E. P. Thompson, *The Making of the English Working Class* (1968 edn).

252 P. O'Brien and R. Quinault, eds, *The Industrial Revolution and British Society* (1993).

253 W. D. Rubinstein, *Capitalism, Culture and Decline in Britain, 1750–1990* (1993).

254 F. M. L. Thompson, *The Rise of Respectable Society: A Social History of Victorian Britain* (1988).

255 R. J. Morris, *Class and Class Consciousness in the Industrial Revolution* SEH (1979).

256 D. G. Wright, *Popular Radicalism: The Working-Class Experience, 1780–1880* (1988).

257 P. Adelman, *Victorian Radicalism: The Middle-Class Experience, 1830–1914* (1984).

258 J. Rendall, *Women in an Industrializing Society, 1750–1880* HAS (1990).

259 J. Belchem, *Industrialization and the Working Class: the English Experience, 1750–1900* (1990).

260 J. Rule, *The Labouring Classes in Early Industrial England* (1986).

261 C. Behagg, *Politics and Production in the Early Nineteenth Century* (1990).

262 N. Kirk, *The Growth of Working-Class Reformism in Mid-Victorian England* (1985).

263 J. Belchem, *'Orator' Hunt: Henry Hunt and English Working-Class Radicalism* (Oxford, 1985).

264 R. G. Wilson, *Gentlemen Merchants: The Merchant Community in Leeds 1700–1830* (Manchester, 1971).

265 R. J .Morris, *Class, Sect & Party: The Making of the British Middle Class: Leeds, 1820–50* (Manchester, 1990).

266 R. H. Trainor, *Black Country Elites: The Exercise of Authority in an Industrialized Area, 1830–1900* (Oxford, 1993).

267 S. D. Chapman, *The Early Factory Masters* (Newton Abbot, 1967).

268 S. Pollard, *The Genesis of Modern Management* (1968 edn).

269 P. L. Payne, *British Entrepreneurship in the Nineteenth Century* SEH (2nd edn, 1988).

270 M. Anderson, *Approaches to the History of the Western Family, 1500–1914* SEH (1980).

271 D. Levine, 'Industrialisation and the proletarian family in England', *P. & P.* 107 (1985), pp. 168–203.

272 L. Davidoff and C. Hall, *Family Fortunes: Men and Women of the English Middle Class* (1987).

273 J. Burnett, *Plenty and Want: A Social History of Food in England from 1815 to the Present Day* (2nd edn, 1989).

274 J. Burnett, ed., *Useful Toil* (1974).

275 J. Burnett, *Idle Hands: The Evidence of Unemployment, 1790–1990* (1994).

276 F. M. L. Thompson, ed., *The Cambridge Social History of Britain* (3 vols, 1990).

277 E. S. Richards, 'Women in the British economy since about 1700: an interpretation' *History* lix (1974), pp. 337–57.

278 A. V. John, ed., *Unequal Opportunities: Women's Employment in England, 1800–1918* (Oxford, 1986).

279 E. A. O. Roberts, *Women's Work, 1840–1940* SEH (1988).

280 J.Walvin, *A Child's World: A Social History of English Childhood, 1800–1914* (1982).

281 E. P. Thompson, 'Time, work discipline and industrial capitalism' *P.& P.* 38 (1967) pp. 56–97.

282 E. H. Hunt, *British Labour History, 1815–1914* (1981).

283 A. J. Taylor, ed., *The Standard of Living Controversy in Britain in the Industrial Revolution* (1975).

284 M. W. Flinn, 'Trends in real wages' *Ec. H. R.* 2nd ser., xxvii (1974), pp. 395–413.

285 P. H. Lindert and J. G. Williamson, 'English workers' living standards during the industrial revolution: a new look' *Ec. H. R.* 2nd ser., xxxvi (1983), pp. 1–25.

286 L. D. Schwarz, 'The standard of living in the long run: London, 1700–1860' *Ec. H. R.* 2nd ser., xxxviii (1985), pp. 24–41.

287 E. H. Hunt, 'Industrialization and regional inequality: wages in Britain, 1760–1914', *J. Ec. H.* xlvi (1986), pp. 935–66.

288 F. W. Botham and E. H. Hunt, 'Wages in Britain during the Industrial Revolution' *Ec. H. R.* 2nd ser., xl (1987), pp. 380–99.

289 A. E. Musson, *British Trade Unions, 1800–1875* SEH (1972).

290 J. Rule, ed., *British Trade Unionism 1750–1850: The Formative Years* (1988).

291 R. Price, *Labour in British Society: an Interpretative History* (Beckenham, 1986).

292 W. H. Fraser, *Trade Unions and Society: The Struggle for Acceptance,1850–80* (1974).

293 J. Stevenson, *Popular Disturbances in England, 1700–1870* (1979).

294 D. Cannadine, *Lords and Landlords: The Aristocracy and the Towns* (Leicester, 1980).

295 H. J. Dyos and M. Wolff, eds, *The Victorian City: Images and Realities* (2 vols, 1973).

296 A. Briggs, *Victorian Cities* (1963).

297 A. Briggs, *Victorian People* (1965 edn).

298 A. Briggs, *Victorian Things* (1988).

299 M. J. Freeman and D. J. Aldcroft, eds, *Transport in Victorian Britain* (Manchester, 1988).

300 J. R. Kellett, *The Impact of Railways upon Victorian Cities* (1969).

301 H. J. Perkin, *The Age of the Railway* (1969).

302 D. J. Olsen, *The Growth of Victorian London* (1976).

303 G. Stedman Jones, *Outcast London: A Study in the Relationships Between Classes in Victorian Society* (Oxford, 1971).

304 G. Crossick, *An Artisan Elite in Victorian Society* (1978).

305 R. Q. Gray, *The Aristocracy of Labour in Nineteenth-Century Britain* SEH (1981).

306 P. H. J. H. Gosden, *Self Help: Voluntary Associations in Nineteenth-Century Britain* (1973).

307 T. Tholfsen, *Working Class Radicalism in Mid-Victorian England* (1976).

308 P. McHugh, *Prostitution and Victorian Social Reform* (1980).

309 W. D. Rubinstein, *Men of Property: the Very Wealthy in Victorian Britain* (1981).

310 D. Rubinstein, ed., *Victorian Homes* (Newton Abbot, 1974).

311 F. M. L. Thompson, 'Social control in Victorian Britain' *Ec. H. R.* 2nd ser., xxxiv (1981), pp. 189–208.

312 P. Joyce, *Work, Society and Politics: The Culture of the Factory in Later Victorian England* (Hassocks, 1980).

313 T. C. Smout, *A History of the Scottish People, 1830–1950* (1986).

314 C.Ó Gráda, *The Great Irish Famine* SEH (1989).

315 S. Gilley and R. Swift, eds, *The Irish in Britain* (1989).

316 R. W. Malcolmson, *Popular Recreations in English Society* (Cambridge 1973).

317 H. Cunningham, *Leisure in the Industrial Revolution, c.1780–1880* (1980).

Index

Abbot, Charles (Baron Colchester)
(1757–1829), 16, 17, 196, 199
Abercromby, Sir Ralph (1734–1801), 83
Aberdeen, George Hamilton Gordon, 4th
earl of (1784–1860), 390–2, 394
French wars diplomacy, 92
foreign secretary, 211–13, 349
attitude to Russia, 349–50
prime minister, 287, 301, 344–6, 350
Accum, Frederick (1769–1838), 164
Adam, Robert (1728–92), 8
Addington, Henry, see Sidmouth
Afghanistan, 212
Africa, 12, 31, 37, 49, 123, 356
agricultural labourers, 10, 108, 128, 138,
147–56, 162, 179, 188, 196, 218
wages, 133, 230–1
work regulated by statute, 289, 407
poor relief, 230–1
nonconformity, 56
trade unionism among, 171, 317
revolt (1830–1), see 'Swing Riots'
agricultural societies, 137–8, 281–2
agriculture, 6–10, 42, 111–12, 115–16,
137–56, 165, 204, 230
improvement techniques, 137–9
in Ireland, 95, 97–9, 379
Agriculture, Board of, 140–2
Albert, Prince Consort (1819–61), 49, 187,
287–8, 291, 295, 341, 353
Alexander I, Tsar of Russia (1778–1825),
88, 91–2, 206–7
Alexandra, Princess (1844–1925), 354
allotments, 152–3, 324
Althorp, viscount (Spencer, John Charles,
3rd earl Spencer) (1782–1845), 138,
227, 230, 250, 257, 390–1
American Independence, war of, 3, 19–20,
26, 31–2, 34–5, 38, 95, 101, 113, 436
Amiens, Peace of (1802), 4, 65, 78, 84–5,
436
Anglicans, Anglicanism, see Church of
England
anti-catholicism, 180, 314, 319–20, 343,
370, 376–9
anti-clericalism, 220, 274, 317
Anti-Corn Law League, 181, 189, 277–84,
290, 346, 362
relations with Chartists, 271
political strategy, 279–81

Anti-State Church Association, 189
Applegarth, Robert (1834–1925), 175, 371
apprenticeship, 5, 69, 114, 120
abolition of compulsory (1813–14), 46–7
'pauper apprentices', 131, 407
arable farming, 10, 137–46, 148, 151, 152–3
in Ireland, 97
Arch, Joseph (1826–1919), 317
aristocracy, 6–9, 17, 48, 137, 145–6, 176–7,
182, 216, 271, 274, 279, 283, 293,
371
attacked in *Rights of Man*, 71, 177
in Ireland, 95, 302
education, 331–2
and industrial investment, 112, 115
and urban development, 306–7, 329
political influence and control after 1832,
223, 225, 257, 280–8, 340–1,
368–9, 370–1, 380–1
sporting interests, 323
'aristocracy of labour', 132–3, 178–9, 274,
329
Arkwright, Sir Richard (1732–92), 118–19,
121, 123, 127
Armstrong, Sir William (1810–1900), 125
army, 6, 18, 29, 149, 349, 412
during French wars, 81–3, 86–92
strengthened in 1802, 85
size, 82, 86, 191, 195, 197, 213, 351
and riot control, 195
demobilization in 1816, 191–2
stagnation in 1830s, 213
weaknesses revealed in Crimean war,
350–1
Arnold, Matthew (1822–88), 289, 297
Arnold, Thomas (1795–1842), 188, 332, 334
artisans,
radical politics, 69–79, 98, 181–2, 196,
268, 273–5, 277, 321, 329, 371
in labour force, 132–3, 174–5
living standards of, 161, 293–4, 295
trade union organization, 166–75
Ashley, Lord, see Shaftesbury
Ashton-under-Lyne, 272
Asia, 123, 209, 211–12, 355–7, 417, 438–9,
441–2
'Association Movement', 73–4
atheism, 321
Attwood, Thomas (1783–1856), 216–17,
220–1, 274

471a